W9-ADV-746

JAMES RUSSELL LOWELL

BOOKS BY

MARTIN DUBERMAN

Charles Francis Adams, 1807–1886

In White America

The Antislavery Vanguard: New Essays on the Abolitionists (*Editor*)

James Russell Lowell

James Russell Lowell

MARTIN DUBERMAN

ILLUSTRATED WITH PHOTOGRAPHS

HOUGHTON MIFFLIN COMPANY BOSTON
The Riverside Press Cambridge
1966

FIRST PRINTING c

LIBRARY OF CONGRESS CATALOG CARD NUMBER: 66–19835
PRINTED IN THE UNITED STATES OF AMERICA

For Case —
and the fortunate strangers

After a man's long work is over and the sound of his voice is still, those in whose regard he has held a high place find his image strangely simplified and summarized. The hand of death, in passing over it, has smoothed the folds, made it more typical and general. The figure retained by the memory is compressed and intensified; accidents have dropped away from it and shades have ceased to count; it stands, sharply, for a few estimated and cherished things, rather than, nebulously, for a swarm of possibilities.

HENRY JAMES, "James Russell Lowell,"
The Atlantic Monthly, January, 1892

ACKNOWLEDGMENTS

SINCE THIS BIOGRAPHY is based largely on manuscript materials, my first debt is to those who made access to such sources possible. Members of the Lowell family have been especially generous. Mrs. H. H. Bundy initially circularized the family in my behalf, and I am grateful for her many introductions. Miss Elizabeth Putnam extended warm hospitality to me and allowed me to examine the valuable collection of family papers she owns, of which the most significant were the letters from James Russell Lowell to her father, Mr. George Putnam, Lowell's nephew by marriage. Mrs. Alfred Lowell has been equally kind; she too owns an important group of papers and gave me free access to it, along with a most friendly welcome. The same cordiality was extended by Mrs. Sherman Baldwin, who let me read the family papers in her possession, of which the reminiscences of Miss Lois Burnett, Lowell's granddaughter, proved of particular value. Dr. Francis Lowell Burnett, Lowell's grandson, placed his large manuscript collection on loan to Harvard's Houghton Library, where he gave me permission to use it, and he answered as well a number of my questions regarding details of family history. Lowell's granddaughter, Mrs. Stanley Cunningham, and his niece, Miss Lois Lilley Howe, granted me interviews in which they gave me the benefit of their personal recollections. Other family members whom I wish to thank for a variety of courtesies are: Mr. Charles L. Bigelow, Mrs. M. Lowell Bigelow, Mrs. Richard Bowditch, Mrs. Lincoln Davis, Jr., Mrs. Pierre Jay, Mrs. James Russell Lowell and Mrs. Henry Lyman.

Besides members of the Lowell family, a number of other

people have given me access or leads to privately owned manuscripts. Mr. Howard Gotlieb put me in touch with Mr. Effingham Evarts, who allowed me to see material relating to his grandfather, William Evarts. Mr. Noel G. Annan and Mrs. David Garnett facilitated my search for the correspondence between Lowell and the Leslie Stephens, part of which is now in The Berg Collection of the New York Public Library. Mr. Albert G. Frothingham not only allowed me to use but in the end made me a present of the John Bartlett papers which he owned; they are now in the Yale University Library. Professor William M. Armstrong searched for manuscript references to Lowell in the extensive collection of notes he has gathered for a biography of E. L. Godkin; his considerable labor went far beyond scholarly politesse and is most appreciated. Miss Barbara D. Simison, Mrs. Louise Hall Tharp and Professor Leon Edel shared the knowledge and notes they had gathered while pursuing their researches, respectively, into the careers of Lydia Maria Child, Julia Ward Howe and Henry James. Professor F. W. Hilles of Yale University allowed me to use certain manuscript letters in his possession which relate to Lowell. Mr. Parkman D. Howe let me examine his collection of first editions of Lowell's works and annotated volumes from Lowell's private library. Mr. Peter de Brant of London let me browse through his large collection of W. W. Story and G. W. Curtis papers, much of which is now at the University of Texas. Mrs. Norman V. Ballou, who is preparing a history of Houghton Mifflin Company and is intimately acquainted with the company's papers and those of Horace E. Scudder, gave me a number of citations and leads. Mrs. David A. Miller sent me an annotated holograph of Lowell's 1884 address to the Browning Society. Mr. C. Waller Barrett, that pre-eminent collector of Americana, gave me the same open access to his huge library of manuscripts and first editions which has put so many scholars in his debt, and his curators, Katherine and William Maas, did everything possible to facilitate my use of the materials; Mr. Barrett's superb collection is now housed in a separate wing of the University of Virginia Library, and its staff members have been generous in checking references and forwarding late acquisitions. Mr. Charles M. Storey gave me free access to the collection he owns of letters to his grandfather, Charles W. Storey, a friend of Lowell's for many years; the collection consists largely of letters from John Holmes, but other correspondents are represented and there are a few significant letters from Lowell himself.

Others to whom I owe thanks for help in locating and gaining access to manuscript materials are: Miss Mabel Abbott, Mr. Thomas E. Andrews, Mr. George C. Clark, Mrs. Nicholas Clifford, Miss Polly Davis, Professor Tilden G. Edelstein of Simmons College, Professor Virginia Harlow of De Pauw University, Professor Gertrude Reese Hudson of the University of Texas, Professor Joseph Jones of the University of Texas, Miss Clara L. Penney of the Hispanic Society, Mrs. Dorothy Verrill Rhodes, Mr. Herbert C. Schulz of the Huntington Library, Mrs. Robert Stevens, Miss Anne D. Snyder, Professor Joshua C. Taylor of the University of Chicago, Mr. Lawrence Terry, Miss Anne L. Thorp, Mrs. Ralph A. Young.

In the many libraries in which I have worked, I have always been given the kindest assistance. In some cases such large efforts were made in my behalf that I would like to make a few special acknowledgments. Dr. John D. Gordan of The Berg Collection in the New York Public Library went out of his way to make their recent acquisition of the Lowell-Julia Stephen and the Lowell-Robert Carter letters available to me at the earliest possible moment. Mr. Thomas de Valcourt of Craigie House, Cambridge, not only made my work there pleasant, but aided me in tracking down manuscripts still privately owned. Miss Eileen Grady of the Yale University Library dug out endless auction catalogues for me and also helped me with genealogical detective work. Miss Carolyn Jakeman of Houghton Library, Harvard, the main manuscript depository for this biography, answered my many queries and requests with her usual patience and helpfulness. Miss Carol D. Goodman, also on the Houghton staff, put considerable effort into helping me locate suitable illustrations. At the Massachusetts Historical Society, Dr. Stephen T. Riley and Miss Winifred Collins gave me the same friendly guide through the Society's rich collections which they have always done in the past. Mr. Donald Gallup of Yale University suggested a number of leads into the University's holdings on American literature. Miss Elizabeth Baer of the Johns Hopkins University made an intensive search for manuscript materials which at first proved elusive. The staff at Columbia University made it possible for me to browse in the stacks which house the immense collections of Stedman and Gay papers, thereby reducing my work by innumerable hours. Mr. Watt P. Marchman, director of the Hayes Library in Fremont, Ohio, gave of his time and energy with a prodigality that has long made him a by-word in the scholarly world.

For a variety of other assists and favors I owe thanks to: Mr. Daniel J. Adams, Mr. Whitfield J. Bell, Jr., Miss Roberta Blaché, Mr. Charles Blitzer, Mr. Michael A. Burlingame, Mr. LeBaron C. Colt, Professor David Donald of the Johns Hopkins University, Mr. Owen Edwards, Professor Enrique Tierno Galván, Professor A. Bartlett Giametti of Princeton University, Rosalyn and Terence Higgins, Dr. Walter Igersheimer, Professor James E. Irby of Princeton University, Mrs. Claire Degener Lord, Mr. Sydney Muirden, Professor Norman Holmes Pearson of Yale University, Mrs. Lee Powell, Mr. Irving Younger, Professor René Wellek of Yale University, and Mr. Walter Muir Whitehill. A Morse Fellowship from Yale University and a Bicentennial Preceptorship from Princeton University, each allowing a year's leave with salary, greatly facilitated the research and writing of this book. I am also grateful to the American Council of Learned Societies for a grant-in-aid to cover a variety of research expenses.

Finally, I owe a great debt to friends who looked over the manuscript of this book. Leo Bersani and James M. McPherson read those chapters dealing with their special fields of interest — respectively, literary criticism and Civil War history. Carolyn Amussen, Richard Poirier, John William Ward, and Craig Wylie of Houghton Mifflin Company each gave the manuscript a line-by-line reading. Though it is difficult to make acknowledgments sound other than perfunctory, I hope these friends will understand how profoundly grateful I am to them for their many valuable suggestions.

M. D.

CONTENTS

ILLUSTRATIONS

INTRODUCTION

WHY JAMES RUSSELL LOWELL? That question has been put to me many times, even politely. To most Americans Lowell's name is now unknown ("Did you say *Robert* Lowell?"), but those for whom it does stir some memory express astonishment that anyone would today care to undertake his biography. For them James Russell Lowell conjures up snatches of bad poetry force-fed in grade school, or some archetypal Fireplace around which he sits with Longfellow, Holmes, Whittier and various other bearded irrelevancies. That Lowell was highly regarded in his own day impresses our moderns not at all. Neither of the components which made up his fame — particular achievements, like *The Biglow Papers*, and the range of his accomplishment as poet, antislavery leader, professor, literary critic, diplomat, public philosopher — any longer carries weight. *The Biglow Papers* has been relegated to dialect humor, and as for Lowell's vaunted "range," quality, not diversity, it is said, arouses the only lasting regard.

To some extent I sympathize with this attitude. Lowell deserves honor for his multiple attainments — he was a fine editor, a successful teacher, an admired diplomat, an honest public commentator — but his achievement as a writer (in which, after all, he invested his greatest energy and his highest hopes) can command only limited admiration. I have found no reason to revise the long-standing consensus which denies him the front rank. There are many moments in his poetry, long sections in his essays, which deserve respect (in some instances more respect than they have found) but they remain incidental; rather than highlighting a consolidated achievement, they call attention to its absence. It has not, then, been the intention or the result of this biography to restore Lowell's stature as a Renaissance figure or a literary giant.

What I have wished to do is to restore him as a man. It is Lowell's qualities as a human being which have most attracted me, and which most warrant rehabilitation. It has long been fashionable to dismiss the "Brahmins" as smug, limited men, ineffectual shadows of their Puritan forebears. I have come to hold a very different view of them, and the purpose of this book is to communicate that view.

Any study of Lowell the man must of course include an analysis of his public career — both for its intrinsic interest and for the way it reveals the emphases and outlines of his personality. Accordingly, I have dealt with all aspects of his career in detail. But the assumption underlying this book is that there is more to Lowell (and to many men) than their "accomplishments" — and more that is of lasting importance. We often validate a man's existence by his tangible product — poems, paintings, novels, etc. But the value of a life can be estimated by its style as much as by its events; by what it was rather than by what it did. This is the standard of measure which Lowell preferred, and the standard by which he can himself be best appreciated today. In speaking of Lowell's human appeal I do not mean to blink away his limitations nor to suggest that I agree with all or even many of his attitudes. I have in mind something at once more general and more personal — not his actions or his beliefs, but his character.

I admire, first of all, the way he treated other people. His deepest loyalties went to individuals, not ideas. The friendships he sustained over long periods of time could transcend (as did that with Leslie Stephen) sharp differences of opinion, could in some measure thrive on them. And he was not shy of expressing his feeling for those he loved. Traditionally we have viewed the Brahmins as a formal lot, embarrassed by emotion or open displays of affection. But for Lowell, at least, this is a caricature. He could indeed be formal, and with strangers or mere acquaintances often was (though the formality was softened by grace and wit). With his intimates, he was quite otherwise. Lowell was capable with family or with close friends like Charles Eliot Norton and John Holmes of a freedom, a lack of self-consciousness in expressing affection, which highlights some surprising inadequacies of our "emancipated" twentieth century.

I admire, too, the way Lowell tried to combine private cultivation and public responsibility, never finding, except briefly, a satisfactory balance between their competing demands, willing to suffer the discomfort of not finding one. His interest in himself did not exclude concern for others. Though he wished to achieve, the wish never became obsessive; he was not a man who placed his own advancement foremost, who pursued self-aggrandizement at the expense of others. He was not, in short, a careerist.

This is not to say that Lowell was invariably agreeable — he could be blunt and opinionated — but only that he tried to be honest. Though his principles were not always deeply explored, he tried to live by them; though he could be too little conscious of complexity, he neither concealed nor defiled his convictions. "It does not matter," he once wrote Grace Norton, "what the duty is, it is the fidelity that makes the measure of the peace." * This sense of probity, of insistent integrity, best sums up Lowell's life and all that we mean by the word "character." Lowell defined it as well as anyone has, when, in his mid-fifties, he wrote to Charles Eliot Norton, "I was long ago convinced that one of the rarest things in the world was a real opinion based on judgment and unshakable by events." **

But all of this is a bit portentous; it makes Lowell sound like George Washington — the Olympian figure of unapproachable rectitude. He had quite another side and one no less appealing:

---

* Letter of July 13, 1877, Houghton Library, Harvard.
** Letter of Jan. 11, 1873, Norton ed., *Letters,* II, 295.

he was a man of warmth and geniality, with a large capacity for enjoying himself and living generously, a man, above all, capable of using his pervasive sense of humor for self-deflation. If Lowell's satirical gifts were liberally spent on public frailties, he always kept some supply in reserve for his own. Perhaps even more unusual, his humor stayed with him throughout life. His personality underwent considerable modification from youth to old age; at twenty-five he was more pungent, more original, more receptive, more self-conscious than he was at seventy, and also less integrated, self-aware, amiable. But his humor, while mellowing, remained with him to the end, a graceful agency for dealing with pain, a rare substitute for querulousness.

Men like Lowell, who have a realistic sense of their own worth — and that of others; who combine conviction with tolerance, holding themselves to strict standards while managing compassion for other men's foibles; who are capable of enjoyment, though sensible enough not to expect it; who insist, despite the demands of personal ambition, on fulfilling public obligations; who are willing to jeopardize their private advantage for the sake of a principle — such men are always in scarce supply. In my opinion mid-nineteenth-century New England had more than its share of them and our own day somewhat less. This, indeed, is the reason why re-acquainting ourselves with James Russell Lowell takes on some urgency. Such at least has been the chief intent behind this biography and must give it what justification it will bear.

JAMES RUSSELL LOWELL

CHAPTER I

CHILDHOOD

ONCE, so we like to believe, there was a time of incorruptible simplicity. Men lived with high purpose, their lives stripped of superfluities, their affections open, their goals clear, their way serene. This vision of a golden age persists because it serves multiple needs: for the discontented it validates disgust with the present, assuring them that theirs is no mere personal failure; for the optimistic, it serves as a promise of the good life — a vision attainable because once attained.

Nowhere can this fantasy of a pristine past find richer play than when one lingers over the New England towns of the early nineteenth century. And within that charmed circle, none is more goldenly suffused than Cambridge, Massachusetts, home of the Brahmin literati, of Longfellow, Holmes and James Russell Lowell. The affection with which these men regarded Cambridge is itself persuasive testimony to its attractions, for though provincial pride and personal association were elements of their regard, these were not men whose judgments were based on merely parochial standards. Charles Eliot Norton's description, "the very pleasantest little oasis of space and time," is, like all superlatives, vulnerable, yet in many ways Cambridge in the first thirty years of the nineteenth century does continue to seem a charmed community.[1]

Its appeal lies in the way simplicities of daily life combined with (perhaps were prerequisites for) intensities of personal character. The simplicities were those of a typical country village, quiet, self-contained, regular. No railroads or trolley cars linked Cambridge to the Boston "metropolis"; so little traffic moved between the two points that one coach sufficed to handle it. Cambridge, in fact, seemed to have but one of everything: one brewer, who made both spruce and ginger beer; one barber, whose shop doubled as a museum full of old prints, engraved whales' teeth and live Java sparrows; one great holiday, Commencement at the College; and one great potentate, the College President (save on artillery-election days when the Governor, splendid in epaulets and buckskin breeches, raised some doubts about academic pre-eminence).[2]

The population shared similar origins and thereby traditions. Almost everyone had been born in New England, and a large proportion in Cambridge itself. Before the Irish began to arrive in large numbers in the 1830's, the town had few foreigners. There were two Scotch gardeners, Rule (whose daughter, Miss Rule, the students nicknamed Anarchy), and Fraser, whom Lowell remembered as "full of bloody histories of the Forty-twa, and showing an imaginary French bullet, sometimes in one leg, sometimes in the other, and sometimes, toward nightfall, in both." The only Irish laborer was a man named Sweetman; in a later day, when the Irish had flooded into Boston, the solitary Sweetman was recalled with extravagant affection — he had always been ready, Norton insisted, "to lean on his spade and put the troublesome schoolboy to a test on the Odes of Horace, or even on the *Arma virumque cano*" (the good Irishman was in every sense singular). These few men, plus the barber, several language teachers at the College and a scattering of the anonymous, made up Cambridge's foreign contingent. It was a group so small as to create little but glamor, almost nothing of hostility.[3]

Thus it was but a slight exaggeration to say, as Norton did, that the inhabitants of Cambridge all knew each other in person, and also "much of everybody's tradition, connections, and mode of life." But homogeneity of origins was not the same as homogeneity of behavior. Individualism was a matter of community pride. Personal peculiarities were thought indispensable, and it was expected, as Lowell put it, that they would be "given the wall." Cambridge was sufficiently sure of the rightness and safety of its norm to cherish even her eccentrics. In later life Lowell lovingly recalled the widow Craigie, sitting in her window as an old woman, her head wrapped in a turban, leaving off her Spinoza only to be sure that no one molested the canker-worms which annually destroyed the leaves on her elm trees. Lowell also remembered the wealthy neighbor who, crossed in love, so shunned contact with the world that when a signature was required for a legal document, he would wrap himself entirely in a blanket, allowing only the hand which held the pen to be seen; late in life this anchorite once more rejoined society; his favorite topic then became Eternity and his favorite charity the giving of annual sleigh rides to the town paupers.[4]

Individualism gained additional protection from existing social distinctions. The more rigid structure of eighteenth-century society was no longer intact, but differences of breeding and culture were still widely accepted as "natural distinctions." No one was so rich or so poor as to excite undue disdain on the one side or undue jealousy on the other, especially since, in this optimistic, mobile society, all could at least share an equality of hope. Moreover, all were aware that the aristocrat held to a communal system of values which mitigated presumption and vanity. The privileged Cambridge boy was taught that those who had been blessed with greater background, intelligence or training were obligated to employ them for the general good. When Horace Mann took as his motto in life, "Be ashamed to die until you have won some victory for humanity," he was echoing the sentiments of his generation. Though Calvin's stark theology had given way in New England to Unitarianism's more cheerful message, there remained the strong moral purpose, the insistence that life was a serious business, that men had the obligation to devote themselves to active usefulness. As Andrews

Norton advised his young son: "above all consider the events of life as intended by God for our discipline, for the formation of our characters." [5]

Thus the physical environment of early nineteenth-century Cambridge — a quiet, homogeneous village — and the intellectual heritage, with its warning against extravagance and pretense, combined to instill the injunction of simplicity. But it was simplicity with an intense purpose — to breed self-discipline, and to instill a sense of responsibility to God and one's fellow men. The severe practicality with which a Cambridge boy was taught to deal with daily affairs, in combination with the abstract purposes to which he was told to devote his ultimate energies, helps to account for the Yankee's "hybrid" character, that strange blend, as Lowell put it, of "calculating-fanaticism . . . cast-iron-enthusiasm . . . sour-faced-humor . . . close-fisted-generosity." [6]

These community values were reinforced for James Russell Lowell by the examples and precepts of his own family. His was the eighth generation in direct descent from Percival Lowle, a successful merchant from Bristol who had settled in New England in 1639. The family had not distinguished itself, either for saints or sinners, until the Reverend John Lowell, great-grandfather of James Russell, achieved a kind of beatification by becoming the first Lowell to attend Harvard, an achievement only mildly augmented in some eyes by his later career as a distinguished divine. His son, Judge Lowell, further solidified the family reputation: he was a member of the Continental Congress, one of John Adams' "midnight appointments" to the bench and Chief Justice of the First Circuit Court. It was part of family lore that as a member of the state Constitutional Convention in 1779, Judge Lowell had written the clause later used to declare slavery in Massachusetts illegal, but in fact the language of the clause had already been used in earlier state constitutions, and its specific incorporation in that of Massachusetts was the work of John Adams. Yet Judge Lowell's other titles to renown are undisputed. He was an eloquent pleader at the bar, a dignified, mild, kindly man (whom Lafayette said he "cherished in [his] heart"), and, no minor claim on posterity, founder through his three marriages of the triple Lowell dynasty.[7]

James Russell was proud of this descent and in later life, when in Europe, he even did a bit of genealogical digging. But his pride was always proportionate and he was able to lampoon the absurdities of ancestor-worship; the first authentic record of his own clan, he once wrote with mock solemnity, was in "the book of Enoch," thirty-first chapter, where it was recorded that "about this time (300 before Adam) flourished Lowell of the Zarrows — a great king over much people"; Eve herself, had she the choice, would have given her hand to a Lowell (who after all "had been noble for many generations"), rather than to Adam, "he which was a *novus homo* & a new Creation." [8]

For his own father, James Russell's affection was too deep for irony. He thought him "the very simplest and charmingest" of men, with "a great deal of the truest magnanimity." This was more than filial piety; it was an opinion of Dr. Charles Lowell widely shared by contemporaries.[9]

The outward events of Dr. Lowell's life were unexceptional. Graduating from Harvard in 1800, he bowed to his father's wishes and began to study law but, when it became clear that he was unsuited for that profession, was finally allowed to pursue his original wish to enter the Ministry. After three years at Edinburgh furthering his theological studies, chiefly under the famed Dugald Stewart, he became Pastor in 1806 of the West Church in Boston, a post he held, in his later years only nominally, until his death in 1861.

In both his theology and his person, Charles Lowell represented the best of a type — the liberal New England minister, optimistic, benign, rational, moralistic. As a theologian he was undistinguished, having none of that interest in speculative problems out of which philosophers are made. He put humanity above creeds and ethics above logic. "The question should not be," he told his congregation, "to what church does he belong? . . . but — What is his *spirit*?" The true Christian was known by his character not his doctrine; he was forgiving, humble, benevolent, never revengeful, never arrogant or unfeeling. "Be careful," he warned his son, "not to become a partisan in theology. Study your bible for yourself, &, without calling yourself a trinitarian or unitarian, orthodox or liberal, let it be your sole aim to be in truth *a christian*. The faith of the *heart* is the only essential faith, & this may be held by christians of every name." [10]

Dr. Lowell believed contention over doctrinal questions unprofitable because unresolvable; imperfect human understanding could never hope to fathom the mysterious ways of Providence. Men had to rely on the certainty that God had designed and still governed the universe, and that he was a benevolent Father. Pain and suffering were mistakenly taken for signs either of His indifference or His malevolence, while in fact they were given in love and mercy, the necessary chastenings of a parent "whose designs are kindest when His dispensations are most severe." The so-called "problem of evil," therefore, was to Dr. Lowell a problem only of limited human intelligence, an inability to appreciate that all was done out of His goodness for our profit.[11]

Thus Charles Lowell, like so many of his clerical contemporaries, managed to be fatalistic and cheerful all at once; to accept present evil as ultimate good, to retain an all-knowing God without turning him into Satan. But this best of all possible worlds was achieved at the expense of intellectual depth and rigor. Earlier New England divines, like Jonathan Edwards, had been less evasive; they had carried the doctrine of God's omnipotence to the logical conclusion of our helplessness. But the new liberal view thought too well of man to take from him all control over his own destiny. It turned God from an all-powerful dictator into a benevolent helpmate, recalling the definition of a Boston Unitarian as a man who believes "in one God — at most." As Charles Lowell put it, "God will not do all. If He did, we should not be free, accountable agents, but mere machines. We must strive to 'work out our own salvation,' and we may then look, with humble confidence, to *GOD* 'to work in us, both to will and to do.' " Man could indeed be ignorant, weak and sinful, but a compassionate Divinity would come to his aid if called upon in a sincere spirit, and if, simultaneously, man utilized his own "innate" instincts for good.[12]

The belief in "innate" human faculties was part of a world view that assumed the existence of fixed essences and self-evident truths. The world "made sense"; it moved with purpose according to His benevolent if inscrutable intention. Like the universe they inhabited, human beings were meant to follow definite laws of conduct. They were able to do so, because in giving man a soul, an instinctive "moral sense," God had endowed him with the intuition to perceive and the strength to pursue that which was immutably "right." If man followed this instinct he would be naturally attracted to "excellence," to all that was benevolent, humble, dignified, sincere, cheerful, diligent, forgiving, devout. Men, of course, had their passions, too, and these could lead them to unworthy ends. But the passions were in themselves neutral, capable of being controlled through reason and prayer. Men could and should guide their conduct by the classical mean of "temperance in all things" and by aiming at spiritual rather than worldly distinction.[13]

To achieve these goals, man had to learn to listen to his inner voice more than to the voices around him. Dr. Lowell firmly upheld the right of private judgment. Men were ultimately accountable only to God; He had revealed distinctly all that was essential — and for the rest, men must be free to differ. The opinion of the community mattered, for man was a social creature with social affections, and his own frailty, moreover, should always make him wary of lightly setting aside established values and institutions. Then, too, every man had the obligation to make certain that his was an enlightened opinion, arrived at through serious inquiry and careful reflection. And finally, in the process of standing up for his own beliefs, he had the obligation to guard against easy condemnation of those who, following their own "internal monitors," might disagree. Yet in the end, the individual had to follow his own conscience. Once sure of the "right," he must pursue it, though all the world unite against him.[14]

Charles Lowell both lived and preached this "higher law." He preferred gentle persuasion to public oratory, but occasionally, when his conviction of "wickedness" proved irresistible, he would speak out forcefully to his congregation. He did so in defense of the temperance movement, in behalf of charity for orphans, and in an effort to solicit relief for refugees from "foreign oppression." Once, when a Massachusetts clerical convention proposed to shut out certain classes of poor persons from its charity, Dr. Lowell "electrified" the gathering by crying out, "their groans shall not disturb my slumber, their blood shall not cleave to the skirts of my garments."[15]

Above all, Dr. Lowell spoke out against slavery — not with the fiery, continuous enthusiasm of some of the younger ministers like Theodore Parker or James Freeman Clarke, for their ardor was antithetical to his own personal style of restraint, but nonetheless with feeling and dedication. Occasionally he joined in public protests, but more characteristically he bore witness against slavery in his pulpit. Sabbath after sabbath, when most of the Boston clergy were silent, Dr. Lowell introduced slavery "decidedly fervently" into his prayers, describing it as a "monstrous iniquity." And his exhortatory powers were considerable. He spoke simply, without straining for effect and without sanctimony, combining the force of sincerity with eloquence. Emerson thought him "a natural orator," and Arthur Hugh Clough, the English poet, meeting Dr. Lowell when he was a deaf old man, was still struck by his "strong clear voice" and his "perfect sentences." Charles Lowell's views on slavery were paralleled in the later abolitionist activities of his son, James Russell, though the two worked out their common opinion in the contrasting styles appropriate to their different generations.[16]

Charles Lowell's insistence on social responsibility pervaded his conception of the ministry. Not only did he voice his views on questions of the day, but directly concerned himself with the condition of his Boston parishioners. He was known as a minister devoted to pastoral offices; one colleague remembered him as going often at night with a lantern into the muddy alleys of the poorer parts of his parish, seeking out those in need. He considered house-to-house visits an essential part of his ministerial function, allowing him to carry to his flock what were to him the indistinguishable comforts of Christianity and human love.[17]

If Charles Lowell could act the occasional social critic, he could never play the rebel; he wished to perfect his society, not reject it. On the whole he fitted comfortably into the world around him, his considerable gifts finding satisfying expression inside of established forms. Nothing within or without pressed with sufficient force to draw forth from him new questions or new formulations. His theology was untortured, almost unexamined, the accepted philosophy of his day. The hard questions — "free will," "evil," the "after-life" — were not for him unsettled problems requiring inquiry and debate, but problems incapable of settlement, and thus better left alone. His temperamental bent was to smooth over, not to unearth, to comfort, not to challenge.

What Charles Lowell may have lost in originality, he gained in benevolence; if he was a becalmed man, he was also, as a neighbor said, a "beautiful" one. Gentle, dignified, compassionate, he managed as both minister and parent to make even his admonitions within a loving context. Thus while arguing that youth needed discipline — for good principles had to be inculcated early, when the mind was fallow — he at the same time insisted that discipline never degenerate into severity; youth must be allowed its natural buoyancy; cheerfulness and ardor were innocent and appropriate in the young, and would soon enough give way before the troubled trials of adulthood.[18]

Understandably, then, James Russell Lowell always thought tenderly of his father. In many ways, he had been an ideal one. He provided humane and generous standards, prescribed them lovingly, and himself strove honestly to live by them. Though he thus made it possible for his son freely to differ, he made it more likely (because he minimized resistance and resentment) that his son would naturally absorb parental precepts. What James Russell later said of Lessing's filial attitude applies equally to his own — "really beautiful in its union of respectful tenderness with unswerving self-assertion." [19]

Charles Lowell's wife, Harriet, was a complex, tortured woman. Her family had come on her father's side from the Scotch Highlands, and on her mother's from the Orkney Islands. She loved the tall tales associated with those regions, and would endlessly repeat their lore and ballads to her children. Later Lowell wrote, and perhaps quite literally meant, that "the passages I love in the poets give me back an hour of childhood, and are like a mother's voice to me." [20]

Harriet Lowell's own person had considerable poetry about it. She was a tiny woman, with size-one shoes, and tight ringlets around her head — willful, vivacious, witty. Contemporaries sometimes doubted if she was well-suited to Dr. Lowell; one, mistaking temperament for origin, referred to her as the Doctor's "wayward little half-French wife," while another, mistaking origin for temperament, insisted that her wild "Celtic blood" precluded compatibility with her serene, dignified husband.[21]

Yet the contrasts between husband and wife were as much complementary as antagonistic. Harriet Lowell's erratic humor could be offset by her husband's gentle stability, just as his dignity could be lightened by her caprice. And they were enough alike, so that points of difference could be the more readily accommodated. For if Harriet Lowell had her impetuous, frivolous side, she was also, like her husband, cultivated, devout, intuitive, compassionate. And like him too, she was devoted to the welfare of their family. James Russell remembered that his mother "schooled & corrected" him from infancy, never letting "a vulgarism pass without rapping it over the knuckles," correcting him with "almost excessive precision." For all her seeming fragility, a family friend remarked that Harriet Lowell's "power and accomplishment" in the home would have made her "a great leader of men, had she been a man herself." Hers was a personality which, in its combination of surface delicacy and underlying authority, was to be repeated in James Russell's wife, Maria White.[22]

Harriet Lowell was more original, more imaginative than her husband, but unlike him could not actively push herself forward, could not find an adequate way of expressing her gifts. She turned inward, gave herself over increasingly to brooding and self-doubt — "we must all labor," she once wrote, "happy those who are qualified for it." Tender, vulnerable, she moved erractically from whimsy and high spirits to anxiety and depression. By middle age, the oscillations of mood became dangerously pronounced, culminating in 1845 in a psychotic break that kept her hospitalized for more than two years and from which she never really recovered. When she died of a stroke in 1850, not even her family could regret her passing; as her daughter-in-law wrote, "the larger portion of her mind had gone before . . . there was some strange derangement . . . a mystery that could not be fathomed." [23]

Though Harriet Lowell's instability did not become pronounced until after her children were grown, it left its mark, in varying degrees, on all five of them. The child most severely affected was the eldest daughter, Rebecca, who never married, but as a shy, peculiar recluse devoted herself in later life to keeping house for her widowed father. The eldest son, Charles Russell, had an equally unhappy life, though the blight, at least superficially, was less directly related to his upbringing. After a promising beginning as a merchant, he lost all his property in the panic of 1837, as well as a large part of his father's, which he had been managing while his parents were temporarily abroad; thereafter Dr. Lowell was forced to live largely within his minister's yearly salary of two thousand dollars. Actual misconduct on Charles Russell's part seems to have been involved — Longfellow, a neighbor, referred to "moral delinquencies" — though Dr. Lowell was "tender in inventing excuses" for his son. The blow was a severe one for the family; James Russell believed that his mother's insanity was brought on by the "disgrace." [24]

Of the other three children, the story is far happier, at least as judged in terms of achievement (though that may be less a measure of contentment than a sign of its lack). The second daughter, Mary, who was nine years older than James Russell, often in charge of him as an infant and close to him throughout his life, was an accomplished woman of considerable learning, intelligence and curiosity (even in heaven, she once said, "I would wish to know who was Secretary of the Treasury"). She was so extraordinary a linguist that once — at least so goes the family story — she calmed a group of Irish immigrants during a stormy transatlantic crossing by speaking a few phrases of Gaelic to them. And when she died, at age ninety, she was just beginning to learn Icelandic, recalling another formidable Boston woman, Sarah Palfrey, who took up the study of Hebrew during her final illness in order "to greet my Creator in his native tongue." Mary Lowell's marriage to Samuel Putnam, at times strained, was later made tragic by the deaths of their two sons, one of cholera and one of wounds in the Civil War battle of Ball's Bluff. During her long life she published a number of volumes of prose and poetry, and at least one, *Records of an Obscure Man*, is still impressive; its learned, sophisticated defense of the Negro was far ahead of its own day, and, in its awareness of past African achievements, of ours. It is not surprising that this remarkable woman was described by Annie Fields, wife of the publisher, as "the first lady of our time," a person of "indescribable sweetness" and "largeness of heart" — and Mrs. Fields, an intimate of the great and near-great, had known most of the likely competitors for that honor.[25]

Closest in age to James Russell was his second brother, Robert Traill Spence Lowell, though so much of his life was spent far away from the Cambridge area that the two had little contact after childhood. R. T. S. Lowell became a considerable personality in his own right. As an Episcopal minister, he served in churches as distant as Bermuda and Newfoundland, while on the side writing poems like "The Relief of Lucknow," still a declamatory favorite, and a number of novels, the most durable of which, *The New Priest at Conception Bay*, his publisher announced as "the best book ever written" in the United States, a claim which would make any praise of its real merits anticlimactic. Later in life, R. T. S. Lowell became headmaster of St. Mark's School for a short time, and then Professor of Latin and Literature at Union College.[26]

James Russell was the youngest child, and something of a petted favorite. His sister Mary, searching her memory late in life, could remember no scene in his childhood which did not tell of happiness. She recalled him as a three-year-old — erect, sturdy, with golden hair (soon to turn reddish brown), and earnest blue eyes; like the man, already ardent, tender, and endlessly curious: he had to know the names of the trees he saw, the seasons and habits of the birds he heard.[27]

Mary would lull her brother to sleep during his infancy by reading musical verse aloud to him, and before he reached the age of three, she and her mother had taught him to read; contrary to the modern fear of "forcing," Harriet Lowell insisted that "the brain, as well as the limbs, required exercise." Yet she was careful to see that learning did not become drudgery; though she demanded strict attention while lessons lasted, she always put them aside before interest began to flag.[28]

Lowell was only three and a half when sent to his first school, under cover "of a broadrimmed white hat with a gold tassel suspended from it by a blue ribbon." The school was the only private one in the area, though not, for all that, very grand:

> *Propt on the marsh, a dwelling now, I see*
> *The humble school-house of my A,B,C,*
> *Where well-drilled urchins, each behind his tire,*
> *Waited in ranks the wished command to fire,*
> *Then all together, when the signal came,*
> *Discharged their* a-b-abs *against the dame . . .*
> *She, mid the volleyed learning firm and calm*
> *Patted the furloughed ferule on her palm . . .*

The "furloughed ferule" was standard equipment; though Lowell collected a drawerful of "rewards of merit" at the school, he could never thereafter pass it without feeling "a certain disagreeable nervousness in my rear." [29]

His second school pleased him more. It dispensed with thrashings, and was run by the accomplished Sophia Dana, granddaughter of a Harvard president and later the wife of George Ripley, founder of Brook Farm. Though the school was meant for girls, Lowell and one other boy were admitted, indeed were placed at head of table on either side of Miss Dana, Lowell made more conspicuous still by his embroidered ruffled shirts with cuffs. Here he began Latin and obtained a fairly thorough knowledge of French, not unusual accomplishments for a Cambridge boy. In poring over French stories at age seven, reading Scott at nine and proudly announcing in the same year that he had already "got quite a library" of his own, he was but exhibiting the intellectual precocity expected for a boy of his time and class.[30]

Again like many of his privileged contemporaries, Lowell attended, from ages eight to fourteen, the famous school run by Mr. William Wells. In later years, grown men were known to tremble — and then to turn violent — at the mere mention of the place. Richard Henry Dana, Jr., who attended at the same time Lowell did, recalled the school with particular horror: most of the thirty boys boarded there, living six or seven to a room, without fires and without lights, except for a few minutes at bedtime. Lowell, a day scholar for most of his six years, was spared this spartan regimen, but was not spared punishment by flogging. Mr. Wells always had a rattan either in hand or lying on his desk, and was quick to lay it upon a boy's back in cases of ill-preparation or disorder. Lowell got a thrashing, which he claimed he didn't deserve, on his very first day, but evened the score thereafter by escaping many which he felt amply warranted. Wells was probably no more severe than other schoolmasters of the time — Thomas Wentworth Higginson insisted that the Wells establishment "was simply a belated old-fashioned English school & not essentially coarser or rougher" than others in the area. And it was agreed, in any case, that outside the schoolroom Mr. Wells was courteous and charming. Nor was there any disputing that he was a fine classical scholar. Earlier, as a Boston publisher, Wells had brought out in twenty volumes the first complete edition of Cicero in America, and then as a schoolmaster, dissatisfied with the standard Latin grammar in use, had turned out his own hundred-page manual. Lowell liked to pretend that he learned little in Mr. Wells' school except "a good deal of proficiency in deviltry of all descriptions," but in his private letters he allowed it to be known that he was at least intermittently diligent.[31]

In preparation for Harvard, the Wells curriculum concentrated heavily on Greek, Latin and mathematics, slighting other subject matter. Nor were athletics allowed emphasis; the school grounds were said to be too confined for the favorite sports of football, handball, cricket and kite flying, though in winter the boys could skate on Fresh Pond and coast on the surrounding hills. On the whole, it was a discipline and a curriculum narrowly conceived, and few looked back on it with much sense of pleasure or profit. But the school did turn out good classical scholars, and Lowell, at age fifteen, successfully weathered the rather stiff Harvard entrance examinations in Latin and Greek. Only a little younger than most of his fellow freshmen, he took his place in the Class of 1834.[32]

CHAPTER II

HARVARD

DURING FRESHMAN YEAR, I did nothing, during Sophomore year I did nothing, during Junior year I did nothing, and during Senior year I have thus far done nothing in the way of college studies" — thus Lowell, on the eve of graduation from Harvard, summed up his official career. It was the familiar pose of a nineteen-year-old anxious to cultivate the image of "free spirit." In truth, as might have been predicted from his upbringing, Lowell paid at least enough attention to his formal studies to maintain respectable academic standing. His best year was his first, when he ranked in the upper third of the class. Thereafter he stayed pretty close to the middle, though he did win a "detur" (a book bearing the college arms, awarded for excellence in scholarship), and in his senior year he was given the academic honor of taking part in a public "exhibition." His record, in other words, though not distinguished, was far from disgraceful.[1]

A youth of Lowell's talent and energy could not have given himself to the prescribed curriculum with much more conscientiousness than he did — not, that is, without burying his talent and leaving his energy unused. For the course of study at Harvard in the 1830's was narrow and mechanical. Soon after Lowell's time, students were allowed in their last three years to abandon Latin, Greek and mathematics for a variety of electives, but in his day the stress was still heavily on the ancient world. As a freshman he had to spend more than two thirds of his class hours on Latin and Greek, and as a sophomore about half his time. Even as a junior, when some electives were allowed in modern languages, science and philosophy, about a quarter of the curriculum was still reserved for the classics. Only in senior year were the students permitted to abandon Latin and Greek entirely.[2]

The average Harvard undergraduate studied not only the languages of the ancient world, but its philosophy, literature and history as well. For someone of Lowell's humanistic and literary bent, such a curriculum held much potential interest, but it could rarely be realized in a system where teaching too often consisted solely of drilling. Discipline was stressed above elucidation; the instructor's prime function was to check that assignments had been completed rather than to inspire interest in them. There were, of course, exceptions, for the faculty boasted such true teachers as John Farrar and Edward Channing, the latter a particular favorite of Lowell's. And even the formal course work held incidental excitements for him: as a freshman he especially enjoyed the study of Rhetoric, as a sophomore was interested enough to do independent reading in Herodotus, Terence and Cicero, and as a junior, found the study of Italian "enchanting."[3]

But if Lowell, despite the blasé indifference he enjoyed affecting, was not wholly alienated by the curriculum, much of his education did necessarily take place outside the classroom. His real love was English literature, and since no such course was then offered at Harvard, he had to read independently and at the expense of his prescribed courses. His parents, meaning to encourage his appreciation (though not his truancy), bought him handsome editions of Milton, Coleridge and Shakespeare. His "editiomania," as he called it, still unsatisfied, he used his own extra money to purchase Butler, Beattie, Cowper and Mary Russell Mitford as well. He also took advantage of the college library; in his senior year alone, a partial list of his reading included Carlyle's *French Revolution* and *Sartor Resartus*, Shelley's *Cenci* ("and most of his other poems"), Beaumont and Fletcher, Coleridge's *Ancient Mariner* (for the "20th time, or so"), Ford's *Plays*, Tennyson and Bunyan. He also followed the literary periodicals, resorting to rhyme at one point to convey his disgust at an article by Carlyle reviewing Lockhart's life of Scott:

> *Carlyle, who's as snarly as a longlegged Tenney,*
> *Because his* own *works wouldn't bring him a penny,*
> *Says that all of Scott's novels are not worth a sou*
> *Why? They fed him & made him a Baronet too.*[4]

Reading was only one outlet for Lowell's energies. Convivial by temperament, he joined clubs, had the standard long talks before the fire (complete with liquor and cigars) and, depending on the season, did some hunting in the fields or went to theater and dances in Boston (where he professed the usual fatigue with the "nonsense" talked by young ladies). In his junior year, he was elected to the Hasty Pudding Club, a society which made an occasional stab at literary or political debate, but whose real purpose was simply to have a good time:

> *Say, why do these grave breth'ren meet? —*
> *To joke, to argue, and — to* eat.

Steaming bowls of hasty pudding — a molasses-rum concoction — would be consumed, mock trials held (member Atkins accused of "eating more than man e'er eat before"), elaborate debates staged (was Aeneas guilty of breach of promise?) and enough hilarity spread around to make the Club seem immensely bright to its members. Lowell was chosen secretary and, in the tradition established by Washington Allston, kept the records in verse, all the while lamenting his labors with an ennui befitting his function:

> *A Record? Lord! it* is *a bore*
> *To tell the same things o'er & o'er,*

And spoil good prose so many times,
By ending all the lines with rhymes! [5]

In his senior year Lowell became one of the editors of *Harvardiana*, the college literary magazine, affectionately known as the "perry," short for "perryodical." Lowell had written nothing for the earlier volumes of the magazine, but as an editor in 1837–1838, he scribbled a variety of prose and poetry. It was poor stuff — as Lowell himself later said, "I was as great an ass as ever brayed & thought it singing" — alternating between high-spirited burlesque, now devoid of almost all humor, and sentimental apostrophes to the "lovers' mournful fate" or "love's youthful dream." If at age eighteen Lowell failed to produce memorable poetry, he did at least demonstrate easy facility with words and a quick eye for the absurd. To his advantage, too, was that he already thought rather well of his powers, self-confidence never being unimportant to the ripening of talent. Lowell's family, in fact, thought his confidence excessive; they feared his gifts came too easily, that he would become careless of his powers and, more dangerous still for a New Englander, of the necessity of using them to build character. "My only wish," his father told him, "is that you may be influenced by proper motive & act with a constant reference to Him from whom you received those powers which render you capable of high attainments, & for the improvement & use of which you must render an account." [6]

Lowell's exuberant self-confidence could sometimes lead him into the kind of egotism which overrides (because it does not apprehend) the feelings of others. He was not always mindful of how easily they could be ruffled, how his jauntiness could be interpreted as mockery, his volatility as sharpness. More than one friend complained of ridicule; they added that Lowell had been derisive "in public" or "to their faces," which suggests that his lapses were at least aboveboard.[7]

Yet his friends loved him — if not for his excesses, for the warm, impulsive temperament of which they were a part. He was capable of deep tenderness towards those close to him; he freely confessed to one friend that he had cried on receiving his long-delayed letter, and reminisced unreservedly about their first encounter — how bashful he had been, how astonished and grateful when spoken to. Such fervid protestations of affection between men came more easily to Lowell's generation than to ours — though their words may now seem to carry more emotional cargo than they in fact did, being to some extent a conventional mode of the day, a conscious modeling on Goethe's ardent Werther. But convention was not solely responsible. It was a generation bred on the classics and thus predisposed to believe that a relationship between two men held greater promise of "lofty purity" than that between a man and woman, necessarily "debased" by physical desire. "What we call Love," Lowell wrote to a close friend, "is not the whole of Love. We straightway, on hearing its name, imagine of a youth & maiden & of a Loveland where music & moonlight & feeling are one. Yet it has often grieved me to think how few women's hearts were so rightly the heirs of this rich birthright as those of the most of men . . . If the hearts be tougher should they not the more toughly Knit & cling together . . . ?" Whether from innocence or security, Lowell and his friends could and did express affection for each other with little self-consciousness, believing such expression a fulfillment, not a denial, of manhood. Though we like to think of ourselves as more liberated than the Victorians, able to deal more openly with more areas of experience, it may only be that we express different, but not less limited, aspects of experience. One can hardly imagine, to give another kind of example, today's college sophomore casually mentioning in a letter to a friend, as Lowell did, that his plants "get through the winter nicely," or promising, as did Lowell after graduation, to send a flower journal to a college friend then living in Virginia, adding the hope that they would "give each other flower journals of our lives in our letters." [8]

Lowell's affection for men and plants inhibited not at all his active interest in women. He took to the ladies easily, well and early, announcing that, like other great poets, he had been desperately in love before the age of ten. He announced, too, with just a trace of pride, that his "animal passions" increased as he grew older. In college he fell "hopelessly in love" at regular intervals, suffering each time pangs of the heart such as none could understand. Some few friends, though, did their best; when, in one contest for the attentions of an indifferent girl, Lowell professed discouragement, a friend gallantly reassured him that had he Lowell's tongue, "prepossessing *bodily form*" and "human face divine," he would never yield the palm, no matter how coquettish the female or wily the opponent. In friends, as is well understood, loyalty counts for more than eyesight; in truth Lowell was no Adonis. He grew handsomer as he grew older, but as a young man he was somewhat undersized, standing about 5′ 8″ at age eighteen, with the typically chunky Lowell body and a somewhat heavy face. He did, though, have fine features and lively blue eyes, and the vivacity of his personality gave special force to his appearance. He was alive and his contemporaries admired him for it. Had he been eccentric, their admiration might have been more qualified, but Lowell was patently one of them, his style in the mode, if the mode accentuated.[9]

His high spirits were not all gain; they were symptoms of an undisciplined as well as a buoyant nature. Though capable of bursts of intense concentration, he had trouble sustaining interest, despite good resolutions and despite family injunctions. Perhaps his restlessness was only an abundance of curiosity and a healthy refusal to confine it; perhaps, as was darkly hinted, the "Spence negligence" associated with his mother's family was asserting itself. In any case, the same capriciousness which helped make Lowell popular as a companion made him delinquent as a scholar, the rambunctiousness which endeared him to his friends put him out of favor with the authorities.[10]

His indifference to college regulations led to a long series of breaches, bringing an equally long series of official reprimands. He began by wearing a hat in chapel though it was the rule that students should remain uncovered; he then several times wore a brown coat on Sunday though a black one was deemed proper. Sartorial violations were matched by academic ones. He was absent from recitations and privately warned; he continued to be absent and was publicly admonished. His father was notified, but the delinquencies continued: omission of themes, speaking out of turn, general inattention in forensics and recitation. The climax came towards the end of Lowell's senior year when the faculty voted, because of his "continued neglect of his college duties," to suspend him until shortly before Commencement. In the interim, he was to be "rusticated" to Concord, there to study Locke's *Essay Concerning Human Understanding* and Mackintosh's *Review of Ethical Philosophy* under the eye of the Reverend Barzaillai Frost, the town minister — a punishment as perfectly New England in its prescription of rational readings as in the careful insistence that they be supervised by a representative of supernatural authority.[11]

The general consensus was that Lowell deserved his fate. But he was unrepentant. "Everybody almost," he protested, "is calling me 'indolent,' 'blind dependent on my own powers' and 'on fate.' Damn everybody! since everybody damns me. Everybody seems to see but one side of my character . . . the worst." That off his chest, Lowell promptly set about seeing the worst side of everyone and everything in "infernal" Concord, regaling his friends back in Cambridge with brashly amusing accounts of life in the provinces.[12]

The "savages," he reported, were "cursed dull," the chief characteristic of the ladies being their failure to clean their nails, of the gentlemen ditto their teeth. Calling on the sisters of a classmate, he allowed that they were good singers ("though they 'sing rather *small*' in *some* other accomplishments"), but deplored their need to "display" themselves. Only one girl in town, Miss Caroline Brooks, won his thorough approval, especially for her "very remarkable black eyes." Lowell vowed he would have married her instantly, but Miss Brooks, alas, was already engaged to E. Rockwood Hoar (later to become a lifelong friend of Lowell's). Thus thwarted, Lowell took (for a poet) logical steps: he wrote, "con amore & currente calamo," a seven-stanza poem commemorating the black eyes, and then, for additional balm, pronounced the poem the best thing he had written in two years.[13]

Though Lowell was something of a lion among the locals ("they *will* invite me, & insist on my going . . ."), they amused him not. To relieve his boredom, he thought briefly of writing for the local paper, but then decided that since "it excelled in its line, being undoubtedly the *dullest* paper" in the state, it was hopeless to try to enliven it. When a commiserating Harvard friend suggested that Lowell try sailing as a way of passing time, he replied grumpily that there were no sailboats, only "some machines that aspire to the elevated station of 'dories' & clam-boats . . . but in most of them there is so much water, & that dirty, that 'twould be cheaper & easier & cleanlier to float about in a basket, or astride of a log." Despairing of amusement, Lowell lamented that he would become a "most melancholy Jacques . . . & be forced like old Hudibras's sword 'to eat into itself for lack of something else to cut & hack.' "[14]

But there were objects enough to "cut & hack" without his turning inward. A favorite target became his guardian and host, the Rev. Barzaillai Frost. Lowell acknowledged that Mr. Frost was "kind and attentive," and he grew very fond of Mrs. Frost, eventually pronouncing her "simply the best woman I ever set my eyes on." Not the least of her wonders, in Lowell's eyes, was that she actually seemed to love her husband, whom Lowell thought a poor specimen. Mr. Frost's chief fault was that he talked too much, with the secondary and related defect of chewing his food too loudly. And he had "views" on everything, endlessly ringing the changes on those "*gret* principles of action" which lay at the heart of the universe. Worse still, he was literal-minded. "If I were to say," Lowell reported to a friend, " 'there's no such thing in the world' or 'under the sun' — B. would begin 'Ah, that you can't be sure of, if we suppose the sun to be, etc. etc.' " The man's basic egotism, Lowell decided, was fatal to conversation, but he was candid enough to add that the egotism was not all on one side: "he loves the sound of his own voice — so do I, ergo, hate *his*." [15]

Lowell's satirical thrusts were not blunted by respect for reputation — as his *Fable for Critics* would later prove. While in Concord, he saw a little of Emerson and his circle, and he pitched into them with the same zest applied to poor Barzaillai Frost. Emerson, who took Lowell on several walks and loaned him books, was acknowledged "a very pleasant man in private conversation," downright "goodnatured," but his talk struck Lowell as too much calculated for effect; "After all I'd heard of him, as an Eagle soaring in pride of place, I was surprised to see a poor little hawk stooping at flies or at least sparrows & groundlings." The young Lowell, more adventuresome in personal style than in opinions, also found Emerson's ideas suspect. He agreed with the sage's "practical opinions (of man's independence etc.)," but was uneasy about his unorthodox religious views. Though Lowell was to develop "transcendental" leanings, he did not then, or ever, give himself over to the "new enthusiasm." [16]

If Lowell had doubts about Emerson, he had none about his followers — they were charlatans, pure and simple. Attending a gathering at Emerson's house, Lowell noted that none of the company except himself and the host made any direct assertions; it was all "wouldn't its?" and "isn't its?" — absurd uncertainties to a positive young man. As for Henry Thoreau, being touted by Emerson as "one of the wonders of the age," Lowell found him a mere carbon copy of the master: "It is exquisitely amusing to see how he imitates Emerson's tone & manner. With my eyes shut I shouldn't know them apart." Even in later life Lowell and Thoreau were to have but limited sympathy for each other.[17]

Elected poet of the Class of '38 shortly before his rustication, it was Lowell's job to compose the class poem, and this became his chief occupation during the weeks at Concord. Traditionally the poem, along with the class oration, made up the Class Day Exercises held in the University Chapel on a day preceding formal Commencement. But since Lowell had been suspended until after Class Day, complications developed. It was first suggested that Class Day take place on schedule, someone else reading Lowell's poem for him. "I'll be damned first," retorted Lowell, though spared that contingency when the faculty formally voted against allowing the poem to be read. The senior class then discussed holding Class Day exercises in the Cambridge meeting house, outside faculty jurisdiction, but the class orator had his heart set on the University Chapel for his performance, others were against changing the ritual in order to suit one whom they thought had deserved suspension, and Lowell, in any case, continued to prefer damnation. The impasse was finally resolved by the oration being delivered on schedule and Lowell's poem being printed rather than read, the costs borne by class subscription.[18]

Lowell professed a low opinion of his poem. It had, he thought, no more than "one or two good things in it"; like most youthful egotists, he hoped for double credit — praise both for his talent and for his humility. There were scant grounds for either. The poem lacked unity of theme or tone, shifting back and forth in its lengthy forty-four stanzas from lampoon to lament, from sharp thrusts at "world-philanthropy" to sorrowful apostrophes for a dead classmate. Yet he did show considerable invention, both in metrical forms, which ranged from heroic couplets to octave stanzas (and in most cases shifting in a manner that suited the changing themes), and in his humorous jibes, aimed especially at the reform impulse then gaining momentum in the country. Most of the current "movements" came in for a share of Lowell's scorn:

Whether you prove war's ills by force of fist,
Make your own ends seem public good by mist,
In zeal to spread your temperance pledges wider
Fell apple-trees to stop the use of cider,
Or fill your purse and show your moral bravery
By suffering eggdom in abusing slavery.

He thought it cant for Northern reformers to attack distant ills such as slavery, especially since they did so in a "zealous" spirit, zealous, that is, as defined by his father's classical mean:

"Be temperate in all *things,"* *Scripture saith,*
And there, there only, will I pin my faith

But like his father, too, Lowell had compassion for the unfortunate, and even while poking fun at the reformers, made it clear that he had at least dormant sympathy for some of their causes:

Not mine the heart that would not keenly feel
A fellow's moans 'neath slavery's iron heel,
Nor mine the eye which could unquivering see
Oppression grind the weak that clasp his knee . . .

And he devoted more than a fifth of the poem to a passionate denunciation of American policy toward the Indians, a despoliation never equaled "except by the Saracen disciples of Mahomet." Though Lowell's temper in his Class Poem, therefore, was conservative to the extent that he distrusted innovation and "enthusiasm," it was a conservatism enough qualified by compassion to help explain how it was possible within a few short years for this "temperate" young man to become actively involved in the abolitionist cause.[19]

In the poem, Lowell bracketed transcendentalism with other misguided modernisms, calling its champions "misty rhapsodists" who

> *. . . having made a "universal soul,"*
> *Forget their own in thinking of the whole;*
> *Who, seeking nothing, wander on through space,*
> *Flapping their half-fledged wings in Reason's face . . .*

For Emerson personally, he showed continuing ambivalence (and continued to misrepresent his views):

> *Alas! that* Christian ministers *should dare*
> *To preach the views of Gibbon and Voltaire!*
> *Alas! that one whose life, and gentle ways,*
> *E'en hate could find it in its heart to praise,*
> *Whose intellect is equalled but by few,*
> *Should strive for what he'd weep to find were true!* [20]

When the poem was published, some of Lowell's friends expressed surprise that having enjoyed Emerson's hospitality and having spoken well of him in private, the young poet should have been so ungrateful as to criticize him in public. Thinking to justify himself, Lowell wrote to Emerson directly, adopting the high line that it had all been in the service of Truth — "for I consider it as virtual a lie to hold one's tongue." He asked Emerson only to acquit him of "uncharitableness," not to "forgive" or to "pardon," and just in case Emerson might have missed the offending passages, Lowell obligingly enclosed a printed copy of the poem.[21]

It was an impudent enough performance, but Emerson replied with immense tact. He thanked Lowell for sending the copy, assured him that he could find no word in the poem "which the license of the occasion" did not more than excuse, and berated *himself* for having lost the chance to be of more service to Lowell while he had been at Concord. He hoped Lowell would come and see him should he again pass through Concord ("I am vain eno' to think that nobody knows so many pleasant walks in it as I"), and he enclosed a copy of his Dartmouth Oration in the hope that Lowell would like it better than the Divinity School Address on which his poetic strictures had been based. Emerson's kindness was not misplaced; the brash youth who criticized him rather than "speak untruth" was to discover in the new truth of his maturity that he loved and honored Emerson well.[22]

CHAPTER III

BEGINNINGS

GRADUATION from Harvard brought no immediate new departure for Lowell; rather, it accentuated his unsettlement. He already knew that he would "love to be able to sit down and do something literary for the rest of my natural life," but literature was then a precarious livelihood, and neither "art" nor "unsafety" carried the compensatory prestige which they now do. Thomas Wentworth Higginson later recalled that when Lowell suggested he might make a career out of poetry, there was much shaking of heads among the elders; Cambridge had produced one poet in Oliver Wendell Holmes, but he had sensibly supported his avocation with the full-time profession of medicine. "Our stout Yankee nation," wrote Lowell dejectedly, "would swap all the poems that ever were penned for a treatise on ventilation." [1]

And so Lowell canvassed the more acceptable alternatives. He thought he might enter the ministry, but soon rejected that idea — professedly out of a belief that a minister needed an independent income if he was to devote himself wholeheartedly to his congregation, but doubtless, also, because he felt the church "is dead nowadays, holds Truth's mirror to her lips & no breath is perceptible." Lowell believed, then and always, in the divine governance of the universe, and believed, too, that the church was its necessary symbol. But he had his father's impatience with creeds and, as a youth, his own special impatience with formal ritual.[2]

A career in business was no more satisfying a prospect. For a few months he tried filling in for his brother in the counting room of a coal merchant, but was soon overcome by the drudgery. That seemed to leave, almost by default, the law. With his father's encouragement he had begun reading Blackstone soon after graduation, but had abandoned it in disgust, announcing he would as leave dig potatoes for a livelihood. But after his experience in the counting room, when he was "miserable with indecision" about his future and had begun to doubt if he was fitted for anything in life but loitering, he finally decided, ten months after graduation, to enter Harvard's Dane Law School.[3]

Under the inspired instruction of Judge Joseph Story and Professor Simon Greenleaf, who taught law as a system of philosophy, Lowell managed sporadic fits of interest. But on the whole law school only confirmed his distaste for the subject. "If I say that I can't study law . . . then they tell me 'so have all young men felt!' Fools! that do not see that this is the strongest argument in my favor . . ." Yet grudgingly he persevered, despite strong doubts that he would ever practice, and with "a blind presentiment of becoming independent in some other way." [4]

He did what he could to make the presentiment come true. Throughout this unsettled two-year period, he continued to write poetry, and tried to establish a reputation by publishing in newspapers and literary magazines. His ambition was matched by his self-confidence. Though at one point he wrote that he rated his ability no higher than "talent," the more characteristic self-appraisal was his exuberant promise to a friend that "before I die your heart shall be gladdened by seeing your wayward, vain, and too often selfish friend do something that shall make his name honored. As Sheridan once said, 'It's *in* me, and' (we'll skip the oath) 'it shall come *out!*' " [5]

Much of this was healthy egotism rather than its counterfeit, vanity — the difference between expressing self-confidence and disguising self-doubt. Of course for a twenty-year-old, the liberation of settled self-respect is apt to lapse into the bondage of narcissism. Thus Lowell, despite his strong assumption of self-worth, could waver in confidence and veer off into the most blatant conceit. In reporting that a poem of his had been called "beautiful," he could grandly acknowledge that "so it was," or, in a still higher flight of self-congratulation, could vow not to hide his God-given powers "in mean clay." But like any well-trained Christian gentleman, aware that humility was one of the signal virtues invented by the church, a required credential, Lowell would periodically groan over his own immodesty, and boasting would give way to self-criticism.[6]

In his more realistic moods he recognized that his actual accomplishment was as yet meager and that most of his poems were of limited worth; he often referred to his poetry as "pottery," and of one piece he said, it was "written too fast to be either very bad or very good . . . I trust I shall gradually get over the fault which belongs to all young writers, and which I should describe as having too many *thoughts* and too little *thought*." He had not yet found an individual voice; his poems tended to be passable copies of current lyrical modes (when he submitted several sonnets to the *Dial*, Margaret Fuller commented that they had "the fault of seeming imitated from Tennyson"). But occasionally he would depart from the romantic postures and themes then fashionable, and strike out into satire. It was then that something of his own person, his directness, zest and, increasingly, his moral earnestness would come through:

Shout too for merry England
Ye factory-children thin,
Upon whose little hearts the sun
Hath never once looked in;
For, when your hollow eyes shall close
The poor-house hell to balk,
(Thank God for liberty of speech)
The parliament will talk.

It would take some years before the satirical voice which suited Lowell so well would mature. Its development paralleled, was perhaps attendant upon, the growth of his concern with social ills, for behind the satirist lies the moralist.[7]

Lowell the moralist, the social critic, *was* beginning to emerge. In college he had shown but a muted awareness of public problems and only a limited interest in their resolution; in this regard he was no more tardy than many others (such as Wendell Phillips or Edmund Quincy) who later became prominent in reform movements. But soon after graduation, Lowell's sympathies began to quicken. Only a few months after decrying the zeal of reformers in his Class Poem, he announced that he was "fast becoming ultra democratic." He gave thought to writing a dramatic piece on Cromwell in order to contrast "those old fiery-eyed, buff-belted warriors, with their deep, holy enthusiasm for liberty and democracy, political and religious" against the "ranting Cavaliers . . . deaf to the cries of the poor and the oppressed . . ." The "enthusiasm" mocked by Lowell the college boy was taking on for him a new, positive connotation. For one of his secure background, developing social conscience can perhaps best be seen as a natural product of increasing maturity, of leaving behind the childish world of self-absorption. But no development is so "natural" that it cannot be arrested or encouraged by outside circumstances; no doubt many a man's fellow-feeling is stunted by personal disappointments which channel his energies into self-pity; no doubt others are helped towards social awareness by an incident which precipitates or a person who encourages the uncertain tendency at a critical juncture. In Lowell's case, his growing interest in social protest has often been attributed to the timely influence of Maria White, though she is more accurately seen as the abettor rather than the originator of his sympathies.[8]

Lowell first met Maria White late in 1839 while visiting her brother, a Harvard classmate; "a very pleasant and pleasing young lady," he insouciantly reported, who "knows more poetry than any one I am acquainted with. I mean, she is able to repeat more." Lowell had probably heard that Maria White was one of those "blue-stockings" who had been meeting with Margaret Fuller to discuss the "questions of the day," the "newness." In any case, after only a few months' acquaintance, Lowell became deeply attached; Maria White was now a creature "pure and spiritlike . . . half of earth and *more* than half of Heaven." His friends predicted that he would fall in love, but still bruised from a wrecked romance of the preceding year he held back ("I should have seen her three years ago," he lamented). Yet the attachment continued to deepen. By the summer of 1840, he paid attention to neither the poem nor the oration at Harvard's Commencement Exercises, for he happened to sit next to Maria and "thought her worth both"; a few weeks later they spent a "glorious" evening alone on the rocks at Nantasket beach; by late summer he dreamt that he saw her walking, strove to overtake her, only to have her vanish and to be told that she had gone down "the happy road"; did this mean, Lowell wondered (with pathetic prescience), "that I shall love M.W. and that she will die?" [9]

By the fall of 1840 they were certain of their love; in a nice bit of romantic rhetoric, Lowell fixed their reading of Wordsworth together as the moment of truth — "the passages that we loved interpreted & interceded between heart & heart." Lowell now looked back on his earlier affair as "no *true* love" — it had not been "built for Eternity." With Maria he felt "the perfect joy of loving & being loved." She was a woman "such as only flowers once in a century." [10]

With less necessity but with equal conviction, most contemporaries agreed that Maria White was a woman of extraordinary presence. "She is truly an angelic creature," thought Edmund Quincy; "the holiest among women," agreed a female friend — descriptions perhaps cloying to modern tastes, but the adjectives of highest compliment a hundred years ago. For women then were not only thought to be different from men, but different in the sense of being made of "finer stuff." Their "spiritual" natures, it was thought, though unequal to the demands of public affairs, made them the depositories and guardians of all that was "sensitive," "pure," "holy." For contemporaries to refer to Maria White as "spiritual," as they did again and again, was therefore tantamount to saying that she embodied all that was best in womanhood.[11]

Her physical appearance seemed a guarantee of other-worldly qualities. Fragile, reserved, delicately beautiful, with astonishingly large, soulful eyes, she suggested an almost incorporeal presence. That she had been educated in a convent and wrote poetry, that her fragile physical appearance gave some hint of tuberculosis, completed the spectral vision. But when friends referred to her "transcendental" quality, Lowell was quick to deny any imputation that she might be unfitted for the "duties of life." She had more common sense, he insisted, than any woman he had ever known. This was not mere defensive pride; Maria White's gentle appearance did in some ways belie her strength of character. As Lowell put it:

> *Not from her weakness hath her mildness grown,*
> *But from a deep, unsounded strength of will,*
> *And a strange earnestness her soul doth fill . . .*

Behind the delicate cameo there was a woman of considerable self-confidence and authority. Lowell continually emphasized her "stedfastness,"

> *. . . a firmness that defies*
> *All shallow tricks of circumstance and time . . .*
> *And where it clingeth never withering . . .*

If she combined the same surface fragility and underlying strength as Lowell's mother, probably the greater attraction still for him was that Maria's consistency was in welcome contrast to Harriet Lowell's capriciousness. Here was a woman, at last, "telling of rest and peaceful heavens . . . a home serene . . ." [12]

Maria White strictly adhered to the prescribed standards of female modesty and never expressed her strength in any overtly assertive or domineering way. In this, as in other respects, she conformed to the norms of the day. Just as her poetic appearance belied her vigor, so it also belied her conventionality. Somewhat undemonstrative, she could be retiring and inhibited, putting a quiet distance between herself and others which did not preclude warmth and intimacy, but which did announce that they must develop slowly.[13]

She and Lowell had much in common. Both shared literary and intellectual interests, both had decided social charm (though hers was more muted by inner reserve), and both believed in "standards" of conduct and character. She was less versatile than he, more disciplined; her "anchored spirit," as Lowell termed it, helped to steady, though also to confine, his more expansive, impulsive nature. As a man who believed "there was enough of woman in his heart to make it capable of true manhood," Lowell was nicely complemented by a woman whose stability and decisiveness, however gently expressed, could be relied upon to take up the "masculine" slack. The balance created by their shared assumptions and complementary strengths might have been what Edmund Quincy meant when he referred to their union as "the very picture of a True Marriage." [14]

They became formally engaged in the autumn of 1840. Maria's father, Abijah White, a leading citizen of Watertown who had accumulated wealth through the cattle trade with the West Indies, opposed an early marriage. That Lowell was not self-supporting was part of the objection, but his "wild" reputation while in college probably contributed further to Mr. White's caution. With consent withheld "until Pegasus should have learned to work in harness," Lowell set about to earn the reputation for steadiness (and to gather the income) which would make an early marriage possible. It was to be four years before the wedding would take place.[15]

During that time Lowell tried to continue his joint career as lawyer and poet. He received the bachelor of laws degree in August, 1840, after only a year of study. This was not uncommon and, as was also usual, Lowell continued to hear lectures at the school during a second year while "reading" in the law office of Charles Greely Loring. As Loring's firm was in Boston, Lowell took a room in Court Street rather than commute daily from "Elmwood," the family home in Cambridge.

In 1842 Lowell was admitted to the bar and opened his own office, announcing, on an engraved card, that he would "perform faithfully any business which may be committed to his care." Very little was. But he preferred to see the humorous side of these "waiting days," and out of his first experiences with the legal life fashioned a fictionalized account full of mock advice to young lawyers. To attract business, he warned them, they had to be sure that their offices showed no sign of comfort or taste, "both of which are generally esteemed incompatible with extensive legal attainments." Should a client appear, they should at once busy themselves with work and refuse to acknowledge his presence, for "men are ever most ready to put their affairs into the hands of those who have too much to do to attend to them faithfully." Even such precautions, Lowell admitted, could not guarantee customers. In his own case, he claimed, the only client to turn up for weeks was a friend who came disguised as a farmer enquiring "if this were Mr. Mortmain's office." And when one day what seemed a genuine "client-like shadow" did appear against his glass door (and his cottage in the country "drew ten years nearer in as many seconds"), the client turned out to be a creditor come to collect on his bill of $11 for painting and lettering the office.[16]

In truth matters were not quite so desperate for Lowell. An occasional client did come, including a Negro sailor cheated out of wages by his captain (Lowell managed to get him his pay but would not take a fee; years later the sailor turned up at Lowell's home in Cambridge and begged him to accept a piece of carved ivory, some gold dust, and a little canoe; "Of course," so Lowell told it, "I couldn't take the gold dust, but I did let him give me the canoe and the ivory"). Lowell even had periodic bursts of enthusiasm for the legal life, but most of his time and energy went into his writing, both because that remained his chief interest and because it soon became clear that he would never be able to support a wife solely on his earnings as a lawyer. Whether he would be able to do so from his pen remained to be seen.[17]

He had managed to place poems in periodicals as early as 1839, but getting paid for them was something else again. His first major outlet, the *Southern Literary Messenger*, a distinguished journal of the day, once sent him five dollars for a contribution, but thereafter held off Lowell's importunities by promising cash "just as soon" as circulation hit three thousand — a nirvana for both parties. The editors hastened to add that they thought his poetry the equal of Bryant's, and that they would welcome a visit at the *Messenger*'s office at Richmond. Though the kind words pleased Lowell, they did not placate him; writing for nothing, he commented, was a bad habit for a poor man to get into.[18]

He realized that one way of opening new outlets — and income — would be to collect his poetry into a volume; if the book was well-received, his future poems would be in demand. Lowell hesitated, but since Maria urged him to it and since her opinion counted, he decided to take the risk. The slim volume published by "C. C. Little and J. Brown" appeared in January, 1841, under the title *A Year's Life*. It was dedicated, with a suggestion of dependency more than figurative, to "gentle Una," she who had led him like "a wondering child" for "her dear sake to fight." Some of the poems in the volume had already appeared in print; few would ever appear again. In later life Lowell found some amusement in "what an inconceivable ass" he had been, but at the time, of course, full of intimations of glory (amply abetted by an adoring fiancée), he thought the volume very good indeed.[19]

And given the reviews, it is hardly any wonder. Two critics cut him up rather badly, but the others were so full of praise, much of it extravagant, that Lowell was able to dismiss the dissenters as men either angered by his liberal views or jealously anxious to put down "a young candidate for the laurels." No less a critic than Orestes Brownson, that pugnacious and independent commentator, predicted that Lowell would become one of the great poets; Margaret Fuller, though far more qualified in her enthusiasm, found "an uncommon felicity of expression" in the poems; Elizabeth Barrett, to whom Lowell sent a copy, wrote him that she found "a natural bloom upon the poems, a one-heartedness with nature, which it is very pleasant to me to recognize"; and Charles J. Peterson in *Graham's Magazine* surrendered all restraint by announcing that in Lowell the country at last had a man capable of writing the great American poem, a work "that shall silence the sneers of foreigners, and write his own name among the stars of heaven." [20]

With such heady praise, even a less cocky young man would have been thrown a little off balance. Lowell complained with mock fatigue that the critics complimented him "ad nauseum," then added in the same breath that there was more in his book than any of them had perceived. But he did retain some perspective. He knew that a few reviews, like those by W. W. Story and C. S. Wheeler, classmates at Harvard, were unthoughtful puffs, tributes to friendship rather than poetry. Besides, Lowell could not ignore the fact that even some of the more favorable reviewers had criticisms to level: they questioned his technical irregularities, his metaphorical extravagance ("an ocean vast of bisons the fair prairie shaking"), his penchant for the didactic and obscure, his occasionally theatrical postures ("My veins are fired with ecstasy!"). Then too, some of the praise had been for content rather than form. Evert Duyckinck, the influential New

York critic, had complimented Lowell more for his "elevated" sentiments than for his poetical gifts. On this point even the hostile critics agreed — Lowell's morality was acclaimed impeccable: he loved nature, truth, humanity and beauty, venerated womanhood and the redeeming power of pure love, believed in God, the soul's immortality and the need to strive for "ideality." As a catalogue of proper nineteenth-century pieties, Lowell's themes were bound to be applauded, but he realized there would have been more cause for gratitude had the critics been as unanimous in praising his talents as his "high thinking." [21]

Yet for a first volume of poetry, all of it written before the age of twenty-two, the reception had been remarkably favorable. Any disappointment Lowell felt was not due to critical reaction but to scanty sales. He had hoped the book might lead to financial independence, and thus to marriage. Following publication, new offers did come from the periodicals — he was especially pleased to be asked to write for one of the "annuals" at the excellent rate of five dollars per page. But the book itself moved slowly; several months after publication only three hundred copies had been sold. Lowell's father offered to pay all expenses towards a second edition should the first become exhausted, but paternal devotion had no such chance to manifest itself.

Yet Lowell was far from discouraged. Though he kept nominally to the law, he increasingly despised it, eager to devote all his energies to writing. He was full of literary projects: he planned an American Tragedy on the trial of Anne Hutchinson, thought of doing a piece on owls, a pamphlet on slavery, an essay on "the philosophical causes of the fact that *Italians* always suffer in convulsions of nature." He had more ideas than time to realize them, though he wrote continuously, buoyed by the new offers and outlets which the critical success of his volume now brought. Some of the best literary journals, including the *Dial*, *Arcturus*, *Graham's* and the *Democratic Review*, began to publish him, though even as they accepted his poetry their editors warned him against writing too rapidly and publishing too much. His fluency, they suggested, might seduce him into pouring out the kind of fugitive verse which already crowded the magazines, and could keep him from the "finer fruits" of which they were sure he was capable.[22]

It was not advice which a young author tasting the first rewards of recognition, and eager for more, was likely to heed. "I try to write carefully and slowly," Lowell confessed, "but I cannot do it . . . I am too young yet . . . My thought always runs far before my pen." Besides, Lowell thought rather well of his productions, rapid-fire though they were; since he tended to think his most recent sonnet always his best to date, it was logical to keep writing new ones. He talked grandly of his "increased power" and of the "mission" he had been entrusted with. This was intoxication, but not wholly self-induced. The very editors who cautioned him against writing too much at the same time tempted him, with praise and money, to write still more. Cornelius Mathews of *Arcturus* told Lowell that his poem, "Rosaline," was "noble," the clear foreshadowing of a great poet, and Charles J. Peterson of *Graham's* reported to Lowell the favorable reaction to the same poem of no less a judge than Edgar Allan Poe. Though Poe deplored Lowell's occasional "ruggedness," he declared that no American poem equaled "Rosaline" in the "higher elements of song." Mixed praise from the exacting Poe was known to be the equivalent of wild cheering from any other quarter.[23]

Still greater adulation came from nearer home. A series of prose articles by Lowell on the "old dramatists," Ford, Webster, Chapman and Massinger, published in 1842 in his friend Nathan Hale, Jr.'s, serious and short-lived new periodical, the *Boston Miscellany*, gained him "an astounding deal of applause and congratulation." And when two sonnets that Lowell had sent to the *Dial* were not immediately accepted, and the poet hinted to Emerson that Hale was interested in them for the *Miscellany*, Emerson wrote at once to say that Hale should not hold out hope of inheriting either sonnet through default: the *Dial* most definitely, and gratefully, wanted them.[24]

If Lowell's fellow authors were becoming respectful, his personal friends were becoming idolatrous. He and Maria were the petted demi-gods of a small circle of talented, high-spirited and earnest young aristocrats, known as "The Brother and Sister Club" (because so many were actually related, and all came to feel "spiritually" so). There was no fixed list of members, just as there were no formal rules, meeting times or rituals, but those who gathered most often included William Wetmore Story, the future sculptor, poet and playwright (now most celebrated as the subject of a two-volume biography by Henry James), and his sister, Mary, who married George Ticknor Curtis, the lawyer and writer; John King and his two sisters, Augusta and Caroline; Maria White and her brother, William Abijah White; Emelyn Eldridge, who later married Story; Maria Fay, cousin to both the Whites and Kings; John Francis and Jane Tuckerman from Salem; and Nathan Hale, Jr., and his beautiful sister, Sarah. The young men in the group generally referred to it as the "club"; the young women, more prone to the binding metaphor, preferred to call it the "Band." "Jaimie" Lowell and Maria White were known affectionately as its King and Queen, a tribute not only to his talent and her beauty, but no doubt also, in that sentimental age, to the fact that they were true lovers who (appropriately) had been thwarted in their union. Indeed their love affair seems to have been something like common property; James' letters to Maria were passed around among the intimates and duly pronounced perfect specimens of their kind — not "silly," but showing all the fervor and "extatification" one would expect from "the most ardent lover."[25]

Being ardent in those days did not mean being overtly sexual. A certain kind and a certain amount of sensuality were thought necessary, the kind which would enrich the soul with "all the delicious impulses which flow to it from without," and an amount sufficient to keep our "animal nature . . . fresh & in-corrupt." But mere "voluptuousness" was to be resisted; the soul must be kept a "fit palace & bridal chamber for God & love to dwell in," receiving only those impulses which were "the pure gifts of a sister's love, or the sweet, retired dalliance of a wife's chaste embraces & not as the gages of a harlot's constant inconstancy." [26]

Changes of style in language can conceal continuing affinities of thought; the transcendental vocabulary with which Lowell's generation described its attitude toward sex, so jarring today in what we like to call its vacuous sentimentality, in fact conveys a bias not uncongenial to the modern view — that lust and promiscuity can prevent more satisfying contact both with ourselves and with others. The Victorians could be foolishly fastidious about sex, and even hypocritical, but they were not mere prudes. By resisting easy promiscuity and immediate gratification in the name of some deeper, more lasting intimacy, the Brothers and Sisters were, after all, acting in what the modern psychiatrist might call a commendably mature manner.

Just as we too easily dismiss the Victorians as prigs, so we too easily assume that they were unrelievedly earnest in their conduct. When the Brothers and Sisters gathered at the home of one of their number, sometimes for as long as a week (for they came from various towns), hilarity and nonsense were more the rule than the exception. There were dancing, cards, sleigh rides, charades, theatricals, singing and a good deal of plain buffoonery, as when Story and Hale went through the pantomime of having just escaped from the Worcester Hospital for the Insane. And Lowell often led the fun. He would extemporize stories about "Mitchell Bonyrotty Angylo," would appear suddenly in a room, face wan and grave, ostentatiously carrying a copy of Burton's *Anatomy of Melancholy*, or would compose and execute an opera "entirely unassisted and, *à la* Beethoven, on a piano without any strings, to wit: the centre-table." One of the Sisters, momentarily forgetting the Band's indissoluble loyalties, once tartly commented that Lowell was weary in any circle where he was not the central figure. But Maria, at least, rejoiced that James' nature was "so exulting, so full of a boy's freedom — that such effluence of life should bless me through one so beloved is a source of daily gratitude." [27]

High spirits were interspersed with quiet talks on the stairs, poetry readings and intense discussions on "questions of the day." Although Lowell's generation was less solemn and staid than is often thought, it did believe in the necessity for "serious living." Gaiety had its place, but the Brothers and Sisters believed in balancing it with "high purpose"; as Maria White put it, "It is not enough to lead sweet lives." [28]

Life was sweet nonetheless. Lowell was finding favor as a poet, was supremely happy in his love for Maria, and was surrounded by a congenial, admiring group of friends. All that was lacking was literary employment profitable enough to allow him to abandon the law and to marry. By the fall of 1842, Lowell thought he saw a way to remove this last impediment, and, in the bargain, to strike a blow for "literature." What he planned was nothing less than to launch The Great American Magazine. At first Maria tried to brake his enthusiasm; she feared an immense circulation would be necessary to make the magazine profitable, and should it not be, she worried lest James' faith in himself or, worse, in his fellow men, should be shaken. Yet she was soon caught by his enthusiasm, and even began to spin a rural fantasy of her own, predicated on the journal's success: with a thousand a year in income from the magazine, they would marry and live with "simple cheer" in the country, with James henceforth having nought to do but "feed his mind with beauty and offer the fruits of his cultivation to all." [29]

Fantasy aside, the current state of periodicals dictated the need, even if not success, for a serious literary journal. It was the *Godey's Lady's Book* era, when colored fashion plates, sheet music, and sentimental fiction flooded the monthlies. The few journals that tried to encourage writers of ability survived at best on a marginal basis. For a time it seemed that Lowell's friend, Nathan Hale, Jr., might manage to make both an artistic and commercial success out of the *Boston Miscellany*, which he had started in 1842. But before long, in a vain effort to hold on, Hale made the usual concessions to popular taste with fashion plates and "factory girl fiction," and although he continued to print material of real distinction, Lowell, for one, had few regrets when the *Miscellany* ceased publication after a few issues.[30]

Lowell was determined that his magazine would proceed and fare differently; he would succeed by boldly challenging dominant taste rather than pandering to it. To avoid the usual business errors of the amateur, he took as a partner Robert Carter, a young man of his own age and sympathies, who had come to Cambridge from Albany only two years before. Carter had worked in a printing office and his experience there, Lowell believed, would save them from those useless expenditures which had often led amateur editors to their doom. That Carter was a kind, learned man, devoted to Lowell, was beyond question; Maria White believed his only object in joining the project was "James' advancement in life, and he will undoubtedly give nearly all the profits to him, as he intends still to retain his place in the Daily Mail office which is quite lucrative and has another editorship to support himself by." But that Carter had the necessary practical competence was less certain — in later life he set out to write a twelve-volume history of the world as told "by a heavenly spirit to a man wandering among the Mountains of the Moon in Africa." [31]

Lowell and Carter issued a prospectus which had all the ring of a manifesto:

> The object . . . is to furnish the intelligent and reflecting portion of the Reading Public with a rational substitute for the enormous quantity of thrice-diluted trash, in the shape of namby-pamby love tales and sketches, which is monthly poured

> out to them by many of our popular Magazines — and to offer, instead thereof, a healthy and manly Periodical Literature, whose perusal will not necessarily involve a loss of time and deterioration of every moral and intellectual faculty.

They dubbed the new periodical *The Pioneer*, reflecting the ardor with which they intended to battle for the new. Lowell informed potential contributors that theirs was to be a "*free*" magazine; it would regard "things and not *names*"; its authors would have *carte blanche* as to what they said instead of being "cut down to the editor's measure"; it would notice "every branch (or twig) of Art" and would comment, too, "on all the great movements of the age"; it would, in short, "keep up with the age & not behind it — nay, if possible it shall run before; as its name would indicate." [32]

Lowell and Carter worked hard to make good these promises. They solicited contributions from the best talent available; Longfellow and Whittier were asked for poems, Hawthorne for stories, John S. Dwight for musical criticism, and Emerson for "anything." The call went out to Europe, too; Elizabeth Barrett was asked not only to send some of her own poems (which she did), but also to solicit something from Tennyson ("alas, alas . . . Mr. Tennyson isn't of my acquaintance — I do not, so 'side the gods!"). To one friend studying abroad, Lowell sent a plea for monthly literary intelligence; to another, in Germany, a request for an account of Schelling's inaugural lecture. And to all went the same message: he, Lowell, intended to have the best magazine in the land, and what was more, to pay his contributors higher fees than did any other periodical — once the venture took hold. His enthusiasm was infectious. Almost everyone responded with something, and Edgar Allan Poe was so interested in the advance reports he heard that he volunteered to become a regular contributor even before Lowell could approach him; he sent, for the first issue, "The Tell-Tale Heart," and subsequently "Lenore" and "Notes on English Verse." [33]

The Pioneer's first number appeared in January, 1843. Along with Poe's tale, it carried contributions by such notables as Jones Very, Elizabeth Barrett, John O'Sullivan and John S. Dwight, as well as by others, such as T. W. Parsons, W. H. Burleigh and John Neal, who were then famous but are now scarcely remembered. Unlike most periodicals of the time, which borrowed half their contents from elsewhere, without pay or permission, Lowell had sought new material and paid for it. "For the present" he could offer only ten dollars per contribution, but aside from exceptional cases like Longfellow, who was paid fifty dollars by *Graham's* for a short poem, *The Pioneer*'s rate was competitive.[34]

Lowell made good the promises of the prospectus in other ways as well. Rather than avoiding controversial issues, as did all but a few reform journals like *The Liberator* (with their miniscule subscription lists), Lowell plunged directly into disputation. He invited contributions from such "inflammatories" as Whittier and Neal; he praised (in a review of Longfellow's *Poems on Slavery*) antislavery pioneers like Garrison and Lydia Maria Child; he called for a *natural* rather than a *national* literature, deploring any provincialism, whether of country, caste or race, which would "put farther off the hope of one great brotherhood," and as if to reinforce this position, wrote a cogent defense of Dickens' severe verdict on the United States in his *American Notes*. The magazine's literary criticism — a good deal of it written anonymously by Lowell himself — was generally of a much higher order than found elsewhere; eschewing the genial puffs which usually passed for reviews, *The Pioneer* dealt in outspoken if not always well-considered opinion. And in a further departure from current practice, the magazine carried criticism of painting and music as well. The first issue was as distinguished for what it omitted as for what it included; there were no colored plates designed to make every woman her own milliner, nor cloying prose to help her cry away the non-millinery interludes. *The Pioneer*, as promised, was a serious journal of literature and opinion, avoiding the vulgar, the mawkish, the sentimental, the safe.

Despite a few dissents, notably by N. P. Willis ("a man of genius [JRL] . . . is a very unfit editor for a periodical"), it was widely agreed that *The Pioneer*'s debut had been auspicious. Poe sent his "delighted" congratulations, Elizabeth Peabody expressed great enthusiasm, and a loyal member of the Band reported, with pardonable partisanship, that "everybody" approved, that there was "only one prophecy & that, success." [35]

But the first cloud appeared before the hosannas had even died away. Lowell, possibly from overwork, came down with a serious eye disease, and had to leave at once for New York City to be treated by the famous oculist, Dr. Samuel Mackenzie Elliot. It was essential that *The Pioneer* come out on a regular basis, for in their contract with the publishers, Lowell and Carter had agreed to a $500 penalty should they be late in presenting copy. And so Lowell was forced to try, by mail, to handle the many editorial chores and petty emergencies which arose during his extended stay in New York, though pain from treatment made writing difficult, and though the doctor warned him that if he persisted, he would prolong his illness and even jeopardize his eyesight. As time wore on, Lowell became increasingly uncertain about Carter's judgment. His sister warned him that Carter was too good-natured to turn down unworthy contributions; she had heard it rumored that a "vision" by Elizabeth Peabody was to be the lead article in some future number, and she feared the vision would "be something very *transcendent* indeed." [36]

The second issue, which appeared while Lowell was still in New York, corroborated his sister's warning. The issue was full of misprints (including one in his own sonnet) and the contents was less distinguished than that of the first number, though it included Hawthorne's "The Hall of Fantasy" and Poe's "Lenore." Lowell angrily called Carter's attention to a poem by T. B. Read which simply would "not do," and to another, by

W. W. Story, which seemed suspiciously reminiscent of one from Lowell's own volume. He also disliked some of the literary notices in the new issue; the unity of tone he had hoped to preserve by excluding conservative reviewers had not been sustained. But, above all, Lowell was disturbed that Carter had printed on the cover excerpts from the favorable critical notices which had greeted the first number. Some of them were personal puffs of Lowell himself, which was bad enough, but worse still was the excerpt from Poe's review, praising all the literary notices in the first issue except the one (written by Lowell!) which had said kind words about *Puffer Hopkins*, the latest novel by the New York writer Cornelius Mathews (Poe's comment: "one of the most trashy novels that ever emanated from an American press"). As Lowell feared, the thin-skinned Mathews let it be known that he was deeply offended at the editors' reprinting Poe's remarks. Personal warfare amongst the New York literati was legendary, almost a staple of life, but Lowell did not enjoy such skirmishes. Mathews fell into a protracted sulk, and ill-feeling between the two men, alternately exasperating and boring to Lowell, was to drag on for years.[37]

Lowell tried to be philosophical about his prolonged entrapment in New York — "poets always are or should be . . . a little beyond the present" — but even aside from the combined anxiety caused by his eyes, by his absence from the magazine and by New York literary sensitivities, he simply did not like the city. There was nothing in it "to match the New England character, or to compare in general enlightenment." The omnipresent "vice & wretchedness" especially appalled him; unlike Boston, where those few in want could count on "the pitying eye & helping hand of some one of the religious or charitable societies," New York's "aristocratic charity" was afraid to soil "the purity of her white raiment." Though there was justice in Lowell's observations, he could be maddeningly parochial, as when he asked Evert Duyckinck (perhaps with calculated innocence), if New Jersey was still a slave state. The next question, mused the astonished Duyckinck, will be whether New Jersey is not a dependency of the Burmese Empire.[38]

The bright spot of Lowell's months in New York was the chance it gave him to enlarge his acquaintance with literary men. The inactivity imposed by his illness left a good deal of time for socializing. Most of his contacts were with the group known as "Young America," those who advocated a new national literature to express that new phenomenon, the American, and who in politics voted with the "locofoco" or radical wing of the Democratic party. The leaders of Young America were Duyckinck, Mathews, William A. Jones, Parke Godwin and John L. O'Sullivan; their chief literary organ was *Arcturus*, until its demise in 1842, and then O'Sullivan's *Democratic Review.*

Duyckinck unhesitatingly welcomed Lowell as "one of the Young Americans," and Lowell did share many, though not all, of their assumptions and goals. Like them, he believed in encouraging a new American literature (much of his own early work, after all, had been first published and praised by Young America), but unlike them he agreed with Longfellow and other literary "conservatives" that "whoever is most universal, is also most national." Like Young America, too, Lowell believed in the necessity of social involvement and reform, though he preferred a radicalism with some roots in tradition:

Safe to its breast the new moon clasps the old
And round it lovingly its arms doth fold,
Forever turning fuller to the sun
Until increase of light hath made them one.[39]

He was perhaps closest to Young America in regarding literature as action. Writers had a redemptive as well as aesthetic function; the poet especially was seer and prophet, for he had special insights into our "moral nature" and a special mission to communicate them. "I believe that no poet in this age," Lowell declared, "can write much that is good unless he gives himself up to this (radical) tendency . . . The proof of poetry is, in my mind, that it reduce to the essence of a single line the vague philosophy which is floating in all men's minds, and so render it portable and useful, and ready to the hand . . . At least, no poem ever makes me respect its author which does not in some way convey a truth of philosophy." Words like "seer" and "prophet" have taken on different values since Lowell's day, now bearing a connotation close to quackery, evoking either amusement or impatience. But the sensibilities of "Young America" are less outmoded than its vocabulary (though in pursuing points of contact there is danger of canceling out real aesthetic differences). When Lowell spoke of the "social" function of poetry, he *seems* to have meant more than that the poet revealed something of the divine intention — though he meant that too. In remarking further that "what a true poet says always *proves itself* to our minds," he also implies — and here is where he is closest to modern sensibilities — that the poet's metaphorical ordering of experience can create a vision of reality so powerful as ever after to affect the way in which we view ourselves. It was what Leonard Woolf meant in *Sowing* when he described undergraduate life before World War I as something out of Henry James' novels; that is, James' view of the importance of the intense moment between individuals shaped the way in which a whole generation sought to express its relationships. In thus manipulating not only his own experience, but that of the future, the writer does in a sense deal in prophecy.[40]

Lowell approved less of the Young Americans themselves than of their ideology. He had some real affection for Duyckinck, and thought W. A. Jones "most amiable," but he cared little for the others. His two best friends in New York were not closely identified with the Young America movement, though like Lowell, they did share some of its assumptions. One of them, William Page, the painter, Lowell had known earlier; the other, Charles F. Briggs, editor and novelist, he met for the first time during this New York trip. Page had a strongly individual personality, a compound of egotism, originality and tenderness: "his creed . . . is his own, worked out by himself for himself, not built upon other men's facts, not deduced from other men's arguments." He and Lowell shared the belief that the artist expressed through his work the Divine Intention, and they regarded their missions in life with high-minded seriousness. Where Page appealed to Lowell's idealistic, romantic side, Briggs complemented his skeptical, ironic one. Brusque in manner, sometimes biting in speech, Briggs' sardonic stance protected a sensitive nature as well as expressing an insistent honesty. As Lowell was to write of him in the *Fable for Critics*:

> *. . . as he draws near,*
> *You find that's a smile which you took for a sneer;*
> *One half of him contradicts t'other; his wont*
> *Is to say very sharp things and do very blunt,*
> *His manners as hard as his feelings are tender . . .*

The three men delighted in each other's company; they were all passionately alive, had the egotism appropriate to "comers," loved to talk and often did so brilliantly, shared an interest in social questions, and attempted in their personal styles to be candid, individual, honest. Despite long separations and occasional misunderstandings, they were to remain devoted friends.[41]

Though pleasure in the company of Page and Briggs made New York tolerable, Lowell rejoiced when after two months he was finally discharged from treatment. But he returned to Cambridge only to discover that disaster had befallen *The Pioneer*. Having no backlog of capital, Lowell had relied on payments from the publishers to keep him even with his creditors until the magazine should become firmly established. But the very first note the publishers gave Lowell was protested for nonpayment. They had, in fact, gone bankrupt, and their default (*not*, Lowell insisted, the lack of subscribers) meant the demise after three issues of *The Pioneer*. Suspension of publication was crushing enough, but Lowell had also been "swindled" (so he put it) out of receipts from sales and left with bills of every description from papermakers, printers, engravers and binders. He was not legally bound to pay these bills, but felt himself bound by honor, and since Carter would have turned over most of the profits to him, Lowell felt an obligation to assume the bulk of the losses — which probably totaled about $750. For a time, the strain was severe; there were at least nine court actions regarding *The Pioneer*, and the sheriff attached Lowell's office furniture for five days until his brother, Charles, and his father loaned him enough money to meet immediate obligations and endorsed promissory notes for the rest. Dr. Lowell bore this "like a hero," for any inroads on a salary as small as his meant considerable retrenchment. Eventually James Russell paid off every cent of the debt through his own meager earnings, though it took him several years.[42]

Such comfort as Lowell could find in the collapse of the magazine came from the general commiseration. "A most severe blow to the good cause — the cause of a Pure Taste," wrote Poe, and Story, echoing, as he put it, the view of "the cultivated public," eulogized *The Pioneer*'s buried hopes: "it really took some stand & appealed to a higher intellectual Standard than our puerile milk o watery namby-pamby Mags with which we are overrun." But good opinions, pleasant though they were, could not help to bring about his marriage, and Lowell remained an anxious lover.[43]

Yet his resilience was such that instead of retreating to safer ground, he promptly moved out into more dangerous territory still: henceforward, he announced, he intended to devote himself wholly to literature. His experience with *The Pioneer* had given him more not less assurance; he had won the plaudits of those who mattered most, and could tell himself that had he not been defeated by a series of unpredictable afflictions and betrayals, the magazine would have been both an artistic and commercial triumph. Sanguine, self-confident, Lowell decided the right moment had come to abandon the law completely. It was a decision of considerable courage in a day when neither Bryant nor Longfellow, far more established and more highly paid than he, had managed to live by their poetry alone. Nathan Hale, hearing of the decision, advised Lowell to leave up his office signs, erasing only the last three letters, thus stating: "J. R. Lowell's Off . . ." He was indeed.[44]

Along with his office, Lowell gave up his room in Boston and moved back to his family's house, Elmwood. This not only allowed him to cut expenses, but put him closer by four miles to Maria's home in Watertown, which meant that he could see her every other day at least. Being at Elmwood meant, too, that he could again be part of the outdoors he loved so well. He went for long walks, gardened, and took special pride in raising a flock of chickens, which as strutters and crowers were the flower of the neighborhood, but as layers gave only promise. Lowell saw no analogue therein with recent events until his father pointed the paradigm by calculating that his son's experiment with poultry was costing approximately one shilling per egg. Except to shave off his prophet's beard and trim his long hair, Lowell gave no sign of penitence.[45]

He had never been happier, though the pressure of his debts remained, and though he claimed "constitutional indolence" kept him from writing as much as he wished. But he was indolent only by a New Englander's definition. In fact he wrote so steadily that within a few months he had accumulated enough poems for a new volume. It appeared in December, 1843, dedicated to William Page: "The sympathy of sister pursuits, of an agreeing artistic faith, and, yet more, of a common hope for the final destiny of man, has not been wanting to us, and now you will forgive the pride in having this advantage over you, namely, of telling that admiration in public which I have never stinted to utter in private." [46]

The new collection showed some advance over the earlier one, which Lowell himself now defined as made up "of rather crude productions in which there is more of everybody else than of myself" — an admission no less useful in announcing his progress as a poet than in establishing his objectivity as a man. But his poetry was still imitative. As Duyckinck put it, Lowell's "words are fine but they are Shakespeares and Miltons and Keats," a judgment which falls short only in that it fails to include Wordsworth and Tennyson. Still, in both form and content, the new work was more varied than that of *A Year's Life.* There were several long narrative poems, ranging from blank verse to *ottava rima,* which, if nothing else, convinced Lowell that he was unfit to write narrative — though Poe soothingly assured him that it was not he who was unfit for the task, but the task for him, indeed for any poet, for "the connecting links of a narration . . . are necessarily prose, from their very explanatory nature." [47]

Though most themes in the new collection were familiar, there was far greater stress than earlier on "activism." Lowell himself characterized the volume as "the poetry of progress, & of the present, not of the past":

> *The hope of Truth grows stronger, day by day;*
> *I hear the soul of Man around me waking,*
> *Like a great sea, its frozen fetters breaking,*
> *And flinging up to heaven its sunlit spray . . .*

The poet's role in this "onward" movement, as Lowell had insisted earlier, was to tell "the age what all its signs have meant," to concern himself with mankind everywhere:

> *Where'er a single slave doth pine,*
> *Where'er one man may help another . . .*
> *There is the true man's birthplace grand,*
> *His is a world-wide fatherland!*

Lowell had no doubt that in the struggle for a better world, good would ultimately triumph. The tone throughout the volume was one of relentless optimism: God was "open-eyed and just, the happy centre and calm heart of all"; man need but become aware of His benevolent purposes in order to establish their dominion.[48]

Some of Lowell's friends worried over his attempt to merge the poet and the philanthropist; the result, thought Duyckinck, was that the poet deferred, Lowell became "one-sided, a preacher in verse and declamatory." (Twenty years later Lowell wrote, "I shall never be a poet till I get out of the pulpit, and New England was all meeting-house when I was growing up.") But congratulations far outweighed criticism. Fanny Longfellow, the poet's wife, found the new volume "full of a pure and Christian spirit," N. P. Willis praised its "vigor, manliness & enthusiasm," and Page wrote from New York that after reading the first few lines of "Prometheus," he had said to himself: "now he has done it." But perhaps the supreme compliment came from young Bayard Taylor, who tremblingly sent Lowell "the first breathings of my soul" (which, translated, meant his poems), though he did not yet dare call himself, he added, "a Brother-Bard." Lowell, it should be recalled, was not quite twenty-five years old, a tender age for veneration.[49]

The reviews confirmed the acclaim of friends. They were, taken as a whole, even more flattering than those which had greeted *A Year's Life.* Such criticism as there was lacked bite because already familiar — it was complained that Lowell's metrics were careless, his stance sometimes cloying or affected, his language insufficiently concise or willfully quaint. A few critics, notably C. C. Felton in the *North American Review,* disagreed with Lowell's antislavery position, but only Poe questioned another of his themes, that the poet's mission was to improve mankind. Poe added, however, that the volume would place Lowell "*at the very head* of the poets of America . . . he has given evidence of at least as high poetical genius as any man in America — if not a loftier genius than any." For the first time, too, Lowell was reviewed in England, with more restraint than shown by the American critics, but with surprising respect, given the general scorn for American letters. With praise so far outweighing criticism, it is no wonder that Willis called Lowell the best-launched poet of his time. But as the young poet was soon to say himself, "the augury of a man's popularity ought to be looked for in the intensity & not the vulgarity of his appreciation." The critical reception of his poetry would never again be so favorable, though his later achievement was to be far more substantial.[50]

Unlike *A Year's Life*, the new volume brought money as well as acclaim. The book went into three editions of five hundred copies each — a large sale for that day — and Lowell received ten cents on each copy. Other offers, moreover, came in the wake of success. The conservative *North American Review*, usually disdainful of those tainted with "Young Americanism," engaged Lowell to do a piece on Frederika Bremer, and Poe suggested, though with no result, that he and Lowell collaborate on a new magazine in order "to elevate without stupefying our literature — to further justice — to resist foreign dictation" (and, somewhat anti-climactically) — "to afford . . . a remuneration to ourselves . . ." *Graham's Magazine* entered into protracted and acrimonious negotiation with Lowell for his exclusive services, offering twenty-five dollars for one poem per month. It was a handsome offer; as Graham pointed out, only Longfellow and Bryant got higher prices, and they had greater standing in the literary world and did not contribute on a regular basis. But Lowell held back. He felt that his new reputation justified and his financial need required that Graham's offer be raised. Longfellow, a neighbor of Lowell's, and aware of his desperate wish to marry, generously intervened, urging Graham to guarantee Lowell a thousand dollars a year in return for one article in each number of the magazine. Graham, "with the air and manner," as Longfellow reported, "of a Drum-major," peremptorily refused, and with anger still to spare, gave Lowell a piece of his mind: "the hardest lesson is to treat all men as bargain-driving, sharpers. I see my dear Lowell, you have learned it early." Lowell rather temperately replied that since he wished to marry, it was his duty, not his desire, to make the most he could out of his wits. There the exchange temporarily halted, with Lowell disappointed at the lost income, but determined not to debase his market value. He was inadvertently encouraged in recalcitrance by Graham's former assistant, Charles J. Peterson (now editing his own magazine) who correctly prophesied to Lowell that all would come right at last, for Graham, though impulsive, was warm-hearted and generous.[51]

In the meantime, other sources seemed likely to make up the needed income. Briggs was starting a new journal in New York, the antislavery papers had begun to ask for contributions, and it even seemed possible that part-time lecturing might serve as an additional means of earning money. The prospects were good enough, and James and Maria were impatient enough, so that they decided at last to set a definite date for their wedding — the day after Christmas, 1844.

Their friends were delighted, and Maria's father rendered at least neutral. He promised to pay for the furnishings of their home but beyond that, though he was wealthy, refused all help. Lowell's father, with less resources but more good will, offered to build them a cottage on a piece of his land if it could be done for about a thousand dollars. Delighted, Lowell christened it in advance "Elmwood Junior." As for daily expenses, Lowell believed his income — potentially — would meet his needs; Graham, he felt (correctly), could eventually be counted on to give him thirty dollars a poem — and without an exclusive contract; the second volume of verse would bring in fifty dollars a year; writing for the antislavery papers would add ten dollars more per month; and finally, another new volume, nearing completion, would pay a hundred dollars for the first edition — if it sold. In a day when Poe lived on an annual income of about $300, and a college professor on about $600, Lowell's calculations were not unreasonable.[52]

The new volume, *Conversation on the Old Poets*, was in fact only partly new. It was a revised, expanded version of the "old dramatists" articles Lowell had begun three years before for Nathan Hale's *Miscellany*, and had then continued in *The Pioneer*. In the few months remaining before his wedding, he set furiously to work in order to complete the volume. He rose early and sat up late, and toward the last few weeks the printers pressed him so for copy that even his visits to Maria had to be limited to two a week. It was typical of Lowell, then and always, to rely on last-minute pressures and inspirations and then to work with furious bursts of energy: "I cannot write anything somehow unless it come to me & haunt me & torment me." Yet this work pattern always made him vaguely uneasy; he retained, like all attenuated Puritans, a lingering belief that work had to be steady to be moral, and in the interims between productive bursts, he would berate himself for indolence.[53]

Written in haste, without time for those final polishings which can mute the forthright or delete the personal, *Conversations* turned out, inadvertently, to be more an autobiographical essay than a work of literary criticism. Both the subjects — Chaucer, Chapman, Ford — and the conversational device used to discuss their works were loose pegs upon which Lowell hung discursive commentary on current topics. The barrage of personal opinion — vigorous, exuberantly defiant, by turns playful and earnest — reveals a great deal more of its author than his subjects, and conveys a distinct portrait of the young Lowell at the crucial juncture when he made his dual commitment to literature and to Maria White.

Now twenty-five years of age, he was no longer as brashly assertive, as self-indulgent, as boisterously confident as when a college boy. All these characteristics, in diminished degree, remained, but there was new awareness of personal insignificance, a sure sign of his developing maturity. The man alone, the man without love, Lowell now wrote, was a man "nailed to the dreadful cross of self without help or hope"; the successes and controversies of the world were alike so many shouted "nothings into the tired ear of the great Silence." This lengthening perspective, though as yet incomplete, indicated a growing composure. The kind of man Lowell increasingly admired (which meant the kind of man he hoped to become) cultivated "plain simplicity . . . a scholarly air of quiet and repose, an easy dignity, and an unstrained grace." Such a model, of course, had always been before him: his description fit Dr. Charles Lowell to the letter. Identifying one's father with virtue is hardly unique, but few fathers survive the godhead beyond their sons' adolescence. That James Russell, in his twenties, could still wish to pattern himself on his father's image is strong testimony to the success of their relationship.[54]

The image was not taken over wholesale, of course. With his different set of experiences, James Russell could never be a mere carbon copy of his father, nor did he wish to be, as he made clear in filling out the details of his ideal man: to be "calm, grand and simple" were high virtues indeed, but other (somewhat contradictory) qualities were no less desirable — earnestness, "rugged heartiness" and "fierce sublimity." Here was the romantic gloss which Lowell, representing his generation, superimposed upon the neo-classic ideal of their fathers. They admired the older model enough so that they preferred to update rather than discard it. In so doing, they wished especially to make room for "enthusiasm" — "abandoned earnestness" — and to repudiate a too great dependence on "rules." "Every great man," Lowell wrote, "is more or less tinged with what the world calls fanaticism." Enthusiasm could be overdone; mere zeal could blind a man to the shortcomings of his position and lead him to substitute intolerance for charity. But at the least, every man should aim at being outspoken and frank. The world had become too polite: "we have grown so delicately decent, that we must need even apologize for nature itself." Men needed to be more natural, unconscious, independent, to surrender to *themselves.* Every man had his "infallible and inexorable monitor within," and it was to this instinctive voice of conscience, not to the verdict of the world, that he must appeal. Rules and codes, whether in literature or in life, had to give way before the higher demands of self-realization.[55]

Thus in poetry it was essential to avoid theories as to what was "proper" verse, for "outward forms of poetry are changeable as those of a cloud" and so they should be — the poet needed to give free play to his "unpruned spirit." He should be open, spontaneous, simple, never the studied, artificial gentleman, never an Alexander Pope, who, whether describing "the cane of a fop, or the speech of a demi-god, the pause must always fall on the same syllable, and the sense must be chopped off by the same rhyme." Unlike Pope, the Elizabethans understood that "the straight line is not the line of beauty," the rude, irregular hand better traced the true outlines of nature. Modern poets lacked the strength, Lowell lamented, to be unconscious. Most of their volumes had "a clipped and suppressed look; and if there be any freedom about them it has a deprecatory and beseeching air, as if it would say, like one of our Governor's proclamations, 'with the advice and consent of the Council.' " It was as impossible to establish rules for criticism as for poetry. Tastes were arbitrary, and the only safe critical method was "to point out what parts of a poem please" and let the rest go; since posterity would reverse judgment in almost every case, it was better to be censured for kindness than for severity.[56]

Just as men were too slavishly devoted to conventions in literature, so they were in life. Christianity had become merely external, "a task ceremony to be gone through with, and not a principle of life itself." True religion, thought Lowell, echoing Emerson in the way Emerson echoed Swedenborg, was natural religion. "All things preach to us"; God's purpose could be read from nature, not literally perhaps, but symbolically:

Let us not think that only here [*church*]
Thy being to our own is near;
But let us find thee every day
Forth in the fields, or by the way . . .
O, let us feel thee every where
As common as the blessed air . . .

Lowell had pronounced Swedenborgian tendencies during these years. Fanny Longfellow, the poet's wife, remembered that when she dined with the Lowells one evening he "talked in a very Swedenborgian way of spiritual sympathies," asserting "most distinctly that he has been long in the habit of seeing spirits, & will not consider it a disease but a very natural phenomenon . . . He says he had a distinct vision one bright afternoon in his easy chair of Maria White's face, & when he saw her was drawn to her by the resemblance." [57]

Lowell's view of the poet was an integral part of this mystical streak, for it was to the poets that God's secrets were especially revealed; they were the "messengers of heaven," piecing together into a coherent whole the average man's fragmentary apprehensions of His meaning. The poet as prophet was a commonplace of nineteenth-century aesthetics; it was a view held by Longfellow no less than Lowell. But Lowell went somewhat beyond common assumptions in the way he mystically linked not only religion, nature and poetry, but also the secular concerns of social reform and even of love between the sexes. What held these disparate elements together, what gave unity to all of life's varied aspects, was love. God was its source; he cared for his creatures, he implanted within their souls the capacity to recognize and strive for beauty and truth, and he transmitted this loving purpose through nature, and secondarily through the poets. Man in his daily life needed to emulate Divine benevolence, to bring the unifying force of love to bear on all his activities. Seen correctly, poetry and natural religion were both "life members of the New England Anti-Slavery Society," for the "high and glorious vocation" of all was to make daily life "more beautiful and holy by the ministerings of heavenly love." In the same way, love between man and woman was not meant merely to serve the selfish delight of pleasure in the beloved: "our love for one is only . . . made pre-eminent, that it may show us the beauty and holiness of that love whose arms are wide enough for all." [58]

It was the heart which should rule men — in religion, poetry and daily life — and not the intellect. Intellect had no conscience, it lusted only for power. Just as the mind had to be held in thralldom to the heart, so man had to be pupil to woman, for women knew the shortest way to the heart. And so it was (for Lowell was relentless in his linkage), that women should be welcomed into reform activities, yes, should even be allowed to speak from public platforms, for the true woman's voice "gushes up from a heart throbbing only with tenderness for our neighbour fallen among thieves." In assigning the "tender virtues" to women, Lowell was again echoing a commonplace of the day, but in giving these virtues clear supremacy over those of the intellect, he was doing something more — he was indirectly acknowledging his dependence on Maria White.[59]

Such views would seem to place the young Lowell solidly in the romantic tradition and a long way from the neo-classicism of his father: he celebrated emotion and intuition over abstract intellectualizing; he put individual freedom above tradition, and social justice above social order; he saw the poet as priestly celebrant of divine mystery, not as secular defender of the Rational City; he believed human love was a gateway to ultimate truth, not merely physical pleasure; he stressed Christian ethics over Christian dogma; he held to the pantheistic belief that God was to be found in all things rather than the deistic belief that God was the impersonal designer, not a continuing participant in the universe.[60]

Yet Lowell's was a restrained romanticism. He emphasized the more domesticated aspects of the Romantic canon, and his views, in their cumulative practicality and caution, reflect his social and personal backgrounds. No romantic writer, of course, wholly fits the rigid categories by which later generations have sought to define the style, but in Lowell's case the variations seem unusually pronounced.

He was too buoyant and unserious, he had had too much success, to indulge except peripherally in the *Sturm und Drang* aspects of the romantic stance. Privately, he had some minor bouts of depression, but he put no special value on such moods; he did not glorify despair by adopting it as a public posture. There was almost nothing in his person of these years, and only slightly more in his poetry, of melancholic introspection, of brooding on the isolation and suffering to which the man of genius was consigned. He could not believe in the authenticity of these attitudes because he could not believe in their necessity. The individual thrown back wholly upon his own self-consciousness presupposed an individual wholly in alienation from society. Lowell was not so constituted. Though believing in the primacy of the individual voice, he did not believe that the individual and his society made up two discrete, necessarily antagonistic units. The hero of European romantic literature, the man of genius, tended to see himself first scorned and then destroyed by the world around him. But for Lowell, the poet-messiah brought the "good news" to society in order to perfect it, and there was reason to believe his message would be heeded:

> *We see the black clouds furling, one by one,*
> *From the advancing majesty of Truth . . .*

By believing the hero able to find fulfillment within rather than apart from society, it followed that Lowell would have little patience with those peripheral romantic myths which derived from an anti-social bias. Thus he found nothing picturesque about "noble savages"; there was such a thing as being *too* natural, of equating "rude ungraciousness of bearing" with honesty, cowhide boots with democracy. Nor could he see the exalting virtue of poverty; actual want, asserted this practical Yankee, was inconsistent with the serenity of mind needed for creativity.[61]

Lowell retained, in other words, something of the eighteenth-century view of cultivated man living in the world, even while eschewing all aspects of that view which suggested artificial cultivations, inequalities or restraints. For Lowell, the past was not automatically outmoded. He held to those aspects of tradition which to him continued to have value, and rejected certain facets of the new which did not. Thus he could ridicule fashionable talk of national "destinies," especially as manifested in national literatures; he thought, like a good *citoyen du monde* of the Enlightenment, that such talk was dangerous twaddle, obscuring "the arcs of one horizon, whose centre is the living heart." He retained, too, some lingering belief in those "general laws" which were part of the Rationalist legacy; the universe "made sense," certain fixed principles did operate, all was not change and flux. Though he agreed with the romantics in dethroning reason from pre-eminence in human affairs, he still liked to think it a prime attribute of divinity; he wished men to be led by their hearts, but the world to move by systematic laws:

> . . . *this huge Minster of the Universe,*
> *Whose smallest oratories are glorious worlds . . .*
> *Whose carved ornaments are systems grand . . .*[62]

Lowell's youthful "world view," in short, was an amalgam of various traditions. He was strongly disposed to those elements in the romantic rebellion which stressed the tender sentiments — he wanted men to feel and to be free, he wanted them to aim at ethical purity, to spiritualize, "make beautiful," transcend, all the mundane and material preoccupations of life. But he had less sympathy with the anti-social, Bohemian, pessimistic tendencies of romanticism. He would not have said with Rousseau, "I am not made like anyone I ever met"; he would never, with Don Juan, have wholly scorned the conventional moralities. Though in these emphases he represented the more restrained American version of the romantic movement, some Americans, like Poe and Melville, did go much further than he toward skepticism, irreligion and pessimism. Lowell, in distinction from his father, mocked the literary regularities of Pope, but he agreed with his father in deploring the personal irregularities of Byron. He could not, like Poe, comfortably assume the mantle of *poète maudit;* he was not the melancholy, demonic, alienated young man, standing "in solitude, where we are *least* alone." He was, instead, the liberal Christian humanist in training.

Though as a twenty-five-year-old Lowell only partly identified with the romantic mode, it was as far as he would ever go in that direction. His later tendency was to move away from, without ever fully discarding, the mysticism, sentimentality and emotionalism of his youth. The classical concern with character would increasingly dominate the romantic glorification of personality; preserving a virtuous integrity before the world would come to seem of greater value than cultivating idiosyncrasies in opposition to it. The mature Lowell would value reason, grace, simplicity and repose above the eager idealities of his youth; gradually, inexorably, he would place pre-eminent value on his father's qualities and example. And so it is that the dedication of the *Conversations* takes on, in retrospect, a special appropriateness:

To
My Father
Charles Lowell, D.D.,
Whom If I Had Not The
Higher Privilege of Revering As A Parent,
I Should Still Have

Honoured As Man And Loved As A Friend,
This Volume,
Containing Many Opinions From Which He Will Wholly,
Yet With The
Large Charity Of A Christian Heart, Dissent,
Is Inscribed, By His
Youngest Child.

CHAPTER IV

MARRIAGE AND ANTISLAVERY

JAMES RUSSELL and Maria were married the night after Christmas, 1844, in a brief ceremony performed by Dr. Lowell at her father's house and attended by family and a few friends. Fanny Longfellow reported that Maria's father "appeared very cordial & happy," but that Maria did not look as charming as expected, for though her dress was exceedingly simple, it was not "well arranged." This apparent unconcern was perhaps deliberate. Maria believed that the formal rites of marriage could mark no significant change for two who had been spiritually wed for five years. Nor did she feel that there was any need at the ceremony to surround themselves with friends; most people had large weddings so that the guests could later certify, after all trace of a real marriage had disappeared, that it had indeed formally taken place. This lofty attitude encouraged sarcasm; as Elizabeth Barrett said (picking up James' uxoriousness as much as Maria's self-satisfaction), Mr. Lowell "seems to have married a supernatural woman without a fault in the world." [1]

After a day and a night at home, the Lowells went to Philadelphia for the winter, hoping the milder climate might rid Maria of a persistent cough she had had ever since a bout with influenza in the summer of 1843. On a previous trip to Philadelphia, Maria had met the abolitionist circle there, and the Lowells now decided to board with one of them, a Quakeress named Emma Parker. For eight dollars a week they got their meals and a small room, third floor back — "quite low enough to be an attic," Maria jested, conscious that they would be expected to conform to a properly Bohemian image. Mrs. Parker, solicitous of Maria's health, plied her with bread and butter, cushions and footstools, but was sensible enough, between motherly ministrations, to leave the Lowells to themselves.[2]

It was as they wished; they preferred to spend most of their time alone, reading or writing, "happy as two mortals can be." Not surprisingly, neither their fellow boarders, nor outside social contacts, nor the city itself, struck them as particularly interesting. Most of the people they saw were in the antislavery fellowship — Sarah, Isaac and Elizabeth Pugh, the Miller McKims and the Edward M. Davises (Lucretia Mott's son-in-law and daughter). Lowell found them pleasant and kind, though somewhat wanting in education; they were "proportionately narrow compared with our New England breadth which God knows is narrow enough." Nor did the city of Philadelphia hold much charm for them. The streets, with their interminable red brick vistas, seemed uncommonly dull, and fashionable society only slightly less so. A distant kinsman took Lowell to the Whister Club, a weekly gathering of scientific and literary men considered the best in the city, but he was "hideously struck with the want of intellect." The Lowells thought better of Boston with every passing day — a frame of mind not uncommon to wandering New Englanders — though like most honeymooners, the Lowells were not exactly geographical-minded.[3]

The uncertainty of Maria's health gave additional reason for restricting their social life. A Philadelphia doctor examined her, offered no decided opinion on the condition of her lungs, but in lieu of diagnosis prescribed an abundance of treatment: tartar emetic plasters and a medicinal compound of sarsaparilla and hydrate of potash — all of which changed the sound and nature of her cough, but not its frequency. Still, she put on some weight and felt "remarkably well," while James grew so rosy in health from their peaceful life that his cheeks looked as if he had "rubbed them against all the red brick walls in the city."[4]

Only one satisfaction was denied them; they might not,

Maria reported with mock alarm, be so *very* poor after all. By March they had accumulated thirty-one dollars, and James teased Maria with the luxurious manner in which he was supporting her. Some of the money came from the success of the *Conversations*; within three months of publication, the first edition of one thousand copies had been sold out and Lowell was $300 richer. Sales had been helped along by a set of good notices. An occasional critic took issue with Lowell's strictures on the church, or with his praise of the abolitionists, and in England especially, sharp rejoinders were made to his brash attack on Alexander Pope. These demurrers aside, the reception was excellent, and within the year a second edition was brought out.[5]

Occasional pieces for the periodicals brought additional income. After the success of the new volume, Graham, as predicted, came around to Lowell's price of thirty dollars per poem. And Briggs invited both the Lowells to write for his new periodical, the *Broadway Journal*. Relations with Briggs, though, became temporarily somewhat strained. Lowell had hoped that the *Journal* would be "a powerful weapon in the hands of Reform" (not least because it would print his own outspoken essays), but Briggs had proved less sympathetic than anticipated. In reviewing the *Conversations* in the *Journal*, he took issue with Lowell's "hot and excited" abolitionism, even while paying extravagant tribute to the book's merits. To "parade" one's antislavery credentials, Briggs wrote, seemed dubious taste: "it smacks of generous bravery to confess to an unpopular virtue, but it is more brave not to confess at all. We should doubt the charity which boasteth itself; or the chastity; or the poverty." Briggs enjoyed being cantankerous, especially with friends, when it could pass for incorruptible honesty, and Lowell, willing to accept it as such, showed no immediate resentment at his friend's strictures. But he did lose his temper soon after when Briggs turned down an article of his against the annexation of Texas. Though Lowell himself had no high opinion of the piece, he was angry that Briggs should reject it as too severe in tone just at the time when the *Journal* was printing an ill-tempered attack by Poe on Longfellow; there was nothing in his own article, Lowell felt, which approached the "grossness and vulgarity" of Poe's. Briggs' desire for large circulation, Lowell sadly concluded, had led him to cater to the public taste for scandal rather than the public need for morality; he had allowed personalities to take precedence over issues. Though he protested continuing love for Briggs, Lowell decided, for the time, not to contribute further to the *Journal*. He felt easier about writing for the *Pennsylvania Freeman*, an abolitionist publication which paid him five dollars for each fortnightly leader. Writing to order was always difficult for Lowell, and prose was not his preferred medium, but he accepted the *Freeman*'s offer out of the double pressure of financial need and the mounting belief that he had a duty to lend his pen to "the cause." [6]

He had been a committed abolitionist for about three years, having come a long way from the college senior who in callow, clever verse had jibed at reformers. It had been a logical progression, for even during college days Lowell had expressed sympathy for abolitionist goals, if not methods. But the methods, too, he came rapidly to approve. Less than six months after graduating, he could firmly declare that the abolitionist party was the only one with which he felt identification, and he later claimed that he had "swore fealty" to it as early as 1839.[7]

If so, his involvement antedated his attachment to Maria, whom he only met for the first time in December, 1839. If she must therefore be denied the credit which she has usually been given for *originating* Lowell's antislavery sympathies, there is no doubt that she did solidify and deepen his commitment, and, even more significantly, was largely responsible for turning it toward active expression. Shortly before his engagement, Lowell confided to Maria that he felt it a mistake to work against the inclinations, and that his were to devote his life to self-culture. Maria replied, with considerable heat and some scorn, that the noblest self-culture was that which gave thought to others — "our good men dream of the perfectibility of human nature, but close their ears to the multitude who cry in every tone for help . . ." She encouraged him to give active witness to his antislavery convictions, to commit his energies as well as his sympathies to the cause.

To some extent the two reinforced each other's reformist tendencies. Thus when Maria was uncertain whether it would be "fitting" for her to present a banner at a temperance rally, and there were many dissuasive voices, "the dearest one seconded my own convictions. Had that disapproved I should have yielded at once, but . . . the inspiration of that beloved voice has always been its sweet accord with every true tone of my own heart." If this was only Maria's subtle way of saying that James never disagreed with her, she was wise enough to make their meeting of minds seem the result of joint discovery rather than one-sided dictation. Not that Lowell was reluctant to acknowledge her paramount influence — her "gentle & holy presence" had "set his spirit free," her "whiter & purer" soul had enveloped his like an "all embracing hope"; it was to Maria, he freely testified, that he owed his "spiritual growth." [8]

Under her tutelage, Lowell's antislavery commitment was rapidly manifested in the early 1840's. Though his first book of poetry, published in 1841, had made almost no reference to slavery, by the following year he was cheerfully admitting to being a "fanatic" on the subject, and Maria's early strictures on self-culture had become his own:

How should we dare to call it ours
This peace that folds our nights & morns?
While just outside our sheltering bowers
Our brother man his brothers scorns?
What profiteth our wreath of flowers
While Truth still wears her crown of thorns? [9]

By 1842 he had begun contributing to abolitionist periodicals like the *Liberty Bell* and the *National Anti-Slavery Standard*, as well as writing antislavery pieces for more conservative journals like the *Boston Miscellany* or the *Boston Courier*. At that juncture, Charles Peterson of *Graham's* felt called upon to give Lowell some "practical" advice: he should be as abolition-minded as he liked, Peterson wrote, but if he hoped to win a national literary reputation, he should at least adapt a more neutral label, like "emancipationist." Lowell thought such caution detestable. His only ambition, he insisted (with no more than a normal amount of disingenuousness), was to do something for mankind. If being an abolitionist jeopardized his literary reputation or cut down the number of potential outlets for his work, he gladly accepted "whatever odium might be attached to a complete identification with a body of heroic men and women . . . whose superiors in all that constitutes true manhood and womanhood . . . never existed." [10]

The strong abolitionist theme in his second book of poetry, published in 1844, did earn him some rebuke from the critics, but despite Peterson's prediction, did not seriously damage its reception. Abolitionism, in fact, no longer carried the onus it had a decade earlier when William Lloyd Garrison had first launched his thunderous challenge to slavery. By 1844 the issues of Texas annexation and of a war with Mexico which threatened to follow had converted many Northerners to the view that more active resistance to slavery was required; otherwise, they feared — as the abolitionists had long insisted — the institution would become ever more entrenched.

Few, however, took up Lowell's advanced position. Though many Northerners had arrived, by the 1840's, at a more determined stance against slavery, only a handful were willing to advocate its immediate abolition. Most preferred instead the intermediate position of "non-extension"; that is, slavery would not be allowed to spread beyond its present boundaries but would not be interfered with where it was already established. The underlying rationale of "non-extension" was that if slavery's expansion could once be stopped it would, in Lincoln's words, be placed "in course of ultimate extinction" everywhere. What the non-extensionists preferred to ignore was that there were still large areas within the Southern states into which slavery might yet expand, that even without further expansion slavery might not cease to be profitable, that even should it cease to be profitable, the South might not feel able, psychologically, to abandon it.

But "non-extensionism," if a chimera, could be more easily assimilated to Northern values than could abolitionism. It was less immediately threatening to certain long-standing, cherished beliefs: the sanctity of private property (and slaves, though men, *were* property, as the Constitution itself seemingly implied); the need, at all costs, to safeguard the federal Union, which meant compromising (or ignoring) divisive issues; and, finally, a widespread conviction that Negroes were biologically inferior, that they lacked the capacity for freedom, certainly for immediate freedom.

Lowell, and a few others of his generation, were impatient with pleas for delay and compromise. He acknowledged that these could be virtues, in their place. But the struggle against slavery, he argued, was not the place. Men mouthed the clichés of moderation to evade responsibility; they flattered prudence in order to lull conscience. Even those who were sincere in counseling a gradual solution were misguided; slavery posed too great a danger for equivocation. Because slavery threatened the very basis on which the nation rested, the very heart of its professed principles, democratic and Christian, it was one of those few issues which could not be dealt with "gradually" or in a "compromising" spirit. As leave tell a man to "go slow" on slavery, so Garrison once put it, as tell him *slowly* to put out a fire destroying the house in which his wife and children lay asleep. "There is something better than Expediency," Lowell wrote, "and that is Wisdom, something stronger than Compromise, and that is Justice." [11]

Lowell, then, was part of the left wing of the antislavery movement, one of the abolitionist "zealots." This kind of rough categorizing, however, does not do justice to the nuances of his position. As Lowell said at the time, but as few have recognized since, abolitionists were "not so unanimous that it is safe to speak for more than one of them at a time"; their ranks, though sparse, contained considerable diversity of opinion.

To speak in the broadest terms first, there were two major camps within the abolitionist movement: those who adopted the leadership and policies of William Lloyd Garrison, and those who did not. Though Lowell did not agree with Garrison on a number of points, he was sympathetic in the main to the Garrisonian position, which is to say he belonged to the more radical wing of the abolitionist movement.

Like Garrison, Lowell was opposed to politics as a vehicle for reform, and he thought the formation in 1840 of the Liberty Party by certain abolitionist groups a decided mistake. To become entangled in party politics would be, he believed, to open abolitionists to the charge of personal aggrandizement, to involve them in the inevitable deceptions and demoralizations of electioneering, to compromise their integrity and moral influence. The ethical purity of the movement would be traded for a dubious share in the spoils of office. Yet unlike some Garrisonians, who looked on every ideological deviation as an act of treachery, Lowell was temperate in his treatment of the "political" abolitionists. Their error, he believed, was only as to "*the best means of bringing about the Right*, and surely [they] deserve more sympathy . . . than those whose creed is *wrong*." His tolerance towards the Liberty Party men was equated by some Garrisonians with acceptance of their position, for at one point it was rumored that Lowell had actually voted for the Liberty ticket.[12]

Lowell was Garrisonian, too, in his willingness to challenge cherished American institutions — the church, the Constitution and the Union. The true remedy for injustice, Lowell believed, was the application of Christianity to life, but in this, unfortunately, there was no greater obstacle than the churches themselves. Secure and formalized, they had proved unable to adapt to new conditions; they had become the great bulwark of "practical Paganism," and as such needed reforming from "foundation to weathercock." Lowell concentrated his attack on the church as an institution; he was careful not to denounce the religious sentiment itself, nor to abuse the clergy as a body. Most clerics, he acknowledged, were "sincere and honest," and some of the younger ministers were actively working to inculcate a spirit of reform. As in his disagreement with the Liberty Party, Lowell tried to separate questions of principle from questions of personality ("I remember when my own eyes were as blind as an owl's to the Sun of Truth, and I learned charity to the blindness of others in the best school"). In this regard he stood apart from Garrisonians like Stephen Foster, Abby Folsom and Parker Pillsbury, but quite in line with others — Edmund Quincy, say, or Samuel Sewall or Ellis Gray Loring. It is no more true to assume that all Garrisonians dealt solely in invective than it is to assume that their opponents spoke only in terms of sweet reasonableness; there were as many modulated voices in the first group as fierce polemicists in the second. Lowell knew that a certain amount of passionate, even shrill, rhetoric was needed to rouse an apathetic public — but he preferred that others use it. When he had begun to write for the antislavery press, his father had begged him to spare nothing in depicting slavery in all of its horror, but to do so in a spirit of love rather than hate, avoiding all that was "harsh, dogmatical, uncharitable, unchristian — do not give to party, what was meant for mankind." In the face of Northern torpor and Southern hostility, it was not easy to maintain the Olympian calm recommended by the reasonable Doctor, but his son did, on most occasions, refrain from mere name-calling. Indiscriminate vituperation — from whatever source — made him uncomfortable; baseness, he insisted, was not merely positive, but declinable — it had its comparative and superlative degrees. And he sometimes sighed over those co-workers whose pitch suggested they had been brought up with the deaf, or near waterfalls.[13]

Lowell's poise was equally evident in his discussions of the Constitution and the Union. If the Constitution did guarantee property in men — which was debatable — why should that piece of parchment be accepted as final moral authority? There was much that the eighteenth century had tolerated which the nineteenth could not; short of repealing the nineteenth century, men would have to recognize that although commonwealths needed constitutions and laws, they did not need strait jackets. Instead of asking "Is it constitutional?" politicians might better ask, "Is it right?" The laws of man should never take precedence over the laws of God, allegiance to the Constitution should never replace allegiance to the Decalogue. When authority served as a shield for wrong, it was time to question the authority; every contract to do an immoral act was void *ab initio* — for surely it was a lesser crime to violate the Constitution of the United States than to violate the Constitution of the Universe.[14]

Like the Constitution, the Union was a man-made convenience, valuable only so long as it fulfilled the function for which it had been designed. It was possible that the "inalienable rights" for whose protection Union had been established might come to be threatened by its continuation; the Union could itself turn into an instrument of tyranny. If so, it would clearly make more sense to reconstitute the government than to abandon the principles on which it had originally been founded. In any case, the Union could never "be stuck together with mouth-glue" if issues of conscience were rendering it asunder; as well try "to stay Niagara with a dip-net, or pass acts against the law of gravitation." But although Lowell would not pay automatic reverence to either the Constitution or to the Union, he refused to follow Garrison when he moved to the active advocacy of dis-Union. Such advocacy, Lowell believed, was "a waste of strength," and worse, an abandonment of the slave. Dis-Union might separate the abolitionists from evil, but would leave the evil itself untouched.[15]

Lowell can be called a Garrisonian not only because of what he was against — politics, the institutional church, excessive reverence for the Constitution and Union — but also because of what he was for — equal treatment of the Negro, the active participation of women in reform and a broad-gauged attack on all aspects of social imperfection. But in the positive no less than negative aspects of his position, he was Garrisonian with a difference.

Lowell recognized that the assumption of Negro inferiority was a national, not a sectional phenomenon. Most Northerners along with almost all Southerners believed the Negro incapable of participating in a free society; he had been a separate, lower creation, meant to occupy a position of servitude. Since doubt about the Negro's capacity for freedom obviously worked against any movement designed to emancipate him, the underlying assumption of his biological inferiority needed refutation. Lowell joined this issue continually. The whites, he argued, had no better foundation for their patent of nobility than "an accidental difference in the secreting vessels of the skin." How easy to deny that Negroes had equal faculties, when, by rigidly excluding them from every path of emulation or ambition, they had been given no chance to develop their faculties. When the whites managed to produce a man like Toussaint L'Ouverture, Lowell remarked, it might then be time to talk of inferior and superior races.[16]

Instead of exonerating the North, Lowell sharply indicted it for anti-Negro prejudice: in the "so-called free states," he wrote, the Negro was degraded by something stronger than laws — by the force of "a depraved and unchristian public opinion." And he quite agreed with the argument that the North should "clean up its own backyard" — not first, but simultaneously. Improving the Negroes' condition in the free states, he argued, should be of prime concern to the antislavery movement; every barrier of "invidious distinction" should be broken down.[17]

In advocating equality of treatment for all races, Lowell did not assume that the races would perform similarly. Like most of those few Americans who denied Negro inferiority, Lowell did not deny Negro "differences." Moreover, he believed that certain differences were innate, not simply environmental — though he stood traditional racism on its head by suggesting that Negroid traits were of a "rarer" quality than Caucasian ones:

> We have never had any doubt that the African race was intended to introduce a new element of civilization, and that the Caucasian would be benefited greatly by an infusion of its gentler and less selfish qualities. The Caucasian mind, which seeks always to govern, at whatever cost, can never come to so beautiful or Christian a height of civilization, as with a mixture of those seemingly humbler, and truly more noble, qualities which teach it to obey.

Assigning inherent characteristics to the races was part of the widespread belief — to be shattered by Darwin — in "fixed essences"; where Lowell and many of his fellow abolitionists stood apart was in their refusal to assume that Caucasian traits were superior to Negroid ones. Indeed, trying to avoid that common fallacy they fell into the opposite one of lauding the "nobler" qualities of the Negro.[18]

Lowell's generation thought of the "gentle, loving" traits such as the Negro was said to have as "feminine." Since these were "noble, Christian virtues," it followed logically that those who possessed them should not be ruled by those who did not — which, of course, applied to women no less than Negroes. The Garrisonians, unlike more conservative elements in the abolitionist movement, insisted that women should have the right to participate freely in reform activities, even to the extent of speaking from the lecture platform. Lowell fully endorsed this position: "in Massachusetts we burn Popish nunneries, but we maintain a whole system of Protestant ones." Women belonged wherever truth was pleaded for; those who were truly chaste would be immune from public indelicacies, those who were not could turn even the House of God into a brothel. In a lighter vein, Lowell waggishly protested that it was no easy matter, even for the well-intentioned male, entirely to avoid slave-holding. He, for one, could never see Maria mending his socks, or a female servant bringing water for his bath, "without hearing a faint tinkle of chains." In the post-Civil-War period, as the cause of female equality advanced and Lowell's radicalism retreated, he was to take a more jaundiced view of women's changing status, clinging, as he put it, to "a prejudice or two as a kind of plank in the general shipwreck" — one being "not to have a man for a wife." Women, he would write twenty-five years later, now understood Greek and political economy and could raise perfect Hell in caucuses, but he still thought a woman showed "her best genius in creating a home & being the heart of it." [19]

The championing of women's rights was but one element in the Garrisonian attack on the "unity of evil." Since any social wrong would be found inextricably connected with every other, it was idle to apply remedies to one while allowing the rest to proliferate. And so Lowell, like the Garrisonians generally, participated in a variety of reform activities. He expressed sympathy for the conditions of the Northern factory worker, wrote sonnets against capital punishment, inclined to the dietary ideas of Sylvester Graham, and became particularly involved in the temperance movement — to the point where an alarmed Longfellow feared Lowell was on the verge of asking him to destroy his wine cellar.[20]

But Lowell's ancillary activities were far more restricted than was the case with most Garrisonians, and became ever more so through time. Most of his side enthusiasms were products of his early twenties, when he was in the full tide of Christian radicalism, eager to apply Christianity to all aspects of life and hopeful that all classes of men might come to know and to love one another. But increasingly he came to believe that thoroughgoing social reorganization could not come overnight, and that since slavery was the nation's most pressing evil, abolitionists should focus their energies on that problem. From the position that only gradual inroads against social injustice could be made, Lowell edged into the belief that the assault itself should be gradual. By the late 1840's he was to give increasing emphasis to healing the world by degrees, and was thereby to move in an opposite direction from the more militant Garrisonians, who increasingly stressed perfectionist goals and utopian means — non-resistance, non-voting, "no human government." [21]

But even after 1845, when Lowell became less sympathetic with the Garrisonian position, he continued to defend Garrison's role. The world, Lowell argued, needed its agitators and "fanatics," its Garrisons; only they, in the simplicity of their vision and the harshness of their tone, could rouse an indifferent public from its corrupt self-satisfactions. God had sent Garrison into the world to criticize, not construct, and he had fulfilled his mission brilliantly. Besides, most of the castigation leveled at Garrison for his failure to present a positive, precise plan for emancipation was cant, disguised hostility to the goal of emancipation itself. Lowell was reminded, he wrote, of the boy whose mother asked him what he would like for breakfast, and was answered: "Just what you ain't got." [22]

Despite Lowell's deep commitment to abolitionism, and despite his identification, however incomplete, with the most radical wing of the movement, he did not occupy his position, even at the height of his enthusiasm, without discomfort. For Lowell, like many other abolitionists, was not a Garrison — not a man unable to admit doubt and uncertainty because unable to tolerate complexity and dissent. Besides, Lowell had varied interests and talents, which meant he necessarily chafed at times under work which confined his wide-ranging curiosities and curtailed his self-expression. Reform could not take up the whole of him; he could tire of controversy, of being relentlessly critical when his temperament was basically appreciative, of having constantly to look forward when he sometimes wished to pause and look about.[23]

Then, too, there was his sense of humor. Lowell once described himself as compounded of two "utterly distinct characters"—one half of him "clear mystic and enthusiast," the other half "humorist." During his long engagement (perhaps making a virtue of necessity), the humorous half had been sublimated in the mystical. Once married, his high spirits again rose and his high seriousness ebbed proportionately. He began to find amusement in the movement's more relentlessly earnest prophets; he privately described one as looking as if "he had relapsed into Presbyterianism, and were just striving to put down an impudent doubt as to whether it were a necessary result of the fitness of things that he should be one of the elect!" Once, when planning to visit Edmund Quincy (who was not one of the self-conscious prophets), Lowell wrote him that he had "half a mind to expend a pint of tar & a pillow" and to hire "a gang of Kelts" to have Quincy "privately martyred" so that he would be jolly when Lowell arrived—though he feared the tarring might make Quincy "almost too hilarious." Lowell's wit hardly isolated him in the movement; there were others, like Quincy, or Sydney Gay, with enough good humor even for self-mockery. Nor did Lowell's wit, of course, compromise his sympathy for the slave; humor and compassion are more likely to be allies than enemies. Still, his penchant for finding (indeed, like all satirists, overplaying) the ridiculous amidst the serious, for seeing the occasional excesses of solemnity, kept him some distance from the pieties of the unquestioning adherent. Yet in this, Lowell probably displayed (if in exaggerated form) the periodic doubts which afflict most reformers; the messianic disciple, free of all hesitations, is more likely to be the exception than the rule.[24]

*

Before returning to Cambridge, the Lowells made a brief stop in New York City to see friends and to mend fences with Briggs. Lowell also took the opportunity to call on Poe. It was the first time the two had met, and both were disappointed. Poe thought Lowell "not half the noble-looking person that I expected to see," and Lowell suggested that perhaps Poe *hadn't* seen, because he was at the time "a little tipsy, as if he were recovering from a fit of drunkenness, & with that over-solemnity with which men in such cases try to convince you of their sobriety." Five years later, after Poe's death, his mother-in-law wrote Lowell a tearful letter, attempting to set matters aright: "Oh if you only knew his bitter sorrow when I told him how unlike himself he was while you were there you would have pitied him, he always felt particularly anxious to possess your approbation." Lowell retained his admiration for Poe's talents, believing that his critical genius had, if anything, been undervalued. But — perhaps affected by their disastrous interview — he thought, too, that by the time of Poe's death "we had got the whole" of him: "Had he possessed conscience in any proportion to his brain, our literature could hardly have had a greater loss."[25]

By spring of 1845 the Lowells were back home at Elmwood and settled in a suite of upper rooms. They looked back with satisfaction on their winter in Philadelphia; they had had the chance to start married life in comparative isolation, Maria's health had seemed to improve, and James, though writing less than he had hoped, had managed to earn enough money to support them. In the next few years, Lowell's major source of income continued to be his antislavery writings, and the bulk of these were done for the *National Anti-Slavery Standard.*

The *Standard* had come into existence following the formal schism in the abolitionist ranks of 1840. At that time the anti-

Garrisonians had split off from the American Anti-Slavery Society and had set up a new organization, the American and Foreign Anti-Slavery Society. For good measure, they had taken with them the old newspaper of the movement, the *Emancipator*. This left the Garrisonian Society without an official paper (Garrison's *Liberator* was a personal organ) — indeed without funds and without the allegiance of most of the state antislavery societies as well — and the *Standard* was established to supply the deficiency. Lydia Maria Child edited the paper for three years, but not happily. Disliking in-fighting and "sectarianism," she tried to avoid intra-abolitionist controversy and to aim the journal at the general public not yet committed to the movement. If the *Standard* simply reproduced the acrimony of Garrison's *Liberator*, she argued, it would, like the *Liberator*, repel all but a limited number. Some of the leading Garrisonians disagreed. Garrison himself gave no indication that he approved Mrs. Child's course, and two of his chief lieutenants, Abby Kelley and Maria Weston Chapman, openly insisted that she bring the paper into "rougher waters." "I am willing," Mrs. Child replied, "to do hard work, but not *dirty* work, for any cause," and in 1843 she resigned.[26]

The American Anti-Slavery Society then established a committee to run the paper, composed of Mrs. Chapman, Edmund Quincy and Sydney Gay. They were an extraordinary trio of talented aristocrats. Mrs. Chapman, niece of Joshua Bates of Baring's in London, overawed contemporaries with her dazzling combination of physical beauty, intelligence and tough-mindedness. Quincy thought her "the most perfect creature"; he admitted it took a little time "to thaw the ice of her exterior," but once melted, he said (perhaps suggesting more than intended), "you are carried away by the torrent." Quincy himself had no mean array of qualities; the son of Josiah Quincy, who had been Mayor of Boston as well as President of Harvard, he was to the manor born — elegant, graceful, ironic and accomplished as both scholar and novelist; Howells remembered him as a man "charmingly handsome . . . his manner was beautiful, his voice delightful." Quincy and Lowell had in common wit, breeding and intelligence, and they became friends as well as colleagues in reform. Many years later, at Qunicy's death, Lowell paid tribute to him:

Much did he, and much well; yet most of all
I prized his skill in leisure and the ease
Of a life flowing full without a plan;
For most are idly busy; him I call
Thrice fortunate who knew himself to please,
Learned in those arts that make a gentleman.[27]

Lowell also found Sydney Gay personally attractive. Like Lowell and Quincy, Gay had a distinguished pedigree of New England ancestors, numbering among them John Cotton, Increase Mather and Governor Bradford of Plymouth. But the Puritan strain took its time in emerging; after a college career cut short by escapades, a sojourn in China as employee of the counting house of Perkins & Co. and an unsuccessful business venture in New Orleans, Gay finally returned to the Boston area, where, at various times, he kept a small school, edited a village paper and then gradually became involved in antislavery work. He was as sensitive as he was clever; Quincy warned that Gay and his wife had to be handled "like a couple of cracked tea-cups." He was also something of a dandy — "from the crown of his French hat to the sole of his French boots," he was always exquisitely dressed, and had "soft winning" manners to match. To see him, Quincy said, you would never dream he was "the working editor of a *nigger* paper." And, unfortunately, some of the rural abolitionists agreed. They complained to Garrison that Gay was doing "great mischief" to the cause, which, on investigation, turned out to mean that his elegant dress and manner had excited provincial suspicions. "We were obliged," Quincy drily commented, "to vindicate the equal rights upon the Anti-Slavery platform of French boots & primrose kids with cowhide brogans & worsted mittens."[28]

Lowell was to be more closely associated in his antislavery work with the group around the *Standard* than with any other, though it was not until the fall of 1845 that Mrs. Chapman suggested he be brought into its operations. The subscription list had been falling, and Lowell's talents, she hoped, might revive it. Besides, it had been rumored that he was thinking of becoming a regular contributor for the *Pennsylvania Freeman*, and that journal had already carried off some of the *Standard*'s subscribers. Gay, who was resident editor of the *Standard* in New York City, and who performed the bulk of the actual work, suggested that Lowell, if willing, take over his job. "Absurd," replied Quincy; Gay had proved himself a "heaven-born editor," and besides Lowell, though certainly able, was as yet "green." Quincy was not alone in questioning Lowell's credentials, the doubt involving his "reliability" as much as his experience. Lowell's "ambivalence" on such questions as the Liberty Party raised uncertainty in some quarters as to his dedication to the Garrisonian position. In making out a list of the American Anti-Slavery Society's Vice Presidents at about this time, some thought was given to including him, but Quincy expressed doubt whether Lowell would welcome the compliment. Gay assured them that Lowell was "as good an abolitionist as you have in Massachusetts"; he may not have been a grass-roots participant, feeling as a literary man that he could best serve the cause through his pen, but give Lowell work to do, Gay said, and he would prove his mettle.[29]

But it was not until the spring of 1846 that Lowell was made a positive offer. By then, the *Standard*'s subscription list had fallen from its peak of 3500 in 1844 to a mere 1400. Part of the trouble had been competition from the *Freeman*, for nearly half the *Standard*'s circulation had been in Pennsylvania, but other subscribers had stopped taking the paper because it seemed increasingly to be a carbon copy of the *Liberator*, and they preferred buying the original. The wisdom of Mrs. Child's earlier policy had become apparent; if the *Standard* was to survive and to have influence, it had to appeal to "outside barbarians" as well as to abolitionists, it had to become a family as well as an antislavery paper — which meant carrying additional literary and miscellaneous reading.[30]

And so Lowell, along with a number of others, like Eliza Lee Follen, The Rev. John Weiss and Dr. William F. Channing, was finally sounded out about making regular contributions. Gay feared, though, that the right moment may have passed for enlisting his services, to the extent, that is, that financial need might have served as an inducement. For Maria's father had died suddenly in September, 1845, and it was rumored that the Lowells were about to be rich. Mr. White's fortune was estimated at $300,000, which meant that each child would probably be able to rely on $30,000; the income from that, Gay speculated, would allow James to spend the rest of his life writing poetry and smoking cigars. As it turned out, Maria's share came to only $18,000, $11,000 of which was in land which yielded no income. Since they resolved not to touch the principal, the Lowells could only count on about $500 a year from her inheritance.[31]

Not that it would have mattered in any case. Lowell felt a duty to devote his pen at least part-time to the antislavery struggle, and financial security would not have erased that sense of obligation. Such doubt as he had about aligning himself with the *Standard* concerned his ability to meet its needs; he disliked writing by timetable and feared he would be unable to contribute with the regularity which the *Standard* required. But if Gay would be content with the unpredictability of inspiration, Lowell wrote, he would send contributions whenever possible. Gay was happy to agree: "you know how you can best work . . . *I* like both your prose & poetry & the more I have of each the better." [32]

Lowell's most active involvement with the *Standard* came during 1848–1849, but in one capacity or another he was associated with the paper throughout the period 1846–1852. During these years he sent the *Standard* parts of *The Biglow Papers*, which is to say, the best poetry he ever wrote, and also, starting in 1848, about forty-five prose articles on various aspects of the antislavery struggle. The articles were sometimes of hasty construction and transient interest — the expected defects of occasional journalism. But more surprising, given the press of deadlines, is that the essays were just as often trenchant and polished, with enough in them of passion and wit to make, if not literature, at least superlative journalism. Lowell, as always, would chafe under pressure and long to be free, but when his connection with the *Standard* did finally end in the early 1850's, he could know that he had given his best. And for the Puritan in public life, the knowledge of duty well done is always worth a little freedom, more or less.[33]

CHAPTER V

1848: ANNUS MIRABILIS

MARIA LOWELL gave birth to a ten-pound daughter on the last day of 1845. When told the child resembled him, James expressed confidence that as she grew older she would have the good sense to look as much like her mother as possible. It had been decided in advance that if a girl, the baby would be named Blanche (i.e. "White"), thus combining in a nice bit of symbolic sentiment the family names of mother and father. Lowell vowed to bring Blanche up "as independent as possible of all *man*kind . . . a great, strong, vulgar, mudpudding-baking, tree-climbing, little wench." [1]

Children were not brought into the world, Lowell declared, "to subject their mothers to a diaper despotism," nor to be viewed by their fathers only after dinner, "as an additional digestive to the nuts and raisins." In part Lowell was putting a good face on necessity, for circumstances required that he take an active hand with Blanche. Maria could not bear the fatigue of continually tending her, and though their enlarged means enabled them to keep a maid, they did not think the baby safe in any hands but their own. And so for the first few months after Blanche's birth, Lowell became, he said, "the personification of the maternal principle." He was quite unself-conscious about the details of baby-care, and by mail freely discussed with his friend Briggs such "feminine" concerns as whether baby should have a wetnurse when teething. Lowell's willingness — his real pleasure — in tending children probably reflected his own needs as much as the mores of his circle. The truest men, in Lowell's view, always had something in them of the "tender feminine virtues"; when searching for the highest terms in which to praise Hawthorne, he wrote:

When Nature was shaping him, clay was not granted
For making so full-sized a man as she wanted,
So, to fill out her model, a little she spared
From some finer-grained stuff for a woman prepared,
And she could not have hit a more excellent plan
For making him fully and perfectly man.[2]

Lowell was certain there had never been a child like Blanche. She laughed all over — you could see it "through her clothes" — and she had the added grace of being exceedingly fond of her father. As this was a taste she could not have brought from heaven, Lowell said, it was yet another "melancholy instance how early the corrupting influences of earth begin their work." [3]

Fifteen months later Blanche was dead. She had suddenly begun to cut four double teeth at once; the doctor prescribed a leech, mustard baths and purgatives, and when the child, not surprisingly, failed to respond, pronounced her disease incurable "dropsy of the brain." Mrs. Longfellow, more simply, reported that Blanche had succumbed to rapid teething. In any case, she was dead, a terrible blow to her adoring family. Dr. Lowell, beside himself with grief, could only repeat over and over that "she was a perfect female infant." James and Maria tried to be philosophical. Earlier, when Briggs had lost a child, Lowell had offered the comfort that death, however cold in touch, was God's angel in disguise. He now tried to embrace the same reasoning, especially for Maria's sake. He talked of the consolation of Blanche's lovely memory, of knowing she had gone to God, of the need for gratitude that they had been allowed to enjoy her for even a short time. Thus armed, the Lowells managed to remain reasonably calm in their affliction, though Maria confessed she could not quite approach the serenity imparted by James' deep faith. Nor could she console herself with the thought of having other children — "I can never have another Blanche:"

The morning-glory's blossoming will soon be coming round,
We see their rows of heart-shaped leaves upspringing from the ground,
The tender things the winter killed, renew again their birth,
But the glory of our morning has passed away from earth.

There was some concern that Maria's health might further deteriorate under the blow. The previous summer the Lowells had gone to the Berkshires, hoping that "higher & purer air" might finally rid Maria of her cough. When she continued to look pale and fragile, they talked optimistically of the cough being merely "constitutional." Longfellow thought it strange that Lowell seemed unaware of how ill his wife was; apparently the prospect of losing Maria was too painful for Lowell to face.[4]

Fortunately, Maria Lowell was already pregnant at the time of Blanche's death, and in September, 1847, gave birth to another daughter, christened Mabel. Delighted with the new baby, Lowell composed an "Elmwood Gazette" recounting details of the birth for friends — and incidentally testifying to the return of good spirits:

From 1 to 2 A.M. Mr. Lowell makes himself generally useful.
From 2 to 3 A.M. Mr. Lowell makes himself generally useful.
At 3 Mr. Lowell asks Dr. Hosmer how he does.
At 1 minute past three Dr. Hosmer observes that he is pretty well he thanks him.
At 3.5′ the ether is administered.
At 3.10′ Dr. H. asks Mr. L. whether his peaches have done well this season.
From 3.10′ to 3.15′ Mr. L. gives a treatise on the culture of that delicious fruit.
At 3.20′ A general feeling of expectation.

At 3.27′ The child is announced as a daughter, to the satisfaction of both father and mother.

From 3 to 3.27′ Mr. L. makes himself generally useful.

At 3.31′ . . . The 'little treasure' wrapt in flannels, where it keeps itself from rusting by continual motion, while the solicitous attentions of all are devoted to the mother.

From 3.31′ till breakfast, Mr. L. is puzzled what to do with his arms and legs and the other parts of his valuable person. During this period he gets in everybody's way and makes himself generally useful.

At 4 A.M. Miss Rebecca L. the aunt of the distinguished debutante is informed of the news.

At 5 A.M. The grandfather is let into the secret and forthwith embraces his distinguished son.

At 6 A.M. A handsome breakfast is served in a style doing credit to the Elmwood cuisine . . .

At 6.30′ Mr. L. lights a little private bonfire of his own and his happy emotions so bewilder him that he does nothing but inhale the smoke and puff it forth again.[5]

With the restoration of good spirits came an outburst of energy; before the end of 1848, Lowell published four volumes of poetry and a large number of articles and reviews. One of the volumes — *The Vision of Sir Launfal* — was only fifteen pages long, and another, *Poems*, 1847, consisted of verse accumulated since 1845. Still, much of the material published in 1847 and 1848 was actually written in that short period, including in *A Fable for Critics* and *The Biglow Papers* the best of his poetic achievement.

The first volume of this "annus mirabilis" was the *Poems*, published late in 1847. It had all of the themes and most of the faults of the earlier poetry. The familiar topics were preached anew: the beauty of Nature and its revelation of God's benevolent purpose; the need to rely on individual conscience above man-made laws and institutions; a deep sympathy for the poor and oppressed; the superiority of the "simple human heart" over the subtleties of intellect; the necessity of striving toward the Ideal; the desirability of subordinating the traditions of the past to the needs of the present.

Once again, too, Lowell did not merely state, but exhorted; he was still the message poet, the prophet, energetically sentimental, demanding active commitment to virtue. Poetry with a didactic purpose, of course, is not inherently defective; by a broad definition, all poetry "teaches." But Lowell was not satisfied to let his art convey his meaning; he had to intrude it explicitly, and in the process the moralist tended to overshadow the poet. Thus in "Ambrose," fearful lest the reader miss his point, Lowell carefully spells it out:

So, from oft converse with life's wintry gales,
Should man learn how to clasp with tougher roots
The inspiring earth; how otherwise avails
The leaf-creating sap that sunward shoots?

Where didactic poetry succeeds, it is through novel thought or novel imagery; the poet either must have something special to say or a special way of saying the obvious. Lowell had neither. The main trouble with his moralizing was not its explicitness, but its banality. He took his ideas and his forms from others, adding little by way of personal signature other than certain faults—the penchant for archaic words ("uncinctured front") or the lapses into cumbersome imagery ("the forest, witched with slumberous moonshine"). Lowell said of himself in *A Fable for Critics:*

The top of the hill he will ne'er come nigh reaching
Till he learns the distinction 'twixt singing and preaching . . .

But this proposition was less an explanation than an excuse for his poetic failures. The preacher *can* sing; successful achievement in poetry is a function of skill not attitude. It may even be that the extent to which Lowell *was* a poet was not in spite of but because of his moralistic urge; without the homiletic drive, Lowell might have written no poetry, or worse poetry still.[6]

Though the themes and the forms of the 1847 volume were too tired to mark any advance for Lowell as a poet, there was enough difference of tone to mark some growth as a man. The rhapsodic, almost strident optimism of Lowell's earlier verse, though still present, was no longer the sole mood. Some tolerance of uncertainty, some recognition that lofty purpose may fall short in action, now occasionally intrudes, even if self-consciously:

Ah, side by side with heart's-ease in this world
The fatal nightshade grows and bitter rue!

For the first time, too, there is a noticeable strain of nostalgia; Lowell now sometimes looks regretfully back as well as relentlessly forward:

O glorious Youth, that once wast mine!
O high Ideal! all in vain
Ye enter at this ruined shrine
Whence worship ne'er shall rise again . . .[7]

Though the dominant mood remained optimistic, personal knowledge of disappointment, doubt and death had widened Lowell's range. He was now able, if only occasionally, to put aside the prophet's stance and write a simple, unaffected lyric such as the one on Blanche's death:

As, at one bound, our swift spring heaps
The orchards full of bloom and scent,
So clove her May my wintry sleeps;—
I only know she came and went.[8]

But with few exceptions, that part of Lowell which was lyrical, mystical, sentimental never found other than stereotypic expression. He had neither the special vision nor, in place of that, the originality of expression to establish an individualized lyric voice. And probably he had only a limited drive in that direction. Lowell may have called himself half-mystic, half-humorist, but since only the humorist part found its personal style, it was almost certainly the more deeply felt, the more essential element of his nature. It may even be, despite the way he chose to see it, that there was little in his make-up which logically cut him out for the role of brooding seer. He was too playful and buoyant, too little given to introspection. Contemporary definitions of the poet's function may have led him to assume the mantle of poetic prophet, dissatisfied with being a "mere" humorist (in a review written in 1845 he commented that "humorous poetry, even where the humor is genuine, is the lowest kind of poetry, if, indeed, it can be rightly called so at all"). It is significant, in this regard, that when Frederika Bremer stayed with the Lowells in 1849, she thought Maria of "more philosophical depth" than he, and was surprised not to find in him that "deeply earnest spirit" which she had expected from reading his poetry — though she did think him "brilliant, witty, gay." And Edmund Quincy, who knew Lowell well, described him as "entirely free from all the real & affected melancholy of poets & even of persons, and seems to be full to overflowing of enjoyment & happiness & fun." There is, in short, much to suggest that the Lowell of the serious poems was more pose than reality, though almost certainly not conscious pose — he had too much integrity for that. Thus, the failure of his "earnest" verse may have been largely the result of attempting to squeeze a joyous temperament into the fashionable prophetic mold. It may have been, in essence, a failure of authenticity.[9]

Lowell was far more comfortable — and original — as a humorist, and it was as humorist, ironically, that he was also most successful as moralist; only his satiric verse was sufficiently individualized to carry his "message" with immediacy and force. He sensed this himself. As soon as he began work in the fall of 1847 on his first extended satirical piece, *A Fable for Critics*, he felt it would "take." (His only earlier such presentiment had come shortly before, in June, 1846, when the first of the satiric *Biglow Papers* had appeared anonymously in the Boston *Courier* and had aroused a good deal of attention.) Briggs expressed surprise that the same public which had been generally indifferent to Lowell's serious poems now seemed so taken with his satire. The real cause for surprise was not, as Briggs had it, that the public had mistakenly ignored serious poetry of great worth, but that in preferring Lowell's humorous work, it had for once chosen the inventive above the derivative.[10]

The *Fable* certainly had its faults. Lowell wrote it impulsively and rapidly, and though this helped to give it all the dash of a *jeu d'esprit*, its hasty constructions led also to forced rhymes, painful puns, rambling digressions. Lines such as

> *My plot, like an icicle's, slender and slippery,*
> *Every moment more slender, and likely to slip awry —*

are so bad as to seem intentional. Many of the digressions *were* deliberate; Lowell would gleefully announce them in advance, with mock apology or none, as much as telling his audience that he was more concerned with indulging his own high spirits than with producing a polished, tightly-knit poem.

And as a spirited romp through contemporary American literature, the *Fable* was a decided success. It had (to modify Lowell's own definition) more wit than humor — that is, designed wholly for laughter, not occasional tears. The portraits were sufficiently generalized, though treating specific individuals, to allow even the non-literary to share the fun. No special knowledge of life among the literati was needed to enjoy Lowell's characterization of the omnipresent pedant:

A terrible fellow to meet in society . . .
You'll be telling, perhaps, in your comical way,
Of something you've seen in the course of the day;
And, just as you're tapering out the conclusion,
You venture an ill-fated classic allusion, —
The girls have all got their laughs ready, when, whack!
The cougar comes down on your thunderstruck back!
You had left out a comma — your Greek's put in joint,
And pointed at cost of your story's whole point.[11]

Those individuals included in the portrait gallery, of course, did find as much cause for tears as laughter. For though Lowell's manner was flip, his judgment was not; the brash, impudent verse conveyed astute, unflinching verdicts. All the portraits (with the possible exception of that of Briggs) were of writers with major reputations. Nothing fazed, Lowell set about separating the wheat from the chaff, and he did so with such acumen that his judgments in large measure still stand. This is the more remarkable because his evaluations often had to be based on careers still in mid-stream, and in several instances ran counter to judgments then current. In general, he was hardest on those whom posterity has also dismissed — Willis, Dana Sr., John Neal, Halleck and Mathews. Even in these cases Lowell made the demolition more palatable by balancing his criticism with some praise. Thus, having put Halleck in his place as a poet, Lowell at least tried to rescue him as a man:

Halleck's better, I doubt not, than all he has written;
In his verse a clear glimpse you will frequently find,
If not of a great, of a fortunate mind,
Which contrives to be true to its natural loves
In a world of back-offices, ledgers, and stoves.

Small comfort, no doubt, to Halleck's self-esteem, but characteristic of Lowell's effort to mingle charity with justice; throughout the *Fable* he tried to salvage something of a reputation, even as he deflated it. To his victims this may have had all the charm of a smiling hangman, but it did rescue the *Fable* from the category of mere malice.

Just as few of Lowell's portraits were entire condemnations, so were few wholly favorable. Even those he greatly admired came in for some share of criticism, and in most cases posterity has confirmed the detraction along with the praise. Few better things have ever been said, certainly never in so succinct a form, as this on Emerson:

All admire, and yet scarcely six converts he's got
To I don't (nor they either) exactly know what;
For though he builds glorious temples, 'tis odd
He leaves never a doorway to get in a god.

No less acute was Lowell's comment that Cooper, having created one truly new character, had then gone on endlessly to repeat it:

His Indians, with proper respect be it said,
Are just Natty Bumppo, daubed over with red,
And his very Long Toms are the same useful Nat,
Rigged up in duck pants and a sou'wester hat . . .

Sometimes in a single line Lowell conveyed a remarkably apt characterization — Orestes Brownson, the convert to Catholicism, "his mouth very full with attempting to gulp a Gregorian bull"; Theodore Parker haranguing his congregation with "the whole tree of knowledge torn up by the roots"; or the reminder, in relation to Longfellow, "that elegance also is force."

Not all Lowell's verdicts were just. With two writers — Briggs and Lydia Maria Child — his personal friendship led him extravagantly to inflate their talent and importance, and with one, Margaret Fuller, his personal distaste led him to pronounce a verdict far below her desserts. These three portraits were among the few not directly identified in the *Fable* by their own names — Briggs was referred to only as "Harry Franco," Mrs. Child as "Philothea" and Margaret Fuller as "Miranda." It is as if Lowell, embarrassed by his exaggerations, tried to clothe them in partial disguises.[12]

The "Miranda" portrait was the most serious lapse of taste and judgment in the poem, and its only wholly negative characterization. One need not admire Margaret Fuller in order to recognize that in drawing her portrait Lowell was needlessly — and uncharacteristically — cruel. Two years before, Miss Fuller had baldly asserted, in an essay on American literature, that "Lowell . . . is absolutely wanting in the true spirit and tone of poesy . . . his verse is stereotyped, his thought sounds no depth; and posterity will not remember him." Given Lowell's output to that point, it would be hard to fault this judgment, yet remembering, too, that he was still in his mid-twenties, her pronouncement was unnecessarily sweeping — especially since she had herself earlier expressed at least limited admiration for some of the poems. At the time, Lowell had professed not to mind the attack, even while admitting that he was tempted to do "a little retaliatory satire." Momentarily he had resisted the temptation, deciding to let time settle accounts, but the *Fable* seemed too good an opportunity to let pass. Even then he hesitated, wondering whether he might not best revenge himself simply by writing better, but when Maria suggested that perhaps after all he ought to give Miss Fuller "a line or two," he gave up the gentlemanly ghost.[13]

Once unleashed, his accumulated sense of grievance overwhelmed his judgment. Even in a day when literary back-biting was acceptable fare, the portrait of "Miranda" could be considered savage:

> *. . . a woman must surely see well, if she try,*
> *The whole of whose being's a capital I:*

She will take an old notion, and make it her own,
By saying it o'er in her Sibylline tone . . .
There is one thing she owns in her own single right,
It is native and genuine — namely, her spite;
Though, when acting as censor, she privately blows
A censer of vanity 'neath her own nose.

Lowell tried to strike the lines about "spite" just before the *Fable* went to press, but it was too late; Miranda was published "spite" and all, and brought down a fair-sized storm.[14]

Lowell believed the general verdict was "served her right," and perhaps it was — Oliver Wendell Holmes, for one, thought the portrait "too good." Yet there were many delighted by the rest of the *Fable* who found the Miranda section distasteful. Thomas Wentworth Higginson expressed warm indignation to Lowell in a private letter: Margaret Fuller, he wrote, had dared, though a woman, "to study, think, talk & write," and though none of this ought to shield her from comment, it should shield her "from undiscriminating solely contemptuous criticism." From Italy, where Margaret Fuller then was living, W. W. Story also sent a protest: "because Fate has really been unkind to her, & because she depends on her pen for her bread & water (& that is nearly all she has to eat), & because she is her own worst enemy, & because through her disappointment & disease, which embitter every one, she has struggled most womanfully & stoutly, I could have wished you had let her pass scot-free." All this upset Lowell. He had not known that Margaret Fuller was poor and ill, only that she had been harsh and dogmatic. "You may be sure," he replied to Story, "I have felt more sorry about it than any one; only I always reflect *after* the thing is done." But Lowell's repentance may not have been genuine, for he retained the offending lines in later editions of the *Fable*, even after Margaret Fuller's tragic death by drowning.[15]

Whether because of or despite the Miranda portrait, the *Fable* met with immediate success. Longfellow thought it was as good as or better than Byron's "English Bards" — "full of wild wit and deviltry, and amazingly clever." Bronson Alcott, whose portrait had been sympathetically drawn, believed "nobody has said better things of Emerson, Parker, Dwight, or Hawthorne," and when John Ruskin belatedly got hold of a copy, he pronounced the poem "in animal spirit & power . . . almost beyond anything I know." [16]

However, there was considerable minority dissent. Some New Englanders objected to the traducing of their gods; some Southerners, like William Gilmore Simms, seemed outraged that instead of being traduced, they were ignored. Poe, who had been treated with a mixture of adulation and derogation ("three fifths of him genius and two fifths sheer fudge"), lashed out in furious, petulant rebuttal, blaming most of Lowell's "distortions" on his ranting abolitionism, and declaring the *Fable* so weak, malevolent and clumsy that it would permanently damage Lowell's reputation. The days of almost unanimous praise for Lowell had gone by, along with the bland, unchallenging verse which had made it possible.[17]

Lowell made a New Year's gift of all profits from the *Fable* to Briggs — a gesture of real generosity considering his own financial need and his presentiment that sales would be high. Three thousand copies were sold as fast as they could be printed, which meant three editions in rapid succession. But sales tapered off rapidly, so that despite Lowell's good intentions, Briggs' net profit apparently amounted to one small silver plate.[18]

If Lowell himself did not profit financially, he gained what for a young author was better — notoriety. The *Fable* had been published anonymously, but it was soon widely known that Lowell was its author, and the poem thus served as advertisement for *The Biglow Papers*, which followed hard upon it. Lowell had in fact worked simultaneously rather than consecutively on his varied projects of this period, switching back and forth between them in accord with his fluctuations of mood. The first *Biglow Paper*, a satiric comment in Yankee dialect on the effort to recruit troops in Massachusetts for the war with Mexico, had appeared in the Boston *Courier* on June 17, 1846, before the *Fable* had even been begun. Lowell apparently gave no thought at that point to an extended series of satirical poems on the Mexican War; in fact more than a year elapsed before a second *Biglow Paper* appeared. Eventually, the pressure of events, plus the enthusiastic public response to the poems, led him to produce nine *Papers*. Each was written rapidly, occasionally at a single sitting, and initially appeared in the *Courier* and the *National Anti-Slavery Standard*, sometimes separated by long intervals. The majority were presented as if from the pen of Hosea Biglow, independent young Yankee farmer, scornful of slavery, politicians and the war with Mexico. Occasional contributions would be offered from two other inhabitants of "Jaalam," Lowell's invented New England village: Increase D. O'Phace, whose name bespoke his sentiments, and Birdofredum Sawin, a volunteer in the war whose disillusions found logical outlet in political ambition. When Lowell collected the pieces into a volume in 1849, he introduced as "editor" of the poems the additional figure of Parson Wilbur, Jaalam's pedant-clergyman, who contributed "explanatory notes" of vast erudition.[19]

The Biglow Papers viewed the Mexican War — and many New Englanders agreed — as a war of false pretenses, in which a squalid attempt to extend the boundaries of slavery was being masked by a variety of high-sounding rationalizations:

They may talk o' Freedom's airy
Tell they're pupple in the face, —
It's a grand gret cemetrary
Fer the barthrights of our race;
They jest want this Californy

So's to lugh new slave-states in
To abuse ye, an' to scorn ye,
An' to plunder ye like sin.

Lowell gave sardonic phrasing to the sanctimonious talk then current of our "manifest destiny" to spread the blessings of liberty and Christianity:

Thet our nation's bigger'n therin an' so its rights air bigger,
An' thet it's all to make 'em free thet we air pullin' trigger . . .

He derided "Anglo-Saxon superiority" as a belief compounded half of ignorance and "t'other half rum," and charged Northerners with no less guilt than Southerners in swallowing the absurd mixture whole. As Birdofredum Sawin put it,

Afore I come away from hum I hed a strong persuasion
Thet Mexicans worn't human beans,—an ourang outang nation,
A sort o'folks a chap could kill an' never dream on't arter
No more 'n a feller'd dream o' pigs thet he hed hed to slarter;
I'd an idee thet they were built arter the darkie fashion all,
An' kickin' colored folks about, you know, 's a kind of national . . .

War, Lowell insisted, should be labeled for what it was: murder, and those who conveniently adjusted their principles in order to defend it should be exposed as contemptible hypocrites. The Increase D. O'Phaces should speak in words which represented their true position:

I'm willin' a man should go tollable strong
Again wrong in the abstract, fer thet kind o' wrong
Is ollers unpop'lar an' never gits pitied

Because it's a crime no one never committed;
But he mus'n't be hard on partickler sins,
Coz then he'll be kickin' the people's own shins . . .

Lowell saved his sharpest barbs for the politicians, men who talked on all sides of every question with equal facility, their only real devotion being to themselves:

I don't *believe in princerple,*
But oh, I du *in interest.*

Though he had no patience with the time-serving of either major party, Whig or Democratic, the Whigs, who gave greater lip service to antislavery sentiments, came in for special excoriation:

Truth is, the cutest leadin' Wigs, ever sence fust they found
Wich side the bread gut buttered on, hev kep' a edgin' round;
They kin' o' slipt the planks frum out th' ole platform one by one
An' made it gradooally noo, 'fore folks know'd wut wuz done,
Till, fur 'z I know, there aint an inch thet I could lay my han' on,
But I, or any Demmercrat, feels comf'table to stan' on,
An' ole Wig doctrines act'lly look, their occ'pants bein' gone,
Lonesome ez steddles on a mash without no hayricks on.

The Northern politicians were encouraged in their desertion of principle by their constituents, for although Northerners "don't sell their children . . . they *du* sell themselves." In the public mind General Scott had the strongest claim to the Presidency because he was said to have "blown to pieces and otherwise caused to be destroyed more Mexicans than any other commander"; his claim would be strongest, that is, until final returns of Mexican killed, wounded and maimed could accurately settle "these nice points of precedence."[20]

Clearly, Lowell's indignation over the war was profound. Yet his outrage was made more palatable for the reader by his artistry, the sharpness of his accusations somewhat softened by the skill of his satire. So inventive was Lowell's invective, so droll his contempt, that even those unsympathetic to his point of view were somewhat disarmed by admiration for his talents; as the *North American Review* said, in reviewing the collected volume, "political opponents as well as friends laughed loud and long . . ." Yet Lowell's audacity in questioning the widely accepted values of "manifest destiny," martial glory and Anglo-Saxon superiority could hardly go unchallenged. Though the *Papers* had considerable — and lasting — popular success, and a fair share of praise from the critics, the reception was on the whole reserved.[21]

A hundred years later, *The Biglow Papers* seem more open to literary than ideological challenge. The chief defect now seems structural — the introduction (in the collected version) of Parson Wilbur, laden with self-importance and antiquarian lore. In conception, the good Parson, earnest, cautious, pedantic, moralistic, may have seemed to Lowell a necessary addition to a volume devoted to exploring and expressing New England character, speech, and sentiment. But in practice, Parson Wilbur's tedious prose interruptions dilute rather than complement the pungency of the verse. Some of his orotund solemnities are amusing ("I would not be understood as questioning in these remarks that pious theory which supposes that children, if left entirely to themselves, would naturally discourse in Hebrew"), but once his character is established, the pontification becomes repetitive and tiresome. In merely transcribing rather than transmuting Parson Wilbur's pedantry, Lowell reproduced all too well his essential tedium.[22]

Where Parson Wilbur's tone does vary, it represents a loss of authenticity, not a gain in range; it means Lowell has lost sight of the character he originally created rather than that he is giving it new dimensions. When warming to a topic, he often forgot or ignored the person of the pompous, oracular Parson, and shifted directly into his own impassioned, sardonic voice. In thus allowing content to overwhelm character, he sacrificed plausibility. In fact, of his *dramatis personae* only Hosea Biglow remained throughout more or less consistently himself. Both O'Phace and Sawin were allowed to express views incompatible with the personalities which Lowell had assigned them. Thus O'Phace, the compromising politician personified, is made to refer to politicians as "humbugs," and Sawin given lines which alternately deflate and glorify the "Anglo-Saxon theory." By these shifts the characters do not gain in complexity but only lose in credibility, for their changing opinions are bald contradictions, not fused ambiguities. Lowell had a fine gift for limning character in a few words, but he could rarely sustain a portrait; perhaps this helps to explain both why he was attracted to the novel and why he was never able to write one, though he did once try his hand. But since Lowell had trouble producing any long work, a novel or otherwise, the more basic difficulty may have been temperamental — his mercurial, impatient nature.[23]

The defects of *The Biglow Papers* detract from but by no means destroy Lowell's achievement. He had found both a mode and a tone congenial to his gifts — the satiric form of the *Fable* had been joined to the earnest temper of his earlier poetry, humorist and enthusiast had been successfully fused. In finding his own voice, Lowell found as well the signature for his region. The New England moment, the mediated passion of its spirit and the angular wit of its speech, had been authentically captured, and since any provincialism, when honestly wrought, transcends itself, *The Biglow Papers* still manages to read like contemporary comment. In all, it remains, as has long been the accepted verdict, Lowell's most striking performance in poetry.

For the last few months of 1848, Lowell was desperately busy. He was correcting proofs for the *Fable* and *The Biglow Papers*, rushing to finish *The Vision of Sir Launfal* in time for Christmas publication, writing a number of short reviews, and trying to keep up the promised contributions to the *Anti-Slavery Standard.* With the publication in December of the *Vision*, the last of his major efforts of this remarkable year was completed.

The last was not the best. Lowell's Christmas message—"the gift without the giver is bare"—was unexceptionable as sentiment, and had, too, some of the innocent charm of a simple morality tale. As he had in earlier poems, like "A Legend of Brittany," Lowell placed his tale in a medieval setting. His aim was to rise above the "merely" realistic, to transcend the mundane. But in giving his *Vision* remote associations, he ran into difficulties. The thirteenth and nineteenth centuries kept getting entangled; anachronism continually edged the poem toward parody. The medieval knight sounded suspiciously like a New England reformer, and the turreted keeps of King Arthur's circle strangely reminiscent of Brattle Street, Cambridge. As Oliver Wendell Holmes gently suggested, the dandelion, though doubtless an excellent herb, was perhaps not entirely suitable as a subject for chivalrous rhapsody, nor the Baltimore oriole exactly appropriate in a knightly tableau. But since anachronisms allow for easy assimilation of the unfamiliar, Lowell's domesticated little medieval tale had by 1851 gone into a fourth edition.[24]

In the midst of these poetic labors, Lowell found time for some occasional prose reviews. Though in themselves minor efforts—Lowell's career as a critic was still largely in the future—these early reviews do prefigure the directions and attitudes which were to mark his mature criticism.[25]

To some degree his special qualities as critic could have been foretold by his poetry. There was the same lack of structural coherence, the same tendency to glide into digression. As in his poetry, too, the informal, almost whimsical framework contrasted with an occasional stylistic "heaviness." Lowell too obviously delighted in his own erudition, intruding rather than integrating his learning; in one page of a review of Whittier's *Poems* he managed to parade "Souters o' Selkirk," Hans Sachs, Jacob Belimere, George Fox, Bampfylde Moore Carew, Ben Jonson, Claude de Saumaise, Alexander More, Charles Lamb and William Gifford. He paraded them sportively, bouncing them on and off the page like some benign literary grandfather — but the accumulated weight was nonetheless overbearing.[26]

Yet if Lowell could clog his prose with allusion or encrust it with learning, he could just as often be succinct and penetrating — such as the reference to Longfellow's *Kavanagh* as "an exact daguerreotype of New England life. We say *daguerreotype*, because we are conscious of a certain absence of motion and color, which detracts somewhat from the vivacity, though not from the truth of the representation"; or the description of Thoreau's *A Week on the Concord and Merrimack Rivers* as "like a book dug up, that has no date to assign it a special contemporaneousness . . ."[27]

Nor could the occasional opacity of Lowell's style conceal, though it might belie, his forthright literary judgments. In criticism, of course, honesty by itself is no special virtue; opinion must be informed as well as sincere. Lowell sometimes ignored a work's structural defects in order to praise its moral, and softened his criticisms out of ideological (Whittier) or personal (Longfellow) partiality. Yet on the whole, he was remarkably straightforward and just in his verdicts. As in the *Fable*, the opinions expressed in his reviews have stood up well with time; we, like Lowell (but unlike some of his contemporaries), are as certain of Hawthorne's eminence as we are of Fitz-Greene Halleck's insignificance. As with all critics, Lowell was to reveal blind spots — notably in regard to Whitman and Thoreau — but the proportion of hits to misses remains impressive.

Yet neither his perceptions nor his misjudgments were ever to reflect a coherent canon of critical taste. He was to be more of an appreciator than an arbiter, more given to expressing his enthusiasms than accounting for them. Even in these early, scattered efforts, we find Lowell employing uncertain, even contradictory critical yardsticks. He praises Thoreau's *Week* for giving "so much pleasure" and for abounding in "fine thoughts," but it is never clear what he takes to be the source of the one or the content of the other. He expresses distaste for "the everlasting flood of romantic slops," but praises Longfellow's *Kavanagh* for those very qualities—"purity of tone, tenderness . . . a story . . . remarkably sweet and touching"—of which "romantic slop" so often consists. Lowell could articulate a more coherent statement of the critical function than in practice he could apply: critics, he once wrote, should not merely ask of a book, "does it interest *me*? and thus make their private taste (or want of it) a criterion of merit, when it should rightfully only decide the question whether they shall read it or let it alone"; the first question they should ask is "what was the author's intention? Then, how has he fulfilled it?" However, in practice, Lowell's private enthusiasms did tend to become the standard (not merely the basis) for his public judgments. And although his instinct for the first-rate was profound, he was always far better in recognizing real achievement than in defining its quality.

Lowell's extraordinary output in this period also included antislavery pieces for the *National Anti-Slavery Standard*. Beginning in the spring of 1848 he sharply stepped up the number of his contributions. When he had become affiliated with the *Standard* back in 1846, Sydney Gay had publicly announced the addition of a constellation of writers "celebrated in the republic of letters." But in the following two years more than one subscriber had remarked that they had seen little evidence of the heralded new talents, and Lowell himself had sent in only an occasional poem. It was Quincy's opinion that Gay had failed to prod the literati into keeping up with their promises, but knowing that Gay was overworked, that on the whole he had done an excellent job, and that he was sensitive to criticism, Quincy had let the matter slide.[28]

By 1848, however, it had become evident that the services of men like Lowell had to be secured on a more regular basis if the paper was to boost its subscription list, and it was therefore decided to introduce an incentive other than conscience. In March, 1848, Lowell was offered a more binding agreement: in exchange for a weekly article — either poetry or prose — he would be paid $500 a year, the arrangement to be terminated whenever either party should wish. Lowell did not like to take pay for antislavery work, but since the offer had been unsolicited, and since he felt his abolitionism had cut him off from more profitable sources, he decided to accept. He did so despite not fully agreeing with the paper's sponsor, the American Anti-Slavery Society. In fact he agreed less than ever with the Society now that it had become more committed to the advocacy of dis-Union, and he feared its tendency to "treat ideas as ignorant persons do cherries — they think them unwholesome unless they are swallowed stones & all."

But differences aside, Lowell continued to think these men and women the best of their generation, the only people willing to grapple directly with the insidious institution of slavery. If Garrison and some of his followers had their faults, who did not? And even some of their faults were those of position rather than personality. Garrison, for example, had become "so used to standing alone that, like Daniel Boone, he moves away as the world creeps up to him, & goes farther *into the wilderness* . . . [He] was so long in a position where he alone was right & all the world wrong, that such a position has created in him a habit of mind which may remain though circumstances have wholly changed." Besides, Lowell still believed that Garrison's infallible cast of mind might well be essential to the work of reform; Luther, after all, had struck no less infallible a pose. At any rate, faults and all, Garrison, in Lowell's eyes, was a "great & extraordinary man." Surely, he thought — he could not have been more mistaken — posterity would forget Garrison's "hard words & remember his hard work." Lowell was glad to be publicly associated with him.[29]

But of course the association had its irritants. The ideological gap between Lowell and the Garrisonians had been widening steadily since 1845. Even aside from the dis-Union question, on which he had always disagreed with them, Lowell had begun to change his mind as well about the utility of political means in the antislavery struggle. He couldn't help but think it a pity that Wendell Phillips, "born and gifted with all the physical requisites for a politician" was voluntarily laying them aside. And when the Free Soil party was formed in 1848, based on the principle of "non-extension," Lowell regarded it as a welcome development, for however narrow its objects, it signaled the break-up of the old parties and the developing conscience of the country: "perhaps it will be wiser for us to be thankful for what they are than to reproach them with what they are not."[30]

None of this was as yet open advocacy of political means, only the same willingness Lowell had always shown to tolerate different paths to the same goal. But by 1850 he had become sympathetic enough with politics to vote that year for the "Coalition" ticket in Massachusetts, a fusion effort by the Democrats and Free Soilers to topple the reigning Whigs from power. Even some Free Soilers thought the arrangement smacked of "politicking" and withheld their support, but Lowell had by then become eager "to achieve some practical result" and was willing to use the levers at hand. The utilitarian Yankee in him had begun to win out over the theoretician. He had grown tired of being "in the wilderness."[31]

Despite this widening ideological gap, Lowell was promised entire freedom of subject matter in writing for the *Standard*. And except on one occasion — when Gay politely refused to print Lowell's kind words about Gamaliel Bailey, a Liberty party editor — direct interference with his opinions was negligible. Yet Lowell had the uncomfortable feeling that the American Anti-Slavery Society was looking over his shoulder whenever he sat down to write. He knew he could and should work in his own way, but also felt that he ought to work in theirs — with the result that he was plagued by the fear of stalemate. Despite these difficulties, he produced a number of strong pieces for the *Standard* (though also some that were hasty and trivial).[32]

Along with the knowledge that he was aiding the antislavery cause, Lowell knew that he was securing a needed source of income. Had he not received money from the *Standard*, he could certainly have managed to live but probably not to keep Maria's property intact, which he hoped to do if at all possible. *The Biglow Papers* (despite a mixed press) had sold well — the first edition of 1500 was gone in a week — but Lowell had absorbed the cost of stereotyping the plates himself, so that his actual royalties, even after a second edition, came to almost nothing. And the proceeds from the land left to Maria by her father totaled no more than $500 annually. After almost three years, one tenant had still not paid Lowell a cent in rent, and he felt unable to demand it — "since it seems to me that the man who tills the land and makes it useful has a better right to it than he who has merely inherited it."[33]

It was true that he and Maria lived rent-free at Elmwood, but in the spring of 1849 Dr. Lowell, no longer able because of increased deafness to carry out all of his ministerial functions, resigned a quarter part of his salary, leaving him an annual income of only $1500. A larger part of the household expenses thereby devolved on James Russell, and at just the time when a supposedly huge inheritance from Maria's father had given the Lowells a reputation for great wealth, thus exposing them to all kinds of additional solicitations. Nor could he easily resist them. What could he do, Lowell asked, when a fugitive slave came begging money with which to purchase a wife or child? One could hold rigidly to the abolitionist principle of "non-compensation" to slaveholders, but that would mean punishing the fugitive for the sins of the master (when one woman asked him for a contribution toward buying a slave's freedom, Lowell replied that as a member of the Anti-Slavery Society's Executive Committee, "I resolutely decline to give you anything, but in my private capacity I send what I can, assuring you that if my poems were more popular my gifts should be larger"). One could legitimately question, too, whether some of those who came begging were indeed fugitives, or indeed had wives, but it was clearly better, Lowell decided, to be occasionally duped than to risk refusing help to those genuinely in need.

And so Lowell gave whenever he had money to give — at one point he left himself with literally three cents to his name — and when he had no money he gave promissory notes to be paid in the future. So long as he had enough to meet his obligations, Lowell cared nothing for money, but there were times when a check from the *Standard* was all that saved him from embarrassment. At such moments, he wrote good-humoredly to Gay, "I become ferociously radical, and look upon Abbott Lawrence [a wealthy Bostonian] with communistic eyes." Perhaps, Lowell suggested, he might piece out his income by poisoning Garrison, then writing his life and supplying Gay, for a vast fee, with advance sheets.[34]

It was thus a real blow to Lowell — in pride as well as pocket — when the *Standard* failed to renew the agreement with him after the first year. In writing Lowell of the decision, Wendell Phillips tried to put it in the softest possible way: grateful though the Society was for his contributions, some of its members wished to see Edmund Quincy writing for the *Standard* as well, and since the Society could not afford to pay both Lowell and Quincy $500, it had been suggested that for the coming year each contribute a fortnightly rather than a weekly piece and divide the money. Phillips assured Lowell that he had fulfilled the Society's "most sanguine expectations" and entreated him to stay on under the new arrangement.[35]

Phillips was putting the best face on it; not all the members of the Society had been pleased with Lowell's performance. When arrangements for the new year had been discussed at the Society's Annual Meeting, two separate propositions had been offered. One, advocated by Francis Jackson and Stephen Foster, was that the *Standard* be given up altogether; it was not, they complained, trenchant enough (Gay, following Mrs. Child's earlier course, had deliberately made the paper less aggressive than the *Liberator* in order to avoid duplication and appeal to a larger audience). But to abandon the *Standard* looked too much like "striking the colors," and Garrison, Phillips and Quincy successfully argued against such a policy. Defeated on this score, Foster and his sympathizers then proposed at least to curtail expenses, and to do so specifically by dropping Lowell from the paper. Lowell's moderate tone had not recommended itself to Foster, a man Lowell had earlier characterized as:

> *A kind of maddened John the Baptist,*
> *To whom the harshest word comes aptest . . .*

(a description which Garrison himself was said to have chuckled over). To forestall Foster's effort to oust Lowell, Gay presented the compromise finally agreed to: divide up Lowell's duties and salary with Edmund Quincy, whose somewhat more aggressive temper would cater to the Fosterites.[36]

Although Wendell Phillips conveyed these new terms as diplomatically as possible, Lowell knew a rebuff when he saw one. He was not surprised at the Foster clique's dissatisfaction. He had warned them from the beginning, he wrote Gay, that Edmund Quincy might better suit their purpose. The cause, Lowell added, needed all kinds of men, and if the Fosters disbelieved in his usefulness, he did not in theirs. All men, though, could not be zealous George Foxes, and he, for one, was content to convert "by our crops, not by drubbing them with our hoes or putting them under our harrows." At any rate, the Society should not worry about offending him; if they now made him the offer to write fortnightly only to "break his fall," he would decline. But if they really wished him to continue, he would agree to the new arrangement. The necessary reassurances were forthcoming, and Lowell decided to stay on as a fortnightly *Standard* contributor.[37]

At the end of the following year, however, he reconsidered, and wrote Gay that he was inclined to resign entirely. Somewhat to his surprise, Gay replied that a resignation might be timely, for the Fosterites were again proposing that Lowell's salary be put to other purposes; he hastened to add that no one was dissatisfied with Lowell's "spirit, or style, or subjects," but there were those who "will cut off expense wherever it can be done." Though hurt at the readiness with which his suggestion had been taken up, Lowell once more offered his resignation, and it was once more decided that he would remain affiliated, though in a reduced capacity, the agreement this time being that he would send in occasional pieces and be paid on a *pro rata* basis. This desultory arrangement was to last until the Lowells left for Europe in the summer of 1852.[38]

Lowell's attenuating relationship with the *Standard* did not mean that he had lost sympathy with abolitionism; in March, 1850, he still referred to himself as a "dreadful fanatic." But although he continued to believe in the cause, he became increasingly unwilling to devote the bulk of his energies to it. One factor in his falling away was doubtless the lack of wholehearted appreciation for his efforts. For every poem he gave the *Standard*, Lowell claimed, he could have gotten four times the amount elsewhere. Since he had not devoted his pen only out of a need for alms, he thought it ungrateful of the Fosterites to grumble if he did not always hold the pen at an angle exactly to their taste. More important, however, in understanding Lowell's lessening activity — and this was his own explanation

— he had simply grown tired of controversy. Reform activity, he had discovered, could not satisfy the varied needs of his personality. He had preached enough sermons, he felt; it was now time "to come down out of the pulpit and *go about among my parish.*" He believed he could do better than he had as a poet, but that a new apprenticeship was called for.[39]

Lowell's disengagement was further accelerated by domestic tragedy. A third daughter, Rose, who had been born in the summer of 1849 and was thought to be the loveliest of the three, died — again of teething — in March, 1850. Only a few weeks later, Lowell's mother, who as Fanny Longfellow said, had been "so long in the world but not of it," also died suddenly. If the death of Mrs. Lowell brought something like relief, that of Rose brought only grief. The family again tried to be philosophical, tried to "thank God for having blessed them with a little life rounded and perfect as a tear drop," but this time consolation was more difficult:

> *Yes, faith is a goodly anchor*
> *When the skies are blue and clear . . .*

Lowell refused to have a funeral for Rose; his father made a short prayer, and then Lowell walked up alone to Mount Auburn cemetery and saw her body laid by her sister's. Death, he wrote to Sydney Gay, "is a private tutor. We have no fellow-scholars, and must lay our lessons to heart alone." The lessons came slowly. For six months Lowell hibernated; pen and ink seemed irrelevant, and even the writing of a letter was burdensome. The Congressional "Compromise of 1850," with its harsh new Fugitive Slave Bill, roused him to write a few poems of protest for the *Standard*. But essentially he was played out.[40]

When, at the end of the year, Maria gave birth to a son, Walter, Lowell began to shed his depression, to lose the terrible fear he had been living with that his only remaining child was in constant peril — the air "full of deadly, invisible bullets flying in every direction, so that not a step can be taken in safety." He began to write again, and to plan ahead. But he still felt that if he was once more to be productive, a change of scene was necessary. He needed distance not only from recent domestic tragedy but also from the slavery issue, which, for the first time (perhaps in part as a reflection of personal sadness), he viewed with discouragement. As the 1850 Compromise demonstrated, the country's mood had turned more conservative, and "such enormities as the Slave Law" weighed him down "without rebound," made him "too restless to work well . . ."[41]

Reluctantly, he and Maria decided to sell some of her property in order to make possible a trip to Europe. William Wetmore Story and his wife, now settled in Italy where he was devoting himself to sculpture, invited them to spend the winter there, and after much hesitation the Lowells agreed. They could live well in Italy, they calculated, on $1500 per annum; that would mean spending at the rate of about ten acres of land a year — "selling our birthrights," as Lowell put it, "for messes of European pottage." "Well," he decided, "Raphael and the rest of them are worth it."[42]

CHAPTER VI

EUROPE — AND AFTER

SINCE THE LOWELLS expected to be in Europe for several years, the Longfellows gave a farewell *petit souper* for a dozen friends. Grouped around a circular table covered with flowers, fruits, ices and vines, they sat chatting and laughing until late at night; it was, thought Richard Henry Dana, Jr., one of the guests, "a golden evening" — the women beautiful, the men agreeable and clever. Several friends noted with alarm, though, how feeble and ill Maria looked; only traces of her once startling beauty remained. Perhaps, hoped Fanny Longfellow, the trip would benefit her: "she is a very lovely creature, & such a union as her's and Lowells ought to be permanent — it will be — but one would like to have its mortal part not too soon sundered." [1]

The Lowells sailed on the bark *Sultana* in mid-July, 1851: Maria and James, the two children, Mabel, now aged four, and the infant, Walter, and a nurse named Mary to assist in their care. There was a final party on ship-board, an affecting farewell from James' father and his sister, Rebecca, and then embarkation, on a sea so smooth and with "such glorious moonlight" that Fanny Longfellow, watching from shore, confessed real envy of the lucky pair.[2]

The trip took five weeks, and barring some fleas left over from a previous cargo of wool, was adjudged a success. There were no storms, no disagreeable fellow passengers, no lack of good food and water, and above all (excepting a mild bout for Mabel), no seasickness. Walter, the baby, gained a pound a week and was full of life from morning to night. Mabel regularly assisted the Captain at the wheel, kept the sailors busy building doll furniture and badly frightened her nurse by insisting she had seen red and blue rats running about the cabin. Maria herself felt no special improvement from the voyage, but was not discouraged; a cough of seven years' standing, she decided, would require at least a year under new conditions before any great change could be expected.[3]

As for James, he was of two minds about the voyage. It had exhilarating moments — a shoal of fish gliding through the phosphorescent water like a stream of northern lights; the sails by moonlight; sunrise in mid-ocean, naked sun meeting naked sea in a classic of nature. Yet none of this was enough to compensate a man of Lowell's energy for five full weeks of imposed idleness. Nothing, he decided, was so desperately monotonous as the sea. He no longer wondered at the cruelty of pirates: "Fancy an existence in which the coming up of a clumsy finback whale, who says *Pooh!* to you solemnly as you lean over the taffrails, is an event as exciting as an election on shore!" During one twelve-day calm, he became so exasperated at the regular slap of the wilted sails as the ship rose and fell with the motion of the sea — slow, smooth, immitigable — that he could think of but one fitting comparison: Wordsworth's Ecclesiastical Sonnets.[4]

Lowell passed most of his time in reading or in the company of the Captain and chief mate. The mate was his special favorite, a man not born in America but whose speech was purest Cape Cod — proof, Lowell thought, of how easily "our omnivorous country assimilates foreign matter, provided it be Protestant . . ." The mate came to think of Lowell ("somehow or other") as a wag, and should he so much as ask for the butter at mealtime would detect an occult joke and burst into laughter. As for Lowell, he delighted in meeting a man who knew just what he did not. It made him doubt the truth of clichés about "the sympathy of kindred pursuits"; such sympathy, he decided, was really more like "the upper and nether millstones, both forever grinding the same grist, and wearing each other smooth." In one of those paroxysms of seaboard camaraderie, Lowell announced that he preferred "the natural grip with which manhood recognizes manhood" to the artificial society of cultivated men. Under more usual circumstances he found the grinding of cultivated Cambridge millstones quite agreeable fare.

The first glimpse of the shore of Spain brought Lowell a "strange thrill," and the need to philosophize: Americans, wanting in background, lacking richness of memory, could not help but feel their inadequacies in sighting a shore so historic. And yet — the optimistic coda — in being thrown back more wholly on nature, Americans might yet produce a literature with fresh flavor; that is, should they once learn to value their difference.

The Lowells went almost immediately to Florence, where they took lodgings at Casa Guidi, temporarily vacated by the Robert Brownings. The rooms were enchanting — close by the Pitti Palace and the Boboli Gardens, and furnished by the Brownings in a combination of English comfort and Italian style. For six rooms and a kitchen, including silver, china and linen, the Lowells paid forty dollars a month. Not surprisingly, they were delighted with their situation.

To make matters still better, they met up with old friends, Sarah and Francis G. Shaw, and also managed to locate the William Pages, who had been living in Florence for a year. Lowell passed Page one day in the Uffizi gallery without recognizing him — the painter had cut his hair short and begun to bald — but when Page stepped back from the Titian he was copying, Lowell caught sight of him, and the two friends were reunited. Page's career had taken giant steps since they had last spent any length of time together, eight years earlier in New York. His technical facility and his penchant for experimentation had grown apace, and he painted increasingly in the dark patina which he believed had originally been used by the Venetian masters. The results had brought him great acclaim; Emerson said that Page's picture of Ruth "imposed silence upon him which is the effect of all great paintings," and William Channing said of the same canvas that it was "the greatest thing that

America has yet done either in painting or anything else!" A more astute critic of art, Charles Eliot Norton, while acknowledging Page's impressive abilities, feared that he lacked judgment (in life and art). Norton was near the truth. As it turned out, Page's technical experiments proved faulty and his canvases suffered rapid darkening and deterioration. Such of his portraits as still exist — psychologically penetrating, almost sculptural in their solidity — display fine gifts, rendering his lost work and reputation still more regrettable.[5]

Much as Lowell admired Page, both as man and painter, he had doubts about his talent for domesticity. Page's second marriage, to the beautiful Sarah Dougherty, was beginning to run into serious trouble at just the time the Lowells arrived in Florence. The painter's absorption in his work apparently exacerbated — and helped to justify — his wife's flirtatiousness. Her involvement with an Austrian officer became such a staple for gossip in the English-speaking community that in 1853 Page was finally to move the family to Rome. But there Sarah again became involved, this time with the handsome, twenty-one-year-old son of the Duke of Cirella; a café brawl followed in which Page inflicted a terrible beating ("Isn't it damnable?" wrote Lowell) and soon after Sarah fled Rome with Cirella, abandoning Page for good. Lowell by no means put all the blame for the break-up on Sarah; when several years later Page told him that he had finally found "his Platonic other half," Lowell wrote Briggs that Page should be discouraged from remarrying — he too soon drained a woman with his continuous demand for "effervescence of sympathy."[6]

In 1851 the Pages' marriage had not yet reached the point of crisis, and together they took pains to acquaint the Lowells with Florence. Maria lacked the strength for extensive touring — though everything she did see delighted her — but James took long walks through the city, amazed at the noise, the beggars, the extraordinary passion continuously invested in the seemingly trivial. Italians exploded at each other on mere contact, not growing warm by degrees but leaping suddenly from calm to white-heat. If asked to name the one universal characteristic of an Italian street scene, Lowell decided it would be "two men clamoring and shaking themselves to pieces at each other, and a woman leaning lazily out of a window, and perhaps looking at something else."

The passion which infused Italian life was exemplified by the style of "bargaining." Lowell was at first astonished that the purchase of tiny earthen pots, valued at perhaps two cents, excited as much debate as might serve for a transaction worth millions. But he soon understood that the metaphysics of "arriving at a price" involved something more than commerce — the sheer excitement of the contest. The elaborate exchange of offers, the volubility (only partly assumed) of the exchanges, all partook of ritual and sport which went far beyond concern with the objects at hand. Though Lowell could laugh at Italian impatience and fury, he felt, too, that such freshness and force were signs of health. Americans, by contrast, seemed to lack vitality, to be spindly, over-intellectual, accommodationist. He couldn't help but wonder if a people who "put up quietly with all sorts of petty personal impositions and injustices, will not at length find it too great a bore to quarrel with great public wrongs."

The Italian style, he found, even carried over into begging. Lowell thought begging had taken on almost an institutional quality, sanctified by the Church when it established mendicant orders, and solidified by an unequal social system which denied the underclasses any stake in their own country. But the Italians had managed to act on necessity with style: when a friend gave too small a coin to a woman, Lowell delighted in her manner of expressing contempt: "Thanks, *signore,* God will reward *even* you!" But Lowell had a way of overdoing the picturesque and underplaying the sordid; though at first "shocked and pained at the exhibition of deformities in the street," he came to see them as tools of the begging trade — "A withered arm they present to you as a highway man would his pistol; a *goitre* is a life-annuity . . ." Lowell was vacationing from reform with a vengeance.

After two months in Florence the Lowells decided to move on to the warmer climate of Rome for the winter. But plans were suddenly unsettled by news from home: Dr. Lowell had had a stroke. The Lowells' first thought was that they must return at once. But it soon became apparent that Maria could neither safely undergo a winter passage across the Atlantic nor be left alone in Europe. There was nothing for it, they decided, "but to hope & pray." More cheerful reports shortly arrived; the danger, it seemed, had been exaggerated, the stroke had not been severe and Dr. Lowell was gradually mending.[7]

Greatly relieved, the Lowells settled into Julia Ward Howe's old rooms in Rome. Though lacking a view, they were warm and pleasant enough, especially at fifty dollars per month, and especially since William and Emelyn Story rented the apartment immediately below. Maria loved the city at once, but James was slower in appreciation. He first thought Rome gloomy, lacking the bustle and life he had become so attached to in Florence. Bad weather contributed to his discontent; for the first few weeks it rained almost literally day and night, to the point where Lowell proposed to friends that they get up a joint stock company to build another Ark — "directors, of course, to have a free passage & to be *found*, no unimportant matter if the Deluge should be sudden."[8]

The appearance of the city was also something of a shock. Lowell had thought of Rome in terms of the ancients, and the approach on the road from Civita Vecchia, with "Via Aurelia" carved on the milestones, had confirmed his preconceptions. He was unprepared for the modern look of the city, and quickly decided that the new additions were unfortunate — mere ostentation, with little splendor and less grace. Then, too, everything was out of repair, "except the humbug, & *that* with its accessories is kept swept & garnished." He did acknowledge, though, that the mountain horizon which shut Rome in on two sides was impressive, not least, perhaps, because the hills reminded him of Brighton, Massachusetts — which prompted Story to remark that in Lowell's mind "America keeps constant pace in growth with the growth of his experiences here." [9]

Bostonians had a way, as Oliver Wendell Holmes once said, of carrying the Common in their heads as the unit of space, and the State House as the standard of architecture. Midway in his trip, Lowell confessed to his father that on the whole his estimate of Americans had not been lowered by his foreign experiences: "Both physically & intellectually they hold their own very well, & in the facility with which they assimilate ideas they are unequalled." Whether or not true of most Americans, ready assimilation was certainly true of Lowell himself, and it was this which continually rescued him from provincialism and discontent. Despite lapses, he did not insistently measure all things European by American standards (themselves unrealistically gauged) but was able to experience Europe for itself, and thereby gain new perspective on things American. "There are two kinds of travellers," Lowell once wrote, "those who tell us what they went to see, and those who tell us what they saw." Lowell wrote about what he saw. Unlike most tourists, he did not prejudge, nor hold fast to first impressions. After an unfavorable initial reaction to the Romans, he not only came to admire their dignity and grace of manner but also to measure his own countrymen by them. He felt that in some ways Americans were peculiarly at home in the Roman milieu, the logical heirs of the old Empire. Like the ancient Romans, Americans thought art and literature to some degree extraneous, shared the Roman instinct for aggrandizement and trade, and also their genius for politics, for law and for colonization.[10]

But Americans had far less in common, Lowell thought, with the contemporary Roman — and it was the American who suffered by comparison. Americans did have a similar independent bearing, but they lacked the natural ease of the Roman manner. The Roman was expert in doing nothing, in giving himself over to the moment. Surrounded by the ruin of centuries, he knew the insignificance of mere hours and days. Time was an endless bounty, to be spent with large style; to the American time was a taskmaster, to be counted out in small change. Italians generally allowed themselves pleasure without worrying about its source, value or duration; Americans, haunted by self-consciousness and the "evil genius of analysis," could rarely enjoy "a day of right Chaucer." They dared not even enjoy their own individuality, but permitted public opinion "to flatten all character to a lawn-like uniformity"; whereas Italians allowed eccentricity its play, knowing that in the "wildest contortions" was often found "something fearfully human." [11]

If Lowell was an open-minded, he was also a didactic tourist. If he had left the Reformer at home, he carried the Moralist ever with him, seeing "lessons" everywhere. Most of them were subtly perceived, nowhere more impressively (for a son of Puritan New England) than in regard to Catholicism. Inverting the usual Protestant emphasis, he found little of appeal in the Church's buildings, much in her psychology. Rome's churches failed to impress him; he thought they looked nearly alike, sharing a kind of clumsy magnificence but lacking the "spring & soar" of Lombard architecture or the "twilight silence" of Gothic. Even St. Peter's, excepting its "noble" interior, suffered from "architectural elephantiasis"; Michelangelo had confused size with strength — he was "the apostle of the exaggerated, the Victor Hugo of painting and sculpture." Church ceremonies, too, had a dreary sameness. The Christmas Day pomp in St. Peter's was dramatic enough, so long as one regarded it as mere spectacle, but if one bothered to reflect on "the servant of the servants of the Lord in cloth of gold, borne on men's shoulders," the spectacle became more sad than exhilarating.[12]

Lowell was not here playing the parochial Protestant, aghast at the empty splendors of harlot Rome. He had a sophisticated awareness of the significance of ritual, and an appreciation of Catholicism subtle enough to transcend theological disagreement. Catholicism to Lowell was the poet among religions; it provided for mystery, imagination, sensuality; it recognized that men do not, cannot, live by reason alone. Rome never made the mistake of Geneva — of trusting herself solely to the intellect; she was too clever to "give over her symbols and images and sacred vessels to the perilous keeping of the iconoclast Understanding." The Catholic Church provided "for the childish in men," for their various wants or, if you will, their various weaknesses.

Lowell toured neither the churches nor the museums with antiquarian thoroughness. He refused to convert Italy, as he put it, "into a Monster Exhibition," stuffing himself full of blurred memories. If one was to know the country, one must learn at the Italian pace, which meant taking time, allowing impressions "to steep themselves in the sun and ripen slowly as peaches." This meant going into churches or museums almost inadvertently, wandering in after a walk on the Campagna or the Pincio, letting the galleries of the street blend gradually into the galleries of art. He was horrified when a book appeared entitled *Rome in Eight Days*; we shall soon, he wrote his sister, "have boys put through college in six hours, washing & meals included." Lowell's leisurely pace allowed him time to discover his own reactions instead of adopting those considered appropriate for the occasion. He did not talk gushingly of the "wonders of art," but specifically of his enthusiasm for Titian; he did not indiscriminately admire all of Titian, but was able to state a precise preference for "Sacred and Profane Love" above any painting in Rome.[13]

The relaxed pace also gave the Lowells ample time for socializing. They preferred not to make too steady a diet of it — as Maria said, they would rather see *things* than people, "since human nature is not greatly different, and educated human nature in the nineteenth century does not amaze one like the Coliseum." But they went out a fair amount. Lowell was especially fond of seeing Walter Savage Landor, and they also enjoyed the Robert Brownings. (Lowell was an early admirer of Browning's poetry — though with reservations; he offered his copy of *Sordello* to anyone who would put his hand upon his heart and swear he understood it. Yet at the same time he encouraged Wendell Phillips to persist in reading Browning despite the "obscurities" — he would soon, Lowell predicted, read himself into "admiration & understanding.")[14]

On Saturday evenings the Lowells were "at home" to friends — and also to relatives. There were fourteen Lowells concurrently in Rome, giving some point to the remark Lowell had made before leaving the United States, that he was going abroad to become acquainted with the family. On Sundays, James and Maria often went to Mrs. Crawford's, who was a great favorite of his. She had been the gentle, beautiful Louisa Ward, younger sister of Julia Ward Howe, before her marriage in 1844 to Thomas Crawford, the sculptor whose "Armed Liberty" still decorates — some would say disfigures — the National Capitol. The Crawfords lived regally on the outskirts of Rome in a huge pile of golden-gray stone known as the Villa Negroni. It was a focal point for the large colony of American artists who were then of necessity living in Rome, where, unlike in their own country, they could find art schools, materials and patrons. The Crawfords were especially fond of private theatricals, and at one such evening Lowell made a great hit with his uproarious playing of Bottom in "A Midsummer Night's Dream" — complete with a prologue full of bad puns which he wrote for the occasion. Throughout his Roman stay, Lowell was apparently at his most charming, a companion, as Story put it, full of "humor & life & freshness & cordiality."[15]

Not only James, but the whole family seemed to be thriving. By mid-winter Maria was feeling so much better that she could take long walks without tiring, and although her cough continued to be "rather noisy," she believed it sounded more superficial than before, as if it came from the throat. Walter, with his "tender ways," beseeching blue eyes and quick intelligence, was developing into an extraordinary little boy — one of that countless number, Lowell wrote his father (striving for objectivity), "out of which the world contrives afterward to make such ordinary men." Mabel rapidly picked up Italian, was getting charmingly fat and had begun to ask the usual incisive questions: when Lowell one day said something about her "Heavenly Father," she gravely countered with, "Papa, have I got a Heavenly Grandfather?" The Lowells were not much in favor of curtailing children, but may have had second thoughts one day when Mabel casually announced, after returning from an afternoon outing, that she had just seen a man hanged. The nursemaid, when questioned, tearfully confessed that having heard of the event in advance, she had rather thought she would like to see it.[16]

In May, after the Lowells had left Rome for Naples, Mabel contracted the measles, and although her case was mild and rapidly over, they feared Walter might catch the disease. But when they arrived back in Rome in mid-May he still seemed in perfect health, and they began to breathe more easily. Suddenly, on the night of May 17, he took ill. Three weeks of intense anxiety followed, constant fear and occasional hope, ending finally in his death. The Lowells were numb; once more a broken promise, once more a lovely child cut off in infancy. "How beautiful & full of promise he was nobody but we will ever know," Lowell told his sister, "& I cannot write about him." Did they dare to think of a future for Mabel? "She is well now, today," wrote Maria, "but I have no certainty for tomorrow."[17]

Lowell thought it more important than ever for Maria that they spend another winter in Europe, but there was also his father to think of. Dr. Lowell had not improved as rapidly as first hoped, and was evidently pining for their return. When a French doctor examined Maria's lungs and found no evidence of tubercular disease — though a good deal of irritation in the bronchial tubes — they decided that they could not justify a longer stay, and so made final plans to return in the fall. With limited time now available, and realizing that activity would be an anodyne, they determined to squeeze in as much hard travel as possible before they sailed. They managed a few days in Venice, about two weeks in Paris, an extensive though hurried tour of Switzerland, and finally, just before sailing, a brief fortnight in England. There were quick impressions, longer memories: the "snow solitudes" of Mt. Blanc; hearing the famous organ at Fribourg; the exquisite pastoral scenes in the Lauterbrunnen valley; the press of fashion in Paris; the ignorance of the English in regard to things American — like thinking the "Free-soil" party was made up of agrarians (Lowell supposed that in retaliation he should write home that the Whig party in England went for the instant revival of periwigs).[18]

They sailed for home October 2, 1852, sharing passage — a final dividend — with Arthur Hugh Clough, the poet, and William Thackeray (who was bound on a lecture tour). They had met Thackeray briefly in London and had found him genial if sometimes rough in manner; to while away the time on shipboard, he made several drawings of Maria and gave them to her, along with some of his other doodles. All that we know of his reaction to the young American couple derives from one ambiguous phrase: "There is an awful superior woman aboard, Mrs. Lowell, with a clever husband, very pleasant . . ."[19]

The Lowells arrived at Boston in mid-November, and were greeted with delight by family and friends. There was general agreement that Maria looked better and that James looked worse: he had shaved his beard (alas, thought Fanny Longfellow, along with it he had removed half the poetry from his face). Dr. Lowell's joy at seeing them was so great that it dissolved any lingering regrets about returning early. They were relieved to find him looking very much himself, though himself a little exaggerated — he shed tears easily, was quickly excited and could not bear to be too long in company. But he had an excellent nurse in constant attendance, and with his children home once more, seemed content with the simple life of daily trips to the Post Office and occasional ventures into town to tend the needs of a parishioner.[20]

Lowell's sister, Rebecca, also seemed well — less excitable and somewhat happier. She soon began to teach Mabel to read, write and sew, and this gave her a greater feeling of usefulness and importance. Mabel was the center of all their lives — she had "such droll little ways with so much dramatic force and sweetness." She and her grandfather were closely attached; the more deaf he became, the more he seemed to cling to the larger writing of a child's world, while she delighted in the adult responsibilities of leading him up and down stairs and carrying him his daily luncheon.[21]

They were a happy family, and in many ways a self-contained one. After the bustle of European travel, James and Maria enjoyed nothing better than quiet evenings at Elmwood, talking or reading in the study. Cambridge, they agreed, was full of pleasant people, but they preferred distant good will to steady fellowship. Not that they were hermits. They saw their neighbors, the Longfellows, with fair frequency, and now and then a friend like Edmund Quincy would come out to stay with them for a day or two. Occasionally, they entertained more elaborately. Lowell gave a supper — men only — for Thackeray, at which ten friends, including Longfellow, Quincy, Arthur Hugh Clough, James T. Fields, the editor, R. H. Dana, Jr., and T. W. Parsons, the Dante translator, sat telling stories and anecdotes from ten until two in the morning. At one point the American West came up, and someone adduced in proof of its wildness that twenty-six school children had been devoured by bears at one place in a single year; Lowell was convulsed by Thackeray's aside: "Ah! — that touches the heart of an Englishman —

twenty-six *eaten* children." Clough thought the Boston fondness for puns dreadful, but Longfellow delightedly copied another sample from the evening into his journal:

> As we were going away Thackeray said, "We have staid very long." "I should say," replied the host, "a long and too short — a dactylic supper." [22]

Lowell went into society more often than Maria, attending those occasional dinners for male worthies which were (and are still) a staple of Boston life. But on the whole he was inclined to stay quiet, to lead a life of domesticity and letters. National affairs could occasionally arouse him — in 1853 he was still quoting with approval one of his favorite passages: "In private and personal wrongs, we do well to put on the meekness of the lamb; *but, when some great public injury is done to virtue, all they are asses which are not lions.*" But he did little to resume an active role, other than occasionally promising himself and Sydney Gay to write something for the *Standard.* His quiescence coincided with the national mood; the Compromise of 1850 had created an uneasy truce over slavery which the election of Franklin Pierce as President in 1852 had further cemented, and the antislavery forces both nationally and locally were demoralized and divided. Lowell's inactivity, though, was less imposed by the discouraging state of public opinion than by the feeling that he "had done his duty" and earned repose. A year's distance from American politics had confirmed his growing disinclination to devote his major energies to transient journalism and the particulars of daily battle: "Nature has provided her Greenwich for all of us, where we recall past exploits rather than project new ones." When Edmund Quincy was asked if it was true that Lowell had fallen from Antislavery Grace, he replied, "I don't perceive any particular difference in James since his return. I never regarded him as a Saint of the first water." But there *was* a difference, if only of degree; when invited to address the "Whole World's Convention," Lowell replied that he sympathized as much as ever with any movement to "elevate man or woman socially or morally" but believed that "the *How* must be left to the care of individual experience." Here was the new note: let each man look within for regeneration rather than taking on the responsibility of being his brother's keeper.[23]

Lowell wished now to concentrate on literature. While in Europe he had written nothing except a few letters and an occasional journal entry. The usual unsettlement following travel compounded the difficulty of re-establishing a writing routine; for a time he was unable to focus on a project. Longfellow met him one day as Lowell was returning from buying a blank book in which to begin a novel, and noting his rather sad manner, Longfellow charitably invited him home to smoke a pipe and to reassure him that once he got "warm in the harness" again, he would write a capital book. Longfellow was wrong; the novel never progressed beyond a first chapter, perhaps, to paraphrase Howells, because Lowell's instincts were to be true to an ideal of life rather than to life itself. Lowell seems to have realized as much; characters in an essay (a form he could work well in) did not demand, he once said, "so much sharpness of outline and truth to every day as is essential in stories of life and the world. In the essay the characters *ought* to be Ideas talking . . ."[24]

Although the novel failed to develop, by midwinter Lowell had finally embarked on a variety of projects. Briggs, in association with George William Curtis and Parke Godwin, had started a new magazine in New York called *Putnam's Monthly*, and Lowell began a series of satiric poems for them on foreign travel. Belabored and arcane, they found little favor, and at Briggs' suggestion Lowell discontinued the series after the third installment. He himself thought well of the poems and had expected that they would make a big hit; such vanity, he told himself, deserved to fail. Yet he regretted the miscarriage as much on Briggs' account as on his own, sensible that the new magazine had needed a popular success ("I thank God for giving me at least this talent — that I love my friends better than I do my own pride, and can almost persuade myself that I love them nearly as well as my interest").[25]

But there were other ventures to take up the slack. He reworked some prose sketches of life abroad and renewed a project started in 1849 to write a sort of New England "Canterbury Tales," in which half a dozen friends would entertain each other during their "nooning" with stories or poems. As with all his large-scale enterprises, "The Nooning" would never be completed; Lowell would return to it off and on for years, and occasionally would publish fragments, but he could not sustain the effort.[26]

What remained of his time during the winter of 1853, he gave to planning a course of lectures which he had been invited to deliver by the Lowell Institute — a tribute to his reputation, not his name, for although the trustee of the Institute, John Amory Lowell, was indeed a cousin, he was also a man of scrupulous integrity. It was a great honor to be invited by the Lowell Institute. Not only did it pay handsomely, but since its inauguration in 1839 it had sponsored a series of "adult education" lectures of the highest caliber: Asa Gray on Botany, Jared Sparks on American History, Charles Lyell on Geology, Louis Agassiz on the Plan of Creation. Lowell was allowed to select his own subject, and he decided on "The English Poets," gaily announcing to Briggs that he would use the opportunity to revenge himself on dead poets "for the injuries received by one whom the public won't allow among the living." As the lectures were not due to be delivered until the following winter, Lowell allowed himself various distractions, including a hiking trip to Maine with his nephew, Charles Russell Lowell (he had a plan, he told Quincy, of "shooting dilemma & bringing home the horns. It is a beast which I fancy may be frequent in those parts, & the antlers hung in my study would have an agreeable effect on disputatious persons").[27]

But preparation of the lectures was to be delayed far longer than Lowell anticipated. His life, though he but little suspected, was about to be broken into pieces. Maria's health had been poor for so long, and yet she had managed to rally so many times, that any new fluctuation was not likely to be thought unduly serious. She had become very ill in the spring of 1853, and took to her bed nearly helpless with exhaustion. But once more she had seemed to mend, and though weak and pale had borne it all with so little complaint that Lowell seemed justified in believing no permanent injury had been done. Besides, the doctors had been telling them for years that there was no evidence of tuberculosis. Friends like Edmund Quincy might be alarmed, might wonder how such a fragile creature still managed to hold on to life, but Lowell would not or could not recognize that Maria had little remaining strength. Suddenly, in early October, he awoke to the danger. Maria's decline had by then become so pronounced, she had grown so frail, that Lowell finally had to face the desperate nature of her illness. "The waters," he wrote Briggs, "have gone over me." An abyss opened before him which he could still hardly bear to acknowledge; when Maria briefly rallied, he talked of her "steadily mending," when she showed the barest signs of strength, he announced that he was "greatly encouraged." Then suddenly it was over; on October 27, 1853, Maria Lowell died — the very day a child was born to their neighbors, the Longfellows.[28]

Friends did what they could, but Lowell was overwhelmed, bewildered, close to shock. He could not stay warm; his thoughts became external and talked *to* him, faster and louder, leaving him dazed. He tried to recall that Maria had died calmly and full of faith, but this gave him no consolation. He tried to remember how beautiful their past had been together, but could not see it for his tears. "By and by," he kept repeating, "by and by," knowing that time would do something for his anguish, knowing he had a daughter for whose sake he must live.[29]

The funeral was held in late afternoon, the sky red with sunset, the trees leafless, no sound but the movement of the mourners as they followed the coffin to a quiet spot on a wooded knoll. The lid was opened for Mabel to see her mother once more. Lowell leaned for a long while against a tree, weeping. Then they returned in the twilight.

And so it was over, the true marriage, the fortunate youth.

CHAPTER VII

BEGINNING ANEW

Were it mine I would close the shutters,
Like lids when the life is fled,
And the funeral fire should wind it,
This corpse of a home that is dead.

LIFE AT ELMWOOD went mechanically on. The unaltered rooms with their familiar objects somehow accentuated the bitterness. Not even Nature gave a sign: "Not a bee stints his hum, the sun shines, the leaves glisten, the cock-crow comes from the distance, the flies buzz into the room . . ." Lowell's immediate family was of little help, his father perfectly deaf, his sister not speaking for a week at a time. Mabel was his only comfort; the tenderness with which she treated her father made her seem older than her years, more like a companion than a child ("She is an unlimited darling," Lowell wrote).[1]

None of his oldest friends were within reach, men like Briggs or Page, who had from the beginning been part of his life with Maria and could best understand the extent of his loss. The Longfellows and Edmund Quincy showed deep concern, and a more recent friend still, the urbane, spare Charles Eliot Norton came to mean much to him during this period; eventually Norton was to become Lowell's dearest friend, his "loving Charles."

But there was little any of these well-intentioned friends could do:

Console if you will, I can bear it!
'Tis a well-meant alms of breath;
But not all the preaching since Adam
Has made Death other than Death.

Everything lacked importance, everything "out of place but silence . . . the only enduring thing on earth is the love we have given away." For the first time Lowell felt old; he had a past, something alien to his present life from which he was now exiled. Sometimes he felt Maria was near him, more often not, and he looked forward with agony to the inevitable time when she would become a memory instead of a presence. At his most desolate, he recalled his faith in a future life, certain that the purity of Maria's soul guaranteed her immortality:

> *But that is the pang's very secret,—*
> *Immortal away from me.*

A future reunion, he felt, depended on his keeping himself worthy of it; he fought off constant thoughts of suicide but felt less certain of his ability to resist "the world & its temptations." "I am not an ass & never could deceive myself," he wrote Briggs three months after Maria's death, "I know perfectly well that my nature is naturally joyous & susceptible of all happy impressions." Therein lay an additional cause for anguish: would he be able to keep himself "pure" enough to deserve a reunion? [2]

For many months he remained almost solitary — an occasional dinner at Longfellow's or at Norton's, an occasional visit from Edmund Quincy. He did his best, when in company, to keep up his spirits, for he did not believe in inflicting private sorrows on others. With close friends he now and then unburdened himself, but he knew that ultimately he must bear his grief alone. His refusal to air his private tragedy indiscriminately, his effort not to turn social occasions into personal purgatives, led to some cruel misinterpretations of his conduct. Francis J. Child, Boylston Professor of Rhetoric and Oratory at Harvard (later a Lowell intimate but in these years a slight acquaintance) reported to Arthur Hugh Clough that though Lowell had been expected to take his loss very hard, he had already, four months after Maria's death, "recovered his ordinary cheerfulness." Child also relayed a remark of Richard Henry Dana, Jr.'s, that Lowell had proven to be "shallow both in his feelings and in his understanding." Dana had accidentally run into Lowell on his way to town, and since Lowell had been "clever, entertaining & good humored" during their walk, Dana decided he was "rather a trifler" — his feelings "cannot be deep." In this same vein, rumors began to fly that Lowell would shortly announce his engagement to Ellis Gray Loring's daughter, Anna, or to Charles Norton's sister, Jane.[3]

Child and Dana were seeing real qualities in Lowell's personality, but drawing false conclusions from them. Because the face Lowell chose to show the world changed but little, men like Dana assumed that beneath the surface all was under control, or rather that his feelings were so shallow that no control was necessary. Those who knew him better realized the desperate struggle he was going through and honored his courage in not forcing it upon others. Quincy thought no man had ever passed "through a stormier tempest of affliction," and Norton believed Lowell's grief, if anything, grew heavier with time. Had those who thought Lowell callow been able to see his private diary, they might have understood the depth of his sorrow:

> Jan. 15 (1854): M.L. anima beata! carissima, ahi de potessi vederti una volta ancora per un momentino solamente!
> Feb. 9: M.L. M.L. M.L. M.L. A sad day — piangeva acerbamente . . . Dearest! dearest!
> Feb. 22: 35 years old today & no better.
> March 10: Dark without & within. M.L. M.L. M.L. . . .
> Oct. 17: Itamane ancora piangera. Sancta Maria, ora pro me!

On many days, he simply wrote "M.L." in large letters across the diary page, too overwhelmed to do more than scratch her initials. Seven months after Maria's death, Longfellow, to whom Lowell would sometimes expose his feelings, found him "low spirited and weary . . . says he would write no more if he were not forced to do it. He has no heart for the task, and is lonely and desolate."[4]

But work, as Lowell recognized, served more than a financial need; he must keep busy, however mechanically. He managed to send an occasional poem to Briggs for *Putnam's* or to W. J. Stillman, whom he had recently met and liked, for his new weekly journal of art and literature, *The Crayon.* But he could not rouse any real enthusiasm for writing poetry. For now he preferred prose, and so began reworking his Italian diary and letters, finished a "Moosehead Journal" about the camping trip he had taken to Maine with his nephew, and started a commemorative sketch on "Cambridge Thirty Years Ago." The three pieces were not to appear in book form until 1864, when they were issued under the title *Fireside Travels,* but the greatest part appeared as magazine pieces in *Putnam's* and *Graham's* during 1854.[5]

Lowell also undertook to do editions of Dryden, Marvell and Donne, and biographical sketches of Keats and Wordsworth, for the *British Poets* series being published by Little, Brown & Co. under the general editorship of Francis J. Child. (Special thought and labor went into the Marvell edition; Lowell believed it would be the most correct available, though he admitted that was saying little.) He even thought of doing an edition of Shakespeare, and also a life of Swift — "I meditate everything, for I must keep busy at work." The project he had his heart most set on, though, was a memorial volume of Maria's poems; in an edition of fifty copies, for private circulation only, it appeared in 1855.[6]

In the midst of these labors, he tried to begin a new "Biglow Paper" for the *Standard.* He was outraged at the recent Kansas-Nebraska Act, which had reopened those two territories to slavery. Lowell felt that every man who hadn't "passed his Master's degree in Black-guardism" ought to speak out; the annexation of Texas had been "white as an angel" compared to the Nebraska "swindle," and Tyler "a Hyperion to Pierce." But this time

Lowell could not convert indignation into poetry. After weeks of attempting a new "Biglow," he had a total of four lines. Somehow, he wrote Quincy, "I have lost the hang of *that* schoolhouse"; only with the Civil War would he again be able to pick up the thread. Gay invited him to write monthly editorials for the *Standard* instead, and Lowell reluctantly promised to try, when and if the spirit came upon him — which it never did. He allowed himself, though, as for years past, to be elected to the Executive Committee of the Massachusetts Anti-Slavery Society; he acknowledged "with shame" that he never did anything, but did not like to be left out — it would make him feel, he told Quincy, as if he had "lost caste." [7]

By the end of the year, he was spending almost all of his time on the series of lectures earlier promised for the Lowell Institute. They were due to begin on January 9, 1855, but by late December, Lowell had still completed only five of the expected twelve; he was, as always, awaiting last-minute pressure and inspiration. But even at the eleventh hour the lectures would not flow as he had hoped, and knowing he had to do an especially creditable job in order to justify having been appointed by a relative, he began to feel desperate. To compound his anxiety, there had been a great rush for tickets, only one applicant in five being supplied, and Lowell, who had never spoken in public before, became lean and sleepless.

As it turned out, the lectures were a great success. There was some grumbling over the soundness of his views, and some feeling that the series as a whole lacked unity, but even detractors agreed that Lowell's performance had been droll and entertaining. Thus Francis J. Child, though thinking the lectures "hasty," acknowledged that their "instantaneous effect" had been delightful — quite the best thing he had ever heard from the "perverse" Lowell, who would "persist in being serious contrary to his impulses and his talents." Others were less grudging in their praise. Longfellow believed the series "admirable," Norton thought the humor in them "as fine & fresh" as Lowell in his best moods, and Charles Sumner wrote from Washington that he had read with delight every word of the series as printed in the *Advertiser*. The most dubious praise came from Mrs. Sigourney, the "sweet singer of Hartford," who had also followed the course via the newspapers, and who wrote to thank Lowell for the "droppings of harmony" which had so cheered her fireside — perhaps what Lowell had in mind when he protested that despite their success, he didn't feel as if he had really gotten himself into the lectures.[8]

While still in progress, the lectures brought forth an unexpected result: the Corporation of Harvard College asked Lowell to replace Longfellow as Professor of Modern Languages. Longfellow had decided to give up the post a year before; he had become tired of the weary round of books, lectures and students, and wished more time for leisure and poetry. To succeed Longfellow (and before him, Ticknor) was considered a high honor. There had been seven applicants for the place, all with excellent qualifications and all friends of Longfellow. Lowell had not applied; when it was proposed that he be a candidate, he refused, and the front runner for some time was thought to be Samuel Eliot or George Ticknor Curtis. But according to Longfellow, Lowell so astonished the town with his lectures on poetry that at the last moment the college offered him the post. Longfellow was sorry for the disappointment to his other friends, but as a lecturer, at least, he thought Lowell the best of the candidates, and was "proud to have such a successor."

As for Lowell, he was delighted. The appointment had come in the best possible way — "the place has sought me, not I, it." The duties, moreover, were to be comparatively light. Unlike Longfellow, Lowell would not do any language teaching — four native speakers, one each in German, French, Spanish and Italian, would handle those chores. Lowell would exercise general supervision over the Department and would deliver two lecture courses a year, the choice of subject his own. The salary, of course, was to be cut in proportion to the diminished duties of the post, but the $1200 income meant that Lowell would have enough to live on without continuously working Grub Street. Besides, Harvard's president, James Walker, made it clear that should Lowell hereafter feel inclined to assume the whole instruction in any one of the languages, his appointment would be changed from a "half" to a full professorship.

There was only one reason for hesitation, hardly insignificant: Lowell feared he was not competent for the post. He felt tolerably able to lecture on Italian literature, and in French he blandly assumed that only further reading was needed, for there was "no French meaning (except Rabelais) so deep that one may not easily get to the bottom of it." But he felt weak in German and Spanish, and German literature especially he considered of prime importance. He therefore suggested to the Harvard Corporation that he be allowed to take a leave of absence his first year so that he might go abroad to master Spanish and German. He felt a year would be sufficient, for he was "naturally fond of such studies" and learned "foreign tongues with ease."

The Corporation consented, and Lowell's appointment was thus settled. Not, however, to everyone's satisfaction. There were misgivings in some quarters about his political, if not his literary qualifications. R. C. Winthrop, the conservative Whig leader, wrote President Walker that Lowell's "ultraisms" did not recommend him; he, Winthrop, should be glad to exchange a little of Lowell's poetry for "more of the practical sense & soundness" of his father, Dr. Lowell. In the final voting at the Board of Overseers, fifteen of the sixteen votes were for confirmation, the sixteenth, a blank, was presumably Winthrop's mute protest.

Once matters were decided, Lowell himself was not overly cheerful about the prospects; he especially dreaded having to leave Mabel for a year. Yet he knew that it was for Mabel, above all, that he had to do it, for the professorship would for the first time give him a financial anchor. Recently, still further drains on his limited income had become necessary. Maria had enjoined him, in case of her death, to hire a governess for Mabel, for she did not wish the child left to the "queerities" of Rebecca Lowell. He had given the position to Frances Dunlap, whose sister had been one of Maria's friends. Miss Dunlap came from a once wealthy family in Portland, Maine, but was now a "reduced gentlewoman," forced to earn her own living. Lowell was to pay her $300 — out of a yearly income of roughly $600 — but she seemed worth the money: "a very agreable person, intelligent, sensible, with several accomplishments." Thus Miss Frances Dunlap, who was to play a sigificant role in his future, quietly entered Lowell's life.[9]

Before learning of the Harvard appointment, Lowell had contracted to lecture through western New York and in Illinois in order to supplement his income. He thus had to spend most of March and April away from home on the lecture trail prior to his June, 1855, departure. He detested it. Lecturing, as he summed it up, consisted of being received "at a bad inn by a solemn committee . . . to have three cold fish-tails laid in your hand to shake, to be carried to a cold lecture-room, to read a cold lecture to a cold audience, to be carried back to your smoke-side," paid, and the three fish-tails once more laid in your hand. Lowell had hoped that seeing the West might at least prove interesting, but he soon decided it was but the East all over again — "dirtier & worse-mannered" in the taverns and on railways, more "openhanded" in private homes. It was all "too new for an old fellow . . . something like eating raw meat." After only a week of it, Lowell was in such low spirits that he tried to beg off from the rest of the trip, but could not get a release and so continued on to the end. Occasionally he did have a pleasant time — seeing Trenton Falls, or meeting ex-President Millard Fillmore, whom he found, to his satisfaction, "one of the stupidest-looking men" imaginable. At any rate, he came home with $600 in his pocket, which in retrospect at least, seemed to make it all worthwhile.[10]

The night before he left Boston for his year abroad, Lowell's friends gave him a bachelor dinner at the Revere House. Many of the Boston notables were there — Longfellow, Emerson, Agassiz, the two Holmeses (Oliver Wendell and John), Benjamin Peirce, C. C. Felton, Quincy, Norton, Dwight, Tom Appleton, Carter. Oliver Wendell Holmes read a poem of farewell and then produced two letters to Lowell, one from the Rev. Homer Wilbur and the other from Hosea Biglow; they were cleverly done and brought shouts of laughter. It was, as Longfellow put it, "a joyous banquet," one of the pleasantest he had ever attended. Lowell was again dined and toasted in New York, where he embarked for Europe. Bryant, still nurturing some grievance against Lowell for his treatment in the *Fable*, was invited to one affair; warned in advance, Lowell set out to captivate him and apparently succeeded. As a friend remarked, Lowell's tact was such that "in society no one whom he desired to interest could resist him." [11]

Amid all the festivities, Lowell looked with apprehension to the year ahead. Cut off from familiar surroundings and friends, his loneliness could, he knew, become acute. And he feared that he would miss his daughter desperately. Under Miss Dunlap's personal charge, she was to live with her uncle and aunt, Estes and Lois (White) Howe; there was little to worry about therefore on her account, more on his. Before sailing, he sent her the good-bye note that appears at the top of page 145.[12]

As Lowell had feared, the year in Europe proved an agony, though it started well enough. He went first to Paris, hoping to meet the Storys, only to discover that they had left for London the day before his arrival. But he stayed on for three weeks, trying to polish his French and touring the galleries. They were rather dull weeks, though he went almost every day to the Louvre and thought it as fine as ever; he discovered his first real pleasure in Rembrandt and renewed his joy in Titian (he took special comfort from one of the Titian portraits, never tiring of sitting in front of it — the face "so young and yet so full of

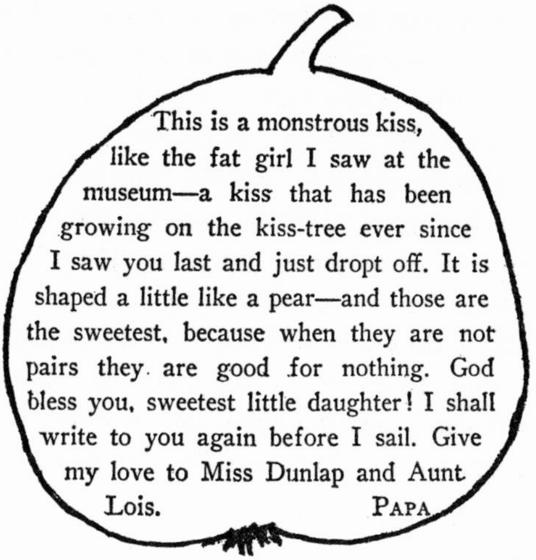

This is a monstrous kiss, like the fat girl I saw at the museum—a kiss that has been growing on the kiss-tree ever since I saw you last and just dropt off. It is shaped a little like a pear—and those are the sweetest, because when they are not pairs they are good for nothing. God bless you, sweetest little daughter! I shall write to you again before I sail. Give my love to Miss Dunlap and Aunt Lois. PAPA

experience, of sadness, and above all, resolve"). There was, too, a glorious day at Chartres Cathedral, its "mossy saints and angels looking down . . . out of that hoary, inaccessible past," the home now of swallows and sparrows "who build upon the shoulders of those old great ones — as we little folks do too, I am afraid." [13]

The only other real pleasure of his Paris stay was meeting with Christopher Cranch, that shy, charming, melancholy shadow, who having fought the good transcendental fight had come to live in Europe, hoping to eke out a living from his varied, unfocused talents as painter, preacher, poet. Lowell called him "The Knight of the Rueful Countenance" and Cranch, in turn, referred to his new friend as "The Knight of the Ruddy Beard" or "Sir Barbarossa" in honor of Lowell's latest red-brown growth. Their friendship progressed rapidly, Cranch's temperamental and Lowell's temporary sadness blending into one; Cranch still further attached, perhaps, by recognizing in Lowell the underlying brass he knew he would always lack, Lowell, by pitying in Cranch that pervasive melancholia which in himself he recognized as transient.

When the Storys tempted Lowell over to London at the end of July he took Cranch with him. Having gone for a day, they stayed a month. The climate agreed with Lowell, it was good to be with old friends, and he felt so much improved that he allowed himself to linger. Together they took excursions to Winchester, Salisbury, Stonehenge, and to Eastbourne on the seashore, toured the art galleries, ate at the Mitre Tavern (where Dr. Johnson's bust "dingy with the steam of many generations of dinner" looked down on them), and spent some time with the literati — Leigh Hunt, Browning and Thackeray. An especially happy occasion was the evening Thackeray took Lowell, Story and Cranch to the Garrick Club for dinner. The cutlets being small, Thackeray advised Story to eat one anyway — "it will make you feel a little hungry at first, but you'll *soon* get over it." Following dinner, the four men went to a room over the "Cyder Cellar" to smoke, and Thackeray read aloud to them from *The Newcomes*, punctuating his recital with parenthetical comments on the characters ("That's my she-devil of a mother-in-law whom I have the pleasure to possess still"). When Lowell objected to the marriage in the book of Clive and Ethel, Thackeray acknowledged that artistically it ought not to have taken place — "But then she needed the sorrow to improve her character and make her a good wife." [14]

From England, Lowell crossed to Antwerp, stayed a day or two to see the Rubenses ("just Paolo Veronese translated into Flemish, but translated by a poet") and to look over the city ("Les Flamandes sont enormement laides. I begin to think that Rubens's second wife was the only pretty one there ever was, and he probably flattered her in his pictures in order to have a quiet home"). [15]

By the end of August, Lowell had arrived at Dresden, expecting to move on to Berlin for the winter — a plan never carried out because of the deep depression which soon overtook him. At first he liked Dresden "well enough." There were pleasant walks, a good art gallery and an excellent theater. And he was comfortably housed with Dr. Reichenbach, a well-known botanist and his wife, who gave him a large ground floor room opening out on an attractive garden. The Reichenbachs were very kind; they presented Lowell with a large case of stuffed and mounted American birds so that, as they put it, he might have some familiar friends. Lowell grew fond of them both. He found the Doctor decidedly individual — learned, simple, whimsical and, in an abstracted way, affectionate — "a great tenderhearted bear." His good-natured wife adored him, proudly calling him her "liebste August," and it delighted Lowell (even while making him sad) to see them acting like betrothed lovers after a marriage of thirty-six years.[16]

Though he had bad intervals from the start, with daily thoughts of "wishing to be out of the world once for all," these first days were the best Lowell was to have in Dresden; summer was still in the air, the novelty of the city had not yet worn off and he had the companionship of his sister, Mary, who had been traveling in Europe with her family and, apparently fearing for her brother's state of mind, stayed on in Dresden with two of her children for almost a month. When she left in late September, and as the desolate winter weather set in, Lowell's real torment began.

He became terribly homesick, and the irregularity of news from Cambridge compounded his anxiety until at times it became all but unbearable. When Mabel did write, her letters brought immense relief, full as they were of a child's naïve charm ("I go to the Episcopal church, and I respond"; "The calf is dead, but the cow did not like her very much. The reason, that the cow did not like her, was because she would not suck, and had crooked legs"). But Mabel confessed that although she "loved her papa very much," she did not like to write, and Miss Dunlap, "excellent person" though she was, did little better in keeping him informed. At one point, however, Lowell began to appreciate that no news could be good news; when he did hear from his sister, Mary, it was only to learn that her eldest son, aged twenty-two, had died of the cholera in Ferrara. She had been on her way to meet him when she had decided instead to linger in Dresden on Lowell's account — and this gave him added anguish.[17]

By November, he had lost his appetite, was sleepless and could hardly bear to be spoken to. He felt less reconciled than ever to his loss of Maria: "a real sorrow is forever at compound interest." He would stare endlessly at his wedding ring; it seemed "as empty as a magic circle after the Prospero is dead who traced it." "My God," he wrote his sister-in-law, "what an enchantress is Memory that she can make it seem better to *have* lived than to live!" The only credit he claimed was that he tried not to bother other people with his troubles, though it might have been better if he had. As his spirits deteriorated, so did his health; he had a nagging, sometimes sharp pain in his side, and when swelling developed, he began to fear liver trouble. His one comfort during this wretched winter, when he was so tormented in mind and body, was that he stayed "faithful in deed and thought" to Maria's memory.

That, and staying frantically busy with his German studies. He held to the most exacting schedule, as if nothing but regular routine could hold at bay the chaos of his emotions. He was up and had breakfasted every day by 8:30. He then fed the sparrows at his window and studied straight through until dinner at one. In the afternoon he studied again, sometimes translating German into English, sometimes exchanging English lessons for Spanish with a young Spaniard also staying in the house. At five he walked in the twilight, often through the great solemn meadow with the long rows of lindens planted by Augustus the Strong; Madame Reichenbach sometimes accompanied him, though it was often too cold for conversation. At seven, he would take an hour's dictation in German from Dr. Reichenbach, followed by a German "tea" of meat and potato salad. He then studied again in his own room, sometimes not retiring before two o'clock in the morning. On Sunday, he allowed himself the "holiday" of writing letters. The only other variations in routine were attending an occasional lecture of the Doctor's (of which he understood little), a few excursions like that to see the fortress at Königstein, skating and, his most satisfying diversion — attending the theater. Lowell thought nothing compared with the Dresden theater for scrupulous attention to detail, even to "the most inconsidered trifles in which so much of illusion consists, and which commonly are so bungled as to draw the attention instead of evading it by an absorption in the universal."

All winter long he lived in the most profound solitude, talking to almost no one other than Dr. and Mrs. Reichenbach, almost always in German or French. His language study, at least, showed the benefits of this concentrated effort. The Reichenbachs assured him that no one had ever learned German so fast, and Lowell was himself satisfied with his progress, fearing only that because his spirits had been too low to go into society, he had not learned enough of the colloquial language. But after four months, he could talk German tolerably well, could read it as easily as French, and could write it as fast as English — with the advantage, he reported, that he could not decipher it afterward. The complexities of the language brought out what reserve of humor he still had: genders in Botany were all well enough, he wrote President Walker of Harvard, but "why the empty distinctions of sex without its privileges or responsibilities" should be conferred upon spoons and forks, he could not understand. And as for the length of German sentences, one got the feeling that one was setting sail "like an admiral with sealed orders, not knowing where the devil he is going to till he is in mid-ocean!"

The language was so demanding that by the end of January, Lowell had decided against his tentative plan to go to Spain — "for I shall not have time, not to say that I have not energy enough just now to undertake any journeyings into the unknown." But some respite from Dresden was needed. And it was

Italy, more and more, that he yearned for — its warmth, its life, the chance to see old friends like Page and recent ones like Norton, who was on an extended tour; surely, he told himself, if for no other reason, he should visit Italy in order to brush up on the language. The lure proved irresistible and at the end of February Lowell left Dresden for the south.[18]

He had gone no further than Trieste when he began to revive. Lilacs and roses were already in leaf and, as he headed slowly down central Italy, bright sunshine followed him everywhere "like a Medea's bath, fit to make an old man young again." With every day his spirits improved. At Orvieto he found Norton and Page, who took him on to Rome, where he met his sister and her family. Then, at her urging, he accompanied them to Naples, promising himself that there his holiday would end. But once in Naples, it seemed a pity not to get a glimpse of Sicily. Three friends, including Norton, were planning a mule trip there, and with little persuasion Lowell agreed to join them. The trip took twice as long as originally planned, and was full of physical discomforts ("I thought a great many times as I hummocked along that if an equal amount of agony had been inflicted on me by the Inquisition I would have acknowledged that the sun went round the earth"). But it was worth every bump. The weather was perfect, the country beautiful and the sense of freedom and companionship immensely restoring.[19]

And so a vacation of one month turned into three. But when Lowell did finally return to Dresden in June, he felt better than he had in years, and his new mood seemed matched by the new season — Germany was full of birds and flowers, as if Italy had followed him north. Although he remained in Europe for two more months, he was generally cheerful, knowing that the end of his exile was in sight. He was even able to summon some energy for worrying about national affairs. So much had happened while he was away, so much that boded ill — the miniature civil war in Kansas, the bloody beating of Charles

Sumner in the Senate, the repeal in Massachusetts of the Personal Liberty Bill — Lowell felt as if he "would like to be kicking somebody." From his remove, America seemed both greater and smaller: "more significant in Idea, & more contemptible in fact." Reading of these events so far away, he felt that he was witnessing the history of a republic "in the last wretched convulsion before absolute dissolution." Yet he took it as a sign of some remaining health that "freesoil" men in Kansas were at least fighting back; their resistance seemed to Lowell the proud echo of Lexington "running down the Future." Perhaps out of such dismaying events "a finer plant of Freedom" might yet grow. But perhaps, too, the Storys had been right in putting the United States permanently behind them.[20]

Of more personal, immediate concern was the problem of where he should live on his return. Much as he loved Elmwood, Lowell dreaded the idea of going back there; memories would be too painful; he feared losing the little ground he had gained toward a more peaceful frame of mind. Yet where else could he live? Well, he thought, a way will be opened, as it commonly was. The important thing was that he was going home.

CHAPTER VIII

PROFESSOR AND EDITOR

LOWELL HAD PREDICTED that friends would find him somewhat changed — not in looks, but in manner, grown more grave, and with an incorporated sadness. The two-year bout with grief, the terrible winter of isolation in Dresden, could hardly help but leave their mark. Something had been precipitated out — a boyish sense of expectation, an exuberant, impatient hope. Lowell was at least fortunate, as many are not, that despair had deepened his tolerance, resignation and grace rather than generating bitterness or belligerence.

To some he seemed much the same as ever — amusing, hearty, quick-witted. And at times he felt like his old self, especially in the first few weeks after his return, caught up in the pleasures of reunion (Cambridge, he reported back to Cranch, "is a great deal better than Paris"). But as he settled into routine, dejection returned. He blamed most of it on "liver trouble" or reassuringly told himself that as "the son of St. Theresa by Dick Steele," he must always be subject to some fluctuation of mood. But by mid-winter, the depression was profound. He was filled with "preposterous forebodings of nothing," the kind of anxiety which *because* unfocused can be peculiarly disabling. His moods prevented him from seeking society, though he always benefited by company when it sought him.[1]

A change in his living conditions contributed to unsettlement. Since Elmwood caused such deep pangs Lowell had decided to board with his sister-in-law and her husband, Lois and Estes Howe (Francis Child found him in his quarters there one day hanging green velvet paper on the walls of his small room under the shade of an elm tree). He paid the Howes $1100 a year for board, which included Mabel and Miss Dunlap — a huge dent in an annual income that was now about $1500. To bring in additional money, he delivered another round of public lectures in the winter of 1856–1857. Again they met with considerable success, and again Lowell hated giving them — he was too lazy, one friend suggested, to enjoy the preparation, and too modest to enjoy the delivery.[2]

These occasional lectures, plus his teaching duties at Harvard, kept Lowell busy enough but he worked with little zest and suffered bouts of indolence, always with him a telltale symptom of depression. Finally he became concerned enough to consult Dr. Holmes, who advised punctual retirement by ten-thirty at night and cold water instead of coffee at breakfast. Soon after, Jane and Grace Norton reported to their brother Charles (still traveling in Europe) that Lowell seemed brighter than he had for a long time, telling stories and joking like his old self.[3]

The Norton sisters were not yet aware that the renewed animation they noticed in the summer of 1857 was due to more than Dr. Holmes' health regimen. Lowell's improved spirits coincided with two major decisions, one personal and one professional, which he was then concluding. Together they were to restructure his life.

When Edmund Quincy visited Lowell in the spring of 1857, he found to his surprise that he and Miss Dunlap had begun to take long walks and to read together. Quincy warned Lowell that he should be more careful — not, he hastened to add, that he thought Lowell in any real danger. Lowell assured him that Miss Dunlap was "not in the least that kind of woman" (Quincy had apparently specified several kinds of danger); he spent as much time with her as he did because she had little or no society except himself and he felt bound to make her residence with them as pleasant as possible.[4]

Whether his initial indifference was pose or reality, Lowell soon came to feel that Frances Dunlap was a woman who suited his varied needs. It was clear, for one thing, that she and Mabel cared deeply for each other; should anything happen to him, Lowell reasoned — and his health had not been good — Mabel would be left in loving hands. But if concern for his daughter's welfare was a real factor in his attraction to Miss Dunlap, it was hardly the only one. The deeper their acquaintance, the more certain he became that she was a woman of "remarkable strength & depth of character & of corresponding gentleness." Though she was not a person of extensive book learning, Lowell felt her education had been complete, for she had had the two best possible teachers, wealth and poverty: "one has taught not to value money, the other to be independent of it." If she had some provincialism of dialect, she had "none of mind or spirit." If she was over thirty and not especially attractive, she had more durable qualities: placidity, directness, simplicity. Above all, Lowell felt entirely comfortable with her, and before long realized that he was profoundly attached.[5]

He had intended never to remarry; in fact he had sworn that he would not. But he could no longer hold to that vow. In telling Maria's sister of his decision, he explained that his "whole disposition & temperament" had been convincing him for some time that marriage was a necessity of his nature, without which he felt only half himself. As if in proof, he had no sooner become formally engaged to Miss Dunlap, than he felt "stronger & better, with an equability of mind" he had not had for years.[6]

Meeting her mother and sisters in Maine made him more certain than ever that he had made a wise choice. They lived in "a little bit of a house on a little bit of a street" directly behind the large home in which Frances had grown up, when her father had been a prospering merchant and her uncle, Robert P. Dunlap, governor of the state. Despite reduced circumstances, no one seemed conscious that they were not welcoming Lowell to a palace; there were no apologies for want of room, no hints at reversals — all was "simple, ladylike & hearty." On September

16, 1857, in a ceremony performed by his brother, the Rev. R. T. S. Lowell, Lowell and Frances Dunlap were married.[7]

That Lowell had decided to remarry at all surprised some of his friends; that he chose Frances Dunlap shocked them. When Fanny Longfellow first met the new Mrs. Lowell, she thought her "very sweetlooking" and reported to George William Curtis that everyone thought her "admirable." But everyone did not. Fanny Longfellow herself, after having the Lowells to dinner, decided that the new bride was "neither pretty nor attractive" and recorded that the general reaction had been one of disappointment. Soon after, meeting the cultivated, charming Jane Norton at a party, Mrs. Longfellow "could not but sigh — 'Oh if she had been Mrs. Lowell!' " Sydney Gay's wife objected to the new match on principle; she could not bear the thought of another in Maria's place, considered it shocking that Lowell should have been consoled so soon, and could not see the new couple without tears. Edmund Quincy claimed that he never knew Frances Dunlap to start a conversation or to do anything more than "smile & assent to what you said," and he did not see how Lowell could bear the comparison to Maria — "that exquisite creature in mind, body & soul." Quincy never considered that in choosing a woman so different from Maria (in all but her emotional strength), Lowell may have been following sound instincts; because Frances would not disturb the earlier image, she would not be forced constantly to compete with it, giving them that much greater chance to develop a separate if no less important relationship.[8]

Lowell took such unfavorable opinions as he heard philosophically; "My second marriage," he wrote Sydney Gay, "was the wisest act of my life, & as long as *I* am sure of it, I can afford to wait till my friends agree with me." Some of his friends never did, especially those who knew Frances Lowell only casually. She was so reserved and taciturn that she almost never made a favorable first impression — and few had either the opportunity or interest to seek out her unobtrusive qualities. Those who did manage to know her better almost invariably came to think well of her. Henry James, not the easiest man to please, found she "improved" much on acquaintance and was a "very sweet and excellent woman." Annie Fields, wife of the publisher, always felt indignant that so few people appreciated Frances Lowell's self-effacing devotion to her husband, her willingness to dedicate herself to his comfort and needs. And William J. Stillman spoke warmly of her "resolute and persistent courage," her serenity, her "extreme sweetness of character." [9]

Ultimately, of course, it is only Lowell's own testimony which can be relied upon in appraising the success of his second marriage, and that testimony makes it abundantly clear that his life with Frances Dunlap was a happy one. If his original motives for marrying her may have been weighted with sober, practical considerations, there is no question that his love for her became profound and his need for her great — so great that when she died thirty years later, Charles Eliot Norton actually expressed the wish that Lowell might die too: "with all his vigour and force of individuality, he was unusually dependent on his wife; his temperament made her essential to him." [10]

The qualities which made Frances Lowell "essential" were not simple ones, however one-dimensional she may have seemed to the outside world. Her reticence could be so massive that it was difficult for strangers to get behind it, her self-effacement so complete that they were not at all sure there was anything behind it to get to. But in the privacy of their home — and she was an immensely private person — Lowell felt her unselfishness, her gentle efficiency, her amiability. He felt, too, her quiet strength. The quality of his reliance on her was perhaps best revealed in a comment Lowell once made on Keats:

> His intellect was satisfied and absorbed by his art, his books, and his friends. He could have companionship and appreciation from men; what he craved of woman was only repose. That

> luxurious nature, which would have tossed uneasily on a crumpled rose-leaf, must have something softer to rest upon than intellect, something less ethereal than culture. It was his body that needed to have its equilibrium restored, the waste of his nervous energy that must be repaired by deep draughts of the overflowing life and drowsy tropical force of an abundant and healthily poised womanhood.

There was a protective, maternal cast to the way Frances cared for him; years later, when temporarily apart from her, he could confess like a little boy, "I miss you every hour of the day, for you know that I always run & hide my face in your lap when I am troubled." When Annie Fields suggested to Frances Lowell that perhaps too large a share of her life was taken up by housekeeping, she simply replied that she had "a sensitive & superior being to care for." But though content to absorb her life in Lowell's, to devote herself to his comfort, she was no mere adjunct. She was a woman of intelligence and culture, able to share a variety of her husband's interests. There is even the bare suggestion of a somewhat less conventional nature than Maria had had, some concealed rebelliousness beneath the imperturbable surface — perhaps what Annie Fields meant when she referred to "a certain smouldering" quality lying behind Frances Lowell's reserve.[11]

Lowell was not interested in analyzing the source of his attachment to his wife; a man nearing forty, he believed, should be wise enough "not to pull *his own* roses to pieces." He was content to feel increasingly in love, to take pleasure in her cheerful, unassuming presence, and, more and more, to rely on her practicality. Within two years of their marriage, he decided that his wife had a better business head than he and thereafter let her handle family finances; as he put it (perhaps suggesting more than he intended), "I am going to put myself wholly in Fanny's hands . . ."[12]

Harmonious though the marriage was, it had its special sorrow, their inability to have children. Soon after they were married, Mrs. Lowell suffered a miscarriage, apparently brought on by jumping from a wagon, though there was a suggestion of organic difficulties. Nor did the marriage entirely free Lowell from sagging spirits. There were still periods (there would always be periods) of feeling "out of place and out of sorts," of being unable to get himself "into right relations with men or things." Within four or five years of remarrying, though, his bouts of depression were much less frequent and intense, and his personal no less than his professional life had become comfortably settled.[13]

Thus the mid 1850's marked a significant transition for Lowell toward a more sober, becalmed life. In part this was the natural development of advancing age, with its expected loss of elasticity. But it was due far more to the necessities earlier imposed by Maria's death. Lowell had then to apply every available control to save himself from the chaos of his emotions, his vulnerability to pain. To some extent the safeguards became habitual; like the nearly-drowned boy who never after goes near the water, Lowell continued to keep up his guard against the free play of feeling, to avoid the sensory edge. Seen in this context, his professorship, his new marriage, his move literally and figuratively from poetry to prose take on an inexorable quality, like the signing of a pact whose terms had earlier been drawn. The choices he made in the critical year 1857 reflect an alteration which had already taken place in his personality; once taken, those choices made the alteration still more irresistible, probably irreversible.

Lowell was aware that he had turned a significant corner, aware and, in regard to the professorship, uneasy. He sensed that the routine of teaching, the easy omniscience, the accretion of detail, might all disable still further his poetic impulses, to say nothing of wholly consuming his time.

Harvard was in stagnant condition, largely unchanged since Lowell's undergraduate days twenty years before (nor would it be rescued from inertia until Charles William Eliot became President in 1869). The college consisted of half a dozen buildings, a total faculty of about thirty, and a total student enrollment of about six hundred. Nearly all studies were prescribed and these mainly consisted of Greek, Latin and mathematics. After freshman year some electives were allowed, but the range of choice was sharply limited — the College offered one course in English literature (Francis Child's Anglo-Saxon), two or three in natural science, all without laboratory work, and some scattered selections in modern languages (though students were deliberately discouraged from taking these by the proviso that although no credit would be given for Spanish or Italian in junior year, they must nonetheless be taken if students wished to get credit for those languages in senior year). Few courses were taught through lecture; reliance was put instead on textbooks, often narrow and outmoded, and on routine recitations. There was little contact between student and instructor, indeed personal relations between the two were considered poor form. Thus the inadequacies of classroom instruction were not redeemed, as can sometimes be the case, by informal exchange; the Harvard student of the 1850's and 60's profited little from either the scholarship of his teachers (and Harvard had some eminent scholars, as, for example, Francis Child and William Watson Goodwin, the classicist) or from their humanity. The professor functioned as an amalgam of high-level disciplinarian and Jovian dispenser of "truth." Edward Everett, who was President of Harvard from 1846 to 1849, summed up the disdain and the disillusion of many when he said, "I supposed I was to be at the head of the largest and most famous institution of learning in America . . . I find myself the sub-master of an ill-disciplined *school*." As befitted the climate, the students rioted frequently and with fervor, and the faculty retreated to their studies and their claret.[14]

After only one year, Lowell seemed to see "all the poetry drying out" of him: "I droop on my rocks and hear the surge of the living waters, but they will not reach me till some extraordinary high spring tide—and may be not then . . ." Eventually he was to find teaching intolerable, and to quit his post. But the early years were not all drudgery; he loved his subject so well, and he had enough success as a teacher, to derive at least peripheral pleasure from the classroom.[15]

He enjoyed least the routine language classes; detailing always bored him, and he neglected it. Beginning with his second year, he did assume some of the burdens of grammar instruction in Spanish (which he studied hard on his own) and Italian. This meant hearing recitations three days a week, two hours each day—and not even the full professor's salary of $2200 could quite compensate for the tedium. Under the monotonous routine, he was known to become abstracted and absent-minded. John Fiske recalled that when he was once down with measles and missed class for six weeks, Lowell forgot all about him and continued to mark him absent after he returned. Nonetheless, even as a grammar instructor, Lowell had fair success for he did what he could to vary monotony by interjecting literary anecdotes and by helping beginners over difficult spots instead of merely harping on their deficiencies. A visiting committee sitting in on Lowell's language classes reported back to the Overseers with astonishment—and rejoicing—that he actually instructed his students, ". . . an uncommon thing. Few teachers . . . consider it their duty to *teach* . . . They simply regard it as their business to act as examiners."[16]

Lowell also lectured once a week on literature, his courses ranging, through the years, from the "classical" books of Germany and Italy to "modern" literature, to aesthetics and criticism. He also gave, on a voluntary basis, advanced classes in Dante (and later in *Don Quixote*), which met two evenings a week at his home. It was here, in his own study, that Lowell was at his best. A wood fire would always be burning, and he would sit to one side of it dressed casually in a loose smoking jacket and slippers, puffing continuously on his pipe. He monopolized most of the talk, switching quixotically from the earnest to the playful, from the beauties of Dante, to the news of the day, to personal reminiscence. His tone was intimate, casual, familiar; he did not try to impress or flatter, and so left no flavor of patronization. "He treated us from first to last," one of his students recalled, "as if we were his equals and were putting him under great obligation." Henry Adams, skeptical as regarded all else about his Harvard education, recalled the "privilege" of reading with Lowell in his own home: "From him the boy got no revolutionary thought whatever . . . but he got good-humored encouragement to do what amused him . . ." Barrett Wendell, a student in the evening seminars in later years, always remembered the "human friendliness" of the gatherings — and also the shock of reading classics as literature rather than as exercises in grammar:

> He never, from the beginning, bothered us with a particle of linguistic irrelevance. Here before us [he would say] was a great poem — a lasting expression of what human life had meant to a human being . . . Let us try, as best we might, to see what life had meant to this man; let us see what relation his experience, great and small, bore to ours; and now and then, let us pause for a moment to notice how wonderfully beautiful his expression of this experience was. Let us read, as sympathetically as we could make ourselves read, the words of one who was as much a man as we; only vastly greater in his knowledge of wisdom and beauty. That was the spirit of Mr. Lowell's teachings. It opened to some of us a new world.

But it was Lowell himself who best summed up his approach to the academic calling:

> True scholarship consists in knowing not what things exist, but what they mean; it is not memory but judgment.[17]

Yet not everyone thought well of Lowell's teaching; whenever a teacher has a coterie of admirers, it is probable he will have a coterie of detractors. Some felt Lowell's choice of lecture topics capricious and his delivery discursive. Others complained of his tendency to treat minor literary figures at undue length, giving more range to his personal preferences than an undergraduate survey warranted. One or two disliked his manner, enumerating grievances which suggest by their triviality (he yawned, he was sometimes cynical, his gloves were excessively nice) that when Lowell talked of his "unfitness" for teaching, the reflection was more on his audience than on himself.[18]

*

Along with a new marriage and a new professorship, the year 1857 brought one other significant departure: the assumption of editorial responsibility for a new magazine, *The Atlantic Monthly*. The inception of the magazine went back to 1853, when F. H. Underwood, a recent arrival in the Boston area, began his efforts to establish a literary periodical. Underwood, a native New Englander who had taught school and studied law in the South, had returned to Boston in 1850 to set up a private law practice and had become clerk of the State Senate. Philadelphia, Underwood reasoned, had *Graham's*, *Godey's* and *Sartain's*, and New York had *Putnam's*, the new *Harper's* and the *Knickerbocker*; surely New England, pre-eminent in literature, deserved at least one reputable monthly of her own. She also deserved, Underwood felt, a journal which would represent such antislavery sentiment as already existed, as well as encourage its further development. Given his double interests — literature and antislavery — it is not surprising that Lowell was Underwood's special hero.

Robert Carter introduced the two men in 1853, soon after Underwood had moved to Cambridge and begun to push his project for a magazine. Lowell thought Underwood a little "cast-ironish" intellectually, and feared his lack of elasticity might be fatal to his success as an editor. But he thought him an attractive human being — hardworking, ambitious and honest, with "nothing of the adventurer in him." Underwood was soon invited to join the "Whist Club," whose members included Lowell, Estes Howe, John Bartlett (of *Familiar Quotations* fame), Robert Carter, John Holmes, the wry, kindly younger brother of Oliver Wendell Holmes, and occasionally Charles W. Storey or Henry Ware (son of William Ware, the author of *Zenobia*). The club met on Friday nights, each member taking a turn as host, with whist more the pretext than the substance of the gatherings. Talk was the main staple, talk on all topics, but especially literature and antislavery — which put Underwood in congenial company. Even late in life, he recalled those Friday night talks as "memorable," and Lowell — perfectly free with none but friends in hearing — as "indescribably" brilliant.[19]

Plans for a new magazine did not proceed smoothly. At first J. P. Jewett & Co., publishers of *Uncle Tom's Cabin*, agreed to back the project but then suddenly withdrew, apparently because of financial troubles. Underwood then concentrated on the house of Phillips, Sampson & Co., which (after Mrs. Stowe and William Lee, a junior member of the firm, had enlisted in the job of persuasion) finally agreed, in 1857, to become sponsor. Delighted and surprised, Lowell wrote Arthur Hugh Clough that "a publisher has gone mad and is willing to sink I know not how much out of pure patriotism. If he be not sent to the Lunatic Asylum before the year's end — I think he will be able to make the Magazine go." [20]

There was reason for thinking Phillips, Sampson & Co. mad. Literary magazines, at least if not compromised by popular sentimental fiction, engravings and the like, had had notoriously short lives. With the addition of antislavery overtones, the new venture would suffer from double jeopardy. But Phillips and Sampson intended to minimize the risks, primarily by lining up in advance a literary stable so impressive that the magazine's prestige would be pre-established. Dinners were arranged at the Parker House in Boston at which literary luminaries were invited to talk over the new project. Those who became most involved were Emerson, Oliver Wendell Holmes, the historian Motley, James Elliot Cabot, Edwin Whipple, the essayist, and, with slightly less enthusiasm, Longfellow.[21]

Apparently Underwood had some expectation of being named editor, but his was too uncertain a reputation, especially after the national depression which had begun in 1857 made it more necessary than ever to guard against speculative arrangements. Emerson, for one, believed success contingent upon Lowell's editorship, and the offer was soon made. Since it carried a salary of $2500 (later raised to $3000), Lowell was glad to accept. He had been "absolutely penniless" for some months, in fact obliged to borrow for his daily expenses. But although the editorship would resolve his financial problems, it would exacerbate others. The new responsibilities, when added to his teaching duties, would leave him almost no free time. And he was well aware that to write, he had to have leisure. He was capable of dashing off some of his best pieces under the pressure of a deadline, but even that required some minimal time in which pressure could accumulate; the new editorship would leave almost none. If there was no conscious abdication from literature in Lowell's decision to run the *Atlantic*, such was nonetheless the final result of his editorship. It was not until 1864 that he amassed enough material to publish a new volume and most of that consisted of pieces originally written ten years before.[22]

Yet in many ways the magazine promised to be worthy of Lowell's labors: the need for it was real, and the list of potential contributors gave hope that the need would be met with distinction. Lowell was excited by its possibilities. He planned for the magazine to be "free without being fanatical," uniting in its pages "all available talent of all shades of opinion." It would speak its mind fearlessly yet without sacrificing a "scholarly & gentlemanlike" approach. He hoped, too, to make the magazine more than a provincial organ; ideally it would include the best of Old and New England, serving as a bridge between the two countries and incidentally establishing, through the generous treatment of its contributors, a decent substitute for the copyright agreement still lacking. Given these international hopes, Dr. Holmes' suggestion that the magazine be named *The Atlantic Monthly* was thought to be just the thing — though the pedants promptly objected to making a noun of an adjective.[23]

In search of an Anglo-American list, Underwood, who had been named assistant editor, went abroad in June, 1857, and Lowell sent off letters of his own soliciting contributions. He asked Clough to be London literary correspondent, which he refused, and also asked him for some of his poetry, which he sent — though Lowell, on reading it, predicted it would prove "caviare to the Generals (of whom, you know, American society is largely made up) and ought to be so." Norton, still traveling in Europe, talked up the new magazine with Rossetti, Morris, Ruskin and Mrs. Gaskell, and his spadework brought some additional contributions. But since Lowell reserved the right of rejection, some Englishmen responded more with contempt than cordiality: "I will never under any circumstances," wrote Charles Reade, "submit a MS. of mine to the chance of any other writer comprehending it and seeing its merit. If therefore *that* is an absolute condition, you will never see a line of mine in the Atlantic Monthly while I live." Mr. Reade understood the proper tone toward colonials.[24]

As Reade's truculence suggests, Lowell's hopes for a transatlantic magazine were only partially realized. Since he would not reprint already published European works (as did most periodicals — usually by outright piracy) and since, promises aside, only a few English authors sent new material, he had to rely for the bulk of the magazine's contents on native talent. And during the years of his editorship, native talent, of necessity, primarily meant that of New England. This opened Lowell, then and since, to the accusation of provincialism —

but unjustly. It *was* New England's day in American literature and had Lowell admitted more writers than he did from the West and South, he would have achieved inclusiveness at the expense of distinction. To the degree consistent with his aim of excellence, he did open the pages of the *Atlantic* to such Southern authors as Paul Hamilton Hayne, Osmond Tiffany, Francis Lieber and J. P. Kennedy. And he did a great deal for that young Westerner, William Dean Howells. Not only did he print Howells' fledgling verses, but wrote a generous review of a joint volume of poetry by Howells and his friend John J. Piatt, managing to make a virtue even of the book's deficiencies: "Dead-ripeness in a first book is a fatal symptom, sure sign that the writer is doomed forever to that pale limbo of faultlessness from which there is no escape upwards or downwards." And when Howells showed up in Cambridge in 1860, Lowell warmly welcomed him and introduced him to the local luminati (Howells was especially eager to meet Hawthorne, so Lowell sent him up to Concord armed with a charming note of introduction explaining to Hawthorne that Howells "wants to look at you, which will do you no harm, and him a great deal of good").[25]

Howells was one of many young authors deeply grateful for Lowell's timely encouragement. Thomas Bailey Aldrich remembered that Lowell was kind to him before they ever met, sending him a generous note just when he was at low ebb, and E. C. Stedman gratefully acknowledged Lowell's "genial & unexpected interest." In printing the work (and boosting the careers) of these and other young writers — Harriet Prescott Spofford, Celia Thaxter, Rose Terry — Lowell may have erred in judgment, but not in intention. If his interest in new talent led him into occasional overestimates, if he was guilty of critical lapses, he was not guilty of parochial indifference, which is the charge more frequently leveled at him. Even the lapses were circumscribed. He made it clear, for example, in reviewing Mrs. Spofford's widely acclaimed *Sir Rohan's Ghost* that her novel showed more promise than achievement, and in welcoming Rose Terry's *Poems*, he objected to the banality of her thought even while praising the verisimilitude of her observation. In encouraging new American authors, Lowell tried to guard against debasing critical standards; he despised the way words were continually deprived of meaning and the way fame was confused with notoriety. Every week, he lamented, one learned that "the most extraordinary book of the age" had just been published; the word "genius" sprang up "like mullein, wherever the soil is thin enough"; and "profound originality" was apparently so plentiful in America that one not knowing better would take it for the most common national product.[26]

Lowell, like so many others, wished for an American literature — for a distinctive expression of his country's special experience — and he encouraged such a literature by making room in the *Atlantic* for the "local-color" fiction then emerging (in 1871 when Bret Harte came East after accepting a $10,000 offer from the *Atlantic* for a year's contributions, Lowell thought the move a great mistake, accurately prophesying that Harte's work would thereafter become sadly diluted — though the move, of course, may have been a symptom rather than the cause of Harte's decline). But unlike so many others, Lowell was not willing to announce an American literature prematurely nor to assume that it could be forcibly manufactured. It made no sense, he argued, to suppose that distinctive physical and climatic conditions were in themselves sufficient to produce a new literature: "enthusiasts wonder, that our mountains have not yet brought forth a poet, forgetting that a mouse was the result of the only authentic mountainous parturition on record." Neither "sublime spaces" nor the fact of democracy was sufficient to make poets; should a man with the gift of words and of imagination appear, "he will be original rather in spite of democracy than in consequence of it, and will owe his inspiration quite as much to the accumulations of the Old World as to the promises of the New." At present, the conditions necessary for developing literary talent were unpromising: "perhaps no country ever offered less encouragement to the higher forms of art or the more thorough achievements of scholarship." Americans needed to learn patience; instead of constantly breaking our eggs to see if they have hatched or pulling up "what we have planted, to see if it have taken root," Lowell believed we would do better to await slow ripening. And in any case, an independent literature should not be looked upon as a chauvinistic weapon; the point in developing a distinctive voice was to express a special, not superior, experience. Good literature transcended national peculiarities even while expressing them; it gave insight into human, not merely geographic, conditions.[27]

Though sound in theory, Lowell had lapses of his own in practice. Indulging some of the very hyperbole he had cautioned against, he could welcome Josiah G. Holland's long poem *Bitter-Sweet* as "purely American," and could do so without pausing to define that quality other than the unhelpful comment that the poem had the local flavor of boyhood: "a kind of sour-sweet, as in a *frozen-thaw* apple." Alternately, Lowell could miss an authentic voice when it did present itself. Critical blind spots are perhaps inevitable, given the usual fallibilities of perception and sympathy, and Lowell, on the whole, had an excellent record in literary judgment. The fact remains that he failed adequately to employ for the *Atlantic* three of the preeminent talents of the day: Melville, Whitman and Thoreau. In all three cases, Lowell's blind spot was not total (though with Whitman it came close to that). Nor was their failure to become *Atlantic* "regulars" entirely Lowell's fault.[28]

Melville's case is the most mysterious. Underwood had written him back in August, 1857, inviting him to contribute, and since Melville had replied that he would be "very happy to," his name had appeared on the back cover of the first issue as one of those "literary persons" interested in the new enterprise. But for some reason—probably because of indifference on Lowell's part—his work never appeared. That Lowell was uninterested in Melville is certain: he is mentioned but once in

The Reverend Charles Lowell. Engraving by H. W. Smith from a miniature by Richard M. Staigg, 1851
Courtesy of Mrs. Alfred Lowell

Harriet Spence Lowell — a portrait by Rand

Maria White Lowell — a crayon portrait
by Samuel W. Rowse
Courtesy of Harvard University

James Russell Lowell at the age of 23 —
a crayon portrait by William Page, 1842
Courtesy of Harvard University

The Harvard Yard in 1821, as painted by Alvan Fisher
Courtesy of Harvard University

Elmwood in Cambridge where James Russell Lowell was born and died
The photograph was taken about 1895
Courtesy of the Society for the Preservation of New England Antiquities

THE PIONEER.

JANUARY, 1843.

EMBELLISHMENTS.

CIRCE GOING TO MEET ULYSSES; from Flaxman's Odyssey; engraved by J. Andrews.

TWO HUNDRED YEARS AGO; engraved by J. Andrews.

THE ROSE; a Ballad, Illustrated on Wood. By J. G. Chandler.

TABLE OF CONTENTS.

The Pioneer is published monthly by Leland & Whiting, 67 Washington Street, to whom all orders, subscriptions, and communications for the Editors, may be addressed, *post paid*.

TERMS.—Three dollars per annum, invariably in advance. Two copies for five dollars. The usual discount allowed to agents.

Title page of *The Pioneer*, January, 1843

William Page — a self-portrait
Courtesy of Henry Page, Esq.

Right: Charles F. Briggs.
From an ambrotype by Brady

Left, below: William Wetmore
Story in later life
Courtesy of Harvard University

Right, below: Edmund Quincy
in later life
Courtesy of Harvard University

all of Lowell's private correspondence (and then only to use the title *Typee* to get off a wretched pun) and but once (again a passing reference only) in the entire body of Lowell's formal writings. Charles Briggs did report to Melville that Lowell had a high opinion of *The Encantadas*: "the figure of the cross in the ass' neck brought tears into his eyes, & he thought it the finest touch of genius he had seen in prose." This reference aside, there is no evidence that Lowell appreciated Melville's literary qualities — perhaps because he was unable to surmount his own temperamental distaste for the "pessimistic." [29]

As for Whitman, Lowell found little in his poetry to like; his opinion was shared by many contemporaries, including Whittier and Longfellow, though Lowell was less admiring than either. *Leaves of Grass*, he felt, aimed too consciously at originality and thereby ended as "solemn humbug." Yet in his capacity as editor, Lowell made an effort to overcome his personal distaste, recognizing that if men like Emerson found unusual value in Whitman's poetry, some place for it should be found in the new magazine. He printed one of Whitman's poems, "Bardic Symbols," and on retiring in 1861 forwarded the manuscripts of three others to James T. Fields, the incoming editor. Two of the poems, he told Fields, could be had for $8 a piece, and the third — "1861" — for $20, but Fields never utilized them. Lowell's opinion of Whitman did not change through the years. Annie Fields recorded a dinner conversation in 1868 in which the talk turned to Whitman: "Mr. Emerson believes in him, Lowell not at all, Longfellow finds some good in his 'yawp' . . ." [30]

Thoreau's *Atlantic* association was brief and explosive. Lowell asked him for an essay soon after the magazine began and Thoreau sent "Chesuncook," meant to be the first of a series. In editing the piece, Lowell, without permission, blue-penciled a sentence in which Thoreau had waxed anthropomorphic over pine tree: "It is as immortal as I am, and perchance will go high a heaven, there to tower above me still." There were mitigating circumstances for Lowell's deletion. The religious press had already charged the *Atlantic* with impiety and though Lowell personally despised truckling to its demands, he felt bound "to have a Captain's fidelity to the interests" of the publishers. Then, too, as any editor knows, the press of deadlines can prevent (especially in one of Lowell's absent-mindedness) those last-minute consultations so precious to authors and so expendable to printers. But although mitigating circumstances existed, and although Lowell intended neither malice nor deception, ultimately there can be no excusing his failure to consult Thoreau on changes in his text. Which is not to say that Lowell's action was so egregious as to deserve the blistering rebuke Thoreau administered. While not charging Lowell directly with responsibility for the deletion, Thoreau insisted it had been made in "a very mean and cowardly manner." He refused to be further associated in any way, he wrote Lowell, "with parties who will confess themselves so bigoted & timid" as to cross out a possibly offending sentence: "I could excuse a man who was afraid of an uplifted fist, but if one habitually manifest fear at the utterance of a sincere thought, I must think that his life is a kind of nightmare continued into broad daylight." [31]

There is no known reply from Lowell, but undoubtedly he viewed Thoreau's outburst as one more symptom of the man's deficiencies of character. From the days of his rustication in Concord as an undergraduate, Lowell had never approved of Thoreau, and his distaste was precisely grounded. Thoreau represented what Lowell had come to consider the worst excesses of romanticism — a sentimentalizing of nature and a concomitant devaluation of human society. The wilderness was all very well, in Lowell's view, "for a mood or a vacation, but not for a habit of life." Those who, like Thoreau, preferred nature to men and seclusion to society were converting their own defects of character into special virtues — namely, their inability to tolerate human imperfections (including their own), to enjoy the pleasures even while regretting the deficiencies of human

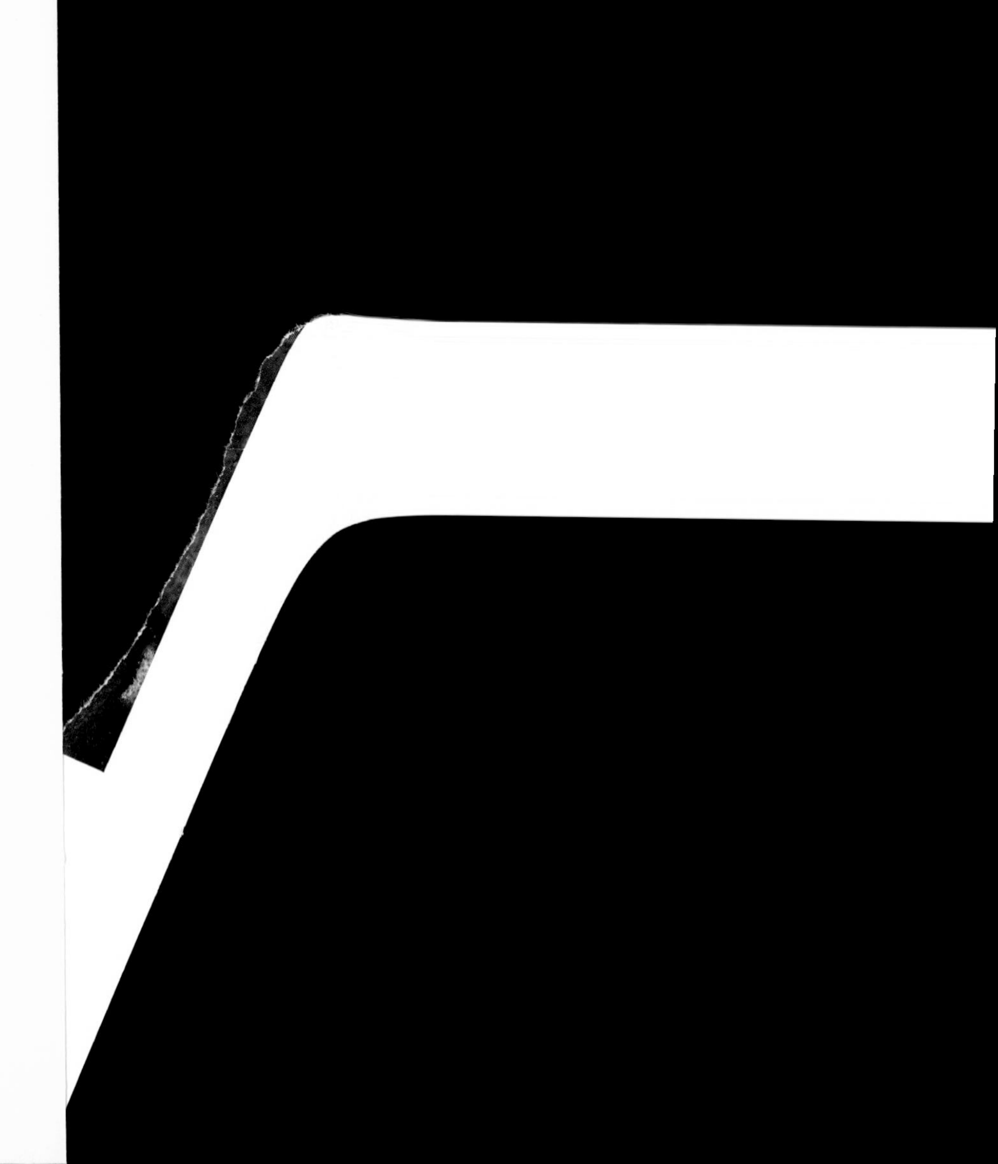

contact. Such men were "solacing an uneasy suspicion of themselves by professing contempt for their kind." And to do so, they had to impute false virtues to the natural world and to exaggerate the failings of the human; or, with equal distortion, to accept in nature what they deplored in men: tolerating the fox but not the fool, shunning the stench of politics, but not of the fungus.

In Lowell's opinion, the most certain way of eluding naturalness was to be forever seeking it: "it is as easy — and no easier — to be natural in a *salon* as in a swamp, if one do not aim at it, for what we call unnaturalness always has its spring in a man's thinking too much about himself." Here was the heart of Lowell's indictment of Thoreau: that his view of the world was wholly egotistical, based on the narrow provincialism of Self. Thoreau continually exaggerated his own importance, he made "his own whim the law, his own range the horizon of the universe." He thought everything in nature *his* discovery, almost his invention, "from moonlight to the planting of acorns and nuts by squirrels." Lowell was always disturbed when he thought he detected an assertion of absolute originality, whether in Thoreau or Whitman; men needed to recognize, he believed, that in both thought and language they owed a certain debt to others. Yet Lowell was shrewd enough to see, and honest enough to acknowledge, that Thoreau's "egotism" had its compensations, that the charge against his character was at the same time a virtue of his writing. Lowell could deplore Thoreau the man, but yet appreciate (within limits) Thoreau the stylist: *because* Thoreau insisted on seeing everything through his own eyes, he could make the familiar appear fresh, his language could hold "an antique purity like wine grown colorless with age."

Lowell's antagonism to Thoreau, in essence, was grounded in the belief that satisfaction and wisdom came from being in the world, not apart from or above it. Even as a young man, attracted to the romantic emphasis on the natural, the irregular, the unpruned, Lowell had never had much sympathy for the romantic hero — the man apart, beating out in lonely isolation the rhythm and purpose of his life. Now, approaching middle age, his own egotism and enthusiasm banked, Lowell found even less appeal in the view that the individual's salvation lay in alienation. He agreed that it was essential for each man to listen to his inner voice, to become as much himself as possible, but this was best done, Lowell believed, through engagement, not detachment. The man who withdrew from his fellows withdrew from their strengths as well as from their weaknesses; he made it easier "to impose on himself when he measures only with himself." Men, for all their imperfections, were more various, more challenging, than trees or squirrels. If we were to judge solitary communin[illegible]h Nature by its effects on character, Lowell acidly c[illegible]ded, Thoreau's case would hardly be reassuring — the [illegible]s with him had not been notably "sanitary or sweet[illegible]" [32]

If [illegible]cure Melville, Whitman or Thoreau for [illegible]nanage to win the services of almost every [illegible] American author, and he often published [illegible]not fugitive, work: Emerson's "Brahma" and [illegible]tier's "Skipper Ireson's Ride" (the dialect of which [illegible] improved upon), Holmes' "Autocrat" series. And in the reviews of their work which he himself wrote for the *Atlantic*, Lowell showed discerning insight into the nature of their talent: he referred to Holmes as a wit "in the earlier and higher sense of the word . . . a player upon thought rather than words," and he commented that Hawthorne, "had he been born without the poetic imagination . . . would have written treatises on the Origin of Evil." [33]

It took no great courage to publish or to praise such established figures, but outcries against their contributions in the *Atlantic* were occasionally raised. Emerson's poetry (especially "Brahma") was ridiculed as incomprehensible, and Holmes was excoriated by the religious press for his "infidelities." Lowell's response to such outside pressures depended on their nature.

Generally he ignored them, but he did occasionally soften or omit passages which might offend the clergy: "we have been denounced from the pulpit on various occasions. This has no great terrors for *me*, but it has (very justly) for [the publishers] . . . since it keeps down our circulation. Harper (God save the mark!) is orthodox & believes in John Knox." Lowell thought it was "a miserable thing, this having to be timid from a sense of duty, to be vicariously pigeonlivered," but he hoped once the magazine became firmly established they could ignore the religious press and "have a *free* magazine in its true sense." [34]

Some of Lowell's editorial changes were in response to pressures within rather than without. He felt the personal need, now and then, to tone down certain kinds of "indelicacies" which threatened his own sensibilities more than the subscription lists. "I have no desire," he wrote one contributor, "to look into dressing rooms, nor to help the steward carry basins, & have no intention that the 'Atlantic' shall encourage that backstair curiosity which is a vice of the country. A man can't blow his nose, but the echo of it runs from one newspaper to another all over the land, as if Jove had thundered." Lowell believed in "realistic" writing, but only to a point; he drew the line at descriptions which were too probingly intimate: "keyholes," he once wrote, "especially such as command the chambers of Death — are not the place for human eyes or ears." [35]

An additional pressure, one Lowell resolutely resisted, was the demand made upon him to "popularize" the magazine — the publishers sometimes leading the cry. They sighed over Lowell's penchant for "heavy" articles, instancing Norton's piece on Roger Bacon as a case in point. Lowell insisted, however, that the standards be kept high; to be "merely entertaining," he argued, would make the *Atlantic* but a carbon copy of "those Scribes & Pharisees the Harpers." But although he was resolved that nothing should go into the magazine which would "merely *do*" and although he tried to read every manuscript himself to insure quality, much of the poetry actually printed was tepid and the fiction mediocre — even if superior to what was being published elsewhere. Charles Reade — he who had refused to allow a mere editor to pass on his work — gave Lowell the English version of a compliment by assuring him that the stories in the *Atlantic* were "no worse" than those in *Blackwood's* or *Fraser's*, the English journals. But Norton let Lowell know that he had heard considerable abuse of the *Atlantic* because of the second-rate quality of its fiction. Lowell was aware of the deficiency, though in continually searching for better material, he did all an editor could do to remedy the situation. Ploughing through the acres of anemic fiction which crossed his desk dampened his spirits but occasionally enkindled his sense of humor; he was sure that he could dictate five sentimental love stories simultaneously without mixing them up — not that it would matter if he did: "Julie gazed into the eyes of her love which sought in vain to escape her inquiring look, while the tears trembled on her long dark lashes — but fell not."[36]

Lowell's editorial courage showed up most strongly not in encouraging unknowns or resisting "popularization," but in his willingness to engage in political controversy. At a time when most periodicals tried to avoid contentious debate, the *Atlantic* announced from the first that it would encourage the discussion of public questions ("A Magazine," its subtitle read, "of Literature, Art, and Politics"). Lowell's own articles, ringing with a vigor and militancy that recalled his earlier antislavery pieces, produced much of the *Atlantic*'s excitement. He had never entirely given up interest in national affairs, though withdrawing for a time from active participation after the terrible personal upheaval following Maria's death. Gradually, his concern with politics had re-emerged. His return from Europe in the summer of 1856 had coincided with the official birth of the Republican party, which, though unwilling to advocate the abolition of slavery, did insist that it be contained within its current boundaries. When the party chose Frémont as its standard-bearer in 1856, Lowell wished him well: should he be elected we might "begin to be a nation at last . . . instead of a clique, as hitherto — and a clique of gamblers, too." Only a few weeks after returning home, Lowell attended a Frémont barbeque, where he thought the talk dry ("dry, at least, to an old Abolitionist") but the day, in total, "glorious." When Frémont went down to defeat at the polls, Lowell was not discouraged. He even managed to find something hopeful in the Supreme Court's Dred Scott decision of 1857 — by giving slavery theoretical permission to exist anywhere in the nation, the Court had opened the lists, "and we shall soon find where the tougher lance-shafts are grown — North or South." [37]

The ferment of public affairs quickened Lowell's capacity for indignation at just the time when the reconstituted stability of his private life once more permitted him to indulge it. The renewal of his career as an active political commentator began almost accidentally. When the *Atlantic* started publication, Lowell invited Parke Godwin to do a series of articles on public affairs; Godwin's political analyses in *Putnam's* and in Bryant's *Evening Post* had gained him considerable reputation. But Lowell thought Godwin's first few articles for the *Atlantic* too tame, and encouraged by Phillips, the publisher, he tacked on to Godwin's analysis of the Buchanan Administration a few outspoken pages of his own. Lowell defended his action to Godwin (who did not appreciate the editorial "improvements") by pleading lack of time for consultation and by insisting that the magazine had to be "aggressive to make an impression." [38]

He shortly followed this debut with an essay condemning the American Tract Society's policy of avoiding the slavery question; in it, he denounced compromise as a "quack cement" which promised to purchase peace at the price of principle. In returning to the rhetoric and arguments he had employed in the early 1840's, Lowell was not, in his own mind, simply duplicating his earlier position. His current stance, he felt, was a more conservative one in that he took heed of the encumbrances and guidelines of the past. Yet if there was a greater respect for the weight and value of tradition, the traditions themselves were defined with a radical militancy very much reminiscent of his earlier writings:

> Christianity has never been concession, never peace; it is continual aggression; one province of wrong conquered, its pioneers are already in the heart of another. The milestones of its onward march down the ages have not been monuments of material power, but the blackened stakes of martyrs, trophies of individual fidelity to conviction.

If the experience of the past had to be valued, prime allegiance was owed not to tradition per se but to its moral continuum — to "the soul and conscience of Man." [39]

Following his blunt article on the Tract Society, Lowell wrote two pieces of stunning intensity attacking Caleb Cushing and Rufus Choate, prominent Northern "doughfaces" who wished to mute agitation of the slavery question. To Choate, who had suggested that the problem of slavery could safely be left to the All-Seeing, Lowell posed a "dilemma": "either God *always* interferes, or *sometimes*: if always, why need Mr. Choate meddle? Why not leave it to Him to avert the dangers of Anti-slavery, as well as to remedy the evils of slavery? — if only sometimes, (*nec deus intersit nisi dignus vindice nodus*) who is to decide when the time for human effort has come? Each man for himself, or Mr. Choate for all?" [40]

Lowell's articles aroused considerable comment. Emerson, for one, thought the piece on Cushing "brilliant," and the thrust at Choate made such a hit that there was serious talk of sending "the political editor" of the *Atlantic* to Congress (until 1862 all articles were printed anonymously, but "identifying *Atlantic* authors" became a popular and easy pastime). As in the 1840's, Lowell had doubts about dealing in personalities, but Norton helped convince him of its necessity: American politics had come to depend so much on the personal character of party leaders, Norton argued, that if a political writer wished to effect change, he could not confine himself "to measures & principles, but must deal his blows at men." Thus Lowell, restored even to the self-doubt that had marked his earlier career as political commentator, was relaunched into the public arena. A few years hence, with the crisis of Lincoln's election and the outbreak of civil war, he was to quicken his output and even to resurrect Hosea Biglow for a new round of satirical verse.[41]

Lowell's reinvigorated public involvement showed itself in other aspects of his editorial policy. He printed articles in the *Atlantic* on a variety of contemporary problems: urban slum life, the deaf and dumb, delinquent boys, the mentally handicapped — and, in line with the magazine's cosmopolitan emphasis, included accounts of European experiments which had been designed to cope with these social ills. Lowell also accepted for *Atlantic* publication the writings of such "notorious" radicals as Thomas Wentworth Higginson, Edmund Quincy and Theodore Parker, though Higginson thought Lowell printed his outspoken piece on women's rights with "a little demurring," and Parker expressed some concern over "mutilations" in one of his manuscripts.[42]

No editor, of course, has ever wholly escaped offending his authors, quick as they always are to deplore suggested changes while alternately resenting the "disinterest" of an editor who refuses to make any. In Lowell's case the trouble was compounded by his failure to attend to detail, or, as Higginson defined his defect, a want of "promptness & business qualities." One of Higginson's pieces, a memorial essay on Theodore Parker, lay under a pile of anonymous manuscripts for two months while Lowell absent-mindedly wondered why it hadn't arrived. Lowell was also known to put a manuscript in his pocket with the intention of reading it at leisure, to carry it home and then promptly to forget all about it. Authors frequently had to inquire after their pieces, requesting, sometimes tartly, that they at least be returned if not found acceptable. When the manuscripts could be located (under that anonymous pile, or in last winter's overcoat) they would be sent back; when they could not be, Lowell would resort to feeble justification ("authors were expected to keep their own copies of short pieces") or, alternately, to total silence. It can at least be said that Lowell did not discriminate between friend and foe. When only one chapter of Story's *Roba di Roma* had been published over a two-year period, despite Lowell's repeated promises that its publication was about to be resumed, Story protested his treatment to Norton as "unfriendly" and "shameful." And Julia Ward Howe had to ask Dr. Holmes to intercede on her behalf when she failed to receive payment for three articles on Cuba and when a poem of hers was neither published nor returned ("Dear Doctor, the sooner we begin to hate our fellow creatures, the better"). Lowell's inefficiencies can be at least partly explained by the extraordinary demands on his time. He described his predicament to a complaining author:

> Before I had won my experience, I had accepted so many MSS. that they have been a millstone round my neck ever since. I am printing them up as fast as I can. Meanwhile, if I receive anything very good, of course I accept *that*, & so my drawers & boxes and pigeonholes don't empty themselves as fast as I would have them. Then, please remember what I have to do. 1st to decide on MSS. 2nd to get ready a number of the Mag. by the 15th of every month; 3rd: to provide literary notices, or for them; 4th: to read all the proofs except Dr. Holmes's; 5th: to answer all queries & settle all doubts from the printing office; 6th: to get worried generally; 7th: to neglect my own private correspondence altogether; 8th: to attend to my college duties.

Though authors could not be expected to know or care, Lowell's schedule was obviously exhausting; at one point he fell into such "dogged despair" over the backlog of business that he actually put his resignation in the publishers' hands — only to be induced to withdraw it.[43]

Lowell's deficiencies as an editor, and the resentment they produced, were real enough, the combined result of temperamental distaste for method and the continual harassments of editorial responsibility. Yet his inadequacies were slight compared to his accomplishments. Judged by a variety of standards, his four years as head of the *Atlantic* must be considered a significant success. He launched a commercially profitable magazine — the first issue of over 20,000 copies sold out and circulation rose steadily thereafter, reaching 30,000 within two years — and at the same time pandered little to popular taste. If the *Atlantic* frequently printed trivial poetry and worse fiction, the fault lay less in Lowell's failure to search for excellence than in his failure to find it. Although he had to rely primarily on established New England authors to maintain as high a level as he did, he was awake to new talents like that of Howells, and to fresh modes like that of realistic "local-color" fiction. He found a place, too, for contemporary English writing, which helped to give some perspective on American achievement, thus curtailing those chauvinistic cheers which elsewhere marked the appearance of every native product. Lowell may have overprinted and overpraised the Harriet Prescott Spoffords while ignoring the far more substantial talents of a Melville, but just as the one was a necessary hazard of the search for new talent, so the other was the unavoidable limitation of any one individual's range of taste. The fact remains that Lowell encouraged many of the more promising new writers and printed most of the established older ones.

Moreover, remarkably little compromise was made with popular taste in order to keep the magazine solvent. Lowell held sentimental fiction to a minimum, printed and wrote critical reviews far more judicious and penetrating than could be found elsewhere, resisted the easy jingoism common to the day and insisted upon making room for controversial discussions of America's ills and inadequacies. Where he failed, it was mostly in detail — an inability, or refusal, to pay adequate attention to those particularities of business and etiquette which, while hardly trivial in net effect, were understandably irksome to him. As deficiencies they seem especially pardonable when placed beside the larger areas of significant accomplishment.

Despite his successes Lowell's tenure as editor ceased in the spring of 1861, a decision not wholly his and the cause of some pain to him. The trouble began late in 1859 with the bankruptcy of Phillips, Sampson & Co. following the death of Mr. Phillips. The *Atlantic* had by then proved itself financially and was in no way responsible for the firm's failure. But the magazine's future was placed in jeopardy. For a time there was talk among Lowell's friends of buying it but the plan never materialized, Lowell himself believing that the *Atlantic* would be safer with a "practical publisher" than with amateurs. Rumors then began to circulate that *Harper's* was about to buy the magazine in order to kill it, or that a Philadelphia firm wished to move the *Atlantic* to that city. Lowell was therefore relieved when an arrangement was finally concluded to sell the *Atlantic* for $10,000 to the Boston firm of Ticknor & Fields; it was, he thought, "the best arrangement possible." Lowell assumed that he would be asked to step down as editor so that James T. Fields, a partner of the new firm, could assume the post, but Fields was in Europe at the time purchase was concluded and Ticknor told Lowell he wished the magazine to go on as before. The old arrangements continued for a year after Fields' return; by then, however, Lowell had become convinced that Fields ("very properly") did in fact wish to be editor, and therefore he resigned in the spring of 1861. Though somewhat reluctant to step down, he bore no ill will toward Fields, even if he had some doubts of his capabilities (earlier he had remarked to Norton that Fields would be best as "dining editor . . . to look after authors when they came to Boston . . ."). At any rate, Lowell continued to send many of his own best pieces to the *Atlantic* and served as an unofficial consultant to Fields after the changeover.[44]

During his editorship Lowell had now and then longed for the day when he could be "vacant to the muses," idling on a fence in the sun. At times he had felt worn down by his labors: "I am muddy and cloggy with the work," he had written Norton at one point, "the feather part of me (curtailed at its best estate) has been torn, nibbled, and otherwise rendered as little suggestive of flight as possible . . ." Some of his closest friends had long been eager for him to give up the editorial post. He was, Francis Child thought, "wasting his time," and when Lowell finally resigned, Norton rejoiced: he knew no one whose next ten years "ought to be worth so much" as Lowell's and he wished to see his path cleared of all encumbrances. The loyal Norton always looked to external circumstances in explaining why Lowell failed to produce a string of masterworks.[45]

It may have been these very expectations, his own and his friends', which had made Lowell hesitate about resigning and then, when he finally did so, find himself vacillating between relief and regret. So long as his time had been wholly consumed by the dual duties of editor and professor, he could bemoan his separation from poetry without having to test his continued fitness for it. In fact he had recently grown uneasy about his future in letters: "Now that I begin to know something," he confided to Sydney Gay in 1858, "the desire for expression is sated." It is not surprising, then, that Lowell's pleasure in being free of the *Atlantic* alternated with rather nervous nostalgia. As he wrote to Fields,

> It is amazing how quickly the waters close over one. He carries down with him the memory of his splash and struggle,

> and fancies it is still going on when the last bubble even has burst long ago. Good-by. Nature is equable. I have lost the 'Atlantic', but my cow has calved as if nothing had happened.

The metaphor of drowning was not inappropriate. Lowell was feeling some desperation at having to prove himself anew, at being thrown back once more on his private resources.[46]

CHAPTER IX

BRAHMIN SOCIETY

LOWELL WAS a social creature in both senses of that phrase, a man who had an abstract belief in community and a concrete need for fellowship. He could criticize society, but with the object of improving it; he could shun companionship, feeling a periodic need for seclusion, but always to seek out once more what for him were its genuine pleasures. Thus while deploring aspects of society, he never rejected the idea of society. Estrangement had little place either in his philosophy or his practice; as he had felt of Thoreau, the individual in isolation was likely to lose rather than to find himself.

Even in his defiant days of active abolitionism, Lowell had never been an outcast. His temperament did not seek ostracism and his society did not demand it. His talents and tastes were varied enough so that he could find close friends both within the movement, like Edmund Quincy, or outside of it, like Briggs and Page. And the movement itself, when Lowell joined it in the 1840's had gained enough respectability so that the Cambridge community at large tolerated, perhaps even secretly admired, those enlisted in its ranks — especially when, as in Lowell's case, they were armed with heredity, accomplishment and personal charm.

By the mid-1850's, Lowell's antislavery views were still too strong for some — Louis Agassiz and Hawthorne, for example — but he had moved enough away from the radicalism of his youth and the intellectual community had moved enough toward it so that what grounds there had been for estrangement were now largely removed. From spokesman for a minority, Lowell had gradually developed into a voice for the New England majority. His recent election to the seats of established authority enhanced this identification. By the late 1850's he was a Professor at Harvard — a sure source of prestige — and the editor of New England's leading periodical — a likely base for influence. If in his youth he had never really severed connections with Boston's elite world, in middle age — because both he and it had changed — he became increasingly its representative, one of the powers that dominated it.

His new position, consolidated by the time of the Civil War, was reflected in his changing social connections. Some of his closest friends continued to be men of small tangible achievement, though (at least in Lowell's mind) creative personalities. Foremost in this regard were the members of his Whist Club: the scholarly, somewhat eccentric Robert Carter, with whom Lowell had earlier edited *The Pioneer*; John Bartlett, the total "Bookman," his long life absorbed in editing, selling, publishing, annotating and anthologizing the words of others; and, closest of all to Lowell, John Holmes, younger brother of Oliver Wendell. (Lowell said he loved John Holmes better than any other man, though there were some, like Norton, with whom he shared a wider community of interests and a deeper mutual reliance.) His ties with these men remained through the years, as did bonds to such older friends as Charles Briggs, W. W. Story and William Page, though these men he now saw less often. In the 1850's new relationships developed, with men of more eminent reputation, and these ties were confirmed in that most famous of all American social gatherings, the Saturday Club.[1]

The Saturday Club had an informal, almost accidental beginning. To the extent that it had a founding father, the credit probably goes to Emerson, who, like Lowell, had come to believe that there was no necessary contradiction between socializing and individual growth — so long, that is, as the socializing was with congenial spirits. As early as 1849, Emerson had helped to form the large, loosely-knit "Town and Country Club" for the purpose of "better acquaintance between men of scientific, literary and philanthropic pursuits." It had included, among many others, Lowell, Longfellow, T. W. Higginson, Edwin Whipple, James T. Fields, John S. Dwight and Theodore Parker — more "radical" representation than was to characterize its successor, the Saturday Club. Not so radical, however, that the Negro leader Frederick Douglass was able to gain membership. Lowell, who had hoped Douglass' presence would help rid "many worthy persons of a very unworthy prejudice," had intended to pay his entrance fee. But opposition developed to Douglass' admittance, and Lowell was astonished at the quarter from which it came. For it was Emerson, at least so Lowell believed, who would have blackballed Douglass had the matter been put to a vote, which it was not (Higginson claimed that Emerson "always confessed to a mild instinctive colorphobia"). Angered at this failure to take in a man "cast in so large a mould," Lowell declared that he, for one, was "an unfit companion for people too good to associate" with Douglass.[2]

In any case, the Town and Country Club was short-lived, probably because of its unwieldy size (it was planned to include at least a hundred members). An informal successor soon followed, though, in casual dinners attended by Emerson, John S. Dwight, Edwin Whipple, and the banker-litterateur Samuel Gray Ward. These were held in the Parker House rooms of Horatio Woodman, a bachelor financier who advised many of the literati on their affairs (a "genius broker," in Dana's acid phrase). It was from this nucleus that the Saturday Club grew. Louis Agassiz, Benjamin Peirce, the mathematician, and R. H. Dana, Jr., were soon invited to meet with the original five, and at this stage some regularity was introduced into the proceedings. It was decided to dine together the last Saturday in every month at the Parker House; there would be no written rules and no records, a unanimous vote would be required to elect a new member, the expense of each dinner would be assessed on those present and guests would be permitted — each man paying for his own guests. Soon after these rules were established, Lowell was invited to join, and then John Lothrop Motley, the historian, and E. Rockwood Hoar, later Grant's Attorney General, unanimous consent being obtained for all three through informal conversation. But thereafter formal votes were held for suggested members and on this basis Oliver Wendell Holmes, Longfellow and C. C. Felton (professor of classics and soon to be President of Harvard) were added. Before the Civil War, the historian W. H. Prescott, Whittier, the widely accomplished James Elliot Cabot (later to be Emerson's literary executor), the businessman-reformer John Murray Forbes, Samuel Gridley Howe, Norton, the scholarly minister Frederick Hedge, Lowell's brother-in-law Estes Howe, and Tom Appleton, the witty brother of Mrs. Longfellow, had also been made members, bringing the list to twenty-three.[3]

It was a distinguished group (and would have been more so, thought the astringent Dana, had not Woodman, Ward and Dwight become members due to the club's accidental origins). But however brilliant, the group did not include, as had the Town and Country Club, the outspoken reformers of the day: Quincy, James Freeman Clarke, Wendell Phillips, Higginson, Parker or Bronson Alcott, men whose attainments and cultivation might ordinarily have qualified them for membership. Lowell and Samuel Gridley Howe represented "advanced opinion," but Lowell was no longer the strenuous abolitionist he had once been, and Howe, though still in the forefront of the antislavery struggle, was not admitted immediately to the club and did not attend with regularity. Lowell carried on a running battle to win admission for Quincy and at one point, in 1868, after Quincy had been blackballed, Lowell and Norton gave serious thought to resigning and forming a new group. But although the "supra-Castilian" delays, as Emerson called them, continued (Quincy was not admitted until 1875, along with

James Freeman Clarke), Lowell retained his membership—he could not give up "what has been good so long." [4]

If from a "radical" perspective the Saturday Club was not sufficiently inclusive, from other vantage points it showed considerable diversity (no group of twenty-odd, of course, could be expected to represent all shades of opinion on all issues; moreover, social congeniality presupposes some limitations and these need not be "malevolent" in intent). In any case, the spectrum of views in the Saturday Club was considerable. Though Lowell, Howe, Emerson, Longfellow and Dana, for example, were all strongly antislavery, they differed widely as to methods and timetables, ranging from Longfellow's apolitical stance, through Dana's participation in the formation of the Free Soil party, to Howe's support of John Brown. And these men, in turn, were separated by leagues from the conservative views of Louis Agassiz, a firm believer in Negro inferiority, and Hawthorne, whose idea of the perfect politician was his personal friend, Franklin Pierce (meeting Lowell at a dinner in 1860, Pierce leaned toward him and said in a confidential tone, "Sir, I glory in your fame! I am proud of every man, sir, who does honor to me country!"; the startled Lowell looked him straight in the face "with the gravity of a Sphinx to whom a traveller should say, 'Sir-Madam, I glory in the perfect unfrivolity of your sienite nature!' "). [5]

The range of temperament was also considerable: Hawthorne, silent and aware, always (when he could be persuaded to attend) something of a rebuke, a judgment, on the high spirits of the club; Longfellow, gentle, modest, sweet-tempered, remarkably free of jealousy and spite, though not of the melancholia so often used to excuse them; Holmes, that miniature Voltaire, ebullient, taut, youthfully egotistical, thrusting from his tiny frame the large intellect and wit which announced to the world his affably combative presence; Agassiz, the most famous scientist of his day, whose denial of Darwinism carried enough weight to delay its acceptance in America, and whose own formidable presence seemed both to himself and others no minor demonstration of that divine purpose which he saw manifested everywhere in nature; Richard Henry Dana, Jr., more successful as lawyer and author than as politician or companion (the first of which roles he coveted, the second of which he scorned), managing to condescend even to his peers, so that as Lowell put it, you could never be with him for very long without having the uncomfortable sense of being patted on the head; Emerson, the radical originality and independence of his youth now modulated into a more placid humanism, poised in unanxious balance above the great questions, like some austere, aristocratic heron, deciding to fly no longer.

With such disparate and developed temperaments, the Saturday Club was hardly the gathering of sedate, parochial graybeards so often portrayed. The dinners were animated, even jaunty affairs, beginning at three in the afternoon, often ambling through seven courses and innumerable bottles of sherry, sauterne and claret. Though conversation was almost always good-natured, full of anecdote, sally, word play, there would be disagreements of opinion and jostlings of personality. Whipple maintained that the club's very success was due to its being "a society based on mutual repulsion . . . It was ingeniously supposed that persons who looked on all questions of science, theology, and literature from different points of view would be the very persons who would most enjoy one another's company once a month . . ." If Whipple overstated the case, real differences did exist, and they produced real tangles. Agassiz and Emerson would contest the merits of Darwin, the scientist upholding man's special creation, the transcendentalist accepting man's common origin with the ape. Politics would cause frequent divisions, often focused around the activities of Charles Sumner, the Bay State's outspoken antislavery Senator; after one prolonged argument between Norton and Hoar, Hawthorne, who had sat quietly by, said in his shy way to Norton, "I'm glad you didn't give in." Tom Appleton especially delighted in opposition. At one dinner he took fire when denouncing the Germans, from the disapproving silence of Samuel Ward: why once, he bellowed at Ward, he and his father had been so rudely treated by a German from whom they had had every reason to expect courtesy, that the elder Appleton had at last burst out, "Sir! Choose which of your features you wish to preserve, and I will take care of the rest!" [6]

Appleton, along with Holmes and Lowell, was one of the club's three great talkers, and each could grow impatient if one of the others spoke at too great length. Once, when Holmes was rippling along in one of those easy, sparkling flows that so mesmerized the club, Lowell kept interjecting critical comments until Holmes, ruffled, decided he had had about enough: "Now, James," he said, without preface or apology, "let me talk and don't interrupt me." [7]

Holmes was the most assured talker, spontaneous, inventive, elegant. Though he made every effort to be courteous, his wish to be clever sometimes overcame his intention to be polite; as Leslie Stephen said, Holmes' "sole aim was to hit the mark if possible, but, if a shot hit a head also, he showed a childlike pride in the achievement." Lowell, more of an improvisor, more fanciful, could sometimes get entangled in his own abundance, though the fascination of the parts usually atoned for the disorder of the whole. Appleton, less versatile than either Holmes or Lowell, knew better than they what Higginson once called "the London art of repression" (though one of Appleton's four-hour torrents left Holmes' mind feeling as his body might after a Turkish bath — "every joint snapped and its hard epidermis taken clean off . . ."). Appleton was also more tactful than the other two, for both Holmes and Lowell could be extraordinarily blunt — as much from periodic insensitivity as from insistent honesty. At a dinner given for the Reverend and Mrs. Stowe, Lowell, at one end of the table, expounded to Harriet Beecher the superiority of *Tom Jones* above all other novels, while Holmes, at the other end, demonstrated conclusively to Dr. Stowe that profanity had originated in the pulpit.[8]

Though Holmes, Lowell and Appleton starred at the monthly dinners, the supporting cast was strong. Most of the club's members, Hawthorne being the major exception, were articulate men who enjoyed conversation, and if the more ebullient trio dominated table talk, they rarely monopolized it. Wit was in especially plentiful supply. Ward was known for his epigrams (he had found out, he once said, why people die — "it is to break up their style"), and Motley for his ability to punctuate his easy flow of conversation with quick asides ("give me the luxuries and I will dispense with the necessaries of life"). Emerson, although too gentlemanly to bore, preach or dictate, contributed his quiet authority (Dana, who could patronize even the Sage of Concord, expressed surprise "to see these transcendentalists appearing well as men of the world"). And even the diffident Longfellow would have an occasional attack of scintillation. In any case, none of the club's members — always excepting Hawthorne — felt so cramped or intimidated as to think of these Saturdays in any but the most agreeable terms. Appleton thought the club would almost surely be remembered and talked of in the future as Dr. Johnson's Club had been, and Lowell, when in his sixties, after years of association with Europe's elite, declared he had "never seen society on the whole so good" as he used to meet on these Saturdays.[9]

Though the distinction of its membership is sufficient to account for the club's brilliance, something more is needed to explain its congeniality. It came from a compound of mutual respect, and shared assumptions about the nature of social occasions. The respect was not perfect — though Emerson admired Lowell, he thought his manner not always "simple" enough; Lowell considered Dana disdainful; Quincy thought Holmes a bore, etc. But where respect could not always be relied upon to forestall antagonism, civility usually could. These men were one in their assumption that there was an obligation at social affairs to be not only interesting, but pleasant. What might be lost in absolute honesty was gained in geniality. Reversing the definitions of our day, Lowell's circle believed it *un*-natural to attempt complete sincerity on all occasions. To do so would be to confuse a necessary distinction between the private and the public. Alone with one's family or with a few intimate friends, the individual could afford, indeed had the obligation, to be sincerely himself. But when men of casual acquaintance were thrown together in a social situation, they had the different obligation to make themselves agreeable. And this could only be achieved by some withholding of personal feelings and opinions. To reveal private intimacies cheapened the intimacies even while embarrassing the listeners; to engage in tenacious debate on public questions ruined what possibilities the occasion offered for relaxation. In short, casual society should be neither a confessional nor an arena.[10]

Social "artificialities," however, did not preclude straightforwardness with intimates, nor even, sometimes, in public print. Lowell once unnerved Longfellow by going up to him at the club and saying straight out, "you ought not to have printed those verses to Agassiz; they are all very well, but it was a private affair." And when formally evaluating a friend's work in a review, Lowell, for one, could be outspoken. In 1863, with Longfellow at the height of his fame and a neighbor as well as friend, Lowell reviewed *Tales of a Wayside Inn* with a judicious combination of firm criticism and respectful praise ("Mr. Longfellow has sometimes mistaken mere strangeness for freshness . . . the Saga [of King Olaf] seems *too* Norse . . . [it] suggests translation with over-much heed for literal closeness"). Lowell's frank evaluation of the *Tales* was not an isolated instance.[11]

The separation these men made between the private and the social helps to explain why they kept their socializing to a minimum. The self-imposed limitations of such occasions might, if too often repeated, unduly contaminate private integrity, just as the obligation to be agreeable could, if too frequently imposed, drain one's limited reserve of public cordiality. Casual socializing was therefore an occasional, not a regular, phenomenon. It was possible in the small Boston world and its even smaller Brahmin circle for John Holmes barely to know Francis Child, and for Oliver Wendell Holmes to confess late in life that although nothing could have been pleasanter than his relations with Lowell, they had "never sat long alone" nor walked a mile in company, for they "did not live within easy reach" of each other. Lowell, in one of his more treasonable moments, described Bostonians as seeming to have but two notions of hospitality: "a dinner with people you never saw before nor ever wish to see again, and a drive in Mount Auburn cemetery . . . Your memory of the dinner is expected to reconcile you to the prospect of the graveyard." Fanny Longfellow, for one, lamented the infrequency of "regular, nourishing" contacts, and thought her husband—"being especially social by nature"—pined away for their lack. It seemed bizarre to her that with "so many men of high culture" about, one lacked the benefit of their company, for "they are too busy, or too domestic, and hardly one of them but Agassiz is to be relied on for any social purposes." Agassiz, Swiss by birth, apparently lacked the native devotion to privacy.[12]

Many Boston wives, along with Fanny Longfellow, felt the isolation more than their husbands, for a fair share of the socializing that did take place was restricted to all-male dinners or clubs; this was perhaps what Julia Ward Howe had in mind when she complained of the "frozen ocean of Boston life." One exception to the all-male gatherings was the irregular meetings of the "Atlantic Club," called by the publishers to allow acquaintance and fellowship among the magazine's chief contributors—and occasionally this meant including Harriet Beecher Stowe, Harriet Prescott Spofford and other female writers. Mrs. Stowe, at one dinner, did little for the cause of female equality by insisting, true to her temperance principles, that no wine be served; Lowell finally teased her out of the ban by regretting aloud how many pleasant dinners she would miss in England (where she was bound) by so self-denying an ordinance.[13]

What women lost in equality, they only partially regained in deference. They were, to be sure, abstractly worshipped as the fountain of all things "spiritual," but in practice their spirituality seems not to have conflicted with a subordinate status, nor to have unfitted them for a fair amount of hard domestic work. Arthur Hugh Clough reported back to England, with some disapproval, that women in Boston did most of the carving at table, that men did not rise when ladies left the dining room, nor open the door for them, except casually. Small wonder that the American female, neither fully enthroned nor fully emancipated, began to agitate for a new status.[14]

With casual socializing held to a minimum, there was more chance to develop deep relationships. One of the poignant attractions of Lowell's generation is that the *particular* friendship had a chance to flourish; time and energy were not so embroiled in multiple activities, nor feelings so dissipated by trivial contacts, that men were unable to pursue the few friendships which held out hope of significance for them. Lowell, while thoroughly enjoying the Saturday Club and other occasional dinners, always preferred the companionship of one close friend; a good talk, he said, was "almost as much out of the question among clever men as among men who think themselves clever." And he added, only partly in jest, that "creation in pairs proves the foreordained superiority of the *tête à tête*." Sometimes, when absorbed in work, Lowell would absent himself almost completely from general society ("solitude is as needful to the imagination as society is wholesome for the character"), husbanding what time he had free for the few people closest to him. Even as a young man he had had friends, like Page and Briggs, to whom he was especially devoted. "Do not think of me ever," he had once written Briggs, "as J.R.L. the author but simply as J.R.L. that loves you. I *will* have two or three quiet nooks into which I can retreat from the pursuit of my own title-pages." He wished to be known, at least to a few, as Lowell the man rather than Lowell the poet, for he hoped he was better than his books — if not, he should "never dream of writing another." [15]

No friendship of Lowell's proved as intimate or enduring as the one he formed, when already in his thirties, with Charles Eliot Norton, almost ten years his junior. Norton came on both sides of his family from a long line of New England clerics. The security of his heritage and the affection of his immediate family gave him a settled self-confidence. Even as a young man he had been so judicious and reflective that when he set off on the grand tour, Tom Appleton quipped that Norton was "going to sow his tame oats." By training and predisposition it seemed likely that Norton would become one more pillar of the over-buttressed Boston community. And in a sense, he did: in his candor, his distrust of the sensuous, his insistence on character, his belief that art should serve a moral and didactic function, he was very much the upright Bostonian, the proper Puritan descendant. But he went further than most of his generation in the urbanity of his outlook and the skeptical questioning of his mind. At the time his friendship with Lowell began to ripen, in the late 1850's, Norton had not gone far toward unorthodoxy, but in later life he outdistanced Lowell in his willingness to probe beyond the commonplace. Lowell as gauged by his manner — his inventiveness, wit, oscillation of mood — may have seemed the less conventional of the two, but by the mid-1850's he had already taken most of his intellectual risks and it would be Norton, grave and sedate in demeanor, who after the Civil War would come more directly to grips with the realities of a post-Darwinian world. It would be Norton more than Lowell who would question, and with rigor, accepted American values — institutional religion, free enterprise, unlimited competition, manifest destiny, the superiority of democracy, the idea of progress, unbridled individualism. And when, in 1869, Norton would say that "society at the present day . . . is not worth preserving . . ." he would sound that pessimistic note far more akin to the generation of Mark Twain and Brooks and Henry Adams than to that of his closest friend, Lowell.[16]

Yet his affinities with Lowell, even in later years, remained substantial: a love of letters and scholarship, a belief in the utilitarian nature and moral purpose of art, an insistence that what men achieved was less important than what they were, a confidence in rationality coupled with a commitment to ideality, a disgust with the pursuit of money and possessions, a large curiosity and intelligence, a belief that although the individual was sacred, he developed within and owed responsibility to his society.

Though Lowell and Norton were in some ways very different, even their differences became mutually supportive. Norton delighted in Lowell's ardor and wit, of which he had little himself, and Lowell found in Norton's stability a safe anchor for his own fluctuations of mood. Norton was Lowell's reliable rock, a man on whom he could consistently count for support — even when he was himself being inconsistent. He was not alone in sensing Norton's constancy; John Ruskin, also Norton's senior by ten years, always thought of him as older and wiser; his last words to him on one leave-taking were, "Good-bye, *papa*." [17]

In his work, too, Lowell came to depend on Norton's steady encouragement and unflagging devotion. "I don't forget, & never shall forget," he once wrote him, "how much you have been to me. I have never done so well as I could & ought, but what I have done has been due to your partiality more than anything else, for you have given me a kind of faith in it." Norton's friendship for Lowell did not prevent — for such men it almost necessitated — frank criticism of his writing, though the criticism was always given with such obvious concern for Lowell's own welfare that it could never be taken for disguised hostility.[18]

The two men cared deeply for each other. Intimacies did not

proceed rapidly in nineteenth-century New England — it took six years for the salutation in Norton's letters to change from "My Dear Lowell" to "My Dear James" — but once developed, the friendship never faltered. And in the privacy of their talks or their letters, they expressed their affection with warmth and openness. They were not afraid to use the word "love" in describing their feeling for each other, and did so with what today seems a remarkable lack of self-consciousness. "Remember always," wrote Norton on one occasion, "how much one person in the world loves you, & how grateful he is for all you are." And it was a love free of sentimentality. With a precision perhaps gratuitous, almost cold, Lowell spelled out his feelings: "When I say you are the best friend I ever had, I mean precisely what I say. I never wrote those words to anybody else. I don't say I love you the most. I never said that. I love you enough, I am sure & you may be sure, but I couldn't love any man more than I do J.H. [John Holmes]." [19]

The willingness of these men to be agreeable in public, in combination with their capacity to be intimate in private, suggests a style far removed from more recent tendencies to define the "interesting" person in terms of his extravagance and to equate awareness with alienation. There was, as George William Curtis said of the Saturday Club, "no Bohemia at that table," none of those furious, anarchic scenes which have come to be associated with the "literary" personality — so closely associated as to merge into a standard of validation. The Saturday Club, with its pleasure in word play and anecdote, its innocent epicureanism, its emphasis on the well-turned rather than the spontaneous phrase, may today seem hopelessly domesticated, prosaic, trivial. Brahmin emphasis on self-restraint over self-indulgence, on the sanctity of one's privacy, on reason and objectivity, and on civic responsibility, place them light years away from the current climate. Which may only mean — *if* one admires their style — that they were more fortunate than we:

nothing in their environment seemed so irremediably distasteful or threatening to suggest estrangement as the only life-preserving path.

It was a style soon to be massively assaulted — in theory by Darwin and Marx, in practice by industrialism and, more concretely still, by the Civil War. In the midst of that holocaust, it would be increasingly difficult to believe in man's rationality, his social nature, his ability to control events or to view his experience objectively. Such values would linger long, but would never again exert the same force; or, it is tempting to say, produce men who combined so much strength with grace.

CHAPTER X

CIVIL WAR

IN 1860, when Lincoln's election symbolized a new departure for the American Republic, Dr. Charles Lowell, who in many ways represented the best of the old, died suddenly after long years of declining health. Shortly before his death, he wrote a farewell letter to his old parish, beseeching its members to love one another. There could have been no more fitting summary for the life (to use Fanny Longfellow's phrase) of this "beautiful old man." [1]

Soon after his death, James Russell moved back into Elmwood, assuming occupancy of his father's house, as through the years he had increasingly come into possession of his father's character. The last six years had been spent, as he put it, "camping out," first with the Estes Howes, then in the anonymous boarding house of a Mrs. Upham, and it had been a time of intermittent poor health and spirits. Back now in the place he loved best, where he had spent thirty years of his life, he hoped to recover something of his former self and of his former inspiration — it had not, he felt, borne "bottling and transportation" very well.[2]

Whatever inspiration and time Lowell managed to salvage from his varied duties, he devoted to political commentary for the *Atlantic*. The rush of national events, the mounting evidence of crisis, called out all his reserves of energy. As the election of 1860 approached, he found himself disagreeing with those abolitionists who held that the Republican party was not truly antislavery, that although its central doctrine of "non-extension" might prevent the further spread of slavery, it would be at the expense of guaranteeing the system where it already existed.

Lowell stressed instead what he took to be the Republicans' underlying animus against slavery, however diluted might be their public policy for dealing with it; the Republicans, he believed, had "an earnest purpose, and the unflinching tenacity of profound conviction." He hoped, in 1860, that the party's Presidential nomination would go to William Seward as representing its advanced antislavery wing — one of the very reasons Seward was passed over. When the nomination went instead to Abraham Lincoln, Lowell, who had read his speeches, was "entirely content." He believed that Lincoln had already demonstrated ability and integrity, that he had had enough experience to become a statesman but not so much as to become a mere politician.[3]

Lowell looked on the 1860 election as a milestone and in this, of course, all agreed, though not necessarily for Lowell's reasons. In his view the question to be settled in 1860 was whether the long history of concession to slavery was to be ended, or whether the country was to continue on its course of compromising human rights "for the sake of a peace that never comes." In an outspoken essay for the *Atlantic*, "The Election in November," Lowell argued that if slavery was to be allowed the right of expansion into the territories, as the South demanded, then the American future would be molded by "an Oriental theory of society." Let slavery into new areas and freedom would flee; extend the principle of property rights in men and human rights would end. The American government had originally been dedicated to purposes higher than cupidity, to interests wider than those of a section or a caste. It was time to recall those other purposes and interests. It was time to remember that labor had rights as well as capital, that Negroes were also men, that the principles of the free states as well as the slave required protection.[4]

It was nonsense, Lowell argued — it had long been nonsense — to say that the North ought not to agitate the slavery question. This was tantamount to telling a man "with the fever and ague on him to stop shaking, and he will be cured." True, the discussion of slavery would produce excitement — no question that cut so deep could be debated, much less resolved, without excitement. But discussion *and* its attendant ferment were the very life of free institutions. Without continual dialogue, first principles fell easy sacrifice to expediency, and the rights of man came to be remembered only by the dead formulas which mocked them. The real danger to the Union, Lowell insisted, was not further debate but further compromise, yet one more concession in a lengthening list that could end by making slavery co-extensive with the national domain; at that point the Union would indeed be endangered, for the simple reason that it would have become "a burden instead of a blessing." Besides, Lowell argued — and here he exhibited a myopia common in the North — the South's threat to secede if Lincoln should be elected was only rhetoric, still another of those false alarms which she had been sounding since the first days of the Republic. As in the past, her threats were made to intimidate the North, to draw forth additional, unwarranted concessions. The "old women" might become frightened at the cry of disunion, but those who recognized that compromise on the territorial issue would fatally damage the American experiment would feel no terror, nor would they flinch. The South's only real grievances were those incapable of solution: she wanted agitation against slavery ended, and her control of the national government continued. She wanted, in short, to repeal the mid-nineteenth century.

Lincoln's success at the polls in November, 1860, delighted Lowell. But the events which immediately followed left him somewhat puzzled. He had predicted that Lincoln's election would pacify the country; seeing that the North was at last in earnest, the South would accept the majority's verdict, talk of secession would recede, and the crisis would have been successfully met and passed. Instead, within a month of the election, every state in the deep South took steps toward disunion, and by March, 1861, seven had formally severed their ties. Lowell, like many in the North who had underestimated Southern resentment, confessed that he did not "well know what to make of the present posture of affairs." But he remained clear on one point: the country had been running "long enough by dead reckoning" and it was time "to take the height of the sun of righteousness." [5]

In another strong article in the *Atlantic*, "E Pluribus Unum," Lowell put much of the blame for the state secessions on Buchanan's want of firmness during his lame-duck tenure: "Mr. Buchanan seems to have thought, that, if to govern little was to govern well, then to do nothing was the perfection of policy." Three members of Buchanan's cabinet were known sympathizers with secession, and their activities, in combination with Buchanan's supineness, amounted in Lowell's eyes to Executive "imbecility" and "moral bankruptcy." Most historians have since echoed Lowell's indictment though in far more measured terms and without his certainty that positive action by Buchanan would in fact have made any difference — without even a clear view of what that action should have been. It was one thing to insist, as Lowell did, that ours was "a government of laws" and that "the sober will of the majority" had to prevail, but quite another to outline and carry through a policy which would command such allegiance. Lowell believed that "firmness" would set matters right: Buchanan should make clear (though the Constitution did not) that the Union was indivisible and perpetual; he should deny the right of separation unequivocably, he should call secession by its rightful name — rebellion — and, if necessary, he should exercise the federal government's legitimate authority. "Firmness in the beginning," Lowell believed, would "save the need of force in the end," though he did not specify how firmness could be differentiated from force, nor how any show of coercion could avoid bringing forth violent counteraction. With hindsight (knowing what happened at Fort Sumter), the line between "firmness" and force may to us seem remarkably thin, but Lowell insisted he was not an advocate of violent measures: "Even if seceding States could be conquered back again, they would not be worth the conquest." The strong assertion of basic principles would alone, he believed, be sufficient to meet the crisis. If Buchanan would make clear that in a democracy the majority had the right to govern and that the American Union was indissoluble, he would give confidence to the unionists of the South, reclaim the wavering, and disconcert the plotters of treason.[6]

Underlying Lowell's position, at the heart of his argument, was the belief — shared by many — that secession had been the work of a discontented few, the fruition of a long-matured plot by an ambitious group of conspirators who had managed to carry along, or ignore, their bewildered fellow Southerners. He believed that "probably a majority, and certainly a powerful minority, in the seceding States" remained loyal to the Union and would assert their loyalty if the federal government would only encourage them to do so. Instead Buchanan, by doing nothing, gave the conspirators the opportunity to work upon the fears and passions of their uncertain neighbors, "luring the ambitious with visionary promises of Southern grandeur and prosperity, and deceiving the ignorant into the belief that the principles and practice of the Free States were truly represented by John Brown." In fact, Lowell insisted (attempting to apply logic to a situation fraught with unreason), there was no real cultural antipathy between North and South, other than that invented by ambitious men to secure their selfish ends. We were basically a nation of one language, one law, one religion. Just as separation was unnecessary, it was also unwise. An independent Southern confederacy could never survive; practical economic difficulties aside, the very theory of secession would destroy it — for how could there be stability in a confederacy whose foundation was the principle "that any member of it may withdraw at the first discontent"? The secessionists liked to compare their movement to the revolt of the colonies against England, but their unreal grievances and their mistaken notions of sectional advantage were in fact a caricature of the Revolution, the parody made complete by a declaration of independence "that hangs the franchise of human nature on the kink of a hair, and substitutes for the visionary right of all men to the pursuit of happiness the more practical privilege of some men to pursue their own negro . . ."

Lowell's view of the secession crisis, widely shared then and since, had much in it that was cogent, part that was open to challenge. His insistence on law, majority rule and the perpetuity of the Union, his denial of the reality of sectional cultural differences, his belief in the enduring strength of Southern Unionism, his conviction of the advantages of continued association and the practical impossibility of separation, were all of a piece with Lincoln's own position, as summarized in his first inaugural address: "Though passion may have strained, it must not break our bonds of affection. The mystic chords of memory . . . will yet swell the chorus of the Union, when again touched, as surely they will be, by the better angels of our nature." Like Lincoln — and so many others — Lowell probably failed to gauge the full depths of Southern resentment, though there are grounds for believing that in the slave states taken as a whole, the majority of the population did not desire secession. In some parts of the deep South, it is true, secession fever was hardly confined to a small group of ruthless opportunists. In South Carolina especially, Union sentiment had long been in decline and no recourse to a "conspiracy" theory is needed to explain the speed with which that state — and several others in the deep South — severed their ties. Elsewhere, though, secessionism seems to have been in uncertain balance with a kind of conditional Unionism — that is, at the least there existed the sort of Union sentiment which was willing to "wait and see," to delay secession until either the federal government should commit overt aggression or until the slave states as a unified whole could agree on separation. This sort of "Unionism," however, was not likely to be encouraged by firm federal measures. Since primary loyalty was probably invested not in the nation but in the state or section, even the suggestion of coercion — as Lincoln learned at Fort Sumter — was likely to precipitate angry retaliation rather than to restore fraternal harmony.[7]

What emerges most clearly from the tangled events of "secession winter" is that diagnosis was, and is, immensely difficult. No single line of policy stood out as promising, all at once, the containment of slavery and the preservation of both peace and Union. Lowell's position, like all those assumed during the crisis, can now be seen to have been faulty, but even now one is hard put to suggest alternative policies which would have been free of error and risk. Paradoxically, it is the very clarity of Lowell's position, more than its particulars, which seems most vulnerable. Given the complexity of events, his analysis now appears too certain, his solutions too clear-cut. Once the passion and confusion of the crisis had passed, Lowell saw as well as anyone that the clarity of his argument had to some extent been at the expense of subtlety:

When I *wuz younger 'n wut you see me now,—*
Nothin' from Adam's fall to Huldy's bonnet,
Thet I warn't full-cocked with my jedgment on it;
But now I'm gittin' on in life, I find
It's a sight harder to make up my mind . . .
The moral question's ollus plain enough.—
It's jes' the human-natur' side thet's tough;
Wut's best to think may n't puzzle me nor you,—
The pinch comes in decidin' wut to du;
Ef you read *History, all runs smooth ez grease,*
Coz there the men ain't nothin' more 'n idees,—
But come to make *it, ez we must to-day,*
Th' idees hev arms an' legs an' stop the way . . . [8]

In the six weeks between Lincoln's inauguration as President and the outbreak of hostilities at Fort Sumter in April, 1861, Lowell chafed at the new President's "indecision." He appreciated the Administration's difficulties and its natural reluctance to assume responsibility for beginning a war, but further temporizing, Lowell believed, was misguided, especially if calculated to hold the border states in the Union — in the long run they could bring little to the rebels by way of money, credit or arms. Given the need to maintain the Union, Lowell believed that Lincoln had to attempt the reprovisioning of Fort Sumter, even at the risk of war, for Sumter had become *the* symbol of national authority — the same conclusion Lincoln himself shortly reached. The only way war could definitely be avoided was by a further attempt at conciliation; yet this would involve "concessions vastly more disastrous than war itself," like allowing slavery into the territories. Further efforts at conciliation, moreover, would seem to "put the party of law and loyalty in the wrong," as if they were the ones who had refused to accept the verdict of the polls. And if conciliation was to be attempted "as a mere matter of policy in order to gain time," it would be a still greater mistake because "it was the rebels only who could profit by it in consolidating their organization." Lowell, in short, had subtly shifted his position of a few months earlier. During Buchanan's last months in office, Lowell had argued that a firm policy would not lead to violence, but to a reinvigoration of Southern Unionism and thereby to a peaceful restoration. Now he was arguing that a firm policy was needed *even* if it led to violence. It was a shift made by many during these months, and made not merely to justify the drift of events, but to readjust to their changed aspect. A firm policy during Buchanan's last months in office had seemed a likely way of avoiding violence; a few months later, firmness seemed just as likely to bring violence on — though no less necessary, even so. Later, however, Lowell decided that Lincoln had after all been wiser than he in delaying the final decision to reprovision Sumter: "Mr. Lincoln . . . though we have sometimes in our impatience thought otherwise, has always waited, as a wise man should, till the right moment brought up all his reserves." [9]

When war began at Fort Sumter in April, 1861, Lowell, again like so many others, South and North, welcomed it with something like relief. It was a generation which knew war as a limited operation for limited objectives, and which assumed, moreover, that the conflict would be brief — just enough grapeshot to bring sense, depending on where you stood, to despots or to rebels. Yet the general enthusiasm for war was so pronounced that finally it can be accounted for only as a convulsive release from decades of sectional hatred and frustration. Even a man like Lowell, he who had written in 1846,

Ez fer war, I call it murder, —
There you hev it plain an' flat;
I don't want to go no furder
Than my Testyment fer that . . . ,

even he could say in 1861 that "no price is high at which the social & political unity of this entire continent (for that is what it means in the long run) . . . can be purchased, nay, that at any price it is not the cheapest bargain that ever a nation bought . . ." Just as Lowell had been ambivalent in advocating "firmness" while deploring violence, so, now that violence had come, he welcomed it as purgative even while lamenting the bloodshed it would entail. If the prospect of Civil War was terrible, the alternatives were more terrible still — to let "this magnificent empire" perish, or to let it become a Southern slave plantation:

Ne'er may war set the trumpet to her lips,
And, with fierce summons, call from forge and field
Our youth that kindle slow and slowly yield;
But oh! fair Freedom, if our choice must be
'Twixt war and craven recreance to thee,
Sooner, dear land, let each manchild of thine
Sleep death's red sleep within the enemy's line . . .

Sooner than brook, what only slaves hold dear,
A suppliant peace that is not Peace, but Fear! [10]

Lowell denied any belief in war as in itself desirable or ennobling; he believed Sidney Smith had spoken well in saying "God is forgotten" in wartime. Yet — his ambivalence was unending — he did assume that war could bring noble results, that "we should be the better for some kind of war to purge the oe'r rank state." As Charles Eliot Norton put it, "we are reaping the whirlwind — but when reaped, the air will be clearer and more healthy"; the principles of majority rule, of the perpetuity of the Union and of freedom for all men would be more firmly established than ever before. Lowell never doubted that the war would produce some radical change in the system of slavery. The guns in Charleston Harbor, he believed, had done more in one day to convert men to abolition than had thirty years of eloquence from Garrison and Phillips: "Whatever other result this war is destined to produce, it has already won for us a blessing worth everything to us as a nation in emancipating the public opinion of the North." Nor did Lowell doubt that the Confederacy would be defeated. What the South had always boasted as its strength would in war prove its weakness: "it has always been commercial & not agricultural communities that have been able to carry on wars successfully, or long, which means the same thing." The contest would prove which was stronger, "an oligarchy built *on* men, or a commonwealth built *of* them." [11]

These high hopes helped to justify the ardor — really the pugnacity — with which humane men like Lowell could greet the onset of hostilities. Norton, when the war was only three months old, declared, "it is a fine thing that . . . Massachusetts blood should be the first shed in the advance of this great army of Freedom. Can we be too glad . . . to be living in these days?" They would be less glad as the carnage increased and as loved ones began to appear on casualty lists. And in the post-war period, with devastation widespread and the "noble results" having turned into mixed blessings, their disillusion would be in direct proportion to their initial zeal.[12]

The almost cheerful earnestness of the war's early days was reflected in a new *Biglow* series which Lowell inaugurated late in 1861 (and which he was to string out into eleven "papers" over a five-year period). During the 1850's he had thought several times of resurrecting Hosea Biglow, but had then been too engrossed by the *Atlantic* to find "brooding" time — with him "as needful a preliminary to hatching anything as with a clucking hen." Finally, after several false starts, he completed the first piece of what was to become a new series late in 1861, and felt "as nervous about it as a young author not yet weaned of public favor." Writing it at all had been against his better judgment, for he claimed not to believe in resuscitations: "we hear no good of the *posthumous* Lazarus." [13]

His misgivings proved justified; the first of the new *Biglow Papers* was a dud. It had a long introduction by the Rev. Wilbur, in his familiar style of arch pomposity, and a still longer contribution in verse by Birdofredum Sawin which, besides being a discursive bore, came distastefully close to being a low parody of the national crisis — not only its jocular tone, but even its loosely structured form seemed mockingly inappropriate to the North's determined mood. Some of Lowell's friends hung back from telling him their poor opinion of the paper; they had continually urged him to take up the Biglow theme again, and now that he had finally done so it seemed churlish to quarrel with its inadequacies. No such nicety bothered Norton. He realized that Lowell needed honest criticism, and that friendship gave him both the right and the duty to express it. He spared Lowell nothing. The people, he told him, were too much in earnest for discursive humor "unless there be a simple, perfectly direct moral underneath." The Sawin poem, in trying to strike ten blows instead of one, had ended by striking none; it was simply too full, suffering from the very abundance of Lowell's powers. Norton advised him to turn his hand to concentrated, powerful, lyrical pieces — it was the lyrics in the First Series, he reminded him, which had become "immortal." Norton even had a specific suggestion: Lowell should try putting into verse the popular resentment against England for her "unsympathetic" reactions to the North.[14]

Lowell followed Norton's advice to the letter. His second try, "Mason and Slidell: A Yankee Idyll," had thematic unity, was pointed in moral and lyrical in tone. The theme, as prescribed, was England's role to date in the American struggle. Lowell excoriated Britain for her haste in extending belligerent rights to the Confederacy, for her peremptory tone in demanding the release of the Southern agents, Mason and Slidell (who had been taken by a Northern vessel from a British packet bound for England), and for allowing Confederate privateers to be fitted out in British shipyards:

You wonder why we're hot, John?
Your mark wuz on the guns,
The neutral guns thet shot, John,
Our brothers an' our sons . . .
We own the ocean tu, John:
You mus'n' take it hard,
Ef we can't think with you, John,
It's jest your own back-yard.

Lowell realized that in some ways he did less than justice to the British position, but when "resenting a slap in the face" one couldn't stop "to be polite & make reservations." His attitude, in fact, was less belligerent than that of the public at large; he did point out that "England ain't *all* bad, coz she thinks us blind," and he welcomed Lincoln's decision to release Mason and Slidell as proof that we had arrived at "years of discretion" — "If courage be the sword, yet is patience the armour of a nation."[15]

Lowell's friends — indeed the public generally — were delighted with "Mason and Slidell." Norton, who could have taken more credit, simply expressed pleasure that the poem had turned out to be "a true Yankee pastoral and lyric." John Lothrop Motley wrote from Vienna, where he was Lincoln's Minister, that there had never been anything "more stinging, more concentrated, more vigorous, more just"; in his view Lowell had condensed into a few pages "the essence of a hundred diplomatic papers and historical disquisitions and 4th July orations." And Christopher Cranch pronounced "Mason and Slidell" a masterpiece, a description safe at least to the extent that it was assuredly one of *Lowell's* masterpieces.[16]

One other poem in the Second Series, "Sunthin' in the Pastoral Line," written in the spring of 1862, also ranks among the best of Lowell's achievements. It is a colloquy of contrasts: the certain new life of spring is set against the uncertain rebirth of the nation; the positive Puritan ancestor debates with his hesitant nineteenth-century descendant, the poem's narrator. Nature and the Past — those two demi-gods of the New England pantheon — are thus brought to comment on the country's crisis. Nature provides the unspoken commentary: its gentle renewal — the bobolink running down, "a brook o' laughter, thru the air" — suggests benevolent continuity in the midst of traumatic change. Yet even as the constancy of Nature brings sustenance, the Past, in the person of a stern Puritan forefather, brings challenge:

God hates your sneakin' creturs thet believe
He'll settle things they run awy an' leave!

The debate between the narrator and his Puritan ancestor, between the contrasting demands of thought and action, continuity and disjunction, delay and haste, come to specific focus in the poem on the question of emancipation. The narrator's uncertainty in regard to that issue was a direct reflection of Lowell's own.

In the first days of the war Lowell had advocated firmness in order to put down "rebellion"; there could be no hesitation or compromise in choosing majority rule over minority tyranny, law over anarchy. In this regard, Lowell's opinion never wavered; he never considered the rebellion itself fit subject for negotiation. But as emancipation came increasingly to the forefront as a wartime objective, Lowell felt less certain about the applicability of a "hard line." He had from the beginning hoped and expected the war to spell the end of slavery, and in the first year of the conflict had even thought the Administration at fault for failing to lift the people "to a higher plane of thought & feeling almost without knowing it themselves." "Prudence," he had written Norton, was certainly "a good drag upon virtue," so long as it didn't completely weight it down.[17]

Yet Lowell preferred emancipation to come as reform rather than revolution; he hoped to achieve justice with as little disruption as possible of order. As advanced sentiment in the North stepped up its demand for immediate emancipation, Lowell came to feel — with Lincoln — that so long as public opinion lagged, it was wiser to be patient a little longer. "I do not believe in that *laissez-aller*," he wrote Motley, "which is commonly nothing more than a lazy trust in *im*-Providence, but I do most firmly believe that we should chasten our hopes, our aspirations even, with our reason & judgment." In the *Atlantic* for December, 1861, Lowell argued that the time had not yet come to turn the war into a crusade against slavery: "To proclaim freedom from the banks of the Potomac to an unarmed, subject, and dispirited race, when the whole white population is in arms, would be as futile as impolitic." Till the North could equip its own army, it was idle, Lowell insisted, to talk of arming the slaves; "and to incite them to insurrection without arms, and without the certainty of support at first and protection afterward, would be merely sacrificing them to no good end." He agreed that the struggle would gain a deeper moral purpose if the government adopted at once an emancipation policy, but that policy would soon falter, he argued, in the face of the practical obstacles to its accomplishment — while at the same time it would add to rebel strength by driving the South to despair.[18]

Lowell's cautionary approach to emancipation horrified radical antislavery men; "it was more than painful," as one of them put it, to find Lowell "limping at such a momentous emergency." The staunch abolitionist, Samuel May, Jr., believed that Lowell had wanted for years to "cut the Abolitionists — having got into the smooth, dignified, self-complacent, and change-hating society of the college & its Boston circles . . . Lowell has gone over to the world, and to 'respectability.' "[19]

Such men were mistaken in taking a shift of tactics for a loss of commitment; Lowell's concern for the slave had not died, only his evaluation of how that concern could best be implemented. Yet he was not himself comfortable with the cautious line he adopted on emancipation. As he wrote in the *Atlantic* piece of December, 1861: "It is a question we have hardly the heart to discuss, where our wishes, our hopes, almost our faith in God, are on one side, our understanding and experience on the other." His anguish was also made clear in "Sunthin' in the Pastoral Line." The poem's narrator is made to speak the counsel of restraint:

> . . . *I want's to heve all* we *gain stick,*
> *An' not to start Millennium too quick;*
> *We hain't to punish only, but to keep,*
> *An' the cure's gut to go a cent'ry deep.*

But his Puritan forebear is allowed a sharp retort:

> *It's Slavery thet's the fangs an' thinkin' head,*
> *An' ef you want selvation, cresh it dead,*

An' cresh it suddin' or you'll learn by waitin'
Thet Chance wun't stop to listen to debatin'!

There Lowell left the issue — in the poem and in himself — the contrasting needs of caution and urgency, of order and justice, remaining in uncertain suspension. Events finally settled the debate for him. In late 1862, Lincoln issued the preliminary Proclamation of Emancipation, and Lowell, profoundly relieved that the knot had been cut, rejoiced that the government (and himself) was at last firmly "on the side of freedom, justice, and sound policy":

Thet's wut we want, — we want to know
The folks on our side hez the bravery
To b'lieve ez hard, come weal, come woe
In Freedom ez Jeff doos in Slavery.[20]

If "Mason and Slidell" and "Sunthin' in the Pastoral Line" were individual successes, the second series of Biglow Papers, taken as a whole, was no match for the original. "Moral satire" was no longer as congenial to Lowell's temper as it had been twenty years earlier, when its blend of earnestness and wit had so perfectly caught the dominant strains of his personality. He was now less radical and less passionate. A new mode was needed to express his changing temperament. But it was a mode he would never find. Such poetry as he was to write hereafter — enough to fill only two volumes in forty years — would lack the personal signature which had once marked his best work. As he deepened in wisdom and grace as a man, he became less distinctive as a poet. It would be possible for him in middle age to speak in the accent of others because their voices would sufficiently express his own.[21]

The central fault of the Second Series was its lack of unity — as if Lowell had trouble sustaining his own attention. Some tenuous thematic links, and the reappearance now and then of a familiar character like Parson Wilbur, did something to bind the separate pieces together, but no single point of view, tone, theme or character dominated sufficiently to integrate the disjointed parts. Not even chronology served as a connector; the series kept doubling back on itself — the topic of secession, for example, surfaced repeatedly in the later papers, usually as an irrelevant aside. New characters like Preserved Doe were introduced for a single paper, only to drop from sight thereafter. And discursive material, that congenital defect of Lowell's, again intruded — Parson Wilbur's long discourse on Runic inscriptions, though more amusing than most of his asides, hardly contributed to pace and focus. In short, the Second Series was more fragmentary and episodic than the first. It contained some of Lowell's finest individual poems and a good deal of incisive political commentary, but the parts did not sufficiently cohere.

Although Lowell wrote the first seven papers in the second *Biglow* series in 1862–1863, the last four were not written until 1865–1866. This two-year hiatus coincided with his assumption of a new editorial position — the joint editorship of the *North American Review*, a journal then all but extinct. Early in the century the *North American* had represented advanced opinion in New England, but after 1830, it had fallen into a dull dignity which had reduced its subscription list almost as fast as its bite. Hoping to reinvigorate the journal, its publishers, Crosby & Nichols, offered Lowell the editorship. He hesitated long, having had his fill while on the *Atlantic* of contending with proofreading, budgets, authors and the like. But finally he agreed to accept if the publishers would make Charles Eliot Norton co-editor, Norton to do the editorial work proper, with Lowell lending his name and writing talents. The suggestion proved agreeable to all concerned, and Lowell thus began his third experiment in practical journalism.[22]

Crosby & Nichols set aside $3000 for the annual cost of

editorial services and authors' fees. Eight hundred went to Norton and Lowell, an amount doubled in 1865 after Ticknor & Fields took over as the *Review's* publishers (Norton, who did most of the hard work, receiving $1200 of the $1600). The journal's previous rate of a dollar a page for articles was retained, but the publishers allowed an extra payment of $1.50 per page for all articles furnished by the editors themselves, and authorized Lowell and Norton to offer the higher rate to other contributors whom they were especially anxious to attract — so long, that is, as the total amount did not exceed $1200 per annum. By modern standards this was hardly a munificent budget, but generous enough a hundred years ago to secure the services of outstanding authors — especially since Lowell and Norton, with or without authorization, sometimes offered still higher fees. They told John Lothrop Motley, for example, that they would allow him five dollars a page and carte blanche as to subject (Lowell added that if Motley agreed to be a contributor, they would henceforward always refer to him as "our amiable and accomplished minister at the Court of Vienna, who unites in himself, etc. etc. etc."; if he refused, there would be inevitable references to the country's misfortune in being represented at Vienna "by a minister as learned in Low Dutch as he was ignorant of high statesmanship").[23]

In assuming control of the *North American*, Lowell and Norton hoped to make it a powerful instrument for affecting public opinion on the great questions then at issue. It was true that the *Atlantic* still flourished, but there was some feeling that Fields' good nature had steered the magazine away from controversy. And certainly the *North American* had earlier been in no position to take up the slack; under conservative editorship it had become, in Lowell's words, "a huge pair of bellows puffing impartially both the just & the unjust." It had not even, in place of disputation, offered its reader sober information; it had not presented the better scholarship of the country nor maintained any impressive standard of literary criticism (in the last number before Lowell and Norton took charge, the words "profound" or "profoundly" had been used to describe more than half the thirty books under review).[24]

Lowell and Norton hoped to change all this. They believed the *Review* could and must be revived as an influential journal of opinion. The opportunity, in Norton's words, had to be seized for stimulating the nation's "better sense, of setting before and holding up to it its own ideal." Lowell was more concise: the *Review* had to be made loyal, lively and opinionated. It would be his own distinguished essays and reviews which would make the major contribution toward those ends.[25]

The first number put out under their joint editorship appeared in January, 1864, and featured a long article by Lowell on "The President's Policy." The piece brought comment from Lincoln himself and helped the issue go at once into a second edition — unheard-of popularity for the staid *North American*. The interest Lowell's article aroused was deserved. Though laudatory, the piece was based not on sentimental or partisan rhetoric but on reasoned argument, the more impressive for containing an open admission that his own earlier impatience with Lincoln had been misguided. In the first year of the war especially, Lowell confessed, he had been eager for more decisive policies, but he now thought Lincoln had been wise in never moving too far in advance of public opinion. In regard to emancipation, the President had correctly seen that his chief object had not been "to proclaim his adhesion to certain doctrines" but "to achieve their triumph by quietly accomplishing his ends." The masses, Lowell argued, are rarely moved by abstract principles of humanity or justice; before they can be brought to defend such principles, some direct infringement of their own rights must take place. When that happens, abstract ideals can be reinforcing, but the ideals alone, without "immediate personal wrong or imminent peril" are an insufficient motive force in politics. Lincoln saw this, and had wisely awaited the development of popular sentiment against slavery instead of attempting to manufacture it by federal fiat. By so doing, he had taken the country with him whenever he advanced, which meant the ground occupied was never in danger of being again yielded. Lowell's defense of Lincoln's policy on slavery was elaborate and cogent, but not wholly persuasive. For one thing, Lincoln's actual emancipation proclamation, limited as it was to areas "in rebellion," did not in fact free a single slave. For another, as we have seen since, a forceful President *can* "manufacture" sentiment, can develop, not merely reflect, public opinion — though the mid-nineteenth century was less ready than we to accept powerful direction from the Executive.[26]

Lowell was as much impressed by the spirit of Lincoln's leadership as by its results. That the North had persevered in the war effort, that in fact its purpose had steadily deepened, he traced directly to the President's personal qualities. Lincoln's large-mindedness had allowed him to see and admit whatever truth there was in opinions different from his own; in his sagacity he had permitted hostile combinations to go so far "as by the inevitable reaction to become elements of his own power"; gentle but shrewd, he had guided public opinion in such a way that he seemed to be following it; he had yielded doubtful points so that he could be firm in essential ones, thus gaining "the advantages of compromise without the weakness of concession." Lincoln was a great leader, in short, because he was a great man. Whether judging political or literary figures, Lowell put character above accomplishment, sometimes even suggesting, as in Lincoln's case, that the one was prerequisite for the other.[27]

When the publishers sent Lincoln a copy of the *North American*, he found Lowell's article so good an analysis of Administration policy that he recommended it to Gideon Welles, Secretary of the Navy, and sent a note of appreciation to Crosby & Nichols. In it, he expressed doubt if he was "quite worthy" of all which Lowell had "kindly said" of him personally, but as an analysis of his policy, he thought the article would be of value to the country. On one point only did he object to Lowell's interpretation. Lowell had written that early in the crisis Lincoln had still labored "under some theory that Secession, however it might absolve States from their obligations, could not escheat them of their claims under the Constitution," a theory, in other words, of letting the South have its cake and eat it too. Lincoln considered this a misrepresentation of his position. He had never held the theory, he wrote, "that secession could absolve States or people of their obligations" and had stated the opposite in his first inaugural address. Indeed, it was because of his belief in the continuation of those obligations that he had been puzzled for a time, "as to denying the legal *rights* of those citizens who remained individually innocent of treason or rebellion." The publishers replied that they would print the President's letter in their April issue in order to remove any erroneous impression as to his policy — and no doubt also (of course left unsaid) in order to puff the *North American.* Lowell was not consulted about printing Lincoln's letter, apparently in the fear (as it turned out, correctly) that he would object to so self-aggrandizing a gesture.[28]

Lowell's article in particular and the January issue in general produced widespread comment and praise. "We all feel," E. C. Stedman wrote Lowell, "like the audience of an Opera when the gas is suddenly 'turned up.'" And in their private diaries (likely to contain their true opinions), Longfellow rejoiced in the *North American*'s "new life," while Evert Duyckinck took heart that it had "waked to a consciousness of the times," that the "Revolution going on in the country" had at last found a voice.[29]

As the Lowell-Norton tenure continued — they held joint editorship until 1868 — the expected number of complaints, open and covert, materialized: this author became annoyed when proofs were delayed, that one by editing which had cut "the heart" from his article, a third by the rejection of a piece solely because of its "advanced views." Others — including Norton himself — feared the tone of the journal remained too heavy ("Nobody but you," he wrote Lowell, "knows how to say weighty things lightly"). And the religious press attacked as blasphemous such pieces as Emerson's essay on "Character." Still, the general view held that Norton and Lowell had restored the *Review* to an influential position and had given voice to significant debate on public issues. This would be especially true during Reconstruction, when Lowell's political essays produced wide discussion. In the post-war years he would also contribute the best of his literary criticism to the *North American*. Taken together, these political and literary articles would, in fact, constitute Lowell's major achievement in prose.[30]

Meanwhile the events of war absorbed most of the energies of the Cambridge community. In a muted way, normal life of course went on, and for Lowell, teaching continued to make up an unhappy share of it. Three days a week went to language drills in Italian and Spanish, which gave him almost no pleasure, and two evenings a week to voluntary seminars in his home on Dante or Don Quixote, which often gave him a great deal. But he was more than ever convinced that he was "not the stuff that professors are made of . . . too sensitive & not quite conceited enough — physically conceited I should be inclined to call it." Lack of sympathetic response in an average class took all the life out of him, while personal adulation from students made him feel more ashamed than pleased. Teaching was not even filling out his income to the extent it once had. Wartime depreciation of the currency and inflationary prices made professors' salaries inadequate, and Lowell had to join in petitioning the Harvard Corporation for an increase in pay. Norton implored him to give up teaching entirely. His influence at the college was doubtless worth much, but a thousand men, Norton argued, could teach Italian and Spanish to undergraduates; Lowell had a larger duty to both himself and the world which was not being fulfilled in the classroom. But with no practical alternatives yet open to him, Lowell had to continue in the traces.[31]

There was little time or inclination during these years for socializing, and entertainment was usually tributary to the war effort; thus in 1862 Lowell helped Francis Child revise his comic operetta, "Il Pesceballo" so that it could be performed to raise money for the United States Sanitary Commission (and later to aid those loyal citizens of East Tennessee who had been impoverished by the war). Only rarely would there be evenings which recalled the high-spirited gatherings of the pre-war years. One such occasion was at Norton's late in 1862, when much amusement was worked up over the billing of a public lecture by Norton as "Pope Innocent III and Hersey" — at last, cried Lowell, justice was to be done to Hersey, the old Cambridge hatter![32]

Such occasions were the exception. The Lowells preferred to stay remote and solitary during the war years. Lowell had recently developed gout, which sometimes made going about painful, but far more important, the death of loved ones came so often in these years that the family was shrouded in almost continuous grief. In October, 1861, his sister Mary's only remaining son, William, was killed at Ball's Bluff. Lowell had been deeply fond of "Willie," and he sadly remembered how handsome and hopeful the boy had looked when they said good-bye at his army camp. There was some consolation in the way Willie had died — springing forward to help his wounded Adjutant — but he was dead nonetheless, and Lowell could hardly fail to recoil from that "heroic purging" which he had earlier welcomed; it was being drawn in his family's own blood.[33]

In 1862, a second nephew, James Jackson Lowell, was killed while attempting to reform his company's lines during the bitter battle of the Seven Days. In 1863, Robert Gould Shaw, the son of old friends, was shot through the heart while leading his all-Negro regiment against Battery Wagner in Charleston Harbor; at the request of his father he was not exhumed from the common grave with his men into which the Confederates had contemptuously thrown him. There is nothing for such a blow, Lowell wrote Mrs. Shaw, "but to bow the head and bear it," but he would rather, he added, that his name be known and blest as Robert Gould Shaw's would be "through all the hovels of an outcast race, than blaring from all the trumpets of repute." [34]

Then, in October, 1864, came the news that a third nephew, Charles Russell Lowell, older brother to James Jackson, had been killed at Cedar Creek. Known as "Beau Sabreur," Charles Russell had been the pride of the family, "by far," said Lowell, "the best thing we had." It was a view widely shared by contemporaries. They thought the young man gifted with all the virtues — gentleness, beauty, brilliance, vitality — and the heroism of his death (leading a charge when mortally wounded) was no more than they had expected of him. His loss was made more poignant still because he had very recently married Josephine Shaw — the sister of Robert Gould Shaw. Lowell memorialized his dead nephews several times in verse, never more movingly than in these lines:

Why, hain't I held 'em on my knee?
Didn't I love to see 'em growin',
Three likely lads ez wal could be,
Hahnsome an' brave an' not tu knowin'?
I set an' look into the blaze
Whose natur', jes' like theirn, keeps climbin',
Ez lon 'z it lives, in shinin' ways,
An' half despise myself for rhymin'.[35]

At least the war was moving to a close. The election of 1864 seemed to Lowell the last major hurdle to its safe conclusion, that is, to a peace which would guarantee the permanent destruction of slavery. He believed the opposition to Lincoln, brought to focus in the Democratic candidate, General McClellan, was "selfish and factious . . . They don't know what they are in favor of — hardly what they think it safe to be against." Lowell argued in the *North American* that McClellan's electoral victory would mean a new effort at negotiated peace, and that concessions would involve the reinstitution of slavery in some form. It was nonsense to talk, as the McClellan Democrats did, of the "unconstitutionality" of Lincoln's Emancipation Proclamation: "If there be no provision in the Constitution for emancipating the negroes, neither is there any for taking Richmond." The rebels had themselves forced Lincoln into emancipation as a war measure by boasting that slavery was their cornerstone and arsenal; they could hardly complain when he took them at their word. Nor was it anything but the cheapest electioneering trick to say that the war had been turned from its original purpose of saving the Union into one designed to free Negroes. What had really happened, Lowell argued, was that the North had gradually come to realize that the underlying cause of the war had all along been slavery, and from that realization had come the determination to "finish the war in the only way that will keep it finished, by rooting out the evil principle from which it sprang." This would be the crucial danger should McClellan be elected — he would allow slavery to remain in some form, thus guaranteeing still further bloodshed in the future: "at a moment when the Rebels would be checkmated in another move, we are advised to give them a knight and begin the game over again." When the returns were in, and Lincoln safely chosen, Lowell felt that democracy had justified itself: although the opposition had appealed "to every base element in human nature," the people had proven their good sense by scorning the appeal.[36]

There was talk after the election of Lowell getting a diplomatic post, in gratitude, so it was rumored, for his pro-Administration articles. Lowell, overworked, tired of teaching, was receptive to the idea. He had been feeling lately as if he had been "altered back from percussion to flint-lock," and he thought an entire change of scene might restore his vitality. Knowing this, friends tried to intercede in his behalf. Emerson wrote to Senator Charles Sumner, pleading Lowell's "great & rare merits. No literary man in the country suggests the presence of so much power as he; with a talent, too, that reaches all classes. Add to this, that he is a person of excellent address, with social & convivial gifts; a man of great spirit, with plenty of resistance in him if need be"; such multiple claims, Emerson thought, commanded attention.[37]

The papers soon picked up the rumors of Lowell's pending appointment — supposedly to Switzerland — and before long Oliver Wendell Holmes was writing to congratulate him "and the Switzers." But congratulations proved premature. Sumner did speak to Lincoln about sending Lowell to Europe, but the President said that he knew of no likely vacancies. Sumner then went to Seward, the Secretary of State (whom Lowell on several occasions had handled roughly in print). Seward pointed out that Massachusetts already had three Ministers, and that it would be impossible to appoint another unless one of the three was recalled. He thought Charles Francis Adams ought certainly to stay as Minister to England until the end of the war, but said he would recall either Motley or Burlingame, the two other Massachusetts men, should Sumner advise it. This naturally embarrassed Sumner, who wrote to Longfellow for advice. "Of course you cannot recall anyone," replied Longfellow, "to make a place for Lowell; and I am very sure he would not desire, nor permit it to be done, if he were consulted." Perhaps, Longfellow added, some vacancy might later occur. So it would — but not for many years.[38]

When news of peace finally came in April, 1865, Lowell felt devoutly thankful. "There is something magnificent," he wrote to Norton, "in having a country to love. It is almost like what one feels for a woman. Not so tender, perhaps, but to the full as self-forgetful." Though somewhat apprehensive about reconstruction, Lowell inclined to think matters would very much settle themselves. It was poor prophecy, as he would shortly recognize, but in the moment of release few had heart for further trepidation, especially when, hard upon peace, came the stupefying news of Lincoln's assassination. Lowell, like many, shed tears for a man he had never seen — "as if with him a friendly presence had been taken away . . . "[39]

It was in this fused mood of exultation at peace and grief over Lincoln's death that Lowell composed his famed "Commemoration Ode" — to be delivered at the Harvard exercises of July 21, 1865, in memory of her graduates killed in war. So rapt did he become in composing the Ode that he lost sleep, appetite and weight. When he recited portions of it to friends, they wept and declared it "noble," and Lowell became convinced that at last he had "written something *really* good." In his nervous exhilaration, he even hoped that the Ode might prove the feature of the day's exercises, despite the fact that the long program would include Holmes, Governor Andrew, Emerson and Phillips Brooks.[40]

Because his hopes were high, his disappointment was great. He delivered the Ode late in a long program, was not listened to with attention, nor distinctly heard. The following day, the newspaper reports made only perfunctory reference to his performance, making it all too clear with their solitary adjectives of bland praise ("eloquent," "graceful") that they had either not heard or not approved. Well, thought Lowell, it served him right for having, like a boy, confused excitement with inspiration. Never again, he vowed, would he be fool enough to think he could write poetry, "a delusion" from which he "had been tolerably free these dozen years." He would be free of it only temporarily.[41]

His friends assured him that he had not misjudged the Ode's worth; Sydney Gay, James Freeman Clarke, T. W. Higginson, E. R. Hoar and Emerson were among those who sent Lowell warm congratulations. It was unlikely they did so merely to be kind, for these men habitually shunned hypocrisy. More likely, the Ode caught the national mood of mixed exaltation and sadness so well that its shortcomings hardly seemed to matter. Thus Emerson, stressing content over form, praised the Ode's "high thought & sentiment," Sydney Gay its "nobility" and James Freeman Clarke its "grandeur of tone." [42]

As identification with the Ode's mood has, through time, faded, its technical faults have become more apparent. It is, like so many of Lowell's poems, derivative, full of echoes (and sometimes even paraphrases) from the works of others, from Milton, Shakespeare, Tennyson. The Ode suffers, too, from another of Lowell's characteristic defects: rhetoric, self-conscious declamation (creating a tone more suitable to this occasion than others, for the Ode, after all, was designed for public recitation). There could be no doubt that Lowell had felt his subject deeply — while writing the poem he had been in a state which could be called overwrought — yet somehow the emotion came out in plaster-cast form, perhaps because he mistakenly settled for stock images, perhaps because these were all he was capable of.[43]

Despite these serious, really fatal defects, there are moments in the Ode when the anguish and pride of the Civil War experience come through with passionate authenticity: Lincoln, "dreading praise, not blame, new birth of our new soil, the first American," or that single line — "Bow down, dear Land, for thou hast found release!" — which seemed to sum up the country's sorrowful gratitude. It was a line which would haunt many during the years of reconstruction, when not release, but a variation on war, was to prove the nation's lot.

CHAPTER XI

THE CRITIC OF POLITICS AND LITERATURE

WILLIAM DEAN HOWELLS recalled a memorable supper one night in 1866 when Lowell read aloud to friends from his final *Biglow Paper*. Howells never forgot the hush which followed Lowell's lamentation for what had begun to seem the waste of heroic lives:

> *I seem to hear a whisperin' in the air,*
> *A sighin' like, of unconsoled despair,*
> *Thet comes from nowhere an' from everywhere,*
> *An' seems to say, 'Why died we? warn't it, then*
> *To settle, once for all, thet men wuz men? . . .*
> *Death, not we, had conquered, we should feel*
> *Ef, she upon our memory turned her heel,*
> *An' unregretful throwed us all away*
> *To flaunt it in a Blind Man's Holiday!* [1]

The Blind Man, in Lowell's view, was Andrew Johnson, President of the United States. He combined "all the obstinacy of a weak mind and a strong constitution," and his course since taking office after Lincoln's assassination made it likely that the results most to be hoped for from the war were to be thrown away. Johnson was willing to have the Southern states come back into the Union with no provision for securing political and civil rights for the Negro and no guarantee that the ex-slave would be protected from mistreatment by his former master. Johnson's view of democracy did not extend to Negroes; he had disliked slavery not because he believed it intrinsically immoral but because it had served as the foundation for that white aristocracy which, as a "yeoman," he had detested. On both tactical and moral grounds, Lowell looked on Johnson's willingness to let the South return with only minimal conditions as an incalculable tragedy.[2]

As early as 1865, in an extraordinarily prescient essay for the *North American*, Lowell argued the necessity of dictating concrete terms. He disclaimed any motive of vindictiveness; the duty of the North was not to punish but to repair, not to weaken but to strengthen the South, not to see that Southern whites suffered more but that Southern Negroes suffered less. He rejected any widespread property confiscation, any rigid rules for readmission. The sole object of reconstruction should be to remove the original source of conflict between the sections — to remove all traces of slavery. Merely freeing the Negro, Lowell argued, was not enough. He had to be helped to overcome the handicaps entailed by generations of oppression and protected from those who would once more reduce him to a condition which would be slavery in all but name. To accomplish this, it was first necessary to make the freedman a landholder. Lowell did not address himself to the problem of how this was to be done (though he made it clear that he disapproved of any wholesale confiscation of rebel property). For the present, he said, he was concerned with outlining general policy, not specific legislation. And in terms of general policy, he was certain that unless the Negro was given some rights in the soil, labor would remain at the mercy of capital, the poor would continue to be subject to the rich and the ancient system of abuses would be reproduced, only in "more specious form."[3]

Making the freedman a landholder would not be enough to protect him. He had to be made a voter as well. At a time when even Thaddeus Stevens was hesitant, Lowell unequivocally advocated giving the ballot to the recently freed slaves. He knew such a policy had its dangers: the freedmen, scarred by centuries of abuse, might not always be capable of those independent, considered judgments which ideally precede the casting of a vote. But few whites cast ideal ballots, either. And besides, any policy other than full enfranchisement held greater dangers still. Should the Negro not be given the vote, Southern whites would have little inducement to educate him; political power, moreover, would remain in the hands of those same pre-war leaders whose misguided policies had been the source of so much grief. But expediency aside, there was also the matter of justice. The war, Lowell insisted, had been waged for the principles of democracy, which did not mean "the impossibility of making one man as good as another," but which did mean "the making of one man's manhood as good as another's" — that is, giving to every human being "the right of unlimited free trade in all his faculties and acquirements." We must rid ourselves of the delusion, Lowell argued, "that right is in any way dependent on the skin." He was willing temporarily to limit the vote to those Negroes who could read or write, but felt it essential to guard against the blacks being excluded as blacks. Any restrictions placed on the suffrage must be applied without discrimination, made to depend on intrinsic capacities, not extrinsic qualities of race or color. Lowell doubted, in any case, whether the freedmen, even if allowed to vote in a body, "would send worse members to Congress than some in whose election merchants and bankers and even doctors of divinity have been accomplices." Men in hovels as well as in palaces could be relied on to vote their own advantage, with the difference that "what is for the interest of the masses . . . is not very far from being for that of the country." [4]

Though Lowell had faith in the principle of universal suffrage, it was not unmixed with apprehension. The Negro's long history of degradation and ignorance did raise doubts about his ability immediately to function within a context of free choices and responsibilities. Lowell's personal experience with recently freed slaves did little to dissolve his misgivings. One of his nieces established a "home" for freedwomen, with the object of placing them as servants with Northern families. The Lowells took in four of them. One ("as black as the darkness in Andrew Johnson's head") was neat and hard-working, but the others proved so intractable that they had to be turned out. He had no hope, Lowell wrote Edmund Quincy, that the first generation of ex-slaves could be used for Northern service — "They are dirty, lazy & lying." He believed that they would — that they must — for a time become the peasantry of the Southern states. Gradually, as their capacities were first restored and then developed (with the aid of federal protection and assistance), they could be expected to rise according to their individual abilities. In the interim, Lowell predicted, the whites, through their "intellectual and traditional superiority" would "retain sufficient ascendancy to prevent any serious mischief from the new order of things." [5]

It might be mistaken to see "racist" overtones in Lowell's statement about "intellectual and traditional superiority," were there not one or two other such suggestions elsewhere in his writings. His characteristic stand rejected any idea of inherent racial inequalities, and such was the overwhelming burden of his writings and actions. But a belief in racial differences (the hallmark of advanced opinion in that day) could shade into a belief in racial inequalities, especially in a country and in a generation so overwhelmingly committed to the assumption of Anglo-Saxon superiority. Though Lowell's view of the Negro's capacity was far more libertarian than that of the vast majority of his contemporaries, this should not be allowed to obscure the fact that even he could occasionally reveal elements of a racist perspective.[6]

If uncertain as to the results of trying to integrate recent slaves into the democratic fabric, Lowell had no doubts that the experiment must be tried. The North had on the battlefield won the prerogative to "Americanize" the South. The rights of the victor should be exercised without exultation and without rancor, but they should be exercised. Indecision would be fatal. Nor should the North flatter itself by misnaming irresolution "magnanimity," for the South would see such behavior for what it was. The moment had to be seized — for the sake of the South no less than the North — to compel substantial changes and guarantees in the treatment of the Negro. Otherwise the war would have been fought for nothing and peace would be temporary: "firmness equably tempered with good-feeling is what we want — not generosity with twitches of firmness now & then." What President Johnson had failed to realize was that civil war was something other than "a more earnest kind of political contest" which leaves both parties free to try again. The Union had been saved by war, but the true unity of the nation could be secured only by making supreme everywhere within it "the national idea that freedom is a right inherent in man himself, and not a creature of the law, to be granted to one class of men or withheld from it at the option of another." [7]

Lowell feared — and as the Southern "Black Codes" were to prove, correctly — that if the South was left to her own devices, as Johnson wished, she would salvage as much as she could of her pre-war system. She could not re-establish slavery, but she could, if not otherwise prevented, find the closest legal substitute possible. The question, Lowell believed, was not whether the North had the right to interfere — her position as victor gave all the sanction needed for that — but whether she dared *not* interfere. North and South had not been able to live together half-slave and half-free; could they succeed better "in trying a second left-handed marriage between democracy and another form of aristocracy, less gross, but not less uncongenial"? Lowell never went so far as Norton did in calling the Southern whites "barbarians varnished with civilization," but he felt certain they could not be trusted to do justice to the Negro. Terms would have to be imposed on them, and if they were not imposed immediately, when post-war unsettlement provided maximum opportunity, the chance might not come again — not, that is, without another war. It was not enough to have conquered the South, she must also be converted, and if the Constitution did not confer the power needed for such work, it should be looked for elsewhere — that, or confess that democracy, "strongest of all governments for war, is the weakest of all in the statesmanship that shall save us from it." It was well that there should always be men to interpret the Constitution by its letter "as interposing a check to hasty or partial action," but in the end it was better to be governed by the Constitution's spirit, "living and operative in the energies of an advancing people." To lose such an opportunity as the post-war situation provided because of Constitutional quibbling "would be as cowardly as unwise." [8]

Lowell did not believe reconstruction should be left solely to Presidential discretion — especially since the President was Andrew Johnson. Congress, representing the people, deserved some voice in deciding peace terms. He was therefore in entire agreement with the Congress when, after futilely attempting to reach a *modus operandi* with Johnson, it took reconstruction into its own hands in 1867. Under the leadership of the Radical Republicans, Congress then established new conditions for the readmission of Confederate states into the Union, including the division of the unreconstructed areas into military districts whose commanders would provide for state constitutional conventions in which persons of color were authorized to vote and which had to adopt Negro suffrage as a permanent feature of their constitutions. Lowell did not believe that these terms could fairly be called harsh. The states kept the right to set conditions on the franchise, and were merely told that the same conditions had to apply to all, regardless of race or color. To do less for the Negro would be "a scandal and reproach," and would mean another "of those fatal compromises which ignore his claims upon us." It was one thing to treat the rebel states with moderation and quite another to let them go their own way on trust: "Moderation is an excellent thing; but taking things for granted is not moderation, and there may be such a thing as being immoderate in concession and confidence."[9]

Committed though Lowell was to establishing justice for the Negro and inclined to side against Johnson and with the Radicals ("we cheerfully accept our share in the opprobrium of the name"), he was not wholly sympathetic to their program. More specifically, he sometimes deplored their tone, even while generally agreeing with their position. He was especially irritated by Thaddeus Stevens and what he took to be his "personal pique." Calling names, Lowell felt, "should be left to children, with whom, as with too large a class of our political speakers, it seems to pass for argument." And when the move began to impeach and try Johnson, Lowell objected to it as folly; it would invest the President's "poor infirmity of nature" with all the harmful dignity of a crime against the state, thereby entangling "in legal quibbles a cause so strong in its moral grounds, so transparent in its equity." He rejoiced when the effort to remove the President failed.[10]

After 1868, Lowell's involvement in political questions sharply decreased, but not because of any displeasure at Grant's accession in that year to the Presidency. Quite to the contrary. Lowell, and most of his circle, at first held high hopes for Grant. They approved all they heard of him — of his magnanimity, honesty and simplicity. Even after Grant's troubles began, Lowell, on meeting him briefly, felt the man's humanity and was struck by the pathos of his face — "a puzzled pathos, as of a man with a problem before him of which he does not understand the terms."[11]

Nor did Lowell back off from political involvement because of disenchantment with the democratic process. Brahmin disillusion did not set in with force until the 1870's, for it was only then, during Grant's second term, that political scandal, reconstruction difficulties and economic depression fully manifested themselves. True, there were already worrisome signs in the late 1860's, especially the emerging power of the "Rings," which

Lowell feared might turn politics into "a huge stock-jobbery," Republicans and Democrats becoming only other names for "bulls and bears." Yet his confidence had not yet been deeply shaken, and his continuing faith in the country was shared by men less temperamentally optimistic than he. Thus Norton could still insist in 1867 that America had "something not only finer in promise but in reality than is to be found in Europe . . . more simplicity . . . more humanity . . . more truthfulness, than has ever before found expression in the world." And E. L. Godkin, also two years after the war, believed that "the value of knowledge in politics is every year more highly estimated . . ."[12]

Lowell felt even more confident than they that the country would come out all right. The "people," he believed, remained sound, "the general common-sense and honest intention of mankind" could still be trusted. And besides, given the benevolent design of the universe, matters could never go too far awry. "I take great comfort in God," Lowell wrote Norton in 1869, "I think he is considerably amused with us sometimes, but that he likes us, on the whole, and would not let us get at the matchbox so carelessly as he does, unless he knew that the frame of his Universe was fire-proof." This confidence in a "fire-proof" Universe had always been and was to remain a constant in Lowell's life — almost the sum of his philosophy. But such confidence was not the equivalent of complacency. God's benevolence did not, in Lowell's mind, nullify human responsibility; faith had to be supplemented with works. Lowell never forswore the necessity of works, but he felt their claim with varying urgency throughout his life. He became most thoroughly engaged when the "rightness" and "wrongness" of public questions seemed clear-cut — as with slavery and secession. For a moralist in politics, such certainty was a prerequisite to acting with force. By the late 1860's, the prerequisite was once more lacking.[13]

New issues had come into prominence — tariffs, "hard" versus "soft" currency, the debt — while older issues, like Negro suffrage, had become linked (fairly or not) with the rise in political corruption. Priorities no longer seemed clear. Was protection of the Negro more urgent than establishing "good government," that is, government based on local rule and civil service reform? Was it more important to hold the South to guarantees of Negro citizenship or to bind up the nation's wounds in order to meet the new economic challenges? With the moralities of public questions now mutually competing in Lowell's mind rather than mutually exclusive, the intensity of his involvement ebbed. Like so many others in the North, his commitment to the Radical program weakened in proportion to the emergence of new public issues, ones whose resolution seemed contingent on burying the old. He began to wonder if the South could ever be reconstructed "except through its own leading men," or if her ties to the Union could ever be reaffirmed until made compatible with her "interest" and "honor." By 1868, he was even finding a kind word, however negative, for "poor old Johnson" — "I have never thought so ill of him as becomes an orthodox Republican. The worst of him was that he meant well." [14]

Though Lowell's feeling of responsibility for public affairs subsided, he did not abandon interest in them, and on occasion after 1868 could still muster considerable indignation. He denounced Benjamin Butler, a recent power in Massachusetts politics as "an unscrupulous demagogue"; and in 1870, he wrote directly to James Garfield in Congress, objecting to high tariffs and high taxes ("The whole aim of our legislation . . . seems to be to make this Country unfit to live in. I mean that its sole object is to increase *material* prosperity at the cost of everything else . . . Our daily increasing tendency is to make a privileged class of the *un*intelligent . . . A promised-land where *want* of training shall be the qualification for office"). But if Lowell's wrath could occasionally be profound, it had, after 1868, no sustained intensity or focus. And his endemic optimism about a "fire-proof" universe continued to moderate such fears about

American democracy as he developed. As late as 1871, he was cautioning Jane Norton not to believe the newspapers that "we are going to the dogs." His attitude in these years was perhaps best captured by a comment he later made about Wordsworth:

> He had made the inevitable discovery that comes with years, of how much harder it is to do than to see what 't were good to do, and grew content to build the poor man's cottage, since the means did not exist of building the prince's palace he had dreamed.

It no longer seemed clear to Lowell, as it once had, that the only way of getting even the cottage built was never to cease insisting on the palace.[15]

*

It looked briefly, in 1869, as if Lowell might receive a diplomatic appointment from Grant. Lowell's chief advocate was Judge Rockwood Hoar, Grant's new Attorney General and the man to whom the second series of *Biglow Papers* had been dedicated. Secretary of State Hamilton Fish was receptive to the idea of sending Lowell abroad, but just when he was being seriously considered for the Spanish mission, Senator Sumner insisted that Motley be sent to England, which led to a general reshuffling of diplomatic chairs, ending with Daniel Sickles being assigned to Spain. As Lowell reported to his daughter, he had come "within an ace of it — or, if I may be allowed a little natural bitterness under the circumstances — within an ass of it." Lowell realized that he had had none of those political claims which count for so much in the distribution of office, nor even (should such minor factors have been admitted), the advantage of diplomatic experience. He did know the language and literature of Spain, but a diplomat who could make himself understood, Lowell acidly remarked, was no doubt "unfit for his business & might do mischief." He tried to make light of his disappointment — surely, he wrote James T. Fields, there was no better place to live and die than Cambridge — but he keenly felt the blow. He had wanted the mission as a respite from routine, hoping to freshen his vision and to salvage a block of time for poetry. Well, he mused, the birds still sing, indifferent as ever to men's affairs and somehow, because of that, comforting. He would concentrate on his vegetables and his chickens, on his Friday night whist club, and on literature.[16]

And so it was to be for a number of years — a routine of small variety, occasional discontent and simple, undramatic pleasures. Cambridge life, Lowell decided (in a tone uncertainly divided between complaint and boast), was chiefly notable for its absence of activity. Perhaps, he thought, it was merely "the collapse of attention that followed the strain of war so that nothing *seems* to happen because one does not take any interest in it." When his daughter Mabel, now in her early twenties, went abroad with the James T. Fieldses in 1869, Lowell (with the same ambivalent mixture of boredom and pride) sent her the accumulated home news: they had a new cook named Christina who made excellent pastry; William, the handyman, was watering the pear trees from the cesspool, and although the trees might like it, he, Lowell, did not; the early potatoes were the best they had ever raised; he had fresh flowers on his table every morning — and oh yes, they had bought a cow.[17]

Lowell's good friend, John Holmes, described Cambridge life in more whimsical terms. The chief local amusement, in his view, were the burglaries — everyone became quite cheerful when it was announced that there had been a "breaking and entering." In summer, when life could get a bit more dull, the city government would enliven the town by instituting repairs on the old burial ground. And then, of course, one could always break the monotony by trips "across the water"; screwing up his courage, Holmes at one point declared that he was leaving his native home, its solitudes and associations, its group of familiar friends, and crossing "the dreary waste of waters to Boston." [18]

Quiet as Cambridge life was, it was not quite so desperately monotonous as these self-mockers liked to pretend. Visits continued to be exchanged with the same (and no greater) frequency as before. Longfellow might wander over for an hour's chat about literature or to lament with Lowell the proposed widening of Brattle Street and the wholesale destruction of the neighborhood's trees. Old friends would come to stay for a few days, like Christopher Cranch, with whom Lowell would have "rhymical debauches," each serving as a "goodnatured, if limited, public" for the other's poetry — "there is always *one* at least who is never bored." (Cranch, though, could make Lowell a little sad — the man had so many gifts and such rare power of invention, yet he had never made a success; Lowell, who claimed "a natural sympathy with the butterflies as against the ants & the bees," thought Cranch's trouble might be that in a "nation of daylaborers," he had not been brought up to work; no doubt one day such men would be put in a "heavenly poor house . . . with the industrious rich to work for them & buy their books & pictures.")[19]

Occasionally Lowell would entertain more formally. He gave a supper for Dickens in 1868 which Edmund Quincy thought as memorable as the one fifteen years earlier for Thackeray (and Lowell thought more memorable because the Dickens dinner featured a home-grown turkey). And in 1869 Lowell gathered a dozen close friends to celebrate his own fiftieth birthday. In inviting Fields, he promised that as was usual with "surprise" parties, a full accounting would be given to the newspapers complete with a "list of gifts (especially in money) and the names of all who *donate*." Page and Briggs came up from New York for the occasion, and Quincy, Fields, the two Holmeses and Estes Howe were also on hand; they had, Quincy reported, "a time, times & half a time."[20]

Some of the guests at Elmwood in these years were more recent friends. Lowell's intimacy with George William Curtis deepened during the 1860's, as did his relationship with William

Dean Howells. With Howells, there were elements of paternalism on one side and of hero-worship on the other, which confined even while intensifying the range of their friendship. "You are the only one that hasn't cheated me by your blossom," Lowell wrote Howells in 1869, "I take a kind of credit to myself in being the first to find you out. I am proud of you." Howells, in turn, treated Lowell with a tender awe beyond ordinary gratitude. "When I reflect," he wrote Norton, that with Lowell's "great gifts to persuade and to make afraid — his poetry and his wit — he has never used them once falsely or cruelly, I feel myself in the presence of a new kind of great man . . ." The two men may not have seen each other wholly in perspective, but this was perhaps prerequisite to the imperturbability of their regard.[21]

There were newer friends still. E. L. Godkin, editor of *The Nation* (a journal Lowell greatly admired but which Godkin had trouble getting him to write for), paid several visits. Godkin thought Lowell at his best when receiving friends in his own home. Meeting him elsewhere, he had sometimes found him too bookish and instructive, but at Elmwood he was always a "delightful host and companion." Another especially welcome guest was the Englishman, Thomas Hughes, author of *Tom Brown's School Days* and the man who had been responsible for the English edition of *The Biglow Papers.* Lowell delighted in Hughes' "simple, hearty, and affectionate" manner and in his ability (so rare, he felt, in contemporary Englishmen) to take America "naturally" and actually to see some good in her. When Hughes left after one particular visit, Lowell was not ashamed to write him that parting had been "like saying good-by to sunshine."[22]

There was only one Englishman Lowell preferred, and that was Leslie Stephen. The two first met during the Civil War, when Stephen, then a young Cambridge don, visited the United States; he presented a letter of introduction to Lowell, they began to talk, the visit extended into two days, and the basis for a lifetime friendship was formed. The two men took to each other so readily because they shared much in common — yet with enough differences to avoid the handicap of a mirror-image. Both were reserved but vigorous in manner, soft-hearted and sensitive underneath; both believed they fronted on the world, facing up without pretension or fear to its "realities" — probably what Stephen meant when he described Lowell as a man who talked "sense," lacked "humbug" and had a healthy dislike for sentimentality. They shared, too, a love of books and learning which disdained preciosity; they believed in a "masculine" life of the mind — a devotion to scholarship which could combine with an interest in raising chickens, a pleasure in books which would not destroy the pleasure of conviviality. Stephen had the more profoundly inquiring mind, for Lowell, as he himself admitted, was not averse to "a judicious shutting of the eyes." In religion the two men diverged with particular sharpness. Stephen's skeptical questioning led him to agnosticism, while Lowell preferred to cling to "the old ship of Faith"; in Lowell's view, Stephen too readily equated conventions with sham, though all were not so "by a good deal, and we should soon be Papuans without them." But Lowell's sarcastic wit gave enough suggestion of skepticism to create at least a surface resemblance to Stephen's more authentically probing mind. In any case, the two men, though able to see each other only infrequently, cherished their friendship over the years.[23]

Not all the visitors at Elmwood were welcome ones. Lowell's reputation was large enough to attract strangers to his door, either seeking favors or bent on silent worship. The favors were easier to deal with, since they allowed for some response, however negative. Thus Mr. Tuckwell from New Bedford, who came bearing a large bundle of his verses, was politely told to send them to the Farmer's Almanac and "to begin a course of assiduous self-culture." But a young lady from Halifax was less easily parried, for her only wish was to gaze at Lowell before returning home. A hundred and sixty pounds of feminine adoration were not easily coped with, especially on a hot July day; Lowell sent her off with an autographed picture, and then memorialized the visit:

> *Graceful nymph from Nova Scotia,*
> *Youth's pale ardor on thy brow,*
> *I had deemed thy land Boetia,*
> *But I find it Attic now!* [24]

Occasionally Lowell would leave his Elmwood retreat: a dinner at Longfellow's, a fishing trip with intimate friends like John Holmes and John Bartlett, a brief vacation at Newport or in Maine, a day rowing on the Concord River with Judge Hoar. When he could be persuaded to socialize, Lowell often proved a charming companion; at Annie Fields' he talked "head & shoulders beyond every body else," mesmerizing the group with his pronunciamentos on literature: the inexhaustible wonders of Calderón, the superiority of Fielding to all other novelists (he read *Tom Jones* once a year) and of Falstaff and Don Quixote to all other characters of literary creation (he scoffed when someone else suggested Pickwick). Or, in a less pontifical mood, Lowell could fool irresistibly, declaiming aloud in broad Yankee dialect or inventing an opera on the theme of "Moses in the Bulrushes" while accompanying himself on an imaginary keyboard.[25]

His most regular outings continued to be the clubs: whist on Fridays and monthly Saturdays at the Parker House. A third club, formed after the war, had more serious intentions. This was the famed Dante Club, though "Club" was something of a misnomer, since it originally consisted only of Longfellow, Lowell and Norton. Soon after the war ended, the three men began to meet on Wednesday evenings at Longfellow's house to go over the final revision of his translation of *The Divine Comedy*. All three were considerable Dante scholars, both in technical mastery and in critical appreciation. Lowell had been giving an advanced course on Dante for years and by 1864 had read him through for the twenty-second time. (Lowell shared his specialist's knowledge not only with Longfellow but with Thomas Parsons, the dentist-poet, who also produced an important translation and who followed nine tenths of the suggestions Lowell made.)[26]

Beginning in October, 1865, Norton, Longfellow and Lowell met weekly to go over the *Paradiso*. Longfellow would read a passage from his translation and the three would discuss it freely, debating a word choice, an obscure passage, an alternate reading. Longfellow either sat apart or stood at his desk pencil in hand, for though he greatly valued the comments of both men, he did not want them to see which corrections he accepted and which he did not. He found Lowell's knowledge astonishing for its accuracy and depth, and Norton, though he had little ear for the construction of verse, made invaluable contributions as a classicist. Now and then one or two other friends, like Howells or Fields, would join the work session, and after it a few guests would come in for supper and talk. The food and wine were always beyond reproach — raw oysters, cold grouse or partridge with salad and paté, or cold game pie and Stilton cheese. But Francis Child, for one, sometimes balked at the conversation: he reported to Clough that Norton and Lowell were so infected with "the Tuscan malady" that they dared classify Milton as a second-rate genius in comparison with Dante or Goethe. As Lowell admitted, Dante's "readers turn students, his students zealots, and what was a taste becomes a religion."[27]

In June, 1866, after thirty-three weeks, they came to the last Canto of the *Paradiso* and Lowell, regretting that the suppers were to end, asked Longfellow if there might not be an Indian epic of a hundred thousand lines which he would like to take on next. Such heroic measures proved unnecessary; meetings were resumed in December, 1866, to read the *Purgatorio* and were then still further extended to include Saturday evenings at Norton's to go over his translation of the *Vita Nuova*, which was to appear as a companion volume to Longfellow's. These ended in the spring of 1867, but fifteen years later the club was once more revived, and today still flourishes. Lowell enjoyed the sessions immensely, though when Longfellow's translation appeared in 1867, did not overpraise it simply because he had had some hand in its revision. He thought of the translation "not as the best possible, by any means, but as the best probable." Ultimately, he believed, poetry could not be translated, and Longfellow, in settling for the "measured prose" of blank verse, had at least rendered the most accurate translation to date.[28]

Except for these activities, the aggregate of which was small, plus a few rounds of lectures — two at Cornell in 1869–1870 and one at Baltimore in 1871 — Lowell was almost continuously at home in these years. He loved Elmwood dearly — and also his family. His life with Mrs. Lowell continued to be placid and happy; he referred to her as "the delight of his life," and Annie Fields noted his "chivalrous tender manner" toward her. Mrs. Lowell and Mabel were also devoted; during the war, when money had been in short supply, Frances Lowell had let her own wardrobe reduce to one gown in order to fit Mabel out in clothes. As for Mabel, she had grown into a handsome, intelligent young woman. When the Fieldses took her along to Europe in 1869, Annie Fields found "real pleasure in her companionship," and Dickens, on meeting her in England, thought her "a charming little thing." Soon after her return from Europe, Mabel became attached to Edward Burnett, the handsome eldest son of a successful businessman-farmer from Southboro, Massachusetts. The elder Burnett had invested some of his profits in a boys' school, which he named St. Mark's, and the first headmaster had been the Reverend Robert T. S. Lowell, James Russell's brother. Very likely Mabel first met Edward Burnett when traveling up to Southboro to visit her uncle. Before long she and Burnett became engaged, and in 1872, when Mabel was twenty-five, they were married. Lowell was "altogether pleased" with his daughter's choice; it was "a queer sensation to have a son extemporised for you," especially one who stood six feet in his stockings, but he rapidly developed "fatherly feeling" toward him.[29]

*

In the immediate post-war years, 1865–1872, Lowell's major energies were devoted to literature. It was one of his most productive periods, the poetry far less distinguished than the prose, but the prose the best of his career, constituting an achievement now insufficiently appreciated.

Most of the poetry Lowell published during this period was in fact not new. No collection of his verse had been made since 1848 and so, encouraged by James T. Fields, his publisher, Lowell decided in 1868 to gather together the scattered efforts of the preceding twenty years. The resulting volume, *Under the Willows*, appeared in 1869 and was dedicated to Norton. All but two of the shortest poems in it had been printed before, the greater number dating back more than fifteen years, and a few from the pre-1848 period. Lowell was not at all happy with the collection. "Gods, how bad they seem now!" he wrote to Fields. "But there they are & I must exploit them. They seem to me just like all the verses I read in the papers — & I suppose they are. Why can't one for once write a *good* poem & be done with it? I am in very doleful dumps indeed. Comfort me, O my Publisher!" There was even trouble agreeing on a title. Fields disliked Lowell's first choice, "The Voyage to Vinland, and Other Poems," and suggested "Elmwood" instead. But the more Lowell thought of that the less he liked it — " 'tis turning one's household gods upon the town, as it were." Finally he hit upon "Under the Willows." It should, he wrote Fields, fill every need — "the basketmakers will buy up the first edition & the gunpowder-makers the second." Should Fields still be dissatisfied, Lowell suggested he try "Under the Billows or dredgings from the Atlantic." [30]

Lowell's evaluation of the volume needs no revising (though he may not have held it in quite the low esteem he professed).

The verse was technically skillful, but as Emerson said, "rather expresses his wish, his ambition, than the uncontrollable interior impulse which is the authentic mark" of new poems and which "is felt in the pervading tone, rather than in brilliant parts or lines." Yet the volume was generously praised, even more by the English critics than by the Americans (George Eliot, for one, remarked in her diary that the glowing notice in the *Spectator* was "a deservedly high appreciation of Lowell's poems"). And the sales of the volume were also gratifying — "The dolts, it appears, begin to value my goods now that they have got an English ticket on 'em." Critics and public, as is so often the way, were atoning for having underpraised the better work by overpraising the lesser.[31]

The only substantial new poem Lowell wrote in these years was "The Cathedral," a meditative poem on science and religion, in more than eight hundred lines of blank verse. It is more noteworthy for the insight it gives into Lowell the man than as a monument to his poetic skills. Originally entitled "A Day at Chartres," the poem is thematically reminiscent (what might be called the American counterpart) of Matthew Arnold's "Stanzas from the Grande Chartreuse." Arnold's

> *Wandering between two worlds, one dead,*
> *The other powerless to be born*

is echoed in Lowell's

> . . . *still lip-loyal to what once was truth,*
> *Smuggle new meanings under ancient names,*
> *Unconscious perverts of the Jesuit, Time.*

But unlike Arnold's, Lowell's questioning and doubt were far more a passing than a pervasive mood. In fact the mood itself seems willed, an intellectual exercise. The narrative voice in "The Cathedral" is that of a man interested in scrutinizing the properties of Doubt, not of a man possessed by it, of an optimist aware that there are grounds for pessimism rather than a pessimist convinced of their validity. Throughout, the tone is self-conscious, clever, unfelt. The glibness with which the narrator's doubts are resolved suggests their lack of intensity:

> *. . . sustained by sure belief*
> *That man still rises level with the height*
> *Of noblest opportunities, or makes*
> *Such, if the time supply not, I can wait.*

The Lowell of "The Cathedral" is to the real skeptic like the man standing in the window of an air-conditioned room on a hot summer day watching perspiration pour off someone in the street — he knows it is hot outside but, gently cooled by the air currents of the room, does not really feel the discomfort. Lowell's comments on Gray's "Elegy Written in a Country Churchyard" apply with force to his own "Cathedral":

> . . . that pensively stingless pessimism which comes with the first gray hair . . . that placid melancholy which satisfies the general appetite for an emotion which titillates rather than wounds.[32]

Lowell's major energies during these years went into prose rather than poetry, and with far more distinguished results. Lowell the poet has been too readily confounded with Lowell the essayist; because the poetry of his middle and later years carries so little interest, it has been assumed that his prose is equally unrewarding. The assumption is unjust. Lowell's contemporaries overvalued his essays (Edward Fitzgerald believed he was "altogether the best critic we have; something of what Ste. Beuve is in French") but the twentieth century has erred more seriously on the other side by too completely ignoring them. Taken as a whole, they constitute, with all their flaws, a substantial body of work. His political and historical essays have received considerable attention both as artifacts and commentary, but his literary essays require further scrutiny. Lowell, as a literary critic, has decided strengths. In the end these are overbalanced by defects which keep him from the first rank, but his virtues, no less than his deficiencies, need explication.[33]

Lowell is perhaps most distinguished as a critic for his "openness," his ability to appreciate a wide variety of excellence — an appreciation made more catholic still by his deep knowledge of several national literatures. He had decided preferences — the pantheon was limited to Homer, Aeschylus, Dante, Chaucer, Shakespeare, Cervantes and Goethe — but even when treating lesser gods, Lowell attempted to isolate their achievement rather than to dwell on their deficiencies. "It is the best rule for happiness in life as well as for soundness of judgment in aesthetics," Lowell once wrote his daughter, "to try & find out why a thing is good rather than why it is bad." It was one of the "schoolboy blunders" of criticism, he thought, which denied one kind of perfection because it was not another; any reader was happiest "whose mind is broad enough to enjoy the natural school for its nature, and the artificial for its artificiality, provided they be only good of their kind." [34]

Lowell quoted with approval Goethe's classic statement that "there is a destructive criticism and a productive. The former is very easy; for one has only to set up in his mind any standard, any model . . . and then boldly assert that the work under review does not match with it, and therefore is good for nothing . . . Productive criticism is a great deal more difficult; it asks, What did the author propose to himself? Is what he proposes reasonable and comprehensible? and how far has he succeeded in carrying it out?" Critics who applied "rules" formulated from a study of past masterpieces failed to understand that art must accommodate itself to the material at hand, to the national traditions in which it works. The climate of opinion always modified ideas and the manner of their expression. To refer constantly to codified statutes of taste was to cramp individual expression and to end by producing — at best — some artificial approximation of past modes. "Correctness" would come at the expense of life, for life was a compound of durable human nature and changing social manners: "Human nature . . . remains always the same, but . . . the habits which are a second nature modify it inwardly as well as outwardly, and what moves it to passionate action in one age may leave it indifferent in the next." Further, if artists were encouraged to copy past forms they would describe sensations they ought to have experienced rather than those they actually experienced. Critics who recommended a slavish imitation of the models of antiquity, for example, failed to see that "between us and the Greeks lies the grave of their murdered paganism, making our minds and theirs irreconcilable." Which was not to say that a contemporary writer could not profit from past achievements, could not have his senses and sympathies quickened by them. One could learn from the Greeks their "virile grace . . . their sense of proportion, their distaste for the exaggerated, their exquisite propriety of phrase," all of which would "steady imagination without cramping it." But there must be no "servile surrender of what is genuine in us to what *was* genuine in them." [35]

"It goes against my grain," Lowell once wrote Howells, "to cut up anything, unless there be some duty involved or some good to be done by it." But if he preferred to concentrate on "productive criticism," to avoid the job of assault, when he did undertake it, he performed with a withering blend of knowledge and scorn. The poseurs roused his special indignation. Falling upon such a man, be he scholar or litterateur, Lowell could be abrasive. He denounced W. Carew Hazlitt's edition of Herrick with a ferocity made more devastating by wit: Hazlitt "seldom clears up a real difficulty (never, we might say, with lights of his own), he frequently creates a darkness where none was before, and the peculiar *bumptiousness* of his incapacity makes it particularly offensive . . . If he who has most to learn be the happiest man, Mr. Hazlitt is indeed to be envied . . ." In reviewing James Halliwell's edition of John Marston, Lowell suggested a new title: "The Work of John Marston, containing all the Misprints of the original Copies, together with a few added for the first Time in this Edition, the whole carefully let alone by James Orchard Halliwell, F.R.S., F.S.A." And Lowell reduced James Gates Percival, who had been touted by some (including himself) as the American Shakespeare, to recognizable proportions: "Percival seems to have satisfied himself with a syllogism something like this: Men of genius are neglected; the more neglect, the more genius; I am altogether neglected, — *ergo*, wholly made up of that priceless material." [36]

Lowell's condemnations were as justified as they were rare. Yet he believed the more difficult test for a critic to be how well he performed the task of appreciation, isolating the elements of a work which accounted for its peculiar power. Dealing as he did almost exclusively with the certified giants of literature, Lowell could not go far astray in his gross judgments; one could hardly quarrel with assigning the label "genius" to Shakespeare or Dante. When it came to detailing the qualities which justified such labels, or assessing the merits of less renowned writers, Lowell had far more qualified success.

In drawing his judgments, he relied heavily on two devices: the precise, summary epigram, and the bland, multi-duty word ("genius," "charm," "manly"). And just as his epigrams, when telling, mark his success as a critic, his tendency to fall back on a vague vocabulary and on vacuous phrases suggests his ultimate defeat.

The epigrams which pervade the essays are usually fair as well as felicitous: Carlyle, who "goes about with his Diogenes dark-lantern, professing to seek a man, but inwardly resolved to find a monkey"; Addison and Steele, "who together made a man of genius"; Richardson, "the only author who ever made long-windedness seem a benefaction"; Coleridge, whose words "have the unashamed nakedness of Scripture, of the Eden of diction ere the voluble serpent had entered it"; *Sartor Resartus,* which "strikes one as might the prophecies of Jeremiah, if the marginal comments of the Rev. Mr. Sterne in his wildest mood had by some accident been incorporated with the text"; Thomson, whose English "is like a translation from one of those poets who wrote in Latin after it was dead." The strain for compression, however, sometimes showed, and what was meant to be a concise epigram turned instead into empty rhetoric: "A great man without a past, if he be not an impossibility, will certainly have no future." [37]

Falling back on the catch-phrase as a substitute for thought was one of Lowell's serious defects as a critic. Thus he would use the word "genius" as a concluding rather than inaugurating remark, as if the word itself carried its own unarguable certification. Or when he did attempt to define it, he could employ terminology so vague (genius is that quality "in whose power a man is") as to allow neither refutation nor agreement. But not even vagueness saved him from contradictions: at one point "genius" was said always to imply "a certain fanaticism of temperament," at another, two separate varieties were acknowledged, that which marked men with force of mind or those with fineness of mind — "for the intensity of conviction that inspires the understanding as much as for that apprehension of beauty which gives energy of will to imagination." Lowell, in fact, recast his definition of "genius" to fit any author who pleased him; he was more concerned with justifying his fondness for a particular writer than with adhering to any fixed position by which all writers would be measured. Thus he could admire Spenser for idealizing and Chaucer for describing, the one for abstracting life, the other for reflecting it — rather than deciding in advance that all poets should either idealize or describe, and then passing sentence on those who failed to meet the definition. This may be taken as a virtue, a symptom of Lowell's catholicity, of refusing to allow his own subjective affinities to metamorphize into objective canons of taste. Searching for what was best in each author, it might be said, Lowell necessarily applauded a variety of qualities, asking only that each be the best of its kind.[38]

But Lowell's varying standards were due to something more than his catholic appreciation; they reflected as well a basic ambivalence in his mind as to the nature and function of literature. He was uncertain if art resulted from inspiration or craftsmanship, if it should primarily instruct or delight, if it should reflect reality or flee it, if it should concentrate on the provincial or the universal, if it should allow the imagination free play or modulate it by "disinterested reason." Most such "problems," of course, are non-problems, the linguistic creations of critics more interested in abstraction than in concrete analysis of a specific work at hand. Moreover, the antithetical terms in which such issues are often raised, needlessly oversimplify. Surely "flight from reality" is a form of it; that which "delights" also "instructs," at least sensuously; and inspiration and craftsmanship are both necessary components of a finished work — whatever "inspiration" means anyway.

Lowell's inability to focus such issues, therefore, can to some degree be taken as one of his critical strengths. He was capable of seeing the unreal dualism of the questions posed and the futility of endless speculation about matters which ultimately rested on personal predilection. "When people jabber so much about art as they do here," Lowell wrote Story from Dresden in 1856, "& have all their terms so cut & dried, they are only playing cards on Art's coffin — just as Aristotle's poetics was the funeral oration of Greek poetry." It is true, too, that Lowell's fluctuations of opinion were in part the result of his ability to reconsider his own earlier views — as in the case of his judgment on Pope.[39]

Nonetheless, it would be a mistake to equate Lowell's contradictions with his common sense or with his flexibility, to put too good a face on his inconsistencies. For he did not so much eschew abstract issues as fail to bring coherence to his spasmodic discussion of them; he did not so much rethink his earlier opinions as simply forget them. He did sometimes introduce "metaphysical" questions in the very antithetical terms which elsewhere he deplored, and further, his changing positions in regard to those questions more often reflect transient moods than careful reconsiderations. His sharp swerves of opinion lack those interconnections which suggest a mind in dialogue with itself. Instead, each pronouncement has the tone of a first consideration, oblivious of its own earlier speculations rather than building on them.

Thus Lowell could in one place distinctly separate the artist from the moralist by insisting that the "aim of the one is to delight, of the other to convince. The one is master of his purpose, the other mastered by it," while at another time, in flat contradiction, he could call for a fusion of the two: "If it be the most delightful function of the poet to set our lives to music, yet perhaps he will be even more sure of our maturer gratitude if he do his part also as moralist and philosopher to purify and enlighten . . ." In the same way, Lowell could refer to the "illuminating common sense" of Lessing, and then applaud Coleridge for helping to emancipate the English mind from common sense's "vulgarizing tyranny." He could praise Lessing for his "hatred of exaggeration," and yet speak elsewhere of "enthusiasm" as "the beautiful illusion" which saves genius "from the baffling quibbles of self-consciousness." He could confess, with one of those genteel winces unjustly thought to be his most characteristic stance, that he had to "hold his nose" through certain "ordures" of Dryden, and yet on the other hand could defend Fielding because he "painted vice when it came in his way . . . as a figure in the social landscape, and in doing so he was perhaps a better moralist than those who ignore it altogether, or only when it lives in a genteel quarter of the town." [40]

If Lowell's literary essays taken together lack internal coherence, they nonetheless do reveal certain definite attitudes. Though willing to change the ground rules to accommodate a favorite, it is nonetheless apparent that Lowell had ground rules, however flexible and uncertain, and that he would have much preferred it if his favorites adhered to them. He may have tried to excuse Fielding's "grossness," but he clearly wished Fielding hadn't made excuses necessary. He admired Chaucer's devotion to the particular, but *ordinarily* believed poetry's prime office was to take us "out of the dungeon of actual life." In general Lowell leaned toward all that was harmonious, simple, disinterested, restrained, and away from that which was particularistic, effusive, eccentric, impassioned. By middle age, in other words, he had come to favor what are usually labeled the "classical" attributes, though the label, especially as applied to Lowell, is at best convenient shorthand. For if he was a "classicist" in regard to the literary qualities he admired, he was a "romantic" (the opposite catch-phrase) in his manner of address to a given work. That is, the "romantic" critic, by generally agreed convention, is more interested in the historical and ideological aspects of literature than in its formal, technical ones; he prefers to talk about content and "ideas" than to discuss, say, poetic diction or the structure of the sonnet. But even here, in terms of critical methodology, Lowell, like most, was far from a consistent practitioner of either major mode; in one essay he could deal at length with the historical context (as in his study of Chaucer), in another he could concentrate on more formalistic considerations (as in his study of Milton).

Such unity as marked Lowell's criticism is to be found neither in the questions he asked of a literary work nor in the assumptions which guided his judgment of it, but rather in regard to a particular leit-motif which emerges from his essays: the concern with "character." Lowell was interested not only in literature but also in the lives of the men who created it. He was not a biographical critic in any gross sense, "explaining" a work by what was known about its author or, alternately, using a literary work as a roadmap for deciphering the private life of its creator. And he specifically warned against entangling the estimate of an author's character with the evaluation of his writing, rebuking Carlyle for his tendency "to confound the moral with the aesthetic standard." Should Shakespeare's memoirs suddenly turn up and reveal him as a contemptible man, they would not, Lowell insisted, affect our judgment of *Hamlet* or *Othello* in the slightest. He realized, of course, that a man's personality would inevitably be reflected in his writing — "character and its intellectual product," as he put it, "are inextricably interfused" — but felt the two should be kept separate for purposes of critical evaluation. Unlike most twentieth-century critics, Lowell was interested in biography as well as literature, but unlike so many nineteenth-century ones, he managed not to confuse the two.[41]

Yet in one curious sense, the two did get entangled. If Lowell avoided denouncing a literary work because he disapproved of its author's character, he did occasionally fall into the related habit of exonerating an individual whose work he approved. Thus he excused Fielding's personal "excesses" partly by attributing them to the vices of the age instead of the man, and partly by denying them: Fielding's known habits "of study and industry . . . are altogether inconsistent with the dissolute life he is supposed to have led." With Coleridge, the rehabilitation was more difficult; Lowell decided that his opium habit had been "congenital," and in any case the poet's faults had been expiated by his suffering. In other words, while admitting in theory that literary genius and impeccable character had no necessary connection, Lowell continued to wish that they had, and his hankering to link his two supreme values could lead him to trim away some of the less lovely aspects of an author's personality.[42]

When he came to a man like Lessing, whose virtue matched his talent, Lowell was clearly delighted. Though avoiding any vulgar effort to establish a causal relationship between the two, he did allow himself to linger lovingly on a description of Lessing's simple, stately, self-reliant manhood: "No scandal was ever coupled with his name, nor is any biographic chemistry needed to bleach spots out of his reputation." If Lowell could not find character and talent linked as frequently as he would have liked, it was comforting to establish the fact that a great author at least *could* be a good man. So comforting was it, that Lowell decided Lessing's "character is even more interesting than his works," that "he had one ideal higher than that of being a poet, namely to be thoroughly a man." [43]

It is at such moments in his essays that Lowell's true hierarchy of values is revealed. He preferred to have literature and character united, but when they could not be, he preferred a good man to a good book — "for surely it is easier to embody fine thinking, or delicate sentiment, or lofty aspiration, in a book than in a life." This hierarchy of values was not stable; when he came to "the *highest* creative genius," Lowell could hedge: "we value character more than any amount of talent — the skill to *be* something, above that of doing anything *but the best of its kind*." And yet when discussing Shakespeare, whom Lowell considered the greatest master of the English language, he explicitly stated that "higher even than the genius I rate the character of this unique man . . ." [44]

Lowell's insistent interest in character was the closest he came to establishing a personal signature as a critic. But the theme was not sufficiently pervasive or conscious to give his criticism unique interest. Ultimately greatness in criticism is established in the same way as is ascendancy in other forms — by a distinctive impress which permeates the fragmentary parts and binds them together. Lowell himself understood that not single qualities but a dominating energy, an identifiable stamp, were the hallmarks of first-rate achievement — he found the main proof of Chaucer's genius in the fact that "he can be so inadequately sampled by detached passages, by single lines taken away from the connection in which they contribute to the general effect." It was this shaping faculty which Lowell lacked, "that exquisite something, as he himself put it, called Style, . . . not . . . a passive mould into which the thought is poured, but . . . the conceptive energy which finds all material plastic to its preconceived design." Perhaps this is the final explanation of why some critics, like Lowell, are essentially "appreciators." Having no central obsession, searching for no particular value, they do not feel the sharp impatience which comes from a thwarted quest. They do not ruthlessly reject authors who fail to meet their needs, because no need is urgently present.[45]

In sum, Lowell's virtues as a literary critic are abundant: wide learning, which could lapse into obscurantism but rarely into pedantry; an ability to cite authorities and allusions in illustration of a point, rather than as self-exhibition; a gift of graceful, epigrammatic expression which encapsulated a subject far more often than caricaturing it; an instinct for the first-rate which might abdicate when dealing with personal friends like Clough or Howells, but which on the whole remained acute; an enthusiasm for literature which managed to communicate itself to the reader; and perhaps above all, a catholic appreciation which was not a cover for timidity or lack of discrimination, but a genuine openness to a wide variety of excellence. These are not inconsiderable virtues in a critic; they endow Lowell's literary essays with enough vitality to warrant more attention than they are usually granted.

Yet finally, Lowell's powers consist of impressionistic insights and perceptive asides. He is not a critic whose distinctive personality is recognizably present — which is to say, the greatest kind of critic (or novelist, or painter, or historian, etc.), the man who, by establishing his world, helps to forge ours. And it is this failure, rather than any incidental defects, which keeps him from the front rank, for when a world is fully imagined even its peculiarities play an integral and thus acceptable part. As Lowell himself said, "there is a kind of gait which marks the mind as well as the body." His own gait was insufficiently defined.[46]

*

Throughout these productive post-war years, there sounded a rising note of discontent; increasingly, Lowell was dissatisfied with his literary achievement and the shape of his career. The modest sales on his books and the limited scope of his reputation bothered him, but these were not the basic sources of disquiet; he had income enough, after all, to live on, and as for reputation, he believed that in the long run "a perfectly just fate" awaits all literature. Here was the real rub. He no longer had confidence that his own work would stand the test of time. A self-depreciating tone becomes increasingly noticeable in these years, and it has a ring of authenticity. "Let us be honest," he wrote Fields, after the publisher had highly praised a poem of his, "the conception of the verses is good; the verses are bad." And while preparing *Under the Willows* for the press in 1868, he found the work "awfully depressing"; there was "a suggestion of something good" in the poems, and they were not "silly," but he confessed to Norton that on the whole he thought them very bad.[47]

Lowell had done worse things in the past and had liked them a great deal better. Perhaps he was now more inclined to think badly of his work because he felt more intensely than before the staleness of his life. He had become, in his eyes, "fat and dull," unable to catch fire. He feared he had permanently lost his chance to be a poet, that he had "suffered a professor change . . . too deep for healing." What "a queer trick of Fate," as he put it, that for thirteen years he should have been doing what grew "harder instead of easier." But the monotony of teaching was not sufficient to account for his failures as a poet. In a day when much of our poetry (and much of the best) emanates from the universities, it is clear that no necessary antagonism exists between the academy and creativity — not, that is, if the talent and the urge to self-expression are sufficiently strong. Somewhere Lowell realized that his ills could not be neatly tied to the classroom. And the realization made his melancholy worse. When he could assign depression to some certain cause — teaching, the reception of a poem, financial burdens — it was less disabling. But when he fell into the dumps for no accountable reason, with only the "apprehension of indefinite evil," then the anxiety was sharpest — it was the undefinable which held the greatest terror. How lamentable, he thought, that a man with "such an immense capacity for happiness" should so often be unhappy; true, he always recoiled "with a pretty good spring," but too much energy was wasted in despondency.[48]

By 1869, Lowell had begun to give serious thought to resigning from Harvard. Poetry, he felt, demanded the whole of a man, and before he got too old he wished to see if he could once more give the whole of himself to it. It was time to find out whether his melancholy was temperamental or occupational, whether his poetic urge had faltered for lack of talent or lack of repose. In most moods, Lowell was convinced that all he needed was time — a year to lie under a tree — in order to recover his imagination; "the fountain is still flowing," he wrote Quincy, "but it will not be dipped by any but the golden bowl of leisure." [49]

The main obstacle to an immediate resignation was financial. Lowell had always lived within his means, but barely within them. Time and again he found himself down to his last few dollars. With the New Englander's tendency to call everything more than necessity a luxury, he liked to refer to himself as a spendthrift. But in fact necessities consumed such a large share of his income that he had small chance to indulge his "rare genius" for being a millionaire. And when he did have extra funds, he tended to give them away — to Cranch under the guise of buying a picture, to the painter Akers, so that he might go to Minnesota for a tubercular cure, to any number of strangers knocking at his door with tales of woe.[50]

But the main drain on his income was Elmwood. The annual taxes on the estate ran to about a thousand dollars, and there was a yearly struggle to meet the bill; Annie Fields feared the constant financial pressure would turn Lowell sour — he seemed to her "like a lion at bay." As early as 1867, he had thought of renting Elmwood and taking a smaller house for himself elsewhere. But he loved the place too well to give it up entirely, and when, in 1870, he finally decided to take some measure to ease his financial plight, it was to sell off land, maintaining the house and two and a half acres for himself. The transaction was completed in the summer of 1871: at fourteen cents a foot, Lowell sold enough land (about $75,000 worth) to bring him an income of over $4000 a year, and Mabel, who owned part of the property, about $1500 more. It was enough, he felt, to provide a substitute for his earnings as a professor, and could be further supplemented, as in the past, with income from his writing.[51]

"I have gone over to the enemy," Lowell wrote Leslie Stephen, "and become a capitalist"; he would now, he added, look for a railroad to steal, so that like Jim Fisk he might further ingratiate himself with his countrymen. At last he had discovered the real Ponce de Leon fountain of youth — it was called an independent income. And it did wonders for his spirits. He had begun to think his low moods constitutional, but with financial anxieties removed, he felt "as light as a bird." As soon as he could set affairs in order, he made arrangements to leave for an extended stay in Europe. His plan was to settle down in some quiet place where he and Mrs. Lowell could live cheaply, and then to give himself to poetry. Whether he would recover "the wholesome mental unrest" which had kept him creative when younger, he did not know, but at least he would not have to print before ready nor "split up the furniture" of his brain in order to keep the pot boiling. He leased Elmwood to the Thomas Bailey Aldriches, resigned his position at Harvard, saw Mabel and her husband well settled in their new home and then on July 9, 1872, sailed for Europe with Mrs. Lowell.[52]

CHAPTER XII

RETURN TO EUROPE — AND POLITICS

THE LOWELLS stayed abroad for two years; for her they were a continuous delight, for him a mixed blessing. Mrs. Lowell's enthusiasm seemed boundless. Since she had never been to Europe before, her vision was fresh, her energy unflagging; in Paris, she reacted with such excitement at her first glimpse of friars that Lowell was sure she expected to figure in an *auto da fe*. Some of her ardor rubbed off on him, but only some. He had not been in Europe a week when he began to feel homesick. He would have periods of contentment, even of marked pleasure, but mainly when he managed to reproduce conditions close to those he had left behind at Elmwood — a home-like hotel, books, a quiet schedule free of events and a friend from Cambridge for company. Lowell had resigned his professorship to recapture poetry, and found that to maintain any sort of serenity he had to recapture his routine instead. Freedom brought not exhilaration but uneasiness.

It was in Paris that he managed most successfully to reproduce Cambridge. The Lowells went there soon after arriving in Europe, expecting to stay a few weeks, but lingering on for seven months. They settled just off the Quai Voltaire in a small hotel decidedly French rather than tourist, thus allowing Lowell to feel that he was carrying out the purpose of foreign travel even as he established a safe little island of domesticity. The days were uniform. He would walk by the river before breakfast, then read, or hunt for bargains in the bookstalls, keeping an eye out especially for works in Old French, which had come to interest him deeply (he bought so steadily that at one point he overdrew his account with Baring's). Then there would be another walk before dinner, preferably with a friend from home who might share cigars and talk in the Tuileries gardens (and would almost surely share Lowell's opinion that a walk along Brattle Street was vastly preferable to one along the Champs Elysées). Yet he enjoyed his Paris walks, and as was his custom in strange cities, covered almost every inch of it by foot, getting to know it better than most natives. In the evenings there would be more study, or perhaps reading French with Mrs. Lowell, who had hired a tutor for daily instruction in the language.[1]

Breakfast and dinner were taken in the tiny hotel dining room, where the fellow patrons were all French. Lowell soon was talking the language fluently enough to hold his place in the conversation but generally preferred to listen — unless American manners came under attack, when he would pitch in with heat and "rout" the opposition. Most of the regular diners at the hotel were veterans of the Franco-Prussian War and there was agitated talk of politics and *patrie*, all of which Lowell found highly entertaining. The conservatives at table far outnumbered the republicans, and they would rage for hours about the need to curtail freedom of the press, to place "Henri V" on the throne and to renew the attack against Prussia. "Stupidity expressed in epigrams," thought Henry James, who occasionally dined at the hotel as Lowell's guest — though James agreed that for 3 francs 50, the talk was the "cheapest entertainment" he had ever known.[2]

Lowell enjoyed the manner of debate so much that he was able to remain calm at its content. But he had his own opinions on French politics. He believed the conservatives, who currently dominated the Assembly, "were sowing reaction of the most poisonous kind"; if the upper classes would only give the French people ("gentle, kindly, patient and industrious") a chance to participate, they would prove themselves admirable citizens. Lowell despaired, though, of any turn for the better in the near future. He thought France as well off with Thiers, then President of the Republic, as not, though observing him at a reception, Lowell was struck by the Frenchman's "intense self satisfaction" — he had "one of those heads that you don't get out of the way without cutting off." When Thiers lost power in 1873, Lowell ascribed it to his egotism more than his policies. Indeed, he believed egotism was a national failing. Though he liked the French, Lowell thought too many of them attached excessive weight to their own personalities. They were like village great men — not really individualistic, but only self-important: "no man can bring himself to get out of the way, even though it is the Country he is blocking." The more Lowell saw of Europeans, the more convinced he became that Americans, with all their faults, were "the happiest and most civilized people on the face of the Earth." [3]

Occasionally the Lowells would break their solitude by an excursion to St. Cloud or Versailles, by an evening at the theater or at some reception which held out special appeal (like that given by the eighty-four-year-old Guizot, whom Lowell found very well informed on American affairs, and with one of the oddest-shaped heads he had ever seen — there was more of it "behind the ears than in front of them, like a quakeress's cap"). But Lowell was indifferent to the large world, and as Henry James put it, "indisposed to make any of the Parisian acquaintances which his 'eminence' would give him admission to." He preferred to read and study, and to save conviviality for those he felt comfortable with — namely, old friends from Cambridge. Emerson and his daughter were twice in Paris ("He grows sweeter if possible," thought Lowell, "as he grows older"), and there was a joyful reunion with Charles Eliot Norton, who had been traveling in Europe for four long years — years which "faded away like a mist" as soon as the old friends met again. There was a reunion, too, with Story, though Lowell found he had grown away somewhat from this friend of forty years, even if their cordiality had not lessened.[4]

With Henry James, it was less a case of renewing an old

friendship than of beginning a new one. The two had known each other only slightly in Cambridge — there was, after all, a twenty-four-year gap in their ages, and almost as wide a margin in their temperaments. But in Paris they struck up what James (with perhaps characteristic irony) called "a furious intimacy." It began with James delivering a message from Norton; the following day Lowell returned the call, the two men began to take walks together, and before long were seeing each other once or twice a week. The encounters were pleasant, but as James put it, more "a truce to the mutual indifference in which we dwelt in Cambridge" than a prelude to "eternal friendship." He thought Lowell "friendly, entertaining & full of knowledge," but too doggedly attached to the uncomplicated. Yet the relationship became affectionate and proved durable, however restricted and intermittent.[5]

Lowell's chief companion during the months in Paris was that specimen of Cambridge incarnate, John Holmes, who lived in the same hotel as the Lowells during much of their stay. Holmes was that "unassimilable" New Englander (as James called him) who when in Venice went every day to one spot in the city because it reminded him of the junction of Broadway and Cambridge Streets back at home. With Holmes constantly at his side, it is hardly any wonder that Lowell felt his homesickness ebbing — he had Cambridge with him. But although immensely fond of Holmes, in Paris Lowell felt occasional irritation with him; he could be such a child, albeit a charmingly odd one, so utterly dependent on the society of others that he gave almost no respite. Lowell could not live without "an occasional draught of solitude," and he saw to it that he escaped for at least some unaccompanied walks.[6]

But Holmes remained a dear friend, and it was he who rushed out for champagne when news arrived from America that Lowell had become a grandfather. Lowell appointed him on the spot "godfather by brevet *in partibus infidelium*," and the godfather proceeded to toast his new position with such zeal that Mrs.

Lowell finally called a halt to the celebration. The birth of a grandson increased Lowell's impatience with foreign travel. He was eager to see the boy: "Do you suppose he will come to me when he sees me?" he wrote his daughter, "or will he roar and ask to see a ring or a birthmark or something to identify me before he acknowledges his ancestor? Will it be Hildebrand and Hadubrand over again, and must I thrash him into recognition?" [7]

Lowell would gladly have returned home. But for the sake of his wife, who thrived on the new life, their "exile" (as he put it) continued. In May, 1873, he crossed the channel alone to say good-bye to Norton, who was finally returning to the United States. It was a visit of only four days but they were full ones. He saw Carlyle, Ruskin, Morris, G. H. Lewes, Thomas Hughes and Leslie Stephen. The meeting between Lowell and Ruskin, long anticipated, was something less than a success. Ruskin was preoccupied and not at his best, while Lowell, whose social gifts could, with strangers, become locked in shyness and sensitivity, also did himself less than justice. But he at least, was glad of the meeting; he felt he understood Rousseau better for having met Ruskin — the man of sentiment "who seeks refuge from a sense of his own weakness in strong opinions (or at any rate the vehement assertion of them) as men reassure themselves by talking aloud in the dark." [8]

Lowell went back to London in June, this time to receive a D.C.L. from Oxford (an honor matched by Cambridge in 1874). The students gave him a roar of welcome when he was presented at the ceremony by James Bryce, public orator at Oxford. Bryce recited Lowell's virtues in Latin, singling out *The Biglow Papers* for special praise (though without attempting a Latin translation of Birdofredum Sawin, an effort Thomas Hughes had predicted might enliven the ceremonies). But the doctoring of Lowell was not unanimously approved. Swinburne, for one, worked himself up into a considerable rage. He wrote the Southern poet, Paul Hamilton Hayne, that Oxford had "disgraced itself . . . degrading the previous recipients of its honours in order to inflict on them the unsavoury society of a vulgar and indecent buffoon . . ." Perhaps Swinburne's fury had been fed by knowledge that Lowell thought little of his poetry, though Lowell had given his opinion only in private correspondence ("I am too old," he had written E. C. Stedman, "to have a painted *hetaira* palmed off on me for a Muse, and I hold unchastity of mind to be worse than that of body"). When Lowell and Swinburne finally met years later, the Englishman was softened by personal contact: making Lowell's acquaintance, he wrote Stedman, had been "a very real pleasure . . ." If Lowell reciprocated, he has left no record of it.[9]

On his way to and from Oxford, Lowell stopped off in London to see the Henry Adamses, who had been fellow passengers on the boat to Europe. When they sounded him out on "his visit to the dons," Lowell admitted that he had been "feasted and flattered and rather enjoyed it," though hearing himself celebrated in Latin had given him "an odd kind of *posthumous* feeling." The Adamses made their own contribution to the festivities by taking Lowell along to a dinner party where for the first time in twenty years he met Robert Browning. He thought Browning "very cordial," but Mrs. Adams, more given to acid, found it "amusing to see Robert Browning's phlegmatic face try to beam." [10]

After his return from Oxford, the Lowells finally left Paris. He had on the whole enjoyed the winter there. Paris, he thought, was surely the handsomest city in the world, and the manners of its citizens attractively civil and ceremonious. Even so simple a matter as buying a cigar turned into an affair of diplomacy, a pleasant change from the United States, "where one had to pad himself all over against the rude elbowing of life." But the French *were* a different breed. He experienced none of that intensity of feeling with which he always regarded the virtues and defects of Americans and Englishmen; he felt no responsibility, no sense of "common blood and partnership" which "makes attraction easier and repulsion more instinctive." [11]

After leaving Paris, the Lowells traveled up the Rhine to Switzerland, accompanied on part of the trip by Leslie Stephen. Switzerland, thought Lowell, would be charming "were it not for the Swiss, all of whom (who are not in the Pope's guard) either keep hotels or beg or offer you rags of soiled edelweiss for money. Where it is chiefly inhabited by mountains it is good company." Yet Lowell liked Geneva so well that they settled in it for two months (whenever he took to a place, he wanted to stay; it was the traveling between places that he hated—"a constant succession of partings, like life"). There was a "certain smack of Calvin & predestination" in the old streets of Geneva that Lowell found bracing. As he grew older his Calvinist leanings grew stronger, though he continued to abhor creeds, claimed no Baedeker for the other world (even while believing in it) and would never think of meddling with the beliefs or lack of them of his friends ("any more than I ask whether they are rich or poor. I love *them*"). Like all creeds, Lowell thought Calvinism had unsatisfactory aspects. He objected especially to the physical notion of hell. For him damnation was a spiritual state, "the very horror of which consists (to our deeper apprehension) in its being delightful to who is in it." Nor did Lowell ever attend church regularly ("I so seldom find any preaching that does not make me impatient and do me more harm than good"). In Geneva he did enjoy the Calvinist services conducted by Bersier, but elsewhere, to the degree that he attended, he preferred the services of the Church of England.[12]

Lowell, then, was neither a dogmatist nor a ritualist in religion, though he clung to the broad outlines of his upbringing: belief in a universe governed by a divine force according to fixed moral laws. He held to this scaffolding firmly, despite "all the science that ever undertook to tell me what it doesn't know . . . When they tell me that I can't *know* certain things, I am apt to wonder how *they* can be sure of that, and whether there may not be things which they *can't* know."

We, who believe Life's bases rest
Beyond the probe of chemic test,
Still, like our fathers, feel Thee near . . .

Lowell preferred to shut out speculation and to "find solace in certain intimations that seem . . . from a region higher than . . . reason." "I suppose," he wrote Leslie Stephen, "I am an intuitionalist and there I mean to stick." He believed that those who discarded all traditional faiths were guilty of elevating private perspective into universal truth. For himself, he thought a belief none the worse for being hereditary, prizing "whatever helps to give continuity to the being and doing of man, and an accumulated force to his character." As the present became more sordid, as standards public and private seemed to disintegrate before the new God of Mammon, Lowell increasingly stressed the value of "roots":

Though all things else should perish in the sod,
Hold with firm clutch thy Puritan faith in God
And the calm courage that deemed all things light
Whene'er the inward voice said, this is right! [13]

*

In October, 1873, the Lowells moved on to Italy. In Venice, surrounded by Tintorettos and Bellinis, Lowell felt "really happy" for the first time since coming abroad. But Florence, their next stop, dampened his mood. The city seemed to him as beautiful as ever, but that part of it which had changed made him feel old, and that which had not made him feel sad. During his first walk in the city, he caught a glimpse of the quarters which he and Maria had occupied twenty years earlier; nothing about Casa Guidi had changed — there was the balcony Mabel used to run up and down, there were the windows from which he and Maria had gazed out upon the city. He had not the heart to go in.[14]

Rome saddened him still more. His associations with that city were peculiarly deep, for his son Walter had died and was buried there — and Lowell was astonished at how little time had dulled those associations. Rome became more unpleasant still because the Lowells stayed with the Storys, who lived at the center of a brilliant society and insisted on whirling them from reception to reception. It was all "rather confusing for wits so eremetical." Lowell always found it difficult to be at ease when feeling his way with people — he was the baby, his wife said, "that won't go to strangers." No, he decided, he was not equal to the *grand monde*. The simplicity of his life in Cambridge had never seemed more appealing.[15]

This was not the Lowell of twenty years earlier, who had taken Europe so jauntily in stride. Traveling now dulled rather than enlivened him. He felt old, listless, "little more than a digestive machine for the consumption of chops," as if nepenthe had been mixed with his wine, "or mandragora, that takes the reason prisoner." He had an occasional return of depression, and since this could no longer be ascribed to the weight of routine, he came back to the idea that his anxiety was constitutional — "the drop of black blood" he had inherited from his mother. "If you knew," he wrote Norton, "how I have sometimes had to struggle against suspicion & distrust of those I love best, you would pity me." If only, Norton wrote in his journal, Lowell had gone abroad ten years earlier — "at fifty-four youth is too far behind one for the hope that any change in life or external circumstance will be such that it can catch up with one again." [16]

Lowell had come to Europe to write poetry, but somehow "couldn't contrive the right kind of solitude":

One mask and then another drops,
And thou are secret as before

Earlier, he had thought the main trouble was lack of leisure. He now added the corollary that *effective* leisure required familiar surroundings; he was "like one of Bryant & May's safety matches which cannot kindle unless when rubbed against their special box," and his was three thousand miles away — in Elmwood alone did writing "come by nature." Now and then, especially when his dreams at night recovered some of their fanciful quality, he hoped he might be on the verge of a new period of creativity. But his few efforts were almost total failures. The only substantial poem he produced during the entire two years abroad (and it was one of considerable merit) was a lengthy ode on the death of Louis Agassiz.[17]

The success of the Agassiz Ode was enough to nurse the hope that his days as a poet were not over. He hadn't realized, he decided, how deeply the professorship had ground its dullness into him. It would take time — more time than he had expected — to work free of its influence. Yet he sensed that this might be whistling in the dark; it was possible he would never again be a poet — no matter how much distance he gained on his professorship. This uneasiness made him susceptible to the idea of going back to teaching, especially since his income no longer seemed adequate. The financial panic in the states which gained momentum in 1873 threatened to cut into Lowell's funds, for some of the bonds in which he had invested had stopped paying interest.[18]

At just this point, word came from America, via Norton, that President Eliot of Harvard was uncertain if Lowell had meant his resignation to be final. Norton also sent word that he had been asked to take Lowell's place should he resign, though he begged Lowell not to let that affect his decision. But of course it did. In answering Norton he acknowledged that he had earlier more than half made up his mind to return to Harvard. The chief incentive, he said, was financial, though he admitted that the salary would be more a convenience than a necessity — a way of helping Mabel and her husband raise the mortgage on their farm. He admitted, too, that he was the less unwilling to resume the treadmill because he had found that "college life had become more a habit than I wish it had, & that my putting the sea between me & it did not emancipate me as I had expected." But now that there was a prospect of Norton succeeding him, such "half-motives," Lowell wrote, were inadequate, and he authorized Norton to submit his resignation "absolutely & unequivocally." [19]

Norton, placed in a difficult position, at once wrote back that it would be "morally impossible" for him to take a place which Lowell might consent to fill — it was wholly contrary to his sense of the comparative services they could render to the college. He then took it upon himself to inform President Eliot that although Lowell had resigned "absolutely," he could probably be persuaded to return. Taking the hint, Eliot wrote directly to Lowell, insisting that the college could not bear to let him go. Norton further eased the way by assuring Lowell that his return would not leave him high and dry, for he had been told that room would be found for him as "Lecturer" in a new department, The History and Literature of the Fine Arts (which proved to be the case). Norton also assured Lowell that he would find Harvard far more tolerable under Eliot's new enlightened regime.[20]

And so it was settled. Less than two years after resigning to reclaim his youth, Lowell decided that he had better accept his middle age instead. The decision to return to teaching was something of a relief; the new round of duties would help to block out the self-doubt which came with unproductive free time. Besides, a return to Harvard became associated in his mind with the anticipated joy of returning to the United States, and thus seemed more appealing. Norton warned him, though, that if Harvard was better than when he left, the country itself was worse.

The scandals and malfunctions of Grant's second term were now in full flower. Norton had been astonished on his own return to the United States in 1873 to discover the extraordinary shift in opinion among his set "from confidence to want of confidence in the principles on which our social & political order rest." At first he thought the pessimism exaggerated: "America & democracy were blamed for conditions which are but expressions of the weak side of modern society, & which under other forms are as visible in England, France & Germany as in America." But within six months Norton had come around to the darker view. The new generation, he decided, was given over to the making and spending of money, was losing the capacity for thought and wanted only to be amused. Those who cared for literature, taste and the "ideal side of life" were becoming every year a smaller minority. "You will not be pleased with America," Norton wrote Lowell, "however fond of her you may be, or however many excuses are obvious for her faults. She is not a pleasing child; and not so hopeful, does not give so good promise as when she was younger." [21]

Even before Norton sent his gloomy accounts, Lowell had himself begun to fear for the country. In Europe he read reports

. . . of public scandal, private fraud,
Crime flaunting scot-free while the mob applaud,
Office made vile to bribe unworthiness,
And all the unwholesome mess
The Land of Honest Abraham serves of late
To teach the Old World how to wait . . .

But he had not lost — could not really lose — faith. He preferred to believe that current excesses were the expected concomitants of a period of stress and transition. Besides, he thought, men of his age "when they looked back to the *tempus actum*" always had a tendency to think the present a period of decline. Change in itself "becomes hateful to us as we grow older, and naturally enough, because every change in ourselves is for the worse." One had to guard against growing "wary" with age, never daring to let oneself go — "what are we good for if our natural temperament doesn't now and then take the bit between its teeth . . . ?"[22]

If most men of Lowell's age confuse their own disintegration with the world's decline, Lowell was suffering from the opposite myopia — equating his own refusal to grow dyspeptic with the country's continuing good health. Three thousand miles from home, of course, it was comparatively easy to remain calm about what he might find on his return, especially since such fears as he had were tempered by the anticipated pleasure of being back at Elmwood; national problems seemed remote, the attraction of his "reeky old den" real. Yet with the end of his "exile" in sight, Lowell thought more kindly of his time abroad. The only apparent results of the trip seemed to be a graying beard and what the doctors called "suppressed gout," but he hoped that once home, some dormant benefits from the two years of travel would emerge.[23]

He had not misgauged the enormous pleasure he would feel at being home again. Arriving in July, 1874, the Lowells had the best possible reception — the new grandson left his nurse's arms to greet them at the door of Elmwood; Lowell decided on the spot that he was "stupidly in love" with the boy. Mabel had already staffed the house with two servants, and John Holmes had sent in a store of "every possible tipple known to gods or man" — and promptly fled to Lake George the next day to escape Lowell's gratitude. The warmest welcomes, Lowell claimed — perhaps because they were the ones he was most apprehensive about — came from his "Irish fellow citizens," who told him it was "plisant to have rale gintleman back to the Ould Pleece agin." Surely Norton had exaggerated the disastrous symptoms of change.[24]

Lowell took up his old haunts and habits with ease. The Whist Club, which had suspended during his absence, reconvened, and at the Saturday Club he was soothingly reassured that there was no noticeable change in his appearance. Lowell knew better. Idleness had made his waist "grow more & more obscure (like many a passage in Browning)," and a waistline was "as important in a poet's economy as in a woman's." But the real decline in his romantic image, he confided to a lady admirer, had been marked by the recent addition of spectacles, and of the worst kind — "the steel-bowed deformity which pale young parsons love." If they had only been "nippers," Lowell lamented, he might have kept some claim to foppishness "and he who is foppish has not yet abandoned the last stronghold of youth, or, if he has, he at least marches out with the honors of war." That steel bow, alas, was "Romance's Candine Forks."[25]

Perhaps the most comforting part of being home was that, as he had hoped, he was once more able to work. For the first few months he continued to spend most of his time reading, especially in Old French and Old English, averaging ten hours a day and often so absorbed that he resented interruption. Much of this was by way of preparation for a return to Harvard, where by the fall of 1874 he was again installed with classes in Dante and Old French. Yet out of this reading came as well new essays — on Spenser, Milton and Dante — which in 1876 were collected, along with two revised pieces on Wordsworth and Keats, as *Among My Books, Second Series*.

As the volume was going to press in the summer of 1875, Lowell fell seriously ill for the first time in his life. "Liver trouble," the doctors announced, with that energetic vagueness usual in cases of uncertain diagnosis. Lowell was wretched for weeks and unwell for months. He was not able to correct proofs with the care he had intended, or to make the additions he had hoped. Often he lost interest in his books once they appeared, but this time he was more disgusted than indifferent. When the new volume came out, it seemed to him a poor thing; compared with the masters, he decided, he was "third-rate." "You would laugh," he wrote Norton, "if I should tell you how much better than I other people seem to me to do things. I think very well of my insight, but the expression of it never appears to me worth the trouble of pen & ink."[26]

Yet these essays, especially the one on Spenser, had much to recommend them. They suffered from Lowell's usual faults as a prose writer — discursiveness, inconsistency, a surfeit of learned citation. But his sympathetic appreciation of his subjects, his common sense and vitality, his play of metaphor and wit, gave a rich texture to the best passages, and to the whole, a tone which pleasantly intermixed gayety with gravity.

The reception of the book, both public and private, was generally favorable. Lowell's reputation had grown during his two years abroad. While overseas, several long evaluations of his work had appeared, and the public had become predisposed in his favor. In England, the reviews of the new volume were less cordial, though they varied wildly as to which were the good or bad essays and why. Lowell at least had the pleasure of Edward Fitzgerald's good opinion; Fitzgerald thought him the only critic capable of doing for English authors what Sainte-Beuve had done for the French. He believed Lowell inferior to the Frenchman in "delicacy of perception, or refinement of style," but superior in humor and extensive knowledge.[27]

Lowell also increased his output of poetry, though in neither amount nor quality was the change appreciable. In one sense, though — the hortatory, indignant tone — some of his new verse did mark a restoration. His willingness while in Europe to suspend judgment on American developments gave way rapidly once he came to view them at first hand. He expressed his shock at the changed aspect of national life in a series of centennial odes and, even more outspokenly, in two poems for the *Nation*:

Is this the country that we dreamed in youth,
Where wisdom and not numbers should have weight,
Seed-field of simpler manners, braver truth,

Where shams should cease to dominate
In household, church, and state?

The scandals which seemed daily to multiply were less alarming than the manner in which the public received them. Instead of wrath at the Belknaps, Goulds and Tweeds, there was banter; instead of condemnation, there was something close to admiration:

With generous curve we draw the moral line:
Our swindlers are permitted to resign;
Their guilt is wrapped in deferential names,
And twenty sympathize for one that blames.[28]

His poems produced a sharp counterattack in the press. Lowell's two years abroad, it was said, had spoiled him for democracy; having mixed with dukes and duchesses and absorbed their values, he was no longer able to appreciate the virtues of his own countrymen. Similar charges were to be leveled at him for the remainder of his life, doing him a grotesque injustice and causing him deep hurt. His belittlers failed to see that his criticism represented not a repudiation of democracy, but a profound commitment to it: "It is no real paradox to affirm that a man's love of his country may often be gauged by his disgust at it." Lowell had reached a point in life (at least so he said), where he would have preferred to be left to his studies rather than become reinvolved with politics. But since he "had attained to some consideration," he believed it a matter of duty to speak out: "I have always tried to tell my countrymen the truth, sometimes even at a sacrifice of poetry." Democracy, Lowell insisted, was an experiment and like any other, had to be judged by its results. In itself it was "no more sacred than monarchy. It is Man who is sacred," and currently Man's duties needed more reinforcement than his rights. "It is honor, justice, culture, that make liberty invaluable, else worse than worthless, if it mean only freedom to be base and brutal." [29]

Earlier Lowell had managed to separate "the people" from the politicians, to regard the one as innocent of and unsullied by the transgressions of the other. Now he was less sure. Massachusetts was currently represented in the Senate by Messrs. Boutwell and Dawes — "the one a chief obstacle to civil service reform (our main hope), the other soiled by the *Credit Mobilier* scandal." In the House, Lowell considered George Hoar the state's only respectable representative — the others were either nonentities or notorieties. The best known was Benjamin F. Butler, a man whose intermingled humanitarianism and demagoguery still make for an uncertain reputation, but whom Lowell considered an unmitigated scoundrel. The disheartening fact to Lowell was not that such a man existed, but that the people had elevated him to public office and had done so with thumping majorities. The inescapable conclusion, difficult as it was for the sanguine Lowell to face, was that "the voters of his district are really represented by him, & till you have cured *them*, you must put up with *him*." [30]

On the national level, the picture was scarcely brighter. Lowell believed Grant personally honest, though compromised by the bad lot with which he had surrounded himself. He appreciated the President's standing by his friends once the scandals broke, but thought it lamentable that he had had such friends in the first place. More was wrong with the Republican party, however, than its larcenies, though those were bad enough. Lowell feared the party's leaders were keeping alive sectional animosities for selfish purposes: not to protect the Negro, but to maintain themselves in power, not for the sake of principle, but for gain. He believed that Radical Reconstruction, the forced conversion of the South, had failed, that the Negro had become prey to spoilsmen, and that those Southern state governments still in Radical hands should therefore be returned to native whites ("We are deliberately trying to make an Ireland of the South, by perpetuating misgovernment there"). The Republican party, in Lowell's view, had bungled the job of reunion, and had done so because of a fallacious belief (which he had once shared) "that human nature is as clay in the hands of a potter instead of being, as it is, the result of a long past & only to be reshaped by the slow influences of an equally long future." Lowell wanted the rights of the Negro guaranteed, but he had now come to feel that this could be accomplished only by turning the state governments back to those conservative Southern whites who had formerly been Whigs, and by then allying with them nationally to restore everywhere good government, prosperity and fraternity. In an Ode composed to celebrate the hundredth anniversary of Washington's taking command of the American army, Lowell used the public occasion to pay a conciliatory tribute to Virginia:

If ever with distempered voice or pen
We have misdeemed thee, here we take it back,
And for the dead of both don common black.[31]

Like so many others who had once been willing to use the strength of the federal government to protect the Negro, Lowell had come to give other values precedence. He might have been willing to continue the struggle longer had he not come to feel that politicians were using the Negro Question for cynical purposes, and had not the issues of local government, national reconciliation, civil service reform and prosperity become entangled with it. Lowell still wished to see the Negro safely settled in his rights but other problems now seemed to him to demand priority. And these could not be heeded so long as energy and attention continued to be focused on "wartime issues"; indeed until good government, prosperity and national reconciliation were accomplished, the Negro problem itself, Lowell believed, could not be resolved. This was a comfortable but, as it turned out, disastrous syllogism. The shift of emphasis in reform circles would end not by solving the Negro's grievances but by submerging them.

Lowell was not content to exhort his countrymen through prose and verse; for the first time in his life he assumed a direct role in politics. His activities centered on the Presidential election of 1876. In the spring of that year a group of young Republicans from the Boston area, dissatisfied with the tendencies of their party, arranged to meet, and they invited Lowell to attend and preside. Though he disliked leading any meeting, political or literary, Lowell accepted; he confessed that he was not as hopeful as he had been thirty years ago, but added that "if there be any hope, it is in getting independent thinkers to be independent voters." The result of the meeting was the formation of a committee of forty, eight from each ward, designed to capture the local caucuses when the time came to choose delegates for the Republican national convention. The main aim of the reformers was to prevent the selection of delegates favorable to the candidacy of Senator James G. Blaine of Maine, considered by them a hopeless demagogue, tainted with corruption.[32]

Their efforts proved successful. Blaine had expected a unanimous delegation from Massachusetts; instead, the Bay State went to the national convention at Cincinnati pledged to Benjamin Bristow, Grant's able Secretary of the Treasury, upon whom the reformers had come to concentrate their hopes. Moreover, the delegation included such noted independents as Richard Henry Dana, Jr., Judge Rockwood Hoar, John Murray Forbes and — James Russell Lowell, who had been chosen to represent the Eighth Congressional District. Mrs. Lowell "used to think it would be a great waste" to put her husband into politics, but now agreed that "nothing less than the best efforts of the best men can save us." [33]

Lowell's journey to Cincinnati brought him new optimism ("as a journey in America always does"). He was impressed with the country's wealth and comfort, with its immense spaces "tremulous with the young grain, trophies of individual, or at any rate of unorganized courage and energy, of the people and not of dynasties." Even if democracy might doom the country "to a dead level of commonplace," might forever inhibit the "higher & nobler things that make a country truly habitable," its material achievements had indubitably meant "a great gain to human happiness." Men capable of such physical feats, such energy, would surely find a way of bringing the country back to first principles.[34]

The proceedings in Cincinnati, ultimately satisfactory to Lowell, at first gave him discomfort. The convention exhausted him physically — the heat was stifling, there was no leisure time and not even an adequate supply of water to keep clean from the coal smoke. He became so "demoralized by the unwonted color" of his fingernails that (so he told it) he kept them carefully hidden lest he be mistaken for a partisan of Blaine's ("the dirtiness of whose hands seemed rather an argument in his favor with many"). It did seem for a time that Blaine might become the party's nominee. On the sixth ballot he had three hundred votes, and when he showed gains on the seventh, Lowell's heart sank. He had never had much hope of nominating Bristow, but the idea of Blaine at the head of the Republican party seemed guarantee that henceforward "vulgarity of character and obtuseness of moral sense" should be the hallmarks of Republicanism.[35]

But after the seventh ballot, breaks came in all directions. New York, Pennsylvania and Indiana withdrew favorite sons and shifted their votes to Rutherford B. Hayes — as did Massachusetts. Though preferring Bristow, the Massachusetts men were content with Hayes. They believed him a man of independent judgment and personal probity, and when he finally succeeded in wresting the nomination from Blaine, they looked on his choice as a triumph for the cause of reform. Lowell proudly announced "that it was New England that defeated the New England candidate."[36]

Later, when Hayes visited Boston, Lowell met him and was confirmed in his favorable opinion. He found him "simple, tender, & sincere," full of those virtues which Lowell had begun to associate with Westerners. During the convention he had been impressed by the delegates from Western states—"they had not the manners of Vere de Vere, perhaps, but they had an independence and self-respect which are the prime elements of fine bearing." They had, too, Lowell believed, a "largeness of apprehension" of which "we victims of the intellectual etiquette of an older civilization are incapable." All this from a supposedly parochial Bostonian! [37]

After his return to Cambridge, Lowell, to his surprise, was pressed to become the Republican nominee to Congress from his district. The local leaders twice offered him the nomination at his home, and later at the state convention (to which he was a delegate) assured him that if he would only allow his name to be used, he could have the nomination by acclamation. He was profoundly touched by this testimonial, but refused all overtures. Nothing could tempt him to accept but a conviction that it was his duty—and he decided it wasn't. He would, he believed, make a very poor member of Congress, and by "that bit of wisdom" held fast. But he could not prevent the state convention from nominating him as a Presidential elector. It seemed too trivial and perfunctory an honor to refuse without appearing ungracious. As it turned out, the office was to prove more significant than could have been anticipated.[38]

Once the campaign got under way, Lowell lost some of his enthusiasm for a Republican victory. The Democrats, in nominating the reformer, Samuel Tilden, made Hayes' election seem less urgent. And besides, the "worst element" of the Republican party, in Lowell's opinion, got hold of the canvass, and was busy waving "the bloody shirt" and stirring up old sectional passions, instead of concentrating on new issues like civil service, tariff or currency. Lowell began to think there was little to choose between the two parties, and almost regretted that Blaine had not been nominated, for that might have led the reform-minded men of both parties into forming a wholly new one. On the state level, Lowell was especially tempted to desert the Republicans, for Charles Francis Adams was running for governor on the Democratic ticket. He was not attracted to Adams as a human being ("there is no great fun in complimenting Adamses, for they come into the world ahead of all praise and only wonder at your inadequacy"), but he did admire the man's accomplishments and integrity. Yet in the end, Lowell voted Republican. He might not trust the party's present managers, but he was "too full of traditional and well-founded doubts of the Democratic party to be a willing helper in the success of its candidates." [39]

The first results in the Presidential contest were indecisive. Tilden amassed 184 electoral votes to Hayes' 166, but remained one vote shy of the necessary majority; the disputed tallies in Louisiana, Florida and South Carolina would decide the final outcome. After considerable jockeying, a fifteen-man electoral commission was set up to review the returns in those states, and by a strictly partisan vote awarded all three to Hayes. Southern Democrats in Congress were persuaded to accept this result by behind-the-scene assurances that the last Federal troops would be withdrawn from the South, that railroad concessions would be forthcoming and that at least one Southern Democrat would be appointed to the Cabinet.[40]

While these negotiations were in progress, a rumor developed that Lowell was going to cast his ballot as a Presidential elector for someone other than Hayes, thus throwing the contest into the House of Representatives and almost certainly assuring Tilden's election. *The Nation* had advised any one of the Republican electors to adopt such a course, and Lowell was thought to be either the object or the abettor of the scheme — one of Hayes' lieutenants sent his chief a telegraphic message that Lowell had himself actually written or revised *The Nation* article. The newspapers descended on Lowell to confirm the rumors, but he quickly squelched them. He had had nothing to do with the article, he told the reporters, and moreover had reached his own decision weeks before that he must vote as directed by his constituents—that is, for Hayes. Possibly Lowell did have some momentary hesitation, some feeling that Tilden had been the actual choice of the people and was being kept from office only by partisan manipulations. But if so, he had soon decided that an elector's function was not to exercise judgment but to carry out the wishes of the party that had selected him. When the electors met to cast their ballots at the Parker House in January, 1877, Lowell's vote for Hayes was greeted with scattered applause, some of it, no doubt, rising from nervous relief.[41]

If Hayes had taken any credence of the rumors, he bore no resentment against Lowell. Soon after the election result was assured, the President-elect sounded him out about accepting a diplomatic appointment. Lowell had been mentioned continuously for the foreign service ever since his return home. In 1874, he had even had a concrete offer. Secretary of State Hamilton Fish, eager to draw men of Lowell's reputation into the Administration in order to improve its tarnished image, had succeeded in getting the Russian mission offered to him (after three others had turned the post down). He had done so despite Grant's hesitation, for the President assumed that since Lowell came from Massachusetts, he must be "a Sumnerite"—that is, a follower of Grant's enemy, Senator Charles Sumner. After Grant's doubts had been quieted, Judge Hoar, at Fish's request, had gone out to Cambridge to discuss the appointment with Lowell, and Postmaster General Jewell had urged the case separately, over dinner. But Lowell had finally declined the appointment. He doubted if the salary would be sufficient, and he would have had to rely on it for expenses, since his personal income had again become reduced when the Western railroad bonds in which he had heavily invested stopped payment. More important still, the critical illness of his wife's sister had made acceptance out of the question. The Grant Administration took care, however, to give the offer publicity; if they could not gain

Lowell's services, they could at least win credit for having sought them.[42]

Two years later Lowell was more receptive. His friends, including Howells, Hayes' relative by marriage, besieged the new President and his Secretary of State, William Evarts, with requests that Lowell be offered a diplomatic post. Norton added assurance that this time Lowell would probably accept — for reasons of health, and "for the sake of relief from long-continued, somewhat uncongenial work." Apparently Hayes, a great admirer of *The Biglow Papers,* needed little if any prodding. In May, 1877, in a handwritten, personal letter carried to Lowell by Howells, the President gave Lowell the choice of either the Austrian or Russian missions. But then, to the chagrin of Howells, who had accepted Norton's assurances at face value and passed them on to Hayes, Lowell declined both offers. In doing so, however, he mentioned off-handedly to Howells that had Spain been suggested, he might have been tempted, for he would love to see a play by Calderón. The indefatigable Howells at once reported the remark to Washington. A few days later, when Evarts was in Boston, he requested a meeting with Lowell, told him the President had been much disappointed by his refusal, but said that an exchange of missions could be arranged whereby Lowell would get the Spanish appointment. After all the trouble taken in his behalf, Lowell now felt he had no choice but to accept, though he doubted if anyone other than old friends would believe with what real reluctance he did so. The salary, at least, was to be $12,000 a year, with an additional $2100 for rent and contingent expenses, so it seemed — mistakenly — that there would be no financial difficulty. Besides, Lowell reasoned, a year or two in Spain — he would certainly not stay longer — might help him with his studies.[43]

In any case, it was now too late for a change of heart. There was a last-minute flurry of arrangements — a trip to Washington for instructions (where he was disgusted with what seemed to him Evarts' "shallow flippancy, pretention & ignorance"), renting Elmwood to Ole Bull, the violinist, correspondence about who should or should not be First and Second Secretaries of Legation, packing, farewells — and then the Lowells sailed from Boston on July 14, 1877. The Cunard agent got up an "ovation" on Lowell's behalf — revenue cutters and the like — which embarrassed rather than pleased him.[44]

He intended to be gone a year, possibly two. As it turned out, Lowell would not again set foot in the United States until 1885.

CHAPTER XIII

MINISTER TO SPAIN

LOWELL'S THREE YEARS in Spain were neither summary nor prelude, neither a leisured respite from concluded work nor the harbinger of a new departure. They were instead an interlude, another in what had begun to look like a series of entr'actes, delays before an uncertain third-act curtain. Lowell himself had little remaining illusion that he could still carry off a major performance; he talked of this trip to Europe not as precursor to poetry, but as a potential aid to his studies. But if hope had diminished, some literary expectation still lingered, enough to make poignant his continuing silence.

The years in Spain were not without incidental pleasures, but the first year was almost entirely disagreeable. Lowell, as always, made slow adjustments, and Cambridge, as always, loomed larger in affection the further it receded from view. But beyond these usual problems, his official situation presented special difficulties.

They began, on a trivial level, almost immediately. The Lowells arrived in Madrid during mid-August heat and had to set out at once to find a house; they could not go about in cabs "like ordinary mortals" but had to be attended by a coachman and footman in livery. Lowell found this rather amusing the first day, but thereafter "a tremendous bore" — he was "too old," he said (he might have added too Yankee), to find ceremonials grateful — though he maintained the forms for the sake of his position. House-hunting took longer than it might because of the Lowells' limited budget. Though his salary had seemed generous, he had to furnish his own residence; with this and other necessary expenses, he had within four months of arrival spent all of his salary except a hundred dollars — as well as $2500 of his own money.[1]

Then too, Lowell was wholly ignorant of ordinary diplomatic business and procedures. And since the diplomatic corps at Madrid consisted mostly of seasoned veterans, he felt very much the neophyte. He was made more conspicuous still by having to appear at court (in line with a long-standing directive from the State Department) in a plain black suit; it made him look, he said, "like the death's head at Egyptian festivals." In combination with the labyrinth of etiquette which marked all procedures at the Spanish Court ("as in some old gardens, if you take a step in the wrong direction, you are deluged with cold water"), it is not surprising that Lowell at first felt as if he were doing the Virginia Reel to a melody by Mozart.[2]

Moreover, he was heir to a somewhat unhappy legacy from recent American Ministers to Madrid. General Dan Sickles had left behind a particularly bad taste, and even Caleb Cushing, Lowell's able immediate predecessor, had been suspected of a personal interest in the Cuban claims he settled. Then, too, Lowell dreaded being known as one of those impractical "literary fellows" — a slander, he believed, on his birthplace no less than his profession. Lowell's being a "literary fellow," however — and his sense of humor — did wonders for this country's Diplomatic Correspondence. When the Spanish government complained that a New York firm, in collusion with a Frenchman named Fourcarde, was illegally smuggling refined oil into the country to avoid duties, Lowell put aside State Department Prose in order to give Evarts the full savor of the occasion:

> The Frenchman . . . established his storehouses in the suburbs, and then hiring all the leanest and least mammalian women that could be found, he made good all their physical defects with tin cases filled with petroleum, thus giving them what Dr.

> Johnson would have called the pectorial proportions of Juno. Doubtless he blasphemed the unwise parsimony of Nature in denying to women in general the multitudinous breasts displayed by certain Hindu idols. For some time these milky mothers passed without question into the unsuspecting city and supplied thousands of households with that cheap enlightenment which cynics say is worse than none. Meanwhile M. Fourcarde's pockets swelled in exact proportion to the quaker breastworks of the improvised wetnurses. Could he only have been moderate! Could he only have bethought him in time of the *ne quid nimis*. But one fatal day he sent in a damsel whose contours aroused in one of the guardians at the gates the same emotions as those of Maritornes in the bosom of the carrier. With the playful gallantry of a superior he tapped the object of his admiration and — it tinkled. He had "struck oil" unawares. Love shook his wings and fled; Duty entered frowning; and M. Fourcarde's perambulating wells suddenly went dry.[3]

Fearing he would prove inadequate, Lowell first tended to magnify his responsibilities, and then to perform them with a conscientiousness that bordered on mania. There were real duties enough, mostly in regard to Cuban claims, customhouse rows and tariff issues (officials in a Spanish port, Lowell commented, "look on it as a duty to suppress trade if they can"), but hardly of a magnitude to warrant the worry he expended on them. He was so afraid at one point of making a blunder over the receipt for a half-million-dollar indemnity that he was awake night after night after having signed it. Some of his anxiety in regard to claims came from a dislike of always having to play "the *dun*" — especially for claims in whose justice he sometimes lacked confidence. He sympathized, moreover, with Spain's difficulty in raising money and with her general "want of aptitude for business." Lowell made life no easier for himself by insisting from the first day on conducting all official business in Spanish. No doubt, as he claimed, this "astonished 'em at the Foreign Office here," but it also multiplied his own difficulties. Though he could read Spanish fluently, he lacked the colloquial forms of speech (and in one sense, even his fluency proved a handicap — he understood everything said to him so well that he paid little attention to the constructions). At first, Lowell later told Mrs. Thomas Bailey Aldrich, he was unable even to offer a chair to a visitor — though he added with a twinkle that he "could have asked him in Old Spanish . . . and had the advantage." [4]

Lowell was aware of his overscrupulousness, but it was only when his health began to suffer that he took himself in hand. Soon after arriving he had had a severe attack of gout, first in one foot and then the other. Between this and overstrain, he sometimes got no sleep for three days on end, which produced new attacks of gout, and also a return of his old devil, depression. "I am *not* reconciled," he wrote Norton, a full eight months after he arrived, "I long for the Charles and the meadows . . . I feel much older in body and mind." [5]

Finally, in April, 1878, Lowell asked for and received a sixty-day leave of absence, and he and Mrs. Lowell took a slow French steamer through the Mediterranean to Athens and Constantinople. The change of scene and pace did him immense good; the Acropolis — "sublime even in ruin" — the Turks, with their "noble bearing even in defeat and even in rags," did something to restore his vision and still more, his perspective. He came back to Madrid in mid-July "a new man," having flung his "*blue* spectacles into the paler Mediterranean." [6]

At last he began to find life in Madrid tolerable, "nay even to enjoy it after a fashion." He turned with enthusiasm to mastering the language, spoke Spanish with a teacher for an hour every morning, and in the intervals worked hard at translation (including a life of Charles Darwin). Before long he felt easier in conversation and even began to try his hand at writing a few elementary poems in Spanish. He also turned his attention to acquiring a knowledge of the broader outlines of Spanish life and politics, instead of exhausting himself on the petty details of ministerial routine. More than a year after his arrival, he finally sent Evarts a detailed analysis of domestic affairs in Spain. The delay had in part been due to proper caution about superficial estimates, but even more, to a misallocation of energies. Now that his obsession with tonnage duties was at an end, Lowell began to develop a shrewd, detailed knowledge of Spanish institutions, heightened in sensitivity by his affection for the Spanish people.[7]

His ministership coincided with a period of relative calm in Spain. In the ten years preceding Lowell's arrival, the country had been torn by Carlist uprisings, a short-lived republic, military coups and provisional governments. But in 1875 the monarchy had been restored in the person of eighteen-year-old Alfonso XII, and in 1876 a new constitution had been accepted by the Córtes, the Spanish parliament. Effective control remained with the king, who chose the ministry which in turn dominated the Córtes, though limited suffrage and a bicameral legislature preserved constitutional forms. There were, however, no recognized organs of public opinion, no well-defined national consciousness. Spanish politics were essentially personal politics, in which private ambitions took the place of public principles and adherents clustered around a chieftain rather than a platform. Though Lowell read the debates in the Córtes every day, he found them uninformative, for they were "not so much expressions of public opinion as of private animosity, masked in parliamentary forms." Outside of the Córtes, there were two major contenders for power: the rejected line of the royal family — the Carlists — and the Republicans. But within the Córtes, the three parties which had any show of strength were all adherents of Alfonso XII, if in varying degrees. There was thus no real opposition in parliament, though ministerial power alternated between the "Liberals" led by Sagasta and the "Conservatives" led by Cánovas del Castillo. Neither, in Lowell's view, recognized "the greatest discovery of modern times, that freedom is good above all because it is safe." [8]

Cánovas del Castillo was in power at the time of Lowell's arrival. Lowell thought him "the ablest politician in Spain," but believed his policy on the whole "a reactionary one" and in danger of becoming more so. Cánovas' main aim, in Lowell's view, was to provide the repose and stability needed to consolidate the monarchy, "to establish a government liberal enough in form to keep the republicans from rising, and repressive enough in fact to keep the tories from plotting." For the moment, Lowell believed, Cánovas had neutralized opposition. But since he had no solid party base for support, ruling instead by a temporary union of incongruous factions, Lowell predicted (and correctly) that Cánovas was likely to fall before rising demands for reform, especially in Cuba. Lowell's temperamental optimism, however, was not confined to things American. Though Spain, "misgoverned for three centuries" was not to be reformed in a day, Lowell believed that with "time and patience" she would establish free institutions, becoming, like France, a conservative republic — one of his more delayed prophecies.[9]

Lowell saw in the Spanish system lessons "full of warning and instruction." With a civil service based on personal favoritism, "the very foundations of public honesty and private independence" had been sapped in the governing class. Leaders represented their own, not public, interests, and once in control of the patronage were difficult to remove from power. Lowell feared that the United States might be moving in a similar direction, though fraud rather than the force of a standing army was the preferred American means for seizing and maintaining power. News from home seemed to confirm his forebodings. Oliver Wendell Holmes wrote that the present "ignoble aspect of the great republic" was enough "to sicken any people of self-government," and Norton flatly asserted that the Hayes Administration had been a failure and politics never in worse condition. Strikes, labor riots, the growth of socialism and communism, the demand for the unlimited issue of Greenbacks and the protest against the resumption of specie payments, all seemed dire symptoms of the country's decay. Norton reported to Lowell that President Eliot of Harvard had been promoting rifle clubs and drilling among the students, feeling the time might soon come when they would be needed for service in the streets.[10]

Lowell, as always, was less pessimistic than his friends. He recognized that "deterioration of national character" always came about gradually and imperceptibly and that there was reason to believe the process had already set in. But he retained "great faith in the good sense of our people." He had been assured so many times in his life that "the bottom of the world had at last dropt out for good and all," and yet had survived "to see it hold water very tolerably nevertheless," that he felt no great alarm at current developments. And when news came late in 1878 that Ben Butler had been defeated at the polls in Massachusetts, Lowell saw confirmation of his trust in the average American, of his long-standing belief that "the upper classes were quite as liable to be influenced by stupidity, selfishness & passion as the lower." [11]

As for the Spanish institution of monarchy, Lowell disapproved its forms even while admiring its incumbent. He first met Alfonso XII when formally presenting his credentials, and was at once impressed by the youthful king's bearing and intelligence (and no doubt charmed when Alfonso recited some of Lowell's poetry, though he realized the king had been primed beforehand). With each subsequent meeting, few though they were and weighted by formal pomp, Lowell's admiration for Alfonso's abilities and good intentions grew. The king's "grace, tact and good humor," he wrote Evarts, indicated "a singularly agile intelligence as well as an amiable character." Lowell did not doubt that if Alfonso had been free to follow his own generous impulses, he would break through the wall of etiquette which shut him off from his people and make himself a genuinely popular figure. Lowell believed the habit of loyalty to the monarch was still strong in Spain, despite the fact that the middle classes had become more conscious of their power, but he feared Alfonso might be too young to take a comprehensive view of his country's needs and too indebted to a group of advisors habituated to personal intrigue to throw off their leadership.[12]

When the king, in 1878, married the seventeen-year-old Princess Mercedes, daughter of the Duke of Montpensier, Lowell attended all the major events, though severely disabled by gout. The "vanity and vexation" of the festivities appalled him — the sense of "anachronism, of decay, and of that unreality which is all the sadder for being gorgeous." Yet he was touched by the young couple "radiant with spirit and hope, rehearsing the idyll which is charming alike to youth and age." He was all the more grieved, therefore, when the young queen, only five months later, was stricken with typhus — a disease so dreaded that her illness had to be officially described as "gastric fever" (otherwise no member of the royal family would have been permitted in the sick chamber). The queen received extreme unction at the very moment the guns were firing a salute in honor of her eighteenth birthday, and four days later the Lowells saw her "dragged to her dreary tomb at the Escorial, followed by the coach and its eight white horses in which she had driven in triumph from the church to the palace on the day of her wedding. The poor brutes tossed their snowy plumes as haughtily now as then." Lowell thought the queen's death was not only a personal tragedy but a national calamity, for she had been amiable, sensible and intelligent, and had she lived might have influenced her husband for the good and given stability to his throne. In a sonnet which he offered to the king, Lowell voiced more than official sorrow:

Hers all that Earth could promise or bestow, —
Youth, Beauty, Love, a crown, the beckoning years . . .

Grim jest of fate! Yet who dare call it blind,
Knowing what life is, what our humankind?

It was not to be Lowell's last — or saddest — encounter with the deadly typhus.[13]

There were several changes of Ministry late in Lowell's tenure, but they were of little consequence to either government policy or Spain's relations with the United States. Lowell's main regret when the Cánovas Ministry lost power in 1879 was that a new Minister of Foreign Affairs replaced Manuel Silvela, with whom he had established agreeable personal relations — initially, by sending Silvela, an avid pipe smoker, some American tobacco to alternate with the blistering home product. Lowell was able to view the changes of Ministry thus calmly because there were no outstanding questions between the two countries, and the minor ones which did exist he had learned to take in stride. The Legation continued to be busy enough throughout his three-year stay, but the business was largely routine. Occasionally a matter of some importance arose — such as the high imposts American citizens had to pay in Cuba — but a more characteristic diplomatic exchange involved the charge laid against the American Consul at Alicante that the mercantile house which he headed had been adulterating its wine with fuchsina.[14]

With his attitude toward his duties in perspective, and no longer constantly wishing himself in Cambridge, Lowell was able to take more pleasure in his surroundings. But he never learned to care much for formal society. The Spanish nobility bored him, he found the hours "frightfully late" and his salary would have prevented his cutting much of a swath even had he wished to. Out of necessity, he attended official functions but could scarcely conceal his impatience with their ceremonial conceits; the cardinals looked to him like "so many disconsolately obese flamingoes hunched on their perch in a zoological garden" and the non-churchmen were so bedecked with medals as to suggest "a discharge of decorations from a blunderbuss." [15]

Given Lowell's horror of official occasions, he awaited with special terror the arrival in Madrid in late 1878 of General and Mrs. Grant. Yet their visit proved easier than Lowell anticipated, largely because the Grants turned out to be as "simple-minded and natural people" as he had ever met. The General went through the required receptions and ceremonials with "a dogged imperturbability" (though after five minutes at the Opera he turned to Mrs. Lowell and asked, "Haven't we had 'most enough of this?"; he could not, he explained, distinguish one tune from another, "knowing only the buglecalls & those after some trouble . . ."). Lowell was especially charmed by Mrs. Grant's equanimity, though he felt that in some part it consisted of naïveté; at one dinner, seated between a French and a Spanish diplomat, and knowing neither language, she blandly went on talking English to them — "her confidence in the language of Shakspeare & Milton as something universally applicable that had triumphed over Babel was sublime." [16]

Though Lowell thought the Spanish vain and parochial, he grew to like them (he liked any people once he came to know them, for his access was never blocked by disabling hostilities or stereotypes). He decided something "Oriental" in his own make-up made him sympathetic with the Spanish genius for "mañana," with their indifference to enterprise and profit and with "the grand way they wrap themselves in their ragged *capa* of a past and find warmth in their pride." They got a good deal out of life without caring about "many things that we are fools enough to care about." There was, in short (for nothing else so well summarized the Virtues), "a flavor of Old Cambridge about 'em, as O.C. used to be when I was young and the world worth having . . ." [17]

For the city of Madrid itself, Lowell had mixed feelings. At first, expecting a *mise en scene* from Calderón, he was disappointed with its modernity, but there was much about it he came to like — the incomparable climate, its variety of fruits, the Campiña ("grander than the Campagna"), the Prado, the Buen Retiro drive. Still, he thought Madrid "a place to get tired of very prettily." It was the noisiest city he had ever known, and noisy without being musical — all the street songs sounded the same, all the voices harsh and nasal. The inhabitants seemed cheerful enough, less grave in fact than he had expected, but he was "struck with the number of deeply furrowed faces," the mark, he assumed, of "hereditary toil." The old porters, tottering under huge loads, especially stirred his angry sympathy; "I turn half communist," Lowell wrote, "when I see them." [18]

He deplored, too, Madrid's lack of learning, cultivated conversation and scholarship. He did attend the theater occasionally, but as for the nation's favorite pastime, bullfighting, his first and last exposure left him shocked at the "brutalising spectacle," all his sympathies on the side of the bull. The major exception to the paucity of cultural life was the Spanish Academy. Lowell was elected a corresponding member late in 1878, and thereafter enjoyed sitting in on the weekly meetings and especially participating in discussions of a new edition of the Dictionary then in progress.[19]

These sessions, and a few friendships, made up the sum of Lowell's social pleasures. "One makes plenty of acquaintances," he wrote Henry James, "but very few friends in Diplomacy." For a man of his solitary tastes, only a few friendships were necessary, and he was fortunate in meeting at least one couple to whom he became genuinely devoted: Juan and Emilia de Riaño. Juan de Riaño, a Senator and a member of the Academy, was a student of archaeology and art history, and his wife, of whom Lowell became especially fond, had had an English mother and had been brought up in England. He originally met the Riaños through her father, Don Pascual de Gayangos, a famous Arabic scholar to whom Lowell had brought letters of introduction. The two families rapidly became friendly, went to the theater, exchanged dinners and books and discussed literature at length. Lowell spent additional time with Señora de Riaño; they talked Spanish twice a week, he helped her with the translation of a fifteenth-century Swabian manuscript written by a traveler in Spain, and with her encouragement (though "blushing like a neophyte") sent her some of the poems he had attempted in Spanish. Through the Riaños, Lowell met enough men of letters (such as Juan Valera, Manuel Tamayo y Baus, and Don Hermenegildo Giner de los Ríos, who tutored him in Spanish) so that his official routine was punctuated by the cultivated conversation he prized. The Riaños were to prove their friendship still more profoundly during a desperate crisis which overtook the Lowells in the summer of 1879.[20]

Frances Lowell had enjoyed Spain — as she did all foreign countries — far more than her husband. Her reserve and formality had found a congenial environment; a newspaper correspondent described her at the king's wedding as "the best dressed and the most dignified person" there, and an American friend reported home that she was looking so "stately and handsome" these days as to rival any competition. Content and in fine health, Mrs. Lowell was pleased when her husband decided in the spring of 1879 (at President Hayes' request) to stay on for at least another year. Lowell had now served his apprenticeship, was held in high regard (a countryman reported hearing daily expressions "of admiration and esteem" for him) and was ready to garner the profits and pleasures of being abroad. He had already found a "new flavor" in Cervantes and Calderón and hoped in the coming year further to perfect his Spanish and to travel more widely in the provinces.[21]

But before settling down for another year or two, Lowell requested and was granted a leave of absence to return home for a visit. They planned to start on the twentieth of June, 1879. Three days before, Mrs. Lowell felt unwell and sent for the doctor. Since she had little fever, he minimized the complaint, but Lowell, remembering that Queen Mercedes' fatal typhus had begun with what was thought to be a cold, was immediately anxious. And with good reason. By nightfall Mrs. Lowell's fever had risen sharply, and a Sister of Charity was brought in to watch over her. Since the nun spoke no English, Mrs. Lowell, whose mind had begun to wander, herself dismissed her after three days and in the dawn of the fourth wrote a note to Señora de Riaño, who came at once and stayed up with her for the next six nights. Her husband, too, came every day, sat with Lowell while he ate his dinner and then got him out for a half hour's walk. After ten days Mrs. Lowell began to rally; Madame de Riaño, Lowell wrote his daughter, "has really saved this dear life to us, for I should certainly have broken down, and her quiet tact, good sense, and experience were invaluable." [22]

But they were far from out of the woods. In the second week of July, Mrs. Lowell had a severe relapse, and there was no longer any doubt that she was a victim of typhus. As her condition steadily worsened, two doctors, one German and one Spanish, took turns in a continuous vigil. The German doctor gave her only two chances in a hundred of surviving and his Spanish colleague, who as head of a Madrid hospital had had considerable experience with typhus, confided to Señora de Riaño that death was inevitable. Twice Mrs. Lowell was thought to be dying and once to have actually died — no breathing could be detected, her hands, feet and nose were cold, her face livid, her lips black. Somehow she got through the desperate crisis and began to rally.

Thus far, Lowell reported home, "the beautiful sweetness & reasonableness of her nature" had persisted through all her suffering. But now followed the cruelest trial of all: for six weeks Mrs. Lowell became "perfectly mad." She believed herself in the time of the Inquisition, insisted that everyone conspired against her and that the walls were full of secret passages through which dreadful shapes entered her room at night to put her on the rack. She said bitter, violent things to her husband — that she would place herself under the protection of the British Legation, since he would not watch over his own wife, indeed that she was not his wife, but Miss Dunlap, and that she would never go home with him. She accused him of speaking ill of her father, of withholding letters from the British Legation, of refusing to write to the Minister of State to have her room cleansed by the police. If Lowell sat up with her, she would insist upon his going to bed, only to reproach him with selfishness for sleeping while she was suffering. Lowell began to fear that he, too, would break down under the terrible strain. He often slept only two hours in twenty-four, night after night lying down on a sofa without undressing so that he might hear her should she moan or need to be turned in order to relieve the pain. His mind felt blunted, though his body — "tough old machine" that it was — bore up well.[23]

The doctors said they had never known a more difficult patient. In her agony, Mrs. Lowell accused them of having broken both her legs — and then insisted on getting out of bed. She slapped the nurses, made impossible demands on them and refused to take any food or medicine, insisting she would live on ice water. Her strength of will in rejecting food was so great that to prevent her from starving the doctors had to introduce a pipe into her stomach and force-feed her. Soon after, she began to gain and intervals of lucidity returned. But there were continual relapses; during one, she talked and gesticulated nervously for twenty-two hours without more than momentary pauses; during another she slept continuously for thirty-six hours. In letters home to his daughter, Lowell tried to minimize the trial; he insisted that despite regressions, "Mama . . . steadily gains more than she loses," but he was deliberately striking an optimistic note for Mabel's sake; she had not been well herself and Lowell wanted to keep her from coming to Madrid, as she wished. To close friends, like the Nortons, Lowell confessed as late as mid-October that he could see little advance in his wife's condition; her legs, especially her swollen knees, caused terrible pain and had to be put in plaster molds, and though she had periods of clarity, her delusions continued.[24]

To make matters still more difficult, the Riaños went off on a trip during one of the periods when Mrs. Lowell seemed to be gaining, which meant that for a time Lowell was entirely without English-speaking companionship other than his secretary, Dwight Reed, who loyally sat up with him night after night. In October the Henry Adamses came to Madrid for a short stay, and Lowell, who had not left the house in four months, found their company a Godsend. They reported home that he "keeps up bravely and is as kind and cheerful as possible to us," but that "there is nothing in her condition to warrant much hope." In November old friends, Mr. and Mrs. John W. Field, arrived and they too were a great consolation — so far as anyone could be, for the condition of Mrs. Lowell's mind gave constant anxiety. When delusional, she kept asking to be taken home, sometimes insisting that she *was* in the United States and could easily enough be driven directly to Elmwood. During periods of clarity, she was hardly less pathetic: "You can't patch me up," she would say, "I can never again be good for anything." [25]

At last, in December, almost six months after the original attack, Mrs. Lowell seemed really better. By Christmas, she had regained "all her old sweetness & gentleness," and with her encouragement Lowell even began dining out occasionally, "& enjoying it, which I can hardly say I used to do." "We are sometimes happier than we ever were before," he wrote Mabel, "& you know that in all these twenty-two years there was never a cloud between us." In the midst of this renewed contentment came an additional piece of good news: on January 19, 1880, a telegram arrived from Secretary of State Evarts informing Lowell that he had been nominated to be Minister to England.[26]

The appointment had been in the works for some time, though Lowell had known nothing of it. Howells, Norton and George

William Curtis had suggested it to Hayes as early as June, 1879, but the President had at that time already put out feelers to F. T. Frelinghuysen, and it was only after he had rejected the post that it became possible to appoint Lowell. The offer took him entirely by surprise and he put in an anxious day before replying. He felt he owed the Administration whatever experience he may have gained but feared the responsibility of the new position and worried, too, whether he would be able decently to support it on a salary of $17,500 (plus about $3500 for contingent expenses). But he had learned in Spain that display added little if anything to one's influence, impressing only the vulgar. Since it was perfectly well known in England that he was neither a duke nor a millionaire, he decided the salary would probably prove adequate. There remained the basic problem of Mrs. Lowell's health. But this, too, seemed a surmountable obstacle. She had been steadily gaining for weeks and the doctor believed she could be safely removed to England within a few months; in the meantime Lowell might go there alone to present his credentials and then return to bring over his wife. Having weighed these matters, he telegraphed Evarts: "Feel highly honored by confidence of the President. Could accept if allowed two months delay." To which Evarts at once replied: "The proposed arrangement will be satisfactory." [27]

But it was not to be so simple. Lowell decided to leave at once for London; he had to present his credentials as soon as possible because his successor to Spain had already been announced and his own house in Madrid was rented only until March 1. Mrs. Lowell had been improving so steadily that he thought it safe to leave her for a few weeks, especially since the Fields were still in Madrid and could keep her company. But then, on the eve of his departure, Mrs. Lowell had a sudden setback. Within a few days she seemed to rally, and with her usual "courage & unselfishness," begged that no fuss be made over her. But soon she was once more helpless and Lowell, who could neither leave her nor move her with safety, was at his wits' end. He feared that if he went to London, it might have a disastrous effect, yet the only alternative was to give up the English appointment. He delayed another ten days and then, with Mrs. Lowell apparently beginning to improve and with further hesitation impossible, he decided to risk a rapid trip to England.[28]

By the time he reached Paris, word came that her condition had worsened; when he got to London, a telegram arrived saying it was "too late & useless" for him to return. Lowell assumed that his wife had died and was plunged into grief. But the next morning a more encouraging cable came and each succeeding one announced improvement. His spirits revived, and when Henry James saw him, Lowell could talk only of his wife — "her beauty, grace, sweetness, cleverness, etc. — in the most touching & tender manner." James thought Lowell looked old and worn, yet relieved to get away from the prolonged vigil of the sickroom: "he has a most childlike temperament in his way of taking troubles, & relief from them." In James' opinion, Mrs. Lowell's death would be an advantage, for he thought her disabled condition would make Lowell's position in London impossible. Even without this impediment, James believed, Lowell would have trouble coping with the big London world: he was too "simple & helpless," the arduous social demands of his position would "bore him to death" and as a result he would shirk them. But James had also mistakenly predicted, shortly after Lowell's appointment to Spain, that he "would not understand half" of what he saw at Madrid.[29]

Lowell got through the required formalities as rapidly as possible; in the round of ceremonials, his heart felt "not so heavy." He briefly met Gladstone, Lord and Lady Ripon and Matthew Arnold, and was everywhere "overwhelmed with kindness." And when he presented his letters to Queen Victoria, she enquired after Mrs. Lowell "with a *human* tone" that deeply touched him.[30]

Arriving back in Spain after a two-week absence, Lowell

found that while he had been away, his wife's life had indeed been despaired of again, and that only her marvelous constitution had saved her. But she was still utterly prostrated, and Lowell decided it would mean certain death for her to remain longer in Madrid; he resolved, against the opinion of the doctors, to remove her at all hazards. When a Mr. and Mrs. J. D. Wheeler of New Haven, with whom Lowell had only the barest acquaintance, offered their house in Biarritz ("with a humanity which is only to be found in Americans"), Lowell accepted. He received leave from the State Department — for with Parliament dissolved, his absence from London would be of little consequence — and on March 22, 1880, Mrs. Lowell was carried to the railroad terminal "on a kind of palanquin." She bore the train journey of twenty hours with "her wonted fortitude," Mr. Wheeler was at the Biarritz station with a covered *fourgon* large enough to receive her chair-bed, and soon she was safely installed in the Wheeler house. The change seemed to do immediate good; her mind cleared, and in a few days she was able to sleep without drugs. But once more, hope gave way to despair. After six weeks of continual improvement, she again had a serious relapse. Nonetheless, Lowell decided to risk transporting her to England.[31]

And so it was that in mid-May, 1880, after a desperate year, Lowell arrived in London to take up his position as Minister. It remained to be seen whether, as Henry James had predicted, Mrs. Lowell would prove a liability and Lowell himself too little a man of the world to cope with his responsibilities.

CHAPTER XIV

MINISTER TO ENGLAND

LOWELL'S APPOINTMENT to the English mission had been widely applauded. "Your path," wrote Henry Adams, "ought to be an easy one, if general good will can make it so." The London press, forgetting or overlooking Lowell's anglophobia during the Civil War, unanimously acclaimed his coming. Almost more surprising, given the built-in suspicions of diplomatic life, was the cordiality of his reception by the staff at the American Legation. If no man is a hero to his valet, Lowell was to prove that one can be to his secretary. From the very start, William Jones Hoppin, First Secretary at the Legation, was charmed by his new chief. Hoppin, a sixty-seven-year-old bachelor who had given up a successful law career three years before to take up the London post, had a good deal in common with Lowell. Both were New Englanders (and strenuous ones) and both were devoted to literature, Hoppin's amateur efforts at poetry and translation predisposing him to adulation of a "master." Yet he came to value Lowell's human qualities more than his literary ones; he spoke admiringly of Lowell's simple unaffected manners, his kindliness, his good temper, his capacity for appreciation coupled with freedom "from all petty jealousies & suspicions." Hoppin's devotion was the greater tribute for not being unqualified. He saw Lowell in perspective, the faults along with the virtues. He came to know well Lowell's carelessness with detail, his willingness to offer opinions on all subjects, sometimes in the form of *dicta* and often on matters about which he knew little. Yet withal, he found Lowell generous, amiable, warm-hearted, a sometimes wayward but thoroughly lovable man.[1]

Lowell's cordial reception augured well for his ministership. And the auguries, for once, proved accurate. His record as a diplomat would have its blemishes, but neither the issues nor the errors would be of sufficient magnitude to mar his larger success as a public figure. His personal popularity in England was to be immense, and since his admirers would include many figures prominent in society and government, these personal triumphs served a real if intangible function in improving his country's image. The United States was to profit from the reflected glory of her representative.

Not that Anglo-American relations were at a low ebb at the time of Lowell's arrival. On the contrary, the Treaty of Washington in 1871 had settled most of the issues outstanding between the two countries and the bitter feeling created by the Civil War had been banked, even if not wholly extinguished. Certainly Lowell's own anglophobia, once so strong that Henry James thought it approached morbidity, had greatly cooled. Even at his angriest, during the war years, Lowell had never entirely lost his admiration for England; it was the only country, he believed, that had succeeded "in combining permanence and the possibility of change," its privileged class had had an instinct for opening its doors at the right moment. Lowell would still be capable during his years as Minister of flaring up at any hint of English condescension, but his fondness for the country progressively strengthened — so much so that he would even praise its climate, an opinion scarcely shared by the English themselves.[2]

The only immediate problem Lowell faced on his arrival was a personal one: Mrs. Lowell's continued poor health. It was decided that she would convalesce more rapidly away from the hectic London scene and she therefore accepted the hospitality of English friends, the William Darwins, who lived in Hampshire. She stayed there the better part of three months; Lowell visited her regularly and for some of the time she had the additional company of Mabel and Edward Burnett, who came over to England for a short visit. At the end of the three months, though still unable to walk, Mrs. Lowell was much improved and her mind again seemed entirely clear. In the fall of 1880 she returned to London, her gains still painfully slow, but her spirit cheerful and her will strong; when Leslie Stephen came to dinner she participated fully (though she had to be carried into the dining room) and he thought he had never seen her so bright and talkative. That whole winter, though, she remained quite helpless, unable to use her legs, and her hands painfully swollen. But by spring she began to move about more freely and gradually expanded her activities. Her frailty had at least the incidental benefit of excusing them from entertaining, and they welcomed the chance to live plainly and quietly in their small house just off Lowndes Street. Hoppin, with obvious approval, noted that no American Minister had ever maintained so unpretentious an establishment.[3]

If Lowell's home life was kept simple, his outside social activities provided a counterpoint of splendor. With his wife's progress unbroken, Lowell's spirits soared — he had the "talk of a lad," Leslie Stephen reported to Norton, full of fun and warmth. As his reputation for geniality and wit spread, invitations began to multiply and Lowell, somewhat to his own surprise, accepted them. While Mrs. Lowell remained at home, slowly convalescing, he dined out almost every day and generally spent one or two days a week visiting at various country houses. His fellow guests at dinner parties often included such luminaries as Gladstone, Froude, The Prince of Wales, Thomas Hardy, Lecky, Millais or Lord Rothschild. Lowell's daily path was "so strewn with stars and garters," he remarked, that skill was required to pick his way. But not all the parties were star-studded and far from all the conversations sparkled. He found the run-of-the-mill dinner partner dull, the talk not nearly so good as that to which he had been accustomed at the Saturday Club. The English made a lion of him, he believed, because he served up the bit of "Worcestershire sauce" required by their "sluggish palate." Yet he would rarely let his mind really "gambol," he claimed, for if he did his fellow diners would look on him "like the famous deaf man at the dancers," wondering to what music he was capering. They called Americans superficial, Lowell wrote Norton, but "thank God, dear Charles, that our nerves are nearer the surface, not so deeply imbedded in fat or muscle that wit must take a pitchfork to us," nor our sensations so unused that we find "Wordsworth's emotion over a common flower so very wonderful." [4]

If the dining-out routine sometimes bored him — in his engagement book he once entered "Witch of Endor" as his hostess for the evening — he obviously enjoyed the social round, the flattery he heard on all sides, the respite from scholarship and the sickroom. Nor is there any doubt that Lowell made a decided hit. Hoppin described him as "a great favorite wherever he goes," and Leslie Stephen believed that no minister had ever been better liked: "I speak of him casually as an old friend, when I want to puff myself a bit." Lowell won a special reputation for graceful, succinct speeches and came to be much in demand at public occasions or for after-dinner toasts, a talent he liked to deny:

When I hear your set speeches that start with a pop,
Then wander and maunder, too feeble to stop,
With vague apprehension from popular rumor
There used to be something by mortals called humor,
Beginning again when you thought they were done,
Respectable, sensible, weighing a ton,
And as near to the present occasions of men
As a Fast Day discourse of the year eighteen ten,
I — well, I sit still, and my sentiment smother,
For am I not also a bore and a brother?

Despite his modest self-appraisal, Lowell was widely compared as an after-dinner speaker to Lord Rosebery, Lord Houghton and Sir Henry Irving, then the reigning masters of the genre, and there were some who thought him the superior of any in the special way he managed to combine felicity and authority, the amusing with the instructive.[5]

Still, Lowell was not quite the universal idol that his friends believed. His popularity was less unanimous in private than in public. Complaints against him were lodged from various quarters. Americans who were resident in London thought Lowell too much attuned to English ways; he preferred hobnobbing with dukes and duchesses, they said, to dining out with fellow countrymen. According to Hoppin, Lowell did decline the hospitality of Americans in London, or, at best, accepted it begrudgingly. But perhaps it was a venial sin to prefer the company of Matthew Arnold, Leslie Stephen or Browning to that of Mr. and Mrs. American-Abroad.[6]

But some complaints about Lowell came from Englishmen. Though he could speak with modesty on subjects about which he was deeply knowledgeable — and there were many — he could also be relentlessly opinionated on subjects about which he knew little, asserting views, without hesitation or qualification, in the donnish tones of a lecturer. And his bluntness or wit, when persistent enough, could shade into rudeness; Mrs. Green, widow of the historian, complained once of Lowell's "brutally chaffing her" at a dinner party by returning endlessly to the charge that American women were superior to English. George W. Smalley, the famed American journalist then resident in London, admired Lowell's conversational brilliance but thought his inability to let a challenge go unnoticed or a pretension go unrebuked produced more than a little fear and trembling in his hosts. The characteristic response to entertaining Lowell, Smalley believed, was this: "I need not tell you how much I like Lowell and how delighted I am to have him here as often as he will come. But from the moment he enters my house till he is gone I am in a panic." Perhaps this occasional pugnacity is what Henry James had in mind when he wrote home to Grace Norton that Lowell was "not a *real* man of the world," not sufficiently acquainted with the subtleties of London attitudes and traditions always to strike the right note (though James, who *was* always aware of his audience, wrote Norton that Lowell was "universally liked & appreciated").[7]

Lowell was most likely to bore or insult a dinner partner if he got off on what had become a favorite topic with him — the Jews. He had come to delight in the bizarre pastime of discovering that everyone of talent was in some way descended from Jewish ancestors, and he would play the game of "detection" with a relish that approached monomania. He based his discoveries less on physiognomy than names; every name which could not be instantly derived from Latin or Anglo-Saxon became "Jewish," resulting, needless to say, in the ascription of Hebrew origins to the majority of people he met. Among others whom he believed descended from Jews were Gladstone, Lord Granville (the telltale family name was *Leveson*-Gower) and, he rather contentedly admitted, himself (that middle name, Russell). Sometimes Lowell relied on still less tangible factors in "proving" the Jewish origins of some noted man. Thus Browning, though he tried to conceal the fact, *obviously* had Jewish blood. Why? Because he *looked* Jewish, because he had once used a Hebrew line in a poem and then canceled it in a later edition, and because whenever you dined with a Jew in London, Browning was sure to be there.[8]

Conscious of his own obsession, Lowell would discuss The Jewish Origins of Practically Everyone with at least occasional drollery. Still, it was difficult for one to know whether he meant his "discoveries" to be taken as compliments or accusations. In fact he was uncertain himself, his admiration for the Jews alternating with stereotypic fears about them. Thus he could describe them as "a people remarkable above almost all others for the possession of the highest and clearest intellect" and yet in an official despatch could ascribe some of the passion of Spanish politics to the large infusion of Jewish blood in the upper and middle classes: "the most intense, restless, aspiring and unscrupulous blood of all." He could speak of the prejudice against Disraeli as "medieval, of a piece with the enlightened public opinion which dictated the legend of Hugh of Lincoln," and yet he could demonstrate some medievalisms of his own by rhetorically asking, "Where would a Jew be among a society of primitive men without pockets, and therefore *a fortiori* without a hole in them?" [9]

Lowell's ambivalent fascination with the Jews reflected the contradictory strains of his divided New England inheritance. On the one side was the Puritan tradition, with its respect for the chosen people of the Old Testament and its direct identification with those upright, austere, sternly moral Israelites who had searched for a Promised Land. But the Puritan view of the Jews conflicted with an image which had become manifest in the late nineteenth century: the degraded immigrant Jew, the vendor, the money changer, the despised outcast. Lowell, even while deploring the conditions under which Jews currently suffered, exhibited some of the mythic fears which helped to justify and perpetuate those conditions — especially the fear (mixed, in his case, with a little hopeful anticipation) of Jewish "domination." His uneasiness was shared, sometimes in more pronounced form, by many of his Cambridge friends. Richard Henry Dana, Jr., in a public speech in 1868 before the Massachusetts legislature, denounced the state's usury law as one benefiting only "the Jews emerging from their alleys." And Norton, in a private letter to Lowell, expressed concern that Jewish students beginning to "inundate" Harvard might "keep the Christian youths away." [10]

Yet Lowell, and most of his friends, were incapable of the harsher anti-Semitism which seized upon such New England aristocrats of the next generation as Brooks and Henry Adams and such patricians of New England ancestry as John Jay

Chapman. By then Jewish immigration had waxed while the Puritan tradition had still further waned. The pessimism, moreover, with which this later generation of aristocrats regarded the country's heightened devotion to materialism found a convenient scapegoat in the Jew. Though the Adams brothers and Chapman also had their share of admiration for certain "Jewish qualities," it gave way, especially as they grew older, to a dislike more virulent than anything known in Lowell's generation. Thus Henry Adams, as early as the 1870's, could write while traveling in Spain, "I have now seen enough of Jews and Moors to entertain more liberal views in regard to the Inquisition, and to feel that, though the ignorant may murmur, the Spaniards saw and pursued a noble aim." And John Jay Chapman, approaching the point of phobia by the 1920's, could laud the Ku Klux Klan for being on "the right track" in recognizing the peril in the Catholic and Jewish Questions.[11]

With Lowell, on the other hand, uneasiness about Jewish "aggression" was offset by respect for Jewish history and for the Jewish commitment to learning and achievement. If he felt some distaste for what he believed the nineteenth-century Jew had become, he also felt some responsibility for that decline. In a public address in 1884, he spoke disapprovingly of the "frenzies of exclusion" which for centuries had denied

> all share in the government of the world . . . to perhaps the ablest, certainly the most tenacious, race that had ever lived in it . . . We drove them into a corner, but they had their revenge, as the wronged are always sure to have it sooner or later. They made their corner the counter and banking-house of the world, and thence they rule it and us with the ignobler sceptre of finance.

Much of Lowell's fear was fantasy, but not fantasy impervious to compassion; he refused to condone any measures of discrimination and repression. And he and his friends at least felt some guilt for such anti-Jewish feeling as they harbored. They could say apologetically with Norton (as representatives of the next generation, like Henry Adams, never could): "My pet prejudices are two, one against Jews, the other against Germans. I hope to outlive them . . ." [12]

If Lowell's discourses on the Jews, his occasional insensitivities, his slighting of the American colony, produced detractors, they were in a decided minority. He was lionized to such an extent that he began to wonder if his sole professional duty would be "to exercise my jaws in mastication." That, and dealing with the flood of Americans who (as in any Legation) rushed to confide their troubles, turning Lowell into a "minister of the Gospel & father Confessor, whose parish includes the entire Union." But he was to have functions other than those of Sybarite or Divine. His diplomatic responsibilities, while never of major significance, proved more substantial, and more personally burdensome, than anything he had experienced in Spain.[13]

Lowell's five years in England coincided almost to the day with the second Ministry of William Gladstone. In the general election of 1880 Gladstone had defeated the Tories led by Disraeli (whom Lowell, on first meeting, described as "uglier than the wildest dream of Gladstone would picture him"). Lowell was to disagree with some of Gladstone's policies, especially British intervention in Egypt, but was in general sympathetic to his administration. And on the Irish Question, the one he became most entangled with in his official capacity, Lowell would approve Gladstone's efforts at pacification even while doubting their sufficiency. On a personal level, the two men apparently cared little for each other, though their contact was limited. Lowell was puzzled and sometimes bored by the apparently equal interest Gladstone took in all subjects, and his tendency to be "diffusively emphatic" about all. He even had doubts about Gladstone's oratorical prowess, though this was much admired. His speeches, Lowell thought, contained little substance; the real secret of his power lay in his ability to improvise convictions.[14]

Lowell was much fonder of Gladstone's Foreign Minister, Lord Granville, with whom he had cordial relations both official and social. Lowell developed admiration for Granville's skill and real affection for his person; "his blandness," Lowell wrote, "was not softness but the amenity of a character strong enough to afford it." When Granville on one occasion wrote Lowell to ask if "the most engaged man in England" would come for a visit, Lowell accepted, and then, when leaving, wrote in the Visitors' Book:

> *The most engaged man he calls* me,
> *A kind of Mormon fate presaging;*
> *I with more verity call* he
> *Of all the most engaging.*[15]

Fortunately, their friendly feeling was never unduly strained by serious diplomatic controversy. The bulk of Lowell's official notes to Granville were hardly such as to provoke heated debate: the patent for a breech-loading carbine, American land claims in Fiji, cattle disease, the whereabouts of John Paul Jones' skull, the protection of American missionaries in Persia. Only two important issues arose during Lowell's tenure: the one involved the North American fisheries and came to a head in 1881, the other concerned the imprisonment of naturalized or native Americans of Irish descent and reached a climax in the spring of 1882. Lowell's handling of the second, and more explosive, issue brought him considerable abuse from home and subjected him to the only real unpleasantness of his five-year stay in England. On both issues, his diplomatic skill was questioned by his superiors. There was some justice in their criticism, but only some — not nearly enough to warrant the extensive blame that was leveled at him.

The North American fisheries question had had a long and tangled history. The major issues regarding it had been settled between the two countries by the 1871 Treaty of Washington.

But it is often the case that international agreements can be jeopardized by local incidents. Just such an incident took place early in 1878 at Fortune Bay, Newfoundland, when native fishermen destroyed the nets of their American rivals and forced them from the coast. They justified the attack on the grounds that the Americans had violated local laws which prohibited certain kinds of fishing. But the American government, taking up the claims of its citizens, insisted that provincial statutes could not compromise rights guaranteed by international treaty, and formally demanded compensation from the British government. Lord Salisbury, just before vacating the Foreign Office in the spring of 1880, declined to entertain any claims for damage. The American fisherman, he insisted, had not only violated local statutes, but by fishing directly from the shore had even exceeded their Treaty privileges. In so doing they had been the "first and real cause of the mischief" which followed.[16]

Thus matters stood when Lowell became Minister. In itself the Fortune Bay episode was of minor importance, but it had produced considerable publicity and ill will in the United States, probably because it gave a focus to the resentment against England which still lingered from the Civil War. And as such, the episode could disturb the improved relations between the two countries which had followed upon the 1871 Treaty. As Edward Thornton, the English Minister to the United States, wrote Lord Granville, "a great deal of soreness and bitterness has been engendered by this affair, and I would venture to suggest whether, taking advantage of the advent of a new Government at home, something might not be done . . . to allay this bad feeling." Thornton made the point, and it could hardly be contested, that even if the Newfoundland fishermen had been justified in law (itself debatable), they had certainly been wrong to take the law into their own hands. Some compensation for the destruction of property, he suggested, might therefore be in order.[17]

Secretary of State Evarts took direct issue with the position

Lord Salisbury had earlier enunciated. International agreements, Evarts insisted, could never be subordinated to local legislation, and the Treaty of Washington had clearly given American fishermen rights to the Newfoundland coast free of all restrictions. Angered at Salisbury's peremptory dismissal of his argument (Evarts was a vain man, Thornton commented, who took diplomatic rebuffs as personal slights), the American Secretary decided on a new tactic with which to exert pressure on the British. He asked Congress to reimpose all duties on products from the Canadian fisheries as they had existed before the Treaty of Washington. In Thornton's view, Evarts had chosen a poor maneuver: some of the principal members of the new English government, including Lord Granville, had been in office at the time of the Washington Treaty, and were likely to be angered by Evarts' efforts to dismember it.[18]

Whether because of or despite Evarts' pressure, Granville did decide to reopen the whole question when he took over the Foreign Office in 1880. And Lowell played some part in bringing him to that decision. He told Granville, in an interview on June 9, 1880, that feeling in the United States on the Fortune Bay affair went far deeper than the British government appreciated. The two men then talked over the possibility of separating the question of damages from the larger issue with which it had become entangled — the interpretation of the Treaty of Washington. It could be agreed, they felt, that the local laws of Newfoundland were not to be put into effect by a mob, even if those laws *were* compatible with the Treaty. Lowell telegraphed news of this breakthrough to Evarts, who expressed pleasure at the friendly disposition of the new government and said the President was ready to entertain any suggestion for resolving the dispute.[19]

No further action was taken for several months. Congress reduced the urgency by adjourning in late June without reimposing import duties (Thornton believed many Congressmen had recognized that such a move would be unfair to the new

British government, which had not been responsible for Lord Salisbury's refusal of damages, and that it might create antagonisms which could actually prevent an agreement). Another reason for the diplomatic hiatus was the onset of a Presidential election in the United States. Lowell's sympathies in the canvass were with James Garfield, the Republican nominee, over General Hancock, the Democrat. But when Garfield won a narrow victory in November, Lowell's enthusiasm was tempered by the problems raised by a change of Administration. He was uncertain, for one thing, if he would be retained as Minister — and he wished to be. Following form, he at once offered Garfield his resignation, but made it clear that he would be glad to remain if the President-elect saw fit to keep him. Lowell heard nothing for a month, but Garfield then sent personal word that barring an emergency which might necessitate a change, he would be gratified if Lowell would stay on.[20]

A second cause for anxiety after Garfield's election, one less readily allayed, was the announcement that James G. Blaine would be Secretary of State in the new Administration. Lowell's relations with Evarts had not been cordial — and they were shortly to worsen — but he could hardly look on Blaine, a man he had long distrusted, as an improvement. The British were no less dismayed by the appointment. Thornton had earlier described Blaine to Granville as "a noisy, mischievous demagogue and most unscrupulous; he hesitates at no falsehood." To this grim estimate Thornton now added that Blaine had no experience in diplomacy and had "a general dislike for all foreigners, and especially the English." [21]

But Blaine was not to take office until March, 1881; time remained, it was hoped, to settle the Fortune Bay affair. Even before the Presidential election, Granville had made a concrete offer. Back in July, he had received a confidential memo from Selbourne, the Lord Chancellor, stating his opinion that although the American fishermen did have to abide by any reasonable local legislation to which native fishermen were subjected, the Newfoundlanders had nonetheless been wrong to take the law into their own hands; if, therefore, the larger question of Treaty obligations could be avoided or postponed, Selbourne advised offering compensation for damages at Fortune Bay. This line of reasoning corresponded exactly to that which Granville and Lowell had earlier outlined together. And so, in late October, 1880, Granville offered £15,000 to cover the Fortune Bay damages (and also two other more recent, minor episodes). Evarts, after more than a three-month delay, accepted the offer and expressed the hope that the two governments could also soon come to agreement on the larger question of which rules and regulations would hereafter govern the fisheries.[22]

Then, on the verge of agreement, the whole negotiation suddenly fell through. At the last minute the English interjected an additional demand — that the £15,000 be accepted for *all* Newfoundland fishery claims up to January 1, 1881. The Americans rejected this new proviso, and a round of mutual recrimination set in. According to Hoppin and Lowell the main culprit was Evarts, who had let Granville's October offer of £15,000 slide until a fortnight before going out of office and then, in a rush to gain credit for settling the dispute, had tried to do so "offhand." Evarts, on his part, accused Lowell of failing to communicate American intentions to Granville with sufficient precision and force, and accused Granville of changing the terms of indemnity after they had been agreed to. Lord Selbourne (showing that larger English impartiality which implicated all Americans in the failure of one) objected to the "grasping" tone of Evarts' despatches — so "characteristic of American diplomacy when international claims (especially money claims) are in question." Granville at least kept his peace, but he was incensed at Evarts' accusations against Lowell and offered to write a despatch to Thornton "saying all sorts of kind things about the discretion and zeal" which Lowell had shown in negotiation — an offer which Lowell graciously declined.[23]

There was some truth to all the accusations, though to the

degree that a tangled situation can be unraveled, Evarts was more at fault than Lowell, and the English government more than either. Evarts did delay answering Granville's October offer until February 4, and Thornton for one (agreeing with Lowell) believed that Evarts, dilatory by nature, had been uncertain for some time what course to take in regard to Fortune Bay and had then "suddenly wished to come to a settlement of the question before he left office." It is also true that the peremptory tone of some of Evarts' despatches had not been calculated to conciliate the English — nor to endear him to his own Minister.[24]

Lowell's responsibility for the breakdown is less evident, at least less tangible. It is true he adopted a pliant tone with Granville and that he withheld all but the sense of one of Evarts' more assertive despatches. But Lowell's moderation was appreciated by the English (which is not, to be sure, any verification of its wisdom), and as for the despatch of which he gave only the sense, Evarts had specifically authorized him to use his discretion when communicating its contents. The more generalized charge that Lowell was inattentive to the details of his duties had some truth, though not as applied to the Fortune Bay episode. Lowell did leave details — sometimes even the writing of whole despatches — to Hoppin. And he admitted as much himself: "You have been the officer of the deck," he once wrote Hoppin, "& I have taken my airing on the quarter-deck & the height of the sun now & then for appearances & my own amusement" (an admission not to be taken at face value; Lowell could be self-deprecating for the sake of graciousness). At any rate, in regard to the Fortune Bay affair he had undoubtedly applied himself diligently. Hoppin insisted that Lowell had shown "great activity and good nature through it all," and since this statement was made in Hoppin's private journal, it could not have been prompted merely by a wish to defend the reputation of a man he admired. Yet Lowell himself was not entirely at ease with the role he had played. He had a nagging sense that *somehow* he had contributed to the breakdown in negotiations; perhaps, he thought, he had misused the discretion given him by Evarts in presenting only part of that despatch; perhaps it was even possible he had misunderstood Granville, that the offer of £15,000 had all along carried larger implications. Lowell was sure he had not — that is, almost sure, for the Puritan conscience is never done lacerating itself, especially when others are insisting that a whipping is warranted.[25]

In any case, the chief responsibility for the diplomatic failure must rest on the English government. Having made an offer of £15,000 and having been notified that Evarts accepted it, Granville then unexpectedly interposed the added condition. His reasons for doing so are unclear, especially since he agreed with Evarts and Lowell that if possible the question should be settled before a "hostile successor" took over the State Department. But apparently the British government had been annoyed at Evarts' tactics and tone, distrustful in general of "grasping" American negotiators and pressed by a Tory opposition which accused them of being timid and truckling in the face of American "belligerence." And so at the last minute, Granville had injected the new condition; he had to guard, he said, against the possibility of additional American demands in the future. The English apparently feared that further claims would later be presented for depredations against American fishermen and that additional compensation would then be demanded.[26]

Evarts was willing to give Granville assurance that the £15,000 would cover all Newfoundland claims thus far presented, but was unwilling to include all claims, whether presented or not. Thornton believed the English government would be safe in accepting this partial assurance, and Lowell thought his government would be just as safe in granting the more inclusive guarantee. But neither country would further modify its stand. Granville believed that the intrinsic value of the Fortune Bay damages was at most £7000 and that the offer of £15,000 was therefore so liberal that it should secure him from the risk of all possible future claims — and he looked on Evarts' unwillingness to give such security as justifying apprehension about later suits. Evarts, on the other hand, did not see how he could sacrifice the rights of unknown parties who might subsequently appear with well-grounded claims.[27]

Thus matters stood in March, 1881, when James G. Blaine took office as Secretary of State. All parties — Evarts, Lowell, Thornton and Granville — assumed that with the new Administration there would be less chance than ever of successfully resolving the controversy. Yet to their surprise Blaine managed to come to terms within a few months — though only by acceding to British demands.

Having received the impression from Evarts that Lowell had bungled his end (Evarts told Blaine that "Lowell was a good poet but a damned bad Minister"), Blaine, with the approval of the English government, transferred the major share of the negotiations to himself and Thornton. In his first interview with Thornton, Blaine assured him that he was not hostile to England, as commonly believed, and that he was eager to settle the dispute. Initially, Blaine felt he could not agree to terms which his predecessor had but recently refused, and for a short time he tried to get the English to throw in an extra £1000 to help him save face. Some of the British Cabinet were willing to go along but Granville stood firm on his last offer, apparently sensing that in any case Blaine would give in. And so he did. After "convincing" himself that no outstanding claims existed anyway, he offered a receipt in full for *all* claims, both presented and unpresented; the larger issue of interpreting the Treaty of Washington was postponed, by mutual agreement, until a later date. In one sense Blaine gave the British even better terms than those they had requested, for he guaranteed all claims up to March 4, instead of only January 1, as they had asked. He did so, he wrote Thornton, "in the hope that you will recognise in it a disposition on the part of the United States to be not merely just, but liberal in dealing with Her Majesty's Government." But if such was indeed Blaine's intention, it was scarcely appreciated. Thornton did credit him with having been amiable, frank and straightforward throughout, but he still felt that Blaine was "an impulsive and dangerous man" and would require "very careful management" in case of any serious question between the two countries. However ungrateful Thornton's comment, it was not without point. Before the year was out, Blaine, in a brusque maneuver, tried to bring about a revision in the long-standing Clayton-Bulwer Treaty. His efforts had no immediate result — other than to reinvigorate British suspicion of him.[28]

Lowell's first major bout with diplomacy did not leave him especially happy. But a sudden turn of events made it seem, in any case, that he would be recalled. On July 2, 1881, President Garfield was struck down by an assassin's bullet and, after lingering for weeks in great pain, died on September 19. Lowell believed Garfield's dignity and fortitude during the last two months of his life could almost be called a political event, for it had done more in England "to make a juster estimate of American character possible" than could years of commercial or social intercourse. As Lowell said in a memorial meeting at Exeter Hall, "it is something that two great nations have looked at each other kindly through their tears. It will at least be more awkward to quarrel hereafter." And he wrote Gladstone that the many letters and expressions of sympathy received at the Legation "go to show that differences are superficial & that the bonds of race & language *do* count for something. Blood is thicker than water after all." If the vocabulary Lowell used to express his belief in Anglo-American unity is now outmoded, the sentiment at least is not.[29]

There had been rumors even before Garfield's death that Lowell would be replaced — by Evarts, it was said, or possibly Grant. Now, with Chester A. Arthur as President, Lowell's position seemed in real jeopardy. And however disenchanted he may occasionally have felt with the diplomatic life, he decidedly wished to stay on; he liked being a salaried lion. Besides, Mrs. Lowell was now greatly improved. She walked more easily, looked (in Lowell's eyes) "young and handsome," and had even developed a new hobby of watercolor painting. Lowell dreaded any abrupt change of scene which might jar her steady progress. But when in October he set off for Italy and Germany on a two-month leave of absence (his wife was not yet well enough to join him), he had still had no definite word as to his future. Finally in Venice, the city appropriately which in his "old age" had come to delight him more than any other, the welcome news arrived — Blaine had telegraphed bidding him to take his house for another year. When Granville was told, he wired Lowell, "delighted to hear the good news. It has given me real pleasure." [30]

Blaine had himself left the Cabinet by the time Lowell returned to London from his holiday. F. T. Frelinghuysen of New Jersey was the new Secretary of State, and even before taking office, he sent Lowell informal word that he meant to retain him as Minister. Lowell, who had chafed under both his former chiefs, welcomed the change of command, though later he lumped together all three Secretaries as having hampered him either with "*insouciance* or imbecility." Frelinghuysen, though long in politics, had had no experience in foreign affairs, and the British thought poorly of him from the first. Their Chargé d'Affaires in the United States warned Granville, with sweeping invective, that Frelinghuysen was "a dried up, pompous, cold blooded man with small brains, little common sense and obstinate . . ." And Lionel S. Sackville West, who replaced Thornton as the English Minister to the United States, cheerfully repeated the rumor that Frelinghuysen owed his appointment to President Arthur's fondness for one of his married daughters. Kinder words were said about J. C. Bancroft Davis, who was coming in as Under-Secretary. He had had wide diplomatic experience, having served in the Grant Administration as Assistant Secretary of State under Hamilton Fish, and the English hoped and believed that Davis would be the actual if not the official head of the State Department.[31]

The new Administration was in office only a few months when the most serious diplomatic controversy of Lowell's career began to take form. Speaking broadly, the issue was Ireland, though in his official capacity Lowell's attention would be absorbed by only one aspect of the problem: the arrest and detention in Britain of native-born or naturalized Irish-Americans suspected of working in behalf of Irish independence. To appreciate the injustice of the charges which were to be leveled at Lowell for his handling of this smaller question, his attitude on the larger must be understood.

Lowell's position on "The Irish Question" was essentially that of the Irish leader in Parliament, Charles Stewart Parnell: that is, Lowell was for Home Rule, a separate legislature for Ireland. If Ireland was ever to be made as loyal as Scotland, he argued, it had to be recognized at the outset that "she is not England and never can be." Lowell's views were thus more radical than those of the Gladstone Administration, which alternated between liberalizing the Irish land laws and passing coercive acts to maintain order. Lowell believed Gladstone genuinely intended that the Land Law of 1881 would improve conditions of rent, tenure and sale, but he believed, too, that in attempting to propitiate both landlords and tenants, the bill had "the weakness inherent in all compromises." As for the most recent "Coercive Act," the 1881 Protection of Person and Property Bill, Lowell thought it both harsh and impolitic. The act declared that any person "reasonably suspected" of "treasonable" activity in Ireland could be arrested and detained for the act's duration without bail or trial. In other words, the act suspended *habeas corpus*, and Lowell unsparingly denounced it to Frelinghuysen as "arbitrary and . . . contrary to the spirit and fundamental principles of the British Constitution." Moreover, in a private letter to Gladstone just before the passage of the act, Lowell, treading like one of those fearless angels, wrote that he was "shocked by the violent measures proposed for the Irish malady . . . We have our Ireland in the Southern States, & *our* heroic remedies have failed as they were sure to do. Ireland is not England & 'fleas are not lobsters.'" Yet Lowell sympathized with Gladstone's difficulties, believed his intentions "just, and even generous," and thought his policy, however defective, had gone to the limit of public opinion in its concessions. The main threat to pacification, Lowell believed, was not the Ministry's lack of good will, but the "passionate selfishness" of the landlords and the "fantastic political theories of the peasantry." Lowell's sympathy for the Gladstone Ministry would be appreciated neither by his own government nor by his Irish-American countryman. His course was not free of error and prejudice, but he would be blamed for mistakes he did not make and accused of attitudes he did not hold.[32]

Lowell became officially involved in the Irish problem over the "Fenians," a group working on both sides of the Atlantic for Irish independence, and specifically over those Irish-Americans imprisoned in British jails under the new Coercive Act. Though Lowell had disapproved of the act on both moral and tactical grounds, once it became the law of the land he felt he had no choice but to accept it. A foreign Minister had no right publicly to criticize an act of Parliament, nor any grounds for expecting that Americans in the British Isles would be exempt from its provisions. He could properly intervene only when a proven American citizen, going peacefully about his private business, was arrested by mistake, or if the act was administered in such a way as to discriminate more harshly against American citizens than against British subjects. When and if such conditions arose, it would be proper and necessary for the American Minister to remonstrate.[33]

From the very beginning of his tenure, even before the issue reached crisis proportions in 1882, Lowell *had* intervened in behalf of imprisoned Irish-Americans. At first he let Hoppin handle almost all the correspondence dealing with arrests but Hoppin was apparently scrupulous in attending to the ten odd cases, though he did so in a temperate tone appreciated more by the

British government than by the imprisoned suspects and their sympathizers in America. The State Department, however, though fully apprised, made no objection to the manner in which Lowell and Hoppin were handling the "suspect" question. With nothing like a reprimand or even a qualification from Washington, they had every right to assume that their procedures were approved and that they were doing all that was necessary. At the same time, it is true that they were apparently doing only what was necessary; they performed their duty, but with little enthusiasm. As Lowell privately wrote to Granville: "I need not say that all I have done (so far as these fellows are concerned) has been *pro forma* merely in case a question should be asked in Congress by some member with too many Teagues in his district." Secretary of State Blaine apparently felt much the same way; he confidentially told Thornton, in regard to one of the Irish-Americans being held prisoner, that he was "a pestiferous fellow and . . . deserved what he had got." It does seem clear that the imprisoned suspects had all been actively engaged in anti-British activity and that the American citizenship of some of them was open to serious question. Thus Lowell's limited intervention in the pre-1882 period seems justified by the nature of the cases that came to his attention; the least that can be said is that his conduct was approved by his own government. In any case, if Irish-Americans had any grounds for claiming that Lowell had not shown sufficient vigor in their behalf, they had none for claiming, as they did, that he was anti-Home Rule and an English toady.[34]

By early 1882, the mounting pressure of public opinion in the United States prodded the American government into a more energetic protest. A confidential message was sent in President Arthur's name asking that the British government either bring the imprisoned Irish-Americans to early trial or release them. The request was made on the basis of expediency, not law, for there was uncertainty (within both governments) as to what grounds, if any, the United States might have for insisting that her citizens be brought to trial when that right was at the same time being denied to British subjects. The American government emphasized instead the pressure building up in Congress to issue a formal demand that the prisoners be tried or released; should such a demand be made, the issue would obviously become far more difficult to adjust.[35]

But the British government had difficulties of its own in acceding to the American request. Like all acts suspending *habeas corpus*, the Coercive Act had been meant as a preventive measure; it had relied on detention rather than trial and punishment to forestall disorders. Moreover, the handful of Irish-Americans being held were apparently all known "Fenians," and some had clearly become naturalized Americans with the sole intention of gaining immunity for their activities. To bring such men to trial, the British argued, would be to discriminate against those of her own nationals who had also been detained. On the other hand, to release the Americans without trial might encourage further subversive activity; Irish-Americans would be tempted to assume that regardless of their deeds, their nationality would henceforward protect them. It was obviously a problem without easy solution, despite the fact that both governments were anxious to avoid complications.[36]

After being instructed to present the American request for trial or release, Lowell held a series of interviews with Granville, Gladstone and W. E. Forster, the Irish Secretary. He pressed the case diligently, urging the expediency (not the legal necessity) of acceding to the American appeal. It is true that Lowell continued to look on the suspects as willing martyrs, men eager to complicate Anglo-American relations. It is also true that in private conversation he made his sympathies with the British position clear, going so far as to tell Granville that he "regretted that his Government should have been induced to make the representations they have done" (not surprisingly, Forster wrote Granville: "Lowell . . . is entirely with us"). Perhaps Lowell was too sweeping in his indictment of the Fenians, too lacking in sympathy for Americans imprisoned without specification of charges against them, too indiscreet in allowing his personal views to be known. But he found it difficult to modulate his indignation against an organization which resorted to dynamite plots, arson and murder, and whose American members often looked upon themselves as "Irishmen who have acquired a right to American protection rather than as Americans who have renounced a claim to Irish nationality." As for Lowell's making known his private views, this could be considered a dereliction only if his acknowledged sympathy with the British position somehow served to compromise the interests of his own country. But the opposite seems to have been true: knowing Lowell to be a friend, the British were the more willing to meet those American demands whose necessity he argued.[37]

And he did argue their necessity (not their soundness) zealously though courteously — the two being incompatible only in the minds of Lowell's critics. He even wrote Granville privately about the issue, stressing that "I cannot say too strongly how full of peril the situation seems to me nor how important I think it is that whatever *can* be done should be done." So strenuously did Lowell press the case, in fact, that Forster thought he was in "unnecessary alarm" about potential consequences. But by late March, 1882, it began to look as if Congress would issue a formal demand for trial or release, and a mass protest rally in New York City had been called for April 3. Personal abuse of Lowell had also risen sharply; a body of trade unionists as well as the New York City Board of Aldermen passed resolutions insisting on his recall, and Irish papers everywhere denounced him for supineness. Lowell thought several times of resigning, feeling that in any case he was likely to be recalled. Hearing of this, Granville sent him a personal letter urging him not to quit; it would, he argued, be tantamount to pleading guilty, and since the President "may not be aware of your excellent position here" he might bow to pressure and accept the resignation — and that, Granville thought, would be a serious misfortune for both countries. Lowell, in reply, thanked Granville for his interest and assured him that he would do nothing rash — that at the least he would await the results of the mass rally in New York.[38]

The crucial breakthrough came in the British Cabinet meeting of March 31, 1882. It was there decided that although the government could not order trials for the imprisoned Americans, it would be in line with its contention that the Coercion Act was a measure of prevention, not punishment, to release the prisoners — on condition that they leave the United Kingdom, not to return. With this major concession, the way seemed clear to a final settlement. Yet one further and serious hitch developed. On hearing of the British decision, Frelinghuysen wired Lowell that the United States could not consent to have her citizens — who were "neither charged with, nor convicted of any offense" — placed under the "dishonorable disability" of a forced and permanent departure from England.[39]

Lowell had already anticipated his government's objection. Even before the arrival of Frelinghuysen's telegram he had had a private interview with Gladstone in which the Prime Minister had agreed that the words "not to return" be limited to the life of the Coercion Act. This modified the Cabinet decision to some extent, but Lowell still hoped to win unconditional release of the Americans, and so on the following day went to see Forster, and Sir William Harcourt, the Home Secretary. They proved willing to go beyond Gladstone and omit the words "not to return" entirely, though they did insist that the prisoners, when released, would have to leave the United Kingdom at least temporarily.[40]

Not realizing the extent to which Lowell had already exerted himself to win a modification of terms, and distrusting his ability to do so, Bancroft Davis, the American Under-Secretary of State, at this point intervened directly and did so in a manner unjust and insulting to Lowell. Davis got his patron, Hamilton

Fish, to wire Sir John Rose, a retired British diplomat whom Fish, when Secretary of State, had known well, asking Rose to do what he could either to win trial for the American prisoners or to have them discharged "quietly without exacting impossible conditions." Rose did enter actively into the negotiations, calling on Forster and sending him a long, able memorandum on why it would be politic to meet the American request. But his efforts produced no concessions beyond those Lowell had already obtained in earlier interviews. The British government would not agree to unconditional release, though Gladstone and Granville were willing to adopt Forster and Harcourt's position that the words "not to return" be dropped completely.[41]

Even then, Lowell did not give up in his effort to win further modification. In private letters to Gladstone, Granville and Forster, he continued to urge that the released Americans not be required to leave the country even temporarily. But this far, he was told, the British government would not go, for to do so would hopelessly compromise its basic position that Irish-Americans had to be treated in the same manner as British subjects. In dropping the words "not to return," therefore, the British had made their final offer, and realizing this, Frelinghuysen accepted it (though he later reargued, and with considerable force, the broader principles at issue). Shortly thereafter the prisoners were freed, and although Fenian operations and arrests continued, the issue never again reached difficult proportions between the two countries.[42]

Lowell's own government never appreciated the role he had played in winning British agreement to drop the "return" clause. Of all his detractors, Bancroft Davis, the Under-Secretary, proved the least generous and the most tenacious. Davis wrote Hamilton Fish that Lowell had "failed utterly" and that only the outside help of Sir John Rose had saved the day; he told Sackville West, the new British Minister in Washington, that Lowell "had not sufficiently insisted on or explained" to Granville the magnitude of the issue in the States, thereby allowing the English to consider the excitement just one more example of American "bluster." [43]

There was little truth in Davis' accusations. Lowell could certainly be accused of lacking sympathy for the Fenians and of performing only the strict letter of his duties in regard to their welfare, but no actual dereliction can be demonstrated. He could be accused, too, of airing his sympathies for the Gladstone Administration indiscriminately — though it is probable that he thereby improved rather than jeopardized his country's position. But Lowell could not justly be accused — as Bancroft Davis accused him — of ineptness in the actual negotiations between the two countries.

Such concessions as the British made were due basically to their wish — the wish of both countries — to avoid a full-blown controversy. But to the extent that individuals do deserve special credit, Lowell would rank far ahead of Sir John Rose. Sir John's efforts were largely after the fact, the basic decision to release the suspects having been made on March 31, whereas the telegram from Fish which first involved Sir John was not even sent until April 1. Possibly the additional pressure Sir John exerted did help in getting the "return" clause dropped, but if so evidence is entirely lacking — whereas evidence is abundant for arguing Lowell's claim to that accomplishment. It is worth noting in this regard that Sir John himself reported back to Fish, who had serious doubts about Lowell's capacity (and even patriotism), that Lowell was working "*most loyally!*" [44]

As for Bancroft Davis' charge that Lowell failed to impress Granville with the gravity of the situation, there is much to prove the contrary. It will be remembered that Forster, for one, had thought Lowell unnecessarily alarmed — and because the British considered Lowell a friend, they took seriously his repeated warnings. It is ironic, in light of the American belief in Lowell's docility, that Sir William Harcourt had actually thought him "defiant" at certain points in the negotiation, (and

Elmwood, July 23. 1849.

My dear Friend,

I agree with you entirely as to the importance of getting Frederick D.[ouglass] quietly into the T. & C. Club. I intended to have paid his entrance fee when I paid my own, but had not the money at that time. But I will see that it is done before the 1st October. I was surprised, I confess, that there should have been any opposition to so entirely desirable a member. Especially was I astonished at the quarter from which it came, for, if I am not mistaken, Emerson would have blackballed him, had it been put to the vote.

I cannot help thinking that the presence of a man cast in so large a mould as D. certainly is, with such a fine tropical exuberance of mental & physical development, will do a great deal in ridding many worthy persons of a very unworthy prejudice. I am quite sure that I, for one, am an unfit companion for people too good to associate with him. Our American chromatic scale is a very complicated affair.

You will be glad to hear that God has sent us another little daughter—outwardly perfect. She was born just a week ago today, & both mother & child are prospering.

As soon as Maria is up again, I am to fulfil my long delayed purpose of paying Levi a visit at the Shoals. I shall hope to see you as I pass through Newburyport.

I remain affectionately yours

J. R. Lowell

Lowell's letter to T. W. Higginson about the probable blackball of Frederick Douglass for the Town and Country Club, 1849

Courtesy of the University of Virginia

The Whist Club: John Holmes, Estes Howe,
Robert Carter, James Russell Lowell

Lowell's three nephews — "Willie," center left; Charles Russell, center right; James Jackson, bottom — with Robert Gould Shaw, all killed in the Civil War

From James Russell Lowell and His Friends *by E. E. Hale, Jr.*

Oliver Wendell Holmes
The Bettmann Archive

John Holmes in later life
Courtesy of Harvard University

Henry Wadsworth Longfellow
The Bettmann Archive

Ralph Waldo Emerson
The Bettmann Archive

Mabel Lowell Burnett in 1869

Leslie Stephen
in academic robes
Courtesy of Harvard University

Henry James
New York Public Library

Emelia de Riaño
The Hispanic Society of America

Charles Eliot Norton
Courtesy of Harvard University

James Russell Lowell
about 1880
The Library of Congress

Frances Dunlap Lowell.
A London photograph
of about 1882

Two contemporary cartoonists' views of Lowell's handling of the Irish Problem

Courtesy of Harvard University and The Bettmann Archive

Lowell's study at Elmwood about 1880

Courtesy of the Society for the Preservation of New England Antiquities

The last photograph of Lowell
Courtesy of Mr. and Mrs. Sherman Baldwin

Bancroft Davis would have been shocked if he had read the letter Harcourt wrote to Granville in the summer of 1882, in which he reported after meeting Davis socially that he found him far more pliant than he had ever found Lowell!). It was rumored that Bancroft Davis, having tired of the State Department, and privately contemptuous of Frelinghuysen's abilities, hoped to replace Lowell in London and was therefore eager to show that he had mismanaged his responsibilities. But it is unnecessary to impugn Davis' motives in order to recognize the flimsiness of his charges.[45]

Most of Davis' criticisms were made privately, but there was considerable public abuse of Lowell as well. In the press, at mass rallies, even in the halls of Congress, he was extravagantly, often savagely, denounced. The New York protest meeting of April 3 came off as planned, and an overflow crowd heard the speakers vie with one another in accusing Lowell of "sycophancy." An ex-Speaker of the House of Representatives, Samuel J. Randall, referred to Lowell's "weak, nerveless, cowardly hands" as ill-fitted "to hold the broad aegis of American protection over American citizens." One resolution was passed damning Lowell directly, and another by unsubtle indirection; the first insisted that his supercilious and servile bearing made his recall imperative, the other denounced the "flunkeyism" of certain "Anglicised circles" in the United States, whose aping of English ways could only be viewed as "bastard Americanism . . . at enmity with democratic institutions." [46]

The demand for Lowell's recall also sounded in the House and Senate. Representative William E. Robinson attacked him repeatedly, and Senator Daniel W. Voorhees of Indiana denounced him so violently that a reporter present thought the Senator must have been laboring under a "morbid nervous condition." Delegations from labor unions and from Irish-American organizations called directly on President Arthur, others sent in petitions to Congress, all with the same theme: Lowell must go.[47]

He was far from being without defenders. The New York

Times, the New York *Evening Post*, *The Nation* and the New York *Tribune*, among others, wrote editorials in support of his actions; friends sent letters of encouragement; and at Commencement Day at Harvard, the crowd rose and gave Lowell three cheers when a toast was proposed in his name. But not even the applause of Harvard could quite assuage the gall. Lowell did his best to keep his sense of humor (he remarked to Granville that he expected momentarily to be sent home in irons), and publicly he remained poised and serene. But he had been wounded by the attacks, and occasionally he allowed his resentment to come through — he remarked to Granville that a good many signatures on the recall petitions were probably crosses; and to several friends he expressed bitterness at being "coached in Americanism" by men who looked on their United States citizenship as ancillary to their Irish allegiance.[48]

Lowell was on the point several times of voluntarily submitting his resignation but decided he could not do so without seeming to confess the justice of the charges against him. For a time he thought it likely that he would be recalled, and the New York *World*, his bitterest enemy in the press, once announced confidently that recall was in fact imminent. But Lowell later learned "on good authority" that the Administration had never thought of such a step, feeling to the contrary that even a resignation would embarrass them. In any case, by summer the clamor for recall died down, and before long subsided completely.[49]

No sooner had the outcry against Lowell begun to fade than a personal crisis replaced the public one: Mrs. Lowell, after months of improvement, suddenly began to show the "nervous symptoms" which had once been all too familiar. She refused food, took to her bed and again became delusionary. This time the trouble seemed focused in her brain, though not even the lack of fever yet made them suspect that this was something more than a typhus relapse. She became listless and melancholy, and Hoppin thought that if not actually insane, she was very nearly so. After two months of little improvement, she was persuaded to go with Lowell's sister and niece to the Isle of Wight — both for "change of air" and, as Lowell frankly admitted, "because we ground into each other." Within five weeks she was back, "remarkably cheerful again," and thereafter she improved so rapidly that by the fall of 1882 Lowell thought her better than at any time since leaving Madrid. Except for a slight halt in her walk and a cramping of her hand, she appeared entirely well, and according to Hoppin seemed "to warm & expand" under Lowell's "devoted & caressing" care.[50]

The way was now clear of both diplomatic and domestic difficulties. The next two years, almost devoid of disruptive events, were among the happiest of Lowell's life — two years of placid routine and cheerful eminence. Now and then the Irish-American problem flared — once Frelinghuysen cabled Lowell that he was in personal peril from dynamite — and occasionally matters of potential significance, like an extradition treaty, were inconclusively discussed. But the vast bulk of diplomatic correspondence related to such minor matters as the recognition of consular officers, the International Inventions Exhibition, the transmission of gold medals to British naval officers who had aided American ships in distress, or the Prime Meridian Conference. Lowell found such routine work distasteful and he allowed Hoppin to assume the bulk. Still, Lowell was kept busy enough, seeing Legation visitors he did not care to see and answering notes "from all manner of people on all manner of subjects" in which he had little or no interest ("It is astonishing . . . how many destitute Americans walk the streets of London just three nights and three days without food — not, I sometimes fancy, without liquid nourishment — before bringing themselves to ask me for help").[51]

He also spent a good deal of time giving speeches. He had by now become something of a public institution, with hardly a week going by without his being asked to preside at a meeting, distribute a prize or offer a toast at a dinner. Much of it he enjoyed, though the trivia and sameness sometimes bored him, and he disliked making any preparation for the more formal addresses he was asked to deliver. On one occasion he felt so miserable at the prospect of having to give a talk on Fielding that he decided it wouldn't be "a bad kind of life to be lying on one's back & trying to read the inscription on one's own tombstone" — though even then there would no doubt be "some bad English or worse Latin to fret one." In any case, his speeches were almost always a great success. Urbane, genial, full of graceful allusions ("at my time of life [my memory] . . . is gradually becoming one of her own reminiscences . . ."), they won him wide praise. Henry James, for example, reported that when Lowell was "doctored" at Edinburgh (along with 120 others) in celebration of the University's Tercentenary, the speech he gave was "far and away the best delivered there." [52]

Lowell almost never made elaborate preparations for his speeches, even the major ones. At Edinburgh the night before he spoke with such success, he wrote Henry White, his new Second Secretary, "tomorrow I must make a speech, & have nothing to say!" An exception to this pattern was the major address he gave in 1884 on "Democracy" — a carefully worked-out effort which caused a great deal of comment, and is at least as revealing of Lowell as of its subject.[53]

The first part of the speech was the best. In it, Lowell defended democracy with a subtlety which allowed recognition of its defects, seeing it as the preferred, not the perfect, system of government. But then, attempting to minimize the very defects he had enumerated — democracy's tendency to vulgarize character and culture, its clumsiness in attempting to arrive at truth by a numerical count — Lowell fell back on stock faith and rhetoric, on "the rooted instinct in men to admire what is better and more beautiful than themselves," on the possibility of appealing to the people's reason, which "has never been known to fail in the long run." [54]

The one defect which Lowell did not minimize, the most

serious danger he saw in the democratic system, was that it might give an entering wedge to Socialism. Lowell did not fear, in fact he approved, that kind of Socialism which meant "cooperation and community of interests, sympathy, the giving to the hands not so large a share as to the brains, but a larger share than hitherto in the wealth they must combine to produce . . ." He approved, in other words, any form of Socialism which meant "the practical application of Christianity to life." But *State* Socialism was another matter. In attempting to equalize conditions and fortunes, State Socialism, he believed, would cut off the roots of personal character — that is, "self-help, forethought, and frugality." Yet Lowell deplored not only State Socialism but also the gross inequalities of condition which that philosophy had been designed to correct. Moreover, he explicitly questioned the ability of private philanthropy to alleviate such conditions; its efforts to build hospitals and schools for the poor were admirable, but "partial and palliative" — like applying "plasters to a single pustule of the small-pox with a view to driving out the disease." Deploring gross inequalities, doubting the adequacy of private philanthropy and the wisdom of public ownership, Lowell yet had no alternate suggestions of his own. State Socialism, he feared, would destroy "character," would create more problems than it solved, but he could offer nothing in its place which might promise fewer risks — and greater hope.

And so he settled — as so often when faced with a difficult dilemma — for bland exhortation. The closing message of his speech on Democracy — it is not too much to say of his life — was that we should "be of good cheer . . . remembering that the misfortunes hardest to bear are those which never come. The world has outlived much, and will outlive a great deal more, and men have contrived to be happy in it." The real solution for the world's ills would come from "the still small voice that speaks to the conscience and the heart, prompting us to a wider and wiser humanity" — though Lowell did not venture to say when the voice might make itself heard or what precisely it might reveal.

He was not a man callous to the misfortunes of the underprivileged, only afraid to minister to them with remedies which he feared would bring worse evils in their train. The warm sympathies of his youth had not disappeared, but they had been diluted by a decreased capacity for risk and an increased willingness to replace logic with faith.[55]

When not giving speeches or attending to Legation routine, Lowell managed a remarkably active social life. Nothing, he claimed, ever puzzled him so much as his popularity in England — but there was no questioning its reality. As Henry James put it, Lowell lived in "social and material clover, the pet of countesses, the habitué of palaces, the intimate of dukes." Leslie Stephen, who remembered Lowell isolated in his study at Elmwood, was amused at his present position as "guest of all the great swells." Stephen thought Lowell had been little changed by it all, except that he now had to wear a good coat and go about with a valet.[56]

Lowell's popularity was not limited to the fashionable world. Late in 1883, the undergraduates at the Scottish University of St. Andrews, in the largest poll ever taken, elected Lowell its Rector. Flattering though the honor was, he had to decline it, for Lord Chancellor Selbourne gave it as his reluctant opinion that since an alien was not amenable to the jurisdiction of any Scottish court, he could not hold the public office of Rector. "How to rob a Scottish University," Lowell mused, "suggests a serious problem." [57]

In their last two years in England, the Lowells did more entertaining of their own. Mrs. Lowell, who had put herself in the hands of a "*rubber* man," could by late 1883 at last walk without a stick, and finally allowed herself to be presented at court. Thereafter, she officially joined society. The Lowells moved into a large, "smart" house, and she began to give weekly afternoon receptions, blossoming out, so Henry James said, "with London conversation & long tails to her gowns." She was even well enough, by the fall of 1883, to join her husband in a two-month vacation in Paris (which they found much the same as ten years before — the roots of the Republic still no deeper, the French still furious at the Prussians, and still as ingratiating).[58]

Pleasant as these years were and willing as Lowell was to prolong them, he knew by late 1884 that his recall was likely. In the Presidential campaign of that year, the Republicans ran Blaine and the Democrats Grover Cleveland, and either, Lowell knew, would almost certainly replace him, the one from personal, the other from political considerations. Though as Minister he officially had no politics, Lowell was entirely in sympathy with those Republican "Mugwumps" who left their party to support Cleveland (he had been a "Mugwump," Lowell quipped, since Lincoln's death). And when Cleveland won the November election, Lowell's satisfaction was undiminished by the knowledge that he would almost surely be removed. He placed his resignation in Cleveland's hands, at the same time making clear to the President-elect that the newspapers had mistakenly reported he would not serve under a Democratic Administration: "I may add without impropriety that I never said anything of the kind, & now mention it only because I wish no misapprehension to exist as to the high respect I feel for your character." [59]

The issue of Lowell's recall hung fire until Cleveland took office in March, 1885. In the interim, Lowell hardly knew whether there were grounds to hope for reappointment, or even whether he wished it. Sometimes he was tempted to resign and have done, for he felt a good deal of his time in England was wasted. But then again, perhaps it wasn't worth saving: "We Yankees have a proverb — 'A hen's time ain't much' — in allusion to her spendthrift way of sitting on addled or mock eggs." Henry James was less uncertain whether Lowell's recall would be a personal blessing or a disaster — it would be pure disaster. For Lowell to give up his position in England, a position "in the highest degree honourable, useful, agreeable — in short perfect," in order to return "to John Holmes & the Brattle Street horse-car," seemed to James "the sport of a cruel & barbaric fortune." Lowell did not at first so view it: "I shall have enjoyed my five years in England, where everybody has been kind to me, and shall find people to be kind to me at home also. It has been my luck to find them everywhere." But he could look thus placidly to the future because he assumed that whatever it brought, Mrs. Lowell would be there to share it — and smooth it.[60]

But suddenly, even as Lowell awaited word of his future, its prospects changed in a way he could not have anticipated. After her best winter in five years, Frances Lowell, in late January, 1885, suddenly had a new attack of "hysteria." It seemed much like the seizure of two years earlier, though more violent, and this time accompanied by epileptoid spasms. A month of horrible insanity followed, during which Lowell was barred from the sickroom because of the agitation his presence produced. The doctors continued to speak confidently of a full recovery, but on February 14, Mrs. Lowell began to sink. The next day she briefly regained consciousness, and Lowell was called to her bed. She put her arms around his neck, and when he asked, "Darling, do you love me?" she nodded. That embrace was an "unspeakable comfort"; four days later, Frances Lowell was dead.[61]

The doctors, in retrospect, decided that her basic trouble had not been typhus, but probably "some permanent lesion of the brain," perhaps a tumor, which had periodically lain dormant. They tried to comfort Lowell by suggesting that if she had recovered from this last attack she would surely have had another, and would probably have been hopelessly insane. But little comfort was possible. Lowell had always taken it for granted that his wife would outlive him, for her strength and serenity seemed so essential that he could not face the possibility of being denied them. His loneliness was almost unbearable at first, but his sister and niece came over from America to be with him, and after two months he could write Norton that the "wound has skinned over now & is not so tender to every breath of air as it was." [62]

He was now at a real loss as to the future. A month after Mrs. Lowell's death, definite word arrived that he had been recalled. Outwardly he appeared philosophical, but he took his removal hard. The Administration kept on some Ministers (including Nicholas Fish, son of the ex-Secretary of State, whom Lowell thought an "ass") and this made his own recall seem a disapproval of his course, especially since the letter which informed him of the decision was "as dry as official formality could compass" — "I should not have cashiered a dog more curtly," Lowell wrote Norton. But he added that he still approved heartily of the new Administration, saying with Job "though he slay me, yet will I praise him." And he was pleased at the choice of his successor, Edward J. Phelps, a Vermont lawyer and Democrat.[63]

But what to do with his own life? He could not return to live alone at Elmwood, yet he could not imagine being content elsewhere. Perhaps he should stay in England, where he had made so many friends; perhaps, as was confidentially proposed, he should allow himself to be a candidate for the Professorship of English Literature at Oxford. But at age sixty-six, the duties seemed too onerous, the alienation from his homeland too permanent. The future, as he put it with pathetic understatement, was "a problem." It would be better, he decided, to take things piecemeal; he would go home at least for a while, and then, having got his bearings, would try to sort out such alternatives as presented themselves.[64]

A week before he sailed for the United States, Lowell unveiled a monument to the poet Gray and he took the occasion publicly to express his gratitude for the consideration which had surrounded both his official and his private life — "to say that while I came here as a far-off cousin, I feel you are sending me away as something like a brother." The compliment was more than returned in kind. When Lowell left England in June, 1885, praises and regrets sounded on all sides. The English newspapers garlanded him with superlatives; the mighty, like Lord Granville, sent personal testaments of their regard; and Charles Hodson, messenger at the American Legation, simply wrote that he would miss the "sunshine." It was something, amidst sorrow and uncertainty, to know that he had left a public record which the powerful could remember with respect and a private one which the humble could remember with affection.[65]

CHAPTER XV

LAST YEARS

A MAN NEARING SEVENTY finds little compensation in his surroundings for the depletions of his personal life; the changes that take place around him underscore rather than offset his private losses, for they always tend to replace the familiar with the new, the landmark with the innovation. For Lowell, away nearly eight years, the accumulated transformations of Cambridge soon made it clear that not he alone, but the remnant of a generation, was in need of solace. Some of his oldest friends, like Edmund Quincy and Jane Norton, had died just before he left for Europe in 1877. Many more had passed away before he returned — in 1882 alone, Longfellow, Dana and Emerson. Looking over the reduced ranks of the Saturday Club, Oliver Wendell Holmes, himself nearly eighty, thought he should probably give up attending.

As life runs on, the road grows strange
With faces new, and near the end
The milestones into headstones change,
'Neath every one a friend.[1]

It was all sad enough, but Lowell struggled against the elegiac mood. He had periods of deep depression — at least twice he thought seriously of suicide — but he was rescued by his disposition and by his standards. Something still remained, remarkably, of resilience and expectation and still more of that stoicism which demanded he go on as well as he could with a minimum of complaint. He knew, moreover, that there was still much to be grateful for. Barring occasional bouts with gout, he had robust health, he was widely admired and sought after, and he had some few people whom he cared for: Norton, John Holmes, and his daughter, Mabel.[2]

It was to Mabel's home in Southborough, Massachusetts, that Lowell went to live on his return from England. The house was spacious and airy, its wide veranda and irregular design gave a feeling of rambling informality. Southborough itself was an unadulterated New England village, full of lovely views and walks. Its solitude contrasted strangely with the glamor and bustle of London, but London already seemed something of a dream to Lowell, an interruption of his natural life, and he had little difficulty adjusting to the village's quiet ways. "I fancy myself happy sometimes," he wrote Norton, "I am not sure — but then I never was for long." [3]

The real novelty of his new life was assuming the role of grandfather. Mabel now had five children, and Lowell set about getting acquainted with them. He claimed no special fondness for children and thought people who did tended also to be indiscriminately fond of puppies. The assorted noises and interruptions of five youngsters could be trying for a man who valued solitude, but the children soon understood that he would not be at their constant disposal; at breakfast, for example, they were allowed to sit with him while the cook prepared his cakes of Scotch oatmeal, but once served he was to be left in peace to read his mail. Lowell was a little disappointed that none of the five seemed especially gifted, though he supposed that "in this Country of Equal Rights" he had no greater call on clever grandchildren than anybody else.[4]

But if he would not automatically adopt the pose of Loving Grandfather, nor assume the superior virtues of his own kin, Lowell did take pleasure in the children and enjoyed repeating anecdotes of their antics. They believed, he wrote Leslie Stephen's wife, Julia, that their grandfather had been overseas as a missionary and were sorry he hadn't been eaten — "it would have been such a feather in their caps." And he repeated with delight his grandson Francis' proud announcement on returning home from school one day: "Mamma, John Smith used bad language, & I told him my mother didn't like me to hear bad language, & — I knocked him down!" [5]

He enjoyed, too, playing preceptor. He read to the children (he recommended Scott for the grandsons — "his wholesomeness & manliness more than make up for any defects he may have"), helped the eldest with his Greek, and taught them about the songs and traits of the birds (the grosbeaks and redstarts were his favorites, but he disapproved of the English sparrows: they were, he said, a fraud and delusion — having been brought to America to eat bugs, they never ate a one, but spent their time quarreling and multiplying). He also taught his grandchildren the "proper" way of handling a book: "Never crack it open. Never leave it face down. Never put a marker in it, because if you weren't interested enough in it to remember where you had stopped you ought not to read it. The most hideous sin of all was to turn down the corner of a page or fold it in." [6]

The lessons his grandchildren least appreciated (at the time anyway) were corrections of grammar. One of them recalled that Lowell had been "like a hawk waiting to pounce" on a confusion between "me" and "I" or "will" and "shall." Certain phrases like "real mean" were forbidden, while correct pronunciation of such twisters as "Janarary (Jan*u*ary), Frebrary (Feb*ru*ary) and Artics (Ar*c*tics that you wear in the snow)" was insisted upon. Lowell was never severe or ill-tempered in his corrections, but he was definite and instantaneous. The children were a little in awe of him; as an old man and something of a taskmaster, he seemed to represent, as one of them later put it, "the infallibility and rightness of God." [7]

But they also loved his humor and his generosity — one granddaughter remembered his open-handedness as his most endearing trait. Mabel tried to save him from being imposed upon by begging strangers, but his answer was always the same: "I would rather give to ten frauds than miss one person in real need." He admitted, though, that with a single exception, none of his loans had ever been repaid; the exception was the poorest man to whom he had ever lent anything. Let his descendants, Lowell said, draw the moral: "If they wish to lend wisely, let them lend to a man who is always and not temporarily poor."

Surrounded by his daughter's family, Lowell tried to be grateful for the semblance of a home. But Elmwood, near in fact and memory, continued to remind him of his displacement. He did venture into the old house once when his need for books became pressing but couldn't bear to stay more than a few minutes — "it seemed so empty & so full." Yet Southborough, for all its contrast with his past and with his recent life, was not unpleasant. Lowell was again close to people he cared about — and also close to nature. He would wander over the hills and the lonely pastures, taking pleasure in the landscape and in the "immitigable sunshine." And if Southborough was a narrow world after London, all worlds, he told himself, were "only as broad as we have the wit to make them." Henry James, hearing the "inscrutable" rumor in London that Lowell was comfortable in Southborough, could not decide whether the world was very blind or very cruel. But James had always projected some of his own horror of provincial New England onto Lowell's more tolerant view.[8]

Besides, Lowell varied the Southborough diet. He visited Norton at his country place in the Berkshires, where they climbed the hills, read together in Dante, listened to the Norton and Curtis girls play piano-violin duets, and delighted in the unspoiled democracy of the little village — everybody as good as everybody else, "but no better, & neither wishes nor pretends to be." He also took an occasional trip: to Philadelphia to visit his niece at the seashore, to Washington with his grandson James in order to make a final report to the State Department and the President.

This last was his "chief adventure" in the first few months after returning. He amused President Cleveland by saying that he came "like St. Denis to make my bow with the head he had cut off under my arm." The brief visit reinforced Lowell's favorable opinion of Cleveland: the President had a good face — kindly and strong — and seemed well-suited to the rough-and-tumble of American politics. He might not be overly intelligent or sensitive, Lowell thought, but even his deficiences could prove useful — the politicians "will not be offended with any sense of his superiority . . . except that of mere strength & can't break his heart as they might one of the more delicate fibre." More important, Cleveland seemed to have nerve, "a backbone with no more *give* in it than that (or the pocket) of John Adams." Lowell was to watch the course of Cleveland's first Administration with close attention and general approval. Within the year, after he was again able to concentrate his energies, he was to give a number of speeches on public questions, in large measure supporting Cleveland's manner of handling them.[9]

But the first year of his return was given over to readjustment, or rather to filling in his time with enough incidental activity so that his changed situation need not be experienced in all of its pain ("We spend most of our days in the past or the future in neither of which is there enough ozone in the air. It is all very well for Horace to advise us jauntily *Carpe diem*. But how if the *dies* be slippery as an eel?"). It did not take New England training to realize that staying busy was at least a partial cure for despondency. He gave speeches at a number of local events (raising money for an Academy at Ashfield, dedicating the Chelsea Library); paid uncharacteristic attention to his correspondence; allowed himself to be appointed chairman of a committee to raise funds for the American Archaeological Society's School in Athens; and even agreed to "a new mode of torture" — readings by himself and Dr. Holmes from their poetry for the benefit of various charities.[10]

Of all his activities he probably held out most hope for pleasure from giving a class in Dante at Harvard, which he agreed to do in the fall of 1885. But instead of reproducing some of the happier memories of the past, the Dante course drove home instead the lesson of his changed condition. He stayed at his sister's in Boston during term and had to hold classes in a bleak room in University Hall — so unlike the warmth and informality of earlier seminars in his study at Elmwood. Not surprisingly, he seemed to one student "rather to be going through a task than to be indulging in a pleasure," and his moods in the classroom shifted more erratically than ever: one day full of whimsy and anecdote, the next formal and almost curt, limiting himself to routine exercises in translation. Judging from the notes taken by one student ("Chaucer very tender, but has not Dante's art"; "Dante's flash sees the important"), Lowell either communicated little or was little understood. By the end of one term he had wearied of the experiment, and decided not to continue it further.[11]

Such free time as remained, Lowell gave largely to reading and to preparing for press a volume of the speeches he had given while in England. These appeared in the spring of 1886 under the title, *Democracy, and Other Addresses*, and as so often in these later years, Lowell looked on the finished product with disgust: the speeches seemed as cold "as Saul on Mount Gilboa." He reacted in the same negative way to generous offers which were made to him to write for various periodicals. When pressed to contribute to the *Atlantic* — a duty, it was said, "to his own child" — he decided they wanted him not for his merit but only for the "abominable notoriety" he had lately achieved. He was not ready to take on new work; with Mrs. Lowell had gone the remaining edge of his ambition:

> *How much of all my past is dumb with her,*
> *And of my future, too, for with her went*
> *Half of that world I ever cared to please.*[12]

After nine months at home, Lowell in April, 1886, returned to England for a summer visit. In doing so, he established a pattern which he would repeat for the next four years: winters with his daughter at Southborough (broken by occasional stops with his sister, Mary, in Boston); summers abroad. There were times when he thought seriously of remaining permanently in England, but a sense of duty always pulled him back — a duty, he would say, to his daughter and her children, but an unspoken duty as well to his own reputation: to stay abroad would have seemed to validate the accusation that he had been "spoiled" for life in the United States. As Henry James put it, Lowell had been bitten deep by London but was "not . . . quite free to confess to the wound." He did admit his need for the cosmopolitanism of English life, though in so doing, tried to excuse America her lack:

> I frankly confess that I like England immensely, I find men of leisure at every turn, men who are profound scholars, who think for themselves, with whom interchange of ideas is an inspiration. Where there is one such man in America there are a dozen here. Do you wonder I like it? The contrast is no fault on the part of our country: it is the consequence of youth and the struggle for material existence.[13]

Aging, footloose, without the love of a wife or the absorption of a routine, without even much interest any longer in "self-expression" ("I am far past the period when I was a constant novelty to myself and eager to communicate it to all and sundry"), Lowell was susceptible to any cycle which promised to provide animation and prolong vitality. In England he could be assured of at least the appearance, and sometimes the reality of both. Since he was able to tell the difference, there was little disappointment from inflated expectations — especially since he was wise enough to accept even the semblance of life as not without its comfort.[14]

He would arrive in London each spring straight from the solitude of Southborough and be swept up at once into a whirlwind of dinners, speeches and receptions. He dined out literally every day, Sundays included, and lunched whenever he was willing (and there were invitations enough to fill each engagement three times over). One day it might be an afternoon garden party at Burne Jones', dinner with Lord Justice Bowen, then to a soirée at Lady Leigh's. On another, it would be the opera with the Misses Lawrence, then on to Rosebery's to meet "a crowd of royalties" (who do not gain "by a near view"). Or he would pay a visit to the Leveson-Gowers in the country (Mr. and Mrs. Gladstone also in attendance, he as "buoyant as a bladder filled with wind"); would give a speech at the Royal Academy (the Prince of Wales complimenting him on his remarks); would dine with John Morley, whose "cheerful fanaticism" was so enlivening; would speak before the Incorporated Society of Authors — mostly composed of American ladies with three names; would attend a formal Drawing Room (where the Queen bestows a smile and announces her pleasure at seeing Mr. Lowell once more in England). Occasionally, there would be some "special" event, like Victoria's Jubilee Day; Lowell, given a card to the Abbey, preferred to watch the spectacle from Lady Margaret Beaumont's in Piccadilly: ". . . the Indian princes . . . made their European competitors smack of Madame Tussaud . . . the procession . . . was well enough, though not comparable to that at the marriage of Don Alfonso . . . The reception of the Queen was hearty and the long roar of the multitude something to be remembered. The crowd was such as only London can turn out and wonderfully good natured and orderly." [15]

It was all dizzying, exhilarating, exhausting, amusing, futile — Lowell experienced the gamut of reactions and denied none of them. He could be dazed by the whirl of new faces, bored by the self-plagiarizing of his own after-dinner speeches ("one runs the risk of a metamorphosis more dreary than any of Ovid's — into a barrelorgan, to wit"), depressed at flying "from perch to perch like a bird in a cage" which instead of enlarging the prison only gave a more accurate notion of its narrow bounds. Ten years earlier Lowell would have abhorred a round of constant socializing and Leslie Stephen still found it "barely credible" that he derived any pleasure from such a routine. But he did, and without decking it in false colors. It was all "rather profitless," he confessed to his daughter, "but perhaps permissible to an old man," for if dining out so constantly could be dreary, dining all alone in lodgings could be drearier still. Motion helped to confound loneliness, flattery to postpone old age.[16]

But summers in England held more substantial satisfactions than the mixed blessings of "the season's" ritual. There was London itself, which Lowell liked better than any city he had ever lived in — "it is so various and amusing and you can get whatever you want or don't want round the next corner." He enjoyed the throng of equipages which made crossing Hyde Park difficult; he liked seeing so many people capable of luxuries, though wondered if he would like it so well if he could not afford to hire a hansom of his own — he half thought he would. To his surprise, he found that the city had a kind of solitude, more poignant even than that of the country; the song of the thrush in the London parks took on a special note, "like a quotation of poetry in a dreary page of prose." And the climate suited him wonderfully. He even liked the fogs; they turned everything into suggestion, making the familiar strange — it was as good "as travelling in the interior of Africa, without the odious duty of discovery, which makes the strange familiar." All in all, he thought England "the most beautiful bit of the earth's surface" he knew, and he marveled "at the strength of mind which sustained" his ancestor Perceval Lowle in his decision to leave it.[17]

Now and then Lowell would have some longing to see Italy again, but the only time he spent out of England was a brief trip in the summer of 1888 to represent Harvard at the eight hundredth anniversary of the University of Bologna. That trip did little to inspire him to further excursions, for the celebration turned into a comedy of errors. Almost no provisions had been made for the guests; Lowell was referred to alternately as "Signor Russell" or, more annoying still, *Professor* Lowell; the printed list of representatives was full of absurd mistakes: South America was put under the heading of Canada, New Jersey appeared as an independent republic, and W. W. Story, after protesting his placement in the South American section, was obligingly reassigned to Australia. To make matters worse, Lowell developed a severe fit of gout which kept him bedded down for three weeks after his return to London.[18]

No, England was his preferred spot. But attached as he was to the country and its people, Lowell was no uncritical admirer. The continued muddling of the Irish problem made him especially impatient. In 1885 Gladstone had been won over to Home Rule, but in the spring of 1886 the measure was defeated in Parliament and a new general election called. During the campaign Lowell found himself quoted on both sides, and the editor of the *Contemporary Review* (at the instigation of John Morley) tried to persuade him to perform "a public service" by writing up his views on Gladstone's policy. Lowell refused, preferring "to keep clear of hot potatoes." But an epigram of his on Gladstone, composed extempore, began to make the rounds:

> *His greatness not so much in Genius lies*
> *As in adroitness, when occasions rise,*
> *Lifelong convictions to extemporize.*

Lowell had repeated the epigram to Lord Acton, and soon after found the last line quoted by Auberon Herbert in a letter to the London *Times*. Luckily Lowell's name was not attached to it, but he considered the episode a warning and regretted it the more because he sympathized with Gladstone's efforts for Home Rule (even while retaining mixed feelings about Gladstone himself). When Gladstone's party met defeat in the 1886 election, Lowell remained convinced that Home Rule would — had to — carry the day. It is "a misfortune and not a crime," he wrote Norton, "to be entangled in an anachronism, but if one won't do what he can to break loose one must share its fate without complaint or hope of compensation." [19]

Though the English failed to grapple with some of their own basic problems, they continued, in Lowell's view, to take annoyingly for granted their superiority over the rest of mankind — especially over Americans. "What a sermon mightn't I preach!" on English civilization, Lowell wrote Julia Stephen, — for example, the debasing moral influence on society of the Prince of Wales, or the "hopeless attempt" of the pre-Raphaelite movement to reproduce by deliberate forethought the "happy inadvertence" of medieval art. But he forbore. Such opinions publicly expressed would be inappropriate, and besides, he was generally fond of the English. There was a "manliness" about them he liked, and every now and then Britain produced "a saint . . . as fair as if they had stepped down from an old painted window." [20]

Lowell was fortunate in believing that his own intimate circle in England consisted largely of such saints: Leslie and Julia Stephen, the George du Mauriers, Thomas Hughes and his wife, and George and Phoebe Smalley. During the height of the "season," with rows of duchesses at his feet, Lowell saw these friends only occasionally. But after the season was over he would spend leisurely weeks with them at the quiet resort towns of St. Ives, or Whitby, in Yorkshire. Whitby was Lowell's special favorite. He had visited the town nearly every summer while Minister, and continued to return to it with undiminished enthusiasm — it was a "delightful combination of moorland, sea, old associations & red tiled roofs." He took lodgings which overlooked the roofs of the old town, with the ruins of Rievaulx Abbey in full view across the river, its gray skeleton alternately "invoking vengeance or begging burial." He would take long walks on moors flushed with heather — "pensively gorgeous like the purple mourning that used to be worn for kings" — or would wander along the beach, hearing in the crash of the surf "perpetual ruin with perpetual renewal." [21]

Whitby was not a fashionable resort, and Lowell rejoiced that the natives lacked the servility which galled him elsewhere in England. The people of Whitby in their simplicity and rigorous honesty reminded him of New Englanders — returning to his boarding house after a year's interval, he found at his first breakfast that the half-bottle of spirits he had left behind the previous year had been carefully placed at his table for him to brew his coffee with.[22]

Lowell also appreciated the lack of activity in Whitby. There was a Salvation Army Band and an American circus, but the only real event was watching the fishing boats come in. That, and walking on the moors and cliffs or lying on the beach. Lowell read a little — Lope de Vega, Dante, Milton — but the weeks at Whitby were mostly mindless and aimless, and he loved them. He felt remarkably healthy there — one day he walked thirteen miles — as happy "as in the nature of things (and my own) I could be." He was especially content when some of his intimate friends were also vacationing there, or when an old acquaintance like Henry James would come up from London for a visit. James thought Lowell appeared to particular advantage at Whitby; he would shed his overcoat "either of cloth or of self consciousness, & that combined with his wondrous good fun & good temper renders him, at his age (& with the Yorkshire airs), miraculous to me." James was always a little shocked at the older man's capacity for enjoyment: "walking, talking, joking, smoking, drinking, playing host & guide in the kindest, gayest, most 15-year old way." Lowell, James concluded, belonged "to a more primitive generation," one he viewed with mixed impatience and nostalgia.[23]

Lowell's greatest pleasure — in Whitby or London — was the company of one of several women with whom he had become particularly close. He had always depended on women both for strength and admiration, and one of the special attractions of England was that there he was fortunate enough to have three such companions: Julia Stephen, Phoebe Smalley and Lady Lyttleton. All were considerably younger than he, all were attractive, accomplished and (especially Mrs. Smalley) immensely devoted to him. "If men were only as good as women," Lowell wrote Lady Lyttleton, only half in jest, "what a delightful world it would be!"[24]

Rumors spread of the amorous involvement of Lowell with two of these friends. Only Julia Stephen escaped — she was simply "noble," "gracious" Julia, apparently immune from London gossip. Lady Lyttleton, perhaps out of deference to her title, was dignified with a rumor wholly decorous: she and Lowell, it was said, would marry. At one point an announcement of their engagement actually appeared in the Boston *Post*, requiring a formal denial by Edward Burnett's father.[25]

Phoebe Smalley, the adopted daughter of Wendell Phillips and the wife of the American journalist, George Smalley, was less favored by the scandal-mongers; she, it was said, was "something more" than a mere friend to Lowell. It was true that she was constantly in his company, and often without her husband (whom Lowell once described as "a hard man, or rather a naturally sensitive man who wilfully hardened himself"). It was true, too, that she was an extraordinarily charming woman; Henry James described her as a person of "very fine nature & . . . very gentle presence." But though Lowell and Mrs. Smalley were deeply fond of each other — love is not too strong a word — there is no evidence of the relationship having been other than Platonic, a term permissibly naïve when applied to a generation not yet made self-conscious about its ambiguities.[26]

At the end of each summer, Lowell would leave England with mixed feelings. Much as he enjoyed his life there, he had doubts as to its "wholesomeness." Except for the weeks at Whitby there was too much living on the surface of things, dazzling enough at times, but to a New Englander not quite "right." His winters in the United States thus provided a useful counterfoil; there, a greatly reduced social life made it possible for him to do some writing and this in turn made him feel easier — in Cambridge self-respect had always been more or less proportionate to the output of work. Lowell's American winters were not productive, of course, by any standard of youthful creativity. Much of his output consisted of earlier work which he now revised or arranged for "collected" volumes: one of political essays from the 1860's, one of poetry (*Heartsease and Rue*) made up largely from material printed in scattered journals during the previous thirty years, and, the most elaborate project, a ten-volume edition of his collected works, which appeared in 1890.

Such new writing as he did in these years consisted mostly of speeches, which after delivery he revised and published. In the period 1885–1889 he made five major addresses which in their widely ranging commentary constitute Lowell's "summing-up." Not that he had come either to a unified or a consistent philosophy; the speeches, like so much of his work, were better for their parts, graceful and epigrammatic, than for any thoroughgoing, systematized statement of principles. Typically, too, they all contained a fair amount of discursive and even contradictory material; as always, Lowell had trouble sustaining a point of view or working through a theme. But he did not look on these speeches, it should be said, as a "legacy" to his countrymen; he had too little pride of authorship left for that kind of self-regarding posture. Indeed, his opinion of his work seemed to decrease in proportion to the amount of praise showered upon it. At seventy, widely considered one of the country's "giants," he confessed to Norton that most of the time he thought of himself as a failure: "I *can't* do my best. That's the very torment of it. Why not reconcile oneself with being secondrate? Isn't it better than nothing? No, 'tis being nowhere." The public might praise, but what Lowell missed was "a comfortable sense of merit" within himself. Months after *Heartsease and Rue* was published, he wrote Norton, "I have never even opened my new book . . . I haven't dared . . ."

Posterity has in large measure validated Lowell's modest self-estimate, which makes his objectivity the more remarkable. It would seem wholly so could we be sure his self-depreciation reflected critical judgment, not merely temperament.[27]

On one level, certainly, Lowell's last speeches warrant only modest interest. There was little of originality in their diagnosis of American life or in their suggested remedies for its ills. The assumptions and arguments of the speeches reflected the standard intellectual baggage of the day, or, to be more precise, the generally agreed-upon hypotheses of New England's "Mugwump" intellectuals. As one of them, Lowell believed certain specific reforms, especially a lower tariff, civil service legislation and "hard" currency, would meet the country's primary needs. He had some sympathy for the plight and working conditions of the farmer and laborer, but none for the remedies they proposed, especially "greenbacks" or the free coinage of silver. And though theoretically in agreement with the organization of labor, Lowell objected to the kind of trade union "coercion" he thought typified by the Knights of Labor. As for increased federal intervention to remedy the hardships of the underprivileged, Lowell believed it should be limited to dealing with evils clearly within reach of the law; the government should never become a distributor of "alms." Individual character and national wealth were both best developed by leaving men as much as possible to their own resources — for the "natural law" of free competition was beneficent in its operations. But embedded within this optimistic context of Natural Benevolence lay an alloy of pessimism: there was no solution for poverty. Though the world as a whole progressed, there would always be those who failed in life's race. The Boston's Mugwumps were compassionate toward such men and gave generously to charities for their support, but finally, the defeated were beyond help; they were the unfortunate but irreducible by-product of an essentially benevolent system.[28]

If many of Lowell's assumptions today seem "old-fashioned,"

some of his incidental insights into American life do not. These alone repay study but his last speeches are also of interest because the personal gloss, the small variations, with which he presented the common "elitist" position of his day, expose the special contours of his own personality. Or rather, the personality of his later years, for these "final views" in some few ways contrast with those he had held earlier; this is especially true of their undogmatic tone and of the stress they place on the obstacles which human nature and human history necessarily (to some extent, happily) put in the path of social change. Yet withal, the continuities of argument in these speeches are more pronounced than the variations. They contain most of the themes which had always absorbed Lowell's attention: an optimistic faith in "the people"; a belief in the necessity of civic responsibility, of active participation in the life of the community; an insistence that character be valued above success, both in private and public life.[29]

The undogmatic tone had certainly not been alien to the younger Lowell, but now it was more consistently maintained. As Thomas Wentworth Higginson (always a qualified admirer) said, Lowell in his last years was "serener in judgment, sweeter in temper, than ever before." Lowell worried that he had reached the point where he was *too* fair to everyone; perhaps, after all, he thought, genius was more "an infinite capacity for being onesided" than for being just. The even temper of his last years is the more impressive for not representing a withdrawal, an abandonment of the world. Lowell remained concerned — not with the intensity he had demonstrated in youth, but with the patient, unruffled composure appropriate to the elder statesman.[30]

Even when arguing the basic axioms of the Mugwump creed, he avoided too rigid a posture. The world was confronted, he said, with "new problems and new conditions"; it would not do to assume that past truths would be applicable to present circumstances. "Old men in general love not change, and are suspicious of it," but they needed to realize, Lowell warned, that change is "the very condition of our being and thriving," just as "deliberation and choice" are the only "secure footholds on the shaky stepping-stones by which we cross the torrent of Circumstances." He warned, too, against any doctrinaire stance, any insistence that "facts shall accommodate themselves to preconceived theory" rather than, as befitted a practical man, deducing theory "from the amplest possible comparison and correlation of facts; in other words, from recorded experience." [31]

Lowell showed similar flexibility in presenting most of the Mugwump canon. As was standard for his group, he lamented the mindless pursuit of wealth, the "barbarizing plutolatry" which was turning the government into "a game of poker among our millionaires." Yet he was "not insensible to the wonder and exhilaration of a material growth without example in rapidity and expansion." Lowell deplored channeling the country's main energies into multiplying creature comforts but he did believe that there was a close relation between the physical and the moral well-being of man — "only when the bodily appetites of man are satisfied, does he become first conscious of a spiritual hunger." Similarly, Lowell could deplore political trends of the preceding twenty years, in which the only difference between the parties had been that "one was *in* and wished to stay there, and the other was *out* and *didn't* wish to stay there," but at the same time could accept the need for parties in a democracy. Through no other channels, he argued, could public opinion be marshaled and expressed (though if politicians were necessary to look after the parties, the "Independents" had to look after the politicians; otherwise considerations of selfish party advantage would wholly replace the discussion of public questions). In the same way, while disapproving of State Socialism, Lowell could admit to a "good bit" of Socialist leaven in himself — though it struggled vainly, he said, with "the dough" of his common sense. The Socialists, he feared, would mend the watch "by taking out the mainspring," and he could not imagine living in a Socialist or Communist world — he would be "bored to death by the everlasting Dutch landscape." Even so, "all well-meaning and humane men," he believed, had to "sympathize with the aims of Lasalle and Karl Marx," and if it was true that too much government interference ran the risk of tampering with the Laws of Nature, he reminded his countrymen that "it is the privilege and distinction of man to mitigate natural laws, and to make them his partners if he cannot make them his servants." [32]

Lowell showed the same elasticity, the same capacity to suspend judgment, when discussing the specific issues then agitating the country. On the tariff question, he applauded President Cleveland for resisting argument on the general, "mainly academic" controversy between free trade and protection, and confining himself instead to specifics. Lowell believed strongly in the need for tariff reform — "for (not to speak of the economical reasons) I believe that the surplus in our Treasury has done more to demoralize the public conscience than anything else within my memory. It has been as fatal as the Nibelungen hoard." But he believed, too, in approaching the problem pragmatically: all that "reasonable men" could currently contend for, he argued, "is the reduction of the tariff in such a way as shall be least hurtful to existing interests, most helpful to the consumer, and, above all, as shall practically test the question whether we are better off when we get our raw material at the lowest possible prices." [33]

Sometimes Lowell's "undogmatic" discussion of a contemporary problem seems to reflect ambivalence more than openmindedness — the difference between shifting erratically back and forth between a variety of viewpoints, and holding them consciously in balance. This was especially true of his views on the immigration question. In one mood, he expressed fear that foreigners pouring into the country might overtax its assimilative powers, "unsteadied" as the immigrants were "by lifelong training and qualifying associations." Yet in another mood, he expressed confidence that democracy had enough "vigor of constitution to assimilate these seemingly indigestible morsels and transmute them into strength of muscle and symmetry of limb." He could even, in this latter mood, manage some sympathy for Irish-Americans whose prime allegiance remained with their native rather than their adopted country; Ireland, after all, was the place around which their lifelong associations and hereditary traditions clustered, and Lowell could not help but admire the "marvels of fidelity and self-sacrifice" which their loyalties called forth.[34]

In any case, there was no doubt in Lowell's mind that the immigrants were to become "bone of our bone, and flesh of our flesh" and the challenge their assimilation represented should be met, he argued, not with nativistic bigotry, but with a broadened system of education. Lowell never sanctioned exclusionist immigration policies nor engaged in the low aspersions and high belligerence favored by the next generation of New England intellectuals — by men like Henry and Brooks Adams. Unlike them, also, Lowell eschewed any romantic (and vicious) glorification of the "Anglo-Saxon" race. He did believe that different "races" (a word he often used synonymously with ethnic or national groups) were endowed with special qualities and aptitudes: the Greeks for art, the Jews for commerce and the "higher divinations of the soul," the Romans for civil and military administration. And occasionally he could speak in a voice which did approximate the more blatant racism of the next generation — he once referred to pure Negroes as "incapable of civilization from their own resources," and to the American Indians as showing "a far greater natural predisposition for disfurnishing the outside of other people's heads than for furnishing the insides of their own." Such views would have been as repellent to the youthful Lowell as they would be congenial to the next generation of Brahmins. But even for the elderly Lowell these were isolated, not representative statements; they bespoke a spasmodic, not a settled prejudice. His earlier libertarianism had indeed become muddied, but was still far from submerged. He remained to the end incapable of the strident bigotry which was so shortly to characterize America's intellectual elite.[35]

When Lowell had delivered his 1884 speech on "Democracy" to an English audience, he had stressed the system's advantages and hopeful portents. Now, several years later and addressing his own countrymen, he paid more attention to its weaknesses and perils — even while reaffirming his belief in its basic efficacy. He feared the idea was spreading that "truth not only can but should be settled by a show of hands rather than by a count of heads." The wholesome democratic ideal that the interest of the many should be substituted for that of the few was becoming confused with the dangerous assumption that the *opinion* of the many should be substituted for that of the few — and the still more perilous tendency to allow concern with the rights of the people to obscure attention to their responsibilities.[36]

There was much else in the recent development of American life which Lowell viewed uneasily: the increased power of the press, controlled more than ever before "by its interests as a business rather than by its sense of duty as a teacher"; the tendency of population toward the great cities; the alienation of the educated from careers in government; the developments in rapid communication which threatened to make public opinion "simultaneous" — "liable to those delusions, panics, and gregarious impulses which transform otherwise reasonable men into a mob"; the tendency in university education toward pedantry, toward putting grammar and philology above literature and philosophy, the means to a livelihood above the development of character, narrow specialization above many-sided culture.[37]

The catalogue of "unexampled problems" facing the nation was formidable enough, but Lowell warned those eager for solutions to proceed with "moderated and controlled enthusiasm." He had once laid the world's imperfections at the door of corrupt institutions; now he was more inclined to ask if the fault might not be in the nature of man — in "the obstinate vitality of human error and human folly." It was possible to restrain, guide, even redirect man's natural impulses but it was prudent to remember that "they are always there and ready to take the bit in their teeth at the first chance which offers." Such improvements as could be made in the conditions of life had to concentrate on building and buttressing personal character: "It was the individual that should and could be leavened, and through the individual the lump. To reverse the process was to break the continuity of history and to wrestle with the angel of destiny." [38]

Lowell meant his argument as a plea for prudence, not inactivity. He asked that we recognize, with Burke, that "human nature was always the text and history the comment," but not that we accept the world's ills as beyond relief. On the contrary, Lowell argued that the greatest weakness in American life was a willingness to acquiesce in "makeshifts and abuses which can and ought to be helped, and which, with honest resolution, might be helped." Democracy was not a machine which would go of itself, and complacency had "made us neglectful of our political duties." What was needed was an active group of citizens who would insist "in season and out of season that we shall have a country whose greatness is measured, not only by its square miles, its number of yards woven, of hogs packed, of bushels of wheat raised, not only by its skill to feed and clothe the body, but also by its power to feed and clothe the soul . . ." Lowell contrasted contemporary indifference to public affairs with the constant vigilance of the Puritan fathers. The Puritan leaders may have been "narrow, ungenial," but they had been statesmen rather than politicians, that is, they had been "not so much interested in the devices by which men *may* be influenced, as about how they *ought* to be influenced; not so much about how men's passions and prejudices may be utilized for a momentary advantage . . . as about how they may be hindered from doing a permanent harm to the commonwealth." The Puritans recognized, too, that men were capable of, indeed required, an ideal outside themselves, and they were zealous in pursuing it. A country worth saving, Lowell argued, was worth saving all the time — and a country like the United States, "with such opportunities and inducements to grow rich, and such temptations to be content with growing rich, *needs* saving all the time." [39]

And he had faith the country could be saved all the time. Could, that is, if men first recognized that human nature and human history put limits on what they could usefully accomplish, and if they then made the most of the potential for change by constant attention to public duties. Lowell believed it was providential that the human skull had a certain resistant thickness — the world was thus saved much rash experimentation — but he believed, too, in the "eventual success of all reasonable reforms." He retained "so much faith in the good sense of the American people as to feel sure that discussion means victory." The progress already made in the "sum total of happiness," he felt, warranted optimism. Progress had not been linear; it had been "a spiral stairway mainly dark or dusty, with loopholes at long intervals only," but it had been progress nonetheless.[40]

The great danger in the United States was that progress might proceed in one direction only — toward a greater accumulation of wealth. Material well-being was an excellent thing for it meant power, leisure and liberty, but if divorced from culture — that is, "from intelligent purpose" — it became a mockery. Ultimately, in Lowell's view, the measure of a nation's success was its ability to produce "not a higher average man, but the highest possible types of manhood" — those who could contribute "to the thought, the moral energy, the intellectual happiness, the spiritual hope and consolation, of mankind." By such a standard, the American democracy had not yet, in his judgment, succeeded; it still complacently confused size with significance. But the verdict was not yet in on the American experiment, and despite dangers and uncertainties Lowell felt the verdict would one day be positive. In 1889 when speaking specifically about American literature, he summed up his general expectations for the country:

> We cannot say that our own as yet suffices us, but I believe that he who stands, a hundred years hence, where I am standing now, conscious that he speaks to the most powerful and prosperous community ever devised or developed by man, will speak of our literature with the assurance of one who beholds what we hope for and aspire after, become a reality and a possession forever.

Eighty of those hundred years have passed, but few speak with the assurance Lowell had confidently predicted.[41]

*

By the end of Cleveland's first term in 1889, some of the Republican Mugwumps had become disenchanted with his cautious policies, especially the limited advance he had made in civil service reform. While Lowell regretted that more had not been done, he continued to think and speak well of the President. He did feel, though, that as matters stood either party was likely to advance reform with equal (and limited) vigor. Thus when Cleveland met defeat in his bid for a second term, Lowell did not view the result as a particular disaster. But when Cleveland was given a dinner by the Merchants' Association of Boston in December, 1889, Lowell, though unable to attend, sent along complimentary verses which were read aloud:

> *Let who has felt compute the strain*
> *Of struggle with abuses strong,*
> *The doubtful course, the helpless pain*

Of seeing best intents go wrong;
We, who look on with critic eyes
Exempt from action's crucial test,
Human ourselves, at least are wise
In honouring one who did his best.

Cleveland was immensely pleased with the poem; he wouldn't exchange it, he said, "for anything that had ever been given him." [42]

Lowell's tribute marked a graceful end to his own active involvement in political affairs. A comment he made in 1886 on the poet Gray helps to define the need Lowell felt for those periodic retreats which had always marked his relationship to politics:

> It may argue pusillanimity, but I can hardly help envying the remorseless indifference of such men to the burning questions of the hour, at the first alarm of which we are all expected to run with our buckets, or it may be with our can of kerosene, snatched by mistake in the hurry and confusion. They devoted themselves to leisure with as much assiduity as we employ to render it impossible . . . one thing I am sure of, that the private person was of more importance both to himself and others then than now, and that self-consciousness was, accordingly, a vast deal more comfortable because it had less need of conscious self-assertion.

Throughout his life, Lowell had been torn by the conflicting demands of active citizenship and private tastes. He knew that he owed something to both, and so never made a final choice between the arena and the cloister, allowing instead the one temporarily to dominate the other whenever the needs of one seemed clearly imperative. Thus his life had been marked by alternating phases of public involvement and secluded privacy.

It was his belief that neither could give way permanently to the other without both suffering damage, for the public and the private were two necessary aspects of the whole man.[43]

*

On February 22, 1889, Lowell reached his seventieth birthday. The event was celebrated by a special issue of the Boston *Critic* with messages and congratulations from Lowell's famous contemporaries on both sides of the Atlantic, including Gladstone, Hayes, Benjamin Harrison, Holmes, George Washington Cable, Story, Whittier, Tennyson and Francis Parkman. Their praises in verse and prose were, as befitted the occasion, munificent, though Harvard's Charles W. Eliot struck a wry note in declaring, "I very much dislike Te Deums before victory & obituaries before death." Lowell was inclined to agree. "I have been employed ever since the 22d," he wrote Julia Stephen, "in thanking people for thanking me for being so virtuous as to reach seventy. It doesn't strike me as very wonderful. I have seen many fools do it & make no fuss about it." [44]

But of course he enjoyed the fuss, and especially a dinner given him at the Tavern Club, with Boston's mightiest in attendance. Norton presided, though not with entire approval of the proceedings (he was willing, he wrote Curtis, that Oliver Wendell Holmes "should live on flattery if he likes, — but ah! not our James. Put me out of the way, my dear George, as speedily as possible, if you ever see me even in secret taking to such a diet"). The evening, in any case, was judged a great success. Judge Hoar, Richard Watson Gilder and Norton, among others, gave speeches, and Oliver Wendell Holmes read a poem he had composed for the occasion:

Once more the health of Nature's favored son,
The poet, critic, patriot, all in one;

Health, honor, friendship ever round him wait
In life's fair field beyond the seven-barred gate!

Writing to Annie Fields the next day, Lowell warned her to be prepared for "a pinch of condescension" in his manner; after listening to his praises for two hours, he had gotten used to the discovery of how great a man he was — "a poison, you know, may be distilled from laurel leaves, and I think the very smell of them goes to the head." Banter aside, Lowell was moved by the dinner, "and indeed none but a pig could have helped liking the affectionate way it was done." Perhaps most touching of all had been a remark of Barrett Wendell's, a former pupil, who told Lowell how much his teaching had meant; Lowell grasped Wendell's hand impulsively and said that he liked hearing that best of all, for he had often wondered "whether in his years of teaching he had not wasted rather fruitlessly time he should have given to literature." [45]

He still hoped that some time for literature remained. And there seemed ground for hope, because he made the decision in 1889 to return once more to Elmwood, the "seat of his inspiration." The house had been let for the past four years, and he had never again expected to live there. But being without a fixed home had become more burdensome each year, though as Norton said, "he is brave, and utters neither complaint nor lament." Lowell hesitated about returning: Elmwood could become a quicksand of memories, and besides, "the edges of a broken life will never quite match, even were there any cement that would knit them together, and who has ever invented that?" [46]

His decision to risk a return hinged on his daughter, Mabel. Edward Burnett had not proved a good businessman and his dairy farm at Southborough had failed to prosper. He had served briefly in Congress (as a Democrat) from 1887 to 1889, but then, defeated for re-election and in search of a livelihood, had taken first to managing and then to building farms for the well-to-do, which required spending most of his time in New Jersey and New York. It therefore served the needs of both father and daughter to set up housekeeping together; Lowell would be solicitously cared for in his old home, and Mabel would have security for herself and her children.[47]

Anxious about the future of his grandchildren, Lowell, who in the past had been so careless of money, now drove hard bargains for his writings. But he needed to exert little pressure. His work was in great demand by the periodicals; the New York *Ledger* sent him a draft for $1000 in return for anything he should choose to send them, and Gilder of *Century Magazine* offered him $12,000 for twelve articles, as short as ten pages each in length. In combination with prospering investments, especially in railroad stock, and about $1200 a year in book royalties, Lowell was free for almost the first time in his life from financial worry. It gave him great comfort to know that he would leave his daughter independent.[48]

Mabel made just enough changes in Elmwood to give it an air of strangeness, and this helped Lowell to keep memories at bay. But renewing life in his old home was at first poignant — "I feel somehow as if Charon had ferried me the wrong way, & yet it is into a realm of ghosts that he has brought me . . ." Slowly, though, he made himself comfortable among them. He loved the "accustomed & familiar" — they gave "a unity to life which trying can't accomplish" — and the two sturdy English elms standing guard in front of Elmwood seemed guarantee against the encroachments of brick sidewalks and new houses. Then, too, there was the immense comfort of being back in his study. He had been separated for years from his library and now he could once more browse among its seven thousand volumes, falling again under the spell of Catullus, Montaigne and those Old French texts which continued to fascinate him even while he worried about their utility — "for I can't see exactly what good it has done me or anybody else." [49]

Lowell would sit near the window in a large, ugly reclining

chair complete with leg rest so that he could keep his foot up during a seizure of gout. His dogs, "Mr. Panks" and "Gobble," old-fashioned brindled bull terriers with long tails and ears, were almost always at his feet. On one side of his chair was a revolving book case, the top of which served as a table for clay pipes and a jar of strong tobacco. Books were everywhere, except in the drawers of the large mahogany desk, which he saved for unripened pears and peaches from the orchard. Around the walls of the study, in oval wooden frames, were photographs and paintings of such friends as Thomas Hughes, Francis Child and Julia Stephen. Safe with his books, shrouded as much as pursued by memory, he could lose himself for days on end, disturbed only by the grating noises of a grandchild practicing some musical instrument. The children soon learned, though, that the study was sacred ground with admission strictly by permission of the chief votary. Now and then they were allowed to enter, and Lowell, indulging his youthfulness as much as theirs, would tell them about the "fairies"—especially the man in gray who often came and stood comfortingly beside his chair. He would have them search for coins which the fairies had left hidden around the room to pay them for keeping their grandfather supplied with spills to light his pipe. Lowell thought the children talked more slang "than is in Grose's dictionary," though he supposed that in the natural course of things, their slang would be "the polite conversation of the next age." But he found it hard to bear in *this*, and was glad to be saved from having to make constant corrections by the arrival of an English governess. Lowell was relieved that she exercised authority, for he found reprimanding the children disagreeable: "I didn't wish to be remembered as a grandfather who was always *pecking*—a form of discipline which even hens reserve discreetly for *other* hen's chickens." [50]

Occasionally there would be visits from friends. Leslie Stephen came over from England to stay for several weeks, but more often, the guests were old familiars: John Holmes, with frock coat and cane, always with a smile and always with a brown paper bag full of nuts, apples and raisins for the children; Charles Eliot Norton, looking a little "too awesome and stern" for the children to do more than peek at from some safe corner. Sometimes Lowell would go out to pay calls or to attend a whist club, but with his hermit instincts once more to the fore, these were only irregular interruptions to a solitary routine.[51]

Though most of Lowell's life had simplified, there were a few elaborations. He was no longer seen in the sack coat or rough suit he used to wear out of doors; now it was a frock coat and high hat, more in the correct London than the usual Cambridge manner. And he even bought a small one-horse Victoria. The carriage was drawn by "The Duchess," actually a large, gray Irish hunter, and driven by one of the local hands, Joe Avord, gotten up in some kind of livery. It was all very grand by Cambridge standards, and on one drive to visit Norton, Lowell found local disapproval voiced from an unexpected quarter: in passing the home of the Harvard philosopher, Josiah Royce, Lowell was suddenly doused by a hose; Joe Avord yelled after the disappearing back of young Christopher Royce, but Lowell laughed and said that Christopher "was just trying to teach him philosophy in a practical way."[52]

Lowell was more content than he had been in years. He even managed to write a few new short pieces, and to put in, as well, considerable hard work on preparing the collected edition of his writings. Occasional attacks of gout aside, he was in fine health. Indeed he felt absurdly young, his gray beard an anachronistic contrast to his ruddy complexion, clear eyes and quick step. Passing a home for "incurable children" one day, Lowell remarked to his companion that he would surely be sent there. "How preposterous that I should be seventy!" he told George William Curtis, and Curtis agreed, for Lowell "seemed no more than fifty, brisk, sturdy, vigorous and chiding Time for his relentless pace." His friends marveled at his ability to renew himself; "he simply *cannot* grow old," Norton wrote to Curtis, "and he resents old age as if it were a wrong." Thus far he had had little to resent.[53]

But he had been back in Elmwood only two months when he became seriously ill. Suddenly, early in January, 1890, he began to void large quantities of blood, which suggested kidney trouble. Despite great pain, he at first refused to go to bed, but when he could sit up no longer, at last relented. For six weeks he was on his back, with intermittent attacks of clotting and one crisis so severe that his physician, Morrill Wyman (himself nearing eighty), watched three consecutive nights at the bedside. But Lowell complained so little and bore the intense discomfort with such serenity that no one, including the doctors, was yet alarmed. They assured him that he would recover completely if he was careful — "which is a bore," commented Lowell, ever impatient of inactivity. But he canceled his plans to go to England that summer and sat back to endure a slow convalescence.[54]

Early in April he was allowed to dress and go downstairs for the first time, but he remained very weak and was easily tired. The doctors insisted that he recline as much as possible, so a chaise-longue was put in the sun, and Lowell tried to make the best of his continuing invalidism: "I am by nature so stolidly content with seeing the things I have seen all my life," he wrote Norton, "and find such a comforting sympathy in them, that I am on the whole satisfied to sit on the veranda and enjoy a vegetative life with my trees, with Panks and Gobble for company." In June he had a slight relapse which was soon over, but it left him apprehensive. The malady seemed to come on with no warning and he feared it might at any time ambush him again.[55]

The whole of the summer of 1890 passed in slow, uncertain improvement. But though languid and inert, Lowell was free of acute symptoms and the quiet months were not unpleasant. The children were off on visits much of the time, and he and Mabel would sit together all day on the veranda or under the trees, reading and talking, sometimes venturing to have a look at the shrubs and flowers. He even managed to write a brief introduction to a new edition of Milton's "Areopagitica," and to plan a short life of Hawthorne which he had earlier agreed to do. Moreover, he began to read again with something like his old zest. One day he went to look up a reference in Rousseau, grew interested and read on in his works for weeks. He read Terence through again, Boswell's *Johnson* for the fourth time and more novels than ever before in his life, finding special pleasure in going over the Waverley series. Oliver Wendell Holmes, paying Lowell a visit, found him reading on the couch; when Holmes asked him how he felt, Lowell answered, "Oh, I suppose I'm in pain; I always am more or less, but look here [holding up his book], I've been reading *Rob Roy*. I suppose it may be for the fortieth time, but it is just as good as when I read it first." When Holmes returned home he got out his own copy of *Rob Roy* but tried in vain to interest himself in it; how in the world, he wondered, could a man in pain lose himself in the book when he could not.[56]

In late summer, as Lowell began to feel like his old self, Mabel suddenly became so seriously ill "as to darken every outlook with foreboding." For four weeks they lay in opposite rooms without being able to see each other. Her disease would turn out to be tuberculosis and would end in her death a few years later; in 1890, though, the symptoms had not yet clarified, or if they had, Lowell chose, as with Mabel's mother forty-five years earlier, not to recognize them.

In any case, by the fall Mabel seemed to be slowly mending, and Lowell's anxiety lost its edge. With the change in the weather his own health seemed to revive marvelously. "After growing younger every day for a fortnight," he wrote Julia Stephen, "I have resolved to draw the line at forty & intrench me there for the rest of my days. 'Tis an age that does not carry me beyond the circle of a woman's interest & so will do very well." He began to walk a little, his spirits improved and even after a new attack he confidently predicted that "the enemy" was but "drawing in his rearguard for a definitive retreat." [57]

Yet he failed to gain in strength. There were intervals when his health seemed as good as ever but languor continued, and then a persistent, bothersome cough developed. He expressed neither uneasiness nor annoyance; he never once asked the doctors for a firm diagnosis nor showed much curiosity about his symptoms; "what will be, will be," he said, "the *name* does not matter." "I don't bother about Death," he wrote Julia Stephen, "but shan't be sorry if he delays as long as he honestly can." [58]

Lowell tried to believe he was only "becalmed," that one day he would be right again. But with the new year came new troubles. In February a severe attack of gout, in June sciatic pain in his left leg. Then his voice began to fail, he could neither sleep for more than a few hours nor eat without nausea, and his strength continued to ebb. Still he made no complaint, but only expressed wonder at the varied symptoms, and weariness at their endless proliferation.

By the summer of 1891, Lowell's doctors faced the fact that he was dying of cancer, the malignancy having started in the kidneys and then spread slowly through the liver and lungs. Friends began to pay their last visits, hopefully telling themselves they might not be the last. When they came Lowell was always up and dressed, awaiting them in the study in his velvet coat, with pipe in hand. William James, who went out to Elmwood several times, reported to his brother, Henry, that Lowell was always "ready to talk and be talked to, alluding to his illness with a sort of apologetic and whimsical plaintiveness that had no querulousness in it, though he coughed incessantly, and the last time . . . was strongly narcotized by opium . . ." The opium began to be administered in mid-July, after the pain had become severe. Under its influence, Lowell's mind wandered and he was only briefly conscious. A few days before he died, Mabel went into his room early in the morning to see how he was. She doubted if he would notice her, for he had not done so in days. But suddenly he opened his eyes, looked at her with a smile and held out his hand. It was his last conscious moment. He died on August 12, 1891.[59]

Funeral services were held in the college chapel. The pallbearers included Norton, Oliver Wendell and John Holmes, Christopher Cranch, George William Curtis, John Bartlett and Francis Child — the few survivors who had marked the milestones of Lowell's life. It was noon of a terribly hot day, with Cambridge apparently deserted for the summer, yet the chapel was densely packed, with hundreds unable to get seats. The overflow crowd remained absolutely silent throughout the simple rites. Lowell had earlier requested "the fixed expression of the English service"; he did not want anybody "let loose over his body." As he was carried from the chapel to Mount Auburn Cemetery, church bells tolled throughout the city. He was buried in a family plot conspicuous for its plainness, unenclosed by granite curbing or by hedges. No monument marks the spot and only small tombstones commemorate the separate graves. "I fancy an honest man easier in his grave," Lowell had once said, "with the bare truth told about him on his headstone." [60]

BIBLIOGRAPHY

I. MANUSCRIPTS

THIS BIOGRAPHY has been written largely from unpublished materials. The most important single depository for manuscripts has been the Houghton Library, Harvard University. It owns by far the largest collection of JRL papers, as well as vast holdings in the papers of JRL's intimate friends, acquaintances and associates. The major collections used at Houghton are as follows:

A. JRL manuscripts: Dr. Francis Lowell Burnett Collection; Esther Lowell Cunningham Collection; James Burnett Lowell Collection; Lowell-Gay Correspondence; C. E. Norton Collection; Mrs. L. B. Rantoul Collection; "Sicilian Journal: C. E. Norton, C. C. Black, J. R. Lowell, J. W. Field, 1856"; JRL to Thomas B. Aldrich; JRL antislavery papers; JRL Business Papers; JRL to Francis J. Child; "JRL to the Family"; "JRL to the Howes"; JRL lectures; JRL notebooks; "JRL to the Nortons"; "JRL Scrapbook"; "JRL to Various Correspondents."

B. JRL letters can also be found in the following manuscript collections: Francis Bowen Autographs; George William Curtis Papers; Edward M. Davis Letters; Ralph Waldo Emerson Papers; E. L. Godkin Papers; William J. Hoppin Papers; William Dean Howells Papers; Henry James Papers; Henry Wadsworth Longfellow Papers; Elizabeth G. Norton Papers.

C. For an understanding of various aspects of JRL's career, attitudes and personal relationships, the following Houghton collections have been invaluable: Francis J. Child Papers; James Freeman Clarke Journal; George William Curtis Papers; Emerson Journals; C. C. Felton Papers; E. L. Godkin Papers; Thomas Wentworth Higginson Papers; Oliver Wendell Holmes Papers; Houghton Mifflin Letter Books and Autograph File; James Family Correspondence; Henry James, Jr., Journals; "Letters from Longfellow"; "Letters to Emerson"; "Letters to Longfellow"; Letters to Robert Carter; Charles Eliot Norton Papers; Norton Family Papers; "Norton to Various Correspondents"; Horace E. Scudder Correspondence and Diary; Scudder "Papers Relating to Lowell Biography";

Bayard Taylor Papers; Samuel G. Ward Papers; George E. Woodberry Papers.

In addition to Houghton Library, I have found useful manuscript materials at the following places:

American Antiquarian Society, Worcester (4 JRL letters; Stedman, Howells, Holmes, Longfellow, Whittier, G. W. Curtis, E. E. Hale Papers)

Bodleian Library, Oxford University (F. J. Child-A. H. Clough letters)

Boston Public Library (29 JRL letters, plus other JRL MSS and family items; Rufus W. Griswold, Weston, May, Garrison Papers; Correspondence of Edmund Quincy and Richard D. Webb, 1843–1872)

British Museum, London (Gladstone, Special and General Correspondence — includes 17 JRL letters; Gladstone Letterbooks; Gladstone Papers, Cabinet Minutes, Official Papers; Sir Charles Dilke Journals; Sir Charles Dilke General Correspondence — includes 8 JRL letters; Sir Edward Hamilton Diaries; Ripon Papers; James Dykes Campbell Literary Correspondence — includes 6 JRL letters; 6 additional JRL letters found in miscellaneous collections: Perabo, Correspondence of Sir Richard Owen, etc.)

Brown University (7 JRL letters, various JRL MSS; G. W. Curtis, G. S. Burleigh Papers)

Colby College (39 JRL letters)

Columbia University (E. C. Stedman, Gay, Moncure Conway Papers; Frederic Bancroft Collection)

Craigie House, Cambridge (12 JRL letters; Alice Longfellow, "The Old Order Changes"; H. W. L. Dana, "Lowell at Elmwood"; Fanny Longfellow Journal and Letters)

Dartmouth College (3 JRL letters; miscellaneous collections for various JRL acquaintances)

Essex Institute, Salem (4 JRL letters; George B. Loring Letters; W. W. Story and Whittier Papers)

Folger Library (13 JRL letters and various JRL MSS and books; miscellaneous collections for O. W. Holmes, Longfellow, G. W. Curtis, Stedman, E. E. Hale)

Harvard University Archives (JRL's Exhibition Part, Oct. 17, 1837; newspaper clippings re: JRL-Bowen controversy of 1850–1851; W. R. Thayer notebook; College Papers, 2nd Series, X, XXI, XXII, XXIV, XXVI, XXVII, XXVIII, XXX; Overseer's Records, VIII, IX, XII, XIII; Corporation Papers; Reports to the Overseers: Academical Series, Instruction Series, Presidential and Fellows Series, Libraries Series, Miscellaneous Series; Faculty Records, XI; Sibley's Private Journal, I; Wendell Barrett Papers)

Hayes Library, Fremont (Hayes Papers, including a few JRL letters)
Hispanic Society, New York City (about 175 JRL letters to Señora de Riaño)
Historical Society of Pennsylvania (15 JRL letters)
Huntington Library (Spence-Lowell Collection; James T. Fields Papers)
Imperial College of Science and Technology, London (13 JRL letters)
Johns Hopkins University (D. C. Gilman Papers, including 11 JRL letters)
Library of Congress (64 JRL letters scattered in many collections; Hamilton Fish Correspondence and Letterbooks; William Evarts, O. W. Holmes, J. G. Blaine, J. C. B. Davis, Frelinghuysen, James Garfield, Henry White Papers)
Macmillan and Company, London (Thomas Hughes letters)
Massachusetts Historical Society (64 JRL letters and various MSS scattered in a number of miscellaneous collections; Horatio Woodman, Dexter, Edmund Quincy, Dana, John W. Field, G. F. Hoar Papers; Quincy Family Autographs; C. F. Adams, Jr., Diaries; Annie Fields Journals)
Middlebury College (15 JRL letters)
Morgan Library (about 50 JRL letters; JRL "Birthday Book"; Letters of Leslie Stephen to Prof. William Knight)
National Archives, Washington D.C. (Series No. 31, Despatches from U.S. Ministers to Spain, rolls 85–89; Series No. 30, Despatches from U.S. Ministers to Great Britain, rolls 135–148; Series 40, Domestic Letters of the Department of State, rolls 84–102; Series 77, Diplomatic Instructions of the Department of State, roll 146 — Spain, rolls 84–86 — Great Britain)
New York Public Library
a. Berg Collection (JRL to Robert Carter — about 45 letters; JRL to Julia Stephen — 124 letters; large collection of JRL MSS and printed works; Stedman letters to Moncure Conway; G. W. Curtis letters to G. B. Briggs; Longfellow, Emerson, O. W. Holmes, J. T. Fields, W. C. Bryant, Hawthorne Papers)
b. Historical Manuscripts Room (folder of JRL "Personal Miscellany," which includes 8 JRL letters; miscellaneous JRL letters and MSS in Bryant-Godwin, Authors Club, Stoddard and Mary S. Harkness Collections; JRL's engagement book while Minister to England; extracts from JRL lectures; J. M. McKim Papers; Century Club Collection; Evert Duyckinck Journal and Papers — includes 10 JRL letters)
Ohio Historical Society (Howells Letters)
Peabody Institute, Baltimore (John Kennedy Pendleton Papers, which include 3 JRL letters)
Princeton University (miscellaneous collections for various JRL acquaintances, including a few JRL letters)

Public Records Office, London (Foreign Office Papers; Lord Granville Papers, including about 35 JRL letters; Lord Tenterden Papers)
Radcliffe Woman's Archives (Loring Family Papers)
Society for the Preservation of New England Antiquities (3 JRL letters; Sarah Orne Jewett Papers, including correspondence of Annie Fields and Mrs. Osgood)
State Library, Albany (E. E. Hale Papers, which includes 16 JRL letters to Nathan Hale, Jr., and miscellaneous JRL MSS)
University of Pennsylvania (20 JRL letters and partial MS for "Blondel")
University of Texas (about 10 JRL letters, various JRL MSS and family items; W. W. Story and G. W. Curtis Papers)
University of Virginia (about 100 JRL letters and various JRL MSS; Howells, O. W. Holmes, Longfellow, Hawthorne, Whittier, G. W. Curtis, T. W. Higginson, Stedman, E. E. Hale Papers)
Vassar College (about 15 JRL letters)
Wellesley College (6 JRL letters; 1611 edition of Spenser annotated by JRL; annotated proofs of "Music. A Lecture in Rhyme")
Yale University
a. American Literature Collection (JRL, R. T. S. Lowell, C. E. Norton, G. W. Curtis, J. T. Fields, Whittier, Longfellow, O. W. Holmes, John Bartlett Papers)
b. Historical Manuscript Room (3 JRL letters; T. D. Woolsey, W. D. Whitney, Evarts Family Papers)

Privately Owned Collections (see Acknowledgments):

Mrs. Sherman Baldwin
Mr. C. Waller Barrett
Mr. Peter de Brant
Mr. Effingham Evarts
Mr. Albert G. Frothingham
Professor F. W. Hilles
Mr. Parkman D. Howe
Mrs. Alfred Lowell
Mrs. David A. Miller
Miss Elizabeth Putnam
Mr. Charles M. Storey

Miscellaneous:

a. I have found ten or fewer JRL letters or MSS in the following depositories: Boston Athenaeum; Boston College; Boston University; Lilly Library, Indiana University; University of Kentucky; University of Buffalo; Lehigh University; Southwest Museum, L.A.; Concord Free Public Library; Swarthmore College; Haverford College; Doheny Library, St. Johns Seminary; Davis Library, Exeter Academy; Wisconsin Historical Society; University of Illinois; Historical and Philosophical Society of Ohio; University of North Carolina; Chicago Historical Society; University of California, Berkeley; Cornell University; University of California, Los Angeles; University of Cincinnati; Duke University Library; New

Hampshire Historical Society; Gray Herbarium, Cambridge; Museum of Comparative Zoology, Cambridge; University of Leeds, England; Keats-Shelley Memorial House, Rome; Koninklijke Bibliotheek, Holland

b. A final source for JRL manuscript material (and a surprisingly fertile one) has been auction house catalogues. These catalogues, in announcing manuscript sales, often print excerpts and where the originals can no longer be located are a valuable if fragmentary source. I found catalogues from the following auction houses especially useful: Anderson, Christie's, Goodspeed's, Libbie, T. F. Madigan, Maggs, Parke-Bernet, Scott & O'Shaughnessy, Sotheby's, Walpole Galleries

II. PRINTED SOURCES

A. PUBLISHED WORKS BY JAMES RUSSELL LOWELL

The edition of Lowell's collected works used for this biography (and the one cited in the footnotes) is the Riverside Edition, *The Writings of James Russell Lowell* (Boston: 1890), 11 vols.: I-IV, Poetical Works; I-VI, Prose Works; I, Latest Literary Essays. A considerable body of Lowell's writing was not collected in the Riverside Edition, and can be found only in scattered publications and manuscripts. I have not attempted to relist these sources, since the footnotes contain full citations. For the *published* items not collected in the Riverside Editon, a guide already exists: George Willis Cooke, *A Bibliography of James Russell Lowell* (Boston: 1906). Though generally reliable, Cooke is incorrect or incomplete in a number of particulars, and his guide should be supplemented by the following more recent additions to Lowell bibliography:

Cameron, Kenneth W., "Harvard Manuscript Resources for Students of Lowell," *Emerson Society Quarterly*, 2nd Quarter, 1960.

Campbell, Killis, "Bibliographical Notes on Lowell," *University of Texas Bulletin*, March 15, 1924, Studies in English No. 4

—— "Lowell's Uncollected Poems," *Publications of the Modern Language Association*, December, 1923

—— "Three Notes on Lowell," *Modern Language Notes*, February, 1923

Clark, H. H., and N. Foerster, *James Russell Lowell, Representative Selections with Introduction, Bibliography, and Notes* (New York: 1947)

Joyce, H. E., "A Bibliographical Note on James Russell Lowell," *Modern Language Notes*, April, 1920

Livingston, Luther S. (largely from the collection and notes of Jacob C.

Chamberlain), *A Bibliography of the First Editions in Book Form of the Writings of James Russell Lowell* (New York: 1914)

Miller, F. De Wolfe, "Twenty-Eight Additions to the Canon of Lowell's Criticism," *Studies in Bibliography*, Fredson Bowers ed., IV, 1951–1952 (Charlottesville: 1951)

White, W., "Two Versions of Lowell's 'Function of the Poet,'" *Philological Quarterly*, XX (1941)

Wilson, Carroll Atwood, bibliography of Lowell in *Thirteen Author Collections of the Nineteenth Century*, limited edition of 350 copies (Scribners, 1950)

Woodress, James L., Jr., "A Note on Lowell Bibliography: The Review of Howells' *Venetian Life*," *Studies in Bibliography*, Fredson Bowers ed., IV, 1951–1952 (Charlottesville: 1951)

Since the Cooke bibliography, various letters and writings of Lowell's have appeared in print or in doctoral dissertations for the first time. The significant items are as follows:

Armytage, W. H. G., ed., "Some New Letters of James Russell Lowell," *Notes and Queries*, May 13, 1950

Beatty, Richmond C., ed., "Lowell's Commonplace Books," *New England Quarterly*, September, 1945

Cameron, Kenneth W., ed., "James Russell Lowell's 'Ancient Epics . . . ,'" *Emerson Society Quarterly*, 1st Quarter, 1961

—— "James Russell Lowell's Undergraduate Verse," *Emerson Society Quarterly*, 3rd Quarter, 1956

Duberman, Martin, ed., "A Brahmin's Self-Laughter" (Lowell's mock genealogy of his family), *Manuscripts*, Summer, 1963

—— "Twenty-Seven Poems of James Russell Lowell," *American Literature*, November, 1963

Duncan, Graham H., "James Russell Lowell's Reviews of American Belles Lettres: An Annotated Anthology," Cornell doctoral dissertation, 1953

Fuess, C. M., ed., "Some Forgotten Political Essays by Lowell," *Massachusetts Historical Society Proceedings*, LXII

Graf, Le Roy, and R. W. Haskins, ed., "'This Clangor of Belated Mourning': James Russell Lowell on Andrew Johnson's Father," *South Atlantic Quarterly*, Summer, 1963

Graham, Philip, ed., "Some Lowell Letters," *Texas Studies in Literature and Language*, Winter, 1962.

Howe, M. A. DeWolfe, ed., *New Letters of James Russell Lowell* (New York: 1932)

Howe, M. A. DeWolfe, and G. W. Cottrell, Jr., eds., *The Scholar-Friends, Letters of Francis James Child and James Russell Lowell* (Cambridge: 1952)

Hudson, Gertrude Resse, ed., *Browning to His American Friends. Letters Between the Brownings, the Storys and James Russell Lowell* (London: 1965)

"Letters of James Russell Lowell to W. H. Furness" (anonymous editor), *Colonial Society of Massachusetts Publications*, VIII (1906)

The Round Table (anonymous editor), early Lowell essays (Boston: 1913)

Smith, Thelma, ed., *Uncollected Poems of James Russell Lowell* (Philadelphia: 1950)

Woodress, James L., Jr., ed., "The Lowell-Howells Friendship: Some Unpublished Letters," *New England Quarterly*, December, 1953.

B. A NOTE ON PREVIOUS LOWELL BIOGRAPHIES

Since my decision to write a biography of Lowell reflects an assumption that existing studies are inadequate, I owe some comment on those studies.

The most elaborate biography of Lowell, by Horace E. Scudder (*James Russell Lowell* [Boston: 1901], 2 vols.) is in some ways a skillful, as it is certainly an earnest, work. But it suffers fatally from having been conceived as a "tribute." Scudder assumes as given Lowell's towering stature, and concentrates on detailing rather than scrutinizing its properties. His book also suffers from being a compendium: large chunks of Lowell's letters and writings are printed without sufficient pre-digestion. Finally, new manuscript materials have now made it possible to fill out or correct Scudder at many points. It should be remembered, however, that Scudder was the first to research Lowell's life in depth, and his considerable efforts turned up basic data on which scholars have ever since relied.

The only other substantial early biographies were by E. E. Hale, *James Russell Lowell and His Friends* (Boston: 1899), and Ferris Greenslet, *James Russell Lowell, His Life and Work* (Boston: 1905). For many years the Hale volume had value as a primary source, for it included lengthy quotations from privately owned manuscripts. But many of these have since become available, notably Lowell's letters to Nathan Hale, Jr., now at the State Library in Albany. With its value as a source book greatly diminished, Hale's study today holds little of interest. It is far too impressionistic and eccentric a book to be relied upon either for its facts or for its judgments.

Greenslet's biography is largely quarried from Scudder and a few other printed sources and suffers from their limitations. Yet in some ways, the Greenslet study is more satisfactory than Scudder: it is better written, more adventuresome in its estimates, less ponderous and conventional. If Scudder remains more authoritative and complete,

Greenslet is more graceful and perceptive. Late in life Greenslet published *The Lowells and Their Seven Worlds* (Boston: 1946), which deals only in small part with James Russell and is throughout most uneven in quality.

There have been only two recent book-length studies of Lowell: R. C. Beatty, *James Russell Lowell* (Nashville: 1942), and Leon Howard, *Victorian Knight-Errant* (Berkeley: 1952). Beatty's book is well (though somewhat lushly) written and uses a few fresh sources, notably Lowell's diplomatic correspondence. But his study is badly marred by a "Confederate" point of view which at several points is so far out of touch with Lowell's frame of reference as to create serious distortions. Leon Howard's volume deals almost exclusively with Lowell's pre-Civil War years. Howard's intention was not a full biography but a study in the use of literary materials for biographical purposes. His book provides much detailed information, though not all of it well integrated; and its speculations sometimes go beyond what the evidence would seem to warrant. As a whole, the greatest value of the Howard volume is bibliographical rather than critical.

The other existing Lowell biographies are slight productions, largely personal reminiscences. Except for an occasional anecdote or detail, they are devoid of value. In this category, the only one worth any mention is Francis H. Underwood's sketch, *The Poet and the Man: Recollections and Appreciations of James Russell Lowell* (Boston: 1893). Far more perceptive than such works are the essays on Lowell by Henry James and William Dean Howells cited in the Bibliography.

C. USEFUL BOOKS, ARTICLES, THESES

I have listed below only those titles cited in the footnotes — in other words, those works which were of use either for a quotation or for direct background information. There would be no point in relisting even these, but they are cited in the footnotes only by short title after their initial appearance, and thus might occasionally be difficult to identify. I have not listed below hundreds of other volumes which I consulted without any special profit. Nor have I listed any newspapers or periodicals, for although these were often of crucial value, the pertinent issues can be easily identified in the footnotes.

Adams, Charles Francis, *An Autobiography* (Boston: 1916)
—— *Richard Henry Dana*, 2 vols. (Boston: 1891)
Adams, Henry, *The Education of Henry Adams* (New York: 1931)
Akers, Charles, "Personal Glimpses of Our New England Poets," *New England Magazine*, 1897, New Series, XVII
Aldrich, Mrs. Thomas Bailey, *Crowding Memories* (Boston: 1920)
Allen, Gay Wilson, *American Prosody* (New York: 1935)

Amory, Cleveland, *The Proper Bostonians* (New York: 1947)
Anderson, Thornton, *Brooks Adams: Constructive Conservative* (Ithaca: 1951)
Arvin, Newton, *Longfellow: His Life and Work* (Boston: 1963)
Auden, W. H., and Norman Holmes Pearson, *Poets of the English Language*, 5 vols. (New York: 1950)
Austin, James C., *Fields of the Atlantic Monthly: Letters to an Editor 1861–1870* (San Marino: 1953)
Bail, Hamilton Vaughan, "James Russell Lowell's Ode," *Papers of the Bibliographical Society of America*, 3rd quarter, 1943
Baker, Paul R., *The Fortunate Pilgrims: Americans in Italy 1800–1860* (Cambridge: 1964)
Barrows, Chester L., *William M. Evarts, Lawyer, Diplomat, Statesman* (Chapel Hill: 1941)
Beale, Howard K., ed., *The Diary of Gideon Welles* (New York: 1960)
Bennett, George N., "William Dean Howells: The Boston Years, 1866–1888. A Biographical and Critical Study," Yale doctoral dissertation, 1954
Beringause, Arthur F., *Brooks Adams: A Biography* (New York: 1955)
Bernard, E. G., "New Light on Lowell as Editor," *New England Quarterly*, June, 1937
Bittner, William, *Poe, A Biography* (Boston: 1962)
Blodgett, Geoffrey T., "The Mind of the Boston Mugwump," *Mississippi Valley Historical Review*, March, 1962
Boutwell, George S., *Reminiscences of Sixty Years in Public Affairs*, 2 vols. (New York: 1902)
Bradley, Sculley, ed., *The Pioneer*, facsimile, with an introduction by Bradley (New York: 1947)
Bremer, Frederika, *Homes of the New World* (New York: 1858)
Brooks, Van Wyck, *Howells, His Life and World* (New York: 1959)
Brownell, W. C., *American Prose Masters* (New York: 1959)
Cameron, Kenneth Walter, ed., "James Russell Lowell's Ancient Epics as Proofs of Genius," *Emerson Society Quarterly*, 1st Quarter, 1961
—— *Undergraduate Verses, Rhymed Minutes of the Hasty Pudding Club* (Hartford: 1956)
Canby, Henry Seidel, *Thoreau* (Boston: 1939)
Clark, George P., "Classical Influences and Background in the Writings of James Russell Lowell," Yale doctoral dissertation, 1948
—— "James Russell Lowell's Study of the Classics Before Entering Harvard," *Jahrbuch fur Amerikastudien*, Band 8, 1963
Clark, H. H., and Norman Foerster, *James Russell Lowell, Representative Selections, with Introduction, Bibliography and Notes* (New York: 1947)
Conway, Moncure, *Autobiography: Memories and Experiences*, 2 vols. (Boston: 1904)

Cooke, George Willis, *John Sullivan Dwight* (Boston: 1898)
Cunningham, Esther Lowell, *Three Houses* (Boston: 1955)
Current-Gracía, Eugene, "Southern Literary Criticism and the Sectional Dilemma," *Journal of Southern History*, August, 1949
Curtis, George William, ed., *The Correspondence of John Lothrop Motley*, 2 vols. (New York: 1889)
de Riaño, Dona Emilia Gayangos, "Mr. Lowell and His Spanish Friends," *Century Magazine*, June, 1900
Dickens, Charles, The Letters of, 1880, 2 vol. edition "edited by his sister-in-law and eldest daughter"
Downer, James Walker, "Features of New England Rustic Pronunciation in James Russell Lowell's Biglow Papers," University of Michigan doctoral dissertation, 1958
Duncan, Graham H., "James Russell Lowell's Review of American Belles Lettres: An Annotated Anthology," Cornell doctoral dissertation, 1953
Dyer, Brainerd, *The Public Career of William M. Evarts* (Berkeley: 1933)
Edel, Leon, *Henry James: The Conquest of London* (New York: 1962)
Edwards, Owen, doctoral dissertation on Anglo-Irish-American affairs in progress at The Johns Hopkins University
Eliot, Charles W., "James Russell Lowell As a Professor," *Harvard Graduates' Magazine*, June, 1919
Elliott, Maud Howe, *Julia Ward Howe, 1819–1910*, 2 vols. (Boston: 1916)
Emerson, Edward Waldo, *The Early Years of the Saturday Club 1855–1870* (Boston: 1918)
Everson, Ida G., "William J. Stillman: Emerson's 'Gallant Artist,'" *New England Quarterly*, March, 1958
Fisk, Ethel F., ed., *The Letters of John Fiske* (New York: 1940)
Fitzmaurice, Lord Edmond, *The Life of Granville George Leveson Gower, Second Earl Granville*, 2 vols. (New York: 1905)
Fredrickson, George M., *The Inner Civil War* (New York: 1965)
Fuller, Margaret, *Papers on Literature and Art* (New York: 1846)
Gilder, Rosamund, ed., *The Letters of Richard Watson Gilder* (Boston: 1916)
Golann, Ethel, "A Lowell Autobiography," *New England Quarterly*, June, 1934
Greenslet, Ferris, *The Lowells and Their Seven Worlds* (Boston: 1946)
—— *James Russell Lowell: His Life and Work* (Boston: 1905)
Haight, Gordon, ed., *The George Eliot Letters*, 7 vols (New Haven: 1954)
Hale, E. E., *James Russell Lowell and His Friends* (Boston: 1899)
—— Prefatory Note, and Walter Littlefield, Introduction, *Early Prose Writings of James Russell Lowell* (New York: 1902)

Hale, Susan, *Life and Letters of Thomas Gold Appleton* (New York: 1885)
Haraszti, Zoltan, ed., *The Letters of T. W. Parsons* (Boston: 1939)
Hardy, Mrs. Thomas, *The Early Life of Thomas Hardy* (London: 1928)
Harlow, Virginia, *Thomas Sergeant Perry: A Biography* (Durham: 1950)
Harris, Frank, *My Life and Loves* (New York: 1963)
Hart-Davis, Rupert, ed., *The Letters of Oscar Wilde* (New York: 1962)
Higginson, Thomas Wentworth, *Old Cambridge* (New York: 1899)
Higham, John, "Anti-Semitism in the Gilded Age," *Mississippi Valley Historical Review*, March, 1957
Holland, Frederic M., "Reading Dante with Lowell," *New England Magazine*, January, 1896
Hovey, Richard B., *John Jay Chapman—An American Mind* (New York: 1959)
Howard, Leon, "The Case of the Sanded Signature," *Manuscripts*, Spring, 1961
—— *Victorian Knight-Errant* (Berkeley: 1952)
Howe, M. A. DeWolfe, *The Atlantic Monthly and Its Makers* (Boston: 1919)
—— *Barrett Wendell and His Letters* (Boston: 1924)
—— *John Jay Chapman and His Letters* (Boston: 1937)
——, ed., *Memories of a Hostess* (Boston: 1922)
—— *New Letters of James Russell Lowell* (New York: 1932)
——, and G. W. Cottrell, Jr., eds., *The Scholar Friends, Letters of Francis Child and James Russell Lowell* (Cambridge: 1952)
Howells, William Dean, *Literary Friends and Acquaintance* (New York: 1900)
Hudson, Gertrude Reese, ed., *Browning to His American Friends* (London: 1965)
Hugo, Howard E., ed., *The Portable Romantic Reader* (New York: 1957)
James, Henry, "James Russell Lowell" (*Atlantic Monthly*, January, 1892), "James Russell Lowell 1819–1891" (*Library of the World's Best Literature*, Charles Dudley Warner ed., 1897), and "An American Art-Scholar: Charles Eliot Norton" (*Burlington Magazine*, January, 1909), all as reprinted in *The American Essays of Henry James*, edited and with an introduction by Leon Edel (New York: 1950)
—— *William Wetmore Story and His Friends* (New York: 1903)
Jayne, H. H. Furness, ed., *The Letters of H. H. Furness*, 2 vols. (Boston: 1922)

Klibbe, Laurence H., *James Russell Lowell's Residence in Spain 1877–1880* (New York: 1964)
Lang, Cecil Y., ed., *The Swinburne Letters*, 6 vols. (New Haven: 1960)
Leyda, Jay, *The Melville Log: A Documentary Life of Herman Melville*, 2 vols. (New York: 1951)
Lowell, Charles, *Sermons: Chiefly Practical* (Boston: 1855)
Lubbock, Percy, ed., *The Letters of Henry James*, 2 vols. (New York: 1920)
McDowell, Tremaine, *The Romantic Triumph: American Literature from 1830 to 1860* (New York: 1933)
McFadyen, Alvan R., "The Contemporaneous Reputation of James Russell Lowell," University of Florida doctoral dissertation, 1955
Mabbott, T. O., "A Review of Lowell's Magazine," *Notes and Queries*, June 29, 1940
Mack, Edward C., and W. H. G. Armytage, *Thomas Hughes* (London: 1952)
Madariaga, Salvador de, *Spain, A Modern History* (New York: 1950)
Maitland, Frederic W., *The Life and Letters of Leslie Stephen* (New York: 1906)
Mann, Horace, Life and Works of (Boston: 1891)
Mendel, Sydney, "A Note on Lowell's 'Ode Recited at the Harvard Commemoration,'" *New England Quarterly*, March, 1962
Miller, Betty, ed., *Elizabeth Barrett to Miss Mitford* (New Haven: 1954)
Mitchell, Robert Earl, "American Life As Reflected in the Atlantic Monthly 1857–1881," Harvard doctoral dissertation, 1951
Monteiro, George, "Howells on Lowell: An Unascribed Review," *New England Quarterly*, December, 1965
Morgan, M. H., "John Bartlett," *Proceedings of the American Academy of Arts & Sciences*, XLI
Morison, Samuel Eliot, *Three Centuries of Harvard* (Cambridge: 1946)
Morse, John T., Jr., *The Life and Letters of Oliver Wendell Holmes*, 2 vols. (Boston: 1896)
Mott, F. L., *A History of American Magazines 1741–1850* (New York: 1930)
Mulhauser, Frederick L., ed., *The Correspondence of Arthur Hugh Clough*, 2 vols. (Oxford: 1957)
Nadal, E. S., *A Virginia Village and Other Papers* (New York: 1917)
—— "London Recollections of Lowell," *Harper's Monthly Magazine*, February, 1916
Nevins, Allan, *The Emergence of Lincoln*, 2 vols. (New York: 1950)
——, ed., *The Letters of Grover Cleveland, 1850–1908* (Boston: 1933)
Norton, Charles Eliot, "Remarks of Mr. Norton at the Annual Meeting of the Dante Society, May 16, 1882," *First Annual Report of the Dante Society* (Cambridge: 1882)

—— "Reminiscences of Old Cambridge," *Cambridge Historical Society Publications*, I (Cambridge: 1906)

Norton, Sara, and M. A. DeWolfe Howe, eds., *The Letters of Charles Eliot Norton*, 2 vols. (Boston: 1913)

Ogden, Rollo, ed., *The Life and Letters of Edwin Lawrence Godkin*, 2 vols. (New York: 1907)

Palmer, George Herbert, *The Autobiography of a Philosopher* (Boston: 1930)

Palmer, R. R., *The Age of Democratic Revolution* (Princeton: 1964)

Pearce, Roy Harvey, *The Continuity of American Poetry* (Princeton: 1961)

Pletcher, David M., *The Awkward Years: American Foreign Relations Under Garfield and Arthur* (St. Louis: 1962)

Poe, Edgar Allan, The Complete Works of, James A. Harrison ed., 17 vols. (New York: 1902)

Potter, David M., *Lincoln and His Party in the Secession Crisis* (New Haven: 1942)

Ramm, Agatha, ed., *The Political Correspondence of Mr. Gladstone and Lord Granville 1876–1886*, 2 vols. (Oxford: 1962)

Ray, Gordon N., ed., *The Letters and Private Papers of William Makepeace Thackeray*, 4 vols. (Cambridge: 1946)

Reilly, J. J., *Lowell As a Critic* (New York: 1915)

Robertson, J. M., "Lowell As a Critic," *North American Review*, February, 1919

Rusk, Ralph L., ed., *The Letters of Ralph Waldo Emerson*, 6 vols. (New York: 1939)

Russell, George W. E., ed., *The Letters of Matthew Arnold 1848–1888*, 2 vols. (London: 1895)

Samuels, Ernest, *Henry Adams: The Middle Years* (Cambridge: 1958)

—— *Henry Adams: The Major Phase* (Cambridge: 1964)

Scudder, Horace E., *James Russell Lowell*, 2 vols. (Cambridge: 1901)

Shaler, Nathaniel Southgate, The Autobiography of (Boston: 1909)

Shapiro, Samuel, *Richard Henry Dana, Jr. 1815–1882* (East Lansing: 1961)

Shepard, Odell, ed., *The Journals of Bronson Alcott* (Boston: 1938)

Smalley, George W., *Anglo-American Memories* (New York: 1911)

—— "Mr. Lowell in England," *Harper's*, April, 1896

Smith, Thelma M., ed., *Uncollected Poems of James Russell Lowell* (Philadelphia: 1950)

Solomon, Barbara Miller, *Ancestors and Immigrants* (Cambridge: 1956)

Stafford, John, *The Literary Criticism of "Young America": A Study in the Relationship of Politics and Literature 1837–1850* (Berkeley: 1952)

Stearns, Frank Preston, *Cambridge Sketches* (Philadelphia: 1905)

Stillman, William James, *Autobiography of a Journalist* (Boston: 1901)
Storey, Moorfield, "Harvard in the Sixties," *Harvard Graduates' Magazine*, V, March, 1897
Taylor, Joshua C., *William Page: The American Titian* (Chicago: 1957)
Thayer, William Roscoe, "James Russell Lowell As a Teacher," *Scribner's Magazine*, October, 1920
——, ed., *Letters of John Holmes to James Russell Lowell and Others*, with an introduction by Alice M. Longfellow (Boston: 1917)
Thoron, Ward, ed., *The Letters of Mrs. Henry Adams* (Boston: 1936)
Trowbridge, John Townsend, *My Own Story, with Recollections of Noted Persons* (Boston: 1903)
Tryon, W. S., *Parnassus Corner, A Life of James T. Fields* (Boston: 1963)
Tyler, Alice Felt, *The Foreign Policy of James G. Blaine* (Minneapolis: 1927)
Vanderbilt, Kermit, *Charles Eliot Norton, Apostle of Culture in a Democracy* (Cambridge: 1959)
Vernon, Hope Jillson, ed., *The Poems of Maria Lowell with Unpublished Letters and a Biography* (Providence: 1936)
Voss, Arthur W., "The Biglow Papers of James Russell Lowell," Yale doctoral dissertation, 1951
Wagenknecht, Edward, ed., *Mrs. Longfellow: Selected Letters and Journals of Fanny Appleton Longfellow* (New York: 1956)
Warren, Austin, "Lowell on Thoreau," *Studies in Philology*, XXVII, No. 3, July, 1930
Wendell, Barrett, "Mr. Lowell As a Teacher," *Scribner's Magazine*, May, 1891
—— *Stelligeri and Other Essays* (New York: 1893)
Whicher, Stephen E., *Freedom and Fate* (Philadelphia: 1953)
Whiting, Lilian, *Boston Days* (London: 1902)
Williams, Stanley T., *The Spanish Background of American Literature*, 2 vols. (New Haven: 1955)
Wilson, Edmund, "Notes on Gentile Pro-Semitism: New England's 'Good Jews,'" *Commentary*, October, 1956
Woodward, C. Vann, *Reunion and Reaction* (Boston: 1951)
Wright, William Aldis, ed., *Letters of Edward Fitzgerald*, 2 vols. (London: 1894)
—— *Letters of Edward Fitzgerald to Fanny Kemble 1871–1883* (New York: 1895)
—— *More Letters of Edward Fitzgerald* (New York: 1901)

NOTES

Abbreviations used in the Notes:

CHSP: Cambridge Historical Society Proceedings

"Harvard": Lowell's address, "On the 250th Anniversary of the Foundation of Harvard University," Nov. 8, 1886

"Independent": Lowell's address, "The Place of the Independent in Politics," delivered before the Reform Club of New York, April 13, 1888

JRL: James Russell Lowell

"Languages": Lowell's address, "The Study of Modern Languages," delivered before the Modern Language Association of America, 1889

"Latest": A posthumous volume by Lowell entitled *Latest Literary Essays* (Boston: 1891)

LC: Library of Congress

"Literature": Lowell's address, "Our Literature," delivered in commemoration of the 100th anniversary of Washington's Inauguration, at New York, April 30, 1889

MHS: The Massachusetts Historical Society

MHSP: The Massachusetts Historical Society Proceedings

MVHR: The Mississippi Valley Historical Review

NAR: The North American Review

NYPL: The New York Public Library

PRO: Public Records Office, London

"Progress": Lowell's introduction to a volume entitled, *The World's Progress* (Boston: 1887)

SPNEA: The Society for the Preservation of New England Antiquities

"Tariff": Lowell's address, "Tariff Reform," delivered at a meeting of the Tariff Reform League, Boston, December 29, 1887

CHAPTER I. CHILDHOOD (pages 1–16)

1 Norton's description is in a letter to S. G. Ward, April 26, 1896, *Letters of Charles Eliot Norton*, Sara Norton and M. A. DeWolfe Howe eds., 2 vols. (Boston: 1913), II, 244.

2 JRL, "Cambridge Thirty Years Ago," first published in *Putnam's Monthly* (April–May, 1853), and then, in a revised version, in *Fireside Travels* (Boston: 1864). The essay can also be found in the Riverside Edition of Lowell's collected works: *The Writings of James Russell Lowell*, 10 vols. (Boston: 1890), *Prose Works*, I, 43–99. Throughout, it is the Riverside Edition of Lowell's Works which will be cited.

Additional useful details on early nineteenth-century Cambridge are in Charles Eliot Norton's "Reminiscences of Old Cambridge," *Cambridge Historical Society Publications* (Cambridge: 1906), I, 11–23.

3 JRL, "Cambridge Thirty Years Ago," *Prose Works*, I, 66 (Fraser); Norton, "Reminiscences," 13 (Sweetman).

4 The Norton comment on "everyone knowing each other" is in his "Reminiscences"; JRL, "Cambridge Thirty Years Ago," *Prose Works*, I, 95 ("giving the wall"), 89 (Craigie), 90 (anchorite).

5 Horace Mann, "Commencement Address, Antioch College, 1859," *Life and Works of Horace Mann* (Boston: 1891), V, 503; Andrews Norton to C. E. Norton, Feb. 15, 1843, *Letters Norton*, I, 21.

This emphasis on "service" may, parenthetically, help to explain both the nineteenth-century enthusiasm for History, which concentrates on man in his social role, and its uncertainty about the utility of fiction, which focuses on "merely" private emotions. The reversal of popularity — and values — in our own day is obvious.

6 Introduction to *The Biglow Papers, Poetical Works*, II, 35.

7 Lafayette to Charles Lowell, Jan. 26, 1825, and Josiah Quincy to Charles Lowell, March 20, 1857, Spence-Lowell Collection, Huntington Library; Charles Lowell to Charles K. Dillaway, Oct. 13, n.y., Washburn Papers, MHS; Charles Lowell to H. G. Otis, n.d., 1846, Otis Papers, MHS; transcript of record in the Bible of Charles Lowell, J. B. Lowell Collection, Houghton.

James Russell believed his grandfather's claim justified, for his Uncle John, "who was quite old enough to remember the matter distinctly," was certain that Judge Lowell had inserted the preamble to the state Bill of Rights with a special view to the rights of Negroes. He remembered, too, that Judge Lowell offered his services as Counsel, without charge, to any Negro who wished to sue for freedom under that preamble. (JRL to Edmund Quincy, Dec. 1866, Yale University.)

8 Lowell's mock genealogy is in the Spence-Lowell Collection at the

Huntington Library. I have published it complete, under the title, "A Brahmin's Self-Laughter," in *Manuscripts*, Summer, 1963.

9 JRL to C. F. Briggs, Sept. 18, 1844, *Letters of James Russell Lowell*, Charles Eliot Norton ed., 3 vols. (Boston: 1904), I, 122.

10 Charles Lowell, *Sermons: Chiefly Practical* (Boston: 1855), 287–297; Charles Lowell to JRL, June 16, 1836, owned by Mrs. Alfred Lowell. Charles Lowell's tolerant spirit is further shown by his friendship with Bishop Cheverus, the first Catholic Bishop in Boston (Charles Lowell to Editors of the *Christian Register*, n.d., MHS.

Though a "liberal," it would not be accurate to describe Charles Lowell as a Unitarian, for he refused formal association with any denomination. Just as he did not belong to the Pastoral Association (Calvinist), so he would not join the Unitarian Association. He described his position as "Congregationalist as it respects the outworks of the house of God, but belongs to no sect as it regards the doctrines of theology, nor has any exclusiveness as it regards his Congregationalism." (Sermon, 1845, as quoted by his daughter, Mary Lowell Putnam, "Charles Lowell," *Memorial Biographies of the New England Historic Genealogical Society* [Boston: 1885], IV [1860–1862], 164.) According to F. H. Underwood, James Russell Lowell used to remark "with evident satisfaction that his father had never called himself a Unitarian; that he was simply pastor of a Congregational Church, and a friend of Channing — nothing more." (*The Poet and the Man, Recollections and Appreciations of James Russell Lowell* [Boston: 1893] 115.)

11 Charles Lowell, *Sermons*, especially the sermons, "The Divine Dispensations Not To Be Questioned, But Submitted To and Improved," 151–163, and "The Goodness of God In The Death of Little Children," 42–49.

12 Charles Lowell, *Sermons*, 88.

13 Charles Lowell, *Sermons*, especially "The Dignity of Human Nature," 50–57, and "Temperance," 261–268.

14 Charles Lowell, *Sermons*, especially "Conscience," 58–63. Mary Lowell Putnam, "Charles Lowell," *Memorial Biographies*, 134–169. The most valuable discussion I know of regarding the "liberal" ethic which Charles Lowell represented is Stephen E. Whicher's superb *Freedom and Fate* (Philadelphia: 1953).

15 C. A. Bartol, letter of Aug. 17, 1891, as printed in the *Advertiser*, Aug. 18, 1891, JRL Scrapbook, I, Houghton Library, Harvard.

16 Charles Lowell to Theodore Parker, June 20, 1854, Theodore Parker to Charles Lowell, June 21, 1854, Wendell Phillips to Charles Lowell, Dec. 27, 1854 — all in the Spence-Lowell Collection, Huntington Library. Further evidence of Dr. Lowell's antislavery activity is in a printed letter, dated April 10, 1855 (newspaper not identified), Boston Public Library. The label of "monstrous iniquity" is in an un-

dated letter to an unknown correspondent (owned by Mrs. Alfred Lowell). He went on to say, in this letter: "I have not been in the habit of keeping back what I deemed it profitable to utter, whether they would hear or whether they would forbear."

Emerson's comment on Dr. Lowell is in a letter to William Emerson, May 27, 1830, *The Letters of Ralph Waldo Emerson*, Ralph L. Rusk ed., 6 vols. (New York: 1939), I, 304. Clough's comment is in a letter to Miss Smith, Dec. 13, 1852, *The Correspondence of Arthur Hugh Clough*, Frederick L. Mulhauser ed., 2 vols. (Oxford: 1957), II, 347–348.

17 Lilian Whiting, *Boston Days* (London: 1902), 261 (muddy alleys); Charles Lowell, *Sermons*, 221; Henry Ware, Jr., to Charles Lowell, Aug. 17, 1828, Spence-Lowell Collection, Houghton.

18 Fanny Longfellow to "Mary," Dec. 10, 1861, Craigie House, Cambridge ("beautiful" man); Charles Lowell, *Sermons*, "Cheerfulness In Youth Sanctioned By Religion, and Should Be Hallowed By It," 31–36.

19 "Lessing," NAR (April, 1867), reprinted in *Prose Works*, II, 182.

20 The comment on "passages I love" is in Lowell's *Conversations on the Old Poets* (London: 1845), 93; see also JRL to his mother, Jan. 28, 1837, Houghton.

21 The "half-French" remark was by a Mrs. Curson, as reported by T. W. Higginson to Horace Scudder, Sept. 28, 1899, Scudder Papers, Houghton; the one about "Celtic blood" is in an anonymous obituary on JRL, *Nation* (Aug. 13, 1891). The details about Mrs. Lowell's personal appearance were given me by Miss Elizabeth Putnam, JRL's grandniece, in a private interview.

22 Very little trace of Harriet Lowell remains — a few manuscript letters and an occasional comment on her in the correspondence of others (I am especially grateful to Miss Elizabeth Putnam for manuscript materials). In order to piece together even an impressionistic portrait, I have utilized the services of two expert graphologists, Dr. Klara Roman (now deceased) and especially Dr. Rose Wolfson. I have incorporated their findings only when corroborated by other data, though in some instances it was their analytical hints which first clarified certain aspects of the documents.

JRL to Mabel Lowell, Jan. 1, 1882, Dr. Burnett Collection, Houghton ("schooled & corrected"); JRL to Mabel Lowell Burnett, Aug. 25, 1878, Houghton ("excessive precision"); letter of C. A. Bartol (colleague pastor of Dr. Lowell), Aug. 17, 1891, as printed in the *Advertiser*, Aug. 18, 1891, JRL Scrapbook, I, Houghton, for Harriet Lowell's "power and accomplishment."

23 Harriet Spence Lowell to Anna C. Lowell, Sept. 9, 1838, owned by Miss Elizabeth Putnam ("we must all labor"); Maria Lowell to

"dear and old friend," April 24, 1850, Cunningham Collection, Houghton ("strange derangement").

There is scant material on which to build a diagnosis of Harriet Lowell's disorder. A tentative diagnosis of "functional mental disturbance" (in contradistinction to an organic brain disease) was independently arrived at by two specialists, Dr. Walter Igersheimer, a psychiatrist, who read over the brief description of Mrs. Lowell's symptoms from the records of the McLean Hospital, where she was confined, and Dr. Klara Roman, a graphologist, who studied her handwriting. The major references to Mrs. Lowell's derangement are in letters of Charles Lowell to JRL, Aug. 8, 1844, April 11, 30, 1845, and May 15, 1845, all in Houghton. The record of Mrs. Lowell's case from McLean Hospital is in the Scudder Papers, Houghton.

In one of Dr. Lowell's letters to JRL (Aug. 22, n.y., Houghton), he expressed the pathetic hope "that the aberration of mind has its origins in the stomach, & is not an affliction of the brain. I desire to trust in God . . ."

24 JRL to Nathan Hale, June 22, 1840, State Library, Albany (in which he talks of 4/5 of his father's property being lost), and JRL to G. B. Loring, June 28, 1840, Norton Collection, Houghton. After 1849, when Dr. Lowell took on a colleague pastor, his salary was reduced to $1500. Longfellow's comment is in a letter to his mother, Feb. 27, 1840, Houghton, and JRL's theory on his mother's resulting insanity is in a letter to C. F. Briggs, Sept. 17, 1844, Norton Collection, Houghton.

Following the debacle, Charles Russell Lowell led a migratory life in search of new prosperity, later settling once more in Cambridge and devoting himself to organizing the card catalogue in the Boston Athenaeum. James Russell was apparently close to him in later life, and greatly admired the way his brother had stood by the wreckage of his life.

25 Annie Fields Journal, Feb. 8, March 8, 1869, MHS; Esther Lowell Cunningham (granddaughter of JRL), *Three Houses* (Boston: 1955), 82, for the anecdote about Icelandic. Sarah Palfrey's remark is in Cleveland Amory, *The Proper Bostonians* (New York: 1947) 140–141.

26 Ferris Greenslet, *The Lowells and Their Seven Worlds* (Boston: 1946), 240–241; JRL to Robert Carter, May 5, 1860, Berg Collection, NYPL.

27 His mother, in a letter to Anna C. Lowell, Sept. 9, 1838 (owned by Miss Elizabeth Putnam), referred to James Russell as her "forlorn hope." Mary Lowell Putnam's recollections of his happy childhood are in a letter to Josephine Shaw Lowell, Dec. 16, 1891, owned by Miss Elizabeth Putnam.

28 Mary Lowell Putnam to Josephine Shaw Lowell, Dec. 16, 1891, owned by Miss Elizabeth Putnam.

29 The descriptions of "a broadrimmed white hat" and "nervousness in my rear" are from Lowell's "autobiographical sketch" written for the Harvard class book of 1838, and dated on the manuscript May 10, 1838, Harvard University Archives. The sketch has been printed by Ethel Golann, "A Lowell Autobiography," *New England Quarterly*, VII (June, 1934), 356–364, but since this printing contains a number of variations from the original, quotations are here made from the manuscript.

The poem is from "*The Biglow Papers, Poetical Works*, II, 23.

30 "Lowell at Elmwood," Random Notes by H. W. L. Dana, April 25, 1950, Craigie House; JRL, "autobiographical sketch," Harvard Archives; Elizabeth E. Dana to Vivien May Norris, Feb. 17, 1900, Radcliffe College Archives (courtesy of George P. Clark, whose doctoral thesis, "Classical Influences and Background in the Writings of James Russell Lowell," Yale, 1948, and article, "James Russell Lowell's Study of the Classics Before Entering Harvard," *Jahrbuch fur Amerikastudien*, Band 8, 1963, also have been most useful). The comment on "quite a library" is from JRL to R. T. S. Lowell, Nov. 2, 1828, Houghton.

31 R. H. Dana, Jr., Journal, I, MHS; T. W. Higginson to C. E. Norton, Nov. 1, 1893, C. E. Norton Papers, Houghton; JRL to R. T. S. Lowell, June 15, 1828, JRL to his mother, Jan. 22, 1830, Houghton.

Even Dana, who detested the school, marveled at the pleasure it later gave him to spend an evening with Mr. Wells, "as nothing could exceed the gratifying character of his conversation & manners." (R. H. Dana, Jr., Journal, I, MHS).

32 The curriculum and athletics are described in R. H. Dana, Jr., Journal, I, MHS.

Lowell's final year of preparatory work before Harvard was spent in the Boston school of a Mr. Ingraham; his basic grounding in the classics, though, came from his six years at the Wells school.

CHAPTER II. HARVARD (pages 17–29)

1 JRL, "autobiographical sketch," Harvard Archives; Rank Scales, Harvard Archives; JRL to W. H. Shackford, Oct. 9, 1835, Norton Collection, Houghton: "I study quite hard this term"; see also letters of Nov. 6, 1835, Feb. 1, 1836; Benjamin Peirce to President Quincy, Oct. 14, 1835, Corporation Papers, Harvard Archives, in which Peirce, the Professor of Mathematics, put Lowell in the third of six categories, namely, "Those who have moderate abilities for Mathematics, but generally appear to study faithfully" (and math was Lowell's most

troublesome subject). For Lowell's college years, G. P. Clark's "Classical Influences" has been especially helpful.

The manuscript of Lowell's Exhibition part, "Ancient Epics as proofs of Genius," dated Oct. 10, 1837, is in the Harvard Archives. It has been reprinted complete by Kenneth Walter Cameron, in *Emerson Society Quarterly*, 1st Quarter, 1961, pp. 63–64. In the piece, Lowell, reflecting current sensibilities, applauded the fact that one may read Homer "without fear of meeting aught that can offend the ear of delicacy or taste," whereas "in a later, & far more refined age, how often do we find the pages of the polished Virgil, and the witty, and no less polished Horace, deformed by instances of coarseness & obscenity."

2 These time allotments are based on the careful estimates of G. P. Clark, "Classical Influences."

3 Samuel Eliot Morison, *Three Centuries of Harvard* (Cambridge: 1946), 260; JRL to William Shackford, Nov. 6, 1835, Jan. 6, April 22, 1836, Norton Collection, Houghton.

4 For Lowell's purchases, see JRL to William Shackford, Jan. 6, 1836, JRL to G. B. Loring, Dec. 26, 1836, Norton Collection, Houghton. The books were read, not merely collected. The Folger Library has the two sets of Shakespeare's Works which Lowell owned in college, and both are marked with numerous marginal comments and queries, showing great familiarity with the texts. He even (as a seventeen-year-old) took learned issue in the margins with some of the editor's notes.

For his reading, see his Commonplace Book, Norton Collection, Houghton.

The rime on Carlyle is in a letter to G. B. Loring, April 15, 1838, Norton Collection, Houghton; beside the word "works" in the manuscript is an asterisk to which Lowell, in a typically bad pun, appended "cursed hard *work* to read some of 'em —."

5 JRL to G. B. Loring, Dec. 23, 26, 1836, JRL to William Shackford, Nov. 6, 1835 — all in the Norton Collection, Houghton; G. B. Loring, quoted in *The Critic*, No. 399, Aug. 22, 1891.

Lowell's rhymed minutes, in the Harvard Archives, have been edited and printed by Kenneth Walter Cameron, *Undergraduate Verses, Rhymed Minutes of the Hasty Pudding Club* (Hartford: 1956). The above lines can be found on pp. 63, 83 of the Cameron edition.

6 JRL to Thomas S. Perry, March 2, 1875, Colby College ("as great an ass"); JRL's verse contributions to *Harvardiana* have been collected and edited, along with much other material, by Thelma M. Smith, *Uncollected Poems of James Russell Lowell* (Philadelphia: 1950); Charles Lowell to JRL, n.d., London, 1837, Rantoul Collection, Houghton. See also Anna Cabot Lowell (sister-in-law) to JRL,

July 3, 1838, Dr. Burnett Collection, Houghton, in which she admonishes him against "blind confidence in your powers & your destiny."

7 G. B. Loring to JRL, Aug. 20, 1837, Eben Wright to JRL, July 12, 1838, Norton Collection, Houghton.

8 JRL to William Shackford, Oct. 9, 1835 (cried at letter), Aug. 14, 1837 (first encounter), Norton Collection, Houghton; JRL to J. F. Heath, Feb. 18, 1841, Berg Collection, NYPL ("What we call Love . . . "; flower journal).

9 JRL to G. B. Loring, April 10, Aug. 23, 1837, JRL to William Shackford, Feb. 1, 1836, G. B. Loring to JRL, Aug. 20, 1837, Norton Collection, Houghton.

10 Charles Lowell to JRL, May 29, 1837, Rantoul Collection, Houghton; G. B. Loring to JRL, April 9, 16, 1837, Norton Collection, Houghton.

11 Records of the College Faculty, XI, Harvard Archives.

Thomas Wentworth Higginson claimed that Lowell's negligence of his studies was only the background for his suspension. The immediate cause, Higginson insisted, was an episode in chapel on the day Lowell was elected class poet. Delighted at being chosen, and having celebrated a little too heavily, Lowell supposedly rose during evening chapel and bowed grandly from right to left in public acknowledgment of his election — thus temporarily disrupting the service. Higginson had this story in writing, many years after it occurred, from a clergyman "of high character & a very accurate person," who claimed to have been only five or six seats away from Lowell when the incident took place (Higginson to C. E. Norton, Nov. 1, 1893, C. E. Norton Papers, Houghton). Higginson later repeated this version of Lowell's suspension in print (*Old Cambridge* [New York: 1899], 156–157), and it was taken up by Ferris Greenslet in *James Russell Lowell* (Boston: 1905), 23, in *The Lowells and Their Seven Worlds* (Boston: 1946), 243, and by Horace E. Scudder (though with cautionary remarks) in *James Russell Lowell*, 2 vols. (Cambridge: 1901), I, 47. The Higginson version is entirely plausible in terms of Lowell's temperament; nor is there any reason to suspect Higginson of malicious invention — indeed he never suggested that the episode involved any "moral depravity." My only reason for distrusting the story, and it is certainly not a conclusive one, is that I have been unable to find any corroborative evidence for it, either specific or veiled, and this despite the fact that in the correspondence of Lowell and his friends details of his other delinquencies are referred to repeatedly. In later years when a teacher himself, Lowell gave still another version of his rustication to one of his Dante seminars (Frederic M. Holland, "Reading Dante with Lowell," *New England Magazine* [Jan. 1896]). This account, which hinges on the ruffled dignity of Professor Edward T. Channing, may well be unreliable; it comes to us third-hand

and only as recalled many years later by one of Lowell's students. At most it probably describes one of many incidents which in combination led to Lowell's suspension.

12 JRL to G. B. Loring, July 8, 1838, Houghton.

13 JRL to G. B. Loring, Aug. 9, Aug. 17 (Caroline Brooks), 1838, Norton Collection, Houghton; JRL to Nathan Hale, Jr., July 14, 1838, State Library, Albany (classmate's sisters).

14 JRL to Nathan Hale, Jr., July 8, 14, 1838, State Library, Albany.

15 JRL to Nathan Hale, Jr., July 14, Aug. 15 (Mrs. Frost), 1838, State Library, Albany.

Ten years later when Longfellow heard Barzaillai Frost deliver a sermon, he commented: "a good sermon, but a bad twang in his pronunciation, which would have spoilt a better sermon than his." (H. W. Longfellow Journal, Nov. 25, 1849, Houghton.)

16 JRL to Nathan Hale, Jr., July 8, 1838 (an Eagle), State Library, Albany; JRL to G. B. Loring, Aug. 9, Sept. 22 (religion), 1838, Norton Collection, Houghton. Lowell was especially hostile to Emerson's Divinity School Address. (JRL to Nathan Hale, Jr., July 23, 1838, State Library, Albany.)

17 JRL to Nathan Hale, Jr., July 8, 1838, State Library, Albany (Emerson's followers); JRL to G. B. Loring, July 12, 1838, Norton Collection, Houghton (Thoreau). For Lowell's later relations with Thoreau, see pages 169–172.

18 G. B. Loring to JRL, June 29, 1838, Eben Wright to JRL, July 3, 1838, Norton Collection, Houghton; JRL to Nathan Hale, Jr., July 8, 1838, State Library, Albany; Mary Story to W. W. Story, n.d., owned by Mr. Peter de Brandt, London, England (deserved suspension).

When Dr. Lowell, traveling in Europe, heard the double news that his son had been suspended from college and chosen class poet he is said to have commented: "Oh dear! James promised me that he would quit writing poetry and go to work." (Walter Littlefield, "Introduction," xiii, *Early Prose of James Russell Lowell* [London: 1902].)

19 JRL to Nathan Hale, Aug. 15, 1838, State Library, Albany (own view of the poem). The Class Poem has been printed in Smith ed., *Uncollected Poems*, 217–248. The three selections above can be found, in order of quotation, on pp. 240, 239, 229, 234 (Saracen).

"I suppose you heard," Lowell had earlier written to a friend, "of the Seminoles massacring, as it is called, those companies of American troops. I think they are in the right of it, by '*they*,' I mean the Seminoles." (JRL to William Shackford, Feb. 1, 1836, Norton Collection, Houghton.)

20 Smith ed., *Uncollected Poems*, 224–225.

21 JRL to R. W. Emerson, Sept. 1, 1838, Norton Collection, Houghton.

22 R. W. Emerson to JRL, Sept. 3, 1838, Rusk ed., *Letters Emerson,* II, 159.

CHAPTER III. BEGINNINGS (pages 30–67)

1 JRL to G. B. Loring, July 22, 1839, Norton ed., *Letters,* I, 56; T. W. Higginson, "Early Recollections of Lowell," CHSP, XXIII; JRL, "Private Journal," Norton Collection, Houghton, dated Sept. 22, 1840, though the entries were obviously made at a variety of times during this period ("ventilation").

2 JRL, "Private Journal," Norton Collection, Houghton.

3 JRL to G. B. Loring, Oct. 1838, Norton Collection, Houghton; JRL to G. B. Loring, March 9, May 20, 1839, Norton ed., *Letters,* I, 44–45, 51.

4 JRL to G. B. Loring, July 22, 1839, Norton ed., *Letters,* I, 56 ("blind presentiment"); JRL to G. B. Loring, Aug. 25, 1840, Norton Collection, Houghton ("strongest argument").

R. H. Dana, Jr., glowingly described the Dane Law School as of "surpassing excellence . . . There was perfect confidence, & yet great deference & respect towards the instructors . . . There was also an abundance of study & honourable competition . . ." (Journal, beginning of vol. 1, MHS.) Dana, however, was far more drawn to the law than Lowell.

5 JRL to G. B. Loring, Jan. 7, 1839, Norton Collection, Houghton ("talent"); JRL to G. B. Loring, Aug. 4, 1839, Norton ed., *Letters,* I, 57 ("before I die . . .").

6 JRL to G. B. Loring, Jan. 2, 1841, Norton ed., *Letters,* I, 73–74.

7 JRL to G. B. Loring, April 29, 1838, Norton ed., *Letters,* I, 45–46 ("too many *thoughts* . . ."); Margaret Fuller to R. W. Emerson, Dec. 6, 1840, Rusk ed., *Letters of Emerson,* II, 363; the poem is JRL's "Merry England," *Graham's Magazine,* XIX, No. 5 (Nov. 1841), 238–239, reprinted in Smith, *Uncollected Poems,* 17.

8 JRL to G. B. Loring, Nov. 8–15, 1838, Norton Collection, Houghton ("ultra democratic"); JRL to G. B. Loring, Sept. 22, 1838, Norton ed., *Letters,* I, 39 (Cromwell).

9 JRL to G. B. Loring, Dec. 2, 1839 (first meeting), May 17, 1840 ("pure and spiritlike"), Norton ed., *Letters,* I, 61–62, 72; JRL to G. B. Loring, August 18, 25, 31, 1840, Norton Collection, Houghton (earlier romance; Nantasket; dream); JRL to Nathan Hale, Jr., July 25, 1840, State Library, Albany.

There are only veiled, though numerous, references in Lowell's correspondence to his earlier romance. We know little more than that the girl was Hannah Jackson, younger sister of Anna Cabot Jackson (wife of Lowell's brother, Charles), that Lowell cared deeply for her, and that the relationship terminated, apparently at her insistence, around the spring of 1839. The break left Lowell feeling like a "bruised reed" and contributed to his general unsettlement during that period. As he wrote to a friend, "Goodbye to 1839 . . . To me it has been a Macpelah cave. There I buried many feelings, many hopes." (JRL to G. B. Loring, Jan. 1, 1840, Norton Collection, Houghton.) Other references to the affair can be found in letters of JRL to Loring of May 9, June 4, 1839, and April 30, Aug. 31, 1840, Norton Collection, Houghton.

Mrs. Henry Lyman, who owns copies of Hannah Jackson's letters and diary, wrote to me that "any personal mention of Mr. Lowell was destroyed when she became engaged to . . . Samuel Cabot." In kindly rechecking the diary on my behalf, Mrs. Lyman did find one cryptic entry for Dec. 1, 1839: "Ah how I wish R.[obert Spence?] & J. Lowell would view life as I do (for I feel as if that were the right way) but they have such a want of faith in men, they have so much more imagination, inspiration & poetry & R. perhaps so much more feeling & less wisdom than I, that I can never do wisdom justice when talking with them & that makes me feel low-spirited."

10 Lowell's comment on Wordsworth is written in the front of a copy of *The Complete Poetical Works of Wordsworth*, 1837, in the possession of Mr. Parkman Howe, who kindly allowed me to examine it. Lowell's pencil note, dated April 13, 1854, shortly after Maria's death, ends "O, saint & martyr pray for both of us — but most for him who needs it most!"

The passages expressing his joy are in letters to G. B. Loring, Aug. 31, Nov. 24, 1840, Norton Collection, Houghton.

11 Edmund Quincy to Elizabeth Neale Gay, May 22, 1851, Edmund Quincy Papers, MHS; Emelyn Eldridge (later Mrs. W. W. Story) to JRL, Aug. 4, 1841, Cunningham Collection, Houghton.

Sample comments: Longfellow: "We called on the Lowells; and saw only Maria, who is gentle and spiritual as ever . . ." (Journal, Nov. 13, 1852, Houghton); T. W. Higginson: "*spirituelle* . . . the French meaning (witty or piquant) was not applicable to Maria White, but the English *spiritual* was" (to Horace E. Scudder, Nov. 12, 1901, Scudder Papers, Houghton).

12 Lowell defended Maria's common sense in a letter to G. B. Loring, Nov. 24, 1840, Norton Collection, Houghton; the first lines of poetry are from "Agatha," dated Sept. 1840, Smith, *Uncollected Poems*, 5, the latter from "Irene," *A Year's Life* (Boston: 1841), 112–117. Proof that "Irene" was modeled on Maria is in JRL to G. B. Loring, Jan. 2, 1841, Norton ed., *Letters*, I, 74.

13 A number of contemporaries referred to Maria White as kindly and charming but "undemonstrative" (e.g. Stephen Allen's reminiscences

in the *Transcript*, Aug. 29, 1891; Emma Forbes Weston to Elizabeth Neale Gay, March 16, 1846, Gay Collection, Columbia: "Pray tell me what sort of a person Mrs. Lowell is, I have scarcely ever heard her speak").

14 The "anchored spirit" reference is from Lowell's poem, "Agatha," Smith, *Uncollected Poems*, 7; Lowell's comment about "the woman in his heart" is from his "Private Journal," dated Sept. 22, 1840, Houghton; Quincy's comment on the "True Marriage" is in a letter to Anne Weston, Nov. 18, 1852, Edmund Quincy Papers, MHS.

15 T. W. Higginson believed that Mr. White's opposition was more precisely grounded still, focusing on the "suspicion of conviviality" which still hung around Lowell's name as a result of the drunkenness in chapel which had supposedly led to his suspension (Higginson to C. E. Norton, Nov. 1, 1893, C. E. Norton Papers, Houghton). "Pegasus . . . in harness" is from an obituary in the *Nation* (Aug. 13, 1891).

16 Lowell's engraved card is in the Cunningham Collection, Houghton. The fictionalized account of his first days as a lawyer is "My First Client," initially published in the *Boston Miscellany* and later reprinted in *Early Prose Writings of James Russell Lowell*, with a Prefatory Note by Dr. E. E. Hale . . . and an Introduction by Walter Littlefield (New York: 1902), 3–15.

17 The account of the Negro sailor comes from Holland, "Reading Dante with Lowell," 576.

18 JRL to G. B. Loring, Aug. 18, 1840, Houghton.

19 The motto Lowell chose for the title page of *A Year's Life* was "Ich habe gelebt und geliebet." JRL to Ticknor, May 3, 1876, B. H. Ticknor Papers, LC ("inconceivable ass").

20 JRL to G. B. Loring, Feb. 18, 1841, Norton Collection, Houghton. The dissenters were G. S. Hillard in NAR (April, 1841), and Charles Gordon Green in the Boston *Morning Post* (Feb. 20, 1841). Hillard, Lowell decided, stood "just in that middle ground of talent where there is the greatest crowd & no one can pass beyond to the more thinly filled region without so jostling as to be felt by the whole mob"; Green, the conservative editor of the *Post*, Lowell simply dismissed as an "ass" (JRL to J. F. Heath, March 12, 1841, Berg Collection, NYPL). For the critical comments cited, see *Brownson's Quarterly Review* (April, 1841); *Dial* (July, 1841) for Fuller review; *Graham's Magazine* (April, 1842); Elizabeth Barrett to JRL, March 31, 1842, Dr. Burnett Collection, Houghton. I have found Alvan R. McFadyen's doctoral thesis, "The Contemporaneous Reputation of James Russell Lowell," University of Florida, 1955, especially useful for this discussion of the reception of *A Year's Life*.

21 JRL to J. F. Heath, March 12, 1841, Berg Collection, NYPL; JRL to G. B. Loring, March 14, 1841, Norton Collection, Houghton.

The charge of "irregularities"—false rhymes, inversions, unusual syllabification and accent—Lowell thought accurate but misguided. The *true* rule of poetry, he insisted, was spontaneity. "All nature," he wrote, "*must* be unconscious. The doing of a good deed or the writing of a good poem should be to us like the act of breathing." (Marginalia in JRL's hand, in his copy of Jones Very's *Essays and Poems*, Houghton.) Lowell's belief in the value of impulse (and its concomitant, irregularity) was part of the "romantic" theory of poetry subscribed to by his generation; his views later underwent revision (see pages 251–252).

22 A sample of JRL's increasing distaste for the law is in his letter to J. F. Heath, Aug. 5, 1842 (as printed in Scott & O'Shaughnessy Inc. auction catalogue, April 12, 1917): "I cannot write well here in this cramped up lawyer's office feeling all the while that I am giving the lie to my destiny & wasting time which might be gaining me the love of thousands."

For the editors' comments: Charles J. Peterson (editor, *Graham's*) to JRL, Jan. 10, 1842, Cornelius Mathews (editor, *Arcturus*) to JRL, Feb. 9, 1842, John L. O'Sullivan (editor, *Democratic Review*) to JRL, Sept. 9, 1842, all in Norton Collection, Houghton.

23 JRL to Cornelius Mathews, Feb. 14, 1842, as quoted in the Anderson Co. auction catalogues for Feb. 17, 18, 1902, and Nov. 22, 23, 1909 ("I try to write carefully . . ."); JRL to J. F. Heath, March 31, 1842, as quoted in T. F. Madigan auction catalogue for Nov. 1928 (his "mission"); Mathews to JRL, Feb. 9, 1842, Peterson to JRL, Nov. 26, 1841, Feb. 8, 1842, Norton Collection, Houghton.

Though "very much obliged" to Mr. Poe, Lowell felt the need to answer the charge of "ruggedness": "If I often want melody it is not from want of ear (in which I am well endowed) but from choice. I love ruggedness & even harshness sometimes. So doth Nature also." (JRL to Peterson, Oct. 31, 1841, Barrett Collection, University of Virginia).

24 Lowell's pieces in the *Boston Miscellany* have been reprinted (along with one or two items from *The Pioneer*) in *Early Prose Writings*, prefatory note by [E. E.] Hale. JRL to J. F. Heath, Aug. 5, 1842, Norton ed., *Letters*, I, 95 ("astounding deal of applause"). The Newark *Advertiser*, for one, said the articles were "full of the inspirations of genius" (JRL to G. B. Loring, May 11, 1842, Norton Collection, Houghton); Emerson to JRL, Dec. 4, 1841, Norton Collection, Houghton.

25 As sample adoration, there is this letter (Jan. 2, 1842, Cunningham Collection, Houghton) from Emelyn Eldridge to Maria White: "You are *so beautiful*, everything about you is so beautiful. I say 'here I must stay I cannot love you more,' but the next moment your own blessed lips move & you speak some new word of truth some

noble thought which only great women can speak, some new encouragement to the weary soul."

The comment on the lovers' letters is in Levi Thaxter to T. W. Higginson, Jan. 19, 1842, Higginson Papers, Houghton.

26 JRL to J. F. Heath, Dec. 15, 1842, Berg Collection, NYPL; JRL to Charles Peterson, Oct. 31, 1841, Barrett Collection, University of Virginia; JRL, *Conversations on the Old Poets* (London: 1845), 77.

27 The portrait I have drawn of the Brother and Sister Club is primarily from the following sources: Maria White to William A. White, Dec. 22, 1841, copy in C. E. Norton Papers, Houghton; Isabella Batchelder James, "James Russell Lowell as I Knew Him," CHSP, XXIII, 1934; JRL to Emelyn Eldridge, April 12, 1842, as quoted in Henry James, *William Wetmore Story and His Friends* (Grove Press ed.), I, 48; JRL to G. B. Loring, April 11, 1842, Norton Collection, Houghton; JRL to J. F. Heath, March 31, 1842, as printed in T. F. Madigan auction catalogue, Nov. 1928; JRL to William A. White, Dec. 9, 1841, Norton ed., *Letters*, I, 79; E. E. Hale, *James Russell Lowell and His Friends* (Boston: 1899), 70–77; W. W. Story to JRL, Feb. 23, 1843, University of Texas.

The Sister's "tart" comment is repeated in T. W. Higginson to Horace E. Scudder, Sept. 28, 1899, Scudder Papers, Houghton; Maria's comment on JRL's "exulting" nature is in a letter to "Kiddy," Oct. 4, 1842, typed copy in Radcliffe College Library, Woman's Archives.

28 Maria White to JRL, n.d. (probably 1840), Dr. Burnett Collection, Houghton.

29 Maria White to "Kiddy," Oct. 4, 1842, typed copy in Radcliffe College Library, Woman's Archives.

30 JRL to J. F. Heath, May 29, 1841, Barrett Collection, University of Virginia; JRL to J. F. Heath, March 31, 1842, Norton ed., *Letters*, I, 81–82.

31 Maria White to "Kiddy," Oct. 4, 1842, typed copy in Radcliffe College Library, Woman's Archives (Carter's object); T. W. Higginson, *Old Cambridge*, 47 (twelve-volume history).

32 A copy of the prospectus is in the Norton Collection, Houghton; JRL to Whittier, n.d., Barrett Collection, University of Virginia; JRL to John Dwight, Oct. 7, 1842; JRL to Charles Briggs, Oct. 7, 1842, as quoted in Joshua C. Taylor, *William Page: The American Titian* (Chicago: 1957), 54.

33 JRL to Longfellow, Nov. 29, 1842, Longfellow Papers, Houghton; JRL to Whittier, n.d., Barrett Collection, University of Virginia; JRL to Emerson, Dec. 16, 1842, Norton Collection, Houghton; JRL to John S. Dwight, Oct. 7, 1842, Barrett Collection, University of Virginia; Elizabeth Barrett to Miss Mitford, Dec. 30, 1842, *Elizabeth Barrett to Miss Mitford*, Betty Miller ed. (New Haven: 1954), 160;

C. S. Wheeler to J. F. Heath, Nov. 14, 1842, Norton Collection, Houghton; Poe to JRL, Nov. 16, 1842, Norton Collection, Houghton; JRL to Poe, Nov. 19, 1842, Norton ed., *Letters*, I, 97–98.

34 Sculley Bradley has edited a careful facsimile of *The Pioneer*, and has introduced it with a detailed, reliable appraisal (New York: 1947); see also F. L. Mott, *A History of American Magazines, 1741–1850* (New York: 1930).

35 Poe to Lowell, Feb. 4, 1843, Norton Collection, Houghton; Emelyn Eldridge to Maria White, Feb. 2, 1843, Rantoul Collection, Houghton; Emelyn Eldridge to JRL, Jan, 2, 1843, Cunningham Collection, Houghton.

Horace Greeley, for one, criticized certain obscurities in Lowell's introduction to the issue, and Lowell thought the criticism deserved — "I owe it to John Neal at whose suggestion I altered the passage which was before as clear as crystal" (JRL to Carter, Jan. 15, 1843, Berg Collection, NYPL).

36 Mary Lowell Putnam to JRL, Feb. 1, 1843, Dr. Burnett Collection, Houghton. "A Vision" did appear in the third issue of March, 1843.

Lowell's letters to Carter have recently been acquired by The Berg Collection, NYPL, and the details of Lowell's New York stay have been taken especially from the letters of Jan. 19, 31, Feb. 2, 4, 1843.

37 Lowell's barbed comment on Story was neither his first nor his last. The previous year he had privately accused Story of plagiarism (JRL to G. B. Loring, April 11, 1842, Norton Collection, Houghton), and although they remained friends throughout their lives, there were periodic outbursts of acid. Lowell apparently retained sincere affection for Story, but distrusted his vanity, competitiveness and sarcasm (e.g. JRL to J. F. Heath, March 21, 1842, Norton ed., *Letters*, I, 82; JRL to Norton, Sept. 13, 1859, Sept. 20, 1861, Norton Collection, Houghton).

For Poe's review, see T. O. Mabbott, "A Review of Lowell's Magazine," *Notes and Queries*, June 29, 1940, 457–458.

The subsequent story of the Lowell-Mathews dispute is one of protracted trivia. Lowell tried to explain to Mathews that no offense to him had been intended, that Carter had merely been anxious to demonstrate his objectivity by printing Poe's criticism along with his praise (JRL to Carter, Jan. 31, 1843, Berg Collection, NYPL). But Mathews was not appeased. Carter then wrote Mathews an apology, and sent it to Lowell with a request that he use his judgment about delivering it. Lowell meant to do so, but mislaid the letter and then forgot it. Mathews, hearing of the letter's existence, wrote angrily to Carter accusing Lowell of having deliberately suppressed it. Carter then became fed up and persuaded Lowell not to attempt further explanations. An additional rebuke, in Mathew's eyes, came when Lowell omitted him from the farewell party he gave when leaving

New York (which Lowell claimed he did only out of deference to W. A. Jones, then quarreling with Mathews). "Is not the whole thing *very* foolish?" wrote Lowell to Evert Duyckinck, "let men who are born with silver spoons in their mouths quarrel — they have time to spare for it. But they who are born with pens in their hands have *nobler* work to do." (Aug. 1843, Duyckinck Collection, MS. Div. NYPL). Lowell's tone of condescension, however much provoked by Mathews' foolishness, lends weight to Duyckinck's reply that Lowell had been "somewhat careless and capricious . . . and particularly culpable in not giving him Carter's letter sooner." Duyckinck to JRL, Aug. 14, 1843, Norton Collection, Houghton; Duyckinck added, in his private diary, that Lowell had a certain "impudent egotism" about him (Duyckinck Journal, March 1, 1843, MS. Div. NYPL).

Lowell did try to make further amends ("I called to smoke the calumet of peace with you & am sorry not to find you" — undated note to Mathews, Houghton), and made a complimentary reference to Mathews in his 1845 *Conversations*. But the affair dragged on for years. Mathews attacked Lowell in print, and Lowell retaliated by drawing a devastating portrait of Mathews in the *Fable for Critics*. But Lowell later confessed to Duyckinck that although Mathews had done him "a great injustice about a matter very trifling in itself," and although "the traditions of literary animosities" more than sanctioned the portrait he drew in the *Fable*, his heart "has never justified it" (JRL to Duyckinck, Dec. 6, 1854, Scudder Papers, Houghton).

38 JRL to Carter, Jan. 15 (charity), 31 (philosophical), 1943, Berg Collection, NYPL; Evert Duyckinck Journal, Jan. 21, 1843, MS. Div., NYPL.

39 Evert Duyckinck Journal, Jan. 13, 1843, MS. Div., NYPL (JRL as one of the Young Americans); H. W. Longfellow Journal, Jan. 6, 1847, Houghton (national is "universal"); holograph poem in the Historical Society of Pennsylvania — the manuscript is dated July 26, 1843, but the poem was first composed in August, 1840.

40 JRL to C. F. Briggs, Aug. 9, 1843, Norton ed., *Letters*, I, 110–111 ("a truth of philosophy"; "*proves itself*").

41 JRL to Briggs, Aug. 9, 1843, Norton Collection, Houghton: Duyckinck is "a good fellow," but O'Sullivan "neither appreciates me nor the tendency of my poetry, nor the true worth of any real poetry."

For details on William Page, see Joshua C. Taylor, *William Page*. The description of Page's "creed . . . his own" is from C. E. Norton to JRL, March 6, 1856, Norton Collection, Houghton.

Briggs, who seems to have been an extraordinary man, has never had a biography; no doubt the destruction of his personal papers is more responsible than his comparative obscurity, for he is interesting enough to have attracted a biographer, had materials been available. In 1834 he published a successful two-volume novel, *The Adventures of Harry Franco,* from which he henceforth took his pen name, and he was later an editor for *Putnam's,* the New York *Times* and the *Independent.* Lowell's portrait of him in the *Fable for Critics* can be found in *Poetical Works,* III, 71–72. In a letter to Briggs of Sept. 17, 1844 (Norton Collection, Houghton), Lowell affectionately accused him of hiding his sincerity "behind an assumed satirical vein, or . . . in the dark corners of *badinage* . . ."

42 JRL to Woodberry, March 12, 1844, Houghton; JRL to Poe, March 24, 1843, Norton ed., *Letters,* I, 104; JRL to Briggs, Sept. 18, 1844, Norton ed., *Letters,* I, 121; JRL to Briggs, March 26, 1848, Berg Collection, NYPL; W. W. Story to J. F. Heath, March 28, 1843, Barrett Collection, University of Virginia (Dr. Lowell "like a hero"); receipts relating to *The Pioneer* are in JRL's Business Papers, Houghton. Lowell described the debt as $1800 or more, but Leon Howard, who discovered the records of the Suffolk County Superior Court, has persuasively demonstrated that this was an exaggeration. The more likely figure as established by Howard was no more than $1000 and probably a little more than half that (Leon Howard, *Victorian Knight-Errant* [Berkeley and Los Angeles: 1952], 131–132, and Leon Howard, "The Case of the Sanded Signature," *Manuscripts,* Spring, 1961, 13–17).

Some money was also owed to authors. Poe, for one, graciously wrote Lowell not to give himself "one moment's concern" about the ten dollars due him; later, in great need, Poe was forced to ask for the money after all, which Lowell then sent (Poe to JRL, March 27, 1843, Norton Collection, Houghton).

43 Poe to JRL, March 27, 1843, Norton Collection, Houghton; W. W. Story to J. F. Heath, March 28, 1843, Barrett Collection, University of Virginia.

44 Nathan Hale to E. E. Hale, March 31, 1843, State Library, Albany.

45 JRL to Briggs, March 6, 1844, Norton ed., *Letters,* I, 116.

46 James Russell Lowell, *Poems* (Cambridge: 1843).

47 JRL to Poe, May 8, 1843, Norton ed., *Letters,* I, 108 ("crude productions"). In "L'Envoi," a poem in the new volume, Lowell "confessed" that in the three years since those "young buds plucked hastily by childish hands," his muse had "seen more of life and men, pondered more . . . and grown a shade more sad." Duyckinck's comment is in his Journal, Dec. 12, 1844, MS. Div., NYPL; Poe's on "narrative," in a letter to Lowell of Oct. 19, 1843, Norton Collection, Houghton.

48 JRL to Theophilus Parsons, 1843, as quoted in Goodspeed's catalogue,

No. 387, July, 1945 ("poetry of progress"); the remaining quotations, in order, are from the poems, "Sub Pondere Crescit," "Ode" and "The Fatherland."

49 Evert Duyckinck Journal, Dec. 12, 1844, MS. Div., NYPL; JRL to Norton, Aug. 28, 1865, Norton ed., *Letters*, II, 105 ("meeting-house"); Fanny Longfellow to T. G. Appleton, Dec. 29, 1843, as printed in Edward Wagenknecht ed., *Mrs. Longfellow: Selected Letters and Journals of Fanny Appleton Longfellow* (New York: 1956), 101; N. P. Willis to JRL, "1844," Norton Collection, Houghton; Page to JRL, Aug. 21, 1843, Norton Collection, Houghton; Bayard Taylor to JRL, Feb. 16, 1844, Houghton.

"Veneration" is not too strong a word. One of Lowell's friends lent a letter of his to an imploring female admirer, which "she kept . . . a long time, and when I saw it again it was about as much worn as a holy relic." (C. W. Scates to JRL, Nov. 18, 1844, Norton Collection, Houghton).

50 For details on the critical reception, see McFadyen, "Contemporaneous Reputation," 40–55. Poe's review (*Graham's Magazine*, March, 1844) can be found reprinted in *The Complete Works of Edgar Allen Poe*, James A. Harrison ed. (New York: 1902), 17 vols., XI, 243–249. Lowell's comment on "the augury . . . of popularity" is in a letter to Hawthorne, April 24, 1851, Berg Collection, NYPL.

51 There is some doubt if Lowell actually got the ten cents per copy due him according to the terms of his contract with John Owen, the publisher (the contract, dated Dec. 15, 1843, is in the Morgan Library, NYC); as late as March, 1844, after eleven hundred copies had been sold, Lowell was still wondering if he would get anything from the book (JRL to Briggs, March 6, 1844, Norton ed., *Letters*, I, 116–117). It seems likely, though, that he *was* paid; for one, he was able to marry and to pay off his debts, for another, he later characterized John Owen as "one of the most amiable men in the world" (JRL to Briggs, Sept. 17, 1844, Norton Collection, Houghton).

Poe's suggestion for a new magazine is in a letter to JRL of Oct. 28, 1844, Norton Collection, Houghton. Lowell apparently did not take up Poe's offer (at least I have found no letters to that effect), probably having had his fill for a time of editorial uncertainties. But he did introduce Poe to his friend, Briggs, who was then starting a new magazine, and the two agreed to co-edit the *Broadway Journal*. At this same time, Poe suggested Lowell as the man he preferred to have write his "portrait" for *Graham's* series on "Our Contributors" (Graham to JRL, Feb. 2, 1844, Norton Collection, Houghton). When Lowell's piece appeared in *Graham's* for February, 1845, Poe thanked him for "all the well-intended flatteries which it contains" (Poe to JRL, May 28, 1844, Norton Collection, Houghton). The piece did contain much praise (no contemporary author had "displayed more varied and striking abilities"), but was not wholly favorable. Lowell had entire confidence in Poe's judgments, he wrote, except when Poe's "one or two pet prejudices" lured him "out of the strict path of criticism"; he singled out Poe's review of Wm. Channing's poems as a case in point (the review, which had appeared in *Graham's* for August, 1843, has been called by Arthur Hobson Quinn in *Edgar Allen Poe, A Critical Biography* [New York: 1941], 399, Poe "at his worst in criticism"). In the article Lowell also made general objection to the low state of American criticism; though Poe was "discriminating, philosophical and fearless," most American criticism could "be best likened to an intellectual gathering of chips to keep the critical pot of potatoes or reputation a-boiling." Before we have an American literature," Lowell wrote, with more of epigram than logic, "we must have an American criticism." The article had a variety of factual errors (Lowell blamed these on Poe, who had supplied him with materials which Lowell, being as "green as Neptune," had accepted at face value — JRL to Woodberry, Dec. 4, 1883, Houghton), but nonetheless was one of the most impressive of Lowell's youthful efforts. A. H. Quinn describes it as "one of the best appraisals he [Poe] received during his lifetime." *op. cit.*, p. 432.)

I have pieced together the discussions with Graham from the following sources: Graham to JRL, Feb. 2, March 2, May 4, 26, 1844, Norton Collection, Houghton; JRL to Graham, May 1, 1844, The Historical Society of Pennsylvania; JRL to Graham, Aug. 6, 1844 (typed copy), Norton Collection, Houghton; H. W. Longfellow Journal, March 28, May 24, 1844, Houghton; Charles Peterson to JRL, May 17, 1844, Norton Collection, Houghton. Graham's reference to "sharpers " is in the letter of May 26. Graham had actually offered Lowell twenty dollars per poem even before his new volume of poetry had appeared (Peterson to JRL, April 25, 1842, Norton Collection, Houghton).

52 JRL to Briggs, Jan. 16, 1845, Norton Collection, Houghton; JRL to Briggs, Sept. 18, 1844, Norton ed., *Letters*, I, 121.

Maria's father was equally difficult in settling money on his son, William (Maria White to "Kiddy," Oct. 4, 1842, Radcliffe College Library, Woman's Archives). In the Burnett Collection, Houghton, there is a contract dated March 13, 1846, between Dr. Lowell and Louis Daly, carpenter, to build a "dwellinghouse with outbuildings" for $400 on Dr. Lowell's estate. A note attached to it, dated May 7, 1846, states that the conditions had been performed to mutual satisfaction.

53 Maria White to Briggs, Dec. 12, 1844, Barrett Collection, University of Virginia; JRL to Mrs. Norton, "1860?", Houghton.

54 The quotations, in order, are all from *Conversations on the Old Poets* (London: 1845), 150, 194, 210 (henceforth *Conversations*).

55 *Conversations,* 151 ("rugged heartiness"), 230 ("fanaticism"), 178 ("delicately decent"), 228 ("infallible monitor within").

56 *Conversations,* 245 ("outward forms of poetry"), 246 ("unpruned spirit"), 8 (Alexander Pope), 61 ("straight line"), 213 ("clipped and suppressed"), 52 ("point out what pleases").

As an older man, Lowell came to hold a far more favorable opinion of Pope. In an 1871 essay on Pope he wrote: "The young demand thoughts that find an echo in their real and not their acquired nature, and care very little about the dress they are put in. It is later that we learn to like the conventional, as we do olives. There was a time when I could not read Pope, but disliked him on principle . . . If I have not come to the conclusion that he is the greatest of poets, I believe . . . the 'Rape of the Lock' . . . for wit, fancy, invention, and keeping . . . has never been surpassed" (*Prose Works,* IV, 26–27).

57 *Conversations,* 80 ("task ceremony"); "Hymn," 1842, in Smith ed., *Uncollected Poems,* 37–38; Fanny Longfellow Journal, November, 1843, Craigie House. For another example of Lowell's "visions" at this time, see his letter to G. B. Loring, Sept. 20, 1842, Norton ed., *Letters,* I, 96. JRL's second wife, Frances Dunlap, was a Swedenborgian.

Many years later Horace Scudder recorded in his diary (Nov. 20, 1891, Houghton), a talk he had had with one of Lowell's friends about the *Conversations:* " 'Very few persons,' said the doctor mysteriously, 'know how real those conversations were.' 'Why,' said I, 'were they held with Story, or Carter or anyone else?' 'They were more than that. Some of them were with Shakespere.' 'Had he then at that time a visionary turn?' I asked. 'He had a very vivid imagination,' said the doctor guardedly. 'He said that the conversations wrote themselves.' "

58 *Conversations,* 11 ("messengers of Heaven"), 135–136 (Anti-Slavery Society), 266 ("love for one").

59 *Conversations,* 140–141 (heart-intellect); 191–192 (women and the heart). For the same reason that Lowell preferred the heart to the intellect, he preferred England to France, "the sturdy honest heart of England" versus France's "monstrous head out of all proportion to the other members." (*Conversations,* 140).

60 The discussions of romanticism which I have found most useful are W. H. Auden and Norman Holmes Pearson, *Poets of the English Language,* 5 vols. (New York: 1950), Introduction, IV; Tremaine McDowell, *The Romantic Triumph: American Literature from 1830 to 1860* (New York: 1933), and Howard E. Hugo's introduction to his *Portable Romantic Reader* (New York: 1957).

61 *Conversations,* 158, 222; "New Years Eve, 1844," in Smith ed., *Uncollected Poems,* 50.

62 *Conversations*, 158 ("arcs of one horizon"); "New Years Eve, 1844," in Smith ed., *Uncollected Poems*, 49.

CHAPTER IV. MARRIAGE AND ANTISLAVERY (pages 68–88)

1 Fanny Longfellow to Mary Longfellow Greenleaf, Jan. 4, 1845, Craigie House, Cambridge; Maria White to C. F. Briggs, Dec. 12, 1844, Barrett Collection, University of Virginia; Elizabeth Barrett to Miss Mitford, April, 1845, in *Barrett to Mitford*, Betty Miller ed., 241.

2 JRL to Briggs, March 6, 1844, Norton Collection, Houghton, ("the cough does not seem to be upon her lungs & I cannot believe that it ever be [*sic*] serious"); Maria Lowell to Sophia Hawthorne, Jan. 16, 1845, Berg Collection, NYPL (attic).

3 JRL to Carter, Jan. 14, Feb. 24, 1845, Berg Collection, NYPL ("happy as two mortals"; Whister Club; Philadelphia abolitionists); Maria Lowell to Lois L. White, Jan. 19, 1845, Houghton; Maria Lowell to Rebecca Lowell, Jan. 17, 1845, Houghton. Lydia Maria Child was much harder on the Pennsylvania abolitionists than was Lowell: "Such a set of fussy, ignorant old women," she wrote, "as the Pennsylvania abolitionists are, I never saw . . . *all* sending me thousands of communications, bad grammar, and detestable spelling." (L. M. Child to E. G. Loring, April 6, 1842, MS. Div., NYPL). But she probably made reference to rural abolitionists, less educated than those of Philadelphia.

4 JRL to Carter, Jan. 14, 1845, Berg Collection, NYPL.

5 JRL to Briggs, Jan. 16, 1845, T. W. Parsons to JRL, March 12, 1845, Duyckinck to JRL, Oct. 11, 1845, John Owen to JRL, April 10, 1845, all in the Norton Collection, Houghton; JRL to Briggs, March 21, 1845, Norton ed., *Letters*, I, 126 ($300); JRL to Carter, Feb. 24, 1845, Berg Collection, NYPL; McFadyen, "Contemporaneous Reputation," Chapter IV.

The sharpest attack on Lowell was made by "Christopher North" (John Wilson, professor of moral philosophy at Edinburgh) in *Blackwood's Edinburgh Magazine* (Sept. 1845); he called Lowell a "Presumptuous youngling" dealing in "monstrous nonsense." Lowell claimed indifference to the attack: "It must be sharper vinegar than he can brew that shall bite me." (JRL to Duyckinck, Oct. 27, 1845, Duyckinck Collection, MS. Div., NYPL).

6 Briggs' review is in the *Journal* for Jan. 18, 1845; JRL to Briggs, Jan. 22, 1845, Norton Collection, Houghton; JRL to Carter, March 16, 1845 ("grossness"), Berg Collection, NYPL; Maria Lowell to Rebecca Lowell, March 17, 1845, Houghton. For additional complaints about Briggs' cantankerousness see J. M. McKim to S. H. Gay, July 9, Sept. 29, 1847, Gay Collection, Columbia.

By spring, 1845, the rift with Briggs had been patched up, and Lowell was once more writing for the *Journal*, reviewing Fitz-Greene Halleck's *Alnwick Castle* for the May 3 issue.

7 JRL to G. B. Loring, Nov. 8–15, 1838, Norton Collection, Houghton; JRL to R. W. Gilder, Feb. 9, 1887, Norton ed., *Letters*, III, 183 ("swore fealty").

8 Maria White to JRL, n.d. (probably 1840), Dr. Burnett Collection, Houghton (self-culture); Maria White to "Kiddy," July 2, 1842, typed copy, Radcliffe College Library, Woman's Archives (temperance banner). JRL to J. F. Heath, Dec. 15, 1842, Berg Collection, NYPL (acknowledging Maria's influence).

9 JRL, "Private Journal," Houghton; the volume is dated Sept. 22, 1840, but entries in it were obviously made over a period of time.

10 C. J. Peterson to JRL, Feb. 17, 1842, Norton Collection, Houghton; JRL to J. F. Heath, Feb. 17, 1842, Berg Collection NYPL (ambition to aid mankind); JRL to Sydney H. Gay, June 16, 1846, Norton ed., *Letters*, I, 158 ("whatever odium . . .").

11 *The Anti-Slavery Papers of James Russell Lowell*, 2 vols. (Boston: 1902), II, 174 (Expediency); see also 17, 70, 120, 170. The citation from Garrison is a paraphrase from his editorial in the first issue of the *Liberator* (Jan. 1, 1831).

12 For his arguments against abolitionists entering politics, see *Anti-Slavery Papers*, I, 3; II, 46–49. His charitable comment on the Liberty men is in a letter to W. A. White, Sept. 19, 1843, Norton ed., *Letters*, I, 112. The rumor that he had voted the Liberty ticket is in E. M. Davis to Mrs. Chapman, Dec. 10, 1844, Weston Papers, Boston Public Library.

13 JRL to Briggs, Aug. 8, 1845, Norton ed., *Letters*, I, 134 (Christianity to life); JRL to Longfellow, Aug. 13, 1845, Norton ed., *Letters*, I, 140 ("foundation to weathercock"); *Anti-Slavery Papers*, II, 23 (formalism; younger clergy), I, 25 (majority sincere); JRL to W. A. White, Sept. 19, 1843, Norton ed., *Letters*, I, 112 ("Sun of Truth"); Charles Lowell to JRL, March, 1845, Dr. Burnett Collection Houghton (love not hate), Charles Lowell to JRL, Jan. 24, 1845, Rantoul Collection, Houghton ("harsh . . ." etc.); JRL to Briggs, Feb. 18, 1846, Norton Collection, Houghton (declinable); H. W. Longfellow's Journal, July 4, 1846, Houghton (waterfalls).

14 *Anti-Slavery Papers*, I, 8–13 ("Is it right?"; Decalogue), II, 179 (*ab initio*), 77 (Universe).

15 *Anti-Slavery Papers*, II, 174 (mouthglue; Niagara); JRL to Briggs, March 26, 1848, Norton ed., *Letters*, I, 173; JRL to Sydney Gay, May 21, 1849, Norton ed., *Letters*, I, 212–214.

16 *Anti-Slavery Papers*, I, 16 ("secreting vessels"); JRL to J. F. Heath, Aug. 5, 1842, Norton ed., *Letters*, I, 94 (L'Ouverture).

17 *Anti-Slavery Papers*, I, 16–21. In 1850, when visiting his brother's

church in New York, Lowell noted with approval that colored persons sat "promiscuously with the rest, which is an improvement on the practice in Boston." (JRL to Dr. Lowell, Sept. 17, 1850, Houghton.)

18 *Anti-Slavery Papers,* I, 22.

19 *Conversations,* 190–192 ("burn Popish nunneries); JRL to Briggs, Feb. 18, 1846, Norton ed., *Letters,* I, 149 ("tinkle of chains"); JRL to C. E. Norton, Dec. 10, 1869, Norton Collection, Houghton ("not to have a man for a wife"); JRL to C. E. Norton, Oct. 30, 1873, Norton Collection, Houghton ("best genius"). See also for his later views on the status of women, JRL to Jane Norton, April 6, 1869, Houghton, JRL to Caroline H. Dall, Feb. 17, 1871, Dall Papers, MHS, and JRL to Miss Stevens, Feb. 26, 1880, LC: "P.S. Prometheus (as a judgment) has his vulture, Boston its woman of superior — Here the pen dropt from the impious hand".

20 JRL to Briggs, Aug. 8, 1845, Norton ed., *Letters,* I, 134; *Anti-Slavery Papers,* I, 14. For JRL's interest in labor, see JRL to J. Miller McKim, July 11, 1845, Garrison Papers, Boston Public Library, and *Anti-Slavery Papers,* I, 10, II, 116. For Grahamism, JRL to Lois L. White, May 24, 1845, Norton ed., *Letters,* I, 127–128. For temperance, H. W. Longfellow Journal, April 15, 1846, Houghton, JRL to G. B. Loring, April 11, 1842, Norton Collection, Houghton, JRL to G. B. Loring, July 6, 1842, Norton ed., *Letters,* I, 89–90.

21 Fanny Longfellow Journal, Jan. 20, 1844, Craigie House, Cambridge (Christian radicalism); *Anti-Slavery Papers,* II, 140 (concentrate on slavery).

22 *Anti-Slavery Papers,* II, 82–88.

23 For examples of JRL's "chafing" see JRL to Sydney Gay, Sept. 1848, Norton ed., *Letters,* I, 193; JRL to Briggs, Jan. 23, 1850, Norton ed., *Letters,* I, 232–234.

24 JRL to Briggs, Nov. 13, 1847, Norton ed., *Letters,* I, 164 (half-mystic, half-humorist); JRL to E. M. Davis, April 16, 1846, Norton ed., *Letters,* I, 155 ("relapsed into Presbyterianism"); JRL to Edmund Quincy, May 15, 1854, Yale (tar and feathering); see, too, Lowell's satiric poem, "Letter from Boston," Dec. 1846, *Poetical Works,* I, 305–312. For a fuller discussion of the inadequacies of the "zealot" stereotype for the reformer (though in another context), see R. R. Palmer, *The Age of Democratic Revolution* (Princeton: 1964), II, in which he concludes that the French revolutionaries, far from being messianic misfits, were in the main well-integrated, solid, middle-class citizens.

25 Poe's impression of Lowell is quoted in William Bittner, *Poe, A Biography* (Boston: 1962), 209, and Quinn, *Poe,* 462, who cautions that Poe's impression of Lowell has come down to us only as reported by T. H. Chivers, who often is "quite untrustworthy as a

witness." JRL to John H. Ingram, May 12, 1879, copy in Ingram's hand, University of Virginia ("a little tipsy"); Maria Clemm to JRL, March 9, 1850, Norton Collection, Houghton; JRL to R. W. Griswold, Oct. 27, 1849, Historical Society of Pennsylvania (Poe's critical ability); JRL to R. S. Chilton, April 20, 1850, copy, Norton Collection, Houghton ("the whole of him"; "conscience-brain").

The year after their meeting, Poe contributed to new tensions between Lowell and Briggs by telling Lowell that Briggs had been talking unfavorably of him behind his back. Briggs angrily denied the story, to which Lowell replied, "But even if you had said so, what matter to me? Suppose you did not love me & thought me moonstruck — I *do* love you & believe you sane. Which has the advantage? Why, clearly I, inasmuch as to love anything is to derive an hourly revenue from it, while to hate it, is to be making it constant payments for no value received." (JRL to Briggs, Feb. 18, 1846, Norton Collection, Houghton.)

26 Lowell's first antislavery assignment after his return home was a series on "Anti-Slavery in the United States" for the London *Daily News* (at 2½ to 3 guineas a column). He published it anonymously, feeling it would do more good if not known to be from the pen of a committed abolitionist, but in any case, the articles disappointed; they were too long and discursive for a daily newspaper, the *News* informed him (John Forster to JRL, Nov. 3, 1846, J. B. Lowell Collection, Hougthon; John Forster to JRL, Feb. 3, June 3, 1846, Norton Collection, Houghton; JRL to E. M. Davis, Feb. 23, 1846, Norton ed., *Letters*, I, 152). The series was discontinued after only four articles; they had appeared Feb.–May, 1846, and had sketched in the history of the movement before the advent of Garrison. The four articles, in manuscript, are in Houghton.

Mrs. Child's tribulations can be traced in her correspondence with Ellis Gray Loring in the MS. Div., NYPL, especially in her letters of Sept. 21, 28, Dec. 13, 1841, Feb. 15, 1842, March 6, 1843, and May 16, 1844. The comment on "*dirty* work" is in the letter of Sept. 28, 1841.

27 Edmund Quincy to R. D. Webb, Jan. 29, 1843, Edmund Quincy Papers, MHS ("most perfect creature"); Lowell, in his "Letter From Boston" (*Poetical Works*, I, 306) referred to Mrs. Chapman's "swift eyes of clear steel-blue, the coiled-up mainspring of the Fair"; for an amusing anecdote regarding Mrs. Chapman, see James Freeman Clarke Journal, Sept. 1840, Houghton. Howells' comment on Quincy is in his *Literary Friends and Acquaintance* (New York: 1900), 129; Lowell's poetic tribute is "Bankside" (the name he gave to Quincy's home), *Heartsease and Rue* (Boston: 1888), 34, reprinted in *Poetical Works*, IV, 128; see also the eulogy Lowell delivered after Quincy's death, printed in MHSP, 1876–1877, XV, 286–287. Unfortunately

Lowell and Quincy, by mutual agreement, destroyed each other's letters; only a few survive in scattered collections, such as that at Yale University.

28 Quincy to JRL, June 3, 1853, Norton Collection, Houghton ("cracked tea-cups"); Quincy to R. Webb, June 14, 1844, Quincy Letterbook, Boston Public Library (Gay's appearance and rural complaints). Some of the details about Gay's early life are from Gay to T. W. Higginson, Oct. 28, 1882, Gay Collection, Columbia.

It might be said here, in passing, that the immense collection of Gay Papers at Columbia University are not only extraordinarily rich as a source for antislavery history, but also one of the few such sources which have not been mined.

29 Gay to Quincy, Sept. 16, 1845 (would relinquish), Feb. 10, 1846 (upholding Lowell's credentials); Quincy to Gay, Sept. 24, 1845 (Lowell "green"), Feb. 4, 18–19, 1846—all in Gay Collection, Columbia. Quincy offered, in turn, to relinquish *his* place in the "triumvirate" to Lowell, but Gay likewise refused to entertain a substitution. Lowell did get an offer around this time from the *Freeman* to write a weekly "letter from Boston," but "without any other compensation . . . than the chance afforded . . . of doing good." (Miller McKim to JRL, Aug. 26, 1846, Norton Collection, Houghton.)

30 Gay to Mrs. Chapman, Jan. 20, 27, 1846, Gay Collection, Columbia; Gay to JRL, May 19, 1846, Norton Collection, Houghton.

31 Gay to Quincy, Sept. 16, Oct. (n.d.), 1845, Gay Collection, Columbia; JRL to Briggs, Jan. 30, 1846, Norton Collection, Houghton; JRL to E. Davis, Feb. 3, 1846, Davis Letters, Houghton.

32 JRL to Gay, June 16, 1846, Norton ed., *Letters,* I, 157–162; Gay to JRL, June 26, 1846, Norton Collection, Houghton.

33 For further details on Lowell's association with the *Standard* see pages 109–116.

CHAPTER V. 1848: ANNUS MIRABILIS (pages 89–117)

1 JRL to Emma Parker, Jan. 1, 1846, Swarthmore College; JRL to Briggs, Aug. 21, 1845, Feb. 18, 1846 ("*man*kind"), Norton Collection, Houghton.

2 JRL to Briggs, Feb. 4, 1846, Norton ed., *Letters,* I, 146–147 ("personification"); JRL to Briggs, Feb. 1, 1848, Houghton; "A Fable for Critics," *Poetical Works,* III, 60 (Hawthorne).

3 JRL to Sydney Gay, April 16, 1846, Norton ed., *Letters,* I, 156–157.

4 Maria Lowell to Sarah Shaw, March 16, 1847, J. B. Lowell Collection, Houghton; H. W. Longfellow Journal, July 4, 12, Aug. 16, 1846, March 14, 1847, Houghton; JRL to Carter, Aug. 10, 1846, Berg Col-

lection, NYPL; the poem is Maria Lowell's "The Morning Glory," Hope Jillson Vernon ed., *The Poems of Maria Lowell, with Unpublished Letters and a Biography* (Providence: 1936), 54; Charles Lowell to JRL, Aug. 14, 1846, Dr. Burnett Collection, Houghton ("constitutional"); Longfellow to Charles Sumner, Aug. 17, 1846, Houghton (JRL unaware).

5 JRL to Emelyn Story, Sept. 10, 1847, Houghton.

6 The quotation from *A Fable for Critics* is in *Poetical Works*, III, 85.
Newton Arvin's comments on Longfellow apply in this area equally well to Lowell: "Nothing, to repeat, could be more sincere than his moral convictions, but they are at second hand; they were not the fruits, as Emerson's (for example) were, of solitary and independent cogitation. He lived by them, as many men have lived by truths they have learned from others; but honorable as they were they had no intrinsic intellectual interest, and they usually do nothing for his poetry but enfeeble it." (*Longfellow: His Life and Work* [Boston: 1962], 69.)
This affinity between the two men may help to explain why Longfellow thought Lowell's new volume "far in advance of his others" (letter to G. W. Greene, April 4, 1848, Houghton), "often soaring into the sublime" (Journal, Dec. 24, 1847, Houghton). The general critical reception, however, was less favorable than it had been to Lowell's earlier volumes (McFadyen, "Contemporaneous Reputation," 73–90).

7 "Si Descendero In Infernum, Ades" ("Ah, side by side . . ."), "Extreme Unction" ("O glorious Youth"), *Poetical Works*, I, 169, 205.

8 "She Came and Went," *Poetical Works*, I, 245.

9 The 1845 review referred to was of Fitz-Greene Halleck's *Alnwick Castle*, in the *Broadway Journal*, May 3, 1845; Frederika Bremer's comments are in her *Homes of the New World* (New York: 1858), I, 130–131; Quincy's remarks are in a letter to R. Webb, July 14, 1846, Edmund Quincy Papers, MHS.

10 Robert Carter to Sydney Gay, June 23, 1846, Gay Collection, Columbia.

11 JRL to Briggs, Nov. 13, 1847, Norton ed., *Letters*, I, 165; *Poetical Works*, III, 26–27.

12 Lowell claimed that he resorted to occasional anonymity in the *Fable* so that "mystery might help the sales" (JRL to Francis Bowen, Nov. 18, 1848, Bowen Autographs, Houghton). But that still leaves unexplained why he chose to mask the particular portraits he did. In two other cases of concealment — Cornelius Mathews and a "critic" — there are grounds for believing that as with Briggs, Child and Fuller, Lowell resorted to disguise out of uneasiness. He later explicitly expressed regret at his treatment of Mathews, which next to Fuller's portrait was the harshest — though unlike it, containing

at least a few hints of praise (JRL to Duyckinck, Dec. 6, 1854, Duyckinck Collection, NYPL; JRL to Stillman, Jan. 11, 1855, Norton ed., *Letters*, I, 294; JRL to R. W. Gilder, Feb. 9, 1887, Norton ed., *Letters*, III, 183). As for the portrait of the "critic," it too involved unpleasantness. The rumor spread that the portrait had been modeled on Francis Bowen, editor of the *North American Review*. Lowell wrote directly to Bowen, denying the allusion, and Bowen replied that such a suspicion had never crossed his mind — which recalls, in a different context, Longfellow's remark that Bowen was "certainly suffering under neutral strabismus" (JRL to Bowen, Nov. 18, 1848, Bowen to JRL, Nov. 20, 1848, Houghton; Longfellow Journal, March 30, 1849, Houghton). Lowell probably had Bowen in mind when, in the preface to the second edition of the *Fable*, he wrote: ". . . a character drawn in pure fun and condensing the traits of a dozen in one, has been, as I hear, by some persons applied to a good friend of mine, whom to stab in the side, as we walked along chatting and joking together, would not be *my* way." In 1850 Lowell became involved in an angry dispute with Bowen over the Hungarian question. Bowen, taking the side of Austria, attacked the published opinions of Lowell's sister, Mrs. Putnam, and Lowell answered him in print, getting very much the better of the argument (Boston *Daily Advertiser*, Nov. 30, 1850, Jan. 2, 1851; JRL to Bayard Taylor, Feb. 18, 1851, Cornell University). It was thought the controversy cost Bowen appointment to the chair of History at Harvard (Sibley's Private Journal, I, 268, Harvard Archives), though later, in 1853, he was given the Alford Professorship of Natural Religion, Moral Philosophy, and Civil Polity — suggesting that when a man is thought unqualified to represent one field, the obvious solution is to allow him to teach three. For the remaining anonymous references in the *Fable*, see E. J. Nichols, "Identification of Characters in Lowell's *A Fable for Critics*," *American Literature* (May, 1932), 191–194.

One other sharp portrait, that of William Cullen Bryant, Lowell also later regretted. It was drawn, some said, in direct retaliation for Bryant's intimation that Lowell's "To the Past" had been suggested by a Bryant poem of the same title. "Does he think that he *invented* the Past and has a prescription title to it?" asked Lowell. In any case, Lowell insisted that he had completed the unflattering part of Bryant's sketch before hearing of the charge, and that all he added subsequently were the closing, complimentary verses (JRL to Briggs, May 12, 1848, Norton ed., *Letters*, I, 181). Lowell was later told that Bryant had been "terribly cut up" by his portrait in the *Fable* (Edmund Quincy to Anne Weston, July 22, 1853, E. Quincy Papers, MHS). See also page 144.

13 Margaret Fuller, *Papers on Literature and Art* (New York: 1846),

132; JRL to E. Davis, Sept. 26, 1846, Davis Letters, Houghton ("a little retaliatory satire"); JRL to Briggs, March 26, 1848, Berg Collection, NYPL (revenge by writing better).

14 JRL to Briggs, Oct. 4, 1848, Norton ed., *Letters,* I, 194 (effort to strike lines).

15 Holmes to JRL, Nov. 10, 1848, Norton Collection, Houghton; T. W. Higginson to JRL, Dec. 5, 1848, Norton Collection, Houghton; Story to JRL, March 21, 1849, University of Texas; JRL to Story, Sept. 23, 1849, as quoted in Henry James, *Story,* I, 181. Other adverse comments on the Miranda section can be found in Bowen to JRL, Nov. 20, 1848, Norton Collection, Houghton; C. E. Norton Journal, May 15, 1873, *Letters of Charles Eliot Norton with Biographical Comment,* by Sara Norton and M. A. De Wolfe Howe, 2 vols. (Boston: 1913), I, 510.

16 Longfellow Journal, Nov. 4, 1848, Houghton; *The Journals of Bronson Alcott,* Odell Shepard ed. (Boston: 1938), 243; Ruskin to C. E. Norton, July 18, 1856, C. E. Norton Papers, Houghton.

17 Simms' review is in *Southern Quarterly Review* (Oct. 1849), Poe's in *Southern Literary Messenger* (March, 1849). See McFadyen for a general summary and generous sampling of the reviews, and for the hostile reception in the South, see Eugene Current-García, "Southern Literary Criticism and the Sectional Dilemma," *Journal of Southern History* (Aug. 1949).

18 JRL to Briggs, Dec. 31, 1847, Berg Collection, NYPL; JRL to Briggs, March 26, 1848, Norton ed., *Letters,* I, 175; Briggs to JRL, Oct. 25, 1848, Houghton. Lowell suggested that should the profits be large, part go to Page in the form of a commission: he would do a portrait of Briggs for Lowell, and one of Lowell for Briggs.

19 JRL to Thomas Hughes, Sept. 13, 1859, Norton ed., *Letters,* II, 39–40.

20 The edition of *The Biglow Papers* from which the above quotations come is in *Poetical Works,* II, 1–50. Useful details on the background of the *Papers* can be found in Arthur Voss, "The Biglow Papers of James Russell Lowell," doctoral dissertation, Yale, 1941, and his article, "Backgrounds of Lowell's Satire in 'The Biglow Papers,'" *New England Quarterly* (March, 1950), 47–64. A thorough discussion of the "dialect" of the *Papers* can be found in James Walker Downer, "Features of New England Rustic Pronounciation in James Russell Lowell's *Biglow Papers,*" doctoral dissertation, University of Michigan, 1958.

21 NAR (Jan. 1849), 187. For further evidence that *The Biglow Papers* was enjoyed even by those disagreeing with its point of view, see George S. Boutwell, *Reminiscences of Sixty Years in Public Affairs,* 2 vols. (New York: 1902), II, 245. For details on the critical reception of the *Papers,* see the doctoral theses, already cited, of McFadyen and Voss.

22 The model for Parson Wilbur was probably an amalgam; there are recognizable characteristics of at least three people — the pedantry of Rev. Barzillai Frost, Lowell's tutor from Concord days; the gentle, cautious qualities of Dr. Charles Lowell; and the moral earnestness of James Russell himself (and to some extent his growing interest in scholarly erudition). On this, see JRL to Thomas Hughes, Sept. 18, 1869, Norton ed., *Letters*, II, 233.

23 There are uncertainties in *The Biglow Papers* other than those of characterization. When, for example, Sawin describes the qualifications needed for office-holding, the satire seems alternately directed at Zachary Taylor and Daniel Webster. For Lowell's efforts to write a novel, see page 132.

24 O. W. Holmes to JRL, Jan. 14, 1849, as printed in *The Life and Letters of Oliver Wendell Holmes*, John T. Morse, Jr., ed., 2 vols., (Boston: 1896), II, 109–111. It should be said that the *Vision* does show considerable virtuosity in handling rhythms and also unusual metrical freedom, probably more so than in any of Lowell's poems (see Gay Wilson Allen, *American Prosody* [New York: 1935], especially 256–258).

25 Most of Lowell's significant short reviews can be found reprinted in Graham H. Duncan, "James Russell Lowell's Reviews of American Belles-Lettres: An Annotated Anthology," doctoral dissertation, Cornell, 1953.

26 The Whittier review appeared in *National Anti-Slavery Standard*, Dec. 21, 1848 (Duncan, "Annotated Anthology," 88–97).

27 The Longfellow review is in *NAR* (July, 1849); the Thoreau review in *Massachusetts Quarterly Review* (Dec. 1849).

28 A copy of the "Standard Extra" of June 26, 1846, announcing the addition of its "celebrated authors," is in the Gay Collection, Columbia. Sample disgruntlement at their subsequent lack of evidence is R. Webb to E. Quincy, March 2, 1847, Webb-Quincy Correspondence, Boston Public Library. For Quincy's attitude to Gay, see Quincy to Webb, March 28, 1847, E. Quincy Letterbook, Boston Public Library, and Quincy to JRL, April 21, 1847, Norton Collection, Houghton.

29 The offer to JRL is in Gay to JRL, March 21, 1848, Norton Collection, Houghton; Lowell's doubts about accepting and his views on Garrison are in JRL to Briggs, March 26, 1848, Berg Collection, NYPL.

Garrison and Lowell seem to have had little personal contact. But as late as 1866 Lowell referred (in an official testimonial, which is not the best gauge of his true sentiments) to the "uniform wisdom" of Garrison's antislavery leadership (Dec. 29, 1866, University of Rochester). Garrison, in reply, chose to remember that Lowell "had flung all worldly considerations and the chance of literary reputation and success to the winds" in joining the abolitionists, rendering a service to the cause "valuable beyond computation" (Garrison to JRL, Jan. 1, 1867, Dr. Burnett Collection, Houghton).

30 JRL to Gay, May 21, 1849, Norton ed., *Letters,* I, 212 (Wendell Phillips); *Anti-Slavery Papers,* 123–127 (Free Soil party).

31 JRL to Gay, election day, Nov. 1850, Norton ed., *Letters,* I, 253.

32 Caroline Weston to Gay, May 17, 1848, Gay Collection, Columbia; Gay to JRL, May 25, 1848, Norton Collection, Houghton (Bailey); JRL to Gay, n.d., Houghton: "Dr. B. did a great deal of service to the cause in Ohio . . . a just mind never forgets past services"; JRL to Gay, Dec. 20, 1848, May 21, 1849, Norton ed., *Letters,* I, 197, 210 (worried about writing his own way).

33 JRL, Business Papers, Houghton (*Bigelow Papers* royalties); JRL to Gay, May 12, 1848, Norton ed., *Letters,* I, 185 (tenant). The First Series of *Biglow Papers* had gone through at least ten editions by 1876.

34 Edward Wheelwright to Horace Scudder, Feb. 22, 1900, Scudder Papers, Houghton (Dr. Lowell's salary); JRL to Gay, May 21, 1849, Houghton (household expenses); JRL to Gay, Feb. 26, 1849, Norton ed., *Letters,* I, 205 (fugitives); JRL to Mary Elizabeth Wormeley, Aug. 1, 1885, Berg Collection, NYPL ("resolutely decline"); JRL to Briggs, May 5, 1848, Norton ed., *Letters,* I, 178 (three cents); JRL to Gay, Feb. 26, 1849, Norton ed., *Letters,* I, 203 (Abbott Lawrence); JRL to Gay, April 30, 1849, Houghton (life of Garrison).

35 Wendell Phillips to JRL, May 24, 1849, Norton Collection, Houghton.

36 Edmund Quincy to R. Webb, Feb. 1, 1849, E. Quincy Papers, MHS (trenchant); JRL, "Letter from Boston," *Poetical Works,* I, 310 (couplet on Foster); Gay to JRL, May, 1849, June 2, 1849, Norton Collection, Houghton.

37 JRL to Gay, May 21, 1849, Norton ed., *Letters,* I, 209–216.

38 JRL to Gay, March 17, April 17, May 19, 1850, Norton ed., *Letters,* I, 235–247. Phillips again begged Lowell to believe that the Society did not undervalue his services, nor had it secretly been hoping to get rid of him (Phillips to JRL, April 22, 1850, Norton Collection, Houghton).

39 JRL to J. F. Heath, March 24, 1850, University of Virginia ("dreadful fanatic"); JRL to Gay, April 17, 1850, Norton ed., *Letters,* I, 242–243 (Fosterites ungrateful); JRL to Briggs, Jan. 23, 1850, Norton ed., *Letters,* I, 233 ("out of the pulpit"); Maria Lowell to J. F. Heath, April 24, 1850, Cunningham Collection, Houghton (tired of agitation).

Though Lowell had welcomed the pay he got from the *Standard,* it is true that in 1850 at least he had had much higher offers — e.g.

$40 an article from *Graham's* and $30 for a short or $50 for a long poem from *Godey's Lady's Book* (Graham to JRL, "1850," Sarah J. Hale to JRL, Jan. 15, 26, 1850, Norton Collection, Houghton).

40 Fanny Longfellow to her father, April 8, 1850, Craigie House ("in the world"); Maria Lowell to J. F. Heath, April 24, 1850, Cunningham Collection, Houghton ("thank God . . ."); JRL to Gay, March 17, 1850, Norton ed., *Letters*, I, 236–237 (poem, "Death," and funeral).

41 JRL to Gay, March 17, 1850, Norton ed., *Letters*, I, 238 ("invisible bullets"); JRL to Gay, election day, Nov. 1850, Norton ed., *Letters*, I, 253–254 ("without rebound").

42 JRL to Gay, April 20, 1851, Norton ed., *Letters*, I, 256.

CHAPTER VI. EUROPE — AND AFTER (pages 118–135)

1 H. W. Longfellow Journal, June 19, 1851, Houghton; R. H. Dana, Jr., Journal, June 19, 1851, MHS ("golden evening"); Edmund Quincy to Elizabeth Gay, May 22, 1851, Edmund Quincy Papers, MHS; Fanny Longfellow to Emmeline Wadsworth, July 14, 1851, Craigie House ("lovely . . . union").

2 Fanny Longfellow to Emmeline Wadsworth, July 14, 1851, Craigie House.

3 Maria Lowell to Mary Lowell Putnam, Sept. 1851, owned by Mrs. Alfred Lowell; Maria Lowell to Lois Howe, Aug. 7, 1851, Houghton.

4 Lowell published his European impressions under the title, "Leaves from My Journal in Italy and Elsewhere," *Prose Works*, I, 100–217. Unless otherwise specified, all the direct quotations in this and the following four pages come from that essay.

5 Sarah and Francis G. Shaw were the parents of Robert Gould Shaw, killed at Fort Wagner in 1863, and of Josephine Shaw, who married Lowell's nephew, Charles Russell Lowell, shortly before he died at the battle of Cedar Creek in 1864 (see pages 220–221). Francis G. Shaw was heir to a mercantile fortune and spent his life in leisure and philanthropy.

JRL to Briggs, Nov. 22, 1852, Norton ed., *Letters*, I, 260–261 (Uffizi); H. W. Longfellow Journal, March 30, 1847, Houghton (comments by Emerson and Channing); C. E. Norton to Samuel Ward, Aug. 5, 1855, Houghton. A further description of Page is in Briggs to Griswold, Aug. 6, 1848, Griswold Papers, Boston Public Library.

6 JRL to Briggs, March 22, 1853 ("damnable"), Sept. 18, 1856, Norton Collection, Houghton; W. W. Story to JRL, Jan. 9, 1855, University of Texas; Taylor, *Page*, 114–140, for additional details on the

marriage. Sarah later had some success in the States as an actress, married Peter B. Sweeney of the "Tweed Ring," fled with him to Paris, then later returned with her son to Cambridge, where she spent her last years.

7 Maria Lowell to Dr. Lowell, Oct. 30, 1851, Houghton; JRL to Estes Howe, Nov. 17, 1851, Houghton; Maria Lowell to Mrs. Francis G. Shaw, Dec. 15, 1851, Houghton.

8 JRL to Estes Howe, Nov. 17, 1851, Houghton.

9 JRL to Maria Fay, Jan. 3, 1852, Houghton (modern Rome); JRL note appended to letter of Maria Lowell to Lois Howe, Dec. 5, 1851, Burnett Collection, Houghton (humbug; Brighton); JRL to Robert Carter, March 6, 1852, University of Cincinnati (mountains); Story to Charles Sumner, Dec. 12, 1851, Sumner Papers, Houghton.

10 O. W. Holmes to J. L. Motley, Feb. 16, 1861, Morse, *Holmes*, II, 157 (Boston as unit of measure); JRL to Dr. Lowell, Feb. 1, 1852, Houghton (estimate of Americans not lowered); JRL's review of Norton's "Notes of Travel and Study in Italy," *Atlantic* (May, 1860), 629 ("two kinds of travellers"—JRL had earlier used the same phrase in his "Leaves from My Journal . . . ," *Prose Works*, I, 127); JRL to John Holmes, March 5, 1852, Houghton (similarities of Rome and U.S.). For the reactions of the more typical American tourist of the mid-nineteenth century (not very different from those of our own), see Paul R. Baker, *The Fortunate Pilgrims: Americans in Italy, 1800–1860* (Cambridge: 1964).

11 JRL to Robert Carter, March 6, 1852, University of Cincinnati (bearing, etc.); "Leaves from My Journal . . . ," *Prose Works*, I, 184 ("evil genius"; "right Chaucer"), 139 ("flatten all"; "wildest contortions"). Maria, too, though more conventional than her husband, found that the "absence of conformity has a great charm for me as belonging to a terribly conforming people as the Americans." (Maria Lowell to Mary Lowell Putnam, Sept. 15, 1851, owned by Mrs. Alfred Lowell.)

12 JRL to Dr. Lowell, Dec. 23, 1851, Dr. Burnett Collection, Houghton ("spring and soar"); JRL to Robert Carter, March 6, 1852, University of Cincinnati (ceremonies).

13 JRL to Maria Fay, Jan. 3, 1852, Houghton. This letter is the source of all quotes in the paragraph except the one about "ripen slowly as peaches," which comes from his essay "Leaves . . . ," and the reference to *Rome in Eight Days*, which is in a letter to Mary Lowell Putnam, May 11, 1852, Dr. Burnett Collection, Houghton.

14 Maria Lowell to Lois Howe, Dec. 5, 1851, Dr. Burnett Collection, Houghton (things not people); William E. Channing to Sarah Hale Whitman, Nov. 21, 1852, Brown University (Landor; Browning); Story to JRL, Aug. 10, 1853, as quoted in Henry James, *Story*, I, 267 (the Brownings, in turn, liked the Lowells); Moncure Conway,

Autobiography: Memories and Experiences, 2 vols. (Boston: 1904), I, 159 (Sordello); Wendell Phillips to Gay, Aug. 1848, Gay Collection, Columbia (read Browning). For a further discussion of the Lowell-Browning relationship, see pages 264, 307.

15 Maria Lowell to Sarah Shaw, Jan. 11, 1852, Rantoul Collection, Houghton (at homes); Edmund Quincy to Elizabeth Gay, May 22, 1851, Edmund Quincy Papers, MHS (acquainted with family); JRL to Maria Fay, Jan. 3, 1852, Houghton (Mrs. Crawford); J. T. Fields to Bayard Taylor, June 5, 1852, Huntington Library (Bottom); J. R. Fields to Longfellow, Feb. 29, 1852, Houghton (Bottom); Story to Sumner, Dec. 12, 1851, Sumner Papers, Houghton (JRL as companion). The prologue Lowell wrote is in the Norton Collection, Houghton.

16 Maria Lowell to Sarah Shaw, Dec. 15, 1851, Cunningham Collection, Houghton (long walks; cough; Walter); JRL to Dr. Lowell, March 3, 1852, Houghton (Walter; "Heavenly Father"); Maria Lowell to Mary Lowell Putnam, Sept. 15, 1851, owned by Mrs. Alfred Lowell (discipline); Cunningham, *Three Houses*, 67 (hanging).

17 JRL to Mary Lowell Putnam, June 11, 1852, owned by Mrs. Alfred Lowell; Maria Lowell to Sarah Shaw, July 3, 1852, Cunningham Collection, Houghton.

18 JRL to Mary Lowell Putnam, Sept. 1, 1852, Dr. Burnett Collection, Houghton; Maria Lowell to Sarah Shaw, Sept. 11, 1852, Rantoul Collection, Houghton; JRL to C. C. Black, Sept. 13, 1852, Morgan Library.

19 Edmund Quincy to Anne Weston, Nov. 1852, Edmund Quincy Papers, MHS (Thackeray); Thackeray to Mrs. Elliot and Kate Perry, Nov. 8–10, 1852, Gordon N. Ray ed., *The Letters and Private Papers of William Makepeace Thackeray*, 4 vols. (Cambridge: 1946), IV, 434.

20 Fanny Longfellow to T. G. Appleton, Nov. 15, 1852, as quoted in Wagenknecht, *Mrs. Longfellow*, 190 (beard), and for a similar comment, Edmund Quincy to Anne Weston, Nov. 18, 1852, Edmund Quincy Papers, MHS. The details on Dr. Lowell are in a letter from Maria Lowell to Mary Lowell Putnam, Feb. 14, 1853, owned by Mrs. Alfred Lowell.

21 Maria Lowell to Mary Lowell Putnam, Feb. 14, 1853, owned by Mrs. Alfred Lowell.

22 Annie Fields Journal, April 23, 1864, MHS ("*eaten* children"); Clough to Miss Smith, Nov. 26, 1852, Mulhauser ed., *Correspondence of Clough*, II, 317; H. W. Longfellow Journal, Jan. 5, 1853, Houghton.

23 The quotation from Fuller about "meekness of the lamb" is in a letter to an unknown correspondent, Jan. 25, 1853, University of Virginia; the saying was a favorite of Lowell's and he used it, in

somewhat different form, in essays and in a letter to Gay, "Elmwood, 1848" (Norton ed., *Letters,* I, 171). The remark about "Greenwich" is in JRL to Dr. Lowell, Oct. 1, 1852, Houghton. Quincy's comment on JRL as "Saint" is in a letter to Anne Weston, March 27, 1853, Edmund Quincy Papers, MHS. JRL's response to the "Whole World's Convention" is in a letter to T. W. Higginson, Aug. 31, 1853, Huntington Library.

24 H. W. Longfellow Journal, Nov. 30, 1852, Houghton; the Howells remark is in Van Wyck Brooks, *Howells, His Life and World* (New York: 1959), 44; JRL to Briggs, Feb. 15, 1854, Norton ed., *Letters,* I, 280 (essay form). Story, hearing of Lowell's intention of writing a novel, thought Thackeray might have put him up to it (Story to JRL, Feb. 11, 1853, University of Texas). The first chapter of the novel still exists, as "item 966" in the Norton Collection, Houghton. Howells, who read and praised it, later expressed the belief that if Lowell had finished the novel, "it would have been a failure . . . He was wholly undramatic . . . He liked to deal with his subject at first hand, to indulge through himself all the whim and fancy which the more dramatic talent indulges through its personages" (*Literary Friends,* 223).

25 The series was published under the title, "Our Own, His Wanderings and Personal Adventures," *Putnam's Monthly* (April, May, June, 1853); it is reprinted in Smith ed., *Uncollected Poems,* 80–104. Lowell later published two stanzas from "Our Own" with the title "Aladdin" in *Under the Willows* (1869), and preserved an additional section, "Fragments of an Unfinished Poem" in his collected works (*Poetical Works,* III, 126–136). The quotation about "I thank God . . ." is in JRL to Briggs, June 10, 1853, Norton ed., *Letters,* I, 267; see also JRL to Briggs, Feb. 15, 1854, Norton Collection, Houghton.

26 For the inception of "The Nooning," see JRL to Briggs, Nov. 25, 1849, Jan. 23, 1850, Norton ed., *Letters,* I, 226–227, 230–231. His renewing of the project is described in a letter to Briggs of June 10, 1853, Norton ed., *Letters,* I, 269, and subsequent references are in JRL to C. E. Norton, Oct. 19, 1866, and JRL to James B. Thayer, Dec. 8, 1868 (in which Lowell lists the various fragments he has published and their titles), Norton ed., *Letters,* II, 133, 184.

27 JRL to Briggs, June 10, 1853, Norton ed., *Letters,* I, 268 (revenge on dead poets); JRL to Quincy, Aug. 9, 1853, Yale ("shooting dilemma"). Lowell subsequently published his Maine experiences, which he thoroughly enjoyed, as "A Moosehead Journal," in *Fireside Travels* (1864).

28 I have traced the details of her final illness primarily from these sources: Maria Lowell to Anna Loring, June 4, 1853, University of Virginia; JRL to Edmund Quincy, June 7, 1853, Yale; Emelyn Story

to Maria Lowell, July 14, 1853, Cunningham Collection, Houghton; Edmund Quincy to Anne Weston, July 22, 1853, Edmund Quincy Papers, MHS; JRL to Briggs, Oct. 6, 1853, Norton ed., *Letters,* I, 271 ("the waters"); JRL to A. H. Clough, Oct. 10, 1853, Mulhauser ed., *Correspondence of Clough,* II, 464–466.

29 Lowell's desperate condition is described in Edmund Quincy to Anne Weston, Nov. 1, 1853, Edmund Quincy Papers, MHS; H. W. Longfellow Journal, Nov. 11, 1853, Houghton; JRL to Briggs, Nov. 25, 1853, Norton ed., *Letters,* I, 273–274. The details of the funeral are taken from Longfellow's Journal, Oct. 29, 1853, Houghton.

CHAPTER VII. BEGINNING ANEW (pages 136–151)

1 The comment on nature comes from an earlier letter when Lowell, trying to comfort Briggs for the loss of a child, speculated about the strangeness of death (Aug. 30, 1844, Norton ed., *Letters,* I, 120). The poem is "The Dead House," *Poetical Works,* III, 218. JRL to Briggs, Feb. 8, 1854, Houghton (father; sister); Norton to A. H. Clough, May 2, 1854, Norton and Howe eds., *Letters Norton,* I, 108 (Mabel's tenderness); JRL to Briggs, Feb. 28, 1854, Norton Collection, Houghton ("unlimited darling").

2 The quotations of poetry are from "After the Burial," *Poetical Works,* III, 216; JRL to Briggs, Nov. 25, 1853, Norton ed., *Letters,* I, 273 (has a past); JRL to Briggs, Feb. 8, 1854, Norton Collection, Houghton ("naturally joyous"). The quotation about "the love we have given away" is from a later letter, when Lowell was attempting to comfort Norton on the death of his own wife (JRL to Norton, March 9, 1872, Elizabeth G. Norton Papers, Houghton).

3 F. J. Child to Clough, Feb. 20, 1854, Mulhauser ed., *Correspondence of Clough,* II, 473–476; R. H. Dana, Jr., Journal, Jan. 28, 1854, MHS. The engagement rumors were reported by Edmund Quincy to Gay (April 26, 1855, Gay Collection, Columbia) and to Hal (?) (May 27, 1855, Edmund Quincy Papers, MHS), but Quincy knew Lowell well enough to add that "Neither report is true, nor likely to be so . . ."

4 Edmund Quincy to Anne Weston, Nov. 26, 1853, Edmund Quincy Papers, MHS; Norton to Clough, "Friday morning" (1853), Norton and Howe eds., *Letters Norton,* I, 100; Longfellow to Clough, March 8, 1854, Mulhauser ed., *Correspondence of Clough,* II, 478–479; H. W. Longfellow Journal, May 23, 1854, Houghton ("lonely and desolate").

Lowell's "private and purely personal" journal is in the Houghton Library; its quotation here recalls Lowell's prophetic remark to Briggs (Feb. 8, 1854, Norton Collection, Houghton): "I cannot write it [his grief] in my journal to be found perhaps hereafter & pried into by dry executorial eyes." The eyes, at least, were not dry.

5 JRL to Miss Norton, April 9, 1855, Norton ed., *Letters,* I, 301.

6 JRL to Duyckinck, Dec. 6, 1854, Duyckinck Collection, NYPL (Marvell); JRL to Briggs, Feb. 28, 1854, M. A. DeWolfe Howe ed., *New Letters of James Russell Lowell* (New York: 1932), 49 (must keep busy).

In 1907 Maria Lowell's *Poems* were reissued in a limited edition of 330 copies, and another edition appeared in 1936, edited by Hope Jillson Vernon, and including letters and biographical data as well (see Bibliography). Maria Lowell's poetry consists largely of sentimental lyrics, a few of which have considerable merit ("The Wreath," "The Sick-Room," "Africa," "An Opium Fantasy"). Amy Lowell is said to have been an admirer of Maria's poetry and believed "An Opium Fantasy" better than anything James Russell ever wrote. Conrad Aiken included Maria Lowell in his anthology, *American Poetry, 1671–1928* (New York: 1929).

7 JRL to Quincy, Feb. 25, 1854, Yale (Kansas-Nebraska); JRL to Quincy, April 19, 1854 (lost the hang), May 15, 1854 (lost caste), Norton Collection, Houghton; Gay to JRL, July 11, 1854, Norton Collection, Houghton.

8 Richard G. White to Horatio Woodman, Feb. 4, 1855, Woodman Papers, MHS (disappointed); F. J. Child to Clough, Jan. 16, 1855, Mulhauser ed., *Correspondence of Clough,* II, 494; Sumner to JRL, Feb. 1, 1855, J. B. Lowell Collection, Houghton; Longfellow Journal, Jan. 9, 12, 20, 27, Feb. 17, 1855, Houghton; Norton to Child, Jan. 25, 1855, Houghton; Mrs. Sigourney to JRL, March 13, 1855, Norton Collection, Houghton. Though James T. Fields urged Lowell to publish the series, he decided not to, at least until he could make them "better" (JRL to Fields, May 21, 1855, Huntington Library).

9 The story of the Professorship told on the preceding pages is taken from the following sources: Longfellow to Clough, March 8, 1854, Mulhauser ed., *Correspondence of Clough,* II, 478–479 (reasons for resigning); Longfellow Journal, Jan. 26, 1854, Houghton (Samuel Eliot); Longfellow to F. Freiligrath, April 25, 1855, as quoted in the Anderson Galleries auction catalogue for sale of Nov. 10–11, 1924 ("astonished the town"); Longfellow Journal, Jan. 31, 1855, Houghton (JRL best lecturer); Longfellow to Sumner, Jan. 31, 1855, Houghton ("proud" of him as successor); JRL to Briggs, Feb. 9, 1855, Berg Collection, NYPL (duties; salary); JRL to President Walker, Feb. 1, 1855, Harvard College Papers, 2d series, XXII, 47, Harvard Archives (feeling incompetent; proposal to study abroad); James Walker to JRL, Feb. 5, 1855, Norton Collection, Houghton (accepts proposal; will raise to full prof.); R. C. Winthrop to Pres.

Walker, March 14, 1855, Harvard College Papers, 2d series, XXII, 77, Harvard Archives; C. E. Norton to Child, Feb. 3, 1855, Houghton (JRL worried); minutes of the Board of Overseers of Harvard College, March 22, 1855, Records of the Overseers, IX, 280, Harvard Archives (vote on confirmation); JRL to Anna Loring, n.d., University of Virginia ("anchor" for Mabel); JRL to Briggs, Feb. 8, 1854, Norton Collection, Houghton ($300 to Miss Dunlap); JRL to Anna Loring, Jan. 19, 1854, University of Virginia (description of Miss Dunlap); Edmund Quincy to Anne Weston, Dec. 23, 1872, Edmund Quincy Papers, MHS ("queerities"); JRL to Norton, Aug. 11, 1855, Norton Collection, Houghton (Miss Dunlap). Maria had wanted her friend Elizabeth Dunlap to care for Mabel, but Elizabeth died soon after Maria, and so the charge passed to Frances Dunlap. W. W. Story suggested that Lowell come abroad to live and let Mrs. Story take charge of Mabel, but the proposal did not appeal (Story to JRL, Jan. 9, 1855, University of Texas).

10 JRL to Miss Norton, April 9, 1855, Norton ed., *Letters*, I, 297 ("bad inn . . ."); JRL to Norton, April 9, 1855, Norton Collection, Houghton (the West); JRL to Mabel Lowell, March 14, 1855, Houghton (Fillmore).

11 H. W. Longfellow Journal, May 29, 1855, Houghton; Norton to Clough, June 10, 1855, Norton and Howe eds., *Letters Norton*, I, 128–129; William James Stillman, *Autobiography of a Journalist* (Boston: 1901), 229 (Bryant).

12 JRL to Mabel Lowell, June 1, 1855, Howe, *New Letters*, 61.

13 Story to JRL, July 9, 1855, University of Texas; JRL to Norton, Aug. 11, 1855, Norton ed., *Letters*, I, 309, 313.

14 After reading, Thackeray gave the copy to Lowell as a present for Lois Howe, his sister-in-law, and Lowell wrote Thackeray's parenthetical comments into the margins. The volume was very kindly shown to me in 1962 by its owner, Miss Lois Lilley Howe.

15 JRL to Lois Howe, Aug. 31, 1855, Howe, *New Letters*, 63–66.

16 JRL to Anna Loring, Oct. 3, 1855, Norton ed., *Letters*, I, 317 (birds); JRL to C. P. Cranch, Oct. 4, 1855, Boston Public Library (Reichenbachs).

17 JRL to Lois Howe, Sept. 24, 1855, Dr. Burnett Collection, Houghton (thoughts of suicide); Mabel Lowell to JRL, Nov. 6, 1855 (Episcopal), May 5, 1856 (calf), Rantoul Collection, Houghton.

18 The direct quotations used in the preceding pages to describe Lowell's winter in Dresden are from the following sources: JRL to Lois Howe, Nov. 4, 1855 ("real sorrow"; "Prospero"; "enchantress Memory"; "faithful in deed"), Howe, *New Letters*, 70–73; JRL to W. J. Stillman, Feb. 18, 1856 (Dresden theater), Norton ed., *Letters*, I, 337; JRL to President Walker, Nov. 4, 1855, Harvard College Papers,

2d series, XXII, 318 (German genders); JRL to Anna Loring, Oct. 3, 1855, Norton ed., *Letters*, I, 319 (German sentences); JRL to Lois Howe, Jan. 28, 1856, Houghton ("unknown").

Additional details for the Dresden winter come from the following: JRL to Cranch, Oct. 4, 1855, Jan. 10, 1856, Boston Public Library; JRL to Anna Loring, Oct. 3, 1855, University of Virginia; JRL to Lois Howe, Feb. 28, 1856, Houghton; JRL to Longfellow, Oct. 14, 1855, owned by Prof. F. W. Hilles; JRL to Mabel Lowell, Oct. 19, 1855, Houghton; JRL to Harriet Lowell, Nov. 22, 1855, Howe, *New Letters*, 75–78; JRL to Norton, Jan. 3, "January, 1856," Norton ed., *Letters*, I, 327–329, 332–333; JRL to W. J. Stillman, Feb. 18, 1856, Norton ed., *Letters*, I, 337.

19 JRL to Lois Howe, April 18, 1856, Norton ed., *Letters*, I, 340 (Medea's bath); JRL to Lois Howe, June 8, 1856, Houghton (Inquisition).

20 JRL to Cranch, July 5, 1856, Boston Public Library (kicking somebody); JRL to John Holmes, Jan. 7, 1856, Houghton ("significant in Idea"); JRL to Estes Howe, June 9, 1856, Norton ed., *Letters*, I, 343 ("wretched convulsion"); JRL to Norton, Jan. 3, 1856, Norton Collection, Houghton (Lexington); JRL to Emelyn Story, July 16, 1856, University of Texas.

CHAPTER VIII. PROFESSOR AND EDITOR (pages 152–182)

1 JRL to Cranch, Aug. 21, 1856, Boston Public Library (Cambridge better than Paris); JRL to Norton, Jan. 30, 1847, Norton Collection, Houghton (St. Theresa; forebodings; seeking society).

2 JRL to Norton, Dec. 31, 1857, Norton Collection, Houghton (Elmwood); F. J. Child to Norton, Dec. 23, 1856, C. E. Norton Papers, Houghton (velvet paper); JRL to Norton, May 22 (?), 1857, Norton Collection, Houghton ($1100); F. J. Child to Norton, March 10, 1857, C. E. Norton Papers, Houghton (lazy; modest).

3 Grace Norton to C. E. Norton, July 5, n.y., Jane Norton to C. E. Norton, July 9, 1857, C. E. Norton Papers, Houghton.

4 Edmund Quincy to Anne Weston, Dec. 23, 1872, Edmund Quincy Papers, MHS.

5 JRL to Norton, Aug. 31, 1857, Norton Collection, Houghton (Mabel; wealth and poverty); JRL to Lois Howe, Aug. 13, 1857, Houghton (character; gentleness); JRL to Norton, Aug. 11, 1855, Norton Collection, Houghton (provincialism).

6 JRL to Lois Howe, Aug. 13, 1857, Houghton ("disposition & temperament"); JRL to Norton, Aug. 21, 1857, Norton Collection, Houghton ("stronger & better"). Lois and Estes Howe did not object to Lowell's second marriage. Such at least is the recollection of their daughter, Miss Lois Lilley Howe, who in a private interview

with me also expressed great personal fondness for "Aunt Fanny." At the time of my interview with her (May, 1962), Miss Howe was ninety-seven years old.

7 JRL to Norton, Aug. 31, 1857, Norton Collection, Houghton (Dunlap family).

8 Fanny Longfellow to Mary Mackintosh, Sept. 29, Nov. 2, 1857, as quoted in Wagenknecht, *Mrs. Longfellow*, 210–211; Fanny Longfellow to G. W. Curtis, Sept. 30, 1857, University of Virginia; Gay to Edmund Quincy, Sept. 12, 1857, Gay Collection, Columbia; Edmund Quincy to Anne Weston, Dec. 23, 1872, Edmund Quincy Papers, MHS.

Years later, at Jane Norton's death, Lowell wrote her sister, Grace: "I was always conscious that she was a woman with whom I might have fallen in love, though she never occurred to me as one who might have fallen in love with me . . ." (July 1, 1877, Houghton.) This may have been disingenuous.

9 JRL to Sydney Gay, Sept. 2, 1858, Houghton ("wisest act"); Henry James to Alice James, Dec. 16, 1872, courtesy of Leon Edel; Annie Fields to Mrs. Osgood, n.d. (1892?), SPNEA; Annie Fields to C. E. Norton, Sept. 18, 1891, Norton Collection, Houghton; Annie Fields Journal, July 30, 1874, MHS; Stillman, *Autobiography*, 275–276.

10 Norton to Leslie Stephen, March 6, 1885, Norton and Howe eds., *Letters Norton*, II, 171.

11 JRL to Frances Lowell, Oct. 25, 1881, Dr. Burnett Collection, Houghton ("run & hide my face"); the quotation on Keats is in an 1854 essay, *Prose Works*, I, 233; Annie Fields Journal, July 30, 1874, MHS ("sensitive & superior being"); Annie Fields to Norton, Sept. 18, 1891, Norton Collection, Houghton ("certain smouldering").

Letters by or comments about Frances Lowell are extremely rare — a posthumous symptom of her self-effacement. In piecing together the above portrait, the following manuscripts (in addition to those already cited) provided clues to her personality: William J. Hoppin Journal, Oct. 3, 1880, Hoppin Letterbooks, Houghton; William J. Hoppin to Anna Dyer, Sept. 30, 1880, Houghton; Emelyn Story to JRL, Feb. 22, 1885, J. B. Lowell Collection, Houghton; JRL to Mabel Lowell Burnett, Nov. 24, 1874, July 15, 1879, Houghton; C. E. Norton to Aubrey de Vere, Oct. 3, 1857, Houghton; Norton to Annie Fields, Sept. 24, 1891, SPNEA.

Additional information on Frances Lowell was given me in interviews with Miss Elizabeth Putnam, Miss Lois Lilley Howe and Mrs. Stanley Cunningham.

Finally, my suggestion that Frances Lowell had an unconventional, if well-concealed, side derives from the joint conclusion, independently arrived at, of two distinguished graphologists, Dr. Klara Roman and Dr. Rose Wolfson.

12 JRL to Jane Norton, July 6, 1859, Houghton ("roses to pieces"); JRL to Norton, Dec. 31, 1857, Houghton (her cheerfulness); JRL to Norton, July 14, 1859, Norton Collection, Houghton (finances).
Frances Lowell's "practicality" was also stressed to me by Mrs. Stanley Cunningham, Lowell's granddaughter; Frances Lowell, she said, "managed everything, which made her perfect for Mr. Lowell."

13 F. J. Child to C. E. Norton, n.d. (but "1857" in pencil), C. E. Norton Papers, Houghton (miscarriage); Stillman, *Autobiography*, 276–277; JRL to Briggs, March 11, 1861, typed copy, Norton Collection, Houghton ("out of place . . ."); JRL to Stillman, Oct. 28, 1857, Norton ed., *Letters*, II, 18.

14 The many recollections of Harvard during this period agree on its drowsy parochialism. See, for example, *Letters of H. H. Furness*, H. H. Furness Jayne ed., 2 vols. (Boston: 1922), I, 2–3; Frank Preston Stearns, *Cambridge Sketches* (Philadelphia: 1905), 25; Charles Francis Adams, *An Autobiography* (Boston: 1916), 35; George Herbert Palmer, *The Autobiography of a Philosopher* (Boston: 1930), 11–13; Ethel F. Fisk ed., *Letters of John Fiske* (New York: 1940), 58–59. For additional details, see Morison, *Three Centuries of Harvard*, 275–319 (the Everett remark is on 278).

15 JRL to W. J. Stillman, May 14, 1857, Norton ed., *Letters*, II, 16 (droop on rocks).

16 In 1869–1870, when the Department of Modern Languages expanded, Lowell ceased to carry any of the duties of elementary language instruction (Charles W. Eliot, "James Russell Lowell as a Professor," *Harvard Graduates' Magazine* [June, 1919], 495); John Fiske to his mother, June 4, 1863, *Letters of John Fiske*, Ethel F. Fisk ed., 103 (when Fiske was hauled up before the faculty for poor attendance, he appealed to Lowell to set matters straight. Lowell apologized, promised to explain and then promptly forgot to do so); Report of the Visiting Committee, Reports to the Overseers, Academical Series, II, 5–6, Harvard University Archives; JRL to President Hill, June 15, 1866, Corporation Papers, Harvard University Archives.

17 Holland, "Reading Dante with Lowell," 575 ("He treated us . . ."); Henry Adams, *The Education of Henry Adams* (Modern Library ed. New York: 1931), 62–63; Barrett Wendell, "Mr. Lowell as a Teacher," *Scribner's* (May, 1891), for details of Lowell's appearance and conversation, reprinted by Wendell in *Stelligeri and Other Essays* (New York: 1893), 206–212; Lowell's comment on scholarship is in "Fragments from the Lectures of Professor Lowell," Part Six, *Harvard Crimson*, May 4, 1894, Harvard Archives. If these "Fragments" from Lowell's lectures are a genuine sample, they were of high quality — an epigrammatic blend of the concrete and the abstract, learned but not pedantic, leading the student into the literature

not into scholarly irrelevancies. For additional evidence, especially on Lowell's courtesy and lack of authoritarianism, see the *Transcript*, Aug. 12, 1891, A. P. Peabody in the *Tribune*, n.d., JRL Scrapbook, II, Houghton, and F. J. Child to C. E. Norton, June 23, n.y. ("1857" in pencil), C. E. Norton Papers, Houghton.

18 Alexander McKenzie in the *Tribune*, n.d., JRL Scrapbook, II, Houghton (minor figures); *Quarterly Review* (July, 1902), 74 (capricious; discursive); T. W. Higginson, *Old Cambridge*, 141 (yawns, cynicism); Stearns, *Cambridge Sketches*, 101 (gloves). The harshest account of Lowell as a teacher is in *The Autobiography of Nathaniel Southgate Shaler* (Boston: 1909), 12. Shaler, a man of Southern background and sympathies, and later a colleague of Lowell's, wrote that as an undergraduate he thought Lowell "the most perfect and most natural poser I have ever known . . . he had a devouring hunger for praise," and also kept his students at a firm distance. Even Shaler, however, remembered Lowell's lectures as "fascinating"; although Lowell read them, he read "admirably," and some of the lectures stayed with Shaler "after half a hundred years."

19 JRL to Underwood, Nov. 23, 1853, Berg Collection, NYPL; JRL to Briggs, Feb. 15, 1854, typed copy, Norton Collection, Houghton (opinion of Underwood); Underwood to Norton, Dec. 1891, Norton Collection, Houghton (1853 plans; Whist Club).

20 JRL to Clough, May 20, 1857, Mulhauser ed., *Correspondence of Clough*, II, 527–528. Reliable, detailed accounts on the launching of the *Atlantic* can be found in M. A. DeWolfe Howe, *The Atlantic Monthly and Its Makers* (Boston: 1919), James C. Austin, *Fields of the Atlantic Monthly: Letters to an Editor 1861–1870* (San Marino: 1953), W. S. Tryon, *Parnassus Corner, A Life of James T. Fields* (Boston: 1963), and John Townsend Trowbridge, *My Own Story, with Recollections of Noted Persons* (Boston: 1903).

21 H. W. Longfellow Journal, May 5, 1857, Houghton.

22 According to Underwood, far from wishing the editorship for himself, it was he, without the suggestion or knowledge of anyone, who proposed Lowell for the job (Underwood, *The Poet and the Man*, 50). Emerson to JRL, May 17, 1857, Rusk ed., *Letters of Emerson*, V, 77; JRL to Norton, May 22 (?), 1857, Norton Collection, Houghton (penniless).

23 JRL to Norton, May 22 (?), 1857, Norton Collection, Houghton ("free," etc.); Howe, *Atlantic Monthly*, 18 (naming of magazine).

24 JRL to Clough, May 20, 1857, Feb. 15, 1858 ("caviare"), Clough to JRL, June 12, 1857, all in Mulhauser ed., *Correspondence of Clough*, II, 527–528, 544; JRL to Fanny Kemble, April 14, 1860, Folger Library (soliciting manuscripts); Norton to JRL, June 20, 1857, Norton and Howe eds., *Letters Norton*, I, 170–171; Charles Reade to JRL, Oct. 10, 1858, Morgan Library.

25 JRL to J. P. Kennedy, April 26, 1860, Kennedy Papers, Peabody Institute, Baltimore; P. H. Hayne to JRL, Dec. 28, 1859, Norton Collection, Houghton (in which Hayne, with more warmth than accuracy, praised the *Atlantic* for never manifesting the slightest "narrow-minded, sectional bitterness"). A generous review of Hayne's poetry was printed in the *Atlantic* issue of Jan. 1860. Lowell's encouraging review of Howells and Piatt's *Poems by Two Friends* can be found in the *Atlantic* for April, 1860. The letter to Hawthorne is in Norton ed., *Letters,* II, 52.

26 T. B. Aldrich to C. E. Norton, March 21, 1892, C. E. Norton Papers, Houghton; E. C. Stedman to JRL, May 24, 1866, Norton Collection, Houghton; C. F. Adams, *Autobiography,* 40–41; Lowell's review of Rose Terry's *Poems* is in the *Atlantic* for March, 1861, and that of Harriet Prescott Spofford is in the issue of Feb. 1860, from which the quotes about "genius," "mullein," etc. come.

27 Annie Fields Journal, Dec. 14, 1870, MHS (JRL on Harte's coming to Boston). In reviewing Harte's *Poems* (NAR, Jan. 1871), Lowell wrote, "Here was our Theocritus at last"; he singled out "purely American" qualities in Harte's work: the "contempt for all received conventions," "a feeling for what is noble in character, and a faith in the final perseverance of humanity under the most adverse circumstances" — perhaps the best, rather than the typical results of democracy. When Harte did arrive in Boston, the two men occasionally met, with some but not entire cordiality.

The remaining quotations in the paragraph are from JRL's review of Bulwer-Lytton's *The New Timon,* in NAR (April, 1847), 460–467, except for the quotation about "original in spite of democracy . . . no country ever offered less encouragement," which is from his piece in NAR (Oct. 1868), 660–663.

28 The review of Holland's poem is in the *Atlantic* for May, 1859.

29 The one mention of Melville which I have been able to find in Lowell's correspondence is in a letter to Sydney Gay, Sept. 1848, Norton ed., *Letters,* I, 193; the one mention in Lowell's works is in a review of Thoreau's *A Week . . . , Massachusetts Quarterly Review* (Dec. 1849); J. Leyda, *The Melville Log,* 2 vols. (New York: 1951), II, 581–582 (Underwood-Melville exchange); II, 584 (name on back cover); I, 487 (letter of Briggs to Melville, May 12, 1854, re *Encantadas*).

30 JRL to Norton, Oct. 12, 1855, Norton ed., *Letters,* I, 319 (conscious originality); JRL to Rev. W. L. Gage, Dec. 7, 1863, Huntington Library ("solemn humbug"); JRL to J. T. Fields, Oct. 8, 1861, Howe, *New Letters,* 101–102; Annie Fields Journal, Nov. 1868, MHS. For another slighting reference to Whitman, see Lowell's review of Howells' *Venetian Life* in NAR (Oct. 1866).

In publishing "Bardic Symbols," Lowell objected to these two lines:

See from my dead lips the ooze exuding at last!
See the prismatic colors glistening and rolling!

Whitman gave him permission to omit the lines (which Lowell did) though expressing the preference that they be kept in (Whitman to JRL, Jan. 20, 1861, University of Virginia). As a student of Lowell's remembered it, Lowell commented late in life (1885) that Whitman's "vogue among the intellectual elite in England was partly due to the fact that they had read him first in a volume of selections skilfully chosen by William Rossetti, who had left out the dreary and tedious catalogues and the grossest of the physiological passages . . . Lowell recognized some of the elements in Whitman's greatness, but I think that on the whole he did not place him among the masters . . . the men who win the long race through the centuries [Lowell said] . . . do not last on the ground that they are adept in the art of startling . . ." (William Roscoe Thayer, "James Russell Lowell as a Teacher," *Scribner's* [Oct. 1920], 480.)

31 JRL to Clough, Dec. 21, 1857, Mulhauser ed., *Correspondence of Clough*, II, 536–537 ("Captain's fidelity"); Thoreau to JRL, June 22, 1858, Norton Collection, Houghton.

32 Lowell wrote two evaluations of Thoreau; one was a review of *A Week on the Concord and Merrimack Rivers* published in *Massachusetts Quarterly Review* (Dec. 1849), the other, more important essay, "Thoreau," was a retrospective view of his life and work first published in Oct. 1865 in NAR and later collected in *My Study Windows* (1871). All the quotations in the preceding three paragraphs come from "Thoreau," except "antique purity," which is from Lowell's review of *A Week*. A perceptive discussion of Lowell's attitude toward Thoreau is Austin Warren, "Lowell on Thoreau," *Studies in Philology*, vol. 27, No. 3 (July, 1930), 442–461.

Annie Fields recorded in her journal (July 23, 1864, MHS) a conversation on Thoreau shortly before Lowell wrote his 1865 essay: ". . . we passed the evening at the Dana's . . . J. R. Lowell and Mr. Dana both consider Thoreau as a man of small genius, indeed they think the word misapplied when directed to him. L. says 'he went in the wrong direction: men would become *pigs* if they continued as he lead!!' I don't believe they either of them ever read his books."

In a "List of books from the library of James Russell Lowell" which Mrs. Sherman Baldwin owns and kindly allowed me to examine, there are two interesting asides on Thoreau. One is a comment written by Lowell in his copy of Thoreau's *Letters to Various Persons:* "Not letters in any sense but sprays, he always carried himself on his back. It is not solitary men, but men who have conversed much with men who have done much. Your solitary aims at being cosmopolitan — the other unconsciously is it. Flint vs. steel." The second comment, written by Lowell in his copy of Thoreau's *A Week,* refers to him as a "Cold Water Rabelais, his love of nature engrafted on him and he does not take the woods in that fine superior way he should, but is a little fussy about them . . ."

33 The remark on Holmes is from Lowell's review of *Elsie Venner* in the *Atlantic* for April, 1861; the comment on Hawthorne is from Lowell's review of *The Marble Faun* in the *Atlantic* for April, 1860 (Hawthorne himself thought highly of this review — see Hawthorne to J. T. Fields, April 26, 1860, Fields Collection, Huntington Library). Other significant reviews by Lowell are those on Longfellow's *The Courtship of Miles Standish* (*Atlantic*, Jan. 1859), on Whittier's *Home Ballads and Poems* (*Atlantic*, Nov. 1860), and on Emerson's *The Conduct of Life* (*Atlantic*, Feb. 1861).

34 For examples of Lowell's cutting or changing passages to avoid clerical criticism, see JRL to Edmund Quincy, Nov. 19, 1857, Yale, JRL to Clough, Dec. 21, 1857, Mulhauser ed., *Correspondence of Clough*, II, 536–537, Stearns, *Cambridge Sketches*, 103–104. The quote about Harper and John Knox is from JRL to C. G. Leland, March 5, 1861, Historical Society of Pennsylvania, and that on being "vicariously pigeonlivered" is from JRL to T. W. Higginson, Dec. 9, 1858, Norton ed., *Letters*, II, 29.

35 JRL to Horatio Woodman, March, 1859, Woodman Papers, MHS ("dressing rooms"); JRL to J. T. Fields, n.d. (1859?), Vassar College ("keyholes").

36 JRL to Norton, Oct. 11, 1858, Norton Collection, Houghton (pressure to popularize); JRL to J. T. Fields, n.d. (1860), Berg Collection, NYPL ("Scribes & Pharisees"); JRL to Norton, n.d. (1857), Norton Collection, Houghton ("merely *do*"); Charles Reade to JRL, Oct. 10, 1858 (?), Morgan Library; Norton to JRL, Nov. 10, 1859, Norton Collection, Houghton (second-rate fiction); JRL to Jane Norton, n.d. (1859), Houghton ("Julie gazed . . .").

37 JRL to Briggs, Sept. 18, 1856, Norton ed., *Letters*, II, 14 (nation instead of clique); JRL to Norton, Sept. 16, 1856, Norton Collection, Houghton (Frémont barbeque); JRL to Norton, March 21, 1847, Norton ed., *Letters*, II, 16 (Dred Scott).

38 Lowell's additions to the Godwin article have been described by E. G. Bernard, "New Light on Lowell as Editor," *New England Quarterly* (June, 1937), 337–341. Bernard prints Lowell's letter to Godwin and expresses the opinion that there was no resentment on Godwin's part. But a letter from F. J. Child to C. E. Norton (March 28, 1858, C. E. Norton Papers, Houghton) suggests the opposite: "Lowell wrote the last few pages of the political article . . . & had a fuss with Parke Godwin about it." Then, too, there is Godwin's

statement to Underwood (as quoted by Henry Seidel Canby, *Thoreau* [Boston: 1939], 376), "I should prefer my writings put before the public without his [JRL's] 'improvements.'"

39 "The American Tract Society," *Atlantic* (July, 1858), republished in *Prose Works*, V, 1–16.

40 The article on Cushing, entitled "A Sample of Consistency," appeared in the *Atlantic* for Nov. 1858, and that on Choate, entitled "The Pocket Celebration of the Fourth," for Aug. 1858, in which the above quotation can be found on 380.

41 R. W. Emerson to William Emerson, Oct. 18, 1858, Rusk ed., *Letters of Emerson*, V, 122; JRL to Jane Norton, Aug. 1, 1858, Houghton (to Congress); Norton to JRL, Oct. 14, 1858, Norton Collection, Houghton (need to attack *men*).

42 A good discussion of the "social consciousness" of the *Atlantic* is in Robert E. Mitchell, "American Life as Reflected in the Atlantic Monthly 1857–1881," doctoral dissertation, Harvard, 1951, especially 186–224. Sample articles on social problems were "Dr. Wichern & His Pupils" and "The Abbé de L'Epée," both by L. P. Brockett (March, April, 1858), and the review of Halliday's *The Lost & Found* (Jan. 1860). Higginson's comment on "a little demurring" is in the *Woman's Journal*, Sept. 12, 1891, JRL Scrapbook, I, Houghton; Parker's on "mutilations" in Oliver Johnson to Theodore Parker, May 6, 1858, Parker Papers, LC. Higginson's complaint must be taken with a grain of salt; Lowell specifically wrote him in regard to the article on women, that he wanted no change in the piece "excepting the insertion of a qualifying 'perhaps' where you speak of the natural equality of the sexes, and that as much on your own account as mine — because I think it not yet *demonstrated*. Even in this, if you prefer it, have your own way" (Dec. 9, 1858, Norton ed., *Letters*, II, 29). But Lowell did gently discourage Higginson from doing a piece on John Brown (Oct. 24, 1859, Norton ed., *Letters*, II, 42). In 1892 Higginson credited Lowell with "kindly & sympathetic interest in the work of individual contributors," though at that late date his resentment may have been softened by Lowell's recent death and his memory blurred by time (Higginson to C. E. Norton, March 30, 1892, C. E. Norton Papers, Houghton).

43 T. W. Higginson to his mother, July 3, 1861, Higginson Papers, Houghton ("promptness"); JRL to Higginson, June 28, 1860, Huntington Library (anonymous manuscripts); newspaper clipping from the *Globe* (1891?), J. R. Lowell Scrapbook, I (ms. into pockets); J. W. Palmer to JRL, April 15, n.y., Norton Collection, Houghton (no answer to letters); JRL to [?], Oct. 27, 1859, as printed in Libbie catalogue for sale of March 3–4, 1915 (keep copies of short pieces); W. W. Story to Norton, Aug. 6, 1859, C. E. Norton Papers, Houghton; Julia Ward Howe to O. W. Holmes, May 14, 1860, Holmes

Papers, LC; JRL to J. W. Palmer, April 17, 1860, University of Virginia (description of his schedule).

44 The details of the Phillips, Sampson & Co. failure and the transfer to Ticknor & Fields have been taken from the following sources: Norton to JRL, Sept. 14, 1859; JRL to Norton, Oct. 11 ("practical publisher"), Oct. 18 (best arrangement possible), 1859; JRL to Emerson, Oct. 21, 1859 — all in the Norton Collection, Houghton. Additional information on the transfer can be found in Tryon, *Fields*, and Austin, *Fields*. Lowell's comment on Fields' "very properly" wanting to be editor is in JRL to R. W. Gilder, typed copy, Feb. 7, 1887, Norton Collection, Houghton; on his being best equipped to be "dining editor," in a letter to Norton of Oct. 18, 1859, Norton Collection, Houghton.

45 JRL to Norton, Oct. 11, 1858, Norton ed., *Letters*, II, 27 ("vacant to the muses"); JRL to Norton, July 12, 1860, Norton ed., *Letters*, II 50 ("muddy and cloggy"); Francis Child to A. H. Clough, Oct. 15, 1860, Mulhauser ed., *Correspondence of Clough*, II, 580 ("wasting his time"); Norton to JRL, Oct. 17, 1861, Norton Collection, Houghton (next ten years).

46 JRL to Sydney Gay, Sept. 2, 1858, Houghton; JRL to Fields, May 23, 1861, Norton ed., *Letters*, II, 58–59 ("the waters close over one").

CHAPTER IX. BRAHMIN SOCIETY (pages 183–197)

1 John Holmes is best recaptured by a reading of the *Letters of John Holmes to James Russell Lowell and Others*, ed. William Roscoe Thayer, with a sensitive introduction by Alice M. Longfellow (Boston: 1917). Information on John Bartlett can be found in M. H. Morgan, "John Bartlett," *Proceedings of the American Academy of Arts & Sciences*, XLI, 2–4, and *The Cambridge Historical Society Publications*, I (Cambridge: 1906), "Reminiscences of John Bartlett," 67–87.

2 Information on the Town and Country Club can be found in Emerson to Dana, Jr., May 12, 1849, Rusk ed., *Letters of Emerson*, IV, 142–143 (where its purpose is stated); Fields to Longfellow, April 3, 1849, Houghton; Samuel Ward to Longfellow, Dec. 18, 1849, Houghton; Higginson to Norton, March 30, 1892, C. E. Norton Papers, Houghton (Emerson's "colorphobia"), JRL to Higginson, July 23, 1849, University of Virginia (Douglass).

Another "social" group, with many of the same members, also came into existence about this same time — the so-called Adirondack Club, which took occasional camping trips. Lowell, Emerson and

Agassiz were among its members, but Longfellow took a jaundiced view of the expeditions; hearing on one occasion that Emerson had brought himself a double-barreled shotgun, Longfellow "respectfully declined" to join the party — Emerson, he thought, would surely shoot one of the members "in trying for a deer" (Longfellow to Sumner, Aug. 12, 1848, Houghton — "respectfully declined"; Fanny Longfellow to Mary A. MacKintosh, Aug. 10, 1858, Craigie House — "trying for a deer"). A useful article on the Adirondack Club is Ida G. Everson, "William J. Stillman: Emerson's 'Gallant Artist,'" *New England Quarterly* (March, 1958), 32–46.

3 R. H. Dana, Jr., Journal, Aug. 6, 1857, MHS. Woodman, so central to the formation of the Saturday Club, has left almost no trace. What does remain is largely unflattering. Norton called him "a bore of the highest class, thoroughly ingenious in the pertinacity of his wearisome offensiveness" (Norton to E. L. Godkin, Oct. 29, 1865, Godkin Papers, Houghton), and Horace Scudder stated, without equivocation, that later in life Woodman "pocketed trust funds." (Scudder to A. Stedman, Nov. 26, 1888, Stedman Collection, Columbia.) Because of these peculations Woodman lost his social and professional standing, and finally took his own life. For a more favorable view of him, see George Willis Cooke, *John Sullivan Dwight* (Boston: 1898), especially 251–253, E. W. Emerson, *The Early Years of the Saturday Club, 1855–1870* (Boston: 1918), 124–127, and C. F. Adams, *Richard Henry Dana*, 2 vols. (Boston: 1891), II, 163, where Adams refers to Woodman as "an amusing story-teller, with a natural eye for character and a well-developed sense of humor . . ."

4 On the fight over Quincy, see JRL to Emerson, Oct. 14, 1868, Norton Collection, Houghton ("good so long"), and Annie Fields Journal, May 2, 1868, MHS. Emerson's "supra-Castilian" remark is in a letter to James Elliot Cabot, Nov. 28, 1860, Rusk ed., *Letters of Emerson*, V, 231.

5 JRL to Jane Norton, June 12, 1860, Norton ed., *Letters*, II, 49.

6 E. W. Emerson, *Early Years of Saturday Club*, especially 121, 215, 219.

7 Annie Fields Journal, Feb. 1867, MHS.

8 Emerson, *Saturday Club*, 154 ("childlike pride"), 77 ("London art"); Holmes to Motley, Sept. 26, 1869, in Morse, *Holmes*, II, 185 (Turkish bath); Higginson, *Old Cambridge*, 89–90, 185–190 (Stowe dinner; the three men as talkers). For further examples of Appleton's geniality and wit, see *Life and Letters of Thomas Gold Appleton*, "prepared by" Susan Hale (New York: 1885).

9 Emerson, *Saturday Club*, 116 (Ward), 92 (Motley); R. H. Dana, Jr., Journal, Dec. 16, 1854, MHS (Emerson as man of the world); Annie Fields Journal, Nov. 5, 1870, MHS (Appleton's comparison

with Johnson's Club); JRL to Norton, April 22, 1883, Norton ed., *Letters*, III, 105.

10 In regard to Lowell's attitude on social relations, the most revealing bit of writing is a holograph fragment in the Norton Collection, Houghton, entitled "The Actual and the Ideal Life," a rewritten version of which appeared in his published essay on Rousseau (*Prose Works*, II, 232–271).

For Emerson's admiration (not unmixed) of Lowell, see Rusk ed., *Letters of Emerson*, V, 87, and Emerson's poem read at a dinner celebrating Lowell's fortieth birthday (Feb. 22, 1859), the manuscript of which is in the Berg Collection, NYPL, and reads in part:

Too well gifted to have found
Yet his opulence's bound,
Most at home in mounting fun,
Broadest joke, & luckiest pun . . .
Logic, passion, cordial zeal,
Such as bard and hero feel . . .

11 Emerson, *Saturday Club*, 382 (Agassiz verses). Lowell's review of Longfellow's *Tales* is in NAR (Jan. 1864), 289–290; in the same issue, Lowell wrote an almost harsh critique of Whittier's *In War Time* ("His rhymes are often faulty beyond the most provincial license even of Burns himself"). For further examples of Lowell's ability to combine criticism with praise when reviewing friends, see his reviews of Bartlett's *Dictionary of Americanisms* in the *Atlantic* (Nov. 1859), 638–644, and of Story's *Roba di Roma*, the *Atlantic* (April, 1863), 515–518.

12 John Holmes to C. E. Norton, Aug. 24, 1897, W. R. Thayer ed., *Holmes-Lowell Letters*, 283; O. W. Holmes to C. E. Norton, Nov. 17, 1893, C. E. Norton Collection, Houghton; JRL to Mrs. S. B. Herrick, April 19, 1876, Norton ed., *Letters*, II, 383 (cemetery); Fanny Longfellow to Emmeline A. Wadsworth, May 15, 1860, as quoted in Wagenknecht, *Mrs. Longfellow*, 221.

13 J. W. Howe to her sister Louisa, Feb. 18, 1853, as quoted in Laura E. Richards and Maud Howe Elliott, *Julia Ward Howe, 1819–1910*, 2 vols. (Boston: 1916), I, 156; JRL to Norton, July 14, 1859, Norton Collection, Houghton (Mrs. Stowe and temperance). Emerson reported a similar episode with Mrs. Stowe five years later (Journal [1864?], Houghton). F. H. Underwood in *The Poet and the Man* (56–57) gives a somewhat different version of the "Stowe dinner"; according to him, Mrs. Stowe stood firm on her ban of alcohol, but wine was secretly smuggled into some of the "water pitchers."

14 Clough to Miss Smith, Jan. 4, 1853, Mulhauser ed., *Correspondence of Clough*, II, 360.

15 JRL to Jane Norton, Oct. 11, 1858, Houghton ("clever men"); JRL

to Briggs, March 26, 1848, Berg Collection, NYPL. The line on "solitude is as needful . . ." is from Lowell's 1868 essay on Dryden, NAR (July, 1868), reprinted in *Prose Works*, III, 132.

16 The best source, in my view, for understanding Norton, in all of his complexity, is in his own letters, many of which have been printed (Norton and Howe eds., *Letters Norton*, 2 vols.). In this collection the most revealing letters are: (in vol. I), to Ruskin, July 17, 1869, June 15, 1870, Dec. 29, 1872; to Meta Gaskell, July 14, Oct. 28, 1867; to JRL, Jan. 13, 1856, Feb. 24, 1870; to Mrs. S. P. Cleveland, May 16, 1850; to Chauncey Wright, Sept. 13, 1870; to G. W. Curtis, Jan. 29, 1869; (in vol. II), to JRL, Nov. 24, 1873, July 24, 1877, Nov. 16, 1884; to John Simon, May 15, 1875; to J. B. Harrison, July 23, 1882; to Edward Lee-Childe, Sept. 29, 1883.

In drawing the above portrait of Norton, I have used too many sources, printed and in manuscript, to give a detailed listing here, especially since the portrait is a composite, impressionistic one. The direct quotations, however, require citation: Appleton's comment on "tame oats" is from Alice M. Longfellow, "The Old Order Changes" (MS), Craigie House, and Norton's comment on society's not being "worth preserving" is from a letter to Chauncey Wright, Dec. 5, 1869, Norton and Howe eds., *Letters Norton*, I, 372.

Recently a much-needed intellectual portrait of Norton has appeared: Kermit Vanderbilt, *Charles Eliot Norton, Apostle of Culture in a Democracy* (Cambridge: 1959).

To my mind the single best description of Norton — in that it beautifully captures the halfway house he occupied — is that by Henry James: ". . . a son of the Puritans the most intellectually transmuted, the most liberally emancipated and initiated possible, could still plead most for substance when proposing to plead for style, could still try to lose himself in the labyrinth of delight while keeping tight hold of the clue of duty, tangled even a little in his feet; could still address himself consistently to the moral conscience while speaking as by his office for our imagination and our free curiosity." ("Charles Eliot Norton," *The American Essays of Henry James*, ed. with Introduction by Leon Edel [New York: 1956], 127.)

17 Ruskin's remark is recorded in Norton's Journal, Nov. 10, 1872, Norton and Howe eds., *Letters Norton*, I, 424.

18 JRL to Norton, Feb. 25, 1876, Norton Collection, Houghton. There are many examples of Norton's encouragement; one may serve as exemplar for the rest: "Do get ready a volume of the poetry that is scattered through the papers and magazines and lying in your portfolio, for the press. And if you will not do it as a duty to the world, do it out of love to some few friends and to me . . ." (letter of Jan. 1, 1857, Norton and Howe eds., *Letters Norton*, I, 161).

19 Norton to JRL, Sept. 14, 1859, Norton Collection, Houghton, JRL to Norton, Feb. 2, 1874, Norton Collection, Houghton.

CHAPTER X. CIVIL WAR (pages 198–225)

1 Fanny Longfellow to "Mary," Dec. 10 (16?), 1860, Craigie House.

2 JRL to C. G. Leland, March 5, 1861, Historical Society of Pennsylvania ("camping out"); JRL to Briggs, March 11, 1861, Norton ed., *Letters*, II, 58 ("bottling").

Mrs. Longfellow feared the old house would be "very gloomy" for Lowell, especially with his "mad sister" Rebecca still in residence (Fanny Longfellow to Tom Appleton, Feb. 1861, Craigie House). Rebecca Lowell lived until 1872.

3 JRL to Gilder, Feb. 7, 1887, typed copy, Norton Collection, Houghton ("entirely content").

4 The précis of Lowell's views which follows in this and the next paragraph (and the direct quotations) are from "The Election in November" first published in the *Atlantic* (Oct. 1860), and later reprinted in his *Prose Works*, V, 17–44.

5 JRL to Charles Nordhoff, Dec. 31, 1860, Norton ed., *Letters*, II, 55.

6 Lowell's 1861 essay "E Pluribus Unum," first published in the *Atlantic* (Feb. 1861) is in his *Prose Works*, V, 45–74. All the quotations in this and the following paragraph are taken from this essay.

7 For a full discussion of "Unionism" in the South at the time of the secession crisis, see Allan Nevins, *The Emergence of Lincoln*, 2 vols. (New York: 1950), II, Chapters XI, XIV. For the difficulties (probably insoluble) in trying to establish Southern sentiment on secession, see David M. Potter, *Lincoln and His Party in the Secession Crisis* (New Haven: 1942), especially Chapter VIII.

8 "Sunthin' in the Pastoral Line," *Biglow Papers*, 2d Series, *Poetical Works*, II, 339. In a similar vein, Lowell wrote:

> . . . as we reach our fortieth parallels
> We reach our temperate zone, if nothing else,
> And threaten judgments less, because we find
> Our own has not been always of one mind.

("The Power of Sound: A Rhymed Lecture," Smith, *Uncollected Poems*, 120.)

For further evidence of Lowell's awareness of the complexities in historical analysis, see his sophisticated comments in the first part of his essay, "The Rebellion: Its Causes and Consequences," *Prose Works*, V, 118–152.

9 Lowell's views on the March–April, 1861, period are best outlined in his essay, "The Pickens-and-Stealin's Rebellion," first published in

the *Atlantic* (June, 1861) and later collected in his *Prose Works,* V, 75–91. All the quotations in the above paragraph are from this essay except the last one, reevaluating Lincoln's career, which is from Lowell's "Abraham Lincoln," *Prose Works,* V, 188–189. On Lowell's later shift of opinion, see pages 216–217.

10 The 1846 lines, "Ez fer war . . ." are from *Biglow Papers,* 1st Series, *Poetical Works,* II, 46. Nor is this an isolated example of Lowell's earlier disapproval of war; in "An Extract," written for *The Liberty Bell,* 1848 (180, 183), he wrote, "Force never yet gained one true victory," and also,

> Those are ill crops whose sickle is the sword . . .
> I never heard that any
> Dared knock at Heaven's gate with his reeking sword,
> Or lift the next life's latch with bloody hands . . .

The comment on "no price is high" is in JRL to Motley, March 27, 1862, Houghton; the poem beginning "Ne'er may war . . ." is from "The Power of Sound: A Rhymed Lecture," Smith, *Uncollected Poems,* 119. See also Lowell's 1861 poem, "The Washers of the Shroud," in which he fears that war may doom the bright promise of the Republic and yet insists "the sheathed blade may rust with darker sin" (*Poetical Works,* IV, 5).

11 Lowell's approval of Sidney Smith's remark is recounted in Moorfield Storey, "Harvard in the Sixties," *Harvard Graduates' Magazine,* V (March, 1897), 338; JRL to G. W. Curtis, "1861," Goodspeed's auction catalogue for Nov. 1935, p. 249 ("o'er rank state"); Norton to Clough, Dec. 11, 1860, Norton and Howe eds., *Letters Norton,* I, 214 ("whirlwind"); JRL to Motley, March 27, 1862, Houghton (agriculture a disadvantage to South); "The Pickens-and-Stealin's Rebellion," *Prose Works,* V, 89–91 (emancipate public opinion in North; "oligarchy built *on* men").

12 Norton to JRL, July 21, 1861, Norton Collection, Houghton ("It is a fine thing . . ."). Longfellow, in his Journal for April 18, 1861 (Houghton), refers to Lowell as being "full of fight." Even as late as 1869, when reviewing the *Life and Letters of Wilder Dwight,* a promising young New Englander killed in the war, Lowell could write that Dwight's giving his life for his country "was nothing less than that most splendid of human achievements, the sacrificing of the seen and calculable to the unseen and uncalculable, the recognition of the ideal as infinitely more real than the actual" (NAR Jan. 1869, 327–328).

13 In 1856 Lowell had thought of resurrecting Hosea to comment on the civil war in Kansas; in 1859 he had had a piece on the slave trade running through his head, and in 1860 he had talked of doing a satire on Buchanan. The quote on needing "brooding" time is in JRL to

Nordhoff, Dec. 31, 1860, Norton ed., *Letters*, II, 56; his "nervousness" is in JRL to Jane Norton, Dec. 9, 1861, Norton ed., *Letters*, II, 68.

The first six of the new papers appeared in consecutive issues of the *Atlantic* from January to June, 1862; then Lowell faltered for several months, until Lincoln's Emancipation Proclamation brought forth the seventh paper. This was the last Lowell wrote until 1865–1866, when he completed the series with an additional four papers and then published the whole in book form, dedicated to Judge Hoar, who of all his friends seemed to him "the most genuine Yankee." (JRL to Fields, June 5, Aug. 2, 1862, Huntington Library; JRL to Norton, Oct. 19, 1866, Norton Collection, Houghton.)

In book form, the Second Series was received with greater favor (and more detailed analysis) in England than in the United States. The first six papers, in fact, had been brought out in London in separate pamphlet form soon after their publication in the *Atlantic*. For details on the reception of the Second Series, see McFadyen, "Contemporaneous Reputation," 221–235.

14 Norton to JRL, Dec. 19, 1861, Norton Collection, Houghton; see F. J. Child to C. E. Norton, Dec. 20, 1861, C. E. Norton Papers, Houghton, for a sample of the feeling that it would be "ungracious" to criticize Lowell too directly.

15 JRL to R. H. Dana, Jr., April 20, 1863, Dana Papers, MHS; JRL to J. L. Motley, March 27, 1862, Houghton ("resenting a slap").

Lowell's attitude toward England, prior to the Civil War, had already shown considerable ambivalence. During his 1852–1853 trip to Europe, he made a number of acid comments on the Englishmen he met — "neat, cleanshirted, short whiskered, always conceited" (JRL to Maria Fay, Jan. 3, 1852, Houghton). They lacked, he felt, genuine refinement of manner, that is, some awareness of the rights of others. He reported to his father that their "brutality & disregard for the feelings of others" made Englishmen "hated all over the continent," and although they imputed a worship of money to the Americans, "we are mere gentiles & heathen compared with them" (JRL to Dr. Charles Lowell, Feb. 1, 1852, Houghton). Yet Lowell acknowledged in the same letter that he was speaking of "superficial characteristics" only, and that such Englishmen as he had come to know well during his travels were "agreable & companionable." During the Civil War, Lowell's anger at England far outpaced his admiration; he was furious at the supercilious tone with which England proffered advice, assuring the North that it should acquiesce in what was in any case the certain dismemberment of the Union. Yet even at the height of his anger, Lowell maintained some appreciation of English virtues (see his essay "Self-Possession vs. Prepossession," *Atlantic*, Dec. 1861, 761–769). Later, when Minister to England, he recovered much of his affection for the country; indeed it ripened to the point where he preferred to spend a good part of his time there in later years (see Chapters XIV–XV).

Lowell's hostility to England before and during the Civil War cannot be linked to literary resentments. It is true that he had not been widely known in England, but he had received a number of complimentary reviews there early in his career, and the First Series of *Biglow Papers* had spread his fame considerably. Both a pirated and an authorized edition appeared in England in 1859, the former inadvertently abetted by Sydney Gay, the latter introduced by Thomas Hughes, of *Tom Brown's School Days* fame. Norton had urged Ruskin (who was a great fan of *The Biglow Papers*) instead of Hughes, as editor, but by the time he made the suggestion Lowell had already concluded with Hughes, for he "did not dream" Ruskin would be willing to take the trouble (Norton to JRL, Sept. 14, 1859, JRL to Norton, Sept. 20, 1859, Norton Collection, Houghton). When Lowell later met Hughes, he was immensely fond of him (see page 238). Ruskin, with the exception of one passage in the preface, thought well of Hughes' editing and predicted the edition would do Lowell "much good." (Ruskin to JRL, Dec. 5, n.y., Rantoul Collection, Houghton.) The prediction proved accurate. A number of printings were run off (and later of the Second Series, too, though these were less admired), the reviews were on the whole excellent, and Lowell for the first time had an international reputation.

16 Norton to G. W. Curtis, Dec. 31, 1861, Norton and Howe eds., *Letters Norton*, I, 250; Motley to Holmes, Feb. 26, 1862, G. W. Curtis ed., *The Correspondence of John Lothrop Motley*, 2 vols. (New York: 1889), II, 66; G. W. Curtis to JRL, May 27, 1862, Norton Collection, Houghton (Cranch's comment).

17 JRL to Motley, March 27, 1862, Houghton (lift the people to a higher plane); JRL to Norton, Sept. 20, 1861, Norton Collection.

18 JRL to Motley, March 27, 1862, Houghton; "Self-Possession vs. Prepossession," *Atlantic* (Dec. 1861), 768–769.

19 Moncure Conway, *Autobiography*, I, 348 ("more than painful"); Samuel J. May to R. Webb, March 26, 1861, May Papers, Boston Public Library ("cut the Abolitionists"). For other animadversions on Lowell for his emancipation views, see Moncure Conway, *The Golden Hour*, 53–55, T. W. Higginson to J. W. Fields, Jan. 20, 1862, Higginson Papers, Houghton, and Frank Stearn's *Cambridge Sketches*, 104–105. The Stearns book, incidentally, is wildly unreliable, and must in all particulars be cross-checked by other sources — which usually turn out to contradict it.

20 "Self-Possession vs. Prepossession," *Atlantic* (Dec. 1861), 769 ("It is a question . . .").

21 A number of critics prefer the Second Series to the First (e.g. Green-

slet, *Lowell,* 157) — as did Lowell himself (JRL to Mrs. S. B. Herrick, June 3, 1875, Norton ed., *Letters,* II, 353).

22 The handwritten contract, dated Oct. 23, 1863, signed by Lowell, Norton, and Crosby & Nichols, is in Houghton Library; Lowell's suggestion of Norton as co-editor is recounted in Norton to Horace Scudder, Aug. 2, 1900, Scudder Papers, Houghton.

23 The new arrangements with Ticknor & Fields are described in J. T. Fields to Norton, June 8, 1865, Houghton; the editors' discretionary powers as to rates can be traced in Crosby & Nichols to Norton, Oct. 15, 1863, C. E. Norton Papers, Houghton, Norton to W. D. Whitney, Oct. 27, 1863, Whitney Collection, Yale, and John Fiske to Abby Brooks, Nov. 1, 1863, Ethel Fisk ed., *Letters of John Fiske,* 108. Lowell's "threat" to Motley is in a letter of July 28, 1864, in Curtis ed., *Correspondence of Motley,* II, 167–168. After Ticknor & Fields took over as publishers, they made Motley the huge offer of $1000 for four articles (JRL to Motley, Dec. 28, 1864, Curtis ed., *Correspondence of Motley,* II, 195–196).

24 T. W. Higginson to C. E. Norton, Nov. 8, 1864, C. E. Norton Papers, Houghton (comment on Fields' editorship); JRL to W. C. Bryant's son, Nov. 23, 1865, MS. Div., NYPL (" pair of bellows"); Norton to Scudder, Aug. 2, 1900, Scudder Papers, Houghton ("profound").

25 Norton to Frederick Law Olmsted, Jan. 24, 1864, Olmsted Papers, LC ("better sense"), courtesy of Prof. W. M. Armstrong; JRL to Motley, July 28, 1864, Curtis ed., *Correspondence of Motley,* II, 167 (loyal, lively).

26 Yet even during the first year of the war, Lowell had not been as impatient as he now (perhaps for purposes of dramatic contrast or catharsis) represented. In his article, "Self-Possession vs. Prepossession," Atlantic (Dec. 1861), 768–769, he did say that ". . . the administration of Mr. Lincoln has sometimes seemed to us over-cautious . . ." but he went on to add that although ". . . in moments of impatience, we have wished for something like the rough kingship of Jackson, cooler judgment has convinced us that the strength of democratic institutions will be more triumphantly vindicated under an honest Chief Magistrate of average capacity than under a man exceptional whether by force of character or contempt of precedent."

27 As Lowell said of Bryant: "Others seem to have celebrated Mr. Bryant as poet chiefly . . . I saw room left for me to speak of a quality which I value even more highly — I mean that granitic temper of mind which keeps him steadfast to principle, buttressed immoveably as one of his own Berkshire hills." (JRL to George Bancroft, Dec. 2, 1864, Bancroft Papers, MHS.)

28 *The Diary of Gideon Welles,* Howard K. Beale ed., 3 vols. (New

York: 1960), entry for Jan. 5, 1864, I, 504; Lincoln's letter to Crosby & Nichols, dated Jan. 16, 1864, has been printed in his *Collected Works,* Roy P. Basler ed., III, 132–133; JRL to R. W. Gilder (typed copy), Feb. 7, 1887, Norton Collection, Houghton (disapproval of reprinting Lincoln's letter).

29 E. C. Stedman to JRL, Feb. 2, 1866, Norton Collection, Houghton; H. W. Longfellow Journal, Jan. 2, 1864, Houghton; Evert Duyckinck Journal, Jan. 4, 1864, MS. Div., NYPL.

The following month Longfellow expressed a little annoyance that a piece by Ticknor had been given fifty pages of space while he "had only a little bone in the backyard. But one's intimate friends are such funny fellows!" (Longfellow to G. W. Greene, Feb. 20, 1864, Houghton.)

30 See Chapter XI for a detailed discussion of Lowell's 1865–1868 writing.

Sample complaints about the *North American* are in G. W. Greene to Longfellow, July 24, 1864, Houghton, and John Fiske to his wife, May 26, 1864, Ethel Fisk ed., *Letters of John Fiske,* 127. Comment on the hostility of the religious press is in Charles Akers to Norton, May 2, 1868, C. E. Norton Papers, Houghton, and G. W. Curtis to Norton, Dec. 18, 1867, Curtis Papers, Houghton. Norton's remark to Lowell about "weighty things" is in a letter of July 7, 1864, Houghton. For a strenuous and intelligent defense of Emerson's essay, "Character," see Norton to Godkin, Feb. 4, 1866, Godkin Papers, Houghton.

Despite their success in other areas, Norton and Lowell never managed to make the *North American* self-supporting; losses reached $5000–$6000 per year (Tryon, *Fields,* 328).

31 JRL to Norton, Oct. 12, 1865, Norton Collection, Houghton ("not the stuff"); a petition signed by thirteen professors (July, 1864[?]), asking for a pay raise, is in the Corporation Papers, Harvard University Archives; Norton to JRL, Oct. 17, 1861, Norton Collection, Harvard (Lowell had a "larger duty").

Norton was not content with exhorting Lowell to give up teaching. He consulted the financier, Samuel Ward, on the feasibility of providing Mrs. Lowell with a $20,000 or $25,000 life insurance policy, so that Lowell's mind might be put at ease at least to that extent about finances. But for whatever reason, the suggestion bore no fruit (Norton to Ward, Jan. 24, 1866, Houghton).

32 G. W. Curtis to C. F. Briggs, Nov. 30, 1862, Berg Collection, NYPL. A dining group formed during these years, the so-called "Dozen Club," was also largely ancillary to the war effort. Apparently the Dozen Club was founded in 1863 as an antidote to the Somerset Club, which was considered lukewarm in its devotion to the Union cause. The dozen members were C. G. Loring, John Murray Forbes,

Lowell, Norton, Dana, S. G. Ward, Dwight Forster (attorney general of Massachusetts), C. W. Storey, Francis E. Parker, Horace Gray, Martin Brimmer and Charles R. Codman. The object of the club, according to Codman, was to bring together once a month or so "a few men who thought alike on the great issues of the day, and who were all believers in Abraham Lincoln" (Charles R. Codman to Moorfield Storey, April 2, 1911 [?], owned by Mr. Charles M. Storey).

33 John Lothrop Motley remembered Willie as a boy in Florence—"most engaging & attractive—full of promise, very studious . . . had devoted himself to the literary profession from his earliest years" (Motley to Thomas Hughes, Sept. 5, 1865, MHS). I have published William Lowell Putnam's touching last letter, ringing with antislavery conviction, in *Civil War History* (Sept. 1963), 325–327; the original of the letter is in the recently acquired Spence-Lowell Collection of the Huntington Library.

34 JRL to Sarah Shaw, August 28, 1863, Norton ed., *Letters*, II, 78–79.

35 JRL to Mrs. White, Oct. 30, 1864, University of Virginia ("by far the best thing we had"); the poem is from the Second Series of *Biglow Papers*.

36 The remark about democracy "justifying itself" is from JRL to J. L. Motley, Dec. 28, 1864, the one about "selfish and factious" is from JRL to J. L. Motley, July 28, 1864, Curtis ed., *Correspondence of Motley*, II, 197, 168–169; the rest of Lowell's argument on the election of 1864, including all the quotations, comes from his essay "McClellan or Lincoln?" which first appeared in NAR (April, 1864) and was later collected in his *Prose Works*, V, 153–176.

37 JRL to [?], May 28, 1865, Berg Collection, NYPL ("percussion"); Emerson to Sumner, Dec. 7, 1864, Rusk ed., *Letters of Emerson*, V, 390.

38 G. W. Curtis to Norton, Jan. 7, 1865, Curtis Papers, Houghton (rumors in newspapers); O. W. Holmes to JRL, March 16, 1865, Norton Collection, Houghton ("Switzers"); Sumner to Longfellow, March 29, 1865, Sumner Papers, Houghton; Longfellow to Sumner, March 13, 29, April 2 ("you cannot recall anyone"), 1865, Houghton.

For an example of Lowell's public treatment of Seward, there is this bit from "Mason & Slidell":

> So Mister Seward sticks a three-months' pin
> Where the war'd oughto eend, then tries agin;
> My gran'ther's rule was safer 'n 't is to crow:
> *Don't never prophesy—onless ye know.*

For one of Lowell's private comments on Seward, there is this remark to J. L. Motley (March 27, 1862, Houghton): "Seward . . . seems to me rather a dilettante than an artist in statesmanship. I don't like your fellows who smoke their cigars & chat cooly over the death struggle of their Country — at least I don't like them at the head of affairs in such a crisis."

39 JRL to Norton, April 13, 1865, Norton ed., *Letters*, II, 100; the remark on Lincoln was appended by Lowell to his earlier essay, "The President's Policy."

40 JRL to Jane Norton, July 25, 1865, Norton ed., *Letters*, II, 101–102.

41 Details on the Ode's reception can be found in Hamilton Vaughan Bail, "James Russell Lowell's Ode," *Papers of the Bibliographical Society of America*, 3rd Quarter, 1943, 169–202.

42 Emerson to JRL, Sept. 17, 1865, Gay to JRL, Sept. 16, 1865, Clarke to JRL, Sept. 21, 1865, all in the Norton Collection, Houghton. It should be noted that all these men commented on the printed rather than the spoken version — which meant the superior one, for Lowell added to the published version those stanzas on Lincoln which are among the most successful parts of the Ode.

G. H. Lewes wrote Lowell that the Ode was "the finest poetical expression of Positivism that had yet found utterance" to which Lowell's astonished reaction was, "Heaven save the mark!" (JRL to Elizabeth Gay, July 6, 1871, Houghton.)

43 For a discussion of some of the derivative qualities in the Ode, see Sydney Mendel, "A Note on Lowell's 'Ode Recited at the Harvard Commemoration,'" *New England Quarterly* (March, 1962), 102–103. Roy Harvey Pearce has some perceptive comments on the Ode in *The Continuity of American Poetry* (Princeton: 1961), 217–218, a fine book that I sometimes disagree with but have read with great profit. See, too, George M. Fredrickson, *The Inner Civil War* (New York: 1965), especially Chapter 12, which not only contains some provocative remarks on the Ode but gives a suggestive reading of the Civil War's effects on Northern intellectuals; though I would quarrel with Fredrickson on a number of specifics, the originality and insight of his book give it unusual value.

CHAPTER XI. THE CRITIC OF POLITICS AND LITERATURE (pages 226–258)

1 Howells, *Literary Friends*, 192.

2 JRL to Leslie Stephen, April 10, 1866, Norton ed., *Letters*, II, 120 (Johnson's "obstinacy").

3 "Reconstruction," first published in NAR (April, 1865), reprinted in *Prose Works*, V, 210–238 (the argument on land is largely on 228).

As early as January, 1865, Lowell had written, ". . . there must be multitudes in the South guilty only of weakness, and who may be wisely pardoned by a country for the first time conscious of its glorious strength" (review of the "Diary of Samuel Curwen," NAR [Jan. 1865], 289).

4 All the quotations in this paragraph are from JRL's essay, "Reconstruction," *Prose Works*, V, 210–238.

In this and other essays Lowell wrote on reconstruction, he prefigured, even to detail, recent "revisionist" interpretations; which is perhaps only to say that the "latest word" in historical scholarship, in this as in so many cases, often represents not a genuinely new departure but a return to an older view recently out of fashion.

5 JRL to Quincy, Sept. 2, 1867, Yale; the other quotations in this paragraph are from JRL's essay, "Reconstruction," *Prose Works*, V, 210–238.

6 For further examples of "racism," see JRL to Norton, Aug. 31, 1858, Norton ed., *Letters*, II, 25–26, and "The President on the Stump," *Prose Works*, V, 279. For Lowell's attitude in later life, see pages 357–358. As counterbalance, and far more typical, is this statement: "We have done everything to get rid of the negro . . . One thing we have not tried . . . We have not acknowledged him as our brother" ("The Seward-Johnson Reaction," *Prose Works*, V, 311).

7 JRL to W. C. Bryant's son, Nov. 23, 1865, NYPL ("firmness equably tempered . . ."); the other quotations are from JRL's 1865 essay, "Scotch the Snake, or Kill It?" *Prose Works*, V, 239–263.

8 Norton's comment on Southern whites is in a letter to Aubrey de Vere, March 25, 1867, Houghton; all the other quotations in this paragraph are from Lowell's "Scotch the Snake, or Kill It?" *Prose Works*, V, 239–263, except the discussion of the letter-spirit interpretation of the Constitution, which is from "The Seward-Johnson Reaction," *Prose Works*, V, 299.

9 All the quotations in this paragraph are from Lowell's essay, "The Seward-Johnson Reaction," *Prose Works*, V, 283–327.

10 The quotations in this paragraph are all from "The Seward-Johnson Reaction," *Prose Works*, V, 283–327.

Lowell wrote E. L. Godkin that impeachment reminded him "of the boy playing at hanging — who finds he has done it all right — only forgotten to cut himself down." (JRL to Godkin, Dec. 20, 1867, Godkin Papers, Houghton.)

11 For Lowell's favorable opinion of Grant as a man, see JRL to Norton, Dec. 30, 1868, and JRL to Jane Norton, Jan. 19, 1871, Houghton. His meeting with Grant in 1870 ("puzzled pathos") is described in JRL to Leslie Stephen, March 25, 1870, Norton ed., *Letters*, II, 255.

12 JRL to Leslie Stephen, April 24, 1869, Norton ed., *Letters*, II, 203 ("stock-jobbery"); Norton to Aubrey de Vere, March 25, 1867,

Houghton; E. L. Godkin to the *Daily News*, Sept. 7, 1867, *The Life and Letters of Edwin Lawrence Godkin*, Rollo Ogden ed., 2 vols. (New York: 1907), I, 321.

13 JRL to E. L. Godkin, July 16, 1869, Norton ed., *Letters*, II, 225 (come out all right); JRL to Norton, Dec. 10, 1869, Norton ed., *Letters*, II, 248 ("common sense"; "comfort in God").

14 JRL to Godkin, Nov. 20, 1868, Norton ed., *Letters*, II, 177 (South); JRL to Leslie Stephen, Nov. 25, 1868, Norton ed., *Letters*, II, 179 (Johnson).

15 JRL to Thomas Hughes, Feb. 7, 1871, Norton ed., *Letters*, II, 271 (Butler); JRL to Garfield, April 8, 1870, Garfield Papers, LC (also a letter of April 14, for further elaboration); JRL to Jane Norton, Jan. 19, 1871, Houghton; "Address as President of the Wordsworth Society, May 10, 1884," *Prose Works*, VI, 102.

16 The story of this episode derives from the following sources: JRL to Judge Hoar, April 14, 1869, University of Virginia ("unfit for his business"); Edmund Quincy to Anne Weston, May 4, 9, 1869, Edmund Quincy Papers, MHS; JRL to Mabel Lowell, May 22, 1869, Houghton ("ace of it"); JRL to James T. Fields, July 13, 1869, Huntington Library.

17 JRL to Norton, Dec. 30, 1868, Houghton ("nothing *seems* to happen"); JRL to Mabel Lowell, May 22, June 14, July 12, Sept. 5, 1869, Howe, *New Letters*, 137–145. Lowell was quite a farmer; Annie Fields reported that he spent $150 a year in manure, and produced "magnificent squashes, potatoes as large a cocoa nuts . . ." (Journal, Aug. 1866[?] MHS.)

18 John Holmes to John Bartlett, Aug. 9, 1868 (kindly sent to me by Mr. Albert Frothingham, and now in the Yale Library).

19 Lowell's circle could discuss the limitations of their community in a serious as well as comic vein; they were not nearly so wedded to provincial loyalty as is commonly assumed. Lowell once wrote Story, for example: "I would gladly subscribe to a reward to anybody who will find a cure for the (*small*) potato-disease with which Boston is fearfully infected" (Jan. 28, 1856, as quoted in Henry James, *Story*, I, 313). And Norton, as early as 1861, frankly stated, "We are provincials, with a very little city of our own . . . A few years hence & Boston will be a place of the past, with a good history no doubt, but New York will be alive" (Norton to JRL, Dec. 19, 1861, Norton Collection, Houghton).

For the social events described above, see H. W. Longfellow Journal, Nov. 13, 1870, Houghton; JRL to Norton, May 30, 1866, Norton Collection, Houghton (Cranch); JRL to Cranch, May 21, 1866, Boston Public Library. Longfellow, after dining with Lowell, Cranch and Fields one night, described Cranch as "a curious, taciturn person. He hardly spoke a word during dinner; but after dinner sang two comic songs, with great effect." (Journal, June 17, 1871, Houghton.)

20 Edmund Quincy to Anne Weston, March 1, 1868 (Dickens), March 29, 1869, Edmund Quincy Papers, MHS; JRL to Fields, Jan. 12, 1869, Howe, *New Letters*, 131.

21 In 1867 Curtis was still addressing his letters to Lowell as "My dear Lowell," but was soon writing "My dear James" and even "My dear Jamie" — an obvious symptom of developing intimacy. For Lowell's relationship with Howells, see G. N. Bennett, "Howells, 1866–1888," Yale doctoral dissertation, especially 96–105, and Howells to Norton, Aug. 29, Nov. 12 ("a new kind of great man"), 1868, C. E. Norton Papers, Houghton. Lowell's letter to Howells ("I take a kind of credit . . .") is dated June 16, 1869, Norton Collection, Houghton; see also the one dated Dec. 21, 1875, in the Hayes Library, Ohio, in which Lowell writes, "I haven't changed my mind about you from the first." For Lowell's laudatory reviews of Howells' work see NAR, Oct. 1866 (review of *Venetian Life*), Oct. 1869 (review of *No Love Lost*) and Jan. 1871 (review of *Suburban Sketches*). For Howell's reviews of Lowell's work, see George Monteiro, "Howells on Lowell: An Unascribed Review," *New England Quarterly* (Dec. 1965), which includes in a footnote a full listing.

22 For Lowell's friendship with Godkin, see Godkin to Norton, Sept. 7, 1868, Ogden ed., *Letters Godkin*, I, 290; for that with Hughes, see JRL to Jane Norton, Oct. 14, 1870, Norton ed., *Letters*, II, 263 ("simple, hearty . . ."), JRL to Hughes, Oct. 18, 1870, Norton ed., *Letters*, II, 267 ("good-by to sunshine"), JRL to [?], Feb. 7, 1871, Norton Collection, Houghton, and Annie Fields Journal, Oct. 18, 1870, MHS. Hughes' perceptive biographers, Edward C. Mack and W. H. G. Armytage, *Thomas Hughes* (London: 1952), describe him as "outspoken," "soft-hearted," "angered by 'flippant scepticism' " — qualities with which Lowell could readily identify.

23 The following sources have been especially useful in analyzing the Stephen-Lowell friendship: Stephen's "short-hand notes" for Oct. 3 and Oct. 4, 1863, as printed in Frederic W. Maitland, *The Life and Letters of Leslie Stephen* (New York: 1906), 118, and his letter to his mother, July 21, 1863, 113–115; Leslie Stephen to Norton, Feb. 2, 1892, C. E. Norton Papers, Houghton, which rehearses at length the story of the friendship; Norton Journal, April 12, 1873, Norton and Howe eds., *Letters Norton*, I, 475; Norton to Ruskin, n.d., 1874, *Letters Norton*, I, 267; JRL to Stephen, Jan. 1, 1874, Norton Collection, Houghton ("ship of Faith"); JRL to Stephen, May 16, 1874, May 15, 1876, Dec. 4, 1876, Norton ed., *Letters*, II, 335 ("judicious shutting of the eyes"), 385–389, 408. Noel Annan's suggestive study of Leslie Stephen (Cambridge: 1952) has given me a number of specific insights, but in my view he misunderstands Lowell at several

points and this has weakened his analysis of the friendship with Stephen.

Lowell became godfather to Leslie Stephen's daughter, the future writer, Virginia Woolf.

24 JRL to Annie Fields, copy, n.d., Norton Collection, Houghton (Mr. Tuckwell); JRL to Jane Norton, July 25, 1865, Houghton (lady from Halifax).

25 Annie Fields Journal, Nov. 19, 1868, MHS; Charles Akers, "Personal Glimpses of Our New England Poets", *New England Magazine*, 1897, New Series, XVII, 447 (Moses).

26 Emerson Journal (MS vol. titled "Gulistan"), April 5, 1864, Houghton (twenty-second time); JRL to Parsons, Sept. 12, 1866, Houghton. In the Jan. 1868 NAR, in an unsigned review, Lowell gave a cordial welcome to Parsons' completed translation of the *Inferno*. Parsons, recognizing Lowell's style, sent his profuse thanks (*The Letters of T. W. Parsons*, Zoltan Haraszti ed. [Boston: 1939], 68).

27 Annie Fields Journal, Jan. 1867; H. W. Longfellow Journal, Oct. 25, 1865, Houghton; Alice M. Longfellow, "The Old Order Changes" (MS), Craigie House; Francis Child to A. H. Clough, April 19, n.y., Oxford University (Milton); the remark on "readers turn students" is in Lowell's essay, "Dante," *Among My Books, Second Series* (Boston: 1876), 39. Norton has given an account of the meetings in *First Annual Report of the Dante Society* (Cambridge: 1882), 17–25 (in which, incidentally, he dates the first meetings from 1863 with a discussion of the *Inferno*).

28 Howells to Norton, June 8, 1866, C. E. Norton Papers, Houghton ("Indian epic"); Norton to Aubrey de Vere, March 25, 1867, Howe and Norton eds., *Letters Norton*, I, 294; JRL to James B. Thayer, Oct. 1867, Norton ed., *Letters*, II, 159–161.

For a modern critical estimate of Longfellow's translation, which sees considerable merit in it, see Newton Arvin, *Longfellow*, especially 250–257.

According to Annie Fields (Journal, Feb. 1867, MHS), Longfellow harbored a suspicion that Norton had passed on notes from their meetings to Parsons; I have found no additional evidence for this assertion and neither the suspicion nor the act would seem in line with either man's character.

29 JRL to Norton, Sept. 25, 1867, Houghton ("delight of life"); Annie Fields Journal, July 25, 1868, MHS (chivalrous manner); JRL to Norton, Aug. 10, 1865, Norton Collection, Houghton (wartime clothes); Annie Fields Journal, Feb. 1867, Jan. 8, 1869, MHS; Charles Dickens to Miss Hogarth, n.d., *The Letters of Charles Dickens* (1880, 2 vol. ed. edited by his sister-in-law and eldest daughter), II, 415; JRL to "Effie" Lowell, July 7, 1871, University of Virginia ("altogether pleased"). Later difficulties in Mabel Lowell Burnett's

marriage are alluded to in Grace Ashburner to E. L. Godkin, Nov. 17, 1891, Godkin Papers (courtesy of Prof. W. M. Armstrong); I have found no other direct references of this kind, but the fact that Mabel and her children later moved to Elmwood, where she kept house for her father, perhaps lends some credence to the suggestion of a difficult marriage. See pages 364–365.

30 JRL to Fields, n.d. (1868) ("Gods, how bad they seem now"), Oct. 6, 1868 ("basketmakers"), Jan. 12, 1869 ("Under the Billows") — all in the Huntington Library.

31 R. W. Emerson Journal, Dec. 9, 1868, Houghton; for the critical reception, see McFadyen, "Contemporaneous Reputation," especially 263–281; George Eliot Journal, Feb. 6, 1869, *The George Eliot Letters*, Gorden Haight ed., 7 vols. (New Haven: 1954), V, 12; JRL to James R. Osgood, May 7, 1869, as printed in Libbie auction catalogue for sale of Nov. 21, 22, 1901 ("the dolts").

32 "The Cathedral" (Boston: 1870); the poem was published almost simultaneously in the *Atlantic* (Jan. 1870). Lowell thought the poem good because he wrote it in a burst, happy in his sleepless obsession — he always believed a thing which "wrote itself" was likely to turn out well (JRL to Mabel Lowell Burnett, Sept. 5, 1869, Houghton). The reviews, however, were mixed, some of the criticism centering on the poem's literary failures, some on its theological unorthodoxies (McFadyen, "Contemporaneous Reputation," 282–298). But many of Lowell's distinguished contemporaries acclaimed the poem. Longfellow thought it was "very beautiful, and will make a great mark" (Longfellow to Sumner, Dec. 17, 1869, Houghton); Ruskin "couldn't lay it down," though he thought it needed "retouching" (Ruskin to Norton, Aug. 12, 1870, Houghton), and Howells believed that "no poem at all equalling it has been written in America, and no poem surpassing it has been written in our generation" (Howells to James M. Comly, Dec. 13, 1869, Ohio Historical Society). It has only recently come to light that Howells anonymously (and glowingly) reviewed "The Cathedral" in the *Tribune* for Dec. 16, 1869 (George Monteiro, "Howells on Lowell: An Unascribed Review," *New England Quarterly* [Dec. 1965]). In later life Howells came to hold the poem in much less esteem (*Literary Friends*, 223). Lowell's comment on Gray's "Elegy" is from "Gray," *Latest Literary Essays*, 32.

33 Most of Lowell's major literary criticism was published in three volumes: *Among My Books, First Series* (Boston: 1870), *My Study Windows* (Boston: 1871) and *Among My Books, Second Series* (Boston: 1876). The large majority of these essays were written in the years 1865–1871; in fact only three of his significant pieces (though a number of minor ones) fall outside these years — the essays on Spenser and Milton, written in 1875, and, perhaps Lowell's

single finest piece (as well as the one most revealing of him personally), the study of Gray written in 1886. The Gray essay and a number of minor pieces can be found in *Latest Literary Essays and Addresses of James Russell Lowell* (Boston: 1892), collected posthumously by Charles Eliot Norton, Lowell's literary executor.

Fitzgerald's remark ("altogether . . . best critic") is in a letter to F. Tennyson, 1878, in *More Letters*, Wright ed., 211. Despite Fitzgerald's good opinion, Lowell, when Minister to England in the 1880's, decided not to visit him at Lowestoft, "for Fitzgerald was the most freakish of creatures, and the surest way to fall out with him was to visit him" (as recounted by Thayer, "Lowell as a Teacher," 478).

There is a considerable body of commentary on Lowell as a literary critic. I have especially profitted from (though I often disagree with) Joseph J. Reilly, *Lowell As a Critic* (New York: 1915), J. M. Robertson, "Lowell As a Critic," NAR (Feb. 1919), 246–262, and the introduction by Harry Hayden Clark and Norman Foerster to their anthology, *James Russell Lowell* (New York: 1947), in which they find even more merit in Lowell's criticism than I do, though in part, I feel, by giving his views on literature a greater coherence than they in fact had. The single most suggestive piece on Lowell as a prose writer is the brilliant if prolix essay by W. C. Brownell in his neglected minor masterpiece, *American Prose Masters* (New York: 1909).

34 JRL to Mabel Lowell, Sept. 30, 1869, Houghton; "Gray," *Latest Literary Essay*, 17 ("school-boy blunders").

35 "Shakespeare Once More," *Prose Works*, III, 67 (Goethe); the remaining quotations in this paragraph come from "Swinburne's Tragedies," *Prose Works*, II, 120–139.

Lowell's opposition to mere "correctness" is also seen in his comments on language. "Our literature," he once wrote, "has to guard against . . . the universal Schoolmaster, who wars upon home-bred phrases, and enslaves the mind and memory of his victims, as far as may be, to the best models of English composition, — that is to say, to the writers whose style is faultlessly correct, but has no blood in it. No language, after it has faded into *diction* . . . can bring forth a sound and lusty book. True vigor of expression does not pass from page to page but from man to man . . ." (review of Bartlett's *Dictionary of Americanisms*, in the *Atlantic* [*Nov.* 1859], 638–644).

36 JRL to Howells, Dec. 1, 1860, Norton ed., *Letters*, II, 53; "Library of Old Authors," *Prose Works*, I, 321, 348 (Hazlitt), 271 (Halliwell); "James Gates Percival," *Prose Works*, II, 148.

37 "Carlyle," *Prose Works*, II, 88 (*Sartor Resartus*), 105 (Diogenes); "Gray," *Latest Literary Essays*, 12 (Addison and Steele; Richardson);

"Coleridge," *Prose Works*, VI, 75 (Eden of diction); "A Good Word for Winter," *Prose Works*, III, 262 (Thomson); "Lessing," *Prose Works*, II, 175 ("a great man . . .").

38 "Gray," *Latest Literary Essays*, 13 ("fanaticism of temperament"); "Rousseau," *Prose Works*, II, 240 ("in whose power"); "Lessing," *Prose Works*, II, 224 (two kinds of genius).

Probably the fullest definition (though not, for that, the more satisfying) Lowell gave of "genius" was in a review of Harriet Prescott Spofford's *Sir Rohan's Ghost*, in the *Atlantic* (Feb. 1860): "genius in Art is that supreme organizing and idealizing faculty which, by combining, arranging, modulating, by suppressing the abnormal and perpetuating the essential, apes creation . . ."

39 JRL to Story, Jan. 28, 1856, Keats-Shelley Memorial Association, Rome, as printed in Gertrude Reese Hudson, *Browning to His American Friends* (London: 1965), 309.

40 "Dante," *Prose Works*, IV, 165 (separation of artist and moralist); "Wordsworth," *Prose Works*, IV, 413 (linking of the two); "Shakespeare's Richard III," *Latest Literary Essays*, 113 (Lessing); "Coleridge," *Prose Works*, VI, 71 ("vulgarizing tyranny"); "Lessing," *Prose Works*, II, 172 (hates exaggeration); "Dryden," *Prose Works*, III, 102 (enthusiasm), 153 (holding nose); "Fielding," *Prose Works*, VI, 60–61 (painted vice).

41 "Carlyle," *Prose Works*, II, 89; "Rousseau," *Prose Works*, II, 241 (Shakespeare's memoirs); "A Good Word for Winter," *Prose Works*, III, 271 ("inextricably interfused"). For a further discussion by Lowell of the relation between genius and character, see his review of Charles Robert Leslie's *Autobiographical Reflections*, *Atlantic* (Sept. 1860), 373–376.

42 "Fielding," *Prose Works*, VI, 58; "Coleridge," *Prose Works*, VI, 76–77.

43 "Lessing," *Prose Works*, II, 187, 192, 194.

44 "Lessing," *Prose Works*, II, 171 ("easier to embody . . ."); "Rousseau," *Prose Works*, II, 257 ("*highest* creative genius"—the italics here and also "*but the best of its kind*" are mine); "Shakespeare Once More," *Prose Works*, III, 94. In paying tribute to John Pendleton Kennedy, Lowell said, "Perhaps we overestimate the worth of mere literary ability . . . It may well be suspected that the power of expressing fine sentiments is of a lower quality than the less obtrusive skill of realizing them in the life and character" (MHSP, 1869–1870, 366).

45 "Chaucer," *Prose Works*, III, 356; "Shakespeare Once More," *Prose Works*, III, 31 ("exquisite something").

46 "Shakespeare's Richard II," *Latest Literary Essays*, 114 (gait).

Curiously, Lowell at a private gathering once claimed adherence to a critical position which in practice he failed to follow. In her journal, Annie Fields recorded a conversation in which Lowell said "that he always looked for certain qualities in writers, which if he could not discover, they no longer interested him and he did not care to read them. He discovered, for instance, in the writers who had survived the centuries the same kindred points, those points he studied until he discovered what the adamant was and where it was founded; then he would look into the writers of our own age to see if he could find the same stuff; there was little enough of it unfortunately" (as quoted in M. A. DeWolfe Howe ed., *Memories of a Hostess*, Boston: 1922, 124). Whatever "kindred points" Lowell may have thought he had discovered, he never elucidated them in his essays.

47 JRL to Godkin, Jan. 24, 1870, Norton ed., *Letters*, II, 252 ("just fate"); JRL to Fields, "Tuesday night," 1868, Norton ed., *Letters*, II, 162; JRL to Norton, Oct. 7, 1868, Norton ed., *Letters*, II, 174.

48 JRL to E. L. Godkin, Sept. 25, 1866, Norton ed., *Letters*, II, 129 ("professor change"); JRL to Fields, Sept. 7, 1868, Norton ed., *Letters*, II, 171 ("fat and dull"); JRL to A. D. White, May 15, 1869, Cornell University ("queer trick"); JRL to Fields, Dec. 20, 1868, Huntington Library ("apprehension of evil"), JRL to Norton, Dec. 10, 1869, Norton ed., *Letters*, II, 247 ("immense capacity").

49 JRL to Edmund Quincy, Nov. 1, 1867, Yale University.

50 JRL to Charles Hazen Dorr, Aug. 12, 1869, Houghton ("skill for spending"); for one of many examples of his charity, see JRL to Carter, July 14, 1871, Berg Collection, NYPL.

51 Annie Fields Journal, Dec. 14, 1870, MHS ("lion at bay"); JRL to Edmund Quincy, Nov. 1, 1867, Yale (renting Elmwood); JRL to Jane Norton, June 30, 1871, Houghton (income).

52 JRL to Leslie Stephen, July 31, 1871, Norton ed., *Letters*, II, 274–275; JRL to Jane Norton, Feb. 17, 1872, Norton ed., *Letters*, II, 281–282; JRL to Norton, Sept. 25, 1871, Norton Collection, Houghton ("wholesome unrest"). Lowell's sister, Rebecca, had died in May, 1872.

Lowell might have settled for a sabbatical, but when Harvard refused his request for two years abroad on half pay, he decided, with some pique, on outright resignation. Paid sabbaticals were not the commonplace then which they have become today, but after sixteen years of uninterrupted teaching, Lowell felt entitled to one.

CHAPTER XII. RETURN TO EUROPE — AND POLITICS (pages 259–283)

1 JRL's Paris routine is most fully described in JRL to Mary Lowell Putnam, May 20, 1873, Houghton; see also JRL to Mabel Lowell Burnett, Oct. 12, 1872, Jan. 7, 1873, Houghton.

2 Henry James to his father (Nov. 1872?), James Papers, Houghton.

3 JRL to Mabel Lowell Burnett, Dec. 19, 1872, ("gentle, kindly . . ."; Americans "happiest"), Jan. 7, 1873 ("sowing reaction"), April 8, 1873 (Thiers at reception), Houghton; JRL to Thomas Hughes, June 2, 1873, Norton ed., *Letters*, II, 311 (Thiers' egotism); JRL to Norton, Dec. 4, 1872, Norton Collection, Houghton ("Country . . . blocking").

4 Henry James to Alice James, Dec. 16, 1872 ("indisposed"), courtesy of Leon Edel; JRL to Mabel Lowell Burnett, Sept. 29, 1872 ("faded away like a mist"), Feb. 6, 1873 (Guizot), Howe, *New Letters*, 162, 181; JRL to Norton, March 18, 1873, Norton ed., *Letters*, II, 296 (Emerson); JRL to Norton, Sept. 15, 1872, Norton Collection, Houghton (Story).

Henry James' reactions to Norton and Story at this time throw them into an interesting perspective. James went to the Louvre with Norton and decided the older man took art "too hard"; James prayed "*not* to grow in discrimination & to be suffered to aim at superficial pleasure." (Henry James to William James, Sept. 22, 1872, James Family Correspondence, Houghton.) As for Story, James thought him "as clever as you please — cleverer! — but not altogether the ripest fruit of time" (Henry James to Jane Norton, Feb. 18, 1873, James Papers, Houghton).

5 For Lowell's relationship with Henry James, see especially Henry James to William James, Nov. 31, 1872, James Family Correspondence, Houghton ("mutual indifference"; "friendly . . . full of knowledge"), Henry James to his father (Nov. 1872), James Papers, Houghton ("a furious intimacy"); Henry James to William James, May 3, 1874, James Family Correspondence, Houghton, JRL to Henry James, Sept. 9, 24, 1878, May 8, 1879, Houghton; and Lowell's favorable review of James' *A Passionate Pilgrim* and *Transatlantic Sketches* (*Nation*, June 17, 1875). See also Leon Edel's analysis of the friendship in his biography of James (vol. II: *The Conquest of London* [New York: 1962], 78–79). Edel has also edited the two important essays which James wrote on Lowell, in *The American Essays of Henry James* (New York: 1956).

6 Henry James to William James, Nov. 31, 1872, James Family Correspondence, Houghton ("unassimilable"); JRL to Mabel Lowell Burnett, Nov. 4, 1872 (Holmes dependent); JRL to Norton, Nov. 6, 1872, Houghton (Holmes a child).

7 JRL to Mabel Lowell Burnett, Feb. 6, 1873 (godfather), Feb. 4, 1874 (Hildebrand), Houghton.

8 C. E. Norton Journal, London, April 2–May 10, 1873, Howe and Norton eds., *Letters Norton*, I, 489–490; JRL to Mabel Lowell Burnett, May 22, 1873, Dr. Burnett Collection, Houghton (Rousseau-Ruskin).

9 Swinburne to Paul Hamilton Hayne, March 20, 1877, *The Swinburne Letters*, ed. Cecil Y. Lang, 6 vols. (New Haven: 1960), III, 302–303; JRL to E. C. Stedman, Nov. 26, 1866, Norton ed., *Letters*, II, 138; Swinburne to Stedman, April 4, 1882, *Swinburne Letters*, Lang ed., IV, 265. See page 465 for Swinburne's reaction in 1877 to a rumor that Lowell was about to be appointed minister to England.

10 JRL to Mabel Lowell Burnett, June 18, July 20, 1873, Howe, *New Letters*, 195–198; JRL to Mrs. Herrick, Oct. 6, 1875, typed copy, Houghton ("*posthumous* feeling"); Marian Adams to her father, June 29, 1873, Ward Thoron ed., *The Letters of Mrs. Henry Adams* (Boston: 1936), 123–125.

Though Lowell had his doubts about Browning (e.g. JRL to George Smalley, March 24, 1883, Howe, *New Letters*, 270), it is clear that Browning had even more about Lowell; there is, for example, this passage from Frank Harris' *My Life and Loves* (New York: 1963), 459–460: "At Lady Jeune's lunch, where he [Browning] showed his disdain for Lowell, who was fêted and honored . . . When he saw that I too felt nothing but contempt for Lowell's poetry, he thawed to me and we walked across Hyde Park together and he took tea at my little house . . ."

11 JRL to Jane Norton, March 4, 1873, Norton ed., *Letters*, II, 295 ("rude elbowing"); JRL to Leslie Stephen, April 29, 1873, Norton ed., *Letters*, II, 301 (different breed).

12 JRL to Señora Emilia de Riaño, Sept. 13, 1879, Hispanic Society; JRL to Mabel Lowell Burnett, Oct. 3, 1873, Houghton (Calvin); JRL to Thomas Hughes, Nov. 25, 1873, Norton ed., *Letters*, II, 318 ("partings"); JRL to Mrs. S. B. Herrick, Sept. 21, 1875, Norton ed., *Letters*, II, 364 (Calvinism growing stronger; "more harm than good"); JRL to Leslie Stephen, May 15, 1876, Norton ed., *Letters*, II, 385–389 (remaining quotations).

13 "An Ode for the Fourth of July, 1876," *Poetical Works*, IV, 100 ("We, who believe . . ."); JRL to Leslie Stephen, May 15, 1876, Norton ed., *Letters*, II, 388–389 ("I *can't* know . . ."); JRL to Leslie Stephen, Dec. 4, 1876, Norton ed., *Letters*, II, 408 (intuitionalist); JRL to Mrs. S. B. Herrick, Nov. 20, 1875, Norton ed., *Letters*, II, 369 (prizing "whatever helps . . ."); "The Power of Sound," Smith ed., *Uncollected Poems*, 116 ("Though all things else . . ."). In this same vein, Lowell later wrote to Huxley, "I can't help being fond of particular scientific men like you & Darwin, but I would trudge over to Smithfield with his Grace the A. of C. to make a bonfire of the rest of 'em all the same. Why wake the Seven Sleepers of Ephesus before their time — especially when their dreams are so pleasant? Not that *I* call 'em dreams, but visions rather." (Nov. 9, 1883, Imperial College, London.)

14 JRL to Norton, Oct. 30, 1873 (Venice), Feb. 26, 1874 (Florence), Norton ed., *Letters*, II, 317, 324; JRL to Mabel Lowell Burnett, Dec. 18, 1873, Houghton (Florence).

15 JRL to Norton, Feb. 26, 1874, Norton Collection, Houghton (Rome); JRL to Jane Norton, March 12, 1874, Houghton ("eremetical"; baby — strangers). Henry James wrote his brother William (May 3, 1874, James Family Correspondence, Houghton) that the Lowells "were very frankly critical of the Storys . . . & seem to have been chiefly busy after the 1st day in inventing subterfuges for getting away."

16 JRL to Jane Norton, Jan. 7, 1874, Houghton ("digestive machine"); JRL to Leslie Stephen, April 29, 1873, Norton ed., *Letters*, II, 300 ("mandragora"); JRL to Norton, Jan. 11, 1873, Jan. 1, 1874, Houghton ("black blood"; "struggle against suspicion"); Norton Journal, April 2, May 10, 1873, Norton & Howe eds., *Letters Norton*, I, 489 ("at fifty-four . . .").

17 JRL to Norton, Jan. 11, 1873, Norton ed., *Letters*, II, 292 ("right kind of solitude"); "L'Envoi. To the Muse," *Poetical Works*, IV, 33 ("One mask . . ."); JRL to "Effie" Lowell, Sept. 1, 1872, Berg Collection, NYPL ("Bryant & May's"); JRL to Thomas Hughes, June 14, 1874, Norton Collection, Houghton ("comes by nature").

Lowell's poem on Agassiz contains, along with heavy-handed sections, some fine passages. It ranks (as he himself believed) among his best verse, and he was delighted with "this renewal of imagination . . . after so many blank years" (JRL to Norton, May 28, 1874, Norton Collection, Houghton). He sent the ode to Norton, who in consultation with Longfellow and Howells doctored a few lines (and also changed the title) before it appeared in the *Atlantic*. Lowell later approved the few changes which had been made, which were indeed for the better (Norton to JRL, March 27, 1874, Norton Collection, Houghton). The poem made a solid hit, and Howells, now editor of the *Atlantic*, was especially enthused over it. Along with $400, he sent Lowell warm congratulations — "it is so like you; it had a sanguine complexion and a mellow voice . . . You seem to me unique for the sort of warm-colored thinking I find in such poems as this and the Commemoration Ode." (Howells to JRL, March 29, 1874, Norton Collection, Houghton.) And Mrs. Agassiz sent word through Norton that the poem had touched her so deeply that she could "hardly speak of it" (Norton to JRL, April 6, 1874, Norton Collection, Houghton).

18 JRL to Mabel Lowell Burnett, Dec. 18, 1873.

19 JRL to Mabel Lowell Burnett, Jan. 1, 1874 (wanted money for mortgage), Houghton; Norton to JRL, Dec. 4, 1873, Norton Collection, Houghton; JRL to Norton, Dec. 24, 1873, Norton Collection, Houghton ("a habit"; resign "absolutely").

20 Norton to JRL, Jan. 15, 19, 1874, JRL to Norton, Feb. 3, 1874,

Norton Collection, Houghton; JRL to Mabel Lowell Burnett, Feb. 4, 1874, Houghton.

Lowell had earlier had some hand in Eliot's choice as President of Harvard. When the canvass for a new President had taken place in 1868, the contest had at first narrowed down to Professor Ephraim Gurney, the "reform candidate" and a personal friend of Lowell's, and the Rev. A. P. Peabody, a conservative who wished the administration of the university to retain a marked religious character. When the contest was at its height, Lowell and Godkin persuaded John Fiske to write an article for the *Nation* in order to advance Gurney's candidacy. As Fiske reported it, his article "probably killed the candidacy of Peabody and at the same time paved the way for a reformer even greater than Gurney." (Fiske to "Mary," Jan. 20, 1869, *Letters of John Fiske*, Ethel Fisk ed., 181). In any case, when the palm did go to Charles W. Eliot, Lowell strongly approved, and gave Edmund Quincy "a very favorable account" of Eliot's qualifications (Quincy to Anne Weston, April 11, 1869, Edmund Quincy Papers, MHS). Lowell further rejoiced that they had succeeded "in keeping the 'clerical element' out of our presidency" (JRL to A. D. White, March 24, 1869, Cornell University).

21 Norton to Ward, June 29, 1873, Houghton ("want of confidence"); Norton to JRL, Nov. 24, 1873, Norton Collection, Houghton ("ideal side"; "not pleased"); Norton to Carlyle, Nov. 16, 1873, Norton and Howe eds., *Letters Norton*, II, 18 (new generation).

22 "Agassiz," *Poetical Works*, IV, 102 (". . . of public scandal . . ."). In its original form, before friends persuaded him to soften it, the poem was stronger still: "the Land of Honest Abraham" at first read "the Land of Broken Promise." JRL to Hughes, March 19, 1873, Norton ed., *Letters*, II, 298 ("*tempus actum*"); JRL to Jane Norton, March 12, 1874, Norton ed., *Letters*, II, 330 (change hateful); JRL to Jane Norton, Jan. 7, 1874, Houghton (growing wary).

23 JRL to Thomas Hughes, Nov. 25, 1873 ("reeky old den"), May 16, 1874 (suppressed gout), Norton ed., *Letters*, II, 219, 335.

24 JRL to Hughes, July 11, 1874, typed copy, Norton Collection, Houghton.

25 O. W. Holmes to J. L. Motley, July 26, 1874, Morse, *Holmes*, II, 211; Annie Fields Journal, Aug. 26, 1874, MHS; JRL to Mrs. S. B. Herrick, April 19, 1876, University of Virginia.

26 JRL to Ticknor, Nov. 10, 1875, B. H. Ticknor Papers, LC (liver); Edmund Quincy to Anne Weston, Nov. 2, 1875, Edmund Quincy Papers, MHS (illness); JRL to Mrs. S. B. Herrick, July 6, 1875, Norton ed., *Letters*, II, 358 ("third-rate"); JRL to Norton, Feb. 25, 1876, Norton Collection, Houghton.

27 Fitzgerald to Elizabeth Cowell, Nov. 13, 1876, *More Letters of Ed-*

ward Fitzgerald, William Aldis Wright ed. (London: 1901), 185 ("delicacy of perception"); Fitzgerald to Norton, Feb. 7, 1876, C. E. Norton Collection, Houghton; Fitzgerald to Fanny Kemble, Feb. 2, 1876, *Letters of Edward Fitzgerald to Fanny Kemble 1871–1883,* William Aldis Wright ed. (New York: 1895), 93–94. Fitzgerald never minced words with Lowell, be they praise or criticism. In a letter of Feb. 28, 1878, he wrote him: "Some one (not you), sent me your Moosehead Journal . . . I did not like the *Style* of it at all — all 'too clever by half.' " (Norton Collection, Houghton.)

For details of the reception of *Among My Books, Second Series,* see McFadyen, "Contemporaneous Reputation," Chapter IV. The volume was dedicated to Emerson, who wrote Lowell that he read it "from the first to the last page with honoring delight . . . your poets have never been so inwardly seen & portrayed . . ." (Feb. 14, 1876, Norton Collection, Houghton.)

28 "An Ode. For the Fourth of July, 1876," *Poetical Works,* IV, 96 ("Is this the country . . ."); "Tempora Mutantur," *Poetical Works,* IV, 240 ("With generous curve . . ."). This last was one of two poems first published in the *Nation*; the other was "The World's Fair, 1876."

In 1877, Lowell's three centennial odes, after having first appeared in the *Atlantic,* were published as a small volume, *Three Memorial Poems* (Boston: 1877), and dedicated to E. L. Godkin, for "His Eminent Service in Heightening and Purifying the Tone of Our Political Thought." As Edward Fitzgerald put it, they were all a little "too uniformly lofty" (Fitzgerald to Norton, Dec. 22, 1876, *Letters of Edward Fitzgerald,* William Aldis Wright ed., 2 vols. (London: 1894), I, 209.

29 For the hostile reaction, see JRL to Joel Benton, Jan. 19, 1876, Vassar College ("some consideration"; "man who is sacred"); and Benton's defense of Lowell, "Mr. Lowell's Recent Political Verse," *Christian Union,* Dec. 10, 1875. The statement, "It is no real paradox . . ." is in JRL's review of Henry James' *A Passionate Pilgrim* and *Transatlantic Sketches* (*Nation,* June 17, 1875); JRL to Ernest Perabo, Dec. 28, 1876, Perabo Collection, British Museum ("countrymen the truth").

30 JRL to Joel Benton, Jan. 19, 1876, Vassar College (Boutwell and Dawes); JRL to E. L. Godkin, Oct. 17, 1874, Godkin Papers, Houghton (George Hoar); JRL to Josephine Shaw Lowell, Sept. 16, 1876, Houghton (Butler).

Lowell could show aristocratic disdain for public opinion — "that is, the judgment of the incapable Many as compared with that of the discerning Few" (to Mrs. S. B. Herrick, Aug. 5, 1875, Norton ed., *Letters,* II, 361). It is significant that many of Lowell's "conservative" views — usually the only ones quoted when discussing his political reactions in these years — are contained in letters to Mrs. S. B. Herrick, a Southerner, an admirer and a woman — all three calculated to bring out Lowell's chivalrous acquiescence.

31 JRL to Hughes, July 2, 1877, typed copy, Norton Collection, Houghton (Grant); JRL to Mrs. S. B. Herrick, Oct. 9, 1876, Norton ed., *Letters*, II, 406 ("Ireland of the South"); JRL to Josephine Shaw Lowell, Sept. 16, 1876, Houghton ("human nature is as clay"); see also JRL to Hughes, July 12, 1876, Norton ed., *Letters*, II, 395–396, and JRL to Mrs. S. B. Herrick, Jan. 14, 1877, Norton ed., *Letters*, III, 4–5; "Under the Old Elm," *Poetical Works*, IV, 89 ("If ever with distempered voice . . .").

32 JRL to Edward P. Bliss, April 4, 1876, Norton ed., *Letters*, II, 379–380.

33 H. S. Noyes to R. B. Hayes, May 12, July 21, 1876, Hayes Library; Frances Lowell to Mrs. S. B. Herrick, May 16, 1876, University of Virginia.

34 JRL to Miss Norton, July 3, 1876, Norton ed., *Letters*, II, 389–390 ("tremulous," etc.); see also JRL to Mrs. S. B. Herrick, July 4, 1876, Norton ed., *Letters*, II, 392–393.

35 Manning Force to Hayes, June 12, 16, 1876, Hayes Library; JRL to Mrs. S. B. Herrick, July 4, 1876, Norton ed., *Letters*, II, 392 (fingernails; "vulgarity of character").

36 Manning Force to Hayes, June 16, 1876, Hayes Library (convention); JRL to Mrs. S. B. Herrick, July 4, 1876, Norton ed., *Letters*, II, 393 ("New England . . .").

37 JRL to Josephine Shaw Lowell, July 3, 1877, Houghton ("simple, tender, sincere"); JRL to Miss Norton, July 3, 1876, Norton ed., *Letters*, II, 390 ("Vere de Vere"); JRL to Grace Norton, July 1, 1877, Houghton ("intellectual etiquette"). For a later comparison of Easterners and Westerners, again flattering to the West, see JRL to Mrs. W. E. Darwin, Jan. 26, 1880, Norton ed., *Letters*, III, 76–77.

38 JRL to Mary Lowell Putnam, Oct. 15, 1876, Berg Collection, NYPL; JRL to Josephine Shaw Lowell, Sept. 16, 1876, Houghton (not a duty).

39 JRL to Mary Lowell Putnam, Oct. 15, 1876, Berg Collection, NYPL (distrust of Republicans); JRL to Thomas Hughes, July 12, 1876, Norton ed., *Letters*, II, 399 (tempted to vote for Adams); JRL to Mabel Lowell, July 1, 1869, Norton ed., *Letters*, II, 216 ("Adamses . . . ahead of praise . . ."); JRL to Mrs. S. B. Herrick, Oct. 9, 1876, Norton ed., *Letters*, II, 405 ("well-founded doubts").

40 For details on the Compromise of 1877, see C. Vann Woodward, *Reunion and Reaction* (Boston: 1951).

41 *The Nation* article appeared in the issue of Nov. 30, 1876; for additional elucidation of its origin and meaning, see the letters of Jan. 5, 6, 1888, from E. L. Godkin to the Editor of the New York

Tribune, as printed, with editorial comment, in the issues of the *Tribune* for Jan. 6, 7, 1888.

The telegraphic message to Hayes was from William Henry Smith, Dec. 4 (?), 1876, Hayes Library; see also Hayes' Diary, July 18, 1890, Hayes Library. The only evidence, slight though it is, that Lowell even hesitated in casting his electoral ballot, is in the unreliable Stearns, *Cambridge Sketches*, 108–109, and JRL to Leslie Stephen, Dec. 4, 1876, Norton ed., *Letters*, II, 408–409, where Lowell's tone, though not his actual words, suggests that had he not felt duty-bound, he might conceivably have switched to Tilden. In a later letter to Hayes, however, Lowell vigorously denied that he had ever entertained such a course, even momentarily (May 26, 1877, Hayes Library).

42 The story of the 1874 offer has been primarily drawn from the following sources: J. L. Cadwalder to Fish, Sept. 28, 1874 (Grant-"Sumnerite"), Fish to J. C. B. Davis, Nov. 15, 1874, Hoar to Fish, Nov. 18, 25, 1874, Fish to Hoar, Nov. 21, 1874, JRL to Fish, Nov. 25, 1874, Fish to Parke Godwin, Dec. 4, 1874, J. C. B. Davis to Fish, Dec. 6, 13, 1874 — all from the Fish Papers, LC; also JRL to Carter, April 13, 15 (Western railroad bonds), 19, 1876, Berg Collection, NYPL, and Carter to Fish, March 30, 1876, Personnel File, National Archives.

43 The story of Lowell's appointment has been traced from the following documents: Howells to Hayes, April 9 (enclosing Norton's letter to Howells of the same date about "uncongenial work"), May 2, May 24, May 28 (chagrin), 1877, Hayes Library; Charles Devens (Hayes' Attorney General) to T. W. Higginson, March 4, 1890, copy, Norton Collection, Houghton, for information that Hayes greatly admired *Biglow Papers*; John Bartlett to Evarts, April 10, 1877, Personnel File, Foreign Affairs Branch, National Archives; JRL to E. L. Godkin, April 25, 1877, Godkin Papers, Houghton; Hayes to JRL, May 18, 1877, JRL to Hayes, May 26, 1877 (two separate letters, same date), Hayes Library; JRL to Mabel Lowell Burnett, June 5 (Evarts talk in Boston), June 16, 1877, Houghton; JRL to Evarts, June 11, 1877, National Archives; JRL to T. W. Higginson, June 16, 1877, Huntington Library; Evarts to JRL, No. 1, June 13, 1877, National Archives (salary details).

Probably a contributing factor to Lowell's feeling a little less pressed financially than he had in 1874 was an agreement he had concluded in 1876 with James R. Osgood & Co., whereby he was guaranteed $1500 per year in exchange for certain rights in his past and future publications (the original handwritten contract is owned by Mr. Charles M. Storey).

44 JRL's reaction to Evarts is recounted in Norton to G. W. Curtis,

Oct. 7, 1877, Houghton; JRL to George Putnam, July 12, 1877, owned by Miss Elizabeth Putnam (Cunard ovation).

Lowell had "a kind of instinct that Mr. Evarts would rather have sent somebody else" (JRL to Mrs. Norton, July 9, 1877, Houghton), but Norton assured him that Evarts, when dining with George William Curtis, had spoken "with a heartiness and fulness of expression which convinced George that you had been absolutely mistaken in supposing that any one else could possibly have been more acceptable to Mr. Evarts" (Norton to JRL, July 24, 1877, Norton Collection, Houghton). In any case, Lowell had slight regard for Evarts. Later, he was to speak in private of Evarts' uttering "pompous platitudes in a solemn manner" and was to complain that during his entire stay in Madrid, "he had never had a dispatch from him which was written by him," for he lacked all attention to detail (as said to J. C. B. Davis and repeated by him in a letter to Hamilton Fish, June 21, 1881, Fish Papers, LC). Norton and Curtis also had low opinions of Evarts (see Norton to JRL, Oct. 31, 1877, Aug. 16, 1878, Norton Collection, Houghton). Even Evarts' sympathetic biographer, Chester L. Barrows, agrees that he "lacked the efficiency of his predecessor," was "dilatory in correspondence and at times negligent of routine," though Barrows concludes that on the whole Evarts administered his duties with "fair success," and with "moderation and sagacity" (*William M. Evarts, Lawyer, Diplomat, Statesman* [Chapel Hill: 1941], 348).

CHAPTER XIII. MINISTER TO SPAIN (pages 284–301)

1 JRL to George Putnam, Aug. 16 (house-hunting), Aug. 22, Dec. 23 (expenses), 1877, all owned by Miss Elizabeth Putnam.

2 JRL to George Putnam, Dec. 23, 1877, owned by Miss Elizabeth Putnam; JRL to Charles W. Storey, Dec. 18, 1877, owned by Mr. Charles M. Storey ("death's head"); JRL to Norton, Oct. 23, 1877, Norton Collection, Houghton; JRL to Mabel Lowell Burnett, Nov. 18, 1877, Dr. Burnett Collection, Houghton ("some old gardens").

Lowell's First Secretary of Legation, Dwight Reed, had considerable knowledge of official routine (and Lowell was personally fond of him), but Reed knew neither French nor Spanish. Lowell had suggested Henry James, among others, for the Secretaryship, but seeing how busy the Legation was, he congratulated James on his failure to get the post — which James apparently hadn't wanted anyway (Leon Edel, *Henry James: The Conquest of London* [New York: 1962], 315).

3 JRL to E. L. Godkin, Feb. 19, 1880, Godkin Papers, Houghton

(Cushing); JRL to R. H. Dana, Jr., Sept. 21, 1878, Dana Papers, MHS ("literary fellows"); JRL to Evarts, Feb. 6, 1878, No. 66, National Archives (Fourcarde).

4 JRL to Charles W. Storey, Dec. 18, 1877, owned by Mr. Charles M. Storey ("suppress trade"); JRL to Norton, Oct. 23, 1877 ("astonished 'em"), April 15, 1878, Nov. 10, 1878 (understood everything; anxiety over indemnity), Houghton; JRL to George Putnam, Dec. 23, 1877, owned by Miss Elizabeth Putnam (sympathy with Spain); Mrs. Thomas Bailey Aldrich, *Crowding Memories* (Boston: 1920), 227.
It should be noted that when Lowell's predecessor, Caleb Cushing, resigned, he complained of the "serious and exhausting" occupations and "the labor incessant" — but Cushing was resident in Spain during a time of far more serious troubles, both foreign and domestic (Caleb Cushing to J. C. B. Davis, March 28, 1877, Davis Papers, LC).

5 JRL to Norton, Oct. 23, 1877, Norton Collection, Houghton (depressions); JRL to Norton, April 15, 1878, Norton ed., *Letters*, III, 38 ("*not* reconciled").

6 JRL to Evarts, March 16, 1878, No. 78, National Archives; JRL to Norton, May 21, 1878 (Acropolis), Aug. 2, 1878 (Turks), Norton ed., *Letters*, III, 43–46; JRL to Mabel Lowell Burnett, April 27, July 26, 1878, Houghton ("new man").

7 JRL to Mabel Lowell Burnett, July 26, 1878, Dr. Burnett Collection, Houghton ("nay to enjoy it"); JRL to Charles W. Storey, Sept. 24, 1878, owned by Mr. Charles M. Storey (improving in Spanish). Miguel Romera Navarro believes Lowell's judgments on Spanish politics were admirable, but is critical of Lowell's understanding of Spanish life and character (*El Hispanismo en Norte-América* [Madrid: 1917], 70–80), while Stanley T. Williams finds Lowell's analyses of Spanish character more acute than anything he produced on Spanish literature; Williams regrets, given Lowell's lifelong devotion to the works of Cervantes and Calderón, that he never produced more than "offhand musings" on them (*The Spanish Background of American Literature*, 2 vols. [New Haven: 1955], II, 199–207). In any case, the shrewdness of Lowell's political judgments is unquestionable. For a modern evaluation of Spain in the late 1870's which corroborates all of Lowell's views, see Salvador de Madariaga, *Spain, A Modern History* (New York: 1950), especially 69–70.

8 JRL to Evarts, April 2, 1878, No. 81 ("private animosity"), Aug. 26, 1878, No. 108 ("freedom . . . is safe"), National Archives.

9 JRL to Evarts, Aug. 26, 1878, No. 108, National Archives. In 1897, when again Premier, Cánovas was assassinated by an Italian Anarchist in revenge for the tortures which had been inflicted on political prisoners at the Montjuich fortress.

10 JRL to Evarts, Aug. 19, 1878, No. 192, National Archives (civil

service analogy); O. W. Holmes to JRL, June 7, 1878, Norton Collection, Houghton; Norton to JRL, May 19, 1878, Norton Collection, Houghton.

11 JRL to Norton, May 4, 1879, Norton ed., *Letters*, III, 69–70 (patronage; "great faith"); JRL to Mabel Lowell Burnett, Aug. 25, 1878 Houghton ("bottom of the world"); JRL to Norton, Nov. 10, 1878, Norton Collection, Houghton ("the upper classes").

12 JRL to Mabel Lowell Burnett, Aug. 24, 1877, Houghton (formal presentation); JRL to Evarts, Feb. 3, 1878, No. 64 ("grace, tact . . ."), Oct. 29, 1878, No. 120 (generous impulses), National Archives.

13 JRL to George Putnam, Jan. 28, 1878, owned by Miss Elizabeth Putnam ("vanity and vexation"); JRL to Evarts, Feb. 6, 1878, No. 65, ("anachronism"; "radiant"), July 3, 1878, No. 95 (gastric fever; national calamity), National Archives; JRL to Mabel Lowell Burnett, July 26, 1878, Dr. Burnett Collection, Houghton ("dragged to her dreary tomb . . ."). The sonnet, "Death of Queen Mercedes," is in *Poetical Works*, IV, 186–187; an earlier, considerably different version (enclosed in a letter to Señora de Riaño, July 13, 1878), is in the Hispanic Society. Alfonso remarried in 1879, to the Archduchess Maria Christina of Austria. He himself died young — in 1886, at age twenty-nine.

14 The Ministerial changes are described most fully in Lowell to Evarts, March 11, May 20, Dec. 15, 1879, Nos. 159, 180, 222, National Archives. Lowell's relations with Silvela are described in JRL to Grace Norton, March 4, 1879, Houghton, JRL to George Putnam, Sept. 9, 1878, owned by Miss Elizabeth Putnam, and Manuel Silvela to JRL, n.d. (in Spanish), Houghton (I am grateful to Sydney Muirden for a translation). Shortly before Lowell's arrival in Spain, the chargé d'affaires, A. A. Adee, had written to Evarts: ". . . all . . . questions . . . have been satisfactorily settled . . . relations have never been more cordial" (May 10, 1877, No. 539, National Archives). The episode at Alicante is described by Lowell to Evarts, May 2, 1879, No. 177, National Archives — one of the longest despatches Lowell wrote that year.

Spanish archival materials have proved of little value in assessing Lowell's diplomatic mission. Mercedes Vera undertook an exhaustive search for me in the manuscript collections of the Spanish Ministry of Foreign Affairs, the library of the Presidencia del Gobierno and the Archivo Histórico. She tracked down as well various leads to periodical materials and to private collections. But all that turned up were rather routine references to formal diplomatic occasions.

15 JRL to Norton, April 15, 1878, Houghton (hours "frightfully late," etc.); JRL to Señora de Riaño, Oct. 10, 1879, Hispanic Society (cardinals; "blunderbuss").

16 JRL to Georgianna Putnam, Nov. 7, 1878, Barrett Collection, University of Virginia ("simple-minded"; "triumphed over Babel"); JRL to Norton, Nov. 10, 1878, Houghton (Opera); for another version of the episode in which Mrs. Grant "triumphed over Babel," see Mrs. Thomas Bailey Aldrich, *Crowding Memories*, 228.

17 JRL to Howells, May 2, 1879, Norton ed., *Letters*, III, 68–69 ("ragged *capa*"); JRL to Thomas Hughes, Nov. 17, 1878, Norton ed., *Letters*, III, 61–62 ("fools enough"); JRL to F. J. Child, April 14, 1878, Norton ed., *Letters*, III 35 ("Old Cambridge").

18 JRL to Henry James, May 8, 1879, James Papers, Houghton (tired of prettily); JRL to Grace Norton, Aug. 11, 1878, Norton ed., *Letters*, III, 48–53.

19 JRL to Evarts, Feb. 6, 1878, No. 65, National Archives (bullfighting); JRL to Greenough, Jan. 9, 1879, University of Virginia (Academy). When inducted as a member of the Academy, Lowell had to return thanks in Castilian; "Fortunately," he reported back to Cambridge, "I was permitted to write it out beforehand & it was received with many *muy bienes* by the courteous audience (JRL to Charles W. Storey, Nov. 22, 1878, owned by Mr. Charles M. Storey).

20 JRL to Henry James, May 8, 1879, James Papers, Houghton; JRL to Señora de Riaño, Sept. 22, 1878, Hispanic Society ("blushing like a neophyte"). Lowell also met Don Hermenegildo's brother, Francisco Giner de los Ríos, and took an active interest in the Institución Libre de Enseñanza, which the two brothers had helped to form in 1876. The Institución was meant to provide a more liberal university education than was available in the stultifying state academies; Lowell was appointed one of its honorary professors. For further details, see Lawrence H. Klibbe, *James Russell Lowell's Residence in Spain, 1877–1880* (Newark: 1964), 110–116.

Lowell's friendship with the Riaños can be traced in the 175-odd manuscript letters and poems in The Hispanic Society, New York City (some of these are in Spanish, and I am grateful to Mr. Richard Kinkade for translations). This manuscript collection has lain almost untouched for many years, and has a curious history. Shortly after Lowell's death, Señora de Riaño proposed printing a volume containing the letters and poems he had sent to her, but she gave up the project when Lowell's daughter and Charles Eliot Norton expressed concern that the letters might be too intimate, especially those written during Mrs. Lowell's illness. Norton, in fact, hoped the originals could be destroyed lest they come into possession by a public library "where they might be open to the inspection of vulgar curiosity." Yet he feared Señora de Riaño's ghost would "not remain quiet until the letters are given to the public," a prophecy fulfilled when The Hispanic Society acquired the letters from the Riaños' son. I have printed the poems from the collection, along with excerpts from those letters containing them, as part of a group of previously unpublished Lowell verse ("Twenty-Seven Poems by James Russell Lowell," *American Literature*, Nov. 1963). Efforts to suppress the correspondence are described in letters of Norton to R. U. Johnson, March 12, 1900, Aug. 15, 1908, Norton to Gilder, May 14, Aug. 11, 1908, and Juan Riaño to Mr. Egan, June 4, 1908 — all in the Century Club Collection, NYPL, and Norton to Annie Fields, March 8, 1902, Huntington Library. Norton's comment on "vulgar curiosity" is in the Aug. 11, 1908, letter to Gilder, and the one on Señora de Riaño's ghost in the letter of Aug. 15, 1908, to R. U. Johnson. An additional source on the Lowell-Riaño friendship is Señora de Riaño's article, "Mr. Lowell and His Spanish Friends," *Century* (June, 1900), 292–293.

21 Annie Fields to unknown correspondent, n.d., SPNEA ("most dignified"); John W. Field to Longfellow, March 3, 1879, Houghton ("stately"; "admiration and esteem"); E. R. Hoar to JRL, March 24, 1879, J. B. Lowell Collection, Houghton (Hayes wishes him to remain); JRL to Henry James, May 8, 1879, Houghton ("new flavor").

22 JRL to Mabel Lowell Burnett, July 3, 1879, Houghton; also JRL to Señora de Riaño, June 18, 19, 20, 21, 27, July 3, 1879, Hispanic Society.

23 JRL to Mabel Lowell Burnett, July 11 ("sweetness & reasonableness"), Aug. 3, 10, Sept. 8, 11, 1879, Houghton; JRL to Grace Norton, Sept. 12 ("perfectly mad"), Oct. 15 ("tough old machine"), 1879, Jan. 8, 1880, Houghton; JRL to Señora de Riaño, July 12, 27, Aug. 5, 1879, Hispanic Society; JRL to J. W. Paige, July 26, 1879, Paige Papers, MHS.

24 JRL to Señora de Riaño, Aug. 23, Sept. 24, 1879, Hispanic Society; JRL to Mabel Lowell Burnett, Aug. 21, 24, Oct. 3 ("steadily gains"), 1879, Houghton; Leslie Stephen to Norton, July 6, 1879, C. E. Norton Papers, Houghton; JRL to Grace Norton, Sept. 12, Oct. 15, 1879, Houghton.

25 Marian Adams to her father, Oct. 19 ("keeps up bravely"), Oct. 26 ("nothing . . . to warrant much hope"), Nov. 2 ("You can't patch me up"), 1879, *Letters of Mrs. Henry Adams*, Ward Thoron ed., 191, 194–198; JRL to Mabel Lowell Burnett, Oct. 30, Dec. 4, 1879, Jan. 29, 1880, Houghton; JRL to Señora de Riaño, Nov. 19, 1879, Hispanic Society.

John W. and Eliza Field were a wealthy, cultivated, childless couple who spent their lives in travel and leisure. Lowell found him "a most delightful companion" (JRL to Mrs. Lowell, Nov. 21, 1881, Houghton; see also Norton to Clough, May 7, 1855, Norton and Howe eds., *Letters Norton*, I, 128, for a sympathetic appraisal of Field).

26 JRL to Mabel Lowell Burnett, Dec. 25, 1879 (dining out), Jan. 17,

1880 ("happier than we ever were"), Houghton; telegram, Evarts to JRL, Jan. 19, 1880, National Archives.

27 Howells to Hayes, Aug. 7, 12, 1879, George W. Curtis to Hayes, Aug. 8, 1879, Hayes Library; Howells to Norton, Aug. 12, 1879, C. E. Norton Papers, Houghton; Frelinghuysen to Evarts, Nov. 24, 1879, National Archives; Evarts to JRL, Feb. 3, 1880, No. 1, National Archives; telegram, JRL to Evarts, Jan. 20, 1880, Hayes Library; telegram, Evarts to JRL, Jan. 22, 1880, National Archives; JRL to Evarts, Jan. 21, 1880, Evarts Papers, LC; JRL to R. H. Dana, Jr., Jan. 26, 1880, Dana Papers, MHS. Apparently the post was also declined by John Jacob Astor and Senator Hoar before being offered to Lowell. Evarts, it seems, hesitated over appointing Lowell; rumor ascribed his reluctance to "the historic Harvard-Yale rivalry," but Chester L. Barrows suggests the more likely reason was his concern over the contrast which would be drawn between "the charming & brilliant, but highly individual Lowell" and his predecessor, "the solemn Baptist-deacon Welsh . . ." (*Evarts*, 393–394).

28 JRL to Señora de Riaño, Feb. 1, 1880, Hispanic Society; JRL to Mabel Lowell Burnett, Feb. 6, 21, 1880, Houghton; JRL to Evarts, Feb. 23, 1880, Evarts Papers, LC; R. H. Dana to Edith Longfellow Dana, March 6, 1880, Dana Papers, MHS.

29 William J. Hoppin Journal, March 12, 1880, Houghton (telegrams re: Mrs. Lowell); Henry James to Elizabeth Boott, Feb. 22, 1880, Houghton; Henry James to C. E. Norton, March 31, 1880, courtesy of Leon Edel (old and worn); Henry James to T. S. Perry, Feb. 22, 1880, as quoted in Virginia Harlow, *Thomas Sergeant Perry: A Biography* (Durham: 1950), 306 ("bore him"); Henry James to his mother, March 9, 1880 (talk with Lowell), Aug. 6, 1877, James Papers, Houghton ("understand half" in Madrid).

30 JRL to Señora de Riaño, March 12, 1880, Hispanic Society ("*human* tone"). Lowell continued thereafter to hold a good opinion of Queen Victoria; he thought her "a *true* person, in all respects" (as quoted by R. H. Dana to R. H. Dana, Jr., Nov. 22, 1881, Dana Papers, MHS).

31 JRL to Evarts, March 31, 1880, National Archives (Wheeler's offer; improvement); JRL to Mabel Lowell Burnett, March 21, 24 (train trip), May 6 (relapse), 1880, Houghton; JRL to Señora de Riaño, May 8, 1880, Hispanic Society (move to England).

CHAPTER XIV. MINISTER TO ENGLAND (pages 302–338)

1 Henry Adams to JRL, Feb. 10, 1880, Rantoul Collection, Houghton; John Russell Young to Evarts, Feb. 23, 1880, Hayes Library (London press). Privately, there was at least some hostile reaction to Lowell's

appointment. Algernon Swinburne, for example, had reacted violently three years earlier to a mistaken rumor that Lowell was about to become Minister to England. The appointment, he thought, would be "a gross insult (possibly not undeserved) to this country by the mission as ambassador . . . of one among the most rancorous and virulent of its revilers." Swinburne added that he thought Lowell "a mountebank of letters in a cash suit of threadbare motley," adducing as evidence one of Lowell's most inept lines: "But Milton is the only man who has got much poetry out of a cataract, — and that was a cataract in his eye"; imagine appointing as Minister, Swinburne commented, "one who chooses such subjects as the blindness of Milton for the mark of his professional jests" (Swinburne to Paul Hamilton Hayne, March 20, 1877, *The Swinburne Letters*, Cecil Y. Lang ed., III, 303). For earlier expressions of ill will between Swinburne and Lowell, see pp. 263–264. Hoppin to Anna Dyer, Oct. 29, Nov. 4 ("petty jealousies"), 1880, Houghton; W. J. Hoppin Journal, Oct. 10, 20, 1880, Houghton. William Jones Hoppin's massive journal and collection of letterbooks in Houghton, have been a most valuable source for Lowell's years as Minister to England; largely unused, the collection is of considerable interest for social and diplomatic historians.

The Second Secretary at the Legation, E. S. Nadal, was also fond of Lowell (see his "London Recollections of Lowell," *Harper's* (Feb. 1916), 366–372, and his *A Virginian Village and Other Papers* [New York: 1917], 148–183). But on his side, Lowell was disappointed in Nadal's casual treatment of his duties; Hoppin, going further, became positively apoplectic at what he considered Nadal's want of attention to Legation affairs (e.g. Hoppin Journal, Dec. 30, 31, 1881; see also George Smalley to JRL, Jan. 1, 1884, Houghton).

2 Henry James to Grace Norton, Aug. 7, 1877, *The Letters of Henry James*, Percy Lubbock ed., 2 vols. (New York: 1920), I, 56; JRL to Thomas Hughes, May 27, 1874, typed copy, Norton Collection, Houghton ("combining permanence . . ."); JRL to Henry James, Sept. 24, 1878, Howe, *New Letters*, 238 (opening its doors).

3 JRL to Mary Lowell Putnam, Aug. 21, 1880, Houghton; JRL to Sara Darwin, June 5, 1880, University of Illinois; JRL to Edward Fitzgerald, Sept. 4, 1880, Boston Public Library; Leslie Stephen to Norton, Sept. 20, 1880, C. E. Norton Papers, Houghton; Hoppin to Anna Dyer, Sept. 30, 1880, Houghton; JRL to George Putnam, April 11, 1881, owned by Miss Elizabeth Putnam; JRL to Mrs. Smalley, Sept. 6, 1880, University of Rochester; Frances Lowell to Señora de Riaño, Dec. 16, 1880, Sept. 11, 1881, Hispanic Society.

4 Lowell's engagement book while Minister to England is in the Berg Collection, NYPL; Leslie Stephen to Norton, Sept. 20, 1880, C. E. Norton Papers, Houghton ("talk of a lad"); JRL to Sara Darwin,

May 24, 1880, Houghton ("daily path"); Hoppin to Anna Dyer, June 3, 1880, Hoppin Letterbooks, Houghton; JRL to Norton, Aug. 18, 1887, Norton Collection, Houghton (remaining quotes). At first, apparently, Lowell accepted few invitations, but gradually, as his shyness waned and his social success waxed, he increasingly joined — and enjoyed — the social whirl (see George W. Smalley, "Mr. Lowell in England," *Harper's* [April, 1896], 788–789).

According to Mrs. Hardy, her husband's opinion of Lowell was that "as a man he was charming, as a writer one of extraordinary talent, but of no instinctive and creative genius" (*The Early Life of Thomas Hardy* [London: 1928], 180–181).

5 Engagement Book, Berg Collection, NYPL ("Witch of Endor"); Hoppin to Anna Dyer, Oct. 29, 1880, Hoppin Letterbooks, Houghton; Leslie Stephen to Norton, June 20, 1881, C. E. Norton Papers, Houghton; Baron Aberdare to JRL, May 22, 1881, Rantoul Collection, Houghton (sample of praise of JRL as after-dinner speaker); "At the Commencement Dinner, 1866, in Acknowledging a Toast to the Smith Professor," *Heartsease and Rue* (Boston: 1888), 209 ("When I hear . . ."); Smalley, "Lowell in England," 794 (felicity and authority).

6 Hoppin Journal, April 29, 1885, Houghton, and Henry Vignaud to J. C. Bancroft Davis, July 9, 1882, Davis Papers, LC, for JRL's ignoring the American colony. Hamilton Fish, the ex-Secretary of State, complained of Lowell's getting a "large salary for making a show of himself & travelling around as a sort of Literary Exhibition" (letter to J. C. Bancroft Davis, July 1, 1884, Davis Papers, LC).

7 Henry James to Grace Norton, May 6, 1884, James Papers, Houghton (Mrs. Green; "not a *real* man"); George W. Smalley, *Anglo-American Memories* (New York: 1911), 206–207, and "Lowell in England," 790; Henry James to his mother, Feb. 7, 1881, James Papers, Houghton (London traditions); Henry James to Norton, Nov. 13, 1880, C. E. Norton Papers, Houghton ("universally liked").

George Smalley's comments on Lowell should probably be taken with a grain of salt. His account of Lowell's ministership in *Anglo-American Memories* is more overtly hostile than any other I have come across, possibly because of jealousy over the fond relationship which developed between Lowell and his wife, Phoebe Smalley (see page 351). Nonetheless Smalley undoubtedly picked up real "failings" in Lowell, for some of his observations are corroborated elsewhere. Theodore Watts, for example, wrote that "Delightful as was personal intercourse" with Lowell, "the charm was not quite undisturbed. Every now and then you felt yourself to be under the microscope of a Yankee naturalist" (*London Athenaeum*, Aug. 22, 1891). And Oscar Wilde described Lowell as one "who barks when he is baited," adding that Lowell was "often mistaken for a lion, at a distance" (Oscar Wilde to Mrs. Alfred Hunt, Feb. 17, 1881, *The Letters of Oscar Wilde*, Rupert Hart-Davis ed. [New York: 1962], 75).

8 Hoppin Journal, Oct. 17, 1880, March 27, 1881, Houghton; E. S. Nadal, "London Recollections," *Harper's*, Feb. 1916; T. W. Higginson, *Old Cambridge*, 195–196 (Browning). Lowell supposedly told one of his students that at his first meeting with Browning he "put to him, with a stand-and-deliver emphasis, the question: 'Where is the Jew in you? You have more passion in your little finger than all the other British dramatists since Shakespeare have in their whole bodies' " (as recounted by Thayer, "Lowell As a Teacher," 478–479).

9 *Anti-Slavery Papers*, I, 20 ("highest and clearest intellect"); JRL to Evarts, Aug. 26, 1878, National Archives ("most intense . . ."); JRL to Thomas Hughes, Nov. 17, 1878, Norton ed., *Letters*, III, 60 (Disraeli); JRL to John W. Field, March 14, 1878, Norton ed., *Letters*, III, 29 ("Where would a Jew . . .").

10 While not always agreeing with the specifics of their analysis, this discussion is much indebted to Edmund Wilson, "Notes on Gentile Pro-Semitism: New England's 'Good Jews,' " *Commentary* (Oct. 1956), 329–335, Barbara Miller Solomon, *Ancestors and Immigrants* (Cambridge: 1956), especially 6–19, and John Higham, "Anti-Semitism in the Gilded Age," MVHR (March, 1957). For Dana's comment, see Samuel Shapiro, *Richard Henry Dana, Jr., 1815–1882* (East Lansing: 1961), 133. Norton's remark is in a letter to Lowell of Oct. 17, 1887, Norton Collection, Houghton. See also W. W. Story to JRL, Dec. 30, 1855, University of Texas, in which he refers to the actress Rachel as "Jewier than ever & tried to skin a flint in Boston . . ."

As a sample of Lowell's sympathy for the current plight of the Jews, see a Memorandum he sent to Blaine (having received it confidentially from Sir Charles Dilke) relating the brutally repressive police regulations against the Jews in Russia (JRL to Blaine, July 25, 1881, No. 227, National Archives).

11 Henry Adams' remark on the Inquisition is quoted in Ernest Samuels, *Henry Adams: The Middle Years* (Cambridge: 1958), 115; see also Ernest Samuels, *Henry Adams: The Major Phase* (Cambridge: 1964), 129–130, 357–359. For John Jay Chapman's attitude, see Richard B. Hovey, *John Jay Chapman — An American Mind* (New York: 1959), especially 281, 287. For examples of Chapman's considerable admiration for the Jews when he was a younger man, see *John Jay Chapman and His Letters*, M. A. De Wolfe Howe ed. (Boston: 1937), 170–171. For Brooks Adams' anti-Semitism, see Arthur F. Beringause, *Brooks Adams: A Biography* (New York: 1955), 135, 155, 175, and Thornton Anderson, *Brooks Adams: Constructive Conservative* (Ithaca: 1951), 60, 63, 73, 215.

12 Norton to JRL, Aug. 4, 1856, Norton Collection, Houghton.

13 JRL to Sara Darwin, May 29, 1880, Houghton ("exercise my jaws"; father Confessor).

14 JRL to Josephine Shaw Lowell, April 4, 1880, Houghton (Disraeli); JRL to Mabel Lowell Burnett, June 19, 1886, Houghton (improvise convictions); Hoppin Journal, April 18, 1886, Houghton (little personal regard).

For Lowell's sympathetic response to the Gladstone Ministry, see JRL to Evarts, Sept. 17, 1880, No. 66, National Archives, and JRL to Gladstone, July 22, 1881, Gladstone Papers, British Museum ("the energy, the eloquence & the good temper with which you have conducted, supported & defended . . . [The Land Bill] are nothing short of marvelous . . . The Bill . . . will be a better monument than any in the Abbey"). For JRL's disapproval of Gladstone's Egyptian policy, see JRL to Norton, Dec. 1884, Norton ed., *Letters,* III, 120–121 (which also contains "diffusively emphatic").

15 JRL to Lady Lyttleton, April 14, 1891, copy, Norton Collection, Houghton (description of Granville); see also JRL to Sara Darwin, n.d. (1880), Houghton; the "Visitors' Books" poem is quoted in Lord Edmond Fitzmaurice, *The Life of Granville George Leveson Gower, Second Earl Granville,* 2 vols. (New York: 1905), II, 131.

16 Background to the Fortune Bay incident can be found in a Foreign Office Memo by F. C. Ford of June 4, 1880, Granville Papers, PRO; in Evarts to JRL, Feb. 4, 1881, No. 110, National Archives; and in the London *Times,* May 19, 1880. The Marquis of Salisbury's position is stated in an official note to Hoppin, April 3, 1880, PRO.

Edward Thornton, the English Minister to the United States, was not convinced that the Treaty denied shore-fishing to the Americans; on the contrary, he believed Article XVIII seemed to allow it (Thornton to Granville, April 19, 1881, Granville Papers, PRO).

17 Thornton to Granville, May 4, 1880 (private letter), Granville Papers, PRO.

18 Thornton to Granville, May 18 (private letter), May 24, May 25 (private letter — Evarts' vanity), June 1 (private letter), 1880, Granville Papers, PRO; "Memorandum for file," British Legation, June 7, 1880, Notes from Foreign Legations, National Archives.

19 JRL to Evarts, June 12, 1880, No. 14, National Archives; Granville to Thornton, June 9, 1880, Granville Papers, PRO; Evarts to JRL, June 11, 1880, National Archives. Lowell and Granville each claimed to have initiated the idea of separating Fortune Bay damages from the interpretation of the Treaty. Lowell made a suggestion of another sort to Gladstone, which the Prime Minister relayed with cryptic humor to Lord Granville: "Lowell this morning gave me his plan for the Fishery difficulty — that we, Newfoundland freely consenting, should cede the Island. I said that in England we had many supersti-

tions" (July 22, 1880, *The Political Correspondence of Mr. Gladstone and Lord Granville*, Agatha Ramm ed., 2 vols. [Oxford: 1962], I, 150).

20 Thornton to Granville, June 15, 22 (private letters), 1880, Granville Papers, PRO; JRL to George Putnam, Nov. 27, 1880, owned by Miss Elizabeth Putnam; Hoppin to Anna Dyer, Dec. 16, 30, 1880, Houghton; JRL to Garfield, Nov. 12, 1880, Garfield Papers, LC; Garfield to JRL, Dec. 11, 1880, Ohio Historical Society.

Grant had intimated to Lowell that if he won a third term as President in 1880, he would offer Lowell the State Department. Though Garfield got the Republican nomination instead, rumors revived after his election that Lowell was to become Secretary of State. They were even printed in the newspapers, but Lowell dismissed them as "utterly absurd" (JRL to George Putnam, June 20, 1881, owned by Miss Elizabeth Putnam).

21 Thornton to Granville, May 4, 1880 ("noisy . . ." etc.), Feb. 8, 1881 (anti-foreign), private letters, Granville Papers, PRO.

22 Confidential memo from Lord Selbourne, July 21, 1880, Granville Papers, PRO; Granville to JRL, Oct. 27, 1880, Granville Papers, PRO; telegram, JRL to Evarts, Oct. 28, 1880, National Archives; Thornton to Granville, Dec. 14 (private letter), Dec. 27, 1880, Granville Papers, PRO.

23 Telegrams, Evarts to JRL, Feb. 19, 23, 25, 1881, JRL to Evarts, Feb. 18, 21, 24, 1881, National Archives; JRL to Evarts, March 5, 1881, No. 138, National Archives; Lord Selbourne to Granville, Feb. 21, 1881, Granville Papers, PRO; Thornton to Granville, telegrams, Feb. 23, 24, 1881, Granville Papers, PRO; JRL to Granville, Feb. 26, Granville Papers, PRO; Gladstone to Granville, Feb. 21, Granville to Gladstone, Feb. 21, 1881, Granville Papers, PRO; Evarts to JRL, March 7, 1881, No. 126, National Archives; JRL to Grace Norton, Aug. 4, 1881, Houghton (Evarts' "offhand" efforts; Granville's offer to write despatch); Hoppin Journal, Feb. 27, 1881, Houghton; J. C. B. Davis, to Hamilton Fish, June 21, 1881, Fish Papers, LC (JRL's accusations against Evarts).

24 Thornton to Granville, Jan. 11, 1881, private letter (Evarts' sudden wish), March 7, 1881 (Evarts dilatory), Granville Papers, PRO. For a sample of Evarts' peremptory tone, see Evarts to JRL, Feb. 4, 1881, No. 110, National Archives, and for sample objections to it, see Granville to Thornton, telegram, Feb. 18, 1881, Granville Papers, PRO, and JRL to Evarts, telegram, Feb. 16, 1881 (in which Lowell stated that Granville had "regretted the tone . . . as more exacting than had hoped, and hardly in unison with conciliatory course of Government of Her Majesty").

25 Evarts to JRL, Feb. 4, 1881, No. 109, National Archives (withheld despatch); Hoppin Journal, Feb. 21, 1881 (Lowell's mildness), Feb.

27, 1881 (Lowell's "great activity"), Houghton; JRL to Hoppin, Oct. 27, 1881, Hoppin Letterbooks, Houghton ("officer of the deck").

26 Confidential notes by Tenterden, Pauncefote and Granville, n.d., Granville Papers, PRO (Granville's contains reference to Blaine as "hostile successor"); Granville's handwritten cabinet opinion, n.d. (pre-March 13, 1881), Granville Papers, PRO (Tory opposition); Granville to JRL, Feb. 26, 1881, Granville Papers, PRO (new conditions); Thornton to Granville, telegrams, Feb. 28, March 5, 1881, Granville Papers, PRO; telegrams, Evarts to JRL, March 1 (two of same date), March 3, 1881, JRL to Evarts, March 1, 2, 3, 1881, National Archives; JRL to Evarts, Feb. 22, 1881, No. 130 (Tories), March 5, 1881, No. 138, Evarts to JRL, March 7, 1881, No. 126, National Archives; Hoppin Journal, March 6, 1881, Houghton.

27 Evarts to JRL, telegrams, March 1, 3, 6, 1881, National Archives; Thornton to Granville, Feb. 28, 1881, telegram, Granville Papers, PRO (safe to accept); JRL to Evarts, Feb. 22, 1881, No. 130 (safe to accept), telegram, March 7, 1881, March 12, 1881, No. 141, National Archives; Granville, handwritten cabinet opinion, n.d., Granville Papers, PRO (intrinsic worth £7000); Thornton to Granville, March 7, 1881 (private letter), Granville Papers, PRO (unknown parties).

28 Blaine to JRL, telegrams, March 9, 14, April 1, 1881, Blaine to JRL, July 30, No. 206, JRL to Blaine, telegram, March 9, 1881, National Archives; JRL to Granville, March 15, 1881, Granville Papers, PRO; JRL to Evarts, April 22, 25, 1881, owned by Mr. Effingham Evarts; Blaine to Thornton, May 6, 1881, F.O. 115/687, PRO ("to be not merely just, but liberal"); Thornton to Granville, private letters, March 14 (Blaine's remark on JRL as good poet, bad minister), April 5, 19, May 10, 17, 1881, telegrams, March 19, April 4, 19, 21, May 5, 1881, Granville to Thornton, telegrams, March 17, April 2, 28, May 27 — all in Granville Papers, PRO; handwritten Cabinet opinions of Granville, n.d. (pre-March 13, 1881); Selbourne, March 1; Kimberley, March 13; Gladstone, March 14; Selbourne, May 9; Northbrook, May 10; Harcourt, May 10; Forster, May 10 — all in Granville Papers, PRO. Also Forster to Granville, March 17[?], 1881, Granville Papers, PRO. At Lowell's death in 1891, it might be added, a reporter asked Blaine to make a statement on Lowell's career as a diplomat, but Blaine "declined to do so" (New York *Times*, Aug. 14, 1891).

Evarts was apparently consulted about, and approved, Blaine's terms with the English. Thornton believed that Evarts in fact encouraged Blaine (though it meant accepting terms he had himself rejected) because he was "personally interested in the affair — a very common practice among lawyers of this country and perhaps not unknown to Secretaries of State" (Thornton to Granville, private letter, March 14, 1881, Granville Papers, PRO). I have come across no evidence to justify this suspicion.

Forster and Northbrook in the British Cabinet were willing to go as high as £16,000 and Lord Selbourne, too, though he disdainfully added: "If the [U.S. Government] . . . think it consistent with their honor and dignity to haggle for 1,000£ more, when they know that we have offered (for mere good will's sake) four or five times as much as we believe to be fairly and justly due . . . I suppose it is not worth our while to keep the question open . . . Although . . . I have some misgivings as to the effect in the long run of the policy of yielding to the screw, whenever it is put upon us" (Cabinet opinions of Northbrook and Forster, May 10, 1881, Granville Papers, PRO; Selbourne, printed memo, April 14, 1881, Granville Papers, PRO).

Even after the Fortune Bay damages were agreed upon, some disturbances continued on the Newfoundland coast (e.g. JRL to Granville, Aug. 19, 1881, F.O. 5/1770, PRO; Granville to Hoppin, Nov. 17, 1881, F.O. 5/1770, PRO). The larger question of whether provisions of the Treaty of Washington could be modified by local legislation was not settled until submitted to the Hague Tribunal in 1909 for arbitration as one of seven questions relating to the North Atlantic fisheries. The arbitrators upheld the British position that the Canadian Provinces could make fishing regulations without the consent of the United States, but also suggested the establishment of a permanent commission to weigh the equity of any provision objected to by the Americans (Brainerd Dyer, *The Public Career of William M. Evarts* [Berkeley: 1933], 213–214; Barrows, *Evarts*, 401).

As for the Clayton-Bulwer episode, Blaine was widely denounced both in England and the United States. In private correspondence Gladstone referred to his maneuver as "an audacious repudiation" (letter to Granville, Dec. 23, 1881, Granville Papers, PRO), Granville described his conduct as "very disgraceful . . . a dangerous rocket" (letter to Gladstone, Dec. 25, 1881, Gladstone Papers, British Museum), and Sackville West, who had replaced Thornton as the English Minister to the United States, called Blaine's diplomacy "as dirty as it is dishonorable . . . simply a vulgar intrigue" (despatch to Granville, Jan. 27, 1882, No. 31, F.O. 5/1785, PRO). In the United States, ex-Secretary of State Hamilton Fish referred to Blaine's "bullying" and his "desperate acrobatic efforts" (letters to J. C. Bancroft Davis, Dec. 15, 1881, Feb. 7, 1882, Davis Papers, LC), and the New York *Evening Post* (March 3, 1882), described the language in Blaine's despatch as "unnecessarily offensive." I have not described the Clayton-Bulwer dispute in detail, because Lowell was but little involved. However, for those interested in the episode, the following documents are of special importance:

In the National Archives, Washington: Blaine to JRL, June 24, Nov. 19, 29, 1881; Frelinghuysen to JRL, May 5, Nov. 22, 1883; JRL to Blaine, Dec. 15, 1881; Granville to Sackville West, Jan. 7, 1882.

In the Granville Papers, Public Records Office: Sackville West to Granville, private letters, Dec. n.d., Dec. 19, 1881; handwritten Cabinet opinions, Dec. 1881, by Harcourt, Selbourne, Kimberley; Bright to Granville, Dec. 22, 1881.

In the Gladstone Papers, British Museum: confidential draft, Granville to Sackville West, Dec. 1881; memo from E. Hertslet, Foreign Office (31 pages), Jan. 6, 1882; Gladstone to Granville, copy, Dec. 25, 1881.

Miscellaneous: telegram, Sackville West to Granville, Jan. 24, 1882, F.O. 5/1790, PRO; Sir Edward Hamilton's Diary, Dec. 24, 1881, British Museum.

See also David M. Pletcher, *The Awkward Years: American Foreign Relations Under Garfield and Arthur* (Columbia: 1962), especially 63–67, 103–106, and for a more favorable though not uncritical view of Blaine's position, see Alice Felt Tyler, *The Foreign Policy of James G. Blaine* (Minneapolis: 1927), 22–45.

29 JRL to Blaine, July 16, 1881, No. 219, National Archives (political event). Lowell's speech on Garfield at the Exeter Hall meeting is in *Prose Works*, VI, 38–46. It was widely considered a triumph of feeling and good taste, not only in its references to Garfield but also in its flattering allusion to the incoming President, Chester A. Arthur (Hoppin Journal, Oct. 1881, Houghton; R. H. Dana to R. H. Dana, Jr., n.d., Dana Papers, MHS: JRL to Mrs. Hill, Oct. 23, 1881, University of Cincinnati). The lines quoted from the speech come from its printed preface, which may not, in fact, have been written by Lowell; such at least was Norton's opinion (letter to Chamberlain, Dec. 5, 1902, Huntington Library). Lowell's letter to Gladstone, July 4[?], 1881, Gladstone Papers, British Museum.

30 Hamilton Fish to Judge Hoar, March 8, 1881, Fish Papers, LC (Evarts rumor); Thornton to Granville (private letter), May 31, 1881, Granville Papers, PRO (Grant rumor); JRL to Señora de Riaño, Oct. 30, 1881, Hispanic Society (love of Venice); JRL to Mrs. Smalley, Nov. 2, 1881, University of Cincinnati (word from Blaine and Granville); JRL to Granville (private letter), Oct. 29, 1881, Granville Papers, PRO.

Mrs. Lowell's improved health is described in: JRL to George Putnam, April 11, June 20, 1881, owned by Miss Elizabeth Putnam; JRL to Mrs. Smalley, Sept. 6, 1881, University of Rochester;

Frances Lowell to Señora de Riaño, Sept. 11, 1881, Hispanic Society.

31 Frelinghuysen sent informal word to Lowell through R. W. Gilder, the author, who had appealed to the new Secretary in the name of "the intelligent young men" in the country to retain Lowell (R. W. Gilder to Frelinghuysen, Nov. 11, 1881, National Archives; JRL to Gilder, Jan. 1, 1882, copy, Norton Collection, Houghton; Gilder to Norton, Dec. 18, 1891, Norton Collection, Houghton). Hamilton Fish was another who had a low opinion of Frelinghuysen, describing him as "constitutionally undecided & wavering" (letter to J. C. B. Davis, July 10, 1882, Davis Papers, LC). But, for a more favorable estimate of Frelinghuysen, see the able studies by David M. Pletcher, *Awkward Years,* and Owen Edwards, doctoral dissertation, in process, at the John Hopkins University.

32 JRL to Evarts, Jan. 7, 1881; JRL to Blaine, June 4, No. 193, 1881 ("just, and even generous"; limit of public opinion; Home Rule); JRL to Frelinghuysen, Feb. 17, 1882, No. 317 ("passionate selfishness"; "fantastic political theories"; Ireland "not England"); the Coercive Act has been quoted as printed in the New York *World,* April 7, 1882; JRL to Frelinghuysen, March 14, 1882, No. 331 (Coercive Act "arbitrary") — all in the National Archives. Lowell's letter to Gladstone about "violent measures proposed" is dated Nov. 17, 1880, Gladstone Papers, British Museum.

33 JRL to Frelinghuysen, March 14, 1882, No. 331, National Archives.

34 Hoppin Journal, Feb. 26, March 19, 23, 1882, Houghton (concurrence of State Department); Hoppin to Anna Dyer, May 26, 1881, Houghton (author of most correspondence); JRL to Granville, Oct. 29, 1881, Granville Papers, PRO ("*pro forma*"); Thornton to Granville (private letter), April 19, 1881, Granville Papers, PRO (Blaine's comment on "pestiferous fellow").

On the pre-1882 cases, see Thornton to Granville, April 10, 16, May 21, 1881, F.O. 5/1753–4, PRO; Harcourt to Granville, June 17, July 3, 1881, Granville Papers, PRO; Granville to Gladstone, June 21, 1881, Granville Papers, PRO; JRL to Blaine, June 4 (the fullest statement of his early procedures on the suspects), June 25, July 15, 1881, National Archives; JRL to Sir Charles Dilke, July 25, 1881, Dilke Papers, British Museum; Sackville West to Granville, Feb. 15, 1882, No. 65, F.O. 5/1815, PRO; Granville to Forster, June 1, 1881, Granville Papers, PRO. For a sample opinion that Lowell had not been sufficiently concerned, see J. Boyle O'Reilly to O. W. Holmes, Dec. 31, 1884, Holmes Papers, LC, and the New York *World,* March 29, April 6, 7, 8, 12, 1882; for a defense of his actions, see the *Nation,* March 9, 16, 1882.

35 For the American request, see Frelinghuysen to JRL, telegrams, March 3, 16, 1882, National Archives; memo, Irish law officers to Forster, copy, F.O. 5/1816, PRO.

Lowell believed the United States had no grounds for insisting that Americans be brought to trial and had early advised that such a request would be futile (JRL to Frelinghuysen, March 14, 1882, No. 311, National Archives; Granville to Forster, June 1, 1881, Granville Papers, PRO: "Lowell . . . privately agrees that such a representation is wrong"; Granville to Sackville West, March 29, 1882 (draft), F.O. 5/1816, PRO). Yet many Americans disagreed, including some who sympathized entirely with Lowell's handling of the Irish problem (e.g. E. L. Godkin to JRL, April 24, 1882, Cunningham Collection, Houghton: "I confess I think the English ground that alien suspects are not entitled to *a trial* simply because the subjects are not, is untenable [and this is] . . . the view most current . . . here among people whose opinion is worth anything . . ."). It was thought the precedent for "preferential" treatment for foreigners had been established by the British themselves during the American Civil War, when their Minister, Lord Lyons, had asked for and received special favors from Secretary of State Seward. But J. C. Bancroft Davis believed the current American demands went "very much beyond anything which Lord Lyons demanded of Mr. Seward" (J. C. Bancroft Davis to Hamilton Fish, June 16, 1881, Fish Papers, LC). For a discussion of the historical precedents, see New York *Times* editorial for April 4, 1882.

Not even the British were as sure as Lowell was about the issue. Lord Harcourt, the Secretary of State, feared that the wording of the 1881 Coercive Act was so obscure that the United States government might be within its right in assuming that the Lord Lieutenant of Ireland could *direct* persons to be tried if he so desired. Harcourt believed, therefore, that it would be unwise to insist on the actual words of the act and advised directing the United States instead to the act's general object, namely, "to supersede and dispense with trial" for aliens and subjects alike (Liddell to Tenterden, March 27, 1882, F.O. 5/1816, PRO). See also Pauncefote to Granville, March 31, 1882, Granville Papers, PRO: "I venture to doubt whether the U.S. Govt. can be put out of Court by the mere assertion of the principle that their subjects are amenable equally with British subjects to the 'Coercion Act.' "

36 For the British position, see the handwritten cabinet opinions of Harcourt, Forster, Gladstone, Granville and Selbourne, March 26–31, 1882, Granville Papers, PRO; Forster to Granville, March 18, 1882, enclosing copies of Liddell (Under-Secretary of State) to Forster, March 8, 1882, and Forster to Liddell, March 18, 1882, F.O. 5/1816, PRO; Granville to Forster, March 20, 1882, F.O. 5/1816, PRO; Forster to Granville, June 4, 1881, Granville Papers, PRO.

37 JRL to Frelinghuysen, March 14, 1882, No. 311, National Archives;

JRL to Granville, May 31, 1881, Granville Papers, PRO (willing martyrs); Granville to Sackville West, March 29, 1882 (draft), F.O. 5/1816, PRO (JRL's regret at U.S. representations). For details on the violence advocated by certain Irish-American leaders and publications, see Pletcher, *Awkward Years*, 235–236, 246.

Lowell did not have a high opinion of Forster; he referred to him as "a man impossible to deal with" (JRL to Holmes, Dec. 28, 1884, Houghton; see also Granville to JRL, "private," April 3, 1882, Dr. Burnett Collection, Houghton). Sir Edward Hamilton's estimate of Forster is probably more just: Forster "has many shortcomings as a Minister . . . his want of decision, his tendency to blunder . . . but there can be no question of the honesty and straightforwardness of his intentions" (Diary, May 4, 1882, British Museum).

38 JRL to Granville, private letter, March 30, 1882, Granville Papers, PRO ("whatever *can* be done"); Forster to Granville, April 2, 1882, Granville Papers, PRO ("unnecessary alarm"); Sackville West to Granville, telegram, March 29, 1882, F.O. 5/1816, PRO (Congress to insist on formal demand); Judge Hoar to JRL, telegram, March 29, 1882, National Archives (Congressional demand); Granville to Sackville West, March 29, 1882 (draft), F.O. 5/1816, PRO (Lowell expected recall); Hoppin Journal, March 23, 1882, Houghton; New York *World*, March 29, 1882 (Aldermen); Granville to JRL, April 1, 1882, Houghton; JRL to Granville, April 1, 1882, Granville Papers, PRO.

39 Sir Charles Dilke Diary, March 31, 1882, British Museum (Cabinet decision); Granville to Sackville West, telegram, March 31, 1882 (draft), No. 16, F.O. 5/1816, PRO; JRL to Frelinghuysen, telegram, March 31, 1882, Frelinghuysen to JRL, telegrams, April 1, 1882 (two), National Archives; Sackville West to Granville, April 1, 1882, F.O. 5/1817, PRO.

40 JRL to Frelinghuysen, April 7, 1882, No. 338, "Confidential," National Archives; Forster to Granville, April 2, 1882, Granville Papers, PRO; JRL to Frelinghuysen, telegram, April 1, 1882, National Archives.

41 Granville to Sackville West, draft telegram, April 2, 1882, No. 19, F.O. 5/1817, PRO; Hamilton Fish to Sir John Rose, telegram, April 1, 1882 (forwarded to Hoppin by Bancroft Davis), National Archives; John Rose to Forster, April 2, 1882, Granville Papers, PRO.

42 JRL to Forster, copy, April 3, 1882, Forster to JRL, copy, April 3, 1882, JRL to Granville, private letter, April 3, 1882, Granville Papers, PRO; Gladstone to JRL, April 3, 1882, Houghton; JRL to Frelinghuysen, telegram, April 3, 1882, Sir John Rose to J. C. Bancroft Davis, April 2, 1882, National Archives; Sackville West to Granville, April 3, 1882, No. 152, "confidential," F.O. 5/1817, PRO;

telegrams, Davis to Hoppin, Frelinghuysen to JRL, April 3, 1882, National Archives; Sir John Rose to Hamilton Fish, April 4, 6, 1882, Fish Papers, LC.

For samples of the continuation of the "suspect" question, though in much diluted form, see JRL to Frelinghuysen, April 22, May 3, July 10, 19, 1882, Nos. 347, 349, 393, 402, National Archives; Hoppin Journal, April 23, 1882, Houghton; Sackville West to Granville, April 28, 1882, No. 195, F.O. 5/1817, PRO. The murder of Lord Frederick Cavendish, the new Chief Secretary for Ireland, in early May, 1882, set off another brief flurry of diplomatic activity, for the British believed that the constant encouragement to violence given by the Irish-American press (especially O'Donovan Rossa's *The United Irishman*) had been no small factor in Cavendish's murder and other atrocities (for this episode, see Sir Edward Hamilton Diary, May 8, 1882, British Museum; Gladstone to Granville, May 9, 1882, Granville Papers, PRO; Granville to JRL, June 24, 1882, Granville to Sackville West, May 10, 1882, West to Granville, telegram, May 12, 1882, private letter of May 16, 1882, PRO). There was also a brief flurry in late 1882 when the British arrested Henry George, but he was quickly released.

43 Davis to Fish, April 9, 1882, Fish Papers, LC ("failed utterly"); Sackville West to Granville, April 4, 1882, Granville Papers, PRO ("had not sufficiently insisted").

44 In my researches into British documents, both public and private, I have not uncovered a single mention of Sir John Rose as an important contributor to the negotiations. In this finding I sharply diverge from David M. Pletcher's view that ". . . Rose's intervention had broken the Anglo-American impasse" (*Awkward Years*, 245; see also similar claims on 243, 253). Sir John's comment on Lowell is in a letter to Fish of April 4, 1882, Fish Papers, LC. On his side, Fish believed the successful conclusion was "wholly due" to the "kind & watchful interest" of Bancroft Davis — at least so he wrote Davis (letter of April 20, 1882, Fish Papers, LC).

45 Harcourt to Granville, Aug. 18, 1882, Granville Papers, PRO; Sackville West to Granville, April 18, 1882, Granville Papers, PRO (rumor about Davis wanting Lowell's job); Hamilton Fish to Nicholas Fish, Aug. 22, 1882, Fish Papers, LC (rumor Davis might replace Lowell); Henry Stevens to Bancroft Davis, July 15, 1882, Davis Papers, LC (same rumor). In the summer of 1882, Davis did resign from the State Department (Fish to Davis, May 3, 1882, Davis Papers, LC; Hoppin Journal, July 30, 1882, Houghton).

46 The meeting is reported in full in the New York *Herald*, April 4, 1882; see also New York *Times*, April 4, 1882. The stage, according to the *Times*, "was crowded with people who are prominent in

local politics and Irish national movements." Mayor Grace presided and among those who spoke were men of more than local reputation: Congressman "Sunset" Cox, General Roger A. Pryor, Representatives Orth of Indiana, Scranton of Pennsylvania and Lord of Michigan, and United States Senator Jones of Florida. Extracts from telegrams and letters were read from Senator David Davis, General Rosecrans, ex-Governor Tilden and, perhaps most unnerving to Lowell, Wendell Phillips.

47 *Congressional Record,* April 15, 26, 1882 (Voorhees speech), April 28, 1882 (Robinson speech); New York *Evening Post,* April 16, 1882 ("morbid nervous condition"). Sackville West believed that the attack on Lowell was only a pretext on the part of the Democrats to assail the Republican Administration (letter to Granville, April 15, 1882, No. 172, F.O. 5/1817, PRO; same, April 18, 1882, private letter, Granville Papers, PRO). For sample petitions: M. Nairy to Pres. Arthur, April 22, 1882, R. T. Ellis to Pres. Arthur, Sept. 30, 1882, National Archives; Sackville West to Granville, April 15, 16, F.O. 5/1817, PRO, encloses and describes others; see also John Boyle O'Reilly to O. W. Holmes, Dec. 12, 30, 1884, Holmes Papers, LC.

48 New York *Times,* April 6, 1882; New York *Tribune,* April 5, 6, June 4, 1882; *Nation,* April 6, May 25, June 1, 1882; O. W. Holmes to JRL, July 2, 1882, Norton Collection, Houghton (toast at Commencement). Harvard conferred the honorary degree of LL.D. on Lowell in June, 1884. W. W. Story to JRL, July 25, 1882, Houghton: "all the good sense of the country is with you"; JRL to Granville, April 17, 1882, "private," F.O. 5/1810, PRO (home in irons); JRL to Granville, May 29, 1882, private letter, Granville, PRO (signatures crosses); JRL to G. S. Smalley, April 17, 1882, as quoted in *American Book Prices Current,* 1918, 903, for sample irritation on being "coached in Americanism."

49 Hoppin Journal, April 9, 1882, Houghton (point of resigning); Leslie Stephen to Norton, July 19, 1882, C. E. Norton Papers, Houghton (couldn't resign); Henry James to Grace Norton, May 25, 1882, James Papers, Houghton (expected recall); New York *World,* April 15, 1882; JRL to Story, Aug. 14, 1882, copy, Scudder Papers, Houghton ("on good authority"); Hoppin to Anna Dyer, March 26, 1883, Houghton (clamor completely over).

50 JRL to George Putnam, June 8, 1882, owned by Miss Elizabeth Putnam; Hoppin Journal, June 17, 1882 (insane or nearly); JRL to Julia Stephen, Aug. 2, 1882, Berg Collection, NYPL ("ground into each other"); JRL to Mabel Lowell Burnett, Aug. 17, 1882, Houghton ("remarkably cheerful again"); Leslie Stephen to Norton, Sept. 29, 1882, C. E. Norton Papers, Houghton (best since Madrid); Hop-

pin to Anna Dyer, Nov. 14, 1882, Houghton ("devoted & caressing").

51 Frelinghuysen to JRL, telegram, Nov. 9, 1884, National Archives; in answer to the warning, Lowell replied, "I have several times received similar intimations here and have never paid the least attention to them. Threatened men, says the proverb, live long . . ." (JRL to Frelinghuysen, Nov. 15, 1884, No. 896, National Archives); JRL to Emma Lazarus, Dec. 10, 1883, Lazarus Papers, Columbia (Legation visitors); JRL to Prof. Knight, April 2, 1884, Morgan Library ("all manner of people"); JRL to George Putnam, Dec. 4, 1883, Howe, *New Letters*, 274 ("It is astonishing . . .").

52 JRL to Francis Child, June 11, 1883, M. A. DeWolfe Howe and G. W. Cottrell, Jr., eds., *The Scholar-Friends, Letters of Francis James Child and James Russell Lowell* (Cambridge: 1952), 55 (public institution); JRL to Hoppin, Aug. 17, 1883, Houghton (talk on Fielding); speech unveiling the bust of Coleridge in Westminster Abbey, May 7, 1885, *Prose Works*, VI, 70 (remark on his memory); Henry James to Grace Norton, May 6, 1884, James Papers, Houghton (Edinburgh); sample speeches given by Lowell when in England can be found in his *Prose Works*, VI.

53 JRL to Henry White, April 16, 1884, White Papers, LC.

54 "Democracy" is in JRL's *Prose Works*, VI, 7–37; all quotations in the following discussion are from this printed version of the speech.

55 Amidst a chorus of praise for the speech's comfortable message, Lowell received only muted congratulations from Norton, who called the address wise, even brilliant, but thought its optimism questionable. He predicted Lowell would learn on his return that democracy had worsened; it "will work," Norton agreed, "but it may work ignobly, ignorantly, brutally" (Norton to JRL, Nov. 16, 1884, Norton and Howe eds., *Letters Norton*, II, 166).

Another minority dissent came from Matthew Arnold. He thought the speech "full of good things," but felt "the want of body and current in the discourse as a whole"; he was "not satisfied with a host of shrewd and well-wrought and even brilliant sayings" (Arnold to Norton, Oct. 8, 1884, *The Letters of Matthew Arnold 1848–1888*, George W. E. Russell ed., 2 vols. (London: 1895), II, 269.

56 JRL to Mrs. Clifford, Nov. 16, 1884, Huntington Library (puzzled at popularity); Henry James to Mrs. E. L. Godkin, Oct. 2, 1884, courtesy of Leon Edel; Leslie Stephen to Norton, Sept. 29, 1882, C. E. Norton Papers, Houghton.

57 JRL to Prof. William Knight, Nov. 17, 1883, Morgan Library; Knight to JRL, Nov. 22, 1883, Houghton; John Tulloch to JRL, Nov. 24, Dec. 10, 22, 1883, Houghton; Lord Selbourne to JRL, Nov. 26, 1883, Houghton; copy of unsigned letter to the Vice Chancellor

of St. Andrews objecting to JRL on legal grounds, Dec. 7, 1883, Houghton; JRL to Francis Child (Dec. 1883), Howe and Cottrell eds., *The Scholar-Friends*, 60 ("How to rob . . .").

58 Hoppin to Anna Dyer, Nov. 28, 1882 (rubber man), March 20, Dec. 18, 1883, Houghton; Henry James to Grace Norton, Jan. 19, 1884, James Papers, Houghton (smart house; London conversation); JRL to G. F. Hoar, Oct. 15, 1883, G. F. Hoar Papers, MHS (Paris). Lowell was always at home for his wife's "Friday afternoons" (JRL to J. Dykes Campbell, May 22, 1884, Campbell Correspondence, British Museum).

59 JRL to G. W. Curtis, Nov. 8, 1884, Curtis Papers, Houghton: "had I been at home of course I should have sided with you"; JRL to E. M. Bacon, March 31, 1890, Norcross Papers, MHS (Mugwump since Lincoln's death); JRL to Grover Cleveland, Nov. 29, 1884, National Archives.

60 JRL to Mrs. W. K. Clifford, Dec. 4, 1884, copy, Norton Collection, Houghton ("a hen's time"); Henry James to Grace Norton, Jan. 24, 1885, James Papers, Houghton; JRL to Mrs. Clifford, Nov. 9, 1884, Norton ed., *Letters*, III, 116 ("kind to me").

61 JRL to Julia Stephen, Feb. 5, 1885, Berg Collection NYPL; Leslie Stephen to Norton, Feb. 15, 1885, C. E. Norton Papers, Houghton; JRL to Mabel Lowell Burnett, Feb. 20, 1885, Houghton (last embrace).

62 JRL to George Putnam, March 2, 1885, owned by Miss Elizabeth Putnam; W. J. Hoppin Journal, Feb. 23, 1885, Houghton; JRL to Norton, April 16, 1885, Norton Collection, Houghton.

63 JRL to Norton, April 16, 1885, Norton Collection, Houghton; JRL to Josephine Shaw Lowell, April 20, 1885, Houghton (Job).

64 Henry James to Grace Norton, March 4, 1885, James Papers, Houghton; JRL to Emelyn Story, March 31, 1885, copy, Scudder Papers, Houghton; JRL to Lilla Perry, May 15, 1885, Colby College ("a problem"); JRL to Smalley, May 21, 1885, Huntington Library (Oxford); JRL to Señora de Riaño, June 6, 1885, Hispanic Society (Oxford).

65 JRL's speech at the Gray unveiling is from an unidentified newspaper clipping in the Norton Collection, Houghton, dated in pencil, May 27, 1885; sample newspaper editorials on his departure are included in a letter from JRL to his daughter, April 24, 1885, Houghton; Granville to JRL, April 14, 1885, Rantoul Collection, Houghton ("Your great reputation in Letters prepared the way for you, but your success was due to your personal qualities"); Charles Hodson to JRL, Dec. 15, 1885, Rantoul Collection, Houghton. On the eve of Lowell's departure, Hoppin, who had worked with him more closely than any other man, wrote in his private journal: "It will be

a great loss & sorrow to me. My friendly intercourse with him has been among the pleasantest experiences of my life" (March 29, 1885, Houghton).

CHAPTER XV. LAST YEARS (pages 339–371)

1 JRL to Norton, March 9, 1872, Elizabeth G. Norton Papers, Houghton; M. Brimmer to Norton, March 26, 1885, C. E. Norton Papers, Houghton (Holmes); the poem is JRL's "Sixty-Eighth Birthday," *Heartsease and Rue* (Boston: 1888), 218.

Lowell was deeply touched that he was one of two people (outside of the family), whom Edmund Quincy mentioned in his will—asking that Lowell be given his first edition of *Tom Jones* (Mary Quincy to JRL, June 3, 1877, owned by Prof. F. L. Hilles; JRL to Mary Quincy, June 5, 1877, Yale). Lowell wrote a memoir of Quincy for the Massachusetts Historical Society (MHSP, June, 1877).

2 For his thoughts of suicide, see JRL to Norton, Nov. 23, 1886, March 30, 1888, Norton Collection, Houghton; for his stoicism, JRL to Mabel Lowell Burnett, July 23, 1887, Dr. Burnett Collection, Houghton.

3 JRL to Norton, July 22, 1885, Norton ed., *Letters*, III, 136.

4 JRL to Misses Lawrence, Jan. 4, 1886, Norton ed., *Letters*, III, 146 (puppies); Esther Lowell Cunningham (JRL's granddaughter), *Three Houses* (Boston: 1955), 69 (breakfast); JRL to Georgianna Putnam, Sept. 20, 1885, Dr. Burnett Collection, Houghton (Equal Rights).

5 JRL to Julia Stephen, July 24 (missionary), No. 9 (Francis), 1885, Berg Collection, NYPL.

6 Lois Burnett, typed manuscript, "A Child's History of a Famous Grandfather," owned by Mrs. Sherman Baldwin.

7 All quotations in this and the following paragraph are from Lois Burnett, "A Child's History," except the maxim on lending, which is in JRL to Mabel Lowell Burnett, Aug. 7, 1887, Howe, *New Letters*, 312.

8 JRL to Moses Coit Tyler, July 1, 1885, Cornell; JRL to Henry White, July 22, 1885, Henry White Papers, LC (visit to Elmwood); JRL to Lady Lyttleton, July 2, 1885, Norton ed., *Letters*, III, 135 ("wit to make them"); Henry James to Grace Norton, Dec. 9, 1885, James Papers, Houghton.

9 JRL to G. W. Smalley, Sept. 10, 1885, Princeton (St. Denis); JRL to Norton, Aug. 13, 1885, Norton Collection, Houghton (can't break Cleveland's heart); JRL to Edward Phelps, Oct. 1, 1885, University of Cincinnati (Cleveland's "backbone"); JRL to Edward Phelps,

March 6, 1886, Princeton (Cleveland's "goodness"). Lowell returned to Washington in January, 1886, to testify in behalf of an international copyright bill, finally passed in 1891.

10 JRL to T. D. Woolsey, Jan. 1, 1886, Woolsey Collection, Yale (Athens school); JRL to Julia Stephen, March 21, 1886, Berg Collection, NYPL ("new mode of torture").

11 The student's notes are those of William Roscoe Thayer, Harvard Archives; the same Thayer, in his maturity, wrote the perceptive article, "James Russell Lowell As a Teacher," *Scribner's* (Oct. 1920), 473–480, from which the above details are taken. Thayer was one of a dozen students in Lowell's Dante course, and also his single pupil in a course on *Don Quixote*.

In 1888 a petition signed by some 500 undergraduates implored Lowell to give a course on the nineteenth-century English poets. Though deeply touched, he refused, pleading age and a variety of responsibilities (Greenslet, *Lowell*, 218–220).

12 JRL to Norton, March 30, 1886, Norton ed., *Letters*, III, 153 (Saul on Gilboa); JRL to R. W. Gilder, Nov. 9, 1885, Norton ed., *Letters*, III, 143 ("abominable notoriety"); "Nightwatches," *Heartsease and Rue* (Boston: 1888), 114 ("How much of all . . .").

13 Henry James's comment is in his *Story*, II, 287; Lowell's statement on life in England is from a clipping from *Kate Fields Washington*, n.d., Norton Collection, Houghton.

Part of Lowell's felt duty to his daughter was financial. Edward Burnett's farm had not been prospering, and Lowell would occasionally help them out with money. Since he didn't feel he could afford two establishments, permanent settlement in England seemed out of the question. "It isn't a bed I have made for myself," he wrote Julia Stephen, "but I must lie in it all the same. After all the only bed in which we sleep soundly is made for us by others, & why should I complain" (letter of Aug. 6, 1886, Berg Collection, NYPL).

14 JRL to Norton, Sept. 24, 1889, Norton ed., *Letters*, III, 252 ("far past the period . . .").

15 JRL to Mabel Lowell Burnett, June 26 (royalty), July 7, 1886, Howe ed., *New Letters*, 290, 310–311; JRL to Mabel Lowell Burnett, May 3, 1886 (Royal Academy), June 19, 1886 (Leveson-Gowers), May 22, 1887 (Morley), July 8, 1888 (Queen), July 26, 1888 (Society of Authors), Houghton; JRL to Henry James, May 17, 1887, Howe ed., *New Letters*, 307 (Gladstone); JRL to Mabel Lowell Burnett, June 26, 1887, Dr. Burnett Collection, Houghton (Jubilee).

16 JRL to Mabel Lowell Burnett, July 26, 1888, Houghton (Ovid); JRL to Julia Stephen, Sept. 19, 1887, Berg Collection, NYPL ("perch to perch"); Leslie Stephen to Norton, May 6, 1886, C. E. Norton Papers, Houghton; JRL to Mabel Lowell Burnett, July 7, 1886 (profitless), July 23, 1887 (dining alone), Houghton.

17 JRL to Mabel Lowell Burnett, July 7, 1886, Howe, *New Letters*, 289 ("various and amusing"); JRL to Mabel Lowell Burnett, May 22, 1887, Houghton ("Great City"); JRL to Mabel Lowell Burnett, May 13, 1888, Norton ed., *Letters*, III, 208 (Hyde Park); JRL to Norton, Nov. 11, 1888, Norton ed., *Letters*, III, 218 (Africa); JRL to Mary Avery, April 7, 1891, Vassar College (Perceval Lowle).

18 JRL to Lilla Perry, July 6, 1888, Colby College; JRL to S. Weir Mitchell, July 15, 1888, University of Pennsylvania; W. W. Story Diary, as quoted by Henry James, *Story*, II, 293–294.

19 JRL to Mabel Lowell Burnett, May 3 (*Contemporary Review*), July 7 (epigram), 1886, Houghton; JRL to Norton, May 26, 1887, Norton ed., *Letters*, III, 189 (anachronism); for further comments by Lowell on the Irish Question, see Hoppin Journal, April 21, Sept. 19, 1886, Houghton.

20 JRL to Julia Stephen, Sept. 29, 1888, Berg Collection, NYPL (sermon; pre-Raphaelites; "saint"); JRL to Norton, Nov. 11, 1888 (manliness), Aug. 18, 1889 (Prince of Wales), Norton Collection, Houghton.

21 JRL to Charles Hodson, Aug. 26, 1886, LC ("delightful combination"); JRL to Mabel Lowell Burnett, Aug. 12, 1888, Howe, *New Letters*, 325 ("invoking vengeance"); JRL to Mrs. W. E. Darwin, Sept. 13, 1889, Norton ed., *Letters*, III, 249–250 ("pensively gorgeous"); JRL to Julia Stephen, Sept. 11, 1889, Norton ed., *Letters*, II, 248 ("perpetual ruin").

22 JRL to Mabel Lowell Burnett, Aug. 29, 1888, Dr. Burnett Collection, Houghton.

23 JRL to Mabel Lowell Burnett, Aug. 14, 1887, Howe, *New Letters*, 314 ("as happy as . . ."); Henry James to Grace Norton, Sept. 22, 1889, James Papers, Houghton (shed overcoat; "walking, talking . . ."); Henry James to William James, Oct. 1, 1887, James Family Correspondence, Houghton ("more primitive generation").

24 JRL to Lady Lyttleton, Oct. 4, 1887, copy, Norton Collection, Houghton.

25 Boston *Post*, Nov. 8, 1886 (Mr. Burnett's denial is in the same issue).

26 Phoebe Garnaut (Smalley), as the orphaned teen-aged daughter of a woman who had nursed Wendell Phillips through an almost fatal illness, had been adopted by the Phillipses in 1849. JRL to Godkin, March 15, 1887, Godkin Papers, Houghton (Smalley "hard"); Henry James to Grace Norton, July 16, 1886, July 23, 1887, James Papers, Houghton.

27 JRL to Norton, March 27 ("I *can't* do my best"), March 30 ("comfortable feeling of merit"), 1888, Norton Collection, Houghton. For Norton's unsentimental efforts to encourage Lowell, see his letters of Dec. 5, 1887, March 30, 1888, Houghton (in the latter, for example, he wrote: "You have not done your *possible* best? Who does? . . . I am indifferent about anything but love from my fellow mortals."

When Lowell was scheduled to deliver a political address in 1887 before the Union League Club in Chicago — to give a concrete example of his lack of self-confidence — he found it so lifeless at the last minute that he substituted an old talk on Shakespeare's *Richard III*. The substitution was not appreciated by the assembled crowd nor approved by his friends Norton and G. W. Curtis, who regretted that Lowell had lost such an excellent opportunity to expound "sound principles." "I suppose," Norton wrote Curtis, "he had his usual fit of despondency concerning his performances, and that he fell into bad hands, and became discouraged. Had you or I been at his side it would have been different; but without a friend to help him, his temperament is very apt to get the better of him, and I am sometimes afraid that it may at last really overmaster him" (Norton to Curtis, March 6, 1887, Houghton; Curtis to Norton, March 4, 1887, Curtis Papers, Houghton). Lowell's explanation for his shifting of the speeches is in a letter to Elizabeth G. Norton, Feb. 18, 1887, Elizabeth G. Norton Papers, Houghton (and disproves, incidentally, the standard explanation given for this episode, namely that he switched to a non-political address at Chicago because he found at the last minute that he was addressing a large, open meeting and not the small, private group he had been led to expect).

28 Speech at the meeting of the Tariff Reform League, Boston, Dec. 29, 1887, *Prose Works*, VI, 183 (Knights of Labor); JRL's testimony before the Committee on International Copyright, March 9, 1888, U.S. 50th Congress, Senate, Committee on Patents, *International Copyright*, 50 (sympathy with labor). I am especially indebted to Geoffrey T. Blodgett's excellent article, "The Mind of the Boston Mugwump," MVHR (March, 1962), 614–634.

29 The five major addresses were: 1. On the 250th Anniversary of the Foundation of Harvard University, Nov. 8, 1886 (henceforward referred to as "Harvard"). 2. At a Meeting of the Tariff Reform League, Boston, Dec. 29, 1887 (henceforward "Tariff"). 3. The Place of the Independent in Politics, delivered before the Reform Club of New York, April 13, 1888 (henceforward "Independent"). 4. Our Literature, at New York Banquet of April 30, 1889, in commemoration of the 100th Anniversary of Washington's Inauguration (henceforward "Literature"). 5. The Study of Modern Languages, 1889, before the Modern Language Association of America (henceforward "Languages"). The first four addresses are printed in JRL's *Prose Works*, VI; the fifth ("Languages") is in a posthumous volume entitled *Latest Literary Essays* (Boston: 1891), included as the last volume in the Riverside Edition of the *Prose Works* (henceforward "Latest"). Aside from these five addresses, there is one other key product of Lowell's pen in these years: his introduction to a volume entitled *The World's Progress* (Boston: 1887), which can also be

found in *Latest Literary Essays,* and will hereafter be cited as "Progress."

30 Higginson, *Old Cambridge,* 194; JRL to Norton, Nov. 29, 1886, Norton Collection, Houghton (*too* fair).

31 "Independent," *Prose Works,* VI, 219 ("new problems," etc.), 193 (doctrinaire-practical man).

32 "Languages," *Latest,* 157 ("barbarizing plutolatry"); "Literature," *Prose Works,* VI, 227 ("wonder and exhilaration"); "Tariff," *Prose Works,* VI, 183 ("one was *in* . . . "); JRL to Henry James, Jan. 11, 1891, James Papers, Houghton (Socialist leaven in himself; "poker among millionaires"); JRL to Hughes, April 20, 1890, Norton ed., *Letters,* III, 270 ("Dutch landscape"); "Progress," *Latest,* 181 ("Lasalle and Karl Marx"; take out mainspring), 183 ("to mitigate natural laws").

In the last summer of his life, Lowell joined the "Social Science Institute"—a society to bring about "a free platform for the study of all sociological questions without fear or favor" (as recounted in a newspaper article by T. W. Higginson, *Woman's Journal,* Sept. 12, 1891).

33 "Tariff," *Prose Works,* VI, 186–187 (Cleveland); "Independent," *Prose Works,* VI, 216 ("least hurtful," etc.). The comment on the dangers of a "surplus" is from a letter to Charles W. Storey, Oct. 17, 1886, owned by Mr. Charles M. Storey.

34 "Independent," *Prose Works,* VI, 205 ("unsteadied"), 219–220 ("marvels"); Address at the Opening of the Free Public Library in Chelsea, Mass., Dec. 22, 1885, *Prose Works,* VI, 98 ("vigor of constitution"); "Independent," *Prose Works,* VI, 219–220 ("marvels of fidelity").

35 Address at the Opening of the Free Public Library in Chelsea, Mass., Dec. 22, 1885, *Prose Works,* VI, 97–98 ("bone of our bone"); "Progress," *Latest,* 175 (Greeks for art . . . , etc.), 177 (pure Negro); "Harvard," *Prose Works,* VI, 148 (American Indian). For the resistance of Lowell's circle to nativism, see Barbara Solomon's *Ancestors and Immigrants,* especially 47–60, 82–83.

36 "Independent," *Prose Works,* VI, 195; "Harvard," *Prose Works,* VI, 175 ("show of hands"); "Progress," *Latest,* 178–179.

As long ago as 1850 Lowell had written in his diary, "Men are aristocrats by nature, & democrats by principle—which is the stronger?" (notebook marked "J. R. Lowell, Aug. 22, 1850," Norton Collection, Houghton). He was less sure than ever.

37 "Harvard," *Prose Works,* VI, 158–163, 172–178.

In his 1866 essay on Lessing, Lowell had made some amusing comments on the German pedantry which he feared was assaulting American universities: "*So* thorough is the German mind, that might it not seem now and then to work quite through its subject, and expatiate in cheerful unconsciousness on the other side thereof?" Lowell rejoiced that Lessing on his deathbed "was at least not haunted by the unappeasable apprehension of a German for a biographer" (NAR, April, 1867).

38 "Harvard," *Prose Works,* VI, 175 (unexampled problems), "Tariff," 189 ("obstinate vitality"); "Progress," *Latest,* 165 ("bit in their teeth"); "Independent," *Prose Works,* VI, 207 ("angel of destiny").

39 "Independent," *Prose Works,* VI, 196 ("may be influenced"), 197 ("human nature"), 206–207 ("makeshifts"; "neglectful"), 220–221 ("in season and out"); "Tariff," *Prose Works,* VI, 188 (country worth saving). "Narrow, ungenial" is from one of Lowell's earlier writings, a review of vol. III of John Gorham Palfrey's *History of New England during the Stuart Dynasty* (NAR, Jan. 1865, 161–176); this review, an extended, perceptive defense of the Puritan fathers, contains (on p. 161) this characteristic statement: "Faith in God, faith in man, faith in work — this is the short formula in which we may sum up the teaching of the founders of New England, a creed ample enough for this life and the next."

40 JRL to Kate Fields, May 15, 1890, Norton ed., *Letters,* III, 278 (providential thickness; "eventual success"); "Independent," *Prose Works,* VI, 215 ("so much faith"); "Progress," *Latest,* 168 ("a spiral stairway"). As Lowell said of tariff reform, "I have no doubt that it will ultimately prevail . . . We are sure of ultimate success" (JRL to H. H. Barrett, et al., n.d., St. John Seminary, California).

41 "Harvard," *Prose Works,* VI, 172–174 ("intelligent purpose"; "higher average"; "consolation of mankind"); "Literature," *Prose Works,* VI, 228 ("We cannot say . . .").

42 For sample Mugwump discontent, see Norton to JRL, June 24, 1888, Norton Collection, Houghton; for JRL's poem and Cleveland's response, see Cleveland to Mrs. Alfred C. Chapin, March 7, 1890, Allan Nevins ed., *Letters of Grover Cleveland, 1850–1908* (Boston: 1933), 219, and R. W. Gilder to JRL, Dec. 24, 1889, Rosamund Gilder ed., *Letters of Richard Watson Gilder* (Boston: 1916), 225–226 ("anything that had ever been given him"), and JRL to Cleveland, Dec. 22, 1889, as printed in Walpole Galleries catalogue for auction sale of Dec. 16, 1916.

43 JRL's comment on Gray is in *Latest Literary Essays,* 9–11.

44 Lowell's "Birthday Book," containing the more notable contributions (in manuscript) from the *Critic,* and stunningly bound and mounted, is in Morgan Library; JRL to Julia Stephen, Feb. 27, 1889, Berg Collection, NYPL.

45 Norton to Curtis, Feb. 22, 1889, Houghton; Holmes' poem was printed in the *Atlantic,* March, 1889; JRL to Annie Fields, Feb. 23,

1889, Norton ed., *Letters,* III, 224; JRL to Julia Stephen, Feb. 27, 1889, Berg Collection, NYPL ("but a pig"); M. A. DeWolfe Howe, *Barrett Wendell and His Letters* (Boston: 1924), 93–94.

46 Norton to Curtis, Dec. 28, 1888, Houghton; JRL to Annie Fields, Aug. 27, 1889, Norton ed., *Letters,* III, 243–244.

47 The information about Edward Burnett comes from an interview with his daughter, Mrs. Stanley Cunningham of May 17, 1962, and a letter from his son, Dr. Francis Lowell Burnett, of April 21, 1962; additional details are in Annie Fields to Mrs. Osgood, 1889, SPNEA.

48 For a sample of Lowell's driving a bargain, see JRL to T. B. Aldrich, Jan. 25, 1887, Aldrich Papers, Houghton, and Aldrich to JRL, Jan. 26, 1887, Houghton. The Gilder offer (not accepted) is referred to in Gilder to Norton, Dec. 15, 1891, Houghton. Further information on Lowell's finances is in Samuel G. Ward to JRL, Feb. 11, 1880, Houghton; Hoppin Journal, Jan. 9, 1881, Houghton; H. O. Houghton to JRL, Oct. 26, 1887, Houghton; Houghton Mifflin Co. to George Putnam, Houghton Mifflin Letterbooks, X, 290, Houghton; and JRL's account book with the Charles River National Bank, Dr. Burnett Collection, Houghton.

49 JRL to Julia Stephen, Nov. 9, 1889, Berg Collection, NYPL (Charon); JRL to Norton, Sept. 24, 1889, Norton ed., *Letters,* III, 253 (Old French). In his will Lowell left to Harvard all the books in his library which the university did not yet possess.

50 Lois Burnett, "A Child's History," owned by Mrs. Sherman Baldwin; Mrs. Stanley Cunningham, *Three Houses,* 69–104; letter to the author from Dr. Francis Lowell Burnett, April 21, 1962; JRL to Julia Stephen, Feb. 9, 1890 (governess), Feb. 4, 1891 (slang), Berg Collection, NYPL.

51 Lois Burnett, "A Child's History," owned by Mrs. Sherman Baldwin.

52 Lois Burnett, "A Child's History," owned by Mrs. Sherman Baldwin. The "hose" incident is probably the original of the tale that Lowell died as the result of a cold caught when John Fiske's sons, unable to resist the top hat, had doused him. Perry Miller told me that this version of Lowell's death is the one still widely repeated in Cambridge circles.

53 JRL to Mabel Lowell Burnett, Oct. 19, 1888, Houghton ("incurable children"); Curtis to O. W. Holmes, Oct. 1891, Holmes Papers, LC; Norton to Curtis, Feb. 6, 1887, Houghton.

54 JRL to S. Weir Mitchell, Feb. 16, April 4, 1890, University of Pennsylvania; JRL to Mary Lowell Putnam, March 25, 1890, Houghton; JRL to Prof. William Knight, April 8, 1890, Morgan Library; JRL to Miss Clarke, May 27, 1890, "Three Letters from James Russell Lowell," *Century Magazine,* Feb. 1896 ("a bore").

55 JRL to Norton, Aug. 23, 1890, Norton ed., *Letters,* III, 287; JRL to S. Weir Mitchell, Sept. 24, 1890, University of Virginia.

56 Mabel Lowell Burnett to Señora de Riaño, n.d. (1891?), Hispanic Society; JRL to the Misses Lawrence, Dec. 18, 1890, Norton ed., *Letters*, III, 309; JRL to W. W. Story, Oct. 2, 1890, University of Texas; Holmes' visit is recounted in Emerson, *Saturday Club*, 79.

Lowell's "Hawthorne biography" had a long history. Soon after Hawthorne's death in 1864, his widow asked Lowell to do the book, but discovering that James T. Fields had given Lowell the manuscript of her husband's "Isle of Shoals Journal" to look over, she was "perfectly aghast" and demanded that it be instantly recovered. Since she would not trust him with the notebooks, Lowell withdrew from the project; he supposed she was "right enough," in case of "fire & what not," but he regretted her attitude, since he "should have liked to do" the biography. Apparently Sophia Hawthorne did not like Lowell personally; at least there exists a letter of hers in which she refers to him as "very unsatisfactory." (J. T. Fields to Sophia Hawthorne, Sept. 17, 1866, Berg Collection, NYPL; Sophia Hawthorne to J. T. Fields, Sept. 19, 1866, Boston Public Library; JRL to Norton, Sept. 25, 1866, Norton Collection, Houghton; Sophia Hawthorne to her mother, Sept. 1, 1850, as printed in Leyda, *Melville Log*, I, 392 ["very unsatisfactory"]). In 1877, John Morley unsuccessfully approached Lowell to do a Hawthorne biography for a series he was editing (Morley to JRL, Nov. 7, 1877, Houghton; Morley to JRL, Nov. 26, 1877, Historical Society of Pennsylvania). But when, in 1889, Lowell was again approached (apparently for a fee of $3,000), he decided to accept. This time his final illness intervened (JRL to Julia Stephen, Dec. 4, 1889, Berg Collection, NYPL; Horace E. Scudder Diary, Nov. 26, 1889, Houghton).

Lowell was thought peculiarly suitable to do the biography because he had been an early, ardent advocate of Hawthorne's work. Though not above criticizing Hawthorne, especially for his "remoteness from ordinary life" (review of *Passages from the American Note-Books*, NAR, Jan. 1869), Lowell believed him "our greatest imaginative genius" (review of *Lyrics of a Day* by H. H. Brownell, NAR, July, 1864). "You are one of the few men in these later generations," Lowell once wrote Hawthorne, "whose works are going to *keep* . . ." (Feb. 26, 1863, University of Virginia). In another letter, congratulating Hawthorne on the triumph of *The House of the Seven Gables*, Lowell claimed to have been a "disciple" as early as his eighteenth year (April 24, 1851, Berg Collection, NYPL). And once Lowell caused a minor eruption at the Saturday Club because of Hawthorne; at Lowell's first club after returning from Europe in 1874, Emerson reminded him that "We have met two great losses in our Club since you were last here — Agassiz and Sumner." To which Lowell supposedly replied, "Yes, but a greater than either was that of a man I could never make you believe in as I did, Hawthorne."

According to Annie Fields, from whose diary the story comes, this "ungracious speech" silenced everyone (Aug. 26, 1874, MHS).

Lowell and Hawthorne were not close friends. There is even a family tradition that they disliked each other — so at least Mrs. Stanley Cunningham, Lowell's granddaughter, remarked to me in a conversation of May 17, 1962. Though some distaste might have been expected from their temperamental differences, I have found no evidence of it. Lowell was active on several occasions in Hawthorne's behalf. He took the lead in raising money for him when he was in desperate straits in 1849–1850 and later went out of his way to arrange private tutoring to help prepare his son, Julian, for entrance into Harvard (on raising money: JRL to Edward Davis, Jan. 13, 1850, Davis Letters, Houghton; JRL to Duyckinck, Jan. 13, 1850, Duyckinck Collection, NYPL. On Julian's tutoring: Hawthorne to JRL, Feb. 22, 1863, Houghton; JRL to Hawthorne, Feb. 26, 1863, University of Virginia; Sophia Hawthorne to Annie Fields, July 8, 1866, Boston Public Library). And after Julian was enrolled at Harvard, Lowell gave him help, privately, with German.

Lowell's favors to Julian, and his fondness for him, met an unhappy reversal late in Lowell's life. Returning from his mission to England in 1885, he welcomed Julian Hawthorne, then writing for the New York *World*, to Southborough, where the two men talked for more than four hours, ranging freely over all aspects of English affairs. Shortly after, to Lowell's astonishment, the "interview" appeared in the *World*, with the headline "Lowell in a Chatty Mood" (*World*, Oct. 24, 1886). "Chatty" was putting it mildly. Among the remarks attributed to Lowell was that the Prince of Wales was "immensely fat," the House of Lords had "a good many fools in it," Secretary Frelinghuysen was "weak," Lord Coleridge, the Lord Chief Justice, was "wanting in tact," and the late Duke of Albany was reportedly "the greatest cad of his day"! No wonder Lowell angrily reported to Julia Stephen that the article made him seem "a toothless old babbler" (Nov. 23, 1866, Berg Collection, NYPL).

Julian Hawthorne insisted that Lowell had known he was being interviewed and that he had been quoted accurately; Lowell, with considerable heat, publicly accused Hawthorne of drawing him out under the guise of a private conversation and then compounding the injury by falsifying the substance of what he said (Boston *Daily Advertiser*, Oct. 26, 1886; the *Critic*, Nov. 6, 1886). There is a wealth of documentation on the episode, but none of it conclusive. It is almost as difficult to believe that Hawthorne would have jeopardized his reputation by "stealing" an interview whose theft was bound to be protested, as it is to believe that Lowell, the soul of public discretion, would have made the comments attributed to him had he known they were for publication. It seems likely that a misunderstanding was at the heart of the matter; Lowell probably did say most of what Hawthorne reported, though never dreaming that he was speaking for the record, while Hawthorne, relying on memory, almost certainly distorted or exaggerated some of Lowell's comments.

In any case, for a "tolerably philosophical old fellow," Lowell was furious. The worst of it, he wrote Thomas Bailey Aldrich, was that the episode was "like a dead rat in the wall — an awful stink & no cure" (Oct. 29, 1886, Aldrich Papers, Houghton). The interview caused wide comment, though the London papers, apparently out of deference to Lowell, carried almost no word of it. Friends rushed to assure him of their horror at Hawthorne's "betrayal." The most overwrought note came from Henry James, who, with that theatricality of emotion which in his correspondence is usually a sign that he is exciting rather than simply expressing his feelings, wrote Lowell that he wished "to throw myself into your arms — or rather to take you, tenderly & healingly, into my own . . ." (Nov. 16, 1886, Dr. Burnett Collection, Houghton).

57 JRL to Julia Stephen, Oct. 7, 1890, Berg Collection, NYPL; JRL to Oliver Wendell Holmes, Oct. 31, 1890, Holmes Papers, LC ("the enemy").

58 Mabel Lowell Burnett to Julia Stephen, n.d., Berg Collection, NYPL ("the *name* does not matter"); JRL to Julia Stephen, Dec. 4, 1890, Norton ed., *Letters*, III, 308.

59 William James to Henry James, Aug. 20, 1891, James Family Correspondence, Houghton; Mabel Lowell Burnett to Julia Stphen, n.d., Berg Collection, NYPL; John Bartlett to Francis Underwood, Sept. 22, 1891, Norcross Papers, MHS. As late as July, John Holmes and John Bartlett, paying Lowell a visit, had thought "his look — his *aspect* . . . quite good and natural." (John Holmes to Charles W. Storey, July 14, 1891, owned by Mr. Charles M. Storey.)

60 G. W. Curtis to John White Chadwick, Aug. 16, 1891, Curtis Papers, Houghton; New York *Times*, Aug. 15, 1891; JRL to Mrs. R. W. Gilder, Jan. 26, 1891, Norton ed., *Letters*, III, 313 ("an honest man").

INDEX

LEE COUNTY LIBRARY SYSTEM